Rome and the New Republic

NOTRE DAME STUDIES IN AMERICAN CATHOLICISM

Sponsored by the
Charles and Margaret Hall Cushwa Center
for the Study of American Catholicism

The Brownson-Hecker Correspondence
Joseph Gower and Richard Leliaert, editors

The Survival of American Innocence:
Catholicism in an Era of Disillusionment, 1920–1940
William M. Halsey

Faith and Fatherland: The Polish Church War in Wisconsin, 1896–1918
Anthony J. Kuzniewski

Chicago's Catholics: The Evolution of an American Identity
Charles Shanabruch

A Priest in Public Service: Francis J. Haas and the New Deal
Thomas E. Blantz, C.S.C.

Corporation Sole: Cardinal Mundelein and Chicago Catholicism
Edward R. Kantowicz

The Household of Faith:
Roman Catholic Devotions in Mid-Nineteenth-Century America
Ann Taves

People, Priests, and Prelates:
Ecclesiastical Democracy and the Tensions of Trusteeism
Patrick W. Carey

The Grail Movement and American Catholicism, 1940–1975
Alden V. Brown

The Diocesan Seminary in the United States:
A History from the 1780s to the Present
Joseph M. White

Church and Age Unite:
The Modernist Impulse in American Catholicism
R. Scott Appleby

Oxcart Catholicism of Fifth Avenue:
The Impact of the Puerto Rican Migration on the Archdiocese of New York
Ana María Díaz-Stevens

Searching for Christ
The Spirituality of Dorothy Day
Brigid O'Shea Merriman, O.S.F.

Rome and the New Republic

Conflict and Community in Philadelphia Catholicism
between the Revolution and the Civil War

Dale B. Light

University of Notre Dame Press
Notre Dame and London

©1996 by
University of Notre Dame Press
Notre Dame, Indiana 46556
All Rights Reserved

Manufactured in the United States of America

Library of Congress Cataloging-in-Publication Data
Light, Dale B. (Dale Beryl)
    Rome and the new republic : conflict and community in Philadelphia
Catholicism between the Revolution and the Civil War / by Dale B. Light.
        p. cm. —(Notre Dame studies in American Catholicism)
    Includes bibliographical references and index.
    ISBN 0-268-01652-6 (hardcover : alk. paper)
    1. Catholic Church—Pennsylvania—Philadelphia—History—18th
century. 2. Catholic Church—Pennsylvania—Philadelphia—History—
19th century. 3. Philadelphia (Pa.)—Church history—18th century.
4. Philadelphia (Pa.)—Church history—19th century.
I. Title. II. Series.
BX1418.P5L54 1995
282'.74811'09033—dc20   95-16520
                                                         CIP

∞ The paper used in this publication meets the minimum requirements of
the American National Standard for Information Sciences—Permanence of
Paper for Printed Library Materials, ANSI Z39.48-1984.

FOR BENG,
WHO MAKES ALL THINGS POSSIBLE

Contents

Acknowledgments

Scholarship is ultimately a cooperative enterprise and in the course of this study I have incurred several debts—more, I fear, than can be cited here. I would particularly like to single out the contributions of Michael Zuckerman, Professor of History at the University of Pennsylvania and former director of the "Transformation of Philadelphia" project. Much of the research for this book was supported by a fellowship administered by that project. Professor Zuckerman has been a perceptive critic of my work as well as an unfailing source of encouragement and good sense. I thank him for all he has done. Portions of this study were also funded by a faculty development grant from Pennsylvania State University.

I would like to thank Richard Dunn and his associates at the Philadelphia Center for Early American Studies. I benefited enormously from the intellectual environment they provided and from participation in their activities. Special thanks to Judith Hunter, whose residency at the Center coincided with my own. We may have disagreed on many issues, but she always made me think deeply about my positions and my work is better for our discussions. Thanks also to Stevie, John, Nancy, Ron, Greg, Avi, Donna, and all the rest who made my stay at the Center memorable and productive.

I have also benefited from the assistance granted by the directors and staffs of several libraries and archival collections. I would particularly like to thank Joseph Casino and his staff at the Archives of the Archdiocese of Philadelphia and Father Thomas, Curator of the Archdiocesan Archives of Baltimore. Their assistance has been invaluable. I would also like to thank the staff at the Historical Society of Pennsylvania, the Library Company of Pennsylvania, the American Philosophical Society, St. Mary's Seminary in Baltimore, the Van Pelt Library at the University of Pennsylvania, the Hesburgh Library at the University of Notre Dame, and especially Wes Loder and his staff at the Ciletti Library of the Pennsylvania State University Schuylkill Campus.

Many thanks are also due to Scott Appleby, Director of the Cushwa Center, and to his predecessor, Jay Dolan. I have gained much from their criticism and comments. I would also like to thank Philip Gleason and the participants in the Catholic Studies Seminar at Notre Dame for their comments on portions of this work. All errors of fact and inter-pretation, of course, are my responsibility alone.

Finally, I want to honor the memory of Dennis Clark, historian of the Irish in Philadelphia. He was a prolific, insightful, and generous scholar and a good friend whose work has influenced mine in innu-merable ways. He will be missed.

Introduction

As a boy growing up in the hills of western Pennsylvania I walked through fields looking for arrowheads turned up by plows and weather. Generations before me had walked those fields with similar purpose. Still, each year new artifacts would rise to the surface to be found— small but tangible remains that connected us, however tenuously, to the Woodlands peoples who had once lived there. Today the fields I traverse are archives and intellectual domains. These too have been plowed and shaped by generations of investigators but have not yet given up all the treasures they hold. Repeated visits over time—after other scholars and intellectual discourse have turned the soil—can still yield insights that connect us in interesting ways to other people and other times.

The narrative core of this study is a series of confrontations between Catholic bishops and dissenters, both lay and clerical, that troubled Philadelphia Catholicism for more than half a century. These episodes of intramural strife are, for some scholars at least, more than twice-told tales. Antiquarians have recounted many of these incidents but presented them as little more than interesting stories or cautionary tales illustrating the chaotic conditions from which Philadelphia's Catholic community emerged. Biographers contributed their accounts, describing episodes of lay and clerical dissent as afflictions visited upon the bishops whose lives they chronicled. Later, institutional historians described in detail the tactics employed by bishops to combat the "evil" of dissent, or debated the canonical justifications for the bishops' actions. Only recently have the attitudes and values of the lay and clerical dissenters themselves become the subject of serious consideration. Today, when American Catholicism is again troubled by widespread dissent, it might prove instructive to view once more these early insurgencies and to reconsider the conditions that produced them.

I have divided the narrative into sections representing three phases in the early development of Philadelphia's Catholic community. In the first of these (stretching roughly from the first years of the new republic to 1815) the traditional community, based on hierarchy, deference, and paternalism, disintegrated under the pressure of various conflicting imperatives—social, cultural, ideological and institutional. In the second period (roughly 1815 to 1830) Philadelphia Catholicity was riven by schism and extreme factionalism, and all efforts to maintain or to create an overarching community structure failed. In the third period (spanning the three decades before the Civil War) a new Catholic community, organized around institutional imperatives emanating from Rome and reflecting the class structures of early industrial society, took form.

I have set this narrative against a broad background that relates the development of Philadelphia's Catholic community to events and transformations taking place in Pennsylvania, in the United States as a whole, and throughout Western culture. In so doing I have found two interpretive frameworks useful. I have located the early phases of the conflicts within the context of a general revolt (brilliantly described by Gordon Wood) against social and political elites whose authority was based in a traditional culture of hierarchy, privilege, and deference. This "radical" transformation of values and perceptions began as an affirmation of the rights of the people against the arbitrary exercise of power and an insistence that an aristocracy of talent and virtue should displace ascribed authority. It evolved into a democratic imperative that challenged the assumption that any group within society could legitimately claim privilege on the basis of disinterest and superior insight.[1]

On a broader scale the Philadelphia conflicts reflected what Martin Marty has called the "Modern Schism." This great cultural and ideological divide has its roots in the scientific revolution of the seventeenth century and the Enlightenment traditions of the eighteenth and it found full expression with the advent of the industrial revolution. The modern schism pitted whose who embraced the "new ethos of industrial enterprise, urbanization and nationalism, accompanied by locally varying programmes or creeds like liberalism, evolutionism, socialism, or historicism" against those who cherished the institutions, values, and beliefs of the "inherited religion of the West." Marty's distinction between modern and traditionalist cultures gives insight into the famous schism that rent Philadelphia Catholicism in the 1820s and provides a useful context for the antebellum development of the city's Catholic community.[2]

In ecclesiological terms the Philadelphia conflicts can best be understood as a competition among several models of church organization. This involved two varieties of "republican" Catholicism (one of them liberal and individualist, the other conservative and corporate) as well as the traditional Catholicism of the peasant cultures of northern

Europe and the ultramontane and tridentine reforms sponsored by the Roman curia.

The interaction of these varieties of Catholic thought was complex and was further complicated by the intrusion of secular ideologies, ethnic antagonisms, class interests, and personal and political rivalries. It is for this reason that I have chosen a narrative approach. By relating abstract and occasionally recondite principles to the statements and actions of the individual actors who participated in the Philadelphia conflicts I have attempted to personalize and give a human dimension to a difficult subject. The reader will judge the extent to which I have succeeded.

PART ONE

The Decline of Community

"Authors of Dissensions & Sowers of Discontent"

In 1787 a group of disgruntled immigrants formed a "German Society" within St. Mary's Roman Catholic Church in Philadelphia. Their purpose was to secure a new pastor for the congregation. Some months earlier the congregation's German-speaking priest had died and the Germans felt that since that time the church's Anglo- and Irish-American leadership had discriminated against them. They petitioned John Carroll, superior of the American mission, to appoint another German clergyman who would represent and protect their interests.[1]

Carroll told the Germans that a priest, Laurence Graessl (Cressler), was already in transit from Europe and urged them to patiently await his arrival. The Germans, though, already had another priest in mind—John Helbron (Heilbron), a young Capuchin friar who had recently entered the United States. They informed the superior of their preference for Helbron and suggested that Lawrence Graessl be assigned elsewhere.[2]

John Carroll saw in the society's attempt to make a separate arrangement with John Helbron a serious infringement of his prerogatives. One day after receiving their request he wrote, "As the Congregation of this place [St. Mary's] never before had the [right of] nomination of the Clergymen appointed to serve, I now see no reason why I should depart from a right which has been always exercised by my predecessors." He confirmed Lawrence Graessl in his post at St. Mary's and banished Helbron, whom he suspected of fomenting the trouble, to circuit duty in the west.[3]

Matters did not rest there. The Germans asked Carroll to "consider further on this matter and not appoint to us a gentleman who would not by any means be agreeable to our wishes." They offered a compromise. "Should it still be your determination to have the said Mr. Cresler [Graessl] appointed against our will, we beg leave humbly to request that you will be pleased to leave us the Rev. Mr. Helbron . . . here, who we will support in all necessaries at our own Expense." They also decided to separate themselves physically from St. Mary's congregation. On February 9, 1788, members of the German Society elected a board of trustees and authorized them to open a subscription for the building of "a new German Roman Catholic church." Twelve days later, Adam Premir, a prosperous grocer, purchased ground on which to build the church and soon thereafter notified John Carroll of the fact.[4]

In his letter Premir attempted to reassure the superior that the Germans were not challenging his authority. They sought nothing more, he wrote, than "to promote God's only and most holy Religion." Premir also contacted Robert Molyneux, pastor at St. Mary's and Carroll's vicar general in Philadelphia, and promised him that the society had "no bad intention." Their undertaking, he said, would "be beneficial to Religion." Once again Premir emphasized that the Germans had no intention of withdrawing from Carroll's jurisdiction and intended to submit for his approval any clergy they might choose, as they meant to "make no schism."[5]

Carroll conferred with his vicar, who assured him that the society's actions posed no great danger to religion. Carroll then gave Premir and his associates approval to build a German church, but with it he issued a strong admonition. He wrote, "As you undertake to raise your church, at your own charge, and with your own industry, it is possible, you may even have it in view, to reserve to yourself the appointment of the clergymen, even without the concurrence of the ecclesiastical superior." Such an action, he warned, "may involve consequences to Religion of the most serious nature." He advised the Germans to "avoid contentions," and to "never assume the exercise of that spiritual power, which can only be communicated to the ministers of Christ." Above all, he concluded, "let the election of pastors in your new church be so settled, that every danger of tumultuous appointment be avoided."[6]

The German Society's separation from St. Mary's congregation was a matter of some import. It marked the first significant breach in the integrity of Philadelphia's Catholic community and it inaugurated a dispute that would continue to trouble the Church in America for decades to come. It also exposed many of the deep currents of conflict that would, in time, disrupt Philadelphia Catholicism and lead to the ultimate disintegration of the traditional Catholic community in that city.

The emerging conflict reflected the ideological enthusiasms of the age. Nationalist feelings ran deep within the German Catholic population. The society's initial petition to John Carroll asking permission to erect their church stated that they were "warm wishers to keep up their respective nation and language." So ubiquitous were references to German nationality and culture that one scholar has concluded that "nationalism . . . was the principle issue at stake, [in Philadelphia] and it lay at the root of all the others." The Germans' goal, he writes, was nothing less than the formation of "a nation within a nation with a right to lead their existence as distinct from the English-speaking community around them as their own German fatherland had been distinct from England."[7]

Nationalism promoted ecumenical ties, forging a bond of solidarity among Germans of all faiths. Early in 1788 the Germans laid the foundation stone for their new church. None of the local Irish clergy from St. Mary's deigned to attend, but German priests from mission stations in the west made the long journey to Philadelphia for the event, and "a large number of German Roman Catholic men, as well as German citizens of other religions, assembled to break ground for the new German Roman Catholic church." Lutherans, in particular, contributed money and labor to the project.[8]

Philadelphia's German Catholics fused nationalist aspirations with liberal principles, producing what one scholar has called "civil nationalism." In all their actions the German Society scrupulously observed democratic forms. They validated their decision to found a separate church through electoral procedures, and their charter of incorporation placed control of the temporalities of the church in the hands of annually elected trustees. When the Germans tried to secure a pastor for their church, they again resorted to democratic means. The trustees proposed three candidates to the congregation who then chose among them. The trustees then informed John Carroll that

> In consequence of the Election of a pastor for the most Holy Trinity Church. . . . Rev. John Carol Helbron was duly chosen by the large majority of the Votes . . . , and we the Subscribers do hereby impower the said Rev. John Carol Helbron to present Himself to the Right Rev. John Carol [sic] for his further approbation.[9]

Time and again the Germans expressed indignation at the arbitrary nature of authority relationships within St. Mary's Church, which was dominated by a conservative clergy and a small coterie of wealthy laymen. The Germans refused to accept direction from men such as these. Patrick Smith, a visiting Irish priest, observed that they would not "submit to what they called the obsolete remains of European barbarism and the blustering dictates of injustice and partiality." "The Germans may be led," Smith wrote, "but they cannot be easily driven." He declared that, "of all countries, America is not the theatre for exercising with impunity coercion or tyrannical measures."[10]

These Germans were not, as Philip Gleason would have it, "conservative reformers." Rather, they embraced a species of republican thought that located ultimate authority within the individual and held that institutional authority derived from the consent of the people collectively expressed through regular elections. This emphasis on popular sovereignty was a common element in early nationalist thought throughout the West, but within the context of contemporary Catholicism it was a radical proposition and it contrasts dramatically with the dominant variant of American Catholic republicanism.[11]

Historians have noted the development of a "republican style" among English and American Catholics that derived from their long experience as a minority group in hostile Protestant cultures. Facing constant pressure from religious antagonists, many Catholics became ostentatiously patriotic and supportive of the dominant civil culture and developed a firm attachment to certain republican principles such as religious toleration, constitutional limits on arbitrary power, and a strict separation of church and state. This conservative, corporate republicanism (which found broad acceptance within the Catholic elite) was ultimately incompatible with the liberal republicanism emerging among Philadelphia's German immigrants.[12]

The Germans' initial petition to John Carroll, asking permission to build their church, began with a reference to "the late glorious revolution in this part of the globe [by which] Heaven has blessed with liberty and free and uninterrupted exercise . . . our most holy religion." Similar paeans to American freedoms sounded through many of their subsequent statements. To these Catholic liberals America was a special place, one in which their hopes, born out of the European Enlightenment, could find fulfillment. In Patrick Carey's words, America was "an open arena—an arena . . . that never really existed in Catholic Europe—for putting Enlightenment principles into practice." Unlike the defensive patriotism of the Anglo-American Catholic elite, the Germans' enthusiasm for America grew out of their hopes, not their apprehensions.[13]

Holy Trinity's Germans sought canonical justification for their liberal principles. John Helbron advanced the argument that the practice of *jus patronatus* (by which lay patrons who had secured land, built a church, and ensured financial support for the clergy, were allowed to nominate or present to their ecclesiastical superiors the name of a pastor to preside at that church) supported the principle of popular sovereignty. This right of presentation was widely recognized in European Catholicism, but there it had commonly been granted to royalty, aristocrats, governmental officials, or town corporations. In Philadelphia the right was being claimed on behalf of a democratically organized association of private citizens. Such "immediate lay involvement as a consequence of newfangled democratic forms," as James Hennesey has noted, was "beyond [the] comprehension" of both Roman and American ecclesiastical authorities.[14]

In response to Helbron's arguments John Carroll explained that, in his view, Philadelphia's Germans were not entitled to the right of presentation because, "in the country of your forefathers, there are very few instances, if any, of [the right of appointment] being in the hands of the people at large." He warned the Philadelphia dissenters against trying to "fix" the right in such a manner. "I desire that a priest be established for the Church of the Most Holy Trinity," Carroll wrote, hoping to end the discussion, "but according to ancient custom and agreement made with me. Beseech the omnipotent God that all things be done rightly and in order."[15]

In this early stage of the conflict moderation prevailed on all sides. Holy Trinity's dissenters were republicans but not radicals. They criticized the monarchic traditions of the Church, but at the same time they repeatedly asserted that they intended to "make no schism." Instead they sought sanction within the canons of the Church for their actions and positions. In their own minds Holy Trinity's Germans were good Catholics seeking merely to defend their rights against the exercise of arbitrary authority. They sought some accommodation between the paternalistic, authoritarian traditions of the Church and their liberal principles.

John Carroll's stance toward the Germans was also moderate. He did not directly object to "the election of pastors" so long as he controlled the selection process. He was quite willing to concede to the congregation the right to choose among clerics approved and presented by him, but reserved to himself the right to select appropriate clergy for all the churches of the American mission. Carroll's position was authoritarian (grounded in the tradition of "apostolic succession") but it was a flexible, moderate, and paternalistic authoritarianism that sought to accommodate, at least in some small way, the liberal sensibilities of the laity.[16]

Carroll was even more willing to indulge the Germans' nationalism. He seems to have had no qualms about granting them permission to erect their own church where they could worship in the manner customary in their homeland. For many years prior to 1788 Carroll had insisted that the international Church must accommodate itself to the cultural tendencies of the various nationalities it embraced and had advanced such arguments in support of his pleas for an indigenous American hierarchy. Now he was extending this general principle to the level of parish government. Just as the peoples of Europe were accorded national church establishments, so were they to be permitted in America to found nationality parishes. The church that Philadelphia's Germans built—Holy Trinity—was the first of these.

Still, Carroll was determined that the controversy should come to an end. In the spring of 1788 he warned the Germans that "the authors of dissensions & sowers of discontent between Pastors & their flock have always been punished by the Church with exemplary Severity, And I should be wanting in my duty, If I did not let her censures fall on them." The superior's warning did not deter John Helbron and the German Society. On November 1, 1789, they announced that Holy Trinity would open in three weeks even without Carroll's sanction. John Helbron declared that he was leaving his mission station for Philadelphia and would take up pastoral duties at Holy Trinity on authority from the general of his order (the Capuchin friars). The young priest did not see this as an act of defiance. Helbron wrote to assure Carroll that he would "never . . . be anywhere placed as an officiating Clergyman without submission & dependence to the Ecclesiastical Superiority," but he also made it clear that he did not recognize the superior of the mission as the proper authority and hinted that if faculties were not soon forthcoming he would "procure me others by way of rome [sic] which I know very well."[17]

John Carroll, seeing danger in the situation, denounced the Germans' "sinful practices . . . so destructive of our religion." No peril was greater, in his eyes, than that posed by John Helbron's attempt to invoke the authority of the superior of his order as an alternative to that of the superior of the mission. To understand Carroll's apprehension, we must briefly recount the profound changes that were taking place in the American church in the last decades of the eighteenth century.[18]

"A Select Body of Clergy"

Throughout the colonial era the American mission had been almost exclusively a Jesuit preserve. The small band of missionaries had become accustomed to ordering their own affairs without much interference from Rome or from members of other religious orders. This arrangement survived the crisis of 1773 when Pope Clement XIV issued the papal brief *Dominus ac redemptor noster,* which suppressed the Jesuits and ordered bishops to assume control of the order's properties in the name of the Holy See. The edict officially placed the American [ex-]Jesuits under the control of the vicar apostolic of the London district, but he had little interest in governing the colonial mission. Instead he appointed the former provincial of the Jesuits as his vicar for "the management of our affairs in North America," and so the American missionaries "remained in their own places and offices . . . , and they continued their manner of life, with the single change of the office of Provincial into that of Vicar General."[1]

After the American Revolution secular clergy and members of other religious orders began to enter the American mission, often traveling on the instructions of their superiors. In the five years prior to 1790 thirty priests took up residence in America; only seven were former Jesuits. These new missionaries complained incessantly about the ex-Jesuit hegemony they encountered and these grievances, real or imagined, came to inform lay protests of the period. "As soon as [conflicts emerge]" John Carroll lamented, they "bring in Jesuitism, & to suggest, that everything is calculated by me for its restoration; & that I sacrifice the real interests of Religion to the chimerical project of reviving it." Carroll's decision to allow St. Mary's Germans to form a separate congregation and to erect their own church was itself largely due to his fear that opposition on his part might "spread the flames of discontent; & . . . raise a clamour, [to the effect] that the Jesuits were determined no churches should be erected, but by their direction." In 1790 the Prefect of the Sacred Congregation for the Propagation of the Faith (*Propaganda Fide*), responding to complaints about the ex-Jesuits, demanded that Carroll employ more priests on the mission who had never been members of the Society of Jesus.[2]

The prefect's communiqué marked an increasing interest in American affairs. As a mission territory the Church in the United States fell under the purview of Propaganda, which in theory wielded almost unlimited authority over the mission; "its decrees had the force of apostolic constitutions and were to be observed inviolably by all persons." In practice the Sacred Congregation's control was far from absolute and had been almost nonexistent prior to 1750. This began to change in 1757 when Pope Benedict XIV issued a decree giving the vicar apostolic of the London district faculties over "all the colonies and islands in America subject to the British Empire." At the same time Propaganda began to request information on the state of the Church in the American colonies.[3]

The mission clergy saw Propaganda's interest as a threat. Not only were they accustomed to "operating more or less independently of episcopal control, and in considerable isolation from Rome," but they also saw Propaganda as hostile to the interests of their society. In response to Rome's inquiries they orchestrated a flurry of cautionary missives from clergymen and lay leaders predicting dire consequences if the Holy See were to attempt to establish its authority in America. They warned that any evidence of Roman interest in the colonies would provoke Protestant opposition and declared that Americans would never tolerate a foreign bishop, especially an agent of Rome, in their midst. The effort was sufficient to convince the vicar apostolic that the American clergy's antipathy to Roman direction would not be easily overcome. "I believe I never told you," he wrote, "how much those gentlemen [the Jesuits] were alarmed, upon hearing the first rumour of a

B[isho]p being designed for North America; and what opposition and subscriptions they procured from the laity there." He concluded that "it will be no easy matter to place a Bishop there."[4]

The suppression of the Society of Jesus in 1773 marked a turning point in the relations between Propaganda and the American clergy. Although the American ex-Jesuits managed for some time to maintain their community and to fend off interference from Rome, their position became more dire with every year that passed. There were too few ex-Jesuits (no more than two dozen in all) remaining in America to meet the needs of the new nation's growing and widely dispersed Catholic population, and no help was coming from Europe. For ten years after John Carroll's return to Maryland, no ex-Jesuits entered the mission. "We are all growing old," Joseph Mosely complained in 1784, "we are very weak handed, few come from England to help us." John Carroll was alarmed. "If they could promise themselves immortality it would be well enough," he wrote, but since the mission priests were mortal, some "form of administration" would be needed "to secure to posterity a succession of Catholic Clergymen, and to secure to these a comfortable subsistence." He determined to do something about the situation.[5]

In June 1783 six of the American missionaries met at Whitemarsh plantation near Baltimore to adopt a "Plan of Organization" that would "put the clergy's affairs on a systematic basis." They adopted a scheme, drafted by John Carroll, that established rules and an administrative framework for what had been an informal community of clergymen. The confreres then adjourned to secure approval for their actions from the rest of the American clergy and agreed to meet again in November. Soon thereafter word arrived that the prefect of Propaganda had initiated negotiations through the papal nuncio at Versailles aimed at placing a representative of Rome at the head of the American church.[6]

The nuncio approached the American minister at Versailles, Benjamin Franklin, and asked him to sound out Congress on the matter. Franklin welcomed the suggestion, seeing in it a way to sever the administrative link between the American clergy and London. Congress responded to the proposal with indifference, indicating that while there was no objection to the establishment of a bishop in America, neither could the government grant permission for such an appointment because "purely spiritual" matters fell outside their jurisdiction.[7]

Propaganda's communications with Congress infuriated the priests on the American mission. They saw the fact that they had not been consulted as proof of "the aversion to the remains of the Society [of Jesus]" that presumably prevailed at Rome. "No authority derived from the Propa[gan]da. will ever be admitted here," John Carroll wrote defiantly. "The Catholick Clergy and Laity here know that the only connexion they ought to have with Rome is to acknowledge the Pope as Spr[itua]l. head of the Church." He continued, "no Congregations . . . shall be allowed to exercise any share of his Spr[itua]l. authority here; [and] no Bishop Vicar Apostolical shall be admitted." If, as seemed inevitable, America should have a bishop, it would not be one sent from Rome, "but an ordinary national Bishop [not a vicar apostolic], in whose appointment Rome shall have no share."[8]

This extraordinary declaration of independence from Rome, inspired by concern for the future of the ex-Jesuit community, drew upon the example of European national churches which in the eighteenth century had operated with little concern for Roman opinion or policy. However, the American mission was not a well-established national church backed by secular power and it was highly unlikely that the Holy See would grant permission to form a national hierarchy independent of the Propaganda. Therefore the ex-Jesuits cast around for some other means of preserving their independence.

In November 1783 the Whitemarsh meeting reconvened and immediately took measures to block Propaganda. They elected John Lewis, the last Jesuit superior, as their spiritual superior and petitioned the Holy See to grant him limited episcopal faculties so that he might in turn grant faculties to clergy newly arrived in the United States. In this way they hoped to forestall any episcopal appointment originating in Propaganda. They also drew up a memorial to Rome making it clear that the American clergy could not accept the spiritual jurisdiction of a bishop or vicar from a foreign state. Of more immediate concern, though, was the disposition of property upon which they depended for their subsistence. In Europe ex-Jesuit properties were being taken over by bishops and it was feared that Propaganda would attempt to seize the order's American properties. John Carroll was determined that if any emissaries of the Propaganda should come to the United States they would, "certainly return empty-handed." Therefore the loose community of American missionaries was reconstituted as a "Select Body of Clergy" that could legally hold and transfer property until such time as the Society of Jesus could be reinstated.[9]

Early in 1784 Cardinal Antonelli, the prefect of Propaganda, acting on the advice of Benjamin Franklin, made a brilliant tactical decision. John Carroll had been the most prominent of Propaganda's foes within the American clergy, so Antonelli petitioned Pope Pius VI to have Carroll appointed superior of the American mission with authority deriving from the Propaganda. The appointment was made on June 9, 1784, and a promise was communicated through private channels that, should matters proceed to Propaganda's satisfaction, Carroll would be elevated to the episcopacy. Yet another private communication hinted that should Carroll refuse the appointment a French bishop would be selected to administer the American mission.[10]

John Carroll was of a mind to refuse the appointment, but first he wished to confer with other members of the American clergy. Their opinions varied. Some were encouraged by the fact that they would be ruled by one of their own, but Leonard Neale saw Carroll's appointment as part of a grand conspiracy on the part of Propaganda to establish, "its infernal influence in this part of the world." Neale agreed with Carroll that, "the S[acre]d. Cong[regati].on ought to be effectively checked in its scheming drift." He disagreed, however, as to the best way to accomplish this.

John Carroll saw the appointment as the first stage in the development of a national church. "To govern the spiritual concerns of this country as a mission is absurd," he argued. The American episcopacy should be granted "jurisdiction ordinary" like that exercised by any other national church. If that were to happen, he wrote, Propaganda would no longer be able to claim any authority over American clergy and the ex-Jesuit community could maintain its independence. Neale, however, felt that if the missionaries were reconstituted into a "National Clergy" their properties might become attached to the national church and would not revert to the society in case of its restoration. Discussions continued through the fall of 1784, and finally on February 17, 1785, nearly four months after he had received official notification of his appointment, John Carroll accepted the post of superior of the American mission and with it not just the leadership of the ex-Jesuit community but also responsibility for all aspects of the American church.[12]

By 1784 many ex-Jesuits had become convinced that only a bishop, properly invested with full episcopal powers, could safeguard their position. However they feared that a bishop chosen by Propaganda might be hostile to their interests and so they were determined to control any such appointment. Late in that year John Carroll sent a circular letter to other members of the American clergy so they could coordinate their communications with Rome and speak with a "most perfect unanimity." In it he laid out the essentials of the argument he planned to advance for placing an American bishop at the head of a national church establishment.[13]

Carroll argued that the American church was not a mission, although the Holy See had designated it as such. "We form," he wrote, "not a fluctuating body of laborers in Christ's vineyard, sent hither and removable at the will of a Superior, but a permanent body of national clergy, with sufficient powers to form our own system of internal government." As a national church, he wrote, the American clergy would not only be free from Propaganda control, but would be able "to choose our own superior [who would be] regularly and canonically chosen by us." "We shall in a few years," he wrote, "stand in absolute need of a Bishop," but he argued, raising once again the bogey of Protestant intolerance, a "Bishop Vicar-Apostolic" (one appointed by and responsible to Rome) would be unacceptable. Rather, "he must be a diocesan Bishop, and his appointment must come neither from his Holiness . . . nor from the Assemblies or different Executives . . . but he should be chosen by the Catholic clergy themselves."[14]

Carroll elaborated these arguments in a subsequent letter to the prefect of Propaganda. He sketched a frightening picture of an embattled Catholic minority barely tolerated by hostile Protestants. "How long we are to enjoy the benefits of toleration and or equal rights," he wrote. "I would not dare to assert. . . . Many of our people . . . fear, that we shall be absolutely excluded from officeholding." He then went on to say that reports that the Propaganda might establish a representative in the United States "filled us with . . . some fear" because Protestants would never allow such an intrusion. He argued that a bishop might be tolerated, but only if the Holy See permitted "the priests who have labored for so many years in this vineyard of the Lord to propose . . . the one whom they deem most fit," would it be possible to allay the "bad feeling" that would otherwise be "excited among the people of this country, Catholic and Protestant."[15]

There are several levels of irony here. John Carroll was seeking to gain for the American clergy the right to elect their ecclesiastical superiors while at the same time he was denying that right to the Catholic laity. He was arguing that the special conditions that prevailed in America justified the abrogation of traditional practices and authority relationships while at the same time he asserted the inviolability of ancient custom. Most significantly, in his efforts as superior of the mission to quell dissent, Carroll was invoking authority derived from Propaganda, the very power he had earlier declared would never be tolerated in America. John Carroll's efforts to create an American national church should be seen as a desperate attempt to resolve these difficulties and ambiguities. He was trying to preserve the integrity of the ex-Jesuit community in America in the face of domestic assailants within the church while at the same time attempting to insure that they would not fall under the dominion of their adversaries in Rome. His only hope, it seemed, was that he, or some other ex-Jesuit, would be allowed to exercise full episcopal authority in America without interference from Propaganda.[16]

In the fall of 1786 the ex-Jesuits met again at Whitemarsh Plantation. The meeting had originally been scheduled for the fall of 1787 but was advanced a year because "Clergymen not of our Body are coming to America. . . . These, as part of the American Clergy, will have an equal right to participate in the ecclesiastical government. Can we tell how soon they may be here in sufficient number to carry measures contrary to our wishes. . . ." The confreres appointed a committee to draft a petition to be sent to Rome asking that the American clergy be allowed to elect a bishop who would serve immediately, subject to the Holy See.[17]

If Rome had approved this plan the American mission would have become the national church that John Carroll envisioned. Instead the Holy See gave permission for the American clergy, "as a special favor and for this first time," to elect one of their own to serve as bishop but refused to allow the mission to be reconstituted as a national church. At Whitemarsh on May 18, 1789, John Carroll was overwhelmingly elected to occupy the new episcopal see. His charge from Rome was to carefully watch for abuses, to make sure that no clergy performed sacred functions without his permission, and to "take care lest quarrels and dissensions may arise from the diversity of character and disposition which generally exists" in a pluralistic institution. Above all, Propaganda urged Carroll to "Impose not lightly hands on any man: but enlist amongst the Clergy only such as have given proof of piety and learning in the Seminary."[18]

"The Preservation of Discipline"

On November 6, 1789, John Carroll received official notice of his appointment as bishop of Baltimore. He had sought enhanced authority in order to counter the cultural, ideological, and institutional pressures that were fragmenting America's Catholic community. Now he moved to assert that authority. When he heard of John Helbron's arrival at Holy Trinity the bishop-elect warned that he "should be wanting to [his] most sacred duty," if he "allowed the intended encroachments, on [his] right of office." Carroll then revoked the priest's faculties in Philadelphia or within ten miles of the city. Undaunted, Helbron presided over the opening of Holy Trinity for divine service on November 22, 1789.[1]

It was a grand event, celebrated "with the greatest solemnity with vocal and instrumental music, to the admiration of a large throng of people," and it bore witness to the ecumenical spirit of the age. Many of the city's most prominent Protestant leaders were present, including several members of Congress, the governor of Pennsylvania, and most of the members of the State Assembly. Notably absent were the "English Roman Catholic clergy & those of Irish descent," from St. Mary's church; their continuing hostility toward the Germans was formally noted and recorded "in everlasting remembrance."[2]

Carroll responded to Helbron's impudence with a flurry of correspondence in which he accused the Capuchin of deserting his congregation at Lancaster, of bearing false witness against and showing contempt for the jurisdiction of his superior, and of bringing rebellion. He threatened to impose "a grave censure" on the refractory priest and demanded from him a public acknowledgment "that no authority belongs to him or to other priests . . . , unless and in so far as they shall have been approved by an Ecclesiastical Superior, whom the Holy See has designated." From the trustees of Holy Trinity he demanded explicit acknowledgment that the right of patronage devolves "from the judgment of the Superior himself." He revoked Helbron's clerical faculties entirely and notified the congregation that he had done so in the interests of "lawful administration," the "preservation of discipline," and the "tranquillity of the consciences of the faithful." He warned them that anyone participating in illegal services would incur a "heavy guilt."[3]

The Germans refused to submit and John Helbron continued to preside over services at Holy Trinity "on the sole appointment of the Trustees of the church." He also threatened to communicate directly with the Holy See to express objections to Carroll's impending elevation to the episcopacy. This threat brought the bishop-elect north to Philadelphia where he confronted Helbron face-to-face behind closed doors. A deal was struck. Two days later at a meeting of the trustees Helbron suggested that "it was better to leave and renounce the Right of patronage to the Right Reverend John Carroll."[4]

Although their pastor was prepared to submit, the lay leaders of Holy Trinity were not. "We cannot" they wrote, "under any consideration cede [this] Right [of Patronage] so graciously granted by our Dear Mother [the Church] in promoting religion in particular in this Country." They listed their conditions for resolving the conflict. They demanded that bishop-elect Carroll and the clergy at St. Mary's publicly retract the various denunciations and slanders they had directed against the dissenters, that Carroll treat John Helbron with respect and kindness, and that he publicly declare "that the differences in Philadelphia were settled." In exchange they offered a general acknowledgment of "the authority of the holy Church" and also "the superiority of the R. R. Mr. Carroll."[5]

John Carroll chose to ignore the implicit challenge to his prerogatives contained in the trustees' demands and instead focused his attention on John Helbron, from whom he continued to require "explicit acknowledgment . . . in writing" that "you cannot exercise any parochial functions till I restore your faculties." This was a crucial point that Carroll could not concede if he was to exercise any authority over the mission clergy. Until it was settled no agreement could be reached on anything. John Helbron was agreeable but he worried about the reaction of the laity. "For God's sake," he advised Carroll, "refrain from saying things which scandalize the people and make them angry." Ultimately he and Carroll agreed to simply ignore the pretensions of the laity and to make peace between themselves.[6]

On the penultimate day of 1789 John Helbron formally capitulated and signed a paper stating that "I acknowledge that neither I nor any other Catholic clergyman in the United States can lawfully administer the Sacraments, preach or perform any parochial function but inasmuch as we are approved by the ecclesiastical Superior whereof." This satisfied the bishop-elect and he immediately confirmed John Helbron as pastor at Holy Trinity. Helbron read the letter of submission from the pulpit of Holy Trinity Church on Epiphany Sunday, January 6, 1790, before the full congregation and its elected trustees as well as several prominent Protestant observers. John Carroll then delivered a sermon on the discipline of the Church and on the necessity of obedience to ecclesiastical superiors. "The matter," he declared, was "closed."[7]

Of course the conflict was not resolved; it was merely deferred. A temporary peace had been restored by the reluctance of all concerned to push matters to a conclusion. Soon both John Carroll and the congregation were preoccupied with other matters and quiet descended over Holy Trinity. The calm, however, was deceptive. The agreement that had been concluded between John Helbron and bishop-elect Carroll left essential matters of principle unaddressed and generated no understanding specifying the prerogatives of the prelate and the rights of the laity. This was a fatal flaw. Any settlement among the clergy that did not take the laity's feelings and aspirations into account could only be temporary.

"Martyr to the Faith"

John Carroll and his antagonists held fundamentally different views of human nature. Despite his republican sympathies, bishop-elect Carroll represented a monarchic institution that was firmly rooted in the *ancien régime* and based its authority in the sanctity of tradition. Carroll was not an autocrat who exercised arbitrary authority—he made some effort to accommodate the sensibilities of the laity and sought to promote collegial relationships with the clergy he directed— but his benevolent paternalism was no less authoritarian for all of that. Carroll had little faith in the capacity of common people to govern themselves. Dissenting layman he considered to be ignorant and erring children in need of instruction and patience, and like children they could not be entrusted with effective power.[1]

Carroll's paternalism was appropriate to a world of patriarchy, hierarchy, and dependency. In that world common people were dependent upon the wisdom, the patronage, and the social leadership of their betters—a hereditary aristocracy. Because they were dependents, common people were assumed to have "no wills of their own, . . . like children they had no political personalities and could rightfully be excluded from participation in public life." The American Revolution, while it had assaulted monarchy and hereditary privilege, had not supplanted this traditional view of society. Many revolutionaries simply substituted for monarchy and ascriptive authority a model of society in which deference was accorded men of conspicuous talent and virtue. In this classical republicanism the role played by common people was restricted and reactive. They were to be jealous guardians of their rights, and their voice should be heard, but authority and responsibility for the direction of society flowed downward from an independent, meritocratic, and paternalistic elite.[2]

John Carroll shared these sensibilities. He embraced "a conservative Federalism committed to the acceptance of religious pluralism but conscious of the need for an aristocracy of virtue and an insistence on the institutions of religion." As a bishop of the Church his view was necessarily hierarchical and informed by patriarchal paternalism. From his clergy Carroll demanded submission and obedience, but he could discount the views and demands of laymen because they in effect had "no political personalities."[3]

None of this placed him outside the major themes of American civil discourse. There was little difference between Carroll's attitude toward Philadelphia's German Catholics and the High Federalist perspective on political movements that sought to gain a voice for common people. When John Helbron submitted to his authority, it was possible for John Carroll to hope that the problems at Holy Trinity were "closed," just as many Federalists hoped that the Federal Constitution of 1789 and George Washington's assumption of the presidency had made of discordant America a classical republic of virtue. Events were soon to disappoint all such hopes.

Benevolent paternalism was not to be the order of the day. In the last decades of the eighteenth century democratic movements throughout the West challenged hierarchical institutions and the traditions on which they were based. In America these imperatives were identified with anti-federalism and Jeffersonian republicanism; in Europe they were associated with revolutionary French republicanism. The immigrants at Holy Trinity, living in the capital of the new republic and carrying memories of their homelands, were influenced by both of these. Steadily through the early years of the decade events both at home and abroad eroded the tenuous peace negotiated by John Helbron and Bishop Carroll and ultimately precipitated a second round of confrontations that raised passions to a new level.

The French Revolution of 1789 was at first universally acclaimed by Americans, who saw in it a reflection of their own revolutionary experience. None was more enthusiastic than John Helbron. So inspired was he by the course of events in France that he decided to participate in them directly. In the fall of 1791 he set sail for Spain and from there traveled north to Bayonne. There he took an oath of submission to the civil authority of the state and was "elected by common votes" *curé* of the *commune d'Anglet*.[4]

James Oellers, a native of Aix-la-Chapelle and the "guiding light" of Holy Trinity's congregation, was also an unabashed Francophile. His hotel, much favored by political figures, catered specifically to republican sensibilities. His assembly hall ("papered after the French taste, with the Pantheon figures in compartments") became a gathering place for Philadelphia's French *émigrés*. Moreau de St. Méry considered it to be the "most beautiful and most comfortable" lodgings in the entire United States; Henry Wansey wrote of meeting Tallyrand there; Edmund Genet was feted there; and the French Republican Society met there regularly.[5]

Philadelphia was a haven for French refugees and political exiles. Henry Wansey estimated in 1794 that one Philadelphian in ten was French and the Comte de Moré met so many of his countrymen there that he felt he was residing in the "French Noah's Ark." In Philadelphia the emigrés began to reconstruct the society they had left behind, complete with its social divisions and political conflicts. Republicans walked the streets attired in pantaloons, laced shoes, and close-cropped hair; royalists wore the full powdered wig, the cocked hat, short clothes, silver shoe buckles, and carried gold-headed canes. The émigré elite joined fraternal societies such as the Société Française de Bienfaisance de Philadelphie and the Société des Grivois. There were also Masonic lodges such as La Parfaite Union and La Reconnaisance. Political conservatives gathered informally but regularly at a bookstore owned by Moreau de St. Méry, the former president of the Paris commune; moderates associated with the Colons de Saint Dominque refugées Aux Etats-Unis, while local Jacobins created the "active and troublesome" Société Français des Amis de la Liberté et de l'Egalité.[6]

While the émigré elite attended St. Mary's and anticlerical radicals erected "altars of freedom," many French Catholics also worshiped at Holy Trinity. By November of 1793 so many French were attending services that a French-speaking priest was appointed to assist the German pastor. Henceforth, even when the preaching was in German, services at Holy Trinity conformed far more to French custom than did those at St. Mary's. The French Revolution thus had a profound impact on Holy Trinity's congregation. Nearly everything changed—the clerical leadership, the ethnic composition of the congregation, even the character of devotions.[7]

John Carroll found the presence of the émigrés disturbing. Writing of the French in Baltimore, he complained "They are everywhere a scandal to Religion . . . , they disseminate, as much as they can, all the principles of irreligion, of contempt for the church." "I find the Emigrants [from France]," he wrote, "uncorrected by the severe afflictions [they have suffered]. . . . Religious principles appear to have never had the least hold of their hearts."[8]

The thought that French radicalism might spread to America terrified Carroll. Like other Federalists, he drew a sharp distinction between "republicanism," which preserved the rule of talented and virtuous men, and "democracy," which he equated with mob rule. He looked to George Washington (whose conservative, pragmatic approach to government he contrasted to that of "the French Theorists") for protection against "the sowers of sedition & wild democracy." "We are threatened here," he wrote in 1793, "with the dissemination of French political errors . . . , and it requires all the firmness and integrity of our great President Washington and the persons acting under him, to withstand the torrent [of infatuation]."[9]

John Carroll strongly disapproved of the "reigning spirit amongst the people" which was "a spirit of independence not only of unlawful . . . but of all authority." He felt that the French experiment in republicanism was a "lamentable catastrophe," and wholeheartedly agreed with Edmund Burke's condemnation of the revolution, particularly with his descriptions of the savagery of the mob. But Carroll was no apologist for Europe's ancien régime. He was critical of both secular and ecclesiastical absolutism, considering them to be inherently unjust and out of step with the "temper of the age." He felt that persons raised under absolutism, never having experienced liberty, were particularly unprepared to exercise a franchise. This, he surmised, was the reason for the failure of French republicanism. "When a person, especially a Frenchman, born under an absolute Government," he wrote, "had got his head full of the sentiments of an English Whig, he is sure to extend them, & push them to excess."[10]

John Carroll's revulsion at the course of events in France placed him in illustrious company. Through the 1790s many prominent Americans, alarmed by the decline of classical republican standards and the rise of democratic sentiment, blamed the French Revolution for all that was wrong with America. Some Federalists displayed an almost hysterical fear that Jacobin principles were infecting America. It would be better that the United States be "erased from existence," Oliver Wolcott, Jr., proclaimed, "than infected with French principles." As in so many other things, then, Carroll's perspectives on the revolution in France and its implications for the Americal republic were not greatly different from those expressed by other Americans of his class and temperament.[11]

There was, however, a distinctively Catholic slant to Carroll's criticism of the French republic, for it was the Catholic Church that felt the brunt of radical rage. Carroll was dismayed by the republic's anticlericalism, which he considered to be a violation of "those rights of spiritual jurisdiction, which being derived from God, and not from men, are not within the competency of any authority merely human." There were good reasons for Carroll's concern. These were illustrated by John Helbron's experience in revolutionary France.[12]

From the beginning the French Revolution had tended toward extreme anticlericalism. One of the first acts of the Constituent Assembly had been to abolish the tithe. Then followed the confiscation of church lands and the suppression of religious orders. Finally, on July 12, 1790, the Civil Constitution of the Clergy reorganized church administration within France, made bishops and other Catholic clergy state employees, and provided for the election and appointment of bishops and priests without prior confirmation by the pope. All this was followed, in the last months of that year, by decrees demanding that all clergymen take the same oath of loyalty to the state required of other civil servants. By the end of 1790 the subordination of church to state was complete and the secular state had assumed all responsibility for ecclesiastical activities in France.[13]

Rome, of course, condemned the Civil Constitution of the Clergy and many French priests refused to take an oath of loyalty. The "November Decrees" of 1791 (issued even as John Helbron was making his way across the Atlantic) declared these refractory priests to be enemies of the state. Thereafter they were subjected to systematic persecution. At first, upon his arrival in France, John Helbron was protected by his status as a "constitutional priest" (one who had taken the oath of loyalty), but in 1792 successive revolutionary regimes imposed ever more stringent restraints on the clergy. In an orgy of anticlerical fervor, huge threatening demonstrations became common, clergymen were massacred by mobs, and thousands were forced to flee the country.

In 1793 the anticlerical impulse reached its peak when the Jacobin leadership instituted a program of "dechristianization" calculated to erase all vestiges of clerical influence in France. The state assumed traditional church functions such as marriage, divorce, and the keeping of civil registers; a republican calendar was constructed in which Sundays were eliminated and purely secular feast days introduced; throughout France churches were closed or torn down, liturgical equipment was looted, and thousands of priests were imprisoned or executed. During the height of this terror John Helbron was ordered by local authorities to close his church. He refused to do so and on November 24, 1793, he was arrested, tried before the local Committee of Vigilance, and promptly guillotined. The Church in France today considers him to be a martyr to the faith.[14]

"The Eye of an Eagle"

John Carroll's political and cultural perspectives were well within the mainstream of American opinion. The same could be said of his antagonists. Holy Trinity's liberals were anything but radicals. In revolutionary France the "will of the people" became the active principle of government, producing a totalitarian variant of republicanism that made popular sovereignty an instrument of repression. By contrast, while American democratic republicans in the late eighteenth century located ultimate decision-making authority in "the people," they did so primarily as a defense against corrupt and arbitrary rule. Rather than directing the government, "the people" in America stood as a check on the abuse of authority. This was certainly the understanding of Holy Trinity's congregation. They did not seek to displace traditional authorities but insisted that the people must check their power.[1]

In the spring of 1793 enthusiasm for the French republic reached a fever pitch in Philadelphia. Demonstrators singing "Ça Ira!" and the "Marseillaise," wearing "liberty caps" and dancing the Carmagnole took to the streets of the city to protest the administration's policy of neutrality. The tricolor republican cockade was everywhere on display. Even the governor and the chief justice of Pennsylvania found it expedient to adopt the title "Citizen." "Ten thousand people in the streets of Philadelphia," John Adams wrote, "day after day threatened to drag Washington out of his house and effect a revolution in the government, or compel it to declare war in favor of the French Revolution and against England." In the midst of this excitement Republican clubs emerged, ominously reminding some of the Jacobin clubs of revolutionary France.[2]

On May 2, 1793 the French frigate *L'Ambuscade*, "armed to defend the rights of men," bearing liberty caps on its foremast and figurehead, came into port. Joyous mobs took to the streets and guns on Market Street wharf fired a salute. She carried word that Edmund Genet, envoy of the French republic, would soon arrive in the Federal City. Two weeks later "Citizen" Genet entered Philadelphia to the cheers of "a great concourse of citizens," that "flocked from every avenue of the city." That night a public meeting of the citizenry chose a committee of leading citizens to organize a proper round of greetings for the French envoy.[3]

Immigrants were prominent in the demonstrations that attended Genet's mission. Among the groups that first met in the spring of 1793 were the French Patriotic Society (comprising "friends of liberty and equality" in Philadelphia) and the German Republican Society (founded to "give that attention and exertion as is necessary to the preservation of civil liberty"). A deputation from the French society met with Genet one day after he arrived and on the following day the German republicans appeared with him to proclaim that "the sovereignty of the people [is] the only security for general liberty and happiness." That night the French Patriots held a "republican dinner" for the envoy at Oellers'.[4]

The liberalism of Holy Trinity's immigrants was not out of place in this republican milieu. Their stubborn refusal to cede what they perceived to be their rights, their suspicion of constituted authority, and their attachment to popular sovereignty were not unlike the protestations of Philadelphia's German republicans who vowed to watch, "with the eye of an eagle to prevent those abuses which never fail to arise from a want of vigilence"; abuses that rose, they said, from "a disposition in the human mind to tyrannize when cloathed with power." In the excitement of those times liberals of every stripe—Germans and Frenchmen, immigrants and Americans, Protestants and Catholics—spoke a common language of civic virtue, liberty, and the equality of man.[5]

In both liberal and conservative forms, then, Catholic republicans articulated values consonant with important elements of American civil culture. The same could not be said for those Catholic clergymen (many of them refugees from revolutionary Europe) who held republicanism in contempt. A substantial number of Catholic clergymen considered lay dissenters to be

> deceivers, drunkards . . . men with little social standing . . . ; poor, simple uneducated men . . . ; wild republicans [who] professed a "fatal [and iniquitous] democracy" . . . ; "an insane and bloody mob of Jacobins" . . . ; only nominal Catholics . . . ; Free Masons . . . deists, Universalists [and] infidels . . . ; "men of the Voltaire school" . . . ; "theoretical lay rebels" . . . ; "thoroughly Gallican" . . . ; [or] devoted disciples of heterodox European Catholics like Justinus Febronius and Paolo Sarpi.[6]

Here was no compromise with republicanism. These churchmen had no significant analogue within the mainstream of American thought, for they repudiated fundamental aspects of the nation's civil culture.When men such as these intruded into Holy Trinity's affairs the tenuous peace negotiated by John Helbron and his superior dissolved into open schism.

After John Helbron's departure from Philadelphia, his elder brother, Peter, became pastor at Holy Trinity. A former chaplain in the Prussian army, Peter Helbron had an authoritarian personality and despised republican innovations. A contemporary described him as "a man of culture and refinement, punctiliously neat and precise in his priestly attire . . . ; sitting on his horse with a military grace and repose." He was less attentive to his duties, though, than to his appearance. On occasion he allowed parishioners to die without administering sacraments, "even though called for repeatedly." Sometimes he disappeared for weeks, taking his gun and hunting hounds, leaving the church in the care of English-speaking priests who could not be understood by some of the congregation. The Germans were clearly dissatisfied with their author- itarian and inattentive pastor, but nothing could be done because, for all his faults, Helbron was preferable to Laurence Graessl and there was no other German priest in Philadelphia.[7]

In 1793 Leonard Neale, a longtime friend of John Carroll's, became pastor of St. Mary's. He also served as Carroll's vicar general and as such was the direct agent of episcopal authority in Philadelphia. Later he was Carroll's coadjutor and successor at Baltimore. Like John Carroll, Neale was born into an illustrious Maryland family, had received a Jesuit education in Europe, and had joined the Society of Jesus prior to its suppression. Both men were conservatives, but Neale was far less tolerant of republicanism than was Carroll.[8]

John Carroll's attitude toward lay dissenters was relatively moder- ate, though at times condescending. He viewed them as erring children who simply did not understand the issues involved. His approach to them, while firm, was more that of an educator than an autocratic dis- ciplinarian. By contrast Leonard Neale saw lay attempts to gain some control over the government of parishes as "a fair inversion of nature, which forbids the head to become the tail." He considered his lay an- tagonists to be "immoral and rebellious heretics," no better than Protestants, and he "absolutely refused" to accommodate their sensibil- ities in any way. Neale's uncompromising absolutism could not coexist with the republicanism of Holy Trinity's lay leadership and his presence in Philadelphia soon raised the pitch of dispute over matters of principle to new and dangerous levels.[9]

"The Rights of This German Catholic Church"

In August 1796 John Goetz, former professor and preacher at the Royal Imperial Academy at Weinerich, Neustadt, arrived in Philadelphia. His eloquence and liberal convictions impressed Holy Trinity's congregation and they decided to hire him as Peter Helbron's assistant. James Oellers wrote to Bishop Carroll informing him that "the votes of the congregation were taken, & . . . they were all in favour of the Reverend John Nepomucenus Goetz." The trustees were therefore "duty bound" to "represent to your Right Reverend the said Revd. John Nepomucenus Goetz for your respected approbation.[1]

Goetz's election was a clear challenge to Carroll's prerogatives, but once again he chose to ignore the pretensions of the laity because the clerics involved had observed proper protocol. Goetz had already petitioned for and received permission to preach in his diocese and Peter Helbron had repeatedly indicated that he would welcome some assistance. So far as Bishop Carroll was concerned, then, the opinions of laymen were of no great consequence; his clergy were well in hand.

Problems developed almost immediately. Peter Helbron resented the fact that Goetz, a superior preacher, was in great demand to officiate at baptisms, weddings, and funerals and so received more of the fees collected for such services. He demanded that Goetz share the income, but the young priest refused to do so and demanded that he be accorded a position, "equal . . . in title and power" to that of the pastor. Helbron complained to Leonard Neale, asking that his assistant be removed, and Neale obliged.[2]

The congregation was shocked. When queried on the matter, Peter Helbron refused to answer, referring all questions to the vicar general. Leonard Neale in turn refused to answer any questions on the grounds that he was not obliged to do so. The laity's part, he said, was to obey their ecclesiastical superiors without asking questions, and "he would as soon be slapped in the face by the [lay trustees] as render them an account of his action." The trustees then engaged a lawyer to question Neale and the vicar gave him the same answer, adding that he might do as he pleased with his priests. Exasperated by Neale's rigidity the trustees invoked their powers under the Act of Incorporation to lay down ordinances governing church affairs. On September 28, 1796, they drew up a "Constitution" consisting of twenty-six statutes, "for the better regulation of divine service, for the prevention of further disputes and as an inviolable rule for the Rev. Clergy of [the] Church."[3]

The specifics of the statutes are unimportant (for the most part they simply stated that the two ministers should share duties and fees) but the principle of independent lay authority they embodied was significant. John Goetz signed the document without hesitation, but Peter Helbron refused, "on the ground that laymen, trustees included, had no right to make rules for their priest, and that he was bound to obey no one but the bishop and his Vicar General." Here, at last, the central issue was joined. Holy Trinity's laymen saw the Church as a unified whole in which authority was shared among the laity, clergy, and bishops within a constitutional framework that limited arbitrary authority at all levels. Leonard Neale and Peter Helbron envisioned a Church in which a rigid distinction separated the clergy and the laity and authority flowed downward through a hierarchical structure free from any constitutional restraints. This was episcopal absolutism—something that Holy Trinity would not accept. Peter Helbron was given a second chance to sign the statutes and when he refused he was dismissed from his post as pastor "with the consent of the community."[4]

On October 5 the trustees met again. Obviously angry at Helbron's obstinacy, they confirmed John Goetz as "sole pastor" of the congregation and agreed that since the dispute among the clergy was "of such great consequence," the trustees, "being ordered, appointed & empowered to examine the business," were willing to use "the rigor of the civil Laws . . . to bring them to proper reason." In a remarkable show of defiance they sent a notice of the meeting to Leonard Neale along with a statement that John Goetz had been "ordered" to conduct divine service alone on the following Sunday and a warning that, if "you or . . . any body else appointed by you shall disturb him during his services, he the disturber shall be turned out of the church by . . . force."[5]

The trustees then called a general meeting of the congregation at the German schoolhouse for October 12. The meeting instructed the board to offer Helbron and Goetz equal salaries and a clear statement of their respective rights and duties. At a second public meeting two days later the trustees reported that Peter Helbron "was pleased to refuse the whole proceedings and refuse to sign his name" to the agreement. He had demanded a written submission and apology from Goetz and would revoke the assistant's salary until he complied.[6]

Angered by Helbron's attempt "to take the powers of the . . . duly elected . . . Trustees," the assembled pewholders resolved "that if there shall [be] any dispute . . . [in the] future, between the clergy or other officers employed in the Holy Trinity Church, . . . the Trustees duly appointed shall be the proper persons & judges to settle all matters in dispute." They ordered the Trustees to "make proper regulations in the church in the services thereof" and stipulated that "such persons not obeying their regulations shall be . . . dismissed or discharged from all future services whatsoever." They explained that, "It was highly necessary to take such steps in order to prevent future abuses & scandels . . . by the Bishop, Irish & English clergy & their constituents in order to deprive us of our church & rights." They closed with a declaration that "no person or persons shall prescribe us Laws much less insult us by impertinent or pretended authorities."[7]

Three days later the trustees of Holy Trinity informed Peter Helbron that, "in consequence of a refusal to sign the resolves," he was, "dismissed and discharged from this day from all future pastoral services and functions in our church." Any resistance, they said, would force them to "make use of the civil Law." They also ordered Helbron to vacate the premises. If he did not comply, leaving all property behind to the congregation, the trustees would "proceed according to the law."[8]

Peter Helbron took refuge at St. Joseph's Chapel, a small church owned by the Jesuits, taking with him Holy Trinity's sacramental register and several other items. The trustees threatened to "take every lawfull steps necessary" to retrieve these articles, but Helbron claimed that as "lawful pastor of Holy Trinity" he was required to keep the register and that the other items were his personal property. He also informed the trustees that he had engaged a lawyer and intended to fight them in the civil courts if necessary.[9]

James Oellers then wrote to William Elling, a German Benedictine who presided over a congregation at Reading, asking him to provide substitutes for the sacramental items. Elling brought the requested articles to Philadelphia, presented himself to the congregation and volunteered to serve as John Goetz's assistant. Meanwhile Holy Trinity refused any normal contact with Peter Helbron or the clergy at St. Mary's.[10]

Now the dissenters at Holy Trinity were in open revolt against Bishop Carroll and many were, in Leonard Neale's words, " in the greatest alarm lest excommunication follow this proceeding." He suggested to Carroll "that the excommunication of the Priests & Oellers would have a good effect with many of them." John Goetz rallied the congregation, urging them to show "resolution, fortitude and constancy to suffer courageously every persecution, to despise all threats and to withstand every noxious invasion, and amongst so many and so great storms of excommunication to walk so peacefully over the thorny paths of the Israelites." He prayed that God might grant the trustees "the resolution to resist powerfully every violent invasion, that the rights of this German Catholic church, obtained with so much labor and sweat, may be defended, guarded, and always maintained."[11]

Leonard Neale ridiculed the trustees and their pretensions. In his view they were incompetent and ignorant. He wrote, "you expose yourselves to the laughter and pity of a discerning public, by spouting forth terms you understand not, and repeating the reveries of an illiterate and factious Leader, who will never reflect honor on you." Neale went on to quote John Carroll as saying that "unless the poor misled Germans can be undeceived and reclaimed soon, they and their Church will soon be separated from the Catholic communion." He warned them that if they continued to support John Goetz they would render themselves "equally guilty with him" and share in his separation from the Church. The Catholic Church, he warned, "cannot long contain within her bosom these deluded children who obstinately fix themselves in opposition to her decisions."[12]

Under Neale's prodding Bishop Carroll hardened his position. On January 22, 1797, he informed John Goetz and William Elling that they were both in danger of excommunication. One month later he issued a pastoral letter branding Goetz a "hireling," a "thief and a robber," guilty of "sacrilegious ministry," "infidelity," "schismatic disobedience," "usurpation," "revolt," and "heretical" doctrines. Goetz and the trustees who hired him were "apostates from the faith." "I say to them," Carroll wrote, "that they are exchanging the doctrines of the Catholic Church for those of

Luther and Calvin; that though they may call themselves her children, yet she will not allow herself to be their mother." On February 23, on the grounds that "he surrendered to the laity ..., the divine and spiritual juris-diction which legitimate pastors of the Church inherit from Christ and his Apostles and countenanced the condemned and heretical doctrine that the power of ecclesiastical ministry and government is derived to pastors from the community or congregation of the people," Bishop Carroll excommunicated John Goetz and his assistant, William Elling.[13]

On March 12, 1797, Leonard Neale ascended the steps of the altar at Holy Trinity and formally pronounced "by bell, book and candle" a sentence of excommunication on John Goetz and William Elling. Henceforth the two, and all who followed them, were to be "shunned and avoided" by all true Catholics and the facilities of all Catholic insti-tutions were closed to them. Holy Trinity's devotion to democracy had carried them beyond the bounds that the Church would tolerate. Now the issues would be joined in another forum.[14]

"The Laws of God & Those of the Land"

In 1796 the trustees of the church brought suit against Peter Helbron to recover title to the church, house, and property he had possessed while pastor at Holy Trinity. Helbron responded that he was still the lawful pastor of the church, and late in 1796, at his and Leonard Neale's request, the Pennsylvania Supreme Court issued a writ requiring the trustees of Holy Trinity to show cause why Helbron should not be admitted as pastor. The case was heard on December 31, 1796. Opening arguments included an affidavit by James Oellers stating that "the German R. Catholicks . . . built themselves a church with no other intention than to choose & appoint ... their Pastor independently of St. Mary's, of the Bishop & all foreign jurisdiction & to govern themselves by the laws of God & those of the land where they lived."[1]

Oeller's statement carried important implications. The first of these was a definition of religious freedom. Differing perspectives on this point separated liberal Catholics from their more conservative coreligionists. To the dissenters, freedom of religion was a right accorded to individuals. Modes of worship and church governance emerged from the aggregated wills of individuals as expressed in regular elections. This perspective, they argued, had been enshrined in the Pennsylvania state constitution which declared that all men had "a natural and unalienable right" to worship according to "the dictates of their own conscience" and held that "no man ought or of right can be compelled to attend any religious worship, or erect or support any place of worship, or maintain any ministry, contrary to, or against, his own free will and consent." Furthermore, the constitution stipulated that "no authority can or ought to be vested in, or assumed by any power whatever, that shall in any case interfere with, or in any manner controul, the right of conscience in free exercise of religious worship."[2]

In the minds of the dissenters this meant that the Church was, in effect, the people who worshiped in it, and the institutions and traditions that gave it form should evolve so as to reflect their sensibilities. In some ways this was not as radical a concept as it seems. John Carroll felt that "the church . . . was the community of those who believe in Jesus Christ" and that there was a fundamental "unity existing between ministers and congregations." Moreover, Carroll was a "religious pluralist" quite willing to adjust liturgical practices to accommodate the wide variety of customs within America's diverse Catholic population. However, there was a real limit to the extent to which he was willing to accommodate republican principles. He was outraged to hear the trustees argue in court that "all distinction between order and jurisdiction was arbitrary and fictitious; that all right to exercise ecclesiastical ministry was derived from the people; and that the Bishop had no power excepting to impose hands on the person whom the people presented as their chosen minister."[3]

John Carroll might have been remarkably liberal with regard to liturgy and forms of worship, but in matters of government he, along with other conservative clergy, interpreted freedom of religion in corporate terms. This meant that each denomination as a corporate entity had the right to organize its worship and governance as it pleased. In the "strong" form of this model standards of behavior and belief and modes of government and forms of worship were defined by tradition and interpreted and executed by an ordained clergy, leaving no independent role for the laity at all. In its "weak" form, advocated by Carroll and some other prelates, the laity's role was extremely limited and essentially passive and the underlying authoritarianism of Church government was meliorated by paternalistic benevolence. Rather than accommodating to the will of the people, then, conservatives, Carroll included, considered that the Church represented a coherent set of institutions and traditions to which members had to conform if they were to be called Roman Catholics.

Through the early phases of the confrontation at Holy Trinity moderation and good will had muted this fundamental philosophical cleavage and accommodations had been sought and achieved within the context of Catholic traditions and canons themselves. Now Leonard Neale's uncompromising absolutism, the congregation's anger, and the willingness of both sides to carry their case into civil court changed both the context and the content of the debate. The question was no longer one of finding some accommodation between liberal principles and Catholic tradition—it had now become a matter of choosing one or the other, and both sides tried to justify their choice through appeals to the American civil tradition.

James Oellers also declared Holy Trinity's congregation to be independent of "all foreign jurisdiction." This marked the beginning of a new and dangerous episode in the history of Philadelphia Catholicism. Previous disputes with John Carroll had mirrored the continuing dialogue between republicans and federalists and had been muted by moderate voices on both sides, but this was something different. The model of church government posited by Leonard Neale ran completely counter to essential features of the American civil tradition and his statements were reminiscent of the ultrareactionary pronouncements of European princes. In the face of what seemed to them to be implacable and arbitrary episcopal absolutism, Holy Trinity's lay leaders took their stand on the Constitution and argued their case not just as Catholics but also as Americans.

The implications of this situation were soon revealed. Opening arguments had been presented on the last day of the court's session in 1796 and further proceedings were continued until March of the following year. At that time Bishop Carroll traveled to Philadelphia, "flattering himself that his presence would restore peace." Scarcely had he arrived in the city when he was "attached by a writ and brought into Court to hear . . . the foulest abuse of [the Roman Catholic Church], its laws, doctrines and government, Pope and Holy Council of Trent, etc., as if they [the dissenters] had ransacked all Protestant libraries to defame it." For three days he heard constant vilification of the Holy See and the Council of Trent. The trustees, he said in a letter to Rome, "ripped [the Council] to shreds with abusive arguments begged from Paolo Sarpi's history." The papal bull creating the diocese of Baltimore they denounced as "un-American" and tyrannical. When Carroll responded by presenting a papal communication authorizing him to appoint clergy in America, the trustees charged that such power was "imposing a yoke on them contrary to the American laws."[4]

The initial confrontations in court were inconclusive. The court ordered Peter Helbron to return the sacramental register and items he had removed from Holy Trinity, but left open the question of pastoral rights. There ensued a long series of suits and countersuits in which each side tried to establish their claim to legal control of church properties, but these were overshadowed by the fatal question that had been raised in the initial confrontation. For Catholic dissenters to cast themselves as defenders of American freedoms against the encroachment of foreign tyranny was a perilous thing for a Roman Catholic Church seeking to establish its legitimacy in a hostile Protestant environment. No less problematic was Bishop Carroll's response, branding democratic innovations as "doctrines of Luther and Calvin." Statements such as these gave credence to the essential anti-Catholic arguments that democracy was a Protestant principle and that the values and institutions of Roman Catholicism ran directly counter to essential features of America's civil culture.

Reuter's Mission

Holy Trinity was not alone in its defiance of episcopal authority. A German congregation in Baltimore had been waging a similar effort under the leadership of Frederick Cesarius Reuter, a German Franciscan. In the summer of 1799 Reuter offered to carry the complaints of both congregations against John Carroll's administration to Rome along with a proposal for the establishment of an all-German diocese in the United States. Holy Trinity's trustees were receptive to Reuter's offer. They granted him conditional approval, agreeing to pay some of his expenses and authorizing him, "to negotiate with the Apostolic See for our German Catholic church and community in the best way possible." However, they agreed to be bound by whatever agreement he might conclude only if it were not, "contrary to the laws of the States or would subject us anew to the yoke of the Jesuits."[1]

Holy Trinity's petition to Rome fused nationalist aspirations with liberal principles. In it the dissenters proposed that the Church in the United States comprise distinct hierarchies roughly corresponding to the national church establishments of Europe. In this pluralistic church German Catholics would be ruled by one of their own. Moreover, local congregations would participate in the selection not only of parish clergy but also of the entire hierarchy. "We have never looked upon John Carroll as anything but an arbitrary bishop," they wrote, "and we have always reserved to ourselves the liberty of electing our own proper German bishop, according to the laws of the state." William Elling in a separate letter asserted that "the congregation of this church never acknowledged Mr. Carroll as their absolute bishop but only as a temporary and conditional one" because of electoral irregularities in the manner in which he had been selected. "The Jesuits," he wrote, "elected [Carroll] without any form of canonical election . . . , nor was any congregation consulted as to the impending election of a suffragan." By 1799, then, Holy Trinity's Germans were claiming the right not only to be governed by one of their own but also the right to participate in the election of their bishop.[2]

The appeal to Rome once again exposed the ambiguity and irony inherent in John Carroll's position. Only a few years earlier he had been elected by the American clergy as their nominee to fill the episcopal chair. Now the Germans in Philadelphia and Baltimore were seeking essentially the same right. Even the basis for their petition was similar to that which brought John Carroll to his position. The ex-Jesuit clergy had argued that only an American could effectively rule an American church and forestall the resentments that a foreign bishop would engender. Now the Germans were seeking a "proper German bishop" to rule the German churches in America and asking that they be allowed to select him "according to the laws of the state."

The Germans' protest also underlined the extent to which John Carroll's early vision of an American national church dominated by ex-Jesuits had become obsolete. As the American clergy became more diverse, Carroll was forced to abandon his earlier partisanship, making allowance for the interests and competencies of non-Jesuits and incorporating into his administration members of other orders. Only in this way could he create a unified institutional framework within which could be contained the increasingly pluralistic American Catholic clergy. One symptom of this shift in perspective, and one that had a marked effect on the conflict at Holy Trinity, was Carroll's decision in 1798 to appoint an Augustinian, Matthew Carr, as his vicar general, replacing Leonard Neale, who assumed the presidency of Georgetown College.[3]

Matthew Carr was quite a different man from his predecessor. Leonard Neale possessed a confrontational personality and viewed the relationship between episcopacy and laity as "a power struggle—a contest for the right to exercise authority in the church's government. He could see the trustees in no other light." Matthew Carr, by contrast, was a peacemaker, assiduously working to resolve disputes between laity and clergy so as to unify the factious Catholic community in Philadelphia. Neale's appointment to Georgetown thus removed one of the greatest obstacles to accommodation between Bishop Carroll and the Holy Trinity congregation.[4]

Carroll saw in Frederick Reuter's mission a possible solution to the Philadelphia problems. In April of 1800 he suggested that all sides suspend court actions until a judgment from the Holy See could be heard. He doubted that the trustees would abide by any unfavorable outcome but agreed to submit to any declaration from Rome. This decision on Carroll's part illustrates yet another significant shift in his thought since he first assumed leadership of the American church. In earlier days Carroll had been an outspoken opponent of Roman influence in America, but now as leader of a pluralistic church establishment he was forced to rely upon the authority of Rome to justify his own actions and decisions. Slowly but surely John Carroll was evolving away from his early partisanship and toward a broader view of his role as the representative in America of the international church.[5]

Peter Helbron and Holy Trinity's dissenters apparently heeded the bishop's urgings; succeeding months show no renewal of the court dispute. For more than a year the impasse continued as both sides awaited word from Rome. Then in the fall of 1801 Frederick Reuter returned to America. The news he brought was shattering; his mission had been a disaster. The Holy See refused to take any action to abridge Bishop Carroll's authority in America. What is more, Cardinal Brancadoro, secretary of the Propaganda, personally declared the Germans' request to be, "entirely absurd and utterly wicked" and "contrary to ecclesiastical discipline."[6]

Propaganda's decision split Holy Trinity's congregation. Some wanted to continue their defiance of Carroll's authority but others, including Adam Premir and James Oellers, the two most influential members of the board of trustees, decided to end the struggle. On October 11, 1801, a few days after hearing Propaganda's decision, Oellers wrote to Carroll opening negotiations to end the schism.[7]

James Oellers' change of heart was crucial to the resolution of the conflict. His wealth and political contacts had made him in the 1790s the mainstay of the congregation. That role ended, though, on December 17, 1799, when Oellers' Hotel was destroyed by fire. Suddenly, Oellers was plunged from prosperity into debt and Holy Trinity, always financially unstable (and especially so since being placed under interdict), was deprived of its strongest financial support. When the decision from Rome went against them, Holy Trinity's leaders were ready to give up their fight over political principles and turn to putting their financial house in order.

Bishop Carroll's first response was a petulant letter addressed to "Rev. James Oellers, the schismatical priest of Trinity Church," in which he listed at length the various abuses and indignities he had suffered. Having vented his rage, Carroll then sent a second letter authorizing Matthew Carr to act as his representative to receive proposals for terminating the controversy. Oellers responded with a formal list of the trustees' conditions for peace. They agreed to avoid future "Difficulties or Law Suits" if, in return, all suits against them were withdrawn. "Unless this condition is met," Oellers declared, "it is impossible to come to a friendly accommodation." The trustees also asserted that William Elling was "a gentleman of good principles" and wished that he be continued as pastor at Holy Trinity. Finally, they asked that the bishop publish a notice in all Catholic churches to the effect that "all variance between your Right Reverence & the Trustees of the Holy Trinity Church are amicably settled." Such a settlement, they concluded, would "reinstate matters without offending or hurting the Feelings of either party."[8]

Bishop Carroll was now in a benevolent mood and once again he took a moderate course toward the dissenters. He immediately agreed to the trustees' suggestions, requiring only that William Elling formally make "acknowledgment and submission to the universally received doctrines of the Church and authority of the Bishop," and that the trustees acknowledge his authority in writing. In order to make matters as easy as possible for the penitent priest, Carroll allowed that William Elling's submission could be made in private. He even appended a personal note to Elling stating, "I was glad to see your handwriting once again."[9]

With Bishop Carroll setting the tone, negotiations proceeded rapidly and with remarkable good will. On January 6, 1802 Elling assured the prelate that he would "always acknowledge in you our Common Father & Bishop, So as I did formerly." He reminded the bishop of a time "in 1791 when at New York you assured me upon your own accord that you would always be a Father to me," and begged "one thousand times pardon, my dear sir." On January 28 Elling made formal submission, stating that he held himself "subject to the authority & jurisdiction" of the bishop and acknowledging that he could not "lawfully and validly exercise any pastoral Function or administer the Sacraments without his express license."[10]

Many in Holy Trinity's congregation, however, were unwilling to abandon their struggle. Early in the negotiations Frederick Reuter met with the trustees in an effort to stiffen their resolve. The meeting made Matthew Carr nervous. "What they are contriving or deliberating upon I am at a loss to conjecture," he wrote, and warned that "a good deal of caution will be required in treating with such people." The results soon became clear; the trustees proposed that if Bishop Carroll should "leave them to go on as in 1795 and six and allow them hereafter to nominate a clergyman" they would become his "dutiful children." They would not, though, make "any publick [sic] avowal or acknowledgment" of their submission to episcopal authority. On December 8, 1801, William Elling wrote to the bishop elaborating on the trustees' position. They promised to "love & revere" Carroll if he would promise not to "disturb the congregation at Holy Trinity in the exercise of their rights, which they claim as Free & independent citizens, Subject to nothing but the laws of God & the land in which they live." He concluded, "If you let them enjoy their rights they will never fall out with you."[11]

Carroll was in a strong position. Civil actions taken against him had proven to be expensive, time consuming, and inconclusive. He expected that future actions would sustain his corporate interpretation of religious freedom. "The laws of Pennsylvania," he informed Matthew Carr, will maintain "all churches in the exercise of their special government and discipline unless these conflict with the constitutions and the laws of the State or of the United States." The trustees' appeal to Rome had failed miserably. Now William Elling was safely in the fold. There remained only the trustees, and their leaders were showing a willingness to compromise. In the circumstances, Carroll could afford to be lenient. A carefully worded act of submission was drawn up by Matthew Carr in which the trustees declared that they held themselves and their constituents, "subject to the Episcopal authority of the Bishop of Baltimore for the time being," and promised to "yield true obedience to the said Bishop conformably to the powers lawfully vested in him."[12]

The key word in the document was "lawfully." Opinions varied as to whether episcopal monarchism could be condoned by American law, but the wording was acceptable to the bishop as well as to James Oellers and Adam Premir, and they moved ahead with the settlement over the objections of other members of the board. Those who favored continued resistance were at a considerable disadvantage. Premir and Oellers had both advanced the congregation large amounts of money in the past. Neither had been repaid. They could therefore exert strong legal pressure on the rest of the trustees. Pennsylvania law at that time provided no limits to the liability of trustees for the debts of a corporation. This meant that the property of individual trustees could be confiscated to pay the congregation's debts. They could even be sent to debtors' prison. Adam Premir and James Oellers were thus in a position to ruin the other members of the board of directors simply by suing for repayment of the money owed them.[13]

Premir and Oellers would brook no opposition. When other members of the board continued to raise objections Premir personally "shut the doors of Trinity Church . . . and assured the other trustees that he would entirely withdraw himself from them unless they complied with the terms required." Then on the evening of January 28, 1802, Oellers personally took the act of submission, already signed by himself and Premir with the seal of the corporation affixed, to the homes of the other members of the board of trustees and one by one secured their signatures on it.[14]

"A Revolution in Our Society"

Soon the accord between Bishop Carroll and the congregation faced its first test. By 1805 William Elling's health was declining and so the trustees wrote to Carroll asking that he appoint an assistant to serve at their parish. They had a candidate in mind—Herman Joseph Stocker, who was then serving as Peter Helbron's assistant at Lancaster. Carroll saw no reason to deny their request and informed them that he would "readily comply with [their] desires" as soon as a German clergyman could be procured to replace Stocker. There should be no problem, Carroll wrote, as he anticipated a "speedy supply of German clergymen." Once one was selected, only Stocker's agreement would be necessary.[1]

This courteous and amicable exchange reflects the determination of all concerned to avoid confrontation on basic principles. The congregation made its wishes known to the bishop but did not insist on a right of presentation; Carroll readily acceded to their desires and did not attempt to force an unwelcome clergyman on them. However, unforeseen difficulties emerged. Herman Stocker soon left the priesthood. Then William Elling was suddenly incapacitated and for several weeks was unable to preach. Adam Britt, a recently arrived ex-Jesuit from Germany, was available but he was advanced in years and physically unfit for the post. More important, he lacked fluency in English and could not be understood by many members of Holy Trinity's congregation. Still, there was no other German priest readily available, and so Adam Britt was sent to Philadelphia as a replacement for William Elling. John Carroll, mindful of the congregation's feelings, apologized for the unfortunate change in plans.[2]

Adam Britt's appointment initiated a new round of conflicts at Holy Trinity. A portent of troubles to come arrived in the person of Peter Helbron. Hearing of William Elling's illness, Helbron returned from the West and demanded reinstatement at Holy Trinity. His presence split the congregation. Forced to choose between Adam Britt and their former pastor, the majority voted to retain Britt, but a group of English-speakers demanded that Peter Helbron be hired. The trustees protested to Bishop Carroll against Helbron's actions and the attempt on the part of "theatrical performers, Drunkers, etc.," to "bring a Revolution in our Society," and Carroll responded by ordering Helbron to return to his mission post. On October 25, 1806, William Elling resigned his pastorship and retired to Bedford in the West. Ten days later Adam Britt succeeded him as pastor.[3]

Adam Britt remained at Holy Trinity for five years. It was an unhappy situation for all concerned. The aging priest was unpopular because of his "strange" and autocratic manner and because his slovenly personal habits were considered not to be in accordance with the "dignity and respect of the congregation." More important, his inability to speak English distressed the non-German elements of Holy Trinity's congregation. Still, most considered him to be preferable to Peter Helbron, who continued to demand reinstatement at the church, and no other German-speaking clergyman was available.[4]

Matters became more complex in 1808 when Philadelphia became an independent diocese under the direction of Bishop Michael Egan, an Irish Franciscan who had been serving for some time as pastor at St. Mary's Church. This institutional reorganization, necessary to cope with the rapid growth of the American church, removed Holy Trinity from John (now Archbishop) Carroll's direct purview. Old habits, though, were hard to break; Adam Britt and the Holy Trinity trustees continued to carry their complaints to Baltimore.

In the fall of 1808 Holy Trinity finally received an English-speaking assistant, Leonard Edelen, a charismatic young Jesuit who was extremely popular, especially with the ladies of the congregation. According to the trustees Edelen was a wonder. He was young and unsure of himself, particularly in the pulpit, but worked hard and was improving, and his zeal for parish work and constant study was admirable. Edelen founded an English school at Holy Trinity, teaching it himself and drawing to it a large number of pupils.

> [He] became acquainted with every Catholic [of note] in the city, he converted several ladies maried to our & other Catholic members, he attended the poor House weekly & often daily . . . , he visited the Hospital, he kept every Thursday catechism to a great number of children, he improved in preaching, & gave great satisfaction to every member of our congregation.[5]

Edelen's enthusiasm infected the board of trustees and the English-speaking elements of the congregation. They made plans to expand the

English school and to add a Latin school, even to open a small seminary as soon as a sufficient number of clergy could be obtained. However, Adam Britt stood squarely in the way of any such plans. The elderly priest resented his young colleague and "traited him worse than a boy." Britt refused to release Edelen's salary and confiscated all stole fees paid to him, then placed him on a strict allowance, so inadequate that the young man reportedly could not afford to have his clothes laundered or to feed himself properly. Eventually, under pressure from the congregation, Britt agreed to allow Edelen to retain the fees he collected, and the young man seemed to be "at last satisfied with his situation." Appearances were deceiving, though. On November 3, 1809, Leonard Edelen left Philadelphia and refused to return. Once again Holy Trinity was without an English-speaking clergyman.[6]

Leonard Edelen's departure brought the potential conflict simmering within Holy Trinity's congregation to a boil. English-speaking members of the congregation resented the young man's treatment and felt that Britt served only the needs of the German speakers. Germans felt that there was a real danger that the congregation might lose its distinctive character. These fears were heightened when the trustees embraced Edelen's proposal for an English school. In the weeks after Edelen left, accusations and recriminations flew back and forth between the English- and German-speaking elements of the congregation. So heated was the atmosphere that early in 1810 James Oellers wrote to Archbishop Carroll pleading for him to procure an English-speaking priest at once, "it being impossible, that our church can remain in the present situation without the Congregation going to entire Destruction."[7]

Frantically, Holy Trinity's trustees searched for a second pastor but to no avail. Finally, in January 1811, Bishop Egan appointed Patrick Kenny, an Irishman, to serve as English pastor to the congregation, assisting Adam Britt. This disquieted the Germans because it further undermined the ethnic character of the congregation. They received another blow when, less than four months after Kenny's appointment, Adam Britt's complaints about his situation in Philadelphia finally induced Charles Neale (brother of Leonard Neale and superior of the Society of Jesus in America) to recall him to Maryland. Once again Holy Trinity was lacking a priest. This time, though, the German-speaking elements of the congregation were bereft, for Patrick Kenny was able to preach only in French and English.[8]

Adam Britt's removal from Holy Trinity precipitated a crisis of authority that reverberated through the American church. Britt had been reassigned by the superior of his order over the objections of both Bishop Egan and Archbishop Carroll. This raised again the question of who had the right to assign regular clergy. Defending his removal of Britt, Charles Neale claimed the right to decide the assignment of all ex-Jesuits in the United States, but only a few months earlier the American bishops, sitting in council, had specifically repudiated this position stating that

> when priests, who are members of secular or regular Congregations have been, with the consent of Superiors, charged with the care of souls, it is our opinion, *judicamus*, that such priests ought not to be at the disposal of their Superiors, and be recalled against the will of the Bishop.

In response to this Charles Neale declared,

> Be it . . . , positively understood, that I mean not to give up any control over any individual subject of our Congregation. . . . It is true that I ought to be reasonable in that respect. But it is equally certain that I have no authority to give up any right that would put the subject out of the power of his Superior.

Carroll's reaction to Neale's challenge was simple and direct. On the back of the superior's letter he penned, "Inadmissible Pretensions." Adam Britt's reassignment brought the issue to a head.[9]

Both Charles Neale and John Carroll appealed to other members of the ex-Jesuit community. Neale denounced both Egan and Carroll as "enemies of the Order," and accused them of attempting to undermine its morale and to obliterate its distinctive character. Carroll "complains that we make our affairs too public," Neale was quoted as saying, "that we style ourselves S.J. &[c], but what is worst of all, he says that the Bishops have no power to ordain our members *Titulopaupertatis*." Neale even claimed that Carroll had attempted to prohibit the ex-Jesuits from wearing exterior marks that would distinguish them from secular clergy. Carroll responded that Neale was "grievously" and "undeservedly" misrepresenting him. He wrote to Thaddeus Brzozowski, general of the Jesuits, charging that Charles Neale was "imprudent" and "not sufficiently exact in his administrative conduct" and stressed that it was necessary for the long-term interests of the society that it appoint superiors who were "acceptable to the bishops of the United States."[10]

Meanwhile, it appeared that Bishop Egan had found a solution to the problem at Holy Trinity. In the early fall of 1811 two young German Jesuit priests passed through Philadelphia on their way to take up duties at Georgetown College. While in the city, they paid a courtesy call on Egan, who then asked Archbishop Carroll to arrange for one of these men, Maximillian Rantzau, to be sent to Holy Trinity. Carroll relayed the request to Charles Neale but the superior refused to release the young priest.[11]

Charles Neale's refusal to reassign Maximillian Rantzau provoked a crisis. Carroll first wrote to Neale trying to persuade him that compliance with Bishop Egan's wishes would be in the best interests of the Jesuits. "You must expect," he wrote, "that your refusal will be complained of to the Pope . . . , and be made a handle of by our enemies to represent our Brethren as desirous of unwarrantable independence." "Remember," he continued, "that, without writing a line of civility to Bishop Egan, you ordered away from Phila[delphia]. Mr. Britt, which left a deep impression. You have had a favourable opportunity for healing that wound; you did not avail yourself of it." "But it is yet in your power," Carroll concluded, "and I depend on your giving the matter another consideration."[12]

Neale held firm. In a letter to Patrick Kenny, he explained that the general had "forbidden [him] to suffer the constitution of the Society to be any ways changed, which would be the case were its members subject to Bishops, and not to their own Superiors." Neale's intransigence infuriated Carroll, who unleashed the full force of his anger. He branded the superior's argument as "a masterpiece of temerity and extravagance." "What language," he raged, "what a spirit of dissension and independence, making the bishops his subjects . . . , I could not believe that he was so ignorant or presumptuous." He warned that "if the General does not make Mr. Neale change his tone, the bishops of America, obliged as they are to maintain the discipline of the Church, and bound by their solemn *oath to obey the orders received from the Congregation of the Propaganda,* will be forced to take very severe measures against him and his adherents" (emphasis mine). He then threatened "to exclude Mr. Neale and all those who act in concert with him from the direction of souls."[13]

The threat of direct action against the Society stirred other members of the Jesuit community to action. They petitioned their general to bring Charles Neale to heel and soon the crisis was resolved. Thaddeus Brzozowski, with apologies to the archbishop and bishops of America, removed Neale from his positions as rector of Georgetown College and superior of the Society and replaced him with John Grassi. This was not the end of disputes between the ex-Jesuit community and John Carroll. Grassi and the archbishop quarreled frequently over the next few years, but a principle had been established—in a direct confrontation between the episcopacy and the Society of Jesus, the interests of the hierarchy would prevail. Through the last years of his life John Carroll time and again reiterated his conviction, to little effect, that the best interest of the Society would be served if the Jesuits adopted a broad understanding of the needs of the pluralistic American church. A few months before his death, Carroll lamented that Jesuits entering America from Europe were "all of them good religious men, but not one of them, possessing an expanded mind, discerning enough to estimate the difference between the American character; and that of the Countries which they left."[14]

The Neale-Carroll dispute resulted in a powerful affirmation of the right of the archbishop to control all elements of the increasingly diverse American clergy, and it is a striking illustration of John Carroll's maturing concept of his role within the church. The same man who had once declared, in defense of Jesuit autonomy, that "no Congregations . . . shall be allowed to exercise any share of [the Pope's] Spr[itua]l. authority here; [and] no Bishop Vicar Apostolical shall be admitted," had now become a vicar apostolic owing obedience to Propaganda and wielding authority derived from Rome to bring the Jesuits to heel. The transition had not been easy; John Carroll lamented the conflict between his "inclination and attachment [to the Society of Jesus] on one side, and duty [to Propaganda] confirmed by oath on the other." But the direction was clear. Inexorably, John Carroll was drawn by the exigencies of his position as the head of the American episcopate to abandon his early emphasis on American particularism and collegiality and to assume a more monarchic and ultramontane system of government that reflected the interests and imperatives of the international church. Whatever his sentiments, Carroll, once established as head of the American church, could never forget his "obligation to be subject to the commands of the Cong[regatio]n. de Prop[agan]da. fide."[15]

The German Party

Charles Neale's downfall cleared the way for Maximillian Rantzau's transfer to Philadelphia and on December 7, 1811, he took up his duties there. Rather than resolving the tensions at Holy Trinity, though, the young priest's arrival exacerbated them. Now the congregation was served by two priests, one who spoke no German and one who spoke no English, and as was so often the case, the two men could not agree. The question was one of authority. Rantzau had been assured by Archbishop Carroll that he would be the primary pastor at Holy Trinity with Patrick Kenny serving as his assistant. However, Kenny was unwilling to accept subordinate status, and in this he was supported by a substantial portion of the congregation. Soon animosity between the clergymen divided the congregation.[1]

Rantzau complained to Archbishop Carroll and threatened to leave Philadelphia if matters were not adjusted to his satisfaction. Carroll replied that Rantzau was perfectly right in his understanding—Holy Trinity was a German church and required a German pastor. At about the same time Bishop Egan, responding to an exodus of parishioners from St. Mary's Church (persons who, driven out by disturbances there, came to Holy Trinity "not only . . . at Mass, but to have baptisms and marriages celebrated there") forbade the German clergy to exercise pastoral functions for persons of other nationalities. In the spring of 1812, then, both Bishop Egan and Archbishop Carroll specifically affirmed the distinctively German character of Holy Trinity. This emphasis on the nationality dimension of the parish encouraged factionalism within the congregation and contributed significantly to the decline of liberal leadership.[2]

Rantzau's triumph left hard feelings within the congregation. Patrick Kenny's supporters resented Carroll's interference in their affairs and soon tempers flared. "Cold language" was directed against the archbishop, the "Dutch" element in the congregation, and the clergy at St. Mary's Church who had attempted to arbitrate the dispute. Animosity built between Patrick Kenny and Rantzau. The two priests began to treat each other with open contempt. Finally, on May 10, 1812,

Kenny asked Bishop Egan to remove Rantzau from Holy Trinity. One week later Egan, despairing of ever seeing an end to conflict while the two priests remained in Philadelphia, relieved Maximillian Rantzau of his duties and wrote to John Grassi, asking him to recall Patrick Kenny.[3]

Rantzau's removal, shortly before the annual election for trustees, was poorly timed. His partisans were infuriated and took advantage of the election to vent their anger. On May 18, 1812, Rantzau appeared at the polling place at the head of a German "party" and proclaimed that "no pew holder but a German should vote." By brute force the "Dutch law breakers," as Patrick Kenny styled them, took the ballots, eliminated all those cast by persons not of German descent, and proclaimed the election of a solid slate of nationalist trustees. This action, so clearly a violation of democratic principles, was an outrage not only to the non-German elements of the congregation but also to the liberal leadership that had managed affairs at Holy Trinity from its inception. Rantzau's coup, Kenny wrote, "threw the last firebrand into the congregation."[4]

Led by James Oellers and Adam Premir, the liberals struck back. They asserted that the election was invalid because the votes of the majority had been disqualified; they refused to resign their offices and called for new elections; they even hired a lawyer and threatened to sue in civil court. "Nothing," Patrick Kenny declared, "will satisfy the insulted people, but the enforcing of the act of Assembly [the church's charter]." Unfortunately for the insulted people the charter contained no provision for challenging elections or for rescheduling them. The legal opinion was that the liberals had little recourse—especially since any civil suit would take more than a year to resolve, and by that time there would be new elections. The lawyer recommended either reconciliation or resignation.[5]

There was little use in appealing to ecclesiastical authorities. Neither Bishop Egan nor Archbishop Carroll had any interest in enforcing democratic procedures at Holy Trinity. Nor could the old republican leadership look for help from the local clergy. The departure of both Maximillian Rantzau and Patrick Kenny opened the way, finally, for the return of Peter Helbron, who was at long last restored to the pastorship from which he had been driven so many years before. Helbron, however, was too ill to long savor his triumph and in 1813 he retired to western Pennsylvania. His assistant and successor at Holy Trinity, Francis Roloff, actively aided and abetted the new German faction, seeing in them the best chance to restore peace and docility to the troubled parish.[6]

The techniques by which the German party established its dominance over Holy Trinity were nothing short of brutal. Through the
summer of 1812 they systematically terrorized other elements of the
congregation in an attempt to drive them out of the parish. On June 28
Rantzau and a "Trustee squad" of Germans interrupted the funeral of
a French child due to be buried in Holy Trinity cemetery. The Germans
filled up the grave, threatened the mourners, and both parties stripped
to fight. Eventually the French gave up and had the child buried elsewhere. On August 2, immediately before high mass, "a Dutch Mob
appeared, & the [new] Trustees sent . . . word . . . , that if [the Irish
priest] attempted to preach [he] should be dragged out of the pulpit."
The reason for the threat was that Bishop Egan had announced that he
would be attending services at Holy Trinity that day and Maximillian
Rantzau, despite having been dismissed from the parish, was determined that the bishop should hear a German service. Patrick Kenny
prudently relinquished the pulpit to Rantzau but took the occasion of
the bishop's visit to tender his formal resignation; within three days he
had settled his accounts and left, as did many of his supporters in the
congregation.[7]

At last, in desperation, James Oellers and Adam Premir resorted to
the same tactics that had proven so successful a decade earlier. On July
6, 1813, the two men appeared at a meeting of the board and demanded
payment of $8,804, which they said was due them. Once again Premir
and Oellers were using the threat of financial ruin to force their will on
the corporation. However, much had changed in the previous decade.
Both men had suffered major business reverses and had little money
with which to conduct a long and expensive contest in court and it
soon became apparent that nothing less would suffice. The trustees
refused to capitulate. They collected all the parish receipts and deeds
and began an investigation into the past conduct of the two men. On
August 18 they informed Oellers and Premir that reexamination of the
accounts revealed that, instead of the parish owing them money, the
corporation was in fact owed nearly fifteen hundred dollars. The
trustees demanded immediate payment and instigated legal action to
collect it.[8]

The investigation had turned up information that was extremely
embarrassing to Oellers and Premir. In 1812, when Premir had been
treasurer, the parish accounts showed a surplus of more than twelve
hundred dollars. Yet the money was nowhere to be found. During the

succeeding year, when Joseph Bartian, a friend of Oellers and Premir, had held the position, another smaller amount had disappeared. Under questioning, both former treasurers admitted that they had allowed James Oellers to use church funds for his private purposes. Premir stated that Oellers had acted "against his will" in the affair. He proclaimed his innocence and declared his insolvency and inability to pay. "If the present trustees should persist in their suit," Premir and Bartian testified in Oellers' presence before the board, "they would be under the necessity of going to Prison." They publicly relinquished any claims against the trustees and threw themselves on the mercy of the congregation. The trustees then forgave Premir and Bartian their debts and declared James Oellers to be "the only debtor of the congregation." They further declared that ambition such as his was "the scourge of all institutions" and that he had "forfeited all rights . . . to the Trusteeship of the Congregation." Premir and Bartian then signed public admissions of their negligence and agreed to pay all court costs that had ensued from the controversy. With this act the liberal era came to a close at Holy Trinity.[9]

Ethnicity and Ideology

The decline of Holy Trinity's liberal leadership can be related to important changes taking place in Philadelphia's Catholic community. In the early stages of the congregation's existence mutually reinforcing resentments (against the Irish and Anglo/American leadership at St. Mary's, against the Jesuit hegemony over the American mission, and against the arbitrary and authoritarian actions of some clerics and ecclesiastical authorities) gave nationalists and liberals a common set of grievances. Potential conflicts of interest were submerged and all could agree on the necessity for the laity to exert some control over clerical appointments, but over time circumstances changed and the unity of purpose that had sustained Holy Trinity through long years of conflict broke down.

One by one, Holy Trinity's external foes diminished in importance. The threat of Jesuit hegemony faded with John Carroll's choice of an Augustinian as his vicar general in Philadelphia and the selection a few years later of a Franciscan as the first bishop of the new diocese. Leonard Neale's departure and John Carroll's determined attempts (after the settlement of 1802) to take lay sensibilities into account lessened the congregation's resentment toward ecclesiastical authorities. All that remained was cultural and ideological antagonism against the lay and clerical leadership of St. Mary's, and that was rapidly fading as Philadelphia's "Irish" church became embroiled in its own revolt against episcopal authority. However none of this brought peace to the troubled congregation, because as external pressures receded internal conflicts began to mount.

Over time Holy Trinity began to lose its distinctively German character. The church's leadership welcomed into their fellowship persons of all nationalities. One decade into the nineteenth century the roll of pewholders at Holy Trinity had come to include "French, Italians, Spanish, Irish, English, Americans, &c." Even among the Germans cultural values were waning, to the consternation of those in whom nationalist feelings ran strong. By the time Adam Britt arrived at the church in 1807 many of the congregation no longer knew enough German to make confessions in that language. Leonard Edelen's founding in the following year of a popular and well-attended English school portended a day when German cultural values would be completely eclipsed within the congregation. By the early years of the nineteenth century, then, those within Holy Trinity's congregation for whom the preservation of German culture was a paramount concern found much to trouble them, and problems of accommodation began to loom large.[1]

It was at this crucial juncture that the lay leadership relinquished their right to order affairs and submitted to the direction of episcopal authorities who had no interest in preserving democracy although they did sanction cultural assertiveness. Statements and decisions made by Bishop Egan and Archbishop Carroll exacerbated cultural tensions. Both prelates affirmed the distinctive German character of the parish and, after William Elling's retirement, sent priests to serve Holy Trinity who were inadequate to satisfy the needs of the increasingly diverse congregation and engaged in a series of petty quarrels that heightened the cultural sensitivities of the laity. The formation of a "German Party" at Holy Trinity was the direct result of one of these appointments and, when the Germans resorted to illegal means to seize control of the board of trustees, episcopal authorities acquiesced in the coup.

In a recent study Liah Greenfield made an important distinction between "civic" and "ethnic" forms of nationalism. In the former case nationalism was strongly associated with liberal ideology and asserted the sovereignty of the people as a defense against arbitrary and established authority. "Nationalism," she writes, "was the form in which democracy appeared in the [modern] world." In the latter instance the idea of the People or *Volk* was elevated to the point where it became the basis for systematic oppression and cultural exclusion and liberal principles were abandoned or submerged. These analytic categories, of course, were not mutually exclusive. Civic nationalists could feel pride in their culture and consider it superior to others while ethnic nationalists could make significant concessions to liberal values. It is perhaps useful, then, to view the two forms of nationalism not as alternatives but as end points on a continuum—a spectrum of sensibility wherein liberal and ethnic values intermingled with varying degrees of intensity.[2]

By this measure the change in leadership at Holy Trinity represented a shift along the spectrum of nationalist sentiment from its civil toward its ethnic manifestation. It did not mean a total repudiation of the liberal values that had so long sustained the congregation. This became apparent in 1813 when the new trustees tried to consolidate their victory by instituting policies that would in the future restrict the franchise within the congregation. They declared all delinquent pews to be vacant and further provided that no fees could be collected on the day of elections. This had the effect of disenfranchising many of the older members who, by custom, had paid their pew rents on election day. The trustees also, at Francis Roloff's suggestion, began negotiations with members of the state legislature to have the charter revised to allow the appointment of trustees by the clergy.[3]

In attempting to amend the charter the German party went too far and provoked a general backlash within the congregation. James Oellers obtained a letter making reference to the negotiations and circulated it through the congregation. So great was the outrage that the trustees were forced to retreat precipitously from their plan. They denied that there had ever been any intent to revise the charter. Their representative, the trustees said, had gone to Harrisburg on strictly private business and his intentions had been misconstrued by the legislators to whom he had spoken.[4]

The ascendancy of Holy Trinity's nationalists thus did not completely obliterate the liberal strains that had for so long provided direction to the congregation. This continuing commitment to popular sovereignty made Holy Trinity a "difficult" congregation to rule, and it provided an enduring link (even at a time when ethnic and Catholic leaders were trying to block the assimilation of immigrants into the American mainstream) binding Holy Trinity's German Catholic community to the broader context of American civil culture.

The "Irish" Church

Through the years while Holy Trinity stood in defiance of John Carroll's authority Philadelphia's "Irish" congregation remained quiescent. From its beginnings in 1765 the members of St. Mary's Roman Catholic Church had prided themselves on their status as one of the most affluent and respectable congregations in America. This reputation was only enhanced during the Revolutionary War when several of St. Mary's members distinguished themselves both in military and political endeavors. This eminent coterie of wealthy Anglo- and Irish-American Catholics formed a conservative and patriotic lay leadership that, together with an equally conservative Jesuit clergy, dominated Philadelphia Catholicism through the early years of the American republic.[1]

Near the end of the eighteenth century an influx of political refugees introduced an outspoken republican element into Philadelphia's Irish community and a swelling tide of Jeffersonian republicanism challenged Federalist dominance in the secular society, but the adamant hostility of Leonard Neale and his lay supporters at St. Mary's kept such sentiments from disturbing the internal politics of the church. An incident early in the last year of the century illustrates the strength of that resistance.[2]

On the evening of Friday, February 8, 1799, Philadelphia's immigrant republicans met to demand repeal of the Alien Act (passed by the Federalist-dominated Congress in the previous summer), which severely restricted their civil liberties. They drew up petitions of protest to be presented to Congress and circulated them for signatures over the weekend. On Sunday Irish petitioners appeared throughout the city at Presbyterian and Catholic churches soliciting signatures. Everywhere matters proceeded without incident—except at St. Mary's.

There a committee of four Irish republicans—Dr. James Reynolds (a prominent physician), Robert Moore (a "gentleman of wealth"), William Duane (a political exile and editor of the *Aurora*), and Samuel Cummings (a compositor on the *Aurora*)—appeared at the entrance to the church before mass and posted notices stating: "Natives of Ireland who worship at this church are requested to remain in the yard after divine service until they have affixed their signatures to a memorial for the repeal of the ALIEN BILL." One of St. Mary's trustees, John O'Hara, confronted the committee, ordered them to leave, and tore the notices from the walls.[3]

Undeterred by O'Hara's hostility, the petitioners simply replaced the signs. They were then challenged by another member of the congregation, James Gallagher, Jr., who again tore down the notices, declaring that "no Jacobin paper had a right to a place on the walls" of the church. When the republicans again refused to leave, Leonard Neale went from pew to pew speaking to influential members of the congregation and urging them to resist the intruders as a group. At last Duane and his friends withdrew. Robert Moore, stating that he had been "a gentleman in Ireland" and still "behaved like a gentleman" in Philadelphia, went home.[4]

Once the republicans were gone Leonard Neale began mass. After delivering his sermon he went out and around the church looking for republican placards. Finding none he went back inside and finished the service. Then, just before mass was over, Duane and his friends returned and replaced the notices. They also spread a copy of their petition on a gravestone and approached members of the congregation as they left the church asking for their signatures. Once again they were challenged. Blows were struck, a pistol was drawn, and the republicans fled the scene while members of the congregation summoned constables. Ultimately

Duane and his friends were tracked down, arrested, and taken before the mayor.[5]

The entire affair became a *cause célèbre.* A "large concourse of people" filled the street for five hours between the mayor's house and that of the Chief Justice, just to glimpse the accused. On February 21 the republicans were brought to trial and charged with causing a riot. Leonard Neale, their chief accuser, testified that he considered the placards and petition to be "an insult to him and the Board of Trustees" because the republicans had not obtained his consent before disturbing the congregation. However, Neale's testimony was rebutted by Matthew Carr, who said that it was a common practice in Ireland to hold public meetings and to solicit signatures on petitions after church services. Faced with conflicting testimony from Catholic priests, the jury returned a verdict of "not guilty" to the charges of inciting a riot but convicted Dr. Reynolds of assault and battery.[6]

The "Irish Riot" at St. Mary's was one of many confrontations between Federalists and Republicans that troubled Philadelphia in the last years of the eighteenth century. In that context it was of little note, but it illustrates a fundamental divergence within Philadelphia's Irish population on matters of political principle, an antagonism that would divide St. Mary's congregation and ultimately precipitate the downfall of the Federalist elite that had long dominated affairs in the church.

For a while the conservative leadership was unchallenged within St. Mary's. Neale's departure created a minor problem because no other clergyman was considered to be of sufficient talent to serve in his place, but a suitable replacement was found in 1802 when John Carrell, a prosperous ironmonger, a staunch Federalist, and a member of St. Mary's board of trustees, met and was impressed by Michael Egan, an Irish Franciscan recently arrived in Pennsylvania who was serving the mission at Lancaster. Carrell recommended that the trustees secure Egan as their pastor. The board then began negotiations with Bishop Carroll that concluded on April 12, 1803, with Egan's appointment as pastor at St. Mary's.[7]

Michael Egan was popular with the elite clique that directed St. Mary's affairs, but the appointment was not universally applauded. Despite its affluence some felt that St. Mary's congregation need not support three priests, especially since many people held the clergy in low regard. "A pew holder" took it upon himself to write Bishop Carroll inquiring whether it would not be "expedient" to effect the "removal" of "the most useless of the three Priests now residing here." Such action, the pewholder claimed, was necessary to "keep the congregation in peace." Bishop Carroll did not reply to this impertinence and the matter was dropped, but concerns about the quality of the clergy and the expense of maintaining them would trouble St. Mary's congregation for years to come.[8]

Michael Egan was a mild and inoffensive man, but some thought him devious. Perhaps the best assessment of his character was made by John Carroll in 1806 and 1807 when plans were being made to create regional dioceses in the United States and Egan was a candidate for the episcopacy. In communications with Rome, Carroll described Egan as "pious," "learned," "religious," "modest," and "remarkable for his great humility," but also lacking robust health, administrative experience, and "firmness in his disposition." These deficiencies in Egan's character were of little importance at the time he assumed the pastorship of St. Mary's, but they were to prove fatal in the time of crisis to come.[9]

Despite his reservations John Carroll considered Egan to be preferable to any other local candidate for the episcopacy and on his recommendation in April, 1808, the Holy See nominated Egan as the first bishop of the newly created diocese of Philadelphia. Bishop-elect Egan delighted the lay leadership at St. Mary's by announcing that he would make it his cathedral church. With eager anticipation the trustees began to make plans to enlarge and embellish St. Mary's to reflect its new status.[10]

In 1809 St. Mary's trustees embarked on an ambitious program of expansion. They opened a subscription to enlarge the church and many of the trustees themselves advanced large sums to speed the project. They also made plans to expand the free school attached to the church and agreed to pay more than any other congregation toward the upkeep of the bishop and his clerical assistants.[11]

At the same time efforts were made to upgrade the quality of the clergy at the cathedral. In the fall of 1808 bishop-elect Egan chose as his clerical assistant a newly arrived Dominican from Ireland, William Vincent Harold. From the beginning, this "eloquent and elegant" man was a sensation. After Harold delivered his first sermon at St. Mary's, "the trustees and several others" congratulated Egan on his choice of assistant, and soon thereafter the bishop made the popular priest his vicar general.[12]

William Harold was a striking personality, "stately" and "venerable" in appearance with a large head, a penetrating eye, and abundant curly locks. He was also a powerful and persuasive speaker with an oratorical style not unlike that of Protestant evangelists of the period. When speaking from the pulpit Harold would begin quietly, "in a manner that was scarcely audible," but soon he warmed to his subject, and "rolled out his periods in tones that could be heard in every part" of the church. "Thumping the pulpit with all the energy in his power . . . , in the most forcible manner he carried conviction to the minds of all who heard him of his great power of language." He was also a contentious man with an overabundance of self-esteem. Mathew Carey described him as "turbulent and domineering" and possessed of an "overweening self-sufficiency and arrogance." These qualities would soon provoke dangerous confrontations within St. Mary's congregation.[13]

William Harold sparked a local revival at St Mary's. His energy and oratorical skills drew many back to the church who had fallen away from the faith while others who had never been observing Catholics swelled the congregation to hear him preach. These new and returned Catholics, many of them working-class immigrants recently come from Ireland, provided Harold with a large and enthusiastic following within the congregation and soon threatened to disturb long-standing relationships among the clergy and laity. Ultimately Harold's evangelical ministry, much like those of his Protestant contemporaries, altered the social composition of the congregation he served and introduced into the church a powerful democratic imperative that posed a challenge to traditional authorities.[14]

"The Laboring Interest"

Troubles first arose over the matter of clerical salaries. Harold declared that he was dissatisfied with his income and demanded more money. If not, he said, he would "abandon the church." The trustees responded that this would be impossible. Because of debts incurred during the expansion of the church there simply wasn't enough money to meet Harold's demands and to maintain the church as well. Harold was unmoved; he assumed a "hostile and overbearing" attitude and told the trustees that they had no right to deny him anything he wanted because "the church belongs to the clergy and with it the whole of the income." The wealthy men who led the congregation could meet his needs, he said, simply "by putting [their] hands in [their] pockets."[1]

William Harold's demands shocked St. Mary's lay leaders, but there was little that they could do because Michael Egan agreed with his assistant. On December 10, 1810, he notified the trustees that the salaries of the clergy were "not sufficient." The trustees then offered a moderate increase which Harold grudgingly accepted. However, the church's financial position was rapidly deteriorating. Income from pew rents had not met expectations, debts were rising, attempts to borrow money failed, and four members of the board offered their resignations. Finally, Philip Smith, an affluent wholesale grocer, personally advanced money to see the congregation through the crisis. Thus ended the first confrontation between William Harold and the circle of men who had dominated St. Mary's since the early days of the republic.[2]

Into this contentious situation came William Harold's uncle, James Harold, an Irish republican priest who had been transported to a penal colony in Australia for his activities during the United Irishmen revolt of 1798. He arrived unexpectedly in Philadelphia in April of 1811 and at his nephew's urging was hired as a second assistant at St. Mary's. Bishop Egan obviously thought that this appointment would calm matters and reported that the younger Harold was now "completely happy." James Harold, though, had a temperament even more volatile than his nephew's and an ambition to match. Soon he stood at the center of controversy.[3]

For decades a small clique of affluent men who cooperated closely with the clergy had held unchallenged dominion over church affairs. "The elections of trustees . . . were generally decided by ten, twenty, or thirty votes—and frequently the board was continued without alteration for many years together." Now the Harolds began to interfere with the elections for trustees, attacking the character of members of the board and enlarging the electorate by paying pew rents for poor persons who had previously been excluded. This new constituency then voted for candidates proposed by the Harolds. By these means William Harold "began to turn [the old trustees] out by degrees and to put his creatures in their places."[4]

Many of the newcomers were unskilled and semiskilled workers and some were not even citizens of the United States. The old trustees boycotted meetings of the board rather than deal with such as these. Then in the Easter election of 1812 they mounted a desperate campaign to reclaim their dominance and won a temporary victory—all were returned to the board.[5]

While the Harolds' machinations divided the congregation, a conflict was also developing among the clergy. Bishop Egan's health was failing. Often he was unable to preach and the two Harolds openly resented having to substitute for him. Through the early months of 1812 relations among the clergy rapidly deteriorated and at one point the argument became so heated that James Harold, asserting that he had ten supporters in the congregation for every one of Egan's, threatened physical violence against the bishop.[6]

One matter, though, united the clergy—their salaries. Early in 1812 the board of trustees recommended that the church dispense with the services of one priest and lower the salaries of the others. Only by doing so, they said, could they ever pay off the church's debts. This solution, of course, was utterly unacceptable to the clergy. To buy time in which to negotiate a settlement, Lewis Ryan, a boot and shoe manufacturer, personally paid the quarterly installments on the clergy's salaries and also paid off a debt "on which a suit of law was threatened." This was only a stopgap, and three months later, after several unsuccessful attempts to borrow money, the church ran out of funds and was unable to pay the clergy. This time Lewis Ryan, toward whom William Harold had behaved "very uncourteously," refused to loan the congregation any more money.[7]

The clergy's response was immediate and immoderate. They indignantly refused any partial payment and published a circular in which they charged that the trustees, by using income to pay creditors rather than for salaries, were guilty of gross malfeasance. "Our rights," William Harold wrote, have been "violated! our feelings tortured! and our character dishonoured! by the caprice or the malice of these individuals." He claimed that the trustees were attempting, "by intrigue and unprincipled misrepresentation," to "[excite] the jealousy of the people against their pastors." No longer, he declared, would the clergy be "the passive victims of Men, who . . . are [bent on] gratifying their own miserable resentment." He called on the congregation to censure the trustees.[8]

The issue of clerical income was not merely an administrative matter (preserving the Catholic Church's rigid distinction between laity and clergy); it had much wider cultural implications. In their insistence on an absolute right to control the income of the church, the clergy were invoking a fundamental distinction that cut through all of traditional society. It was, in Gordon Wood's terms, "the great horizontal distinction . . . between extraordinary and ordinary people, gentlemen and commoners."[9]

In this dispute over incomes Michael Egan and his assistant were hearkening back to a world in which secular and religious authorities lived, not on the fruits of their own labor or business activities, but on the income guaranteed them by virtue of their position in society. In Egan's view the clergy were a superior order of persons entitled to special privilege and empowered to exercise extraordinary authority and responsibility. If the clergy could not control church revenues, Egan argued, they could not enjoy the independence of action and judgment appropriate to their station and responsibilities. This was a commonplace of prerevolutionary thought and reflected a world in which both secular and religious elites were expected to be "independent in a world of dependencies, learned in a world only partially literate, and leisured in a world of laborers."[10]

The republican revolutions of the late eighteenth century, though, brought such situations into disrepute in both Europe and America. Patriots, in their assault on the traditional social order, insisted that persons who held positions of power and influence derive their rank "naturally from their talent and from below, from recognition by the people." "Even God," Wood writes, "was losing his absolute right to rule." In revolutionary France clergy were reduced to the status of civil servants. In postrevolutionary America "any position that came from any source but talent and the will of the people . . . seemed undeserved and dependent . . . all the fine calibration of ranks and degrees of unfreedom of the traditional monarchical society became absurd and degrading." Michael Egan's insistence that he control church revenues was thus seen by some as an unseemly presumption. Priests, many felt, like all who claimed exalted status, should justify their claim through utility. Thus the suggestion, made when Egan assumed his pastorship at St. Mary's, that the church save money by divesting itself of the most useless of its pastors.[11]

If Bishop Egan's perspectives hearkened back to those of the prerevolutionary elite, the Harolds were very much in tune with the democratic imperatives of their day. A new generation of democratic leaders, many of them immigrants, emerged in Philadelphia in the early decades of the nineteenth century and developed a broadly based following among the lower levels of society. Like the Harolds, these "DEMOCRATIC-Republicans" assaulted the revolutionary elites and the institutions that supported them. Also like the Harolds, these precocious democrats and their supporters were denounced by respectable Philadelphians who saw themselves as a natural aristocracy of talent entitled to the deference of the multitudes.[12]

From the time he arrived in America, William Harold had assiduously courted lay support and had achieved it not only through the conspicuous display of talent but also through diligent attention to the needs and desires of his parishioners. The Harolds were, one contemporary claimed, "Zealous Pastors, who left nothing undone" to promote the cause of religion among the common people of the congregation. William Harold in particular was considered to be the "ablest advocate" of the poor and downtrodden. His claim on the loyalty of many members of St. Mary's congregation was thus based not on merely the traditional status of the clergy, or upon his considerable abilities, but also on his efforts in their behalf. In the emerging democratic culture of early nineteenth-century America the last of these carried the most weight.[13]

The revolutionary generation of the 1770s had assaulted monarchic privilege in the name of a "natural aristocracy," and the founders of the republic had carried in their minds a vision of a hierarchical social and political order in which deference would be accorded leaders based upon their virtue and talent. By the early nineteenth century, though, even this aristocracy of virtue was under assault from common citizens who substituted for virtue and honor the dignity of labor. In the democratic republic "the new moral value given to labor tended to override all mere legal titles . . . and brought aristocratic leisure into contempt and turned labor into a universal badge of honor." It is in this context that we can begin to understand not only the outraged insistence of the Harolds that Bishop Egan, despite his infirmities, perform his fair share of pastoral duties, but also the anonymous demand that "useless" clergy be discarded.[14]

Democratic exaltation of the dignity and moral value of labor did more than challenge the rights of ascribed authority—it also became the cultural basis for new social categories and political action. "All who lived by their labor, whatever their dissimilarities in our modern eyes, did feel as one," sharing "common resentments of a genteel world that had humiliated them and held them in contempt from the beginning of time." This "laboring interest" was by no means confined to the working classes. "Despite all the apparent differences between wealthy mule merchants, small shoemakers, and big manufacturers, socially and psychologically they were all the same." All, workers and business-men alike, joined with the Jeffersonian Republicans "in a democratic attack on all those gentlemen 'who do not labor.' "[15]

The democratic assault on traditional values, privilege, and ascribed authority thus embraced a large and diverse portion of the population of the new republic. This was certainly the case at St. Mary's. James Harold bragged that he and his nephew had ten supporters in the con-gregation to every one who supported Bishop Egan and the dispute over salaries, which pitted the congregation as a whole against the elite trustees, showed a similar imbalance. The traditional values that had sustained St. Mary's lay and clerical leadership for so long found few adherents in the increasingly democratic world of the early nineteenth century.

Because of their differing perspectives Bishop Egan and the Harolds were unnatural allies. Still the matter of clerical salaries united them. To Bishop Egan the inviolability of clerical income was a matter of princi-ple. Any attempt on the part of laymen to control clerical incomes was "not only an act of injustice but an invasion of his right in the govern-ment of his church, which could not be opposed too soon, or too strongly; especially as it might lead to further innovations totally sub-versive of Catholic discipline." The Harolds viewed the matter differ-ently. Like democratic political leaders they saw their position less as a sacred trust than as a career and they expected to be paid well for their efforts. Still the Harolds' ambitions coincided with the bishop's princi-ples to an extent that allowed them to present a united front against the lay trustees who sought to diminish their incomes.[16]

When the trustees of the church declared that they could not pay the clergy's salaries in full, Bishop Egan called a meeting of all the pewhold-ers to discuss the matter. It was a "riotous" and "disorderly" affair char-acterized by many "pernicious" and "antichristian" charges and accusa-tions. "Threats of violence were reciprocated. Clenched fists were held up in the faces of different persons active on the occasion—and one severe blow was given and received." The Harolds came prepared with a list of resolutions approving their own conduct and censuring the trustees; these were passed without debate. When the trustees attempted to defend their actions they were shouted down and silenced. John Carrell attempted to speak and was "several times threatened to be knocked down, by some of the fellows who were placed in different parts of the house, to intimidate everyone that ventured to speak in behalf of the Trustees." "My life," Carrell complained, "was threatened by an Irish porter."[17]

The disturbances at St. Mary's in the late summer and early fall of 1812 came shortly after several episodes of ethnic violence at Holy Trinity Church and resembled them in many ways. In addition to the obvious overtones of class resentments displayed by the Harolds' partisans, there was a strong ethnic component to the confrontations. Although St. Mary's Church was popularly known as Philadelphia's "Irish" church, many of its wealthier members were of old Anglo-American Catholic stock. Such men had been prominent in the coterie of individuals who had traditionally provided leadership to the congregation. Now they were singled out for anonymous threats.

Several of the trustees received letters "threatening their lives, and the burning of their property." A letter was thrown into Charles Johnson's house. It warned, "Lookout dam you—you got a great manny Houses take care of them fire an faggot is your portion if you dont let the Clergy alone—look out black ball." On the following day he received a second threat, this one decorated with crudely drawn shamrocks. It read, "Charley my dear look out you joined the tories, if you ever met them again you will be sorry mind your black ball and your grog and dont mind the Clergy . . . lookout my dear fellow look out." John Ashley received a similarly decorated note saying, "Look out sharp Jack, or you will get a home Spun coat of Kind dam you doe you think that we wil Sufer an English Torry to run down our Clergy. . . . Death is your portion if you dont behave your self keep your self quiet and—and nobody will touch you."[18]

These were the traditional tactics of the Irish countryman used against hereditary enemies, and their appearance in Philadelphia testified to the depth of the cultural animosites that divided the city's Catholic community. Charles Johnson was terrified. On September 8 he asked to be excused from the board of trustees because "a sense of duty to my family and my own peace of mind, prevents me from ever having any thing to do with St. Mary's Church Directly or indirectly." John Carrell saw the entire series of incidents as an effort "to inflame the minds of the people against the Trustees, in order to remove them and put in Men, who are mostly of a class to be dreaded in any society, violent Jacobins, and nearly strangers among us." Such men, he prophesied, though they might be controlled by the Harolds now, would eventually "tyrannize over the Clergy and the people." Should such an end come to pass, he predicted that "most of the respectable members will leave the Church." Not surprisingly, William Harold took a quite different view of the affair; he was jubilant. "The verdict of the congregation," he wrote, "has stung our board of liars more sorely than I imagined. Their address has given universal displeasure and disgust."[19]

Through violence and intimidation, then, the Harolds had carried the day, but the nature of Philadelphia Catholicism had been forever changed. At St. Mary's, just as at Holy Trinity, the years before the War of 1812 saw the emergence and exploitation of class and ethnic antagonisms that had long been submerged. They would not be easily restrained. Something of importance had been lost too. The wrangling over salaries and the blatant attempts to control elections had the inevitable consequence of diminishing the status of the clergy and of the Church itself.

"The Instrument of Unprincipled Men"

In traditional society priests enjoyed special status in large part because they were widely accepted among the laity as moral arbiters, unswayed by worldly interests. This disinterested authority was the aristocratic ideal of the world that had existed prior to the republican revolutions of the eighteenth century, but in the aftermath of those revolutions it was widely seen as a utopian dream, never to be achieved in human affairs. In the civil sphere debates over the salaries to be paid public officials revealed them to be "something other than virtuous leaders" and by the early nineteenth century officeholders were no longer considered to be "specially qualified gentlemen who stood apart from the whole society with a superior and disinterested perspective." A similar shift in perspective was occurring in Philadelphia Catholicism. The unseemly spectacle of priests electioneering and squabbling over salaries could only spawn cynicism and lead many to agree with James Oellers who, after a dispute with William Elling over the terms of his pension, declared that "*all the clergymen are rascals.*"[1]

The uproar over clerical incomes alerted many in the congregation to the financial problems plaguing the church, and donations poured in to pay the priests' salaries, but this brought no end to the affair. The trustees had been publicly humiliated and were determined to regain their honor. They complained to Archbishop Carroll, asking him to personally intercede, but he demurred. They issued a pamphlet putting forth their case and published a list of sixty-seven pewholders who approved their actions. William Harold found their efforts amusing. The trustees, he wrote, "are now begging about for a character. The insurance offices are ransacked for names to keep them in countenance. They are soliciting the dray men for an expression of their confidence. Any name they can come at by influence of any kind is tacked to a paper which they are hawking about laughed at by the city." Bishop Egan refused all appeals for mediation and declared that he would accept from the trustees nothing less than "an unconditional submission and publick disavowal" of their position. Finally, frustrated and desperate, the trustees drew up a petition to the state legislature for an amendment to St. Mary's charter banning clergymen from sitting on the board of trustees.[2]

The threat of an appeal to civil authority brought an immediate response from Bishop Egan. He called and personally chaired a second public meeting, "to refute the calumnies" in the trustees' public statements. One hundred eighty-seven pewholders crowded into St. Joseph's chapel to hear William Harold "harangue [them] in the most inflammatory manner for a considerable time." Then, with near unanimous votes they passed resolutions charging the trustees with "gross falsehood and misrepresentations," of slandering the character of the clergy, of making "indecent and illiberal" statements, and demanding that the trustees "make public and adequate satisfaction to [the clergy], and to the congregation for the unjust aspersions on their character." Faced with overwhelming opposition, the trustees capitulated. At a private meeting with Bishop Egan they agreed to withdraw their petition to the state legislature and promised to moderate their language in the future. Bishop Egan then declared that "all things" were "amicably adjusted to our mutual satisfaction." He apologized for the immoderate statements made by his fellow clergymen and did not require the trustees to make any public admission of their error. He also confided to them that he intended, as soon as possible, to send James Harold out of Philadelphia.[3]

The controversy over salaries had disturbed Bishop Egan. He had been forced to make common cause with men he despised and had alienated his natural constituency—conservative members of the lay elite. In a letter to Archbishop Carroll he confided that he regretted his part in what he called a "dirty work." The inflammatory remarks that had precipitated the breach, Egan said, were written by the elder Harold and he was sorry to have signed them. He also disapproved of the fact that the Harolds had attempted "to interfere in the election of Trustees by influencing the members of the congregation to vote for a ticket of their selection." Such practices, Egan declared, would come to a halt. The incident also convinced Egan that he would have to assert himself against his assistants. "It is my intention," he wrote, "to have Mr. Harold, Senior, removed."[4]

Bishop Egan found that it was not easy to dislodge James Harold. The elder Harold was not popular, but his nephew, William, had a large following and was soon able to rouse a chorus of indignation against the bishop. "A report . . . is in circulation," a member of the congregation informed Egan, "that you have signified your intention of depriving one of your clergy of his trust, without any cause." Such actions, the writer charged, were taken "to appease those [the elite trustees] who are known to be hostile" to the Harolds, and were "unjust" and damaging to the bishop's reputation, for they made him, in the eyes of many within the congregation, "the instrument of unprincipled men" motivated by "diabolical malice."[5]

The letter by "a Catholic" illustrates the extent to which the internecine conflict within St. Mary's had diminished Bishop Egan's status. Rather than being the unquestioned ruler of his diocese he was now being identified as the tool of a specific interest within his cathedral congregation. Through the early months of 1813 the situation deteriorated even further. Finally, Egan ordered James Harold to leave Philadelphia and to assume pastorship of a church in Pittsburgh. When the elder Harold refused the transfer Egan threatened to dismiss him from the diocese. At that point William Harold denounced Egan as a tool of the trustees and threatened to resign from St. Mary's in protest. A letter written in William Harold's support made clear the contempt that many Catholics had for their bishop. It warned that, should Harold be forced to resign, "the poor of St. Mary's would be deprived of their ablest advocate," and it would be difficult to find another priest who would not "lay down his integrity and independence at the feet of that portion of the Congregation who may happen to have wealth or influence, however profligate or unprincipled."[6]

The Harolds then made a fatal error—they publicly announced that they were resigning their positions. Bishop Egan immediately and "gladly accepted." The Harolds apparently had expected that their offer to resign would be refused and greeted Egan's statement with "astonishment and dismay—and were quite thunderstruck." The congregation was stunned and resentful. "The people were inflamed to the highest pitch against the Bishop and Trustees." A "meeting of the congregation" held soon thereafter denounced the unwonted influence of the trustees and the "mortifying" and "imperious" actions of Bishop Egan. Five hundred thirty-four persons who attended the meeting signed a petition delivered to Archbishop Carroll asking him to restore their favorite priest.[7]

What most offended the protesters was Egan's arbitrary manner and the "veil of mystery" that hung over the bishop's affairs. They reported that, when asked by parishioners why he refused to reinstate the Harolds, Egan responded with "rather a harsh refusal" and further comments to the effect that he, as bishop was "the only judge of [the congregation's] wants." They also denounced Egan's proclamation that "Peace and Harmony were restored" between himself and the trustees. Clearly, the Harolds' partisans presumed, Egan had reached a private accommodation with the trustees at the expense of the popular priests. To check the bishop's arbitrary authority they established a watchdog committee that would meet from time to time and consult with the people on matters concerning the congregation as a whole.[8]

John Carroll was sufficiently impressed by the outpouring of protest to urge that William Harold be reinstated at St. Mary's, but Egan was obdurate. He felt that the Harolds were "dangerous persons" whose efforts to rouse public protest were a terrible "stab to Religion," for they were introducing the "spirit of Presbyterianism" into Philadelphia Catholicism. Egan declared his "fixed determination never to receive the Harolds as subjects of my Diocese." William Harold finally relented. Early in April 1813 he appeared before the bishop and asked to be allowed to return to St. Mary's—he even agreed to arrange for his uncle's return to Ireland, but Egan simply said that he had already provided other clergymen for the church.[9]

William Harold's supporters continued to protest. They held mass meetings and passed resolutions condemning the bishop and the current board of trustees. Soon they began to lock up their pews. They saw in the upcoming election for trustees an opportunity to express dramatically the will of the congregation. In the days before the election the Harolds made "domicilary visits" to many members of the congregation to plan their strategy and to solicit votes against the incumbent trustees. Bishop Egan, they speculated, was "possessed of a devil" and "would be a curse to the congregation." Egan's supporters, they said, were "all of them . . . a nest of scoundrels," and their leader had a "soul as black as hell."[10]

The Easter elections expressed the new democratic spirit that raged through St. Mary's congregation. Voting was restricted to pewholders but the Haroldites expanded the electorate by paying rent on a number of pews and then distributing receipts to their supporters. Thus they "gained additional votes by a manner not before availed of." Bishop Egan was shocked by the character of the new voters. James Harold, he wrote, "has descended so low as to meet and confer with numbers of dray porters on the wharves and others of that description." These people, armed with receipts for pew rents, "formed such a multitude and secured so completely the access to the windows that the respectable part of the congregation was prevented from approaching the officers appointed to receive tickets."[11]

John Carrell confirmed Egan's impressions. The "partizans" of the Harolds, he wrote, were "of the lowest class of society, chiefly Aliens and Strangers, with a very few well-meaning men" among them. On the day of the elections a tumultuous "rabble collected round the Window where the votes were taken . . . crowding and shouting for Mr. Harold's ticket" and insulting the "decent persons" who sought to vote. The outcome was a clear victory for the Harolds; a solidly "Haroldite" board of trustees was elected by a margin of three to one. A few days later the defeated "bishopites" met to consider appealing the election, but so overwhelming was the vote for the Haroldites that "despairing of success" they decided to take no action.[12]

Gordon Wood has discussed the consequences for civil society of the decline of traditional authority. Democracy was inevitable, he argues, once the leaders of society (whether hereditary or natural aristocrats) ceased to be seen as disinterested umpires and were identified with specific interests. "If men were all alike," he writes, "equal in their rights and in their interestedness, then there were no specially qualified gentlemen who stood apart from the whole society with a superior and disinterested perspective. All people were the same: all were ordinary and all were best represented by ordinary people. That was democracy."[13]

Such was certainly the case at St. Mary's. Not only were the traditional lay leaders of the congregation discredited in the Haroldite affair, but Bishop Egan unwittingly had allowed himself to be identified with their specific interest. Once that perception had lodged in people's minds it was no longer possible for the bishop to pose as an impartial moral arbiter. Instead, the members of the congregation began to look to themselves and to democratic processes to protect what they perceived to be their own interests.

"Innovators on Established Governments"

The rhetoric accompanying the election of 1813 clearly shows that the Haroldites considered themselves to be defenders of "the People" who had been "injured, insulted, and provoked," by the actions of a "wicked few" among the congregation. Bishop Egan they considered to be the "accomplice" of this cabal, acting to "carry their designs into effect." The removal of both Harolds had deprived the congregation, they said, of their "Zealous Pastors, who left nothing undone" to promote the interests of the many against the few. What was most significant, though, was the conclusion reached by many of the congregation that because traditionally constituted authorities could not be trusted, institutional safeguards would have to be raised to protect the people and the lower clergy. Therefore, like their coreligionists at Holy Trinity, the democratic "Haroldites" at St. Mary's set about to redefine Catholic church governance.[1]

The newly elected trustees, "invested with . . . the confidence of their fellow members by the votes of three fourths of the Congregation," assumed the mantle of defenders of the people formerly worn by the Harolds. They proudly proclaimed their "duty to receive their instructions" from the people, and "to direct the power vested in us to promote such object as they may have in view, by such means as they shall recommend." The trustees promised to "convene the people, and take their opinion and advice on such new measures as we may find necessary from time to time to adopt." These radically democratic innovations they justified as being in accord with the American civil tradition and warned that, "The power of Bishops should always be applied with a most delicate hand," because the arbitrary exercise of authority, even if "just and necessary," was repugnant to Americans who would consider it "absolute tyranny."[2]

The split with episcopal authority came quickly. On May 4, 1813, the new trustees met to discuss church finances. The congregation had no more than $700 to meet expenses and debts were high and overdue. Adding to the financial distress was the fact that the Haroldites had promised to lower the pew rents and funeral fees (which they considered exorbitantly high, but which were major sources of income) so as to make full participation in the church community affordable to all classes. To ease the financial pressure the board voted, as an emergency measure, to restrict the salary of the clergy. Bishop Egan attempted to rule the vote out of order but the board refused to accept this. Egan and his new assistant, Patrick Kenny, then stormed out of the meeting.[3]

Immediately the trustees voted to replace Egan as president of the board, dismissed the sexton of the church (Egan's brother-in-law), and adjourned. They refused to meet again until February of the following year. During these months Bishop Egan disdained all payments from the trustees, interpreting their action as an "unconstitutional" attempt to starve him into submission so that the Harolds might be reinstated. Instead he relied on the charity of the "respectable members" of the congregation. He also asked for and received from Archbishop Carroll permission to refuse absolution to the trustees and all who voted for them. Finally, on July 18, 1813, Bishop Egan formally condemned the trustees and excluded them from the sacraments of the church.[4]

One week later the trustees issued a circular protesting Egan's actions. It was intolerable, they argued, that the bishop could make "the salvation of any portion of his flock" dependent upon satisfying his opinion of how much money he should receive. The trustees emphasized that they were not merely quarreling over money. If they acquiesced to the bishop's demands, they said, they would be "guilty of a treacherous surrender" of the "rights" of the congregation that had elected them.[5]

The trustees' justification of their actions placed them squarely in the mainstream of contemporary democratic thought. It was important, they argued, that they retain control of the bishop's income lest the congregation be placed be at the mercy of his arbitrary power. The only "consecrated fund" that should be available to the bishop, they declared in a letter to Archbishop Carroll, "is in the hearts of the People." Bishop Egan, of course, refused to negotiate with the trustees over this essential matter of principle. In response the trustees threatened open schism. They declared that if the Harolds were not to be reinstated at St. Mary's, "a church should be built for them" where they could preach without interference from Bishop Egan.[6]

In October the trustees, representing, they said, "the poor, the pious, the disconsolate families of our congregation," carried their case to Baltimore. In their remonstrance the trustees attributed their difficulties and those of the Harolds to an elite conspiracy: a plan "impregnated" with "poison" launched by "an implacable vindictive spirit." The plot, they charged, had affected even the archbishop who, surrounded by "unfit" advisors ("absolute infidels in the eye of religion") had unwittingly compromised the integrity of his office and become the instrument of the "busy agents" who swarmed around Bishop Egan.[7]

The conclusions that the Haroldites drew from this were nothing short of revolutionary within the context of the Church's monarchic traditions. They identified Bishop Egan and his supporters with the monarchs and aristocrats of Europe who demanded "absolute unconditional obedience." Such demands, they argued, were not justified unless the bishop, in the judgment of the people, embodied Christian virtue. "We do not hold it among the duties of a Catholic," they wrote, "to consider any dignitary of the Church virtuous, merely because he ought to be virtuous."[8]

In Haroldite eyes Egan's removal of William Harold confirmed Egan's absolutist tendencies, his abuse of power, and his unfitness to rule. The bishop and his lay allies, they alleged, were determined to "permit no clergymen to remain among us who would not become subservient to all their views and wishes." Egan, they wrote, was "trifling with our dearest interests . . . , sporting with our most sacred rights . . . ,

[and] wounding us in our tenderest part." "Your Grace may rest assured," they wrote, that no American congregation "will tamely submit to be trampled on by a monopoly prepared to sacrifice every thing sacred and profane to the very worst of purposes. . . . Neither will the episcopal authority supporting these men, ever create such a submission. On the contrary . . . , they will become more determined by opposition."[9]

Harold's partisans challenged Archbishop Carroll to give them and their ideas a "fair trial." Let the matter be put to a vote of the congregation, they promised, and they would gladly abide with the result. Carroll, though, was by no means willing to allow the parishioners to resolve the conflict through recourse to democratic procedures, nor was he anxious to intervene in Egan's affairs. In his responses Carroll repeatedly expressed his admiration for William V. Harold and his abilities as a preacher but also insisted that it would be impossible to reinstate him at St. Mary's over Bishop Egan's objections.[10]

The confrontation continued through the waning months of 1813 but pressure for accommodation was beginning to mount on both sides. Harold's supporters became increasingly frustrated as they found no official sanction within the Church for their actions and they lacked the resources to found an independent church. Moreover, their justification for cutting the clergy's salaries was losing force since Bishop Egan and his assistants had refused all payments and as a result surplus revenues had begun to accumulate. Michael Egan was in a difficult financial position. For months he had depended on loans from wealthy parishioners, but as church revenues accumulated his benefactors began to insist that Egan come to an agreement with the trustees so that they could recover the money they had advanced.[11]

Elections in April of 1814 produced results much like those of the previous year; the Haroldite trustees were all returned to office. Bishop Egan protested that the trustees packed the church with so many of the rabble that respectable people could not reach the polls. Because there were no funds to pay them, the assistant pastors were sent away to other churches and Egan, whose health was rapidly declining, declared that he was too distressed to hold services without assistance. A final plea for compromise by Mathew Carey was ignored by both sides and soon the church was nearly abandoned. In May of 1814 John Carrell observed that: "Bishop Egan has only a Spanish priest with him, and we are often without a sermon on Sundays. Our morning service does not occupy an hour, the church is very thin of people in the morning and almost empty in the afternoon."[12]

The continuing conflict took a toll on the bishop. By the summer of 1814 he was dying. In his last months Egan eked out a lonely, poverty-stricken existence in a small house owned by the Jesuits attached to St. Joseph's chapel. His two assistants had been sent away, as "for peace's sake" were his sister who had served him at the rectory and his brother-in-law who had acted as sexton. Early in July he suffered "an alarming hemorrhage of his lungs, succeeded . . . by copious bleedings, cupping and blisters, [and] by a pain in the left breast that baffles all medical art." On July 6 Egan made out his will. Sixteen days later, attended by John Grassi and Patrick Kenny, Philadelphia's first bishop expired at the age of fifty-three. Twelve days before his death his former assistant, Patrick Kenny, proclaimed Egan "a Martyr of the . . . truly Catholic principle: That the laity never had nor ever will acquire by any means the right of nominating and appointing their priests as Pastors, in defiance of the will and approbation of a Catholic Bishop." On the day Egan died, Kenny hailed him as "the first Victim of Episcopal rights."[13]

Bishop Egan was not the only casualty of the Haroldite insurrection at St. Mary's. The church itself would never be the same. The arrival of the Harolds shattered the united front that had been maintained there, by the clergy and influential laymen, against democratic innovations. They instituted a popular style of preaching that drew new members into the church, and they actively recruited into the congregation people who had previously been excluded. "Never before," John Carrell complained, had "such Men [as the Haroldites] . . . presumed to interfere in the affairs of the Church." He felt that "Mr. [William] Harold has much to answer for in bringing [them] forward," for he has "shewn them their strength."[14]

That the Harolds did all of this in the service of their own considerable ambitions is beside the point. The Harolds by the summer of 1814 had transformed St. Mary's from a elitist, Federalist stronghold, properly docile and submissive to episcopal authority, into a factionalized congregation "split into two distinct parties, as much at enmity, as if the possessions of one had been plundered by the other." In this divided congregation the majority faction formed a "phalanx of opponents to church authority," committed to the principle that "Episcopacy must bend & bow low to the purse strings of a corporate body." By the summer of 1814 "Laymen" were "so fully initiated into . . . Clerical affairs that . . . nothing has been transacted without their advice & their directions." So sweeping were these democratic innovations that Patrick Kenny was of the opinion St. Mary's had ceased to be a church and had become, in effect, a "Lay department."[15]

"Paltry Intrigues"

Bishop Egan's death removed from the troubled diocese the last vestige of episcopal authority. Diocesan affairs soon dissolved into a welter of contending parties. Matters were not much different at the national level. Archbishop Carroll was aged and infirm and his control over the mission was slipping. Suffragan bishops, clerics, and laymen fought and conspired over episcopal appointments, and the archbishop's desires were little heeded. At the international level, too, chaos reigned. The disruptions attendant on the Napoleonic Wars, the pope's flight into exile, and a host of other problems made Propaganda's efforts to exercise its authority over the American mission only intermittently successful. Still, within the chaos, traces of a new, emergent order could be discerned.

In Philadelphia attention was focused on the question of who would succeed Bishop Egan. Almost immediately Harold's supporters began to press for his return. On July 24, 1814, St. Mary's trustees implored Archbishop Carroll to restore their "most worthy and beloved pastor," whose exile they blamed on the "Unprincipled Intrigues of a few Men" who had evinced a "Spirit of malevolence" toward their pastor and had reduced the congregation "to a State of distraction and desolation far Surpassing whatever the most timid could forebode, or the most pious deprecate." Carroll, the Haroldites hoped, would never lend his support to such men and would soon sanction William Harold's return. If he did not, they warned, and like Egan "disappointed" the "Just

Expectations" of the congregation, "more serious calamities" would surely ensue.[1]

Carroll of course responded in the negative. He warned the trustees against introducing "party politics" into church affairs. The Haroldites then charged that Carroll was attempting to "inflame and aggravate the existing animosities amongst us which are already but too raucorous." Like Bishop Egan, they wrote, the archbishop had allied himself with "those who have brought so much misery upon this congregation," and gave "countenance and support . . . only . . . to those who coincide with [his] political views." Should Carroll persist in his opposition to William Harold, they promised, it would be "necessary for us to have recourse to . . . other authority," and they warned that if those extreme measures became necessary Carroll's continued "subservience of the episcopal authority . . . to the improper views of a few men, would be as fatal to religion in our day as it was in those of Henry 8 and Elizabeth."[2]

John Carroll's rejection of their appeal thus reduced him, in the eyes of the Haroldites, from the status of disinterested moral arbitrator to that of spokesman for a specific interest. By contrast the Haroldites saw themselves as the true moral force in Philadelphia Catholicism, articulating the needs and desires of common men and women in a continuing struggle against arbitrary authority wielded in the service of social, political, and religious elites. Like democratic insurgents in the civil sphere, they legitimized their opposition to constituted authority through reference to the principle of popular sovereignty and asserted that power must always be exercised in accord with the will of the people broadly defined.

Once again the conflict between democracy and constituted authority carried dangerous overtones. The Haroldites were beginning to identify their grievances and principles with the spirit of the Protestant Reformation. Nor were they the only participants in the controversy to make such a connection. In his response to the trustees' demands Carroll himself confirmed this linkage. "The Catholic Church," he thundered, "will never admit the principles and practice [of the] Presbyterians." He expressed his absolute "disapprobation of ecclesiastical democracy," which he defined as "an overbearing interference of the people, in the appointment of the Pastors," and he advised the Haroldites to "leave . . . the gov[ernmen]t. of the Church & appointment of its pastors, . . . in the hands of those, where the laws of Cath[olic]. discipline have constituted them."[3]

The democratic rhetoric and threats of schism advanced by the Haroldites convinced Archbishop Carroll that William Harold must never return to Philadelphia. Harold's presence there, Carroll argued,

> would be a signal for rancour, religious and political; religious between the friends of the holy deceased Bishop and partisans of Harold; political between the opponents of previous democracy and innovators upon established governments, or rather those who are always for innovation, glossed over with the fair pretexts of the *rights of the people.*[4]

The Haroldites were baffled by Carroll's stance. They felt that Bishop Egan's death had removed the most important obstacle to Harold's return. They noted that the archbishop had repeatedly praised Harold in the past and had expressed a strong desire for his "continuance in Am[eric]a, and even at Phil[adelphi]a, in preference to any other Nation." Carroll had even written that Harold's departure was one "of the greatest misfortunes that can befall [Philadelphia] and the American church generally." The archbishop's change of heart, they felt, was evidence of the same elite conspiracy that had suborned Bishop Egan. What the Haroldites did not understand was that, by the fall of 1814, William Harold and John Carroll had become embroiled in a confrontation that reached all the way to Rome.[5]

Carroll's remarks had been made several months before the death of Michael Egan when Harold had decided to leave America and to return to Ireland with his friend and fellow Dominican, John A. Ryan. Once away from America, though, Harold and Ryan had run afoul of the archbishop. On their way to Ireland they stopped in London and there delivered a scathing critique of the ex-Jesuit community in Maryland based on the fact that many of the missionaries there derived their income from lands worked by slaves.

This criticism offended Carroll because Harold and Ryan were raising a difficult issue at an inopportune time. Negotiations were going on in Russia and Rome that would soon lead to the restoration of the Society of Jesus, and the ex-Jesuits were sensitive to anything that might impede that process. On learning of the criticisms, Carroll wrote to Bishop Moylan of Cork denouncing Harold and Ryan and accusing them of misrepresenting the condition of slaves on the Jesuit plantations. The two Dominicans stood by their objections to slavery on clerical estates, made copies of all the correspondence relating to the controversy, and sent them to the prefect of Propaganda.[6]

The controversy over slavery reinforced John Carroll's determination to oppose Harold's return to America, but a larger issue was also involved—William Harold wished to succeed Michael Egan not only as pastor but as bishop. In October 1814, James Harold wrote to the Holy See recommending his nephew for the Philadelphia post. He also secured a recommendation from the bishop of Bordeaux. Meanwhile William Harold sought and received recommendations from a number of Irish prelates, apparently including Archbishop Troy of Dublin.[7]

Harold's pursuit of the mitre marked a change in the relationship between Rome and the American church. Ever since 1788 control of episcopal nominations had, with one exception, remained in America. In 1792 Propaganda had asked John Carroll to nominate his coadjutor, and the archbishop chose Lawrence Graessl, who died before he could assume the post. Carroll then suggested Leonard Neale for the position and in 1795 Rome issued the bulls confirming Neale as coadjutor. In 1808, when the American mission was divided into separate dioceses, Rome again accepted Carroll's nominees to fill most of the newly created sees, although it rejected his recommendations with regard to the diocese of New York and appointed Luke Concanen (a Dominican) to be bishop there. Bishop Concanen died before he could leave Italy and so the newly created see of New York remained vacant. Thus by 1810 all of the sitting members of the American hierarchy had been nominated either by American bishops or by the American clergy. In that year, at the first conference of the American hierarchy, the bishops sought to make permanent this privilege when they "respectfully suggested to the [Pope] to allow the nomination for vacant dioceses to proceed solely from the Archbishop and Bishops of this Ecclesiastical Province."[8]

Through all of this Propaganda had been careful to emphasize the fact that ultimate power over episcopal appointments resided in the Holy See. In 1788 the congregation extended the privilege of electing a nominee "as a special grant and favor for this time only." In 1808 Propaganda honored Carroll's recommendations, but the bull establishing the American dioceses specifically stated that future bishops were "to be elected and constituted by us and the Apostolic See, etc." The American bishops' suggestion that they be allowed to choose their successors was simply ignored. Neither was there any response to Archbishop Carroll's attempt in 1814 to control the appointments to fill the vacancies in New York and Philadelphia.[9]

On August 23, 1814, little more than a month after Michael Egan's death, John Carroll asked his suffragan bishops and the administrators of Philadelphia and New York to propose candidates to fill the vacancies. Carroll then selected two from among the suggested candidates and forwarded the recommendations to the Holy See. Because of unstable conditions in Europe at the end of the Napoleonic era he took the precaution of sending several copies of his recommendations, two of them carried by "safe persons." Nevertheless, when Carroll asked some months later why there had been no response to his proposals, Propaganda replied that none of his letters had been received. Carroll found this hard to believe, especially since he had confirmation that two of the letters had been received by the papal nuncio in Paris. He saw the fine hand of the Harolds and the Irish bishops at work and concluded that "Intrigue has been very active."[10]

There was no real conspiracy. The Holy See had simply determined to take a more active role in American affairs. Propaganda was well aware of the antipathy that had developed between William Harold and Archbishop Carroll and early in 1815 asked Archbishop Troy to sound out Carroll on the matter. On the same day the prefect informed Carroll that John Connolly (a Dominican and a longtime associate of Bishop Concanen) had been appointed bishop of New York, despite the archbishop's preference for Ambrose Maréchal in that post. Carroll thought he saw in the New York appointments and Harold's ambitions an Irish plot to exert influence over the American church. Charles Plowden agreed with him. "I have long known," he wrote, "the wonderful activity of Irish Friars [Dominicans] to get their heads into mitres, and I have often been amazed at the success of their paltry intrigues."[11]

Angrily John Carroll fired off a letter to Archbishop Troy denouncing Harold and John Ryan. "The manner in which Messrs. H[arold]. and R[yan]. left this country," he wrote, "indisposed my R. R. B[ishops]. & myself" to recommend Harold as Egan's successor. Harold's recourse to an "irregular agency" (securing recommendations from European prelates) outraged Carroll. "Would it not be resented," he asked Troy, "as a very improper interference, if we the B[isho]ps in the U.S. should presume to suggest to the Holy See the persons to be appointed to fill the Vacant Sees of Ireland?" To Propaganda he complained that Harold had spoken "openly and most contumaciously" against Bishop Egan and had lied repeatedly about the American Jesuits. "For these reasons," he wrote, the possibility that Harold would return to America, "clothed with a new dignity, . . . greatly disturbed" the American prelates and would "result in arousing the gravest dissension." Three months later he again wrote to Rome complaining about William Harold's "insulting and improper" conduct. He predicted that Harold's return would provoke "many and serious dissensions, even among the laity." At last Carroll was satisfied that he had thwarted the Dominicans. To Charles Plowden he wrote, "Notwithstanding the irregular interposition & recommendation of the friends in Ireland of Mr. Harold, and even of Archb[isho]p Troy & other prelates there, I do not, & probably shall not hear of his appointment."[12]

Carroll also moved against the Haroldites. A few days before his death Michael Egan had nominated Louis DeBarth, who served the Conewago mission, as his vicar general. The nomination had not been accepted or confirmed, but it gave Carroll an important opening. On July 27, 1814, he informed St. Mary's trustees that DeBarth was entitled, under canon law, "to exercise all the authority of the deceased." No alternatives were possible, he said, because DeBarth held this authority "immediately in virtue of the power, of the Pope himself, and he holds it dependently on the Pope alone." No ultramontane zealot could have advanced a more extreme position with regard to papal power, and the fact that it issued from John Carroll shows how far his thinking had evolved from the days when he defiantly rejected the authority of Rome over the clergy of the American mission.[13]

Louis DeBarth was an Alsatian aristocrat out of place in the new republic. He was a man of limited intellect ("unable to bear study, reading and very little writing") and his temper was "very warm; his passion sudden." Nonetheless John Carroll considered that DeBarth had the correct political attitudes. The émigré priest, absolutely repelled by the liberal tendencies of the age, was a staunch defender of monarchy who urged laymen to adopt the stance of "faithful and obedient children" toward episcopal authority. This, Carroll thought, was exactly the kind of man who would serve him well in Philadelphia. He described DeBarth as a man with "firmness of mind . . . well qualified to withstand a turbulent party at Philad[elphi]a," and as "A firm man [who] will execute orders."[14]

Louis DeBarth, though, had no ambitions, no taste for controversy, and no intention of moving to the city. He refused the appointment as Egan's successor and on July 24 notified the archbishop that he should

"consider this Diocese as having no Vicar General." Carroll was determined that DeBarth fill the post. He ignored the priest's decision and
ordered him to take up his duties in the city. DeBarth responded with
a dramatic plea. "I write upon my knees. Do not, Most Revd. Father,
drive me into Despair, Death would not be so frightful to me as
Philadelphia, where I would soon follow my Bishop. Order me to quit
Conewago I will obey . . . , but do not order me to go to Philadelphia."
Should Carroll insist on the appointment, DeBarth asserted, he would
be forced, "notwithstanding the repugnance I feel" toward France, to
return there. Carroll was not moved. On July 29 he appointed DeBarth
administrator of Philadelphia with "all the authority of the deceased
until the Holy See appointed a new Bishop." Reluctantly, Louis DeBarth
bowed to the wishes of his superior and traveled to Philadelphia and
there took up residence.[15]

"The Present System of Ecclesiastical Mismanagement"

In December 1815, John Carroll died and an era in the history of
American Catholicism came to an end. During Carroll's episcopacy the
American clergy had grown from a collegial band of equals into a hier-
archically organized, pluralistic, ecclesiastical bureaucracy in which
authority was progressively monarchized. Through all of this Carroll
had attempted as much as possible to preserve the informal relationships and collegial customs that had prevailed in the colonial church.
Although a fierce defender of episcopal prerogatives, Carroll generally
maintained a nonpunitive stance toward the lower clergy and laymen
who challenged him. His approach, in Patrick Carey's words, was "firm,
but conciliatory."[1]

Carroll's successors, though, were far less forgiving and far more
absolutist in their understanding of episcopal authority than was he. As

Jay Dolan put it, "the clergy failed to step boldly into the future and fashion a church in tune with the republican spirit of the new nation. Rather, they looked to the past, to the European tradition of Roman Catholicism, for their model of the church." For Leonard Neale, Carroll's coadjutor and immediate successor, challenges to episcopal prerogatives were the work of "immoral and rebellious heretics" with whom no compromise was possible. Neale's successor, Ambrose Maréchal, was equally inflexible. To him lay and clerical dissenters were "enemies of the church of Christ," besotted with the "drunkeness of ambition," and possessed of "the same customs, principles and turbulent passions which imbued those impious men who tried to overthrow the altars of Christ in the abominable French Revolution." Such adamantine inflexibility aggravated existing tensions in Philadelphia and contributed significantly to the conflicts that erupted there in the 1820s.[2]

Carroll's death also initiated a period of instability in the American episcopacy. His successor as metropolitan of Baltimore was Leonard Neale. Archbishop Neale, aged and infirm, ruled for little more than a year. Ambrose Maréchal, who succeeded Neale, was a capable administrator but his regime was plagued by internecine conflict between French and Irish clergy. This instability and conflict, along with the breakdown of even the limited collegiality of John Carroll's later years, produced terrible strains that exacerbated existing conflicts between the episcopacy and Catholic dissenters. It also invited an ever greater degree of Roman interference in American affairs.[3]

Already in the last years of Carroll's regime Propaganda had begun to take control of episcopal assignments. The appointments of Luke Concanen and John Connolly to the see of New York originated in Rome and were made without input from the American bishops. "Mr. Connolly is appointed," Carroll complained in the spring of 1815, "with whom none of us are acquainted; nor has any one in this country been consulted. I wish this may not become a very dangerous precedent." The archbishop's wishes were not heeded. Six months later, little more than a week after Carroll's death, the cardinals of Propaganda, faced with conflicting claims, decided to ignore all the recommendations from Europe and America and nominated Ambrose Maréchal to become the second bishop of Philadelphia.[4]

Maréchal never served in Philadelphia. In February 1816, unaware of Rome's decision, Leonard Neale suggested Maréchal as one of two candidates to serve as his coadjutor in Baltimore. Two months after that Maréchal himself wrote to the prefect of Propaganda saying that he could not accept the Philadelphia appointment. The Sacred Congregation refused to accept Maréchal's refusal and ordered him to the city, but when the bulls naming him bishop arrived, Maréchal simply declined to accept them.[5]

Shortly thereafter Propaganda altered its decision with regard to the vacant diocese. On August 17 the prefect suggested that Archbishop Neale make Maréchal his coadjutor. This was what both men desired and they leaped at the opportunity. On December 20, 1816, Neale formally requested Maréchal's appointment to Baltimore. At the same time he suggested that Louis DeBarth be nominated bishop of Philadelphia. Propaganda had already been considering just such an action and so on the same day (May 19, 1817) that Ambrose Maréchal was nominated as coadjutor bishop of Baltimore Propaganda extended an informal invitation to Louis DeBarth to accept the mitre of Philadelphia.[6]

Louis DeBarth was no more willing to accept episcopal responsibilities in 1817 than he had been two years earlier. He ignored Propaganda's offer and when bulls arrived naming him bishop he refused them in the most dramatic terms. If the nomination to the episcopacy is not withdrawn, he warned Bishop Maréchal,

> I will not accept, but will kneel down and devoutly put the bulls in the fire, as we do with fragments of articles that have been blessed. Then I will make out testimonials for myself, signed in my real name, as Vicar-General, and give myself another name in the body of the paper, and then farewell, Monseigneur. Neither you nor any one else shall ever know the corner of the globe where I shall vegetate the few years still left me to live.[7]

Through all these months of maneuver and intrigue the Haroldites continued to hope for their pastor's return and at each stage in the complicated series of appointments they renewed their petition. Soon after John Carroll's death they asked Archbishop Neale to return Harold to them. Leonard Neale refused the request. When Ambrose Maréchal succeeded Archbishop Neale, the Haroldites renewed their petition. "We . . . humbly beg leave to lay before you Most Rev. Sir, our Prayers and Desires. . . . We . . . implore you, Most Rev. Sir, to make use of your influence to have the Rev. William V. Harold once more restored to the congregation at St. Mary's."[8]

In response to the Haroldites' petition Ambrose Maréchal wrote that he was "not sufficiently acquainted with [William Harold] to pronounce whether it would be advantageous or not to Religion to invite him to Philadelphia." He had only "been once or twice in [Harold's] company during a few hours" and the Irish priest had "certainly left a favorable opinion in [his] mind." But, he continued, "the heavy complaints which the good and venerable Bishop Egan and the illustrious Dr. Carroll have made against [Harold], are sufficient reasons for me never to make use of my influence to draw him over to this country, . . . where he might be the cause (although innocent) of new troubles and disturbances."[9]

The Haroldites saw in the archbishop's denial of their petition evidence of anti-Irish bias. Maréchal was indeed prejudiced against the Irish. He considered them to be turbulent, drunken, devious and ambitious by nature, and subversive of authority. These attitudes did not endear him to his colleagues of Irish descent, one of whom was John Connolly, the bishop of New York. By 1818 French émigré bishops already controlled the dioceses of Baltimore, Louisiana, Boston, and Bardstown, and DeBarth's appointment would add yet another. Connolly saw Maréchal's attempts to orchestrate DeBarth's nomination as part of a French conspiracy to dominate the American church, and to counter this supported William Harold's attempts to secure the Philadelphia appointment. He asked his agent in Rome to spread the word in Propaganda that Harold was "most worthy of that vacant See" and followed this with a letter recommending Harold in the most favorable terms.[10]

To buttress his case for Harold's appointment Bishop Connolly solicited testimony from the laity in Philadelphia. True to their principles, the Haroldites scrupulously followed democratic procedures in their response. They called a meeting of the congregation which elected a committee to petition the trustees to call a second meeting that would pass resolutions to be sent to the Holy See. At that meeting the Haroldites deplored "their loss and privation by the retirement of their former beloved pastor—the Rev. Wm. V. Harold," and resolved, "that as all applications [for his return] to the Church authorities . . . [have] been in vain, the Trustees are requested to make direct application to the Sovereign Pontiff for obtaining that object."[11]

The language of the petition clearly reflected Bishop Connolly's influence. "Our Congregation," they wrote, "as well as the far greater part of the Roman Catholics throughout the Union . . . are . . . Migrators from Ireland and the Descendants of such." These people should be served by clergymen who had shared their "three hundred years of mutual sufferings and privations for the cause of our Holy Faith" and who could preach to them in their accustomed "Language, Idiom, and Pronunciation." They accused Maréchal of "partiality to his native Country" which caused him to favor the Frenchman, DeBarth, over the Irishman, Harold. They appealed to Rome for the return of Harold, who would be a benefit to religion, for he could furnish "from his known character and connexions in Ireland a constant supply of Priests . . . who would be identified with ourselves in origin kindred, languages and Sensations."[12]

The appeal failed. In July 1818, Propaganda informed Bishop Connolly that William Harold could not be considered because the decision had already been made to elevate Louis DeBarth. However when DeBarth refused the nomination Bishop Connolly again urged Propaganda to consider William Harold for the vacancy. The Haroldites followed this effort with a second petition in June 1819. Once again the influence of Bishop Connolly is unmistakable although the language is not what he would have chosen. In a cover letter attached to the petition the Haroldites declared that the appointment of an Irishman to the episcopacy was necessary "to defeat the designs of a French Jesuitical faction; who seem so anxious to possess themselves of our Churches and Church livings here."[13]

The Haroldites' second petition again fused ethnic and liberal imperatives with institutional rivalries within the Church. They strongly protested the "present system of ecclesiastical mismanagement in this country," which they blamed on "men actuated by views of gratifying their ambition." They complained about "the Archbishop of Baltimore, who is a Frenchman" as well as "a particular order [the Jesuits], primarily instituted for the promotion of their best interests, at the shrine of their own aggrandisement in power and wealth." These nefarious interests, the Haroldites claimed, were seeking to introduce into America "a race of clergymen foreign as well to the feelings as [to the] language of the people."[14]

Should these conditions not be corrected, the Haroldites predicted a general revolt throughout American Catholicism. "A great number of souls," they declared, were determined not to "surrender their rights, their honor and their conscience by permitting clergymen to be forced upon them, whom they knew to be both incompetent and immoral." They predicted that a "convention of Delegates from the several Catholic Congregations of the United States" would soon meet to "devise a remedy" for "the state of our ecclesiastical affairs," and they urged the Holy See to prevent such an occurrence by instituting a policy of "reasonable compliance with the request of the people, and a just respect for their rights."[15]

As the cardinals of Propaganda contemplated their response to the Haroldites' petition, further communications came in from interested parties. Archbishop Maréchal wrote to say that the dissenters' complaints were "sheer pretexts." He pointed out that similar protests had occurred under Bishop Egan, an Irishman, and during times when St. Mary's had been served solely by Irish clergy. Maréchal, betraying again his prejudices, suggested that the true cause of the disturbances was "the turbulent spirit of the Irish, enjoying for the first time in many centuries of their history an independence they were not ready for." From John Ryan came a letter indicating that Harold was aware of the problems in America and willing to return to Philadelphia in order to settle the disorder there.[16]

A second letter from Ryan, in December 1819, summarized and sought to explain the arguments of Harold's supporters. He recounted the dispute between the Harolds and Bishop Egan and the controversy over Jesuit slaveholding, presenting each as a misunderstanding; he cited John Carroll's early praise for William Harold; and he raised the specter of a "systematic plan," headed by "Doctor Marechall" and his advisors, "for the exclusion from the Church of America, of every clergyman who is not a native of France." This, he said, was a matter of great concern to all American Catholics. Ryan also raised the possibility of civil action. Since they were invested by the laws of the United States with "an undoubted right to elect their clergy," he wrote, the laity had the legal means to correct the French drift within the episcopacy. Should the Holy See not act to block the French by placing Irish prelates, such as William Harold, in vacant sees, then the American Catholics might be tempted to use "this legal right," which would be injurious to "the essential spirit which pervades the discipline of the Catholic Church."[17]

All these efforts in Harold's support failed. The years of controversy surrounding William Harold, the veiled and sometimes explicit threats of his supporters, and the opposition of the American archbishops rendered him unfit, in Propaganda's opinion, for the post he sought. On

September 11, 1819, the prefect wrote to inform Maréchal that an appointment would be made to Philadelphia and that it would not be William Harold. Propaganda also informed St. Mary's petitioners that fears of French dominance were misplaced since it had made ample provision for Irish bishops. Two new dioceses (Richmond and Charleston) had been created and both were to be ruled by Irish bishops, and an Irishman, Henry Conwell of Armagh, had been chosen for Philadelphia. Moreover, Propaganda declared, the presumption in St. Mary's petition, that the laity had a right to nominate their own candidates for episcopal offices, was contrary to the laws of the Catholic Church. Finally, on November 20, 1820, Propaganda formally pronounced that William Harold "did not possess those qualities which are necessary for a Bishop and therefore on account of Religion he should not be promoted to that dignity."[18]

"A State of Confusion"

While episcopal authorities bickered among themselves, the Philadelphia diocese verged on general revolt. A letter written in 1818 reported that "The Catholics of [Philadelphia] did not wish . . . to hear about the discipline of the Church or about Canon law, and many of them held that only the civil law of the States should prevail in ecclesiastical affairs. The author of the letter feared that if some concessions were not made to the American Catholics, the Church [in Philadelphia] would be extinct in twenty years." Louis DeBarth agreed. He declared in 1818 that the Haroldites at St. Mary's "will soon shut the door on lawful ministers." One year later Francis Roloff, the pastor at Holy Trinity, complained about the "phrensied minds" of many Philadelphia Catholics. "The Proceedings and plans of these Strange Catholics cannot but strike every reader with abhorrence," he wrote, "notions of religious independence, and hierarchical Tyranny have taken possession of many a deluded head."[1]

Louis DeBarth was totally ineffectual in this situation. He disliked Philadelphia and spent as little time there as possible, returning often to the western missions and leaving the pastoral duties at St. Mary's to his assistant. It was his habit in any crisis to procrastinate, hoping that the arrival of a bishop would lift the burden of responsibility from him. Under DeBarth "pastoral affairs simply drifted along. Discipline, never much enforced . . . , became more and more relaxed" and dissent spread widely. Outside the city of Philadelphia two German priests, one at Conewago and another at York, raised revolts against the administrator and were relieved of their faculties (both soon left the Catholic Church). By 1820 congregations in Lancaster, Lebanon, York, and Conewago were "in a state of confusion."[2]

This turmoil was not confined merely to Catholic congregations. These years witnessed throughout Pennsylvania, the nation, and even through much of the hemisphere, the final dissolution of a traditional social and political order based on a culture of hierarchy and deference. Everywhere ancient standards and institutions were giving way to new modes of social, political, and cultural organization and the Haroldite insurrection at St. Mary's Church was but one episode in this general pattern of decline and transformation.

The general contours of change that accompanied Philadelphia's growth from a commercial entrepôt into an industrial metropolis are well known. In a remarkably short time the bulk of the city's commerce shifted from foreign to domestic trade, the population swelled dramatically, and manufacturing displaced commerce as the economic base on which the city's prosperity depended. These were momentous changes and together they dramatically altered the social and cultural landscape of the city. In the process the social context of religious dissent and the values attached to it were substantially transformed.[3]

In the first two generations after the American Revolution Philadelphia's population mushroomed—from less than 24,000 in 1775 to more than 80,000 at the turn of the century, to nearly 190,000 in 1830. As the city grew, it spread out and the "walking city" of the eighteenth century gradually dissolved into a number of discrete neighborhoods, each with its unique social, cultural, and economic character. In this complex urban mosaic various elements of the population pursued increasingly disparate existences. Of particular importance to the Catholic community was the emergence, in a "ring" around the periphery of the center city, of several industrial neighborhoods. In these working-class communities, residents, both Protestant and Catholic, developed and sustained patterns of behavior and belief that were quite different from those of the city's emerging bourgeoisie and industrial elite.[4]

The social structure of industrializing Philadelphia bore little resemblance to that of the traditional world. The mercantile elite that had dominated the preindustrial city gave way to new entrepreneurial and professional classes while a nascent bourgeoisie began to displace the old "mechanics interest" that had once dominated the middle ranks of society. At the workplace the old solidarity of artisanal labor broke down as the traditional master-journeyman bond increasingly evolved into an employer-employee relationship, and at the bottom of the occupational ladder a "floating proletariat" of young, unskilled and semiskilled workers flowed through the city looking for steady work. Finally, by the 1820s, in what had once been the "best poor man's country" in the world, a permanent indigent population had become an ineradicable feature of the urban environment and was beginning to pose a problem of significant proportions.[5]

Philadelphia's Catholics participated in and were profoundly affected by this general restructuring of social and economic relationships, and the tensions generated by rapid change were reflected in the Catholic community. One prominent focus of resentment was the emerging bourgeoisie. Reminiscing about his boyhood years in early nineteenth-century Philadelphia, Father Patrick Jordan noted that many of the city's Catholics "had been very successful in commerce and in mercantile pursuits, and, with the acquisition of wealth put on the airs of the parvenu." Father Jordan was contemptuous of these "new made gentlemen and women," particularly "the fashionable Catholics of East Fourth Street . . . *et hoc genus omne*." He identified them as the foremost enemies of the Church—those who fostered the "spirit of independence, or more properly speaking insubordination," that kept Philadelphia Catholicism in turmoil through the 1820s.[6]

These "fashionable Catholics" were among the most conspicuous beneficiaries of social change. Others were not so fortunate. For many immigrants life was difficult and even desperate. Often work was uncertain. Seasonal and cyclical changes in the business environment produced frequent rises in unemployment, especially for unskilled and semiskilled workers, while mechanization and more efficient ways of organizing production rapidly destabilized traditional crafts. The result was a huge pool of workers, many of them immigrants, who floated from job to job seeking permanent employment and who were frequently unemployed and hard-pressed to support themselves.[7]

The Haroldite revolt had enjoyed wide support within St. Mary's congregation. Immigrant laborers and the new-made men and women had cooperated in an assault on tradition. It was a remarkable confluence of liberal resentments against an authoritarian regime, Irish ethnic assertiveness, and class-based antagonism against the elites that had traditionally dominated Philadelphia Catholicity, but this unity of interests could not hold for long. The processes of change that had brought down the old order continued to operate, and in the years after William Harold's departure from Philadelphia class antagonisms and cultural divergence drove an ever widening wedge into the city's Catholic community.

Members of the resident Catholic clergy played a role in fomenting and sustaining these antagonisms. Many of Philadelphia's priests were ethnic "traditionalists" who sought to maintain in urban America the values and relationships that prevailed in rural Ireland. In some cases they were simply retaining and defending the traditions they had known in their youth, but at times more complex psychological processes were involved. By far the most noted of these traditionalists was Michael Hurley, O.S.A., pastor at St. Augustine's Church. A large, burly man with a florid complexion and impressive rhetorical abilities, Hurley emerged in the years after William Harold's departure from the city as "the leading priest" in Philadelphia and the chief spokesman for this ethnic traditionalist faction within the local clergy.[8]

From his pulpit at St. Augustine's Hurley launched an unrelenting assault on the Catholic bourgeoisie. He "laughed at and ridiculed their airs, and took delight in violating their rules of etiquette, and in generally shocking their sensibilities." His speech and mannerisms were "brusque and unpolished" and he often affected an almost impenetrable Irish brogue. He drank heavily—it was said that often he was so disabled by the previous "night's frolick and singing" that he was "unable . . . to descend down stairs," and was forced to hear confessions "in his bed chamber." He associated publicly with disreputable characters from the Southwark slums (it was charged that Hurley "kept no society but that of singers and gamblers") and generally delighted in "shocking the sensibilities of the elite," both Protestant and Catholic. On one notable occasion, in full view of a horrifed audience of respectable Catholics, he publicly humiliated Robert Wharton, a leader of Philadelphia's Quaker community.[9]

Although Michael Hurley posed as an almost stereotypical Irish immigrant of the lower classes he was actually a product of the very social environment he so assiduously attacked. Alone among the resident clergy he was born in Philadelphia. His father, Thomas Hurley, had emigrated from County Tipperary shortly after the American Revolution and found employment in Philadelphia first as an upholsterer and then as a paperhanger. An ambitious man, Thomas Hurley soon went into business for himself, hiring others to hang paper while he opened a shop and ultimately built a manufacturing establishment "of large size" in Southwark where he produced his own line of paper. Success in business brought social acceptance. After the death of his first wife (Michael's Irish-born mother) Hurley married a Protestant lady of good family. At the time of his death in 1817 Thomas Hurley was a man of considerable affluence and much of his wealth passed to his son, who served as administrator of the family estate. Thus, during Michael Hurley's formative years his family had experienced precisely the same trajectory of achievement and assimilation he so vehemently denounced in others. No less than the targets of his scorn, Michael Hurley was a new-made man.[10]

It is tempting, but probably fruitless, to speculate on the psychological forces that shaped Michael Hurley's career. As a boy he had worked for his father, preparing to take over the family business, but after his mother's death and his father's remarriage he turned to religion. His family's wealth bought him an excellent education in Italy and it was there, not in Ireland, that he studied for the priesthood. In his early twenties Hurley returned to Philadelphia where he joined Matthew Carr at St. Augustine's Church. There he distinguished himself as a preacher and an administrator. His talent, his education, and his family's social standing all recommended Hurley to the lay leadership at St. Mary's, and after William Harold's departure the Haroldite trustees even considered offering him the position of pastor there, but nothing came of it, perhaps because Hurley's intemperance, unpolished manners, and lower-class associations offended some influential members of the congregation.[11]

Philadelphia's Catholic bourgeoisie reciprocated the contempt leveled against them by the traditionalist clergy. "This congregation has always been looked upon as highly respectable," a "Layman of [St.

Mary's] congregation" wrote in 1821, "but we owe this respectability, ·
not to the priests who have occasionally been sent out to us." William
Harold was remembered as a man of "talents, good education and a
gentlemanly conduct," attributes that the other clergy "had only heard
of . . . , but by name." With their ethnic affectations, their lower-class
associations, and their authoritarian manner the traditionalist clergy
were disdained as mediocrities at best and a disgrace to the church.
They were, we are told, in the habit of "delivering sermons unintelligi-
ble to the majority of the congregation . . . , and associating with the
very lowest dregs of society." At times, it was said, these "reverend gentlemen" boasted "of having carried one another out of the room, when
in a state of intoxication!" Men such as this, it was argued, "from associating with people as illiterate as themselves, and sunk equally as low
in society, procure for themselves the contempt and obloquy of the
more refined part of its members."[12]

Eventually the fashionable Catholics at St. Mary's found a pastor to
suit their tastes. William Hogan, a native of Limerick who took up duties
as assistant pastor in April 1820, was an immediate sensation. Like
William Harold before him Hogan effected within the congregation a
revival as impressive as any wrought by contemporary Protestant ministers. Before Hogan's arrival, we are told, St. Mary's had been "in a state
of somnolency; the fire burnt feebly in the bosoms of many Catholics;
defection was manifesting itself; coldness and indifference to public
worship had appeared; the Catholic children were not instructed in the
principles of their religion." Hogan "broke the lethargy that was pervading the congregation," and "fed the fire of faith with the oil of religion;
defection was changed into enthusiastic attachment; coldness and indifference was changed into ardor and interest for the religion of their
ancestors."[13]

There was much to admire in William Hogan. He was pleasant and
handsome, "of pleasing address"—"the embodiment of manly beauty." It
was his custom, we are told, "after morning services to mingle with the
congregation, and visit their pews conversing with the ladies and patting
the children on the head with almost parental fondness." His geniality
and social graces made him "a decided favorite . . . with the ladies and
children" of the congregation and particularly, Father Jordan tells us, he
"gained much favor with the so-called 'first families.'" Not only Catholics
enjoyed Father Hogan's company. His circle of friends soon extended
even into the highest levels of Philadelphia society. He was entertained in

the homes of such luminaries of the social world as "the Ingersolls, Sergeants, Prices, Bories, Binneys, Cadwalladers, and Chews."[14]

Hogan applied himself zealously to charity and mission work and, significantly, mobilized respectable members of the congregation to assist him. Each Sunday afternoon "from six to seven hundred children assembled . . . to be instructed in the principles of their religion, by a society of ladies and gentlemen, who charitably volunteered their services." Hogan also revitalized St. Mary's Sunday school, founded by the Haroldites in 1816, which had previously been in "a sickly and expiring state," and attracted to it "four or five hundred indigent children." He also preached several charity sermons, raising funds "to clothe [the children of the poor] during the inclemency of the winter." This was "a practice that had never before prevailed in the congregation." Hogan even went so far as to preach regularly in the alms-house. Altogether, we are told, he was "ambitious in the discharge of his duty, in instructing the ignorant, in feeding the hungry, and in clothing the naked."[15]

William Hogan was by no means the only Catholic clergyman to evince concern for the immigrant poor, but he was distinctive in that his interest was as much didactic as sympathetic. Unlike other members of the resident clergy Hogan actively sought to modify the behavior and values of the immigrants. Mathew Carey, who extravagantly praised Hogan's efforts, explained the purpose of such instruction as Hogan provided specifically in terms of moral uplift. The Sunday school, he wrote, was designed to produce "salutary effects, on the morals and manners of the rising generation." It promoted "habits of docility and order, which cannot be too highly appreciated in their effects on future life." Another member of the congregation explained Hogan's accomplishments in similar terms. The dynamic young priest, he wrote, "snatched [immigrant children] from vice, and led them into the path whereby they might become useful members of society."[16]

From the outset William Hogan clashed with traditionalist elements of the clergy. At St. Mary's Church he and his colleagues fought over clerical duties and the allocation of income from collections. At the "priests' house" where St. Mary's clergy lived, they quarreled over a number of petty matters. At last Hogan, saying that he "could not live in the midst of filth, comfortless and unlike a gentleman," requested separate accommodations. When the trustees, constrained by a lack of funds, did not act on Hogan's request, a public meeting of the congregation voted a stipend that allowed him to live alone.[17]

Hogan's decision to separate himself from his colleagues and his marked preference for the company of affluent laymen and Protestants were fatal. Like antibodies reacting to an invasive virus, the resident clergy, whatever their personal differences, closed ranks against him. Through the spring and summer of 1820 they conducted an insidious whispering campaign directed against Hogan and his supporters. The "dapper" young priest "paid due respect to all the requirements of dress"; for this they styled him a "dandy" and a "fop." Over time the charges became more specific and more vicious. It was said that Hogan attended midnight revels at the homes of wealthy Catholics where he drank heavily, danced with the daughters, and behaved obscenely. He was alleged to be carrying on clandestine affairs with several female members of the congregation and supposedly had attempted to seduce many others. Hogan's demand for separate quarters was interpreted as an effort to conceal his sins from the other clergymen.[18]

In July of 1820 Louis deBarth returned from mission work to find the Philadelphia clergy abuzz with rumors about Hogan. Michael Hurley, leader of the traditionalist faction, had emerged as the most implacable of Hogan's foes. He made "the 'Limerick boy'" a staple of each Sunday's discourse and "made the walls of St. Augustine's resound with denunciations of 'the fop who had made himself a priest.'" As usual, DeBarth equivocated. He made the rounds of lay leaders advising them against inviting "a bad and dangerous man" into their homes, but other than that he did nothing. DeBarth, a Frenchman, seems to have considered conflicts among the Irish clergy to be of no great moment. To one complainant he said, "[Hogan is] Irish and the new Bishop [Henry Conwell who was en route to America] is Irish; let the Irish settle it among themselves." Hearing this, Michael Hurley responded, "St. Michael may be here tomorrow and St. Michael may be here the next day, but Lucifer is here today."[19]

To escape what was becoming an increasingly difficult situation, William Hogan made plans to leave Philadelphia. He wrote to Bishop Flaget in Kentucky and Archbishop Maréchal in Baltimore seeking permission to relocate to their respective dioceses. Both men accepted Hogan's applications, but Maréchal made it clear that he preferred that Hogan remain in Philadelphia because the priest was far more valuable where he was. "What truly would become of the congregation of St. Mary's Church," he asked, "were you to withdraw from it?" Without the administrator's permission Hogan could not leave Philadelphia and, as with most things, DeBarth delayed making a decision. As a result, William Hogan, angry and frustrated, was still in the city when the new bishop, Henry Conwell, arrived on December 2, 1820.[20]

PART TWO

Schism

"That Absolute Power"

When Henry Conwell came to Philadelphia he was already more than seventy years of age and had served for a quarter of a century as vicar general of Armagh in Ireland. He was unknown in the United States and his appointment once again illustrated the fact that Rome was directing appointments to the mission with little regard for the interests or desires of the American prelates. Philadelphia had been something of a consolation prize for Conwell. He had sought but been denied the episcopal chair of Armagh. To soothe his feelings and to reward his long years of service Propaganda had offered the aged priest a choice: he could become bishop of either Madras or Philadelphia. He chose the latter and so was consecrated as the second bishop of Philadelphia.[1]

Bishop Conwell was an intelligent and imposing figure. Father Jordan describes him as "tall, straight and muscular" despite his more than seven decades. In his portrait he appears dour and somewhat aloof. At times, especially when angry, he was "not deficient in dignity." In addition to his quarter-century of administrative experience Conwell had the benefit of an excellent education and was something of a linguist. "His Latinity was classical. . . . He was a Greek Scholar." He "spoke French fluently and Spanish and Italian with but little difficulty." In short, he conformed to a traditional aristocratic ideal that by the second quarter of the nineteenth century in America had become obsolete.[2]

Henry Conwell had come of age in the waning years of the *ancien régime.* He was in his thirties when the American Revolution turned the British world upside down; he was in his forties when the French and associated revolutions toppled the crowns of Europe; and in his fifties he witnessed the "Year of the French" when tides of liberal revolt washed over Ireland. Henry Conwell was the product of a world that was rapidly fading. The Irish Church in which he had lived was insular, authoritarian, patriarchal, steeped in peasant traditions. It was a world in which the bishop, as Conwell had told the public when he first arrived in Philadelphia, *was* the Church—the lord of his domain. In Philadelphia Henry Conwell tried to recreate the world that he knew, acting the part of a "Prince of the Church," surrounding himself with "servants and innumerable nephews and cousins," building a loyal coterie among the traditionalist Irish clergy, and attempting to rule by aristocratic fiat and consultation with his episcopal colleagues.[3]

At first Bishop Conwell attempted to take a position above the contending factions that troubled the diocese. His perspective was rooted in the prerevolutionary culture of paternalism, subordination, and dependency, and he sought to assume the traditional aristocratic role of an impartial moral arbiter whose superior status and sensibilities could be relied upon to preserve order. When he addressed the laity it was in the "language of a father to his children" urging them to a dutiful obedience and deference to his will. He distanced himself from the ethnic factions within the clergy and laity by pointing out that, although he was Irish, he had lived for several years in France, had traveled extensively in the German states, and was consecrated in England. "So you see," Conwell said, "I may be called an Englishman as well as a Frenchman, a Dutchman or an Irishman; Indeed it is hard to say what countryman I am, so you see I can have no prejudices."[4]

From his clergy Conwell demanded dutiful obedience and disinterestedness. He denounced in no uncertain terms "speculating adventurers among the clergy, who forgetting their duty, endeavored to mislead the people." These men, rather than standing above and directing the laymen in their charge, "made it their chief study to court popular favor, to excite a revolutionary spirit among all ranks and principally to gain the friendship of such gentlemen as commanded the purse of the congregation." By such means, he explained, leaders of mere factions prospered while legitimate ecclesiastical authorities were "left destitute of support" and unable to fulfill their proper duties.[5]

Henry Conwell brought a sense of urgency to his post. Rumors in Ireland had alerted him to the "great deal of dissensions" in Philadelphia. He had been warned, by Archbishop Maréchal and Propaganda, that the Church in America was rapidly approaching a crisis.

Philadelphia, he had been told, "was in great confusion, and . . . anarchy prevailed in many places: . . . suspended priests were in the exercise of ecclesiastical functions, and seduced many into their errors, and . . . a schism, in consequence of this was apprehended, and was actually impending." Conwell was not exaggerating the extent or tenor of Rome's concern. John England, another recent appointment to the American hierarchy, reported that before assuming the mitre of Charleston he "had a letter from Rome, representing the Catholic Church in America to be in imminent extinction from the uncanonical usurpation of the laity in some places, and the unprincipled conduct of a few of the clergy who in place of upholding the discipline of the Church, misled the people and involved them in schism."[6]

Based on information given him by authorities in Ireland, Rome, and Baltimore Henry Conwell judged that strong and decisive action was needed; almost immediately he found an opportunity to assert himself. On his second day in Philadelphia Conwell attended mass at St. Mary's and there heard William Hogan deliver from the pulpit a "severe and sour attack" on Louis DeBarth. We have no record of Hogan's exact remarks, but both the administrator and the bishop found them to be insulting and offensive. Mathew Carey described Hogan's performance as "a display of a domineering spirit—of peevishness—of petulance—and of high temper unbecoming a clergyman." Conwell moved quickly to discipline the fractious priest. He upbraided Hogan for his speech and behavior and ordered him to move back to the "priests' house," but Hogan, obviously angry, refused to comply.[7]

Bishop Conwell took Hogan's refusal as a personal affront and an open defiance of his authority. Hogan, he complained, "will conduct the congregation without advice or instructions from the Bishop. He said he disregarded [the bishop] in everything relating to church affairs or what concerned his duty as a clergyman." Conwell thought moreover that he saw in Hogan's actions a plot to topple episcopal authority and feared that "further delay would bring [the conspirators'] project to perfection." Obviously, he felt, decisive action was needed. One day later, on December 12, 1820, Bishop Conwell formally revoked William Hogan's faculties.[8]

William Hogan's suspension precipitated a crisis in Philadelphia Catholicism that would reverberate throughout the American mission and even to Rome, but there was little indication at first of the troubles to come. Hogan and his friends repeatedly sought some accommodation with the bishop. Hogan wrote to Conwell offering to revoke any remarks derogatory to episcopal authority and to make proper apology for them. Twice, through lay intermediaries, Hogan stated that he was willing to return to the clerical residence. He even offered to leave Philadelphia on the condition that it not be under duress and that he be given an opportunity to clear his name. In a letter to Archbishop Maréchal written two days after his suspension, Hogan laid out his position. "I am satisfied," he wrote, "to do anything to prevent Scandal, if [Bishop Conwell] would even allow me to resume my faculties for a time . . . I would shortly resign quietly & retire from this City to some other mission."[9]

Conwell, however, was determined to be rid of of Hogan. When one of the priest's lay supporters proposed a reconciliation, Conwell reiterated his position that "he would not have [Hogan] here [in Philadelphia]; because should he restore Mr. H[ogan], he would only use his influence to make himself more popular." On another occasion Conwell expressed his fear that Hogan's popularity was such that, should he remain in Philadelphia "he would [in effect] be Bishop." Hogan, he said, "had a light pair of heels, and a clean pair of breeches, and the world was wide for him." When pressed for an explanation, Conwell refused to give any account of his actions or make any formal charges against the priest, in the hope (he later admitted) that the ambiguity surrounding the situation would leave Hogan "no room for appeal."[10]

Appeal Hogan did, but to no effect. In his own defense he tried to invoke various canons protecting the rights of parish clergy in Europe. "Why did the church institute a code of canon law?" he asked, "was it not to protect her Bishops in the conscientious and just exercise of their authority, and the priest, in the pious discharge of his duty . . . ? Is it not the only weapon which the priest has, to oppose to the cruelty of the ecclesiastical tyrant, whose arm is ever ready to crush him?" He wrote to Archbishop Maréchal, arguing that Conwell had suspended him uncanonically. When Maréchal failed to respond, Hogan wrote again asking the archbishop to convene an ecclesiastical court "to see & know why and for what reasons Dr. Conwell has deprived me of my living." "If he can show just cause for suspending me in his diocese," Hogan wrote, "I shall not only submit but even retire; But if not I call on you to act toward him and me as the Laws & Canons of the R[o]m[an]. Catholic Church direct."[11]

William Hogan's demand that episcopal authority be constrained within a framework of law found no support at Baltimore. Archbishop Maréchal refused to respond to the priest's letters and instead wrote to Bishop Conwell declaring that Hogan had "disgraced the Church of God" and no longer had "any right whatever to call on me as Metropolitan. No! not even under the vulgar pretext of [his] being innocent and persecuted." In addition he warned Hogan's supporters that any actions taken by them in support of the priest carried a terrible risk of involving themselves, their families, and their friends "in guilt, and a boundless spiritual misery."[12]

Maréchal's response to Hogan's appeals reflected the absolutist nature of the American episcopacy in the early decades of the nineteenth century. That was a time when bishops sought to "rule their dioceses with an iron rod," ceding few, if any, rights to members of the lower clergy or the laity. "Each bishop," John England noted, "had practically greater power in his own diocese than the Pope had in the Universal Church." American bishops did their will "without any Congregation, or Council or established discipline, to limit their exercise [of power]." Clerical appointments and jurisdictions were assigned by the bishop and were held at his pleasure, and there existed no institutional mechanisms, short of an appeal to the Holy See, whereby a priest who felt he had been wronged could challenge or seek redress from episcopal decisions. William Hogan's plight made clear to many Catholics just how arbitrary episcopal authority had become and the extent to which, in his words, the "second order of the Clergy," had become little more than "slaves in a land of civil and religious liberty." "It would appear," St. Mary's dissenters complained to Archbishop Maréchal, "that each Prelate in his own diocese is sovereign and independent of all authority short of His Holiness, and may act as uncharitably, as inconsiderately, even tyrannically, as his inclinations may impel him."[13]

Perhaps the most extreme statement of episcopal authoritarianism was made by Henry Conwell himself in his "Charge to the Congregation" delivered early in 1821. On that occasion Conwell betrayed an absolutist sensibility worthy of Louis XIV. "I am the church for I am bishop," he said. "I was sent here by the Pope with extraordinary powers to act in a papal way as my conscience directed me." In response to Hogan's claim that as pastor of St. Mary's he was entitled to due process, Conwell was reported to have said, "*I as being the church, that* is the representative of the church, am and can be the only Pastor in this diocese." Conwell flatly denied that the laity had any say in the matter. There have been and will be protests, he noted, but they will avail Hogan nothing, "for I am Bishop and I must act as my conscience bids me."[14]

Other voices joined in to affirm the essentially absolutist nature of Church government in America. Writing in support of Conwell's position, Benedict Flaget cited "that absolute power invested in bishops by the wisdom of the Council of Trent, whereby (for the good of religion and the occasional correction of their subjects) they may withdraw their spiritual power." Clerical faculties, Flaget explained, "are always revocable at will, particularly in a missionary country like America, for any conscientious reason, even of a hidden crime, even without trial." The bishop's power over the "inferior ministers in [his] diocess," in Flaget's view, was without limit. "So absolute and necessary is the power vested in bishops," he wrote, "that . . . no power on earth can oblige them to give faculties to those whom they conscientiously consider unworthy." Nor, he continued, could any authority "bring them to account for withdrawing spiritual powers" from any inferior minister. Nor was there any possibility of redress. Since the decision of the Council of Trent, Flaget wrote, "from such an exercise of episcopal power no appeal could be made."[15]

Mark Frenaye, a prosperous merchant of French descent and a stalwart defender of episcopal prerogatives, further elaborated the absolutist position. In a pamphlet circulated to St. Mary's congregation he presented a detailed exegesis of the canons pertaining to a mission territory like the United States and concluded that "a Prelate has power to suspend a clergyman, even for a *hidden crime,* and without entering into a judgment . . . and . . . no appeal is granted from that sentence, otherwise [a priest] could be restored to his functions against the will of his Prelate." The Bishop, Frenaye continued, "can suspend clergymen, for reasons known to himself . . . and . . . *is not even obliged to manifest the cause of suspension, or the misdemeanor, to the delinquent himself, but only to the Apostolic See.*" Moreover, he added, not only was there no appeal from the bishop's decision, but a clergyman lodging a complaint against a bishop "*immediately becomes irregular.*" Nor did a priest have any right to face his accusers, because "This would, in many instances, betray those who lodged the information against his conduct, and cause hatred, persecutions, &c." In conclusion Frenaye charged that William Hogan was animated by a Protestant spirit and warned that those who chose to support him would find themselves, before they realized it, "as far from catholicity, as he is from piety."[16]

William Hogan and his supporters also protested Bishop Conwell's Actions on the grounds that they violated the principles of due process and popular sovereignty, both essential elements of the American civil tradition. With regard to the evidence amassed against him by the bishop, Hogan asked, "Should such [*ex post facto*] proofs be admitted in a civil court?" Obviously not! "Why not give me a fair trial . . . ?" Hogan repeatedly asked. "In vain have I asked why I have been deprived of my living, in vain have the congregation asked why thay have been deprived of my preaching, in vain have I appealed to the Metropolitan . . . , in vain have I protested against the precipitancy and injustice of such proceedings against me." Conwell's actions, he concluded, constituted nothing less than "ecclesiastical despotism" and a clear violation of the "rights of Man."[17]

Mathew Carey, writing two days after Hogan's suspension, advanced the position that in America the men and women of the congregation were "entitled to respect and attention." He warned that "their opinions and their wishes cannot be treated with neglect and slight, without producing consequences which every good man would studiously avoid." John T. Sullivan bluntly informed the bishop that "he ought to listen with attention" to "the voice of the congregation." Conwell himself summarized the laity's position as being "that no Bishop Can Suspend a Priest without Satisfying the public that he has a just cause which they are to be the Judges of."[18]

Through decades of conflict Philadelphia's Catholics had developed a rhetoric of dissent and forms of expression based on the principles of popular sovereignty and the sanctity of fundamental rights under the rule of law. Once again they invoked long-familiar mechanisms through which the "opinions and the wishes of the people" could be heard. One day after Hogan's dismissal a "large and respectable portion" of the congregation held a public meeting at St. Mary's schoolhouse to discuss the matter. At the meeting sentiment ran overwhelmingly in the priest's favor. Mathew Carey tells us that a substantial majority expressed their support for Hogan and denounced Bishop Conwell's precipitate action. Three days later, at a second public meeting, "250 of the most respectable" members of the congregation affixed their signatures to a memorial in protest of the bishop's actions.[19]

The petition itself consisted mainly of a panegyric to William Hogan's talent and character, but it also contained a threat. "Perhaps you will not think it irrelevant," they wrote, "to state that St. Mary's Church is the property of the laity and the clergy are supported by them." They then went on to predict that, "refusal" to reinstate Hogan would produce "lamentable consequences" that would affect the bishop's "individual peace and support." This, of course, was the same threat that had been used against Bishop Egan during the Haroldite insurrection of recent memory and it was one of the practices against which Bishop Conwell had been warned prior to his coming to America.[20]

The wording of the petition only confirmed Henry Conwell's conviction that matters in Philadelphia had come to a dangerous head and required firm action. He denounced as "error" attempts to apply American principles of civil law and administration to religious matters. It had often been argued, Conwell wrote, that because of "the nature of the constitution of the United States . . . Bishops could not exercise authority in this country"; that "the clergy were subject to no control"; and that they had "a right to subvert all order, by defying and despising the Bishop, and bringing his authority into contempt and ridicule." In his mind the lay demonstrations and demands were the beginning of a "revolutionary movement" that, if allowed to grow unchecked, would effectively destroy the Catholic Church in America. He declared his determination to persevere, even to suffer persecution, rather than yield an inch to Hogan and his supporters. Compliance with their wishes, he said, "would produce the worst possible effects and consequences." Should he neglect his duty on this occasion, Conwell averred, the result "would unhinge the hierarchy, undermine church government, destroy subordination, and subvert all rule and order in the church here and elsewhere throughout the United States."[21]

Bishop Conwell understood that much more was at issue at St. Mary's than the fate of one priest. The conflicts that disturbed that congregation in the 1820s were a distant echo of titanic controversies that rent all of contemporary Western culture. Martin Marty has termed this international confrontation "the Modern Schism." It had its roots in the scientific revolution of the seventeenth century and the Enlightenment traditions of the eighteenth and found full expression with the advent of the industrial revolution. The modern schism pitted those who embraced the "new ethos of industrial enterprise, urbanization and nationalism, accompanied by locally varying programmes or creeds like liberalism, evolutionism, socialism, or historicism" against those who cherished the institutions, values, and beliefs of the "inherited religion of the West."[22]

The modern schism carried special meaning for nineteenth-century Catholics because of profound changes that were taking place in the Church. Roger Aubert has described what he calls a "religious counterrevolution" that swept through the Catholic Church in the wake of the French Revolution and the restoration of the papacy to Rome. This "shift in the intellectual climate" of Catholicism represented a turning "away from the modern ideas of progress and back toward a tradition rooted in the Catholic Middle Ages." Catholic reformers promoted an idealized vision of the "golden days of Christianity" when the international Church dominated the affairs of men and nations, and they repudiated the social and cultural perspectives associated with the heritage of the Enlightenment. In this climate no significant compromise with modernity was possible. For most influential churchmen, Aubert writes, the "only uncertainty was whether the counter-revolution was to be conducted implacably or with a limited tactical flexibility." Thus, in the decades after the fall of Napoleon, and the restoration of the papacy, the Catholic Church emerged not only as an international bulwark against the modernizing forces of liberalism, nationalism, and secularism but as a militant counterrevolutionary force actively attempting to reshape Western culture.[23]

In America a generation of émigré priests, many of them refugees from European revolution, embraced this antimodernist perspective. Repudiating liberalism and other modern doctrines, they systematically promoted what Jay Dolan has described as a "culture of authority" in which "being Catholic meant to submit to the authority of God as mediated through the church—its Pope, bishops, and pastors . . . ;" where "Catholics were taught to be docile and submissive . . . ;" and "obedience and docility, not dissent and independence, were the ideals cherished." Unlike an earlier generation of "Enlightened Catholics" who were willing to make some accommodation to republicanism, the new leaders of the Church in America actively sought confrontation with liberal and other modernizing elements within the church.[24]

For American Catholics the conflict between modern and traditional sensibilities took on special resonance. This was because Rome and the United States occupied antipodal positions in the imaginations of those who were engaged in the great ideological confrontations of the age. The Catholic culture of authority stood in direct contrast to the liberal imperatives that were becoming ever more prominent in American political culture. So, too, the ultramontane vision of a unified Christendom directed from Rome ran directly counter to the nationalist enthusiasms of the new republic, and the romantic nostalgia for medieval Europe (with its stable social ranks and Christian communalism) that inspired so many Catholic leaders stood as a moral indictment of the individualistic, competitive, and progressive values of industrializing America. Rome, after the restoration of the papacy, and the new republic both symbolized what many hoped would be a *novus ordo seclorum*, but the visions informing each were diametrically opposed.

What is more, Roman Catholic and American civil cultures were diverging. At a time when the United States was becoming more nationalistic, more committed to the idea of secular progress, and when an increasing number of Americans accepted as a fundamental tenet the proposition that political authority ultimately resides with the people, the institutional structure of the Roman Catholic Church was becoming more monarchic, more committed to a supernatural interpretation of human affairs, and more imbued with a romantic vision of universal medieval christendom. Modernists within the church, then, increasingly found the values embodied in American civil culture more congenial than those emanating from Rome, while Catholic traditionalists of all kinds, repelled by a republican culture that was antagonistic to and even destructive of the values and standards they held most dear, increasingly sought comfort in the church community.[25]

This discrepancy between "modern" and "traditionalist" sensibilities powerfully informed the continuing controversy that troubled St. Mary's Church in the 1820s. It cut across the class divisions that had previously polarized the congregation, creating new political alignments, new points of conflict, and new meanings for Catholic dissent. This is not to say that Bishop Conwell was an ultramontane zealot, assiduously promoting a counterrevolution directed from Rome. Nor were his opponents violent Jacobins, though Conwell saw them as such. But the confrontation that was building in Philadelphia did resonate to many of the principles and positions that informed the great political and ideological struggles that were convulsing contemporary Europe and Latin America.[26]

Hoganites

—————»-◊-«—————

William Hogan's strongest support came from the "fashionable Catholics" so disdainfully described by Father Jordan. These men and women had welcomed the young priest into their hearts and homes and now they stood by him in his time of trials. Their passionate involvement in Hogan's cause was important for they introduced into the debate perspectives that marked a significant shift in the social context of dissent in Philadelphia Catholicism.

Hogan was not a democrat. He specifically rejected the leveling tendencies that had previously informed dissent at St. Mary's. Virtue, not equality, was his touchstone. "Far be it from me" Hogan wrote, "to wish to level all distinctions, or deprecate relative superiority in any department civil or religious; on the contrary, I consider superiority a noble and glorious prerogative." But authority and status, in Hogan's view, were not legitimate unless they were grounded in virtue. "My opinion is, has been, and shall be," he proclaimed, "that superiority in any department, should be . . . a tribute due to preeminent virtue, transcendent talents, unsullied sanctity and unaffected devotion." For Catholicism to succeed in America, Hogan felt, the hierarchy had to "learn that talents and elevated stations, unless supported by virtue and a strict regard for the rights of others, so far from conferring honour on him who possesses them, only render him an object of contempt."[1]

William Hogan in the 1820s was once again invoking classical republican ideals that had informed America's revolutionary struggle half a century earlier. Like the leaders of that effort he was no leveler or democrat—virtue for him was not located in "the people." Rather Hogan envisioned a society purged of corruption and interest in which a disinterested elite of talent, virtue, sanctity and devotion would rule benevolently in the name of the people and be accorded all due deference by them. Like many American revolutionaries he categorically rejected the idea of absolute and ascribed authority based in tradition, but wished to substitute for it an aristocracy of merit based in achievement and conspicuous virtue.[2]

Though William Hogan invoked classical republican concepts he applied them to the rapidly industrializing world in which he lived. His primary constituents were creatures of commerce and industry—upwardly mobile individuals, mostly immigrants, who were seeking a place in the new social order commensurate with their accomplishments and talents. They rejected the ascribed authority of the traditional world that would have fixed them in their places and blocked their upward progress. So, too, they denied the leveling tendencies of democrats that would have reduced them to the status of their less ambitious and accomplished countrymen.

Emphasizing virtue as a legitimating principle resolved a fundamental discrepancy in the positions taken by William Hogan's supporters. While they denied the moral authority of the clergy and their bishop, at the same time time they articulated a moral imperative that required instructing the poor, raising their moral consciousness, and instilling in them qualities of docility and order that would make of them useful citizens. Defiant rebels in one context, the Hoganites were paternalistic authoritarians in another. Their insistence upon the legitimacy of social and political hierarchies ill-matched their contempt for constituted ecclesiastical authority. An emphasis on virtue (which, in their eyes, was conspicuously lacking in both the ecclesiastical hierarchy and the immigrant working classes) reconciled the tensions inherent in the Hoganite's position, but it carried dangerous implications.

The Hoganites were defining themselves against two groups that shared a common characteristic—they were seen as alien to the American environment. This led Hogan's partisans to articulate positions usually associated with Protestant nativism. They held that the bishops and the unruly immigrant workers both represented the outmoded values of a corrupt and obsolete European social and political order. Time and again Hogan and his supporters stated their belief that, in modern America, the promise of the Enlightenment was being fulfilled and the standards of the European past no longer applied. To illustrate their point they drew a sharp contrast between the freedom enjoyed by American citizens and the authoritarian and repressive regimes that ruled Catholic Europe in the age of the Holy Alliance.

Mathew Carey articulated this belief in American exceptionalism at the beginning of the Hoganite crisis. He explicitly repudiated the authoritarian traditions and practices upon which the Restoration

Church predicated its reforms and contrasted them with core values of the American civil tradition. "The regime that prevails," he wrote, "in Catholic countries on the continent of Europe, as well as in England and Ireland, does not exactly quadrate with the practice in this country." In Europe, he noted, "the civil authority on emergency is always in requisition to support the hierarchy. . . . And in England and Ireland," where civil authority did not support the Church, ages of "horrible oppression and tyranny" had "produced [among Catholics] a subserviency of the laity to the clergy, which operates as effectually as the dread of the civil authority does on the continent. . . . A different order of things prevails in this country," Carey warned:

> The extreme freedom of our civil institutions has produced a corresponding independent spirit respecting our church affairs, to which sound sense will never fail to pay attention, and which it would be a manifest impropriety to despise or attempt to control by harsh or violent measures. The opinions and wishes of the people require to be consulted to a degree unknown in Europe.[3]

America, the Hoganites believed, embodied the political and cultural imperatives of the Enlightenment, and for this it was to be exalted rather than reviled. Time and again Hogan and his partisans expressed their faith that an "enlightened public" would see the truth of the matter at hand and repudiate what they styled episcopal despotism. "I once indulged [a hope]," William Hogan wrote, "that [the] dark times . . . of ecclesiastical tyranny and despotism . . . were gone by . . . , down, never to rise"; and that "the state of society, and progress of civilization in this enlightened country [America]," would provide a model for Catholics throughout the world. But men like Bishop Conwell, "a prelate, on whose intellect a ray of science never seemed to have beamed," represented an obsolete and repressive regime. They were ignorant of the "progress of science and religion in this country," and so attempted to perpetuate here the archaic religion of their homeland [Ireland]—a "land of bondage . . . [a] land of slavery."[4]

For William Hogan and his supporters the sins of old Europe were made manifest in the plight of contemporary Ireland. In their minds Ireland was a terrible and desperate land, made so not just by an oppressive civil authority, but also through the complicity of the Church. "In Ireland," a "Layman of the Congregation" wrote,

> that oppressed, unhappy country, the priests are generally
> the corrupt tools of a more corrupt administration; the
> labouring class of people are kept in utter ignorance of their
> religion; they are taught to repeat a few "Pater nosters and
> Ave Marias," they are instructed in a *blind* submission to
> their pastors, (be their conduct right or wrong).

By contrast, he continued, in America immigrants could find the church "shining with pure lustre," its "true tenets" expounded freely by those Catholics who "having minds superior to the generality of their brethren, cannot brook the idea of fettering religion to be subservient to the acts of a despotic administration." "This is not Ireland," another layman warned the bishop, "Ever bear that in mind hereafter" and remember that in America "all men are equal in the scale of humanity."[5]

No one posed the contrast more dramatically than William Hogan. "When," he cried, "are we unfortunate Irishmen to be rescued from the chains of civil and religious slavery? Are we no sooner disentangled from the former [through emigration to America], than the latter are flung around us . . . ?" He charged that Bishop Conwell was "a despot, who having spent his life in ignorance and poverty, in want and slavery, is now incapable of living in the pure air of freedom and independence." Such representatives of an archaic and oppressive order, Hogan argued, had no place in America. "Are we," he asked, "in the nineteenth era of the Christian religion, to be encumbered with the existence of such a man among us?" "No," he replied, "if such an evil were tamely submitted to, in vain have we fled from our native country in search of freedom, if such an evil be tolerated [in America], why did we not rather submit to it in the land of our birth."[6]

From here it was but a short step to acceptance of the essential nativist proposition that Catholic institutions and traditions, as manifested in post-Napoleonic Europe, not only embodied values antithetical to those of American civil culture but were a palpable threat to the republic itself. "Here," Hogan wrote,

> a system of religious slavery is attempting to be introduced,
> by which, an ascendancy will be acquired over the physical
> and mental powers of one-fifth of our population, and if
> tolerated, will ultimately degrade a large portion of a noble,
> proud and generous nation who have fought for their rights
> and enjoy them.

Americans, he concluded, "will not tolerate tyranny; such a people will not submit to despotism, civil or religious." Mathew Carey agreed. To him the traditionalist clergy were the products of an alien culture, to whom America was a "strange country," and Americans "a people whose habits, manners and disposition," they could not comprehend. "They have come," he opined, "from a country [Ireland] in which too frequently the relations between the pastor and his flock partake of the nature of extravagantly high-toned authority on the one side, and servile submission on the other." "The attempt," he wrote,

> to carry such a system into operation here, is not consistent with religion or morals . . . , our citizens will never submit to it. They . . . will revolt at, resist, and defeat any attempt to "drive" them even with armed lictors. Their respect for their clergy . . . is sufficient surety for all the obedience that can be required. This may be unpalatable doctrine, but it must be swallowed.[7]

Like Bishop Conwell, the Hoganites viewed their situation in apocalyptic terms. Should their opponents triumph, Hogan wrote, they "would prostrate justice at the shrine of interest, establish despotism amid a free people, and ultimately raise the standard of tyranny in a land of civil and religious freedom." He called on the Americans, a people "foremost in every art where genius can be shown, in every science where talents can be displayed, in every field where glory can be won, or despotism crushed, or tyranny trampled, or persecution prostrated," to rise against this threat. "They will not," he hoped, "behold the cause of religion fall a victim to caprice, despotism, ignorance and intolerance," for if such things "be tolerated, the angel of liberty, both civil and religious, will no longer wave her all-protecting wings over us; no, she will retire to the tomb and weep where her rights have been buried."[8]

Behind these statements lay no simple confrontation between "American" and "European" cultures, but rather a much more profound ideological engagement that cut across national, ethnic, and religious boundaries. It was Martin Marty's "Modern Schism"—the continuing dialogue between those who accepted and exalted the promise of the Enlightenment and those who rejected and sought to reverse its effects. American culture, in the minds of the Hoganites, was distinctive and precious because it embodied in its institutions and customs the principles and promise of the European Enlightenment. They found the monarchic and ultramontane tendencies of the Restoration Church, as well as the ethnic posturings of the traditionalist clergy, to be offensive because they represented a repudiation of those principles. Bishop Conwell's troubles ensued, not simply because he was administratively and personally maladroit or because he was unable to "adjust" Catholic doctrine to the distinctive values of American republican culture, but because he and his antagonists personified opposing ideological movements, each of which sought to shape the modern world.[9]

"Day of Tryal"

The Hoganites were not alone in their dissent. From the first, the embattled priest enjoyed broad support within the congregation. He was, by Mathew Carey's account, "the most popular clergyman who had been in St. Mary's for many years." His removal and the arbitrary way in which it was effected ignited an impassioned storm of protest from the laity. "All ranks," John T. Sullivan testified, "were attached to [Hogan]." His cause thus divided both the immigrant working classes and the Catholic elites, pitting modernist elements of both against their traditionalist counterparts.[1]

Many former Haroldites, offended by William Hogan's treatment, came to the priest's defense. For years Harold's partisans had scorned traditionalist members of the resident clergy, whom they considered vastly inferior to their hero, and had agitated for his return to Philadelphia. At every turn, though, they had been frustrated by episcopal authorities and their resentment against the unresponsive hierarchy began to mount. What is more their influence within the congregation was declining. In the 1813 elections for trustees the Haroldites elected a solid slate of candidates and for three years after that they maintained their domination of the board, but beginning in 1817 new men (sponsored by the traditionalist clergy) sought and won election.

By 1819 the Haroldites elected only five of the eight lay trustees. Thus, although they constituted a majority of the lay trustees, the Haroldites were a minority on the full board because the clergy cast three votes. It was in this situation of mounting despair and declining influence that the Haroldites launched a determined effort to limit the temporal power of the clergy at St. Mary's.[2]

In February of 1820, one month before William Hogan's arrival in Philadelphia, a committee of Haroldite leaders petitioned the Pennsylvania legislature for permission to amend St. Mary's charter. Authorization was finally granted, subject to judicial review of the proposed amendments, more than a year later. The intervening year had been an eventful one. In the Easter elections of 1820 the Haroldites had lost two more seats on the board of trustees, leaving the traditionalist clergy and their lay allies with a solid majority. In December the new bishop (a disappointment for those who hoped for Harold's return) arrived, and shortly thereafter William Hogan's suspension threw the congregation into turmoil. All of this imparted a special significance to the effort to amend the church's charter. On April 7, 1821 (with the Easter week elections looming ahead), a public meeting at Washington Hall voted to propose amendments barring clergy from sitting on the board of trustees, to restrict the franchise to citizens and pewholders, and to select an interim board of trustees to govern the temporalities of the church until elections could be held under the new charter.[3]

The meeting at Washington Hall was a momentous occasion. It marked a fusion of the two major dissenting elements within St. Mary's congregation, the Haroldites and the Hoganites. The proposal to exclude clergy from the board of trustees spoke to the frustrations and needs of the Haroldite faction while the attempt to ban noncitizens from voting reflected the nativist tendencies of the Hoganites (and, incidentally, suggested a major source of opposition faced by the dissenters). The slate of "interim" trustees elected by the meeting included leaders of both factions. From the Hoganite camp came men such as John Leamy (president of the Marine Insurance Company), John Ashley (president of the Philadelphia Insurance Company), Joseph M. Doran (a wealthy "gentleman"), and Richard W. Meade (a prosperous merchant and former U.S. consul in Cadiz, Spain); while the Haroldites included John Doyle (a grocer), John Dempsey (an iron and bread dealer), Augustine Fagan (a printer and bookseller), and Joseph Dugan (a printer who had served his apprenticeship with Fagan). Together these men spoke for a broad segment of the congregation. An enemies list compiled by Bishop Conwell notes among those who attended the meeting and voted for the proposals several draymen, carters, and other unskilled workers as well as a publican, a grocer, a bottler, a soap manufacturer, and other small businessmen and professionals.[4]

William Hogan thus enjoyed the support of much of the congregation. His strongest partisans were rising members of the middle classes who shared his proto-whiggish views on society and politics, but he also attracted Haroldite democrats who may have disagreed with the Hoganites' social and political biases but were equally alienated by their experience with episcopal authority. In addition to these Hogan gained support from a large and somewhat amorphous group who, while lacking the intense commitment of the partisans, were still disturbed and offended by the arbitrary nature of Bishop Conwell's actions and pronouncements. He even seems to have enjoyed considerable support (or so his enemies claimed) of many non-Catholics. The series of meetings at Washington Hall in which the dissenters articulated and organized their protest were said to have attracted "strangers of every denomination."[5]

Bishop Conwell, however, was not without resources. In addition to strong support from other members of the episcopal hierarchy his position was also sustained by traditionalist members of the clergy and their lay allies. Many of these "bishopite" laymen were immigrant aliens (hence the attempt on the part of the Hoganites to exclude such individuals from the franchise) but their leadership was drawn from another source.

On April 19, 1821, a "Committee of Pew holders" wrote to Archbishop Maréchal denouncing the Hoganites and their allies as "persons devoid of true religion" engaged in a "deep, and foul conspiracy against a *Pastor.*" The correspondents proclaimed their loyalty to the bishop and claimed that they spoke for a majority of the congregation. "We unanimously opposed any further prosecution of the measures, relative to Mr. Hogan," they wrote, "and on a division we had a majority—if the strangers present and those who had no right to vote on the concerns of the Congregation, were taken from their numbers." Prominent among these bishopite spokesmen were several former trustees—members of the clique that had dominated the congregation prior to the Haroldite insurrection and had been driven from office in the elections of 1813.[6]

Through the second decade of the century these old-guard conservative Catholics, like the Federalists in the civil sphere, had tried to bridge the ever-increasing gap between the old culture and the new. Their position had become increasingly untenable over time. They were, in effect, trying to reconcile the irreconcilable—clinging to a hierarchical order that made sense only in a society based on dependence and deference while all around them that traditional order was being extinguished. They watched in dismay as, in the absence of any effective episcopal authority, democratic values, ethnic assertiveness, and class consciousness overwhelmed instruments of constraint throughout the diocese. They longed for a return to the certainties and stability of the past and hoped for a champion who could restore them. Now they rallied to Bishop Conwell as they once had to Bishop Egan.

In the wake of the legislative decision permitting amendments to St. Mary's charter, these members of the old elite protested to the Pennsylvania Supreme Court that the changes proposed by the public meeting at Washington Hall did not represent the will of the corporation. Their petition proved to be instrumental in shaping a court ruling (issued one week before the annual election for trustees) that the proposed amendments could not be allowed. Undeterred, the Haroldites, supported by William Hogan's partisans, pressed again for a charter change. Once again the Pennsylvania state legislature responded with an act authorizing amendments, and in response Bishop Conwell's supporters issued a petition of protest. Thus matters stood on April 24, 1821, when St. Mary's congregation held their annual election for trustees.[7]

The election of 1821 was an important test of strength between the Haroldites and their old antagonists, the bishopites. For William Hogan and his partisans the stakes were far higher. Quite early in the conflict the Hoganites, recognizing the fundamental incompatibility of their views and those of the bishop, had contemplated a complete break with the existing ecclesiastical hierarchy. They even went so far as to rent a Methodist church where Hogan intended to preach and say mass for "a people to be called Independent Catholics." But this plan was never put into effect. Instead the Hoganites announced early in February 1821 that the suspended priest would conduct services at St. Mary's. Bishop Conwell responded to this declaration with a formal monition against Hogan threatening to excommunicate not only the priest but anyone who attended such services.[8]

The threat of excommunication brought pause to the Hoganites, and William Hogan himself seems to have suffered a temporary failure of nerve. He asked his representatives to make one last attempt at reconciliation. On March 13, 1821, a committee of laymen wrote to Archbishop Maréchal, denouncing the slanders against Hogan and protesting that he had not been given a fair trial, but also offering to submit to the bishop's authority. Hogan, they declared, "craves pardon and forgiveness" and is "ready to make any submission . . . which may be prescribed and in a manner the most public, in the pulpit if required." Maréchal refused to accept any submission and branded Hogan "a most abandoned character." He warned the members of the committee that they, their families, and their associates were in danger of involving themselves "in guilt and boundless spiritual misery."[9]

Archbishop Maréchal's response to their attempted capitulation stung the Hoganites and confirmed their determination to separate themselves from the control of the American hierarchy. This in no way, they argued, meant that they were abandoning the Catholic Church. They denied that they were schismatics, "openly and sincerely" declaring themselves to be "Roman Catholics, born and baptized in the Church." They declared that they "uniformly acknowledged His Holiness the Pope as the Viceregent of Christ on earth," but, cognizant of "the unwise, uncharitable and persecuting dispositions of some of [the Church's] unworthy ministers" they intended to take actions to protect themselves and William Hogan from injustices perpetrated by members of the American episcopacy. "We deeply regret" the necessity of such action, they said, "but we shall always carry with us, even to our graves, the pleasing consolation that we have done our duty as Children of the Church"[10]

The elections of 1821, then, would not only determine which faction controlled St. Mary's Church, but also promised to bring about the ecclesiastical revolution so feared by Bishop Conwell and other members of the American hierarchy. In the weeks leading up to the election, tensions mounted and tempers flared as all of the major participants assumed increasingly provocative stances. "There are political meetings here on this Subject every night." Bishop Conwell complained, "Sunday is a day of great confusion and alarm. Yesterday [April 1] the parties came to blows." Soon the conflict spread beyond the bounds of St. Mary's congregation. There were at least two public meetings of St. Augustine's congregation and the last of these was also the occasion of "great disorder." "These times," Bishop Conwell wrote with despair, "appear like those of Luther in Germany or John Knox in Scotland."[11]

Bishop Conwell was shocked at the breadth of support William Hogan enjoyed in St. Mary's congregation, but was undeterred. He denounced his lay opponents as "bad men styling themselves Catholics," as "libertines and people of bad fame," as "those deluded people . . . wicked miscreants," even as agents of the "powers of darkness." In an attempt to drive a wedge between Hogan and his lay supporters Conwell, finally revealed the accusations that had convinced him to suspend the priest. "I am delicate and ashamed to mention them," he said, "but as I am brought to it I must tell you . . . that I would not think it safe for me in my conscience, to allow any of my females, I mean any of my young girls into the same room with this person."[12]

The charge of sexual improprieties backfired on the bishop. At two meetings at Washington Hall "large and respectable" crowds cheered speakers who denounced the bishop for his attempts to "intimidate the friends of justice" and what they interpreted as "indecent imputations . . . upon the character of our wives and daughters." Several outraged women of the congregation confronted the bishop in his home and had to be expelled by force. With popular sentiment running in his favor, William Hogan succumbed to the temptation to taunt his adversaries. Each Sunday, "both fore and afternoon," he and "a great mob of small & large children" would gather near the clerical residence to shout abuse at the bishop and the traditionalist clergy. To counter this, supporters of the bishop filed the first of many legal actions. "We were obliged to [file the suit]," Bishop Conwell's agent explained, "or give the [church] property to the mob."[13]

As the election approached, it became apparent that the dissenters would carry the day. "The day of tryal [sic] is fast approaching," Bishop Conwell despaired, "The new Trustees will be elected on Easter Tuesday and I am greatly afraid that the Enemies of the Church will prevail." Anticipating defeat the probishop trustees (who were still in a majority) took out a large mortgage on the church property and paid the clergy their salaries in advance.

Once again election day violence seemed likely. Joseph Snyder wrote, "I am fearful we shall have a great deal of trouble . . . at the election." Tensions were certainly running high. Francis Roloff made note of a "most turbulent" meeting at Washington Hall "where some came off with bloody heads and the whole was broken up by the Mayor of the city." Mathew Carey wrote of "unholy strife," "discord and confusion"—"old friendships" sundered and replaced by "deadly hostilities." In his decision denying the petition to amend the charter, State Supreme Court Justice William Tilghman made reference to "intimations of alarming emergencies" that would attend an election held while "the present ferment in their minds" disturbed the congregation. A few days before the election Tilghman and two other justices prepared a pamphlet, widely distributed in the congregation, containing a clear explanation of the legal provisions governing the election. As an added precaution several "judges of election," representing all the contending parties, were appointed. On Easter Tuesday, to the surprise of many, the elections were held without incident. Not surprising, though, were the results. The dissenters carried the day, electing a solid slate of candidates.[14]

"The Interesting Catholic Question in America"

In the spring of 1821 matters at St. Mary's quickly moved toward open schism. Shortly before the Easter elections Bishop Conwell and his assistants abandoned the cathedral church and took up residence at nearby St. Joseph's Chapel, where they ministered to a small band of faithful. Then, hoping "that the fear of being excommunicated might operate on [Hogan] and perhaps detach some of his adherents from him," Conwell issued a monition against the priest threatening to excommmunicate him and any who supported him. The threat, however, only provoked resistance.

At a public meeting held at Washington Hall on May 10 the congregation overwhelmingly voted to restore Hogan as pastor of the church. The defiance was intentional. The trustees issued a public announcement, printed in several newspapers, that they considered it "an imperious duty" to resist Conwell's monition and declared excommunication to be "a proceeding equally disgraceful to the age and country in which we live, as it is libelous and injurious to the Religion of which we are members." They promised to keep St. Mary's Church closed until they could find a pastor who "properly appreciate[s] what is due to religion and common decency." Three days later William Hogan was proclaimed pastor of St. Mary's. A series of actions taken on May 28 completed the separation of St. Mary's from ecclesiastical control. On that day the trustees voted to vacate the clergy's chairs on the board and to bar them from future meetings, ordered the removal of all episcopal insignia from the church, and dismissed the church organist, the sexton, and the teacher at St. Mary's school (all of whom had been loyal to the bishop) and replaced them with dissenters.[1]

Bishop Conwell was baffled and outraged by the resistance. "The new Jacobinical trustees," he wrote, "have made an outrageous beginning—They have usurped and exercised even the power which belongs exclusively to the holy See . . . by which they . . . incur *ipso facto* The Major Excommunication." Once again Conwell expected that the threat of excommunication would undermine Hogan's lay support but again he was disappointed. Rather than being intimidated, the dissenters threatened the bishop with civil law suits should he proceed. Faced with determined resistance from the laity, Conwell retreated and stopped making any reference to general excommunication.[2]

Finally, on Sunday, May 27, 1821, Bishop Conwell took the pulpit at St. Augustine's Church and there publicly read a form of excommunication against William Hogan. In it he charged the refractory priest with "causing confusion in the Church, and endeavouring to establish a schism"; with "exercising priestly functions . . . in direct violation of [a] . . . pastoral mandate, forbidding him in express terms" to do so; and with seducing and leading astray many Catholic laymen and women, thus threatening their souls and bringing "a curse on themselves and [their] families."[3]

Conwell explained to Archbishop Maréchal that the situation at St. Mary's afforded him an opportunity to directly challenge the practice of electing lay trustees which he considered to be "the bane of Religion in this Country." He and his attorneys planned to argue in court that the dissenters, because of their support for William Hogan, had separated themselves from the Church and were not true Catholics and therefore had no right to control the properties of the Church. Conwell fully expected to win his case and in doing so to establish in civil law the principle that obedience to episcopal authority was a defining element of the Roman Catholic religion. Bishop Conwell thus viewed the loss of the election and the subsequent actions of the trustees as events that would eventually operate to confirm episcopal authority. "The Success of these Jacobins," he wrote, "will ultimately enable us to crush the System." They "have so far exceeded and transgressed every kind of law that they are become actually odious to all thinking men."[4]

Conwell looked forward to "a most important trial" that would "determine whether the doctrine and discipline of the Catholic Church are to be protected and supported, or whether adverse denominations may come into our Churches and banish us out of them." He even expected that it would finally settle the question of dual allegience— "whether we may not be forbidden by the Spirit of the law to acknowledge the Pope's Supremacy," for this issue would certainly "be debated by the Hoganites or Huguenots." This case, he confidently predicted, "will become the interesting Catholic question in America, and may fill volumes."[5]

The bishop's lay allies were of a like mind. They wrote to Ambrose Maréchal of the intended suit "for legal redress against the usurpations of the lay Trustees of St. Mary's church, for the restoration of the Bishop and Clergy and the removal of Mr. Hogan from the church. The force of this trial," they declared, "will be important to the whole Catholic Church in the United States; we are determined to spare neither pains nor expense in the prosecution of it." Maréchal responded with approval, declaring that "the unfortunate trustees who have introduced [Hogan] into [Conwell's] cathedral, and expelled [the bishop] from it, instead of being the defenders and supporters of the Catholic religion, . . .are in reality the enemies and persecutors of it."[6]

Like the bishop and his supporters the dissenters were determined and optimistic. They had failed to gain any satisfaction from either Bishop Conwell or Archbishop Maréchal, but several other avenues of appeal were open to them and they intended to make use of them all. Through years of agitation on the behalf of William V. Harold, many of the dissenters had gained some familiarity with the internal politics of the international Church. Now they sought relief through those channels.

Even before the election a committee of laymen had composed a "Memorial and Protest" to be sent directly to Rome. In it they denounced Bishop Conwell and the members of the resident clergy in

Philadelphia, complained of Archbishop Maréchal's refusal to heed their appeals, and effusively praised William Hogan and his work. They predicted that, unless the Holy See immediately removed Bishop Conwell and replaced him with a worthy prelate (a man "cultivated with moral, physical, and metaphysical science"), the result would be "a more awful, scandalous, and disgraceful scene of Bloodshed."[7]

On June 11 the newly elected trustees sent a second petition to the Holy See asking "for the removal of the present bishop of this diocese" because of his "rash and improper conduct" and charging that Hogan had been excommunicated for "frivolous and absurd" reasons. They denied that they in any way sought to cast doubt on the legitimacy of episcopal prerogatives, saying "It is only to the abuse of episcopal authority we are opposed," and they charged Conwell with the most "essentially injurious" form of abuse—"oppression and injustice toward the inferior clergy." Once again, the situation in Philadelphia became a topic of consideration within the Propaganda, and on July 28, 1821, the congregation wrote to Bishop Conwell demanding that he send all available documents on the Hogan matter to Rome.[8]

Once again dialogue within Philadelphia Catholicism bore witness to the great fault line that separated those who embraced Enlightenment ideals and those who clung to the traditions of "inherited religion." Excommunication, the dissenters declared, was a meaningless ritual of no concern to them—a relic of "the days of sorcery and witchcraft." It was, they said, "an ecclesiastical monster . . . , that stalked through the earth, from the tenth to the sixteenth century, the scourge of Christendom . . . , spreading terror and desolation" and provoking "all the horrors of war and extermination." But science, they wrote, "by expanding the human mind, and disenthralling it from the slavery of superstition, [had] enabled mankind to look this monster in the face; and unable to bear the scrutiny, it slunk to its den, execrated and despised." They declared that it was shocking that "in the nineteenth century, in the United States of America," this archaic horror "should have been again brought to light."[9]

St. Mary's dissenters articulated a "whiggish" view of history that celebrated the progressive establishment of individual freedoms. To them the Enlightenment marked a great divide, a time when "the genius of civil and religious science," overwhelmed "the darkness of religion, superstition and priestcraft." They confidently expected that, though "the serpent" of Catholic despotism had again risen "to disturb the happiness of the children of God, in their second paradise [America]," mankind was "*now*, too far advanced, in the science of God, and of true religion, to allow the serpent, under any *shape* or *form*, to interrupt his happiness." Freedom, they felt, advanced with the inevitability of natural law. It was "truly ludicrous," they said, to suppose that "the course of nature, has been interrupted, that a physical law has been suspended, and disorganized in its operations, to further the views of Henry [Conwell]."[10]

Once again St. Mary's dissenters drew a sharp contrast between Catholic traditions and American civil culture. It "is a subject of astonishment to enlightened individuals of every religious class, in the community," stated the "Friend of the Civil and Religious Liberties of Man," that "in an age when the liberties of man are so well understood, and in a country in which those liberties are so well protected, . . . daring attempts . . . have been made to *trample* on your religious rights, and pervert the civil laws of this happy land." Richard Meade proclaimed that "The Bishop and a foreign monk, [William V. Harold, who had entered the fray on Bishop Conwell's side] can have no more right to usurp the rights of citizens of the United States, than they have to establish in this country the INQUISITION." It was the desire and the duty of the trustees, he asserted, to effect "an exclusion of foreign monks and priests from meddling in the affairs of their church, and the rights of the laity."[11]

Recalling the American revolutionary tradition, Meade likened the bishop's actions to British tyranny, calling his attempt to control the Church's revenues a "new foreign stamp-act, or tax on us." He made it clear that the authoritarian form of Catholicism represented by Bishop Conwell and Archbishop Maréchal was alien to American civil culture. Their doctrines, he wrote, "are not adapted to the atmosphere of the United States; [though] they might have answered in the 12th and 13th centuries, in Europe, before this happy and now free soil was discovered." Another layman wrote that Bishop Conwell's action "savors too much of the inquisition to [accord] with the Constitution of the United States." He continued, "The beams of reason have too long illumined the minds of the citizens of the United States, not to have eradicated the glooms of superstition. . . . This is a land of Liberty, conscience here is unshackled . . . , and . . . too much of our fore-fathers blood was spilled on the altar of Liberty," for Americans "ever to crouch under the tyranny of a foreign power." "Americans will never tolerate oppression . . .", he warned, "this is not Ireland." Noting that the pope's "power is rapidly declining in Europe and South America," he predicted that soon attempts to assert episcopal authority would produce a like effect and "give the vital power of Rome its death-wound in Philadelphia."[12]

Once again themes usually associated with Protestant nativism emerged in the rhetoric of Catholic dissent. "The Catholics of this country" one Hoganite wrote, "have suffered too much from the despotism of bishops, and ignorance of curates, not to see the necessity of checking the one, and removing the other." "It is only now," he warned, "before they obtain a perfect ascendancy, that the evil can be remedied." Only the strongest and most decisive measures would do. "If the Catholics themselves," he wrote, "are not united in putting a stop, to the tyranny and despotism of bishops, in this great and free country, the government will have to interfere." "But let even the government take heed," the warning went, "lest its interference should be too late. When despotism reaches to a certain height, but particularly ecclesiastical despotism, it is almost impossible to impede its progress."[13]

In the dissenters' minds not only the fate of their congregation, but that of the whole republic was at stake. "The fabrick of ecclesiastical despotism," a "Member of St. Mary's" argued, "is invariably raised on the ruins, and total prostration of the powers of the human soul." For this reason, he explained, the overthrow of despotism "becomes almost impossible; as oppressed man, wants that energy of mind and perspicuity of intellect, necessary to show him the loss he has sustained, and the privileges he is entitled to." He argued that, "It has been the policy of ecclesiastical tyrants, at all times, to keep the great and majestic mass of the people, in ignorance and darkness," and he warned that such a policy, "is attempted to be practiced among us, and if we tolerate it . . ., we and our children will have to lament the consequences." He predicted a political apocalypse should his warning not be heeded. "The Roman Catholics of this country," the writer [himself an Irish immigrant] observed, "are averaged at the rate of one fifth of its population, and were the spirit of despotism, to be introduced into so large a portion of the community, what would the consequence probably be? perhaps, the total overthrow of our political institutions."[14]

"The Majesty of the People"

Bishop Conwell and his opponents were fully aware of the broader contexts within which their struggle took place. Their apocalyptic statements might seem extreme today, but we must remember that the troubles in Philadelphia were taking place even as liberal revolutionaries were challenging, often successfully, monarchic regimes in Europe and Latin America. Revolutionary republican movements terrified Philadelphia's Catholic conservatives, but they inspired some of St. Mary's dissenters who saw their own small struggle as part of a great international movement. One person so inspired was Richard W. Meade.

Richard Meade was the scion of one of Philadelphia's oldest and most distinguished Catholic families. His grandfather was reputed to have attended the first Catholic service held in Philadelphia and his father had contributed to the construction of St. Mary's Church and served as trustee there for many years. The family was affluent, well-connected, and influential in local and national affairs. Richard Meade's politics, though, bore little resemblance to the conservative republicanism usually associated with the Anglo-American Catholic elite. This was because he had experienced an absolutist regime firsthand.[1]

Meade's formative political experiences had taken place in Spain. While living there he had been strongly influenced by the continuing struggle between republican revolutionaries and the Catholic monarchy. In 1812 and again in 1816 he was imprisoned for publishing criticisms of the government and in neither case was he allowed the benefit of due process. Instead he was, in his own words, the victim of an arbitrary legal system in which "punishment most generally proceeds from private information, without any examination or notice to furnish evidence to the accused, or any confronting of witnesses." The parallels between Meade's treatment and William Hogan's fate at the hands of Bishop Conwell were obvious, and upon Meade's return to Philadelphia he embraced the priest's cause with a heartfelt fervor.[2]

To support their efforts Meade and his associates drew upon personal and professional contacts in Spain and Latin America. To counter the canonical pronouncements of Bishop Conwell and his clerical allies they solicited opinions from liberal clergymen forced by the political and ideological conflicts of the age to flee their homelands and even, in some cases, to abandon the Church. One of these was John Rico, a native of Valencia, Spain. During the Peninsular Wars Father Rico had been a prominent liberal partisan, but with the failure of the Constitutional movement and the restoration of a reactionary Bourbon regime in 1814 he had been arrested and imprisoned. Escaping with the assistance of his friend Richard Meade, Rico fled to the United States and settled in Philadelphia where he pursued a career as a manufacturer and vendor of cigars. Then in 1817, with the financial backing of affluent friends in Philadelphia's Catholic community, Rico purchased land in the Alabama territory on which he cultivated Spanish vines and olive trees.[3]

On January 1, 1820, a military junta rose against the Bourbon monarchy and proclaimed the liberal Constitution of 1812 to again be in effect. In the months that followed, expatriate Spanish liberals flocked back to Spain; one of those who intended to return was John Rico. In the spring of 1821 he traveled north to Philadelphia to take ship for Spain.[4]

Upon his arrival in Philadelphia Rico met with Lewis Clapier (local agent for the revolutionary Cortes and a prominent Hoganite), his old friend Richard Meade, and other dissenter leaders. They offered him the pastorate of St. Mary's, but Rico had no interest in remaining in America and declined. Then, on May 2, two days before he embarked for Spain, Rico submitted to an interview in which he strongly supported William Hogan's interpretation of canon law. Bishop Conwell, Rico felt, had clearly violated Hogan's right to due process and was therefore in violation of the canons. The Hoganites gleefully publicized Rico's statements and used them to counter the bishop's argument that those who opposed episcopal authority were not true Catholics.[5]

John Rico was not the only radical clergyman who sanctioned the dissenters' cause. Throughout Latin America liberal insurgents were challenging Spanish rule and many radical clergy had joined the cause of independence. One of these was Servandus A. Mier (Servando de Mier), "a liberal priest and scholar of international repute." Mier had been politically active in "defense of the rights and liberties of his native country" and in consequence of his "writings in vindication of the sovereignty of

the people" had spent three years in the "dungeons of the Inquisition."
Upon his release in 1820 Mier fled Mexico and sought refuge in
Philadelphia. There he was welcomed by Richard Meade and his associ-
ates at St. Mary's.[6]

His experience as a revolutionary had alienated Mier from the
Church hierarchy. He denounced the bishops who "established cru-
sades against the [Mexican] patriots, commanding them in person
under the rank of colonels," who "approved the war of extermination,
and exhorted the people to it in their pastoral charges or letters," who
pronounced "excommunications on cities and whole provinces," and
whose "fanaticism made a most horrible carnage." Were it not possible, Mier wrote, "to distinguish the *church* from the *bishops,* and *religion* from its *abuses,*" the revolutionaries "should have apostatized
from catholocism [sic] as England did." This was precisely the argument that the dissenters at St. Mary's were making—that fidelity to the
Catholic Church could be separated from obedience to the dictates of
the hierarchy—and they happily embraced Servando Mier and his
views.[7]

Some of St. Mary's dissenters advertised Mier's arrival in the secular press, styling him a bishop, and they even suggested that he was a
papal nuncio, sent to America "to regulate the affairs in the U.S. and
sanction its Independence." Mier, of course, would have none of this,
but he did attend mass at St. Mary's in company with Richard Meade
and other lay leaders and, like Father Rico before him, he submitted to
a well-publicized interview in which he supported the dissenters'
claim that Bishop Conwell had no right to suspend William Hogan
without granting him due process. Further, he maintained that
because Bishop Conwell was in violation of the canons his excommunication decree had no force. Before leaving Philadelphia Mier warned
Bishop Conwell and his ecclesiastical allies that "if in the midst of so
much information and so many liberal ideas, the reverend bishops do
not become more moderate, and only adhere to that tissue of inepti-
tude and despotism, which they call the new right of the decretals, . . .
they will destroy the church."[8]

John Rico and Servando Mier were participants in a great international confrontation between republicanism and absolutism; between
nationalists and proponents of a universal moral order; between those
who accepted the Enlightenment ideal of rational, secular progress,
and those who cherished the medieval ideals of social stability and

authority grounded in faith and tradition. Many among St. Mary's dis-senters drew inspiration from and saw themselves as actors in that same struggle. To them Bishop Conwell and the "Reverend Junta" that supported him were merely the local manifestation of a great evil that threatened all of Western civilization. "Let us open the pages of the history of France," they urged, where "ecclesiastical intrigue, and despotism, have been the source of all the misfortunes that have fallen that country." "Look to Spain," they cried, "and behold to what a level of degradation, ecclesiastical intrigue and despotism have reduced her." "Take alarm," they said, and "behold, even at the present moment, the stand and struggle which religious fanaticism, fanned into a species of madness, by clerical intrigue, is making against freedom and inde-pendence."[9]

Against this clerical despotism, the dissenters asserted, stood only the will of the people. For generations, they declared, "the people bowed their necks to the yoke and submitted to their remorseless tyrants, not because they approved the conduct of their spiritual rulers, but because they could not, and dare not resist." But in the modern age liberty beckoned, as "evil pressed on evil, and acts of injustice were reit-erated to such a degree" that they could no longer be tolerated, and "oppressed and insulted humanity arose" to throw off their masters. "So," proclaimed a member of St. Mary's—who styled himself the "Friend to the Civil and Religious Liberties of Man"—"did the majesty of the people rise in Germany, in England, in France; and in our own day, in Spain and Portugal; and will ere long in Italy, hurl back the insults upon their oppressors, with redoubled force."[10]

A Republican Church

St. Mary's dissenters did more than protest. They proposed to create in America a Catholic church, commensurate in status with the national churches of Europe but organized on a liberal, constitutional basis. "Almost every country, within the pale of the Catholic church," a "Member of St. Mary's" congregation complained, "has its concordat with the Holy See, and is by virtue of it, entitled to certain privileges, [but] We [in America] alone . . . are doomed, to the fatal necessity of being obliged, to receive any bishop, whom the junta of Fide propaganda, please to send us." "The Irish," he noted, "have a concordat with the court of Rome, they elect their bishops . . . ; the English elect theirs . . . ; in France, they are appointed by the government; in Spain they are also appointed by the government." But American Catholics, "have not a voice, either of ourselves, or through our government, in the selection or appointment of our bishops." What was needed, he concluded, was an American "concordat, or some understanding, or agreement with the Holy See, by which the reciprocal rights of the clergy and laity, may be known and defined."[1]

On June 18, 1821, a committee including leaders of all the dissenting factions at St. Mary's issued a call "to Their Brethren of the Roman Catholic Faith Throughout the United States of America." In this remarkable document they pointed to "Sundry Abuses" in the administration of the church and to "the numerous and scandalous scenes" which they attributed to "the arbitrary and unjustifiable conduct of certain foreigners, sent among us by the Junta or Commission, directing the Fide Propaganda of Rome." These persons, the dissenters declared, had "uniformly shown themselves hostile to our institutions, and completely ignorant of our country." They had made unjustified claims to the ownership of church property, had attempted to introduce "superstition and ignorance" into true republican religion, and had "constantly fomented . . . divisions and parties [among us] in order to rule with greater despotism." Rather than using this power responsibly, they asserted, the foreign bishops and clerics had exercised it "in too many instances, in a despotic and arbitrary manner." As a result a situation had developed in Philadelphia and elsewhere "such, as neither our education nor principles can sanction."[2]

The dissenters called upon American Catholics to free themselves from the "direction of [the] Junta . . . called the Fide Propaganda," which, they claimed, was incompetent to order affairs in America and to judge the quality of the prelates sent there. The dissenters were careful to note that this was not to be interpreted as an attempt at schism—

they still "acknowledge[d] the Pope" as their "spiritual chief"—but they were determined to separate themselves from the control of the corrupt clerics "who surround his Holiness, and who frequently make religion a pretext for deceiving him." These clerical deceivers, they clearly felt, included the cardinals of Propaganda.[3]

The dissenters hoped that once freed from Roman control American Catholics could establish "some general system—an uniform system— . . . whereby our rights can be secured." They envisioned a constitutional church within which "the reciprocal rights of clergy and laity, may be known and defined." It would be an American church. Instead of receiving "foreigners of every class and kind, to direct and command" them, American Catholics would "claim the exclusive right which always belonged to the church, of electing our own Pastors and Bishops." Once elected, the American bishops would be "ordained in this country, and receive the Bull, or approbation from Rome, as a matter of course." In this church the powers of bishops over the lower clergy would be constitutionally limited. Once "having been regularly chosen, by the respective Parishes, and inducted into the Church," no priest could "be suspended by the Bishop, without a fair and impartial trial" by a board of his peers. In order to guarantee lawful rule all regulations governing the clergy and the congregations would be "clearly defined and published" for all to know, and after his trial a suspended priest could appeal the judgment to the archbishop and then to Rome.[5]

The church envisioned by Philadelphia's dissenters was thus a constitutional, democratic, and uniquely American establishment. This insistence on the new church's national character was not a simple assertion of American nationalism nor was it, as some historians have claimed, rooted in the historical experience of an Anglo-American Catholic elite, which sought to distance themselves from Rome so as to blunt Protestant hostility. Rather, it was a prophylactic measure, designed to protect a bastion of republican enlightenment from the monarchic, ultramontane spirit that was spreading through the Restoration Church. "We wish to preserve our religion unchanged and free from the superstition and ignorance which has attempted to be introduced among us," the committee declared. "A Layman of the Congregation" echoed their sentiments. The American church, he wrote, should be "devested [sic] of all pomp, outward show, and processions, which in some countries in Europe, serve only to blind the ignorant and create a spirit of superstition in them." The dissenters drew inspiration from the primitive Christian church, a community of faith shorn of elaborate ritual and hierarchy. Their "only object," St. Mary's trustees proclaimed, was "to preserve the doctrine of [the Catholic] Church in its primitive purity, and to sustain their rights as citizens of this country, against the pretensions and despotism of a few foreigners."[5]

Education was important in the republican church. It was necessary, the dissenters believed, to promote and to control education at all levels so as to foster rational, republican values in both laity and clergy. They asserted control over St. Mary's parish school, dismissing the bishopite teacher and replacing him with one who shared their sentiments. The Sunday school, so important for instilling proper republican values in the working class, they strongly supported. To ensure that children learned proper republican values in their religious instruction, Hogan revised the standard catechism, altering the sections on confession and indulgences. The dissenters even projected the establishment of a seminary wherein candidates for the priesthood would be "brought up among us and educated under our immediate inspection." The dissenters also expanded their charitable efforts, founding in October 1822 St. Mary's Beneficial Society for the relief of the sick and distressed, and one month later they established the first Catholic newspaper in the diocese, the *Catholic Herald and Weekly Register*.[6]

The bishopites saw in the proposal for a republican church proof that St. Mary's dissenters were no longer Catholics. In pamphlets and from the pulpit they unleashed an unrelenting stream of scorn and vilification. Conwell declared that the authors of the "infamous Heretical pamphlet," were "Infidel Jacobin[s]." A "Layman of St. Mary's Congregation" likened the dissenters to "Turks or Pagans" and branded them men who would "disgrace Paganism itself." They are "schismatics and heretics," he wrote, "Not one drop of Catholic blood warms the heart, nor one ray of Catholic faith enlightens the understanding of those who penned the Address." Francis Roloff, the pastor at Holy Trinity, styling himself "A True Catholic and No Traitor," wrote a series of satiric pamphlets in the form of a "Last Appeal" to the congregation. "*The Independent Catholic Church*, which [the dissenters] are about astonishing the world with," he declared, is "worth the song of a future Milton." William Hogan, he wrote, is "a founder of a new religion, the independent catholic church. He will out-do Henry the VIII and make [his followers] as independent as the English church is from the Roman see." Another bishopite who published under the pseudonym "The Detector," likened the public meetings of St. Mary's congregation to a "conventical of bats [congregating] to remonstrate against the sun." He declared that "all laical interference [in ecclesiastical affairs] is preposterous and unjustifiable . . . , for the words of Jesus Christ are not directed to them, but to the apostles and their lawful successors."[7]

The bishopite attacks raised once again a fundamental question: could a church infused with liberal principles be tolerated within the milieu of Restoration Catholicism. Although the answer of most members of the American hierarchy had been a resounding "No!" the dissenters saw some promise in the person of John England, the bishop of Charleston, of whom William Hogan wrote, "A star has risen in the south, the lustre of whose brilliancy will disperse those clouds of unmanly envy, low jealousies, and provincial prejudices, that have for so long a time lowered over our religion in this Country, and impeded its progress." Hogan hoped that England would sympathize with his cause. On March 26 he proposed to Bishop Conwell, "Send for the Rt. Rev. Dr. England of Charleston, and the Rt. Rev. Dr. Chevereux [Cheverus] of Boston, let a plain statement of facts and circumstances be laid before them and let you and me be bound to abide by their decision."[8]

The ecclesiastical trial never took place. Bishop Cheverus, on hearing of Hogan's proposal, immediately gave notice that he fully supported Henry Conwell's actions. England, too, in a private letter informed Bishop Conwell that he had "been horror-struck at reading the publications which Mr. Hogan and his associates have disseminated." He wished to have no part in the affair. Gleefully, Bishop Conwell published both of these letters, prompting William Hogan to criticize Cheverus and England for having prejudged a case about which they had little information. England's response to Hogan's criticism was equivocal. "I never wrote or expressed a condemnation or acquittal of Mr. Hogan," he protested. "At this moment," he continued, "I do not . . . , clearly understand the state of the dispute." He expressed disapproval of both principals (Hogan for his extreme and unorthodox pronouncements and Conwell for making public what was intended as a private communication) and he again expressed his desire to avoid entering the conflict.[9]

The Star of the South

John England was something of an anomaly within the American hierarchy. Alone among his contemporaries he made a serious effort to adapt Catholic institutions and principles to the "American republican mentality." In his ecclesiological writings Bishop England tried to argue that the Church itself embodied republican values. "Her institutions," he argued in a famous passage, "are eminently republican. Her rulers are chosen by the common consent—her officers are obliged to account strictly to those over whom they preside—her guide is a written constitution of higher force than the will of any individual. What can you call this?" he asked, "Aristocracy? Monarchy? It is republicanism." England argued for a constitutional church in which papal authority was shared with that of a general council of bishops. Only when the bishops and the pope spoke with one voice, he felt, did they represent the true values of the Church and only then were their rulings infallible. Even then the assembled hierarchs were not free to legislate arbitrarily. They were still bound within a vast constitutional tradition that included the writings of the Church fathers, the scriptures, the "whole of revelation." This elaborate system of constraints, he held, was essentially republican.[1]

England also argued for a decentralized church in which each nation and locality could determine its own customs, so long as they did not violate general principles of doctrine and discipline. He called for regular provincial councils of the American bishops to regulate church discipline and also to demonstrate that episcopal authority was not arbitrary but the result of careful and consultative deliberations. "Law and system" would thus replace "arbitrary power" and "episcopal mandates." England also felt that each bishop should meet regularly with his diocesan clergy and with prominent laymen in liturgical and consultative sessions that would demonstrate the unity of the Church. At the level of the individual congregation, England urged priests to consult regularly with prominent laymen and recognized that in some matters of financial administration the priest's wishes should bow to those of the vestrymen. He was even willing to tolerate the existence of elected lay trustees so long as they confined their actions to management of the temporalities of the parish and did not challenge monarchic traditions of church government.[2]

Bishop England's view of the Church was a remarkable departure from the absolutist and ultramontane tendencies that dominated Restoration Catholicism but it was also quite limited. England "shared many of his colleagues' perceptions on a monarchical episcopacy." His church was a paternalistic structure in which the bishop functioned as a "father who embodied all the legislative, judicial, and executive powers in the diocese." In contrast to the dissenters' assertion that episcopal authority must be legitimated by popular approbation and conspicuous virtue, or that it must be subordinate to the dictates of the state, England declared that

> The authority to preside and to teach in the church of God is not derived from talents, nor from wealth, nor from worldly power, nor from popular choice, nor even from the piety and virtue of the individual, but from his having been regularly assumed to the apostleship, and ordained therefore by some successor of an apostle who has thereby received his authority from Jesus Christ.

England might consult with laymen but held fast to the principle that "the laity had no power or authority in the government of the church." He felt that the claims of lay trustees to the right of patronage were "the primary cause of all the unfortunate schisms in the church in the United States" and expressed the view that the canons which supported such a right were "very bad."[3]

Bishop England's concessions to republicanism, then, were minimal, but even these limited concessions were firmly rejected by his colleagues in the American hierarchy. When the bishops finally met in 1829 for the first provincial council of the American hierarchy they took advantage of the occasion, not to establish constitutional limits on their power, but to confirm episcopal rights while severely restricting clerical and lay rights. England's peers overwhelmingly mistrusted his "radical" and "innovative" procedures in church government, and some even accused him "of following Protestant principles and practices in establishing his constitutional system of church government." Ultimately, in Patrick Carey's assessment, Bishop England's attempts at administrative innovation "had the ironical effect of implanting an episcopal aristocracy" rather than recasting the American church in a conservative, but vaguely republican mold.[4]

John England's involvement in the Philadelphia schism was brief and of little consequence, but it points up the discrepancy between his limited concept of Catholic republicanism and the more extreme perspectives of St. Mary's dissenters and of Bishop Conwell. While on a trip to New York, England granted an interview to William Hogan during which the unhappy priest tried to distance himself from the increasingly radical views of his supporters at St. Mary's. He had "never intended to oppose the Bishop," Hogan said, but "the Trustees prevailed upon him to do so." Hogan repudiated and expressed contrition for the pamphlets he had authored and claimed that his participation in the schism had been motivated by "dread of [the dissenters'] vengeance and exposure." The whole experience at St. Mary's, he said, had been "to him the worst species of slavery, . . . from which he was anxious to escape."[5]

Bishop England was sufficiently impressed with Hogan's account to offer him a place in his diocese and to write a letter on his behalf to Bishop Conwell asking for permission to lift the priest's excommunication. At the time Conwell was away from Philadelphia so the letter was opened and read by members of the resident clergy. They were astounded. They had taken earlier statements by Bishop England to indicate his "most pointed disapprobation" of Hogan but now, in what seemed to them to be a "truly wethercock-like" reversal, the "Bishop of the South" had apparently decided to support the "Schism of the North" and to enlist in the "army of the Wrong." Fearfully, they sent out letters and emissaries begging Bishop Conwell to immediately return to the city.[6]

If England's letter caused "the greatest confusion" among the clergy, it had the opposite effect at St. Mary's. There the dissenters obtained the original of the letter and held it "sacredly," until it could be personally delivered to Bishop Conwell. The Hoganites were jubilant. At long last, it seemed, they had found episcopal sanction for their cause. John England's clerical envoy even went so far as to assist Hogan at mass, an act that the dissenters took to confirm "the legality of their proceeding" and "the rumor was bruited about that the Bishop of Charleston had taken the side of [the dissenters] and had promised to carry their fight against Dr. Conwell to Rome." To celebrate their victory the dissenters organized a procession "of 30 Carts with white flags flying and the horses curiously adorned to haul sand and stone to their Church to enlarge it in order to give more place for pewholders of their party."

Extra pews were certainly needed. As word of Bishop England's letters spread through Philadelphia's Catholic community, "the church of St. Mary's [began] again to fill, like a Balloon sometimes inflates anew at the sudden heat of the approaching earth." Anxiously, the elated congregation began to prepare for Bishop England's expected arrival. They appointed a "grand Committee to receive him and lay the State of the Church before him."[7]

Meanwhile Bishop England met with Henry Conwell in New York and there the two men hammered out an agreement. Conwell would not grant Hogan a trial nor would he allow anyone to mediate the quarrel, but he gave England power to lift the censures if Hogan left Philadelphia, did penance, and publicly condemned his "infamous pamphlet." On October 15 Bishop England traveled to Philadelphia. There he met with Hogan and began negotiations to effect the priest's withdrawal from the diocese.[8]

On October 17 Bishop England met with William Hogan and induced him to sign a letter requesting admission into the diocese of Charleston, in which he agreed "to abide by [England's] decision and that of the Holy See upon his previous conduct." England then formally welcomed Hogan into his diocese. At this point three of Hogan's supporters were called into the room, where the bishop astonished them by denouncing Hogan for the "complete irregularity" of his actions. Even if he had been wronged by Bishop Conwell, England said, "it was only by an appeal to Rome, and not by irregular opposition, [that] redress could be had." Then, relenting a bit, England promised that "if [the dissenters] conducted themselves as Catholics and had causes of complaint [he] would not only forward their statements [to Rome], but if [he] found them supported by evidence [he] would aid them to obtain redress."[9]

This remarkable statement was guaranteed to alienate everyone involved. Hogan and his friends were offended to be told that their actions were "completely irregular." England's statement also seemed to place him in the position of offering to judge Bishop Conwell's conduct, a prospect that would outrage not only Conwell but other members of the American hierarchy who fiercely guarded their episcopal prerogatives. Finally, England's assertion that only the Holy See could grant redress for episcopal abuse seemed to be an extreme ultramontane position, very much out of character with his pronouncements in other forums. It virtually invited Rome to become involved in the settlement of local disputes.[10]

The laymen then queried Bishop England as to how they would replace Hogan, for now they were without a pastor. England replied that the decision was Bishop Conwell's to make, but when the dissenters said that "their objections to receiving those whom [Conwell] had appointed were insuperable," England promised to ask Conwell for permission to select a suitable pastor for St. Mary's. The lay committee then "expressed themselves satisfied if this were granted" and left, whereupon Bishop England had William Hogan kneel before him and profess, before clerical witnesses, that he belonged to the diocese of Charleston, that he was true to the Roman Catholic faith, that he was contrite for his improper publications, and that he promised to abide by the injunctions of the Holy See and his bishop's judgment and decision upon his case and conduct. England then absolved Hogan from all censures and the two men sat down to dinner together.[11]

St. Mary's lay leaders were not satified. They felt that Bishop England had betrayed them. They insisted that Hogan remain at St. Mary's until a suitable replacement was found but England forbade the priest to say mass and ordered him to leave the city as soon as possible or face a reimposition of his sentence of excommunication. He advised the laity to await action from Bishop Conwell. England then offered to appear at St. Mary's to explain to the assembled congregation their error. Here we see a marked difference between Bishops Conwell and England. Instead of simply issuing orders to the laity, England was willing "to give them an explanation." This consideration was, however, essentially a matter of style rather than substance. England was conceding nothing in the way of authority to the laity.[12]

William Hogan wavered, then yielded to his friends' demands and said Sunday mass at St. Mary's. Outraged, Bishop England denounced Hogan and reimposed on him the sentence of excommunication. When asked for an explanation, England remarked that, as far as he was concerned, William Hogan had by his actions renounced his allegiance to both Philadelphia and Charleston. "Now," he said, "Mr. Hogan is under censures, without jurisdiction, belongs to no Diocese, and is incapable of being employed for any ecclesiastical purposes, according to the discipline of the Roman Catholic Church."[13]

Shortly thereafter John England left Philadelphia for the south. His efforts in the city had in all instances failed and he had roused acrimony everywhere. John Powers, England's secretary, reported that "Philadelphia is torn to pieces." Bishop Conwell was furious at England for having meddled in his diocese and the traditionalist Catholic clergy saw him as a dangerous innovator whose only effect had been to exacerbate existing difficulties. Patrick Jordan reflected this opinion when he wrote that before England's arrival "the Trustees [at St. Mary's] knew they were insubordinate, but when they gathered from the Bishop that they were on an equality with their diocesan and ought to, not *might* or *could* appeal to Rome, offering himself to be appointed their agent, their conduct became insupportable."[14]

St. Mary's dissenters were also disillusioned and resentful. They felt that the "Star of the South" had betrayed them, revealing beneath his republican facade a soul as despotic as that of any other prelate. England, they wrote, was not "acquainted with the progress of the human mind in this great and vast country." His experience had been in Ireland, among "convicts, and cells and gallows." Never, they said, had he "looked at the fairer side of human nature, or never seen the bright and progressive aspect which the human soul wears when it breaks through the fetters of slavery, and shakes off the encumbrances of ignorance, despotism, and superstition, as it has done in this country."[15]

Bishop England shared in the general atmosphere of resentment and recrimination. He denounced all the participants in Philadelphia's controversy. "The Bishop," he wrote, "is not exactly in his place. Hogan is without faith, principle or information, habituated to sacrilege, and supported by envenomed anti-Catholics under the disguise of the Catholic name." Once back in Charleston, England launched a long series of virulent attacks on St. Mary's dissenters. They were, he wrote, men and women who, "never discharged a single duty of those principally obligatory on Catholics." Their proposal for an American church he branded "the strongest blending of folly, and fallacy, and falsehood that ever fell under our observation." Their apologetic pamphlets were "disgusting collections of broken concords and bad divinity, of garbled law and misquoted Scripture, of foppish arrogance and petulant vituperation, of false statements and imbecile sophistry." Hogan was a "vampire, crawling forth from the graves of the respected dead, with his head smeared with gore, his entrails filled with corruption, and the air around him fetid and contagious." "There is not," England proclaimed, "on the continent of America a body of persons professing Christianity, who are more palpably, and we fear more inexorably opposed to the doctrine and discipline of the Roman Catholic Church, than the congregation of that once Catholic Church."[16]

Bishop England blamed the troubles in Philadelphia on the institution of trusteeism. "Hogan is not the author of this evil," he wrote, "though he should leave Philadelphia, the evil would not be removed." Rather the schism was "the natural consequence of the system [trusteeism] upon which Catholicity has been established in Philadelphia." Repeatedly he urged Archbishop Maréchal to call a synod of all the American bishops so as to develop a strategy to destroy the practice. "The system is horrible," he wrote, and . . . Catholicity will make no progress where it will exist. I look upon every new church erected under Lay Trustees as a curse, and I would as soon burn my hand as bless it."[17]

Many historians have accepted Bishop England's assessment, holding the practice of trusteeism to be the cause of the dissensions that troubled the American church in the years between the Revolution and the Civil War, but trusteeism in itself did not cause dissent. St. Mary's dissenters did not learn their liberal principles through the exercise of the electoral franchise. Rather trusteeism simply afforded them a mechanism by which they could put their democratic beliefs into practice. What John England encountered in Philadelphia was a confrontation between diametrically opposed sensibilities, and his failure to effect a reconciliation there can be understood as a consequence of his attempt to mediate between irreconcilable points of view. Bishop England, who sought a middle ground between republican principles and the monarchic traditions of the Church, stood apart from and was therefore mistrusted by both the Philadelphia dissidents and their episcopal antagonists. His failure confirmed the growing suspicion that liberalism and Catholicism, even in its most modern aspects, could not be reconciled.

Anti-Catholics

On December 2, 1821, William V. Harold returned to Philadelphia under circumstances that once again bore witness to the influence that

Rome exerted over affairs on the American mission. Having heard of the troubles at St. Mary's, Harold had traveled to Rome and asked that his "entire case be reopened and that everything be made the subject of a new examination." When the General Congregation met to consider the matter, Harold asked that he be allowed to return to St. Mary's. Despite Archbishop Maréchal's explicit opposition to Harold's presence on the American mission, Propaganda designated him an "honorary missionary" and approved his request. Once more Maréchal was reminded "that his jurisdiction was being systematically disregarded and that the wishes of his suffragans were being ignored in the . . . Propaganda Fide."[1]

Despite a personal dislike for Harold, Bishop Conwell saw in him a useful tool, one that might split the dissenters and precipitate their downfall. He immediately installed the Dominican as his vicar-general. For several weeks after his arrival Harold kept a low profile, preaching only occasionally at St. Joseph's Chapel and then only on noncontroversial subjects, while he judged the situation. Then, on January 6, 1822, he finally took the pulpit at St. Mary's and delivered a sermon on the schism.

For weeks Philadelphia's Catholic community had been abuzz with speculation as to Harold's intentions. More than twelve hundred people crowded into the church that day to hear him. All factions were in attendance, as were several Protestants who had been invited to hear the famous man speak. His words threw the congregation into turmoil. Harold began by asserting a claim to be the rightful pastor of the congregation. Then he launched into what some called the "most inflammatory sermon" they had ever heard. "*The Prince of Darkness,*" Harold said, "*had stretched out his arm to mislead Mr. Hogan and his followers.*" Hogan's good works, he claimed, were nothing but a "stale trick" undertaken "in order to gain popularity." He declared that Hogan was the source of all turmoil in a congregation that had previously enjoyed total "peace and harmony."[2]

Harold's "inflammatory tirade" set off a violent round of denunciations. "THE GRAND MELO-DRAMA OF SATANIC INTRUSION" produced "melancholy and disastrous and disgraceful consequences" within the congregation, and reignited passions that had begun to abate. Harold continued his assault from the pulpit and in print on St. Mary's dissenters. Hogan's apologists, he claimed, were paragons of "ignorance, insincerity and fraud," their reasoning on religious subjects "might have been put down by a child." Their minds, he said, were "deranged by passion." He declared them totally incompetent to interpret the canons—their citations of canon law he dismissed as mere "index learning" so ludicrous as to make them the "subject of general amusement."[3]

Harold's attacks on the dissenters changed both the tenor and the ideological context of the conflict at St. Mary's. He took up a point, first articulated by Bishop England, that the dissenters had not only separated themselves from Catholicism, but had actively enlisted on the side of the Church's enemies. Hogan's defenders, he said, were nothing less than anti-Catholics, as menacing as any Protestants. He asked, "Is the *no popery* yell, which the blindest bigot in England would blush to utter, to disgrace the land of liberty and the city of the liberal Penn?" In Harold's eyes the dissenters constituted a "no popery party" that sought to destroy rather than to reform the church.[4]

Harold's charge was repeated by other defenders of episcopal authority. A Catholic "Of the Olden Time" declared that the schism was not a legitimate dispute over principles among Catholics but a clash "between the supporters of the catholic church and the enemies of that church—between the maintainers of catholic discipline and the destroyers of that discipline." It constituted nothing less than an "Anti-catholic conspiracy." He denounced the "ignorance" and "infidelity" of the dissenters, proclaiming their actions and statements to be "unnatural and monstrous." "If a man be a Jew," he wrote, "let him be a Jew in all the sense of the word—if he be an episcopalian, let him comply with the tenets of that creed. . . . If he be a presbyterian, let him be one in word and deed. . . ." But it was sheer absurdity, he felt, for the dissenters to call themselves Catholics. "This may be *republicanism*," he thundered, "but it is not *catholicism*."[5]

Once more the fatal question had been raised—whether the Roman Catholic Church could accommodate liberal principles—and once again the answer was an emphatic "No!" This in itself was a perilous position for the Church to take in the new republic, for it lent credibility to nativist rhetoric, but other more subtle themes had also emerged. Now Catholic clergymen had begun to define their lay opponents as anti-Catholics—as Protestants—and in doing so they specifically identified republicanism with Protestantism.

Implicit in William Harold's (and Bishop England's) charges was a new appreciation of the role of laymen in Catholic dissent. Whatever the differences, and they were many, between John Carroll and the prelates who succeeded him, all were products of a paternalistic and aristocratic regime wherein common people were considered to be a dependent class and accorded little or no independent political identity. This prejudice colored their views of Catholic dissent. Rather than seeing their lay antagonists as independent actors, Catholic prelates tended to view them as errant children, misbehaving because they had been misled by clerical adventurers. Because they were fundamentally irresponsible, acting out of delusion or ignorance, lay dissenters were still deemed to be Catholics, however misguided. By 1822, though, it was becoming increasingly difficult to hold this view of dissenting laymen. At St. Mary's and elsewhere laymen were clearly acting on their own, independently of clerical leadership, and nobody understood this better than William V. Harold. In his view the lay dissenters had to be addressed directly. Their statements could no longer be ignored. For this reason he vigorously engaged the lay leaders of St. Mary's congregation in an extensive and vitriolic pamphlet war and tried to define them as being outside and even antagonistic to the Catholic community.

These tactics and charges shocked the dissenters. Many had hoped that Harold, who in his struggle against Bishop Egan had encouraged lay interference in church affairs, would rally to William Hogan's cause, but Harold now emerged as the most articulate and formidable proponent, his critics said, of "the monstrous doctrines of the frantic *ultra-Montanists* or of the artful and fanatic Dominican Friars." To the dissenters Harold's "*volte-face*" smacked of cynical opportunism. William Meade declared that Harold was "a man devoid of every principle of Christian charity, with no other object in view but that of seizing on the revenues, and living at the expense of a congregation who despise him." Harold's sermons and writings he characterized as "a continued series of barefaced falsehoods, circulated with a view of deluding his ignorant and fanatic followers," and motivated by his own inordinate ambition and chimerical projects of obtaining possession of the temporalities of St. Mary's church."[6]

Many former Haroldites agreed with Meade's assessment. Augustine Fagan declared that experience had "taught us how erroneous were the ideas we had formed in regard to the nature of the dispute" that had divided the congregation in the days of Bishop Egan. Now many of his former followers attributed the troubles of 1812–13 entirely to William Harold's ambition. They noted with disgust the fact that Harold's former opponents, the traditionalist elites, were now his strongest allies.

Such betrayal, they concluded, could only be evidence of overweening ambition and a base character. "Mr. Harold," they said, "has sanguine hopes of succeeding to the mitre," and has shown, "that while he can pursue his victim with the fell and unrelenting malignancy of a Portuguese inquisitor, he can also seek the attainment of a favorite object with all the refined duplicity of an Italian intriguer." "The people" they declared, had once been "the cause of William Vincent Harold . . . it is now only that of a young priest by the name of William Hogan.[7]

William Harold was an opportunist, but there was far more to him than mere ambition. There were serious ideological and ecclesiological foundations for much of what he said and did. In 1810, when he spoke on the occasion of Bishop Cheverus's consecration, Harold delivered a paean to hierarchy, a form of government that he considered to be ordained by God and sanctified by the sufferings of the Church Fathers. But Harold's support of hierarchy was conditional. Bishops, he pointed out, wielded great power, but he held that it was absolutely imperative that a bishop "support the authority by a blameless sanctity of life." "The fire of heavenly charity," Harold declared, "must glow in his words, and be visible in his actions; for if the world can contrast the life of a Bishop with his doctrine, from that moment he has lost the power to save." Harold warned, "Instead of encouraging the growth of virtue and co-operating with heaven to save the immortal soul, [such a bishop] kills every feeling of good, . . . confirms the doubts of the unbelieving, and hardens the obduracy of the impenitent."[8]

William Harold's insistence that episcopal authorities display virtue in their lives and actions resembled William Hogan's belief that authority must always be legitimated by conspicuous virtue. In both cases the insistence on consistently virtuous behavior could and did become the basis for challenges to episcopal authority, but there was a significant difference in the priests' understanding of what constituted virtuous conduct. William Harold defined virtue in traditional religious terms, specifically mentioning "sanctity of manners," "unimpeachable integrity," and "heavenly charity," while St. Mary's dissenters and the revolutionary clergy insisted that virtuous conduct be based in rationality, respect for individual rights, and responsiveness to the will of the people. These different understandings, as so many other perceptions, were based on disparate reactions to the Enlightenment.

In his Baltimore sermon William Harold made explicit his revulsion for the Age of Reason. His view of society was Hobbesian, not

Rosseauian. "Whatever can restrain the lawless passions of man," he said, "whatever can counteract his inordinate propensities, that is the parent of human happiness." Harold rejected the Enlightenment premise "that civilization can supply the place of Religion, and assume the guidance of human actions," and declared that "no force but the force of the Gospel can save man from the passions of man." "To what other hope can we recur?" he asked, "Is it to law?" The answer was no. "Law has forbidden the commission of crimes . . . [but] it has scarcely thinned the numbers of the guilty. The arm of violence is still uplifted. The robber still infests society." "It may perhaps, be affirmed," he said, "that civilization can supply the place of Religion, and assume the guidance of human actions." But, pointing to the revolutionary violence of contemporary Europe he said, "it has been reserved for our own days, and for our instruction, to see how civilized men can act when withdrawn from the salutary restraint and benignant influence of Religion. They have acted. The voice of unutterable confusion has echoed back their deeds." The peoples of Europe, he proclaimed, "have broken the chain that bound them to the Deity, and they have sunk the dupes and victims of a proud, shallow, presumptuous philosophy. The storm of almighty vengeance has burst over their heads."[9]

In William Harold's estimation spiritual authority could never be compromised. His insurrection against Bishop Egan in 1812–13 was, at least in part, motivated by his belief that the bishop had compromised the integrity of his office by allowing a clique of influential laymen too much of a voice in the management of the church (especially in the matter of clerical salaries). Any bishop who "listens to any other command than the dictate of conscience," he maintained, "he is a wicked man." Although Harold made use of democratic mechanisms and stirred class resentments to advance his interests, he was by no means a champion of ecclesiastical democracy or of the common man. Harold asserted that he had "deprecated [in 1812] and will ever deprecate, the employment of secular influence in a spiritual government" and declared that in no case whatever could a bishop allow his judgment to be swayed by "the arrogance of faithless men or the yell of a depraved rabble." He had mobilized public support, he maintained, in order to protect, rather than to compromise, clerical prerogatives.[10]

Ultimately, then, William Harold (like John England) stood on the far side of the great cultural divide that we called the "modern schism." This was a bitter disillusionment for many among St. Mary's dissenters.

For years they had cherished the memory of a liberal priest whose cause had been "the freedom and welfare of the people." They had seen Harold as a sympathetic figure who might bring about a reconciliation between the warring factions within the congregation, but when he returned to Philadelphia it was in the service of a regime that had consistently rejected in no uncertain terms the fundamental ideological principles upon which St. Mary's revolt was predicated. William Harold's return made it clear that in the diocese of Philadelphia no reconciliation between episcopal absolutism and liberalism could be effected.

Clubs against Cudgels

William Harold's return altered the cultural and social dimensions of the conflict at St. Mary's as well as the ideological. Many remembered his earlier success in mobilizing immigrant workers to physically intimidate his opponents and, as the Easter-week elections of 1822 approached, rumors of impending "riot and confusion" were rife. "It was publicly reported," Edward Barry testified, "that the ensuing elections would be attended with much confusion, and in all probability bloodshed." As vicar-general William Harold took charge of organizing the bishopite efforts and, along with several of the traditionalist clergy, made careful preparations to control the outcome. To swell the bishopite ranks they sent for people "from the country within 40 or 50 miles of this city."

> Some came from pleasant Wilmington,
> And some from Brandywine,
> From Dover far, and New Castle —
> Not Newcastle on Tyne.
> To banish Hogan from the Church,
> And drive his friends away.[1]

On the evening before the election several of the bishopite pewholders met at St. Joseph's chapel and remained there through the night. At
sunrise they rose, armed themselves with cudgels, pinned green and
white ribbons to their lapels, and received a blessing from Bishop
Conwell. They then marched to St. Mary's and took possession of the
premises. John Maitland, a close friend of William Harold's, placed a
lock and chain on the gate giving access to the church. Soon they were
joined by "young men and buxom maids," who came "trudging in from
Germantown, Manayunk and Chester, and Darby, and even from over
the waters [in Delaware and New Jersey], to do and die, for Bishop and
for Church."

> They bore in hand their cudgels stout,
> For swords may cut too deep,
> The gate secured with bolt and bar,
> And thus their watch did keep.

At 6:00 A.M. Hogan's partisans began to gather on the street in front of
the church. When ordered in the name of the trustees to open the gate,
John Carrell, a bishopite leader, responded that "every man on the
ground was a Trustee on that day."

> Now when the morning dawn appear's
> The Hoganites drew nigh,
> With many a faithful Irishman,
> Who for his priest would die.

After an exchange of insults and threats the dissenters armed themselves with "stones and bricks" and tried to force their way onto the
church grounds. The church was enclosed by a four-foot brick wall
topped by a six-foot cast iron railing, and the dissenters began to press
against it. "The iron rail swayed backwards and forwards, like a reed
shaken by the wind, and at last fell with a crash."

> And now the barriers prostrate lay,
> In rush the impetuous crowd,
> While man to man, and hand to hand,
> They fight with tumult loud.[2]

The fight went on for "about 10 or 15 minutes," during which "perhaps
200 persons were wounded." All in all, there would seem to have been
"800 or 1000 combatants."

> Clubs against cudgels brandished were,
> Bricks flew 'gainst flying stones,
> Some had their noses broken there,
> And some had broken bones.

William Hogan and some of his friends watched the fray from a nearby dentist's residence. Most of the resident clergy gathered at a nearby street corner while Harold and one other priest marched up and down through the ranks of the rioters "*spiriting* up their friends." The wounded were taken into nearby homes and to two drugstores on Fourth Street. There they were treated and some returned to the fight.[3]

Soon after the battle began the mayor of the city arrived on the scene accompanied by several peace officers. Both parties at once quit fighting and under police supervision the election proceeded. The votes were then tallied separately by each side and both factions claimed victory. Each side immediately accused the other of tampering with the count and each slate of candidates claimed to be the legally elected trustees of the church. At one point William Harold stood on a pew with the intention of announcing the election of a bishopite slate of trustees, but he was shouted down by the dissenters. Finally, after much confusion and mutual recrimination, the bishopites quit the field and returned to their homes. The dissenters rejoiced and claimed victory:

> The Bishopites did fly, the people cried
> The Hoganites forever,
> They have gained the day, lets all huzzah,
> Saint Mary's Church is their's forever.[4]

In the aftermath of the affray both sides took their cases to the public, each claiming irregularities on the part of the other. The dissenters protested "the violence of an armed, lawless mob" while bishopites argued that the outcome of the election was of little importance since the dispute "was a contest between true Catholics and schismatics." Finally, both sides agreed to refer the matter to an impartial arbitrator and chose General Thomas Cadwallader, one of Philadelphia's most distinguished citizens, to render judgment. General Cadwallader carefully surveyed the pewholders at St. Mary's and on June 22 declared victory for the dissenters.[5]

This did not end the violence at St. Mary's. Two months after the election Harold's friends made a second effort to physically take the church. "A large number of persons friendly to Bishop Conwell" marched to the church "and took possession of it." This time they carried, in addition to cudgels, "guns, blunderbusses, pistols, [and] swords." The armed men intended to "keep possession of the church until the Sunday following, and then give it up to the Bishop," but constables intervened and dispersed the intruders "amidst shouts loud and long," from "crowd upon crowd of spectators . . . , among whom epithets of all kinds were freely circulated."[6]

After this William Hogan and Bishop Conwell, both clearly disturbed by the tumult and violence, came to an agreement whereby they would share the church. On the following Sunday they attempted to put this plan into effect but the clergy began quarreling, and when Hogan accused the bishop of lying the service disintegrated into "a scene of confusion." Men shouted at and threatened each other and at the priests and bishop. "Women too, joined in the confusion, and several with uplifted hands and uttering vehement exclamations, threatened vengeance upon their opponents. Children were crying, pew backs were creaking, the Bishop stood aghast, while Hogan seemed utterly confused." Shaken by his experience, Bishop Conwell departed and his supporters dispersed, leaving St. Mary's again in the possession of the dissenters.[7]

The battles of St. Mary's marked an important shift in the social and cultural context of the dispute. Not only had violence erupted but the nature of the argument had changed. In an attempt to rouse the Irish working class William Harold began to recast the situation at St. Mary's within the framework of ethnic antagonisms. "To answer his purposes," Mathew Carey protested, Mr. Harold "has endeavored to persuade Catholics at a distance, that the whole affair is a struggle of the Protestants to expel the Catholics." Augustine Fagan complained that Harold attempted "to enlist [the immigrants'] prejudices, feelings, and recollections, on the side of episcopacy." Harold played on ethnic themes, attacking Hogan and the dissenters as anti-Catholic nativists indistinguishable from Protestant bigots and Orangemen. Early in 1823 Harold even founded an ethnic magazine, *The Catholic Advocate and Irishman's Journal,* the declared purpose of which was "to defend our ancient and holy religion from the pestiferous breath of heretical innovation; to cling to the same faith and the same hope in which our fathers lived and died, and not be led astray by the wicked machinations of base and irreligious intruders."[8]

Other bishopites joined in. Shortly before the Easter week elections, "An Irish Catholic" took pen to urge his countrymen to compare the candidates for office. Our ticket, he wrote, "is not filled with the names of Englishmen, of those who for centuries have trampled on the rights, and sacrificed the interests of Ireland, and oppressed even unto death its inhabitants. Our ticket is made up of other materials." The "Irish Catholic" even went so far as to express an apprehension that "some of our Protestant brethren should be prevailed upon to interfere in our election," and in the wake of the riots bishopite spokesmen argued that the arrival of the mayor and sheriffs to quell the violence was just such a case of Protestant interference.[9]

The passions that could be tapped by ethnic appeals were shown in a series of letters published in 1823. They were written in response to a proclamation purportedly issued by three revolutionaries named "Capt. John Firebrand, Patrick Fury, and Timothy Bloodsucker," all of whom were "sworn to walk knee deep in Orange blood." The proclamation was widely printed in the Irish press then reprinted in the *Charleston Mercury*, which cited it as an example of Catholic intolerance. John England responded to this incendiary article by declaring it a forgery designed to stir anti-Catholic passion. "I know the Roman Catholics of Ireland," he wrote, and the Catholic "is not a furious monster, plotting the death of his Protestant neighbor." Never, he declared, in years of association with Irish revolutionaries, could he recollect "that any one of the unfortunate creatures thought that his religion sanctioned his crimes."[10]

William Hogan objected. He wrote in response to England's assertion, "How can the bishop of Charleston even insinuate that the outrages in Ireland, are not sanctioned by the Roman Catholic church?" "I will go further," he declared, "and contend that all the excesses and barbarities committed in that country, are to be attributed solely to the amalgamated system of faith and discipline to which the deluded Irish Catholics conceive themselves bound to submit." Hogan sketched a parallel between Catholic intolerance in Ireland and his treatment in Philadelphia. Here, he wrote, we have seen "a fatal instance of the influence of the Roman Catholic religion . . . on the moral [and] political conduct of its members." He was referring, of course, to the influence of "an overbearing, domineering, licentious monk of the name of W. V. Harold, hired and imported for the purpose," who incited immigrant workers to "rush headlong regardless of all consequences, into the most shameful excesses." "Were it not for the paucity of their numbers, and activity of our police," he wrote, "Heaven only knows to what lengths their fanaticism might carry them."[11]

Hogan then attacked traditional Irish Catholicism. He declared that many Catholics of his acquaintance "thought it is no crime to murder a Protestant, a Proctor, or a Guager." Truly, he wrote, "the *priest-ridden* peasantry of Southern Ireland, [are] "literally firebrands, furies and bloodsuckers." Such, he felt, was the effect of a "system of discipline at present adopted by the Court of Rome, that disobedience to the laws of the Pope and his Court of Cardinals, not only excludes a man from Salvation, but subjects him to forfeiture of all civil rights." "There never was a braver, never a more generous people" than the Irish, he wrote, "but while in Ireland, while influenced by priestcraft, they cannot be depended upon; they cannot, nor do they depend even upon each other."[12]

Traditional Irish Catholicism, Hogan felt, left the emigrant working classes without a moral compass. "There are some of them" he wrote, "who never saw a bible until they came to this country, who never heard a sermon or exhortation except at Christmas and Easter; and what was it ever then, a vulgar dissertation on the obligation of the laity to pay their pastors, accompanied with a threat, that if they did not, they should do public penance, or incur the odium of a ludicrous excommunication, which the poor people are taught to consider the greatest of all evils." Hogan warned his readers that the American bishops were now attempting "to establish in this country, the same system of church government upon which they now act in Ireland." This, he argued, was the source of religious dissension in the new republic. The bishops, he concluded, have to be made to realize that "their authority is purely spiritual, and that they are bound to love their neighbor, whether Protestant, Presbyterian, or Jew, as they love themselves."[13]

Hogan's letter prompted a torrent of ethnic vituperation from his opponents. "An Irishman" wrote to the *Democratic Press*, "to redeem my country, my religion and its professors, from the foul stigma which [Hogan] would cast upon them." He pointed out that Hogan was "Imported" and lived off the "hard earnings and scanty pittance" of other "imports." These, he said, were a people of "faith and fortitude" who fled Ireland to escape religious persecution and continued to "adhere to the faith and the discipline of their Fathers!" Hogan was a "Hypocrite . . . who . . . heats the iron and cuts the letters and stamps 'Imported' on their foreheads"— who levels "against them the powerful artillery of Prejudice." "Let me tell you, sir," he wrote, "that there are hundreds of Irishmen in this city who would chastise you for your falsehoods and your insolence, but that *they* reverence that which it would seem you disregard—the cloth you wear." A "Lady" wrote to the *Columbian Observer* to charge that Hogan's "principle [is] Protestant, and [he] wishes to overthrow the religion which [he] profess[es], giving scandal to the land of [his] birth and mine." "If you do not quit the city in less than one month from this date," she threatened, "your days will be short, and put an end to by me, either by poison or fire."[14]

Another letter from "An Irishman" declared Hogan's statements to be "barbing and poisoning the arrow, which . . . is aimed at the heart of Ireland and Irishmen." "*The Orangemen*," he wrote, "the *sworn* foes of Ireland, will be delighted with Mr. Hogan's letter. . . . It is a justificatory manifesto for them; sanctioned by the name of a Catholic Priest. . . . Let every Irish Catholic who knows how cruel are the tender mercies of the Orangemen, reflect how *they* will rejoice and be encouraged, by the manifesto of Mr. Hogan, to torture and kill the people of Ireland." It seems, he mused, that Hogan, though "from that section of Ireland he so unblushingly libels . . . , has become a citizen of the world, and soars above those vulgar and ignoble prejudices which attach men to their family and friends, and to the country of their birth." He warned Hogan that the Irish "love their friends; but . . . despise and hate those who libel and slander them."[15]

The power of ethnic sensibilities to shape perceptions can be seen in Patrick Kenny's account of the 1822 election riot. Despite all evidence to the contrary, Kenny believed that William Hogan had instigated the riot. "Hogan," he wrote, "the butcher of character and this day the butcher of men, slaughtered by the hands of his vile anti-Catholic party, a number of valuable persons." "Philadelphia," he wrote, "disgraced itself forever: its mob vociferated the sentiments of its inhabitants and its courts of law, 'Down with the Pope and Popery!' and stoned to death its Catholic citizens." "O Penn," he cried, "the . . . apostates and their olive-branch Orangemen or Free Masons, *soi-disant* Catholics, have set all your philanthropy at defiance." "Philadelphia," he concluded, was "worse than Derry for Catholics."[16]

Unlike the polemics cited above, Patrick Kenny's impressions were inscribed in his personal diary and were not intended for publication or any public forum. We may presume, therefore, that they reflect his honest understanding of what he had witnessed. What is notable about them is the fact that, instead of seeing a dispute between Catholic factions, Kenny associated St. Mary's troubles with ancient ethnic antagonisms (Orangemen against Irish Catholics) and contemporary European ideological confrontations (Freemasons against the Church). His view was that of the Irish country priest, locked in a bitter struggle against hereditary Protestant foes, English landlords, and the insidiously corrosive strains of revolutionary republicanism. He, like many other immigrant Catholics, both lay and cleric, preserved in America the cultural perspectives and antagonisms of the countries from which they came and fought resolutely against anything that threatened to disturb the patterns of behavior and belief to which they had been long accustomed. Hogan and the Hoganites were just such disturbers.

The battles at St. Mary's bear witness to the extent to which the disputants inhabited a transatlantic intellectual, institutional, and cultural milieu. Participants in the Philadelphia struggles all linked their experiences to conflicts on the far side of the Atlantic. Patrick Kenny railed against the Freemasons and Orangemen, Bishop Conwell likened the dissenters to Reformation Protestants, "Carbonari," and "Jacobins," and St. Mary's lay leaders quite explicitly compared their cause to that of liberal revolutionaries in the Catholic lands of Europe. The battles also bore witness to the power of those broader perspectives to shape the context of dissent. The distinction between modern and traditional cut across the class spectrum. Now working-class democrats were firmly allied with bourgeois Hoganites while traditionalist workers sided with the old Catholic elite. Each of the forces that contended in St. Mary's churchyard included all levels of Philadelphia's social order—wealthy and respected pillars of the community fought side by side with common farmhands or laborers. The conflict also sundered ethnic ties. Irish "imports" were arrayed on both sides. The Philadelphia disputes in the 1820s may have been informed by class and ethnic imperatives, but ultimately they represented a confrontation between competing perspectives on the modern world.

But the alignments produced by the modern schism, because they overrode class and ethnic distinctions, were inherently unstable. The alliance of democratic workingmen with bourgeois whigs masked profound conflicts of interest, as did that linking traditionalist workingmen with the Catholic elite. What is more, the fact that bishops enjoyed the support of ethnic traditionalists in their struggle with the inheritors of the Enlightenment by no means reflected a broad and inclusive identity of interest or perception between the bishops and their loyal subjects.

We must remember, for instance, that Bishop Conwell publicly declared on his first day in the diocese his determination to eschew all ethnic or national particularism, and there is nothing to indicate that he ever indulged in ethnic characterizations or appeals. Conwell was well aware of the complaints made by bourgeois Catholics against the traditionalist clergy, and in an attempt to woo them away from Hogan even went so far as to employ as an assistant Samuel Sutherland Cooper, an American convert to Catholicism and "a man of wealth and refinement," who, he felt, might be more acceptable to Hoganite sensibilities. The bishop's points of reference throughout the conflict were the institutional needs of the Church, the Protestant Reformation, and the revolutionary turmoil of contemporary Europe, not the ancient rivalries and ethnic pride invoked by the traditionalists. Ultimately, as we shall see, the institutional imperatives of the restoration church were every bit as corrosive of ethnic traditions as the enlightenment Catholicism they opposed. This inherent tension, however, was not yet manifest in Philadelphia in the 1820s and the bishop, at least for a time, enjoyed the solid support of ethnic traditionalists, both lay and clerical, against a common foe.[17]

Courts of Appeal

The controversy at St. Mary's could not be contained solely within the Catholic community. From the beginning both bishopites and dissenters made use of the secular press and published pamphlets that were widely distributed to Protestants as well as Catholics. Both sides also took their case to court. The most important of these court actions involved attempts to establish legal control of the church grounds, but in these there was no clear resolution. There were also several nuisance suits, none of which seemed to have much merit. "Innumerable . . . law-suits" grew out of the violent episodes in St. Mary's churchyard. Others were in the nature of slanders on the principals in the conflict. Twice in 1823 William Hogan was charged with sexual improprieties and on another occasion a woman instigated a paternity suit against Bishop Conwell. As suits and countersuits dragged on through the court system without clear resolution, legal expenses mounted. By January of 1822 Bishop Conwell was complaining that legal battles against the trustees "have involved us into great expenses." None, however, resolved the conflict.[1]

Far more important than the legal proceedings were attempts to amend the charter of St. Mary's Church. There had been several such efforts, dating back to 1805, but none had been in any way successful until three Haroldite members of the board of trustees petitioned the Pennsylvania state legislature in 1820 for amendments that would exclude clerics from sitting on the board. This time the legislature approved the changes subject to review by the State Supreme Court. The court, however, rejected the amendments because the three petitioners did not represent the will of either the board of trustees or the congregation as a whole. In 1821 newly elected Hoganite trustees renewed the petition and again the legislature approved the suggested amendments and sent them on for review by the Supreme Court.[2]

Early in 1822 the decision of the Court was announced. Once more the trustees' petition was denied, this time on the grounds that the clergy had been illegally excluded from the deliberations that produced the appeal. The majority decision read by Chief Justice Tilghman was an important triumph for the bishop's party. "Every church has a discipline of its own." Tilghman wrote, "It is necessary that it should be so, because, without rules and discipline, no body, composed of numerous individuals, can be governed." He reasoned that an individual could be subjected to discipline—he could be "admonished, reproved, and finally ejected from the society." He could, if dissatisfied, "retire from it, at his own free will" but the clergy as a body were an integral element within the corporation and must have a say in its administration. The lay trustees, therefore, had no right to exclude the clergy from their deliberations.[3]

Tilghman also remarked on the nativist implications of the dissenters' arguments. "Something was said," he wrote, "of the danger of a foreign head of an American Church. But our laws have expressed no apprehension of any such danger." Regarding the doctrine of apostolic succession, which held that "the power of conferring or withdrawing the sacred rights of the Clergy has been handed down in sure succession from the Holy Apostle St. Peter to the present pontiff," Tilghman stated that "the people of the United States of America have seen nothing in this belief either criminal or dangerous." Moreover, he asserted, there was no indication that Catholics "have been less patriotic than their fellow-Christians of other denominations."[4]

Bishop Conwell was elated by the court's judgment. He wrote, "One material point is determined in favour of authority and ecclesiastical discipline, that is, that the Supreme Court will maintain and support every church and sanction exclusions [excommunications] when proceeded in according to the respective laws or canons of the church or sect, be it what it may." He opined that "*Now is the time* . . . , the case has come to a *crisis*. . . . It is necessary to defeat the *Jacobinical* disposition, which prevails among a certain class of citizens in the United States, otherwise Religion will be lost there forever." "When they are conquered," he wrote, "they will never attempt the like again." In another letter Conwell expressed his opinion that the cause "of the Church will triumph, and much good will be derived from these *procès* to the Catholic Church universally throughout the United States and eventually elsewhere."[5]

Tilghman's decision heartened the bishopites but it did not daunt the dissenters. They took encouragement from a minority opinion by Justice John B. Gibson that the church had been chartered as a lay corporation and the trustees were therefore civil officers. The clergy, he felt, could not be accorded a status within the corporation different from that of other trustees; if they were, their presence would be indispensable to the operation of the corporation and they could effectively dissolve it by withdrawing their services.[6]

Justice Gibson's opinion also gave sanction to the nativist elements in the trustees' arguments. He noted that Catholic clergy "were bound" to follow their bishop and that bishops in turn were bound "on the same terms of unconditional submission to the Papal See." "Here then," he wrote, "is a foreign jurisdiction, in its nature political as well as ecclesiastical, holding and exercising the power of appointing to offices, created by the government of Pennsylvania for purposes entirely civil and domestic." "Far be it from me," Gibson wrote, "to counsel the Catholics to shake off their spiritual allegience to the Pope; that is their concern, not mine, but I do protest against a right of appointment to a civil office incautiously granted to a foreign potentate, being considered irrevocable by the government of our own country." He dismissed the theory advanced by Bishop England that the Catholic Church was essentially republican. He wrote,

> With me it is of no consideration that the catholic Bishop is elected by the catholic clergy here or elsewhere: both he and they acknowledge the supremacy of the Holy See as the source from which they derive all their authority and the power to which alone they are responsible. It is enough for me that our citizens here, whose interests are involved in the government of the corporation, have no voice, either in nominating or rejecting, the pastors who are introduced into the church.[7]

Justice Gibson's opinion shaped the dissenters' response to the court's decision. On January 15 they published a reply to Chief Justice Tilghman's assertion that St. Mary's corporation was composed of two classes, clergy and laity, each deriving their authority from different sources. If the clergy were an integral element in the corporation, they argued, then they would have the power to destroy it by removing themselves. By this means "the Pope becomes invested with the power of disfranchising all the incorporators.... So a foreign power is enabled to do what the sovereign power of this country . . . cannot do. For no power in this country, without crime and without trial, could disfranchise a corporation or deprive an individual of his rights or his estates." In following months the dissenters alluded time and again to the foreign influence represented by an immigrant clergy and denounced their claim to special status within the church. Thus, the decision of the Pennsylvania Supreme Court early in 1822 inadvertently called attention to and served to accentuate the nativist implications of the dissenters' position.[8]

Judgment also came from the Court of Rome. Already there had been several complaints to the Holy See from all sides. Finally, early in 1822 the Sacred Congregation met to review the Philadelphia situation. Their decision, released in a papal brief on August 24, 1822, was a disaster for the dissenters. The brief denouncd the "incessant discord and dissensions," the "schisms" and the "perverse doctrines" that plagued Philadelphia Catholicism. "These disorders," the brief stated, originated in William Hogan's "senseless arrogance . . . , nefarious . . . [and] execrable deeds," as well as the lay trustees' "abuse of power." The Holy See expressed "astonishment" and "indignation" that Hogan "could find many followers, supporters and defenders of his pride and contumacy" and warned the dissenters that "not those only who do evil, are to be considered and treated as guilty, but those who give their assent to them, and . . . procure them assistance, counsel or protection."[9]

"It belongs not to laymen," the brief continued, "to meddle with ecclesiastical judgments, which are reserved to the Bishop." In conclusion the Holy See urged Philadelphia's quarrelsome Catholics to render to the bishops, "that respect, honour, and obedience which belongs to them: to receive them as their fathers and the directors of their souls; to lend a willing ear to their admonitions; to supply them with the subsidies necessary for their support; to harbour no other ministers . . . but those who have been approved by them; finally to embrace with pleasure and with readiness whatever they may judge conducive to establish regular order and discipline, and to rest in peace."[10]

The papal brief and accompanying correspondence from the Holy See marked a significant expansion of Rome's presence in the American church. Not only did the Holy See act "to restrain the sacrilegious audacity of the priest Hogan," but it also intervened to ensure Bishop Conwell's income, granting him "*in commendam* . . . the parish of St. Mary at Lancaster." The brief also denounced the "immoderate and unlimited right, which trustees . . . assume, . . .of [supporting as] pastors, priests destitute of legal faculties . . . , and also of removing them at their pleasure, and of bestowing the revenues upon whom they please." This, the Holy See declared, is a practice *new* and *unheard of* in the church." Should it be allowed, "the Church would be governed, not by Bishops, but by laymen, the Shepherd would be made subject to his flock, and laymen would usurp that power, which was given by Almighty God to Bishops."[11]

In conjunction with the brief, Propaganda issued "certain regulations and instructions concerning the choice and direction of trustees" that were to be applied in all dioceses. In the future bishops should attempt to influence the election of trustees so as to elect only those people who would be properly subservient to episcopal authority and who would recognize the freedom of clergymen from lay control. When new churches were constructed bishops were to secure title to all church property so as to erect legal barriers to lay interference in church affairs. If a congregation insisted on having a board of trustees, the bishop should require a legal contract that would guarantee episcopal prerogatives. Should the parishioners object, the bishop was instructed to refuse to bless the church or to assign it a pastor. These "Regulations for the management of Church concerns" were kept secret rather than being promulgated, because it was felt that they would rouse popular resistance. "Time enough to disclose the Pope's Regulations," Bishop Conwell wrote in the spring of 1823, "when our pending causes shall be determined and brought to a successful issue." Such micro-managing from afar was a direct consequence of the failure of American hierarchs to successfully quell dissent within their realm and it marked a significant trend toward greater involvement of the Holy See in the internal affairs of the American church.[12]

Rome's decision devastated William Hogan. He repeatedly attempted to negotiate a settlement that would allow him to leave Philadelphia without carrying the stigma of censure, but Bishop Conwell and his vicar-general rejected every proposal; as they did, Hogan's resentment and suspicions grew. On December 14, 1822, William Hogan finally decided not to submit. He declared that the papal brief was inauthentic since it contradicted the canons of the Church. Such a document, he held, could not represent the judgment of the pope, nor could the brief's "harsh invectives" against him and his followers have ever issued from the person of the pope. Even if the brief were authentic, Hogan argued, it could not be obeyed: the principles expressed in the brief, "may suit the meridian of the Roman State, but they will always meet with the decent but firm resistance of American Catholics." "I am forced to say . . . ," he wrote, "that I foresee great evils to arise to the American Churches from this rash attempt to establish here a monkish system of discipline and to enforce antiquated pretensions in matters of church property."[13]

Three days later Harold and Hogan clashed openly at St. Mary's Church. Hogan had already entered the pulpit to begin the service when Harold arrived and commanded him in the name of the bishop to leave the pulpit. Hogan replied, "I will not, Sir. I am preaching to my congregation." Harold again ordered the priest to leave and he again refused, stating "I shall not do so for you or the Bishop. This is my congregation, and I will recognize neither. I am preaching to my congregation and they will sustain me." Harold then pronounced an anathema against Hogan and left the church. Once again matters stood at an impasse and the bishop's hopes for a quick resolution of the schism were dashed. Benedict J. Fenwick, who was assisting Conwell, wrote shortly thereafter that "Mr. Hogan . . . still continues in possession of St. Mary's and bids defiance to every authority. The Bishop . . . still continues to officiate at our little chapel of St. Joseph's and I think is likely to end his days there. . . . He has already seen much but I am persuaded he will yet see a great deal more."[14]

Early in January 1823 William Hogan published in several local papers an extended defense of his position. In it he reiterated his earlier arguments that Conwell's actions were irregular, that his censures were illegal and carried no force, and that no human action could divest him of priestly powers sanctioned by God. He declared the pope alone was incompetent to judge the conflict between him and Conwell for it involved a disagreement over matters of faith and discipline and these, he held, could be decided only by a general council of the Church. Ironically, in support of this position he cited Bishop England's writings on the conciliar tradition in the Church.[15]

Then, addressing himself to the civil context of his situation, Hogan made his final break with the administrative structure of the Church. He argued that the pope could have no jurisdiction in America. "It matters not," he wrote, "whether the Pope interferes in our temporal concerns directly or through his agents in this country. The evil may be the same, and it is our duty to guard against its consequences." Should papal power expand in America, he claimed, the result would be the same as in other countries such as France, where clerical intrigues had "so often divided and distracted the . . . nation"; or in "our sister country, South America," where Roman authority had caused "intellectual degradation"; or in Ireland, where "the reciprocal intrigue and corruption of her clergy, Protestant and Roman Catholic" were the source of endless misery.[16]

By the end of 1822, then, William Hogan had carried his defiance to the point of an open break, not just with his bishop and the American hierarchy, but with the Holy See itself. The bishopites saw this as a conclusive point in their favor, and anticipated imminent victory not only in the hearts and minds of Catholics, but in the civil courts. William Harold put the bishop's case plainly in a letter to the dissenting priest. He began by asserting that Hogan and those who followed him in defiance of Rome were no different from Protestants and could no longer be considered Roman Catholics. "St. Mary's Church," he wrote, is "specially reserved to Roman Catholics, and for Roman Catholic worship. . . . If the Bishop shall succeed in proving that St. Mary's is at this moment not a Roman Catholic

Church . . . , he will find his remedy not in the power of the Pope . . . but in the laws which are impartially administered to all who have the happiness to live under our admirable constitutions."[17]

Appeals to Rome and to the American civil courts thus pushed both sides in the Philadelphia dispute toward extreme positions. More and more the dialogue between the disputants sounded nativist and ethnic themes. Civil contests led the dissenters to emphasize the alien elements of Catholic tradition while the content of American civil law led the bishop and his supporters to insist that their opponents were beyond the pale of the Catholic community and to deny them any standing at all within that community. The result (which had the full approval of Rome) was an extremely narrow and overtly authoritarian definition of Catholic faith and community that confused dogma with discipline and excluded more than it included.

The Catholic Bill

Condemnation from Rome meant that St. Mary's dissenters could find sanction for their positions only through recourse to civil institutions. They were optimistic in that regard. Many Hoganites were well-connected politically and, despite their many defeats at the hand of constituted authorities, the dissenters' numbers were growing. The initial resolution of support for William Hogan in December of 1820, immediately after his suspension, had garnered 250 signatures; in the spring elections of 1821 the dissenting trustees received 453 votes; one year later their vote totaled 497; and now, in the last month of 1822 when the board of trustees once again petitioned the state legislature for amendments to the charter that would exclude the clergy from any say in managing the temporalities of the church and would enshrine in civil statute the laity's right to choose their pastors, 579 "Pew and seat holders" affixed their names to the petition.[1]

In preparing this petition St. Mary's trustees took care to meet the objections to previous efforts. They were careful not to exclude members of the clergy from their deliberations and diligently recorded the priests' protests in the minute book of their meetings. The pewholders' signatures served as evidence that the memorial really did represent the will of the congregation. Having thus disposed as best they could of technical objections to their efforts, the memorialists went on to lay out the ideological and legal arguments for charter change. They proposed that revisions to the charter were necessary in order to account for the "progressive advancement in knowledge" since it was first issued and to bring the church into correspondence "with the liberality, and intelligence, and spirit of advancement of the [present] age." They asked that the legislature amend the charter so as to grant the board of trustees power "to select pastors for St. Mary's Church from among the body of regularly ordained Roman Catholic Clergy," contending that in so choosing they were not attempting "to set aside the regulations of a system of faith which they revere." They assured the legislators that they would "receive no other pastors but those who have received the sanction of the head of the church," and only hoped to "enjoy a privilege, common to all other worshippers, to select from the persons duly ordained those to whom they are to be allied in one of the closest of social relations." This, they argued, was a reasonable compromise between democratic principles and Catholic traditions of government.[2]

To justify their petition the dissenters invoked once again an individual, rather than a corporate, concept of religious liberty. "The great end of every religious association" they wrote, "is to receive instruction in points which concern the spiritual welfare of the members. Each individual has therefore a deep and vital interest in the selection of those to whom the important duty of instruction is confided." This, they argued, was the "universal practice" of churches in America, with the "mere exception" of some portions of the Catholic Church. In Philadelphia, they complained, they were "compelled blindly to submit to receive spiritual instructors whom they did not choose, and whom the united voice of the members has not the power to remove."[3]

These pastors, "generally sent out from a foreign country," were "without any knowledge" of the "abilities, morals, or disposition" of the congregation, and were therefore incompetent to instruct them. Nevertheless these clerics were accorded special status within the congregation. "The interested opposition of an individual," they wrote, "who happens, without the approbation of any part of the [congregation], to exercise pastoral functions, under a foreign domination, will defeat the attempt; and the will of the whole body of worshippers may thus be made subservient to the wishes of a single person." They declared that the injustice of this situation, and the dangerous intrusion of foreign interests, compelled them to request that the charter also be amended so as to require that the trustees be selected only from the lay pewholders and additionally that they be citizens of the United States.[4]

Previous petitions had been approved by the state legislature as a matter of course and then referred to the State Supreme Court. This time, though, the "Catholic Bill" (as the petition came to be called) became a hotly contested political issue that engaged the attention and participation of people throughout the state. This was a momentous occasion in the political history of the Commonwealth because for the first time Catholic authorities decided to exert their considerable influence to challenge legislation of which they disapproved.

Senate committee hearings on the dissenters' petition began on January 7, 1823, and "the subject excited considerable interest." The committee room was "full to overflowing" with "members of both branches of the Legislature." Dissenters and bishopites were both well represented. "The debate . . . continued till after candle-light" and through the following day. The speakers were frequently interrupted by questions from members of the committee. So pointed were these that at least one experienced observer was sure the bill would never reach the floor of the Senate. Nevertheless, on January 11 the bill was reported out of committee despite being opposed in "warm debate" by some members.[5]

The intensity of the debate and the interest of the spectators testify to the importance of this bill in a gubernatorial election year. State politics of that period has been called a "game without rules" and 1823 was particularly fraught with peril for ambitious politicians. The Republican "caucus" that had dominated state affairs for nearly a quarter of century was rapidly disintegrating but no effective structure had yet risen to take its place. In Philadelphia the "Old-School," DEMOCRATIC-Republican faction that had long provided the major opposition to the Republican caucus was dissolving too. Adding to the uncertainty was the fact that the popular governor, Joseph Heister, announced that he would not be seeking reelection in the fall, setting off a confused and intense struggle among Pennsylvania's Republicans for the nomination. It was during this period of political maneuvering leading up to the Republican convention in March that the Catholic Bill was being argued in the legislature. All concerned were well aware that Governor Heister had enjoyed strong support from the state's immigrant workers in the 1820 elections and all feared to antagonize this important element of the voting public.[6]

This was the situation when Bishop Conwell, William Harold, and their supporters organized opposition to the Catholic Bill. "Our present struggle is highly important," the bishop proclaimed, "The object of our enemies is to reject Ecclesiastical authority *in toto*, to regulate the Discipline by lay Trustees, to permit Clerical intemperance, to chuse & reject The Clergy & change every thing which they may Chuse to Consider." Determinedly he and his vicar-general launched a massive protest against the proposed legislation. In the weeks after the Catholic Bill was reported out of committee, "petitions rained in upon the legislature, and every means was adopted to have it suppressed." Memorials came from Roman Catholic congregations in "York, Carlisle, Elizabethtown, Conewago, Lancaster and other places."[7]

The bishopites also solicited petitions from Catholic authorities and congregations in other states. William Hogan "is no longer a Catholic Pastor," an association of New York Catholics opined, the "Trustees of St. Mary's, with their adherents . . . , have ceased to be Catholics, [and so] . . . unjustly retain possession of St. Mary's Church." They urged the legislature to reject the petition, saying that its passage would set "a dangerous precedent, rendering the tenure of all church property insecure to its founders." An association of Maryland Catholics declared that the schism at St. Mary's was "alone attributable to the anti-catholics and rebellious conduct of the pretended pastor of said church, and the blind infatuation of his followers." They denounced the trustees' petition "as subversive of a fundamental principle of the Catholic Church." Bishop Conwell's actions, they said, were "in strict conformity with the canon law, and the established usage and discipline of the Catholic Church throughout the world." Even the venerable Charles Carroll condemned the dissenters and praised efforts "to repress the turbulence and schism prevailing in Philadelphia."[8]

The bill passed the House of Representatives without amendment, but in the Senate debate continued intermittently through February and into March, even as major political factions were choosing their candidates for the fall election. Positions taken by persons on both sides illuminated parallels between conflicts in the civil and in the religious realms. Thomas Earle, arguing for the dissenters, made the connection explicit. "The cause of these petitioners," he wrote, was ". . . decidedly the cause of religious liberty," for all Americans had a right "to determine for themselves, . . . by whom they will be instructed in the truths of religion." People, he argued, "have a natural and unalienable right, to choose who[m] they will have to rule over them, as well in religious as in civil matters. They are as much under the dominion of detestable tyranny, when *compelled* to forego the one right, as the other."[9]

Apologists for the dissenters took a radically individualistic view of political and religious affairs, asserting the unalienable rights of individuals to absolute freedom in both realms. To them the principles supporting episcopal authority were like those sustaining all undemocratic institutions. When opponents of the Catholic Bill pointed out that the State Supreme Court had already ruled the principles embodied in the bill unconstitutional, two senators turned the occasion into an assault on the idea of an independent and appointive judiciary. In doing so they were hearkening back to ancient battles between Federalists and Republicans that had been an important continuing theme in American civil discourse. Thomas Earle, editor of the *Mechanic's Free Press*, chimed in arguing that "It is aristocracy and despotism, to have a body of officers, whose decisions are, for a long time, beyond the control of the people." The Supreme Court, he declared, was just such a body. On another occasion a senator stated that only the legislature could guarantee the rights of the people because it served as a check on the despotic power of the other branches of government.[10]

The dissenters and their supporters also argued for strict majoritarian rule. Should the bishopites prevail, they argued, a minority whose "superstition and ignorance fit them to become the passive instruments of the clergy" would determine the "religious rights and duties" of the community and make them "obligatory upon the majority." One senator even went so far as to introduce a bill that would have expanded the provisions of St. Mary's petition into a general statute affecting all denominations.[11]

Once again the dissenters related their struggle to recent and contemporary liberal insurgencies throughout the West. "In one age," Earle wrote, the pope was recognized as "the proper authority to determine who should be the kings and emperors of nations," but his authority "in the present enlightened age, even in catholic countries," is often disdained.

> He directed the catholics of France to disobey Napoleon, but they did not heed them; those of Naples to submit to a despotic king, but they were influenced more by Austrian bayonets than by the pope; those of Ireland not to circulate the Bible, but they still distribute it: those of South America to submit to Spain, but they still maintain their independence; and, those in Spain, herself, to preserve the revenues of the clergy, and submit to absolute authority in the beloved Ferdinand: but they have curtailed the income of monks and still keep the king under control of the Cortes.

"How preposterous would it be," he concluded, "if catholics were compelled, by the government and laws of the freest country on earth, implicitly to obey the pope, or lose their property and privileges;—while in all other countries except his own narrow domains, they are permitted to disobey him, and avail themselves largely of the permission."[12]

The dissenters and their supporters also sought to portray episcopal absolutism as a clear and present danger to the republic. They "dinned into" the ears of their opponents the proposition that "in conceding the point of the power of the Bishop to appoint pastors, we are admitting the existence of the exercise of a foreign Jurisdiction by the Pope, incompatible with the freedom of our political institutions, and derogatory to the character of our republican government." They pointed to the petitions pouring in from Catholic congregations throughout the state as evidence of "this foreign influence, operating through the medium of the Roman Catholic priests stationed in these several places."[13]

Opponents of the bill countered these arguments with a ringing defense of minority rights. Senator Stephen Duncan, in a speech later printed and distributed by Bishop Conwell, extolled the United States as a "land of freedom [that] had always and justly been considered the asylum of the oppressed, as a haven of rest and religious tolerance to the Jew as well as the Gentile; the Episcopalian and the Roman Catholic." Immigrants, he said, came to America and "contributed their labor to the improvement of the state" in the expectation that "their indefeasible and natural rights to worship God agreeably to the dictates of their consciences" would be guaranteed by the Constitution. The proposed amendments, Duncan held, violated the rights of "members [of the congregation] in unity with the Catholic Church" to have pastors "duly appointed" in conformity to Catholic doctrine. The rights of the faithful minority must be protected against oppression by an impious majority. If the principles embodied in the dissenters' petition were granted, he argued, "every religious society was liable to abrogation, and the constitution would go abroad with a lie on its face."[14]

Senator John Wurts spoke too in opposition to the Catholic Bill. He argued that its passage would make St. Mary's, in effect, a Protestant church, and this manifestly was not what the original incorporators intended. Moreover, it "would be taking away, by legislative enactment, rights, liberties, franchises, and even property . . . , now vested in the clerical members of the Board of Trustees . . . , and placing them at the disposal of others, who at present have no control over them." This, he argued, would be unconstitutional since both the federal and the state constitutions specifically prohibited the state from depriving citizens of their rights or property without due judicial process.[15]

The debates over the Catholic Bill exposed deep conflicts of principle and illuminated the political difficulties posed by such a controversial piece of legislation in an election year. Senator William R. Smith argued that serious principles and issues (not to say votes) were at stake that outweighed the fact that he knew and admired St. Mary's dissenters and felt that they had been wronged by Bishop Conwell. He asserted that the rights and privileges of the clergy as specified by the act of incorporation were being violated and Catholics throughout the commonwealth had a vital interest in the outcome because essential articles of faith were being questioned. Ultimately, Smith argued, all citizens had reason for concern because the principles embodied in the dissenters' petition threatened the integrity of the constitution.[16]

"All power," Smith declared, making explicit the ideological underpinnings of his argument, "is inherent in the People, and springs from them. But the people, as well as an individual may give up certain rights for the purpose of better securing others." If the Catholic Bill was passed the integrity of the Constitution would be compromised. Twice, he noted, the State Supreme Court had ruled petitions from the dissenters to be unconstitutional. To pass a third such petition would be to reject the validity of the court's judgment and might even be interpreted as an attempt on the part of the legislature to assume judicial powers. This, Smith argued, would be an unpardonable infringement upon the constitutionally defined role of the Supreme Court and could not be sustained, even if the will of the people demanded it. The Constitution must be protected even against the claims of popular sovereignty and individual rights.[17]

The Catholic Bill had thus become entangled with long-standing disagreements over matters of political principle that had been a persistent feature of American, and indeed of all of Western, political culture. On one level the rights of individuals were posed against those of corporations and the sanctity of contracts; on another the principle of popular sovereignty was countered by assertions of the rights of minorities and a defense of established institutions against a tyrannical majority.

This latter formulation provided the ideological basis for a political alliance that has long puzzled historians of the period—the emergence of the "Federal" or "Independent" Republican movement which united immigrants with the remnants of the old Federalist party in common resistance to the Republican "Caucus." Usually explained as a matter of political expediency (two marginal groups pooling their efforts) this movement, which was of particular importance in Philadelphia and other urban areas, actually represented ideological agreement on the principle that minority interests (whether economic or culturally based) must be protected by institutional safeguards that could be implemented even in the face of overwhelming popular opinion to the contrary. Both at St. Mary's and in the broader civil culture traditional elites that had been displaced by liberal reformers in the early nineteenth century found common cause with immigrant workers who wished to preserve in America the standards of behavior and belief that had prevailed in their homelands, and both sought to protect minority rights by elevating corporate rights and constitutional safeguards over the majoritarian interests of the people, broadly defined. Once again, as at Holy Trinity and in the earlier Haroldite insurrection at St. Mary's, we see that the political and ideological imperatives driving the internal discourse within Philadelphia's Catholic community were broadly consonant with those that prevailed in the broader civil culture.

"An Interested Union
of Religion and Politics"

For most members of the legislature practical political considerations were more important than matters of principle. They tried to water down the measure so as to quiet the public outcry from all quarters. On March 17, 1823, these moderates, led by John Shulze (since March 4 the Republican Caucus candidate for governor), joined with opponents of the Catholic Bill to remove its "objectionable features." A sizable majority of the Senate rejected the provisions of the bill that would have excluded clerics from the board of trustees and allowed election of pastors. They then approved a provision governing elections for trustees that would make it difficult for William Harold to pack the voting rolls with persons who were not members of the congregation, as he had often done in the past. This was the only substantive point that the dissenters gained in the long debate over the Catholic Bill, and the entire episode constituted a significant defeat for them. More disappointments loomed ahead. The attorney general submitted an opinion that declared the provisions of the bill to be an "alteration" in the "essential character" of the corporation so substantial as to be a violation of the contract implied in the corporation's charter and therefore unconstitutional. The provisions of the bill, he judged, would "possibly destroy the peace, the order and good government of the Church of St. Mary's, subvert her most valuable rights and inflict incurable wounds upon the Roman Catholic persuasion." He recommended that the governor veto the bill.[1]

On March 27, 1823, Governor Heister took the advice of his attorney general and vetoed the Catholic Bill. In his veto message Heister noted that the amendments contained in the bill carried implications that "subvert or disturb fundamental articles of faith" and that they were adopted "without the full consent of the congregation and at a time of great excitement." He also considered the act to be an unconstitutional intrusion by the state into the affairs of a religious body. Heister suggested that no changes should be made "until peace be restored to the society, and the disorders which now prevail cease to exist, unless the alteration be asked for by the society in a spirit of conciliation and brotherly love, or at least shall not be remonstrated against by a considerable portion of the members."[2]

The debate over the Catholic Bill continued long after Governor Heister vetoed it. Shulze's opponents charged that his vote was evidence of anti-Catholic bias and used the issue to solidify support in Philadelphia for the "Independent Republican" candidate, Andrew Gregg. Some Republicans quickly distanced themselves from the vote. Senator Eichelburger declared that although he had first supported the bill he had since "learned from his constituents that its provisions were more injurious than he had first believed." Others refused to apologize. In his defense Shulze stated that the bill for which they voted had been amended so as to remove its most "obnoxious" feature—the right of the laity to elect their priests—and therefore was not an assault on Catholic faith. In an attempt to forestall criticism and to correct "the erroneous impression that the . . . Legislature [had] interfered with the religious rights of Roman Catholics . . . and violated their chartered privileges," Shulze's supporters ordered that the text of the amended bill be printed "at full length" in the journals of the Senate.[3]

This, of course, did not quiet criticism. The outpouring of Catholic solidarity orchestrated by the bishopites had impressed politicians throughout the state and many sought to take advantage of it. In Philadelphia the "Old-School Democrats" (remnants of the old "DEMOCRATIC-Republicans") now in alliance with former Federalists, hectored Shulze and his supporters mercilessly on the issue. For decades Philadelphia's Democrats had carefully balanced ethnic appeals to their immigrant supporters with a determined commitment to Jeffersonian principles. Now they drummed away on ethnic themes almost to the exclusion of everything else and in the process abandoned their traditional opposition to hierarchy, privilege and the concentration of power in unrepresentative institutions.

They skillfully played on ethnic fears. On June 16 the party organ, *Aurora,* printed "A Catholic Democrat's" announcement of an incipient plot on the part of the mainstream Republicans to disenfranchise Catholics "on account of their religion." One week later in the same paper "A Catholic" referred to "an attempt . . . made during the last session of the Legislature to trample upon our religious rights, which we are determined to protect." Shulze, he wrote, was "a man who has attempted grievously to injure us; and requires only the power [of the governorship] to annihilate our privileges . . . both civil and religious." On July 8 the *Aurora* charged that Shulze had "injured and insulted" Philadelphia's Catholics and "endeavored to take from them an important constitutional right." On August 1 the *Aurora* declared that "It has become a political necessity for Shulze's friends to blacken the character of Roman Catholics, to arouse bigotry etc." In September the *Aurora* publicized the charge, made by two prominent bishopites, that Senator Shulze had made a blatantly anti-Catholic speech during the debate over the Catholic Bill. And so it continued right up to the election.[4]

What lent plausibility to such charges was the fact that several of St. Mary's dissenters had openly joined the Shulze campaign and were using it as a forum to project their views into the political arena. "The Trustees or Liberals," Bishop Conwell complained, "still hold the revenues of the church and apply them to political purposes, as they please." On June 19, 1823, Archibald Randall, secretary of St. Mary's board of trustees, spoke at a Shulze rally and proclaimed his detestation as a republican Catholic to the appearance of a "Roman Catholic combination for the avowed purpose of affecting political objects through religious excitements." He denounced this "interested union of religion and politics of Church and State" and declared that it was "incompatible with Civil liberty." Less than a month before the elections the trustees of St. Mary's addressed a pamphlet to "Their Fellow-Citizens" in which they charged that the "Catholic combination," by taking a position "in the approaching election of a chief magistrate of this state" was "attempting to blend religion with politics, and, in fact, endeavouring to introduce into our happy country, all the horrors of those religious disputes, which have drenched Europe with blood."[5]

The bishopites treated these charges as nativist assaults. "Enemies say that Catholics cannot be trusted, they are subservient to a foreign power. Absurd!" The issue of the pope's supremacy, they claimed, was nothing more than a "political bugbear calculated to awaken prejudice" against Irish Catholics, who had on many occasions proved their loyalty. The dissenters, they said, were repeating in America the "threadbare arguments of Europe. . . . They are loaded with every epithet that intolerant Europe can supply." What was most disgusting was that such libels issued from the mouths of "many who have fled from the lash of suppression and made America their home."[6]

On March 18, 1823, Washington Hall on Third Street, the scene of so many dissenter rallies, burned to the ground. Its smoldering ashes serve as an apt metaphor for the fate of St. Mary's congregation. Their appeals to religious and civil courts rejected, defeated in the legislature, heavily in debt, and facing the prospect of long and costly litigation to come, the dissenting movement was on the brink of collapse in the spring of 1823. Bishop Conwell was cautiously optimistic. On March 19 he wrote that "the object of the Jacobins of Philadelphia was defeated in the Legislature—at Harrisburg—which will be Serviceable to us on approaching tryals [sic] against the lay Trustees for Mismanagement in the discharge of their Trust." He continued, "Our case is not so bad as formerly . . . , and [events are] coming gradually to a conclusion in our favor." All in all, he considered that the disturbances over the Catholic Bill "may turn out [to be] the most propitious occurrence [that has] ever happened towards propagating the Catholic religion" in America. Patrick Kenny was jubilant. He rejoiced in the veto of what he called the "Nag's Head Bill" and crowed, "God has defeated these living pests and their Buck Parson, and gallinipper followers." The Catholic congregation in Carlisle, south of Harrisburg, hailed a grand victory over "Rabid fanaticism and frenetic bigotry." But the spark of defiance had not yet been fully extinguished.[7]

Pastor of St. Mary's

On April 1, two days after the announcement of Governor Heister's veto of the Catholic Bill, St. Mary's congregation once again held elections for the board of trustees. As in the previous year, the results of the election were contested and both factions claimed victory. Once more the bishopites attempted to take control of the church by force (breaking down the doors, occupying the church property, and making "a great dirt and filth" therein) but were finally removed by civil authorities. The failure of the bishopite coup left the dissenters in possession of St. Mary's, but their support was rapidly dwindling. The record of pew rents shows a significant turnover and defection within the congregation at this time. At last the beleaguered trustees opened negotiations with Bishop Conwell aimed at ending their long dispute.[1]

Early in June 1823 the dissenters offered a set of "Conditions on which the Trustees and Congregation worshipping at St. Mary's Church . . . , are willing to enter into an amicable accommodation of all their differences with the Right Rev. Bishop Conwell." The bishop was reluctant to negotiate but several members of the old Catholic elite insisted that he do so. The reason was that by the spring of 1823 respectable Catholics on both sides of the dispute had begun to feel threatened by the ugly turn that affairs had taken. The nativist overtones in the dissenters' statements, the blatantly ethnic appeals of William V. Harold and the traditionalist clergy, the projection of intramural conflicts into the political arena, and most of all the rising levels of "tumult and disorder" were disturbing to many respectable Catholics. At last, under pressure from his advisors, Bishop Conwell relented enough to respond to the dissenters' overtures. "If I had refused," he wrote, "much [would] be said by the good Catholics who still adhere to me that I was the occasion of keeping them out of their Church by my obstinacy."[2]

Bishop Conwell's terms for reconciliation were fairly mild. He absolutely refused to compromise episcopal authority. "If ever Catholic worship is to be reestablished in The Cathedral Church of St. Mary's" he wrote, "The Church must be opened on Catholic Principles—on which Principles The Bishop cannot annul his own right of Pastorship or Trusteeship nor that of his Successors, nor alienate the right vested in him of removing or appointing Pastors." He was also adamant that "Mr. Hogan, . . . Shall never appear in St. Mary's Church." But he was willing to consult the laity in the matter of clerical appointments. "Never," Conwell wrote, would he "obtrude a Priest on the Congregation whom He shall [discover?] to be Scandalous or disagreeable to the body of the People whose inclinations He shall endeavor to please in this respect." Conwell further agreed that "all pending Suits at law Shall be given up & quashed on either side." But he absolutely refused to cede to the laity any right of presentation. He wrote, "My lawyers and [John] Keating a Catholic, wish me, if possible to concede to [the dissenters] the *jus patronatus*. I answered that this is impossible. They asked me, under existing circumstances, might not the Pope consider this? I replied He could not."[3]

From a number of "personal conferences" among lay leaders emerged an understanding that "something in the shape of a reconciliation might be effected" if William Hogan should leave St. Mary's. In the fall of 1823 the arrival in Philadelphia of the Rev. Mr. Angelo Inglesi, already "well known to many of the most respectable men in [the] city," afforded the trustees an opportunity to effect this change. At the time Bishop Conwell was out of Philadelphia and had entrusted diocesan affairs to William Harold. Inglesi presented himself to Harold and received from him written permission to officiate as a priest in the diocese. Shortly thereafter Inglesi met Richard Meade and agreed "to use his influence towards the attainment of the long wished for reconciliation," and to "accept . . . , and perform the duties of Pastor of that Church." Overjoyed, the trustees hailed him as "the instrument of the future tranquillity and harmony of the congregation."[4]

Inglesi's appointment must have been a terrible humiliation for William Hogan but he took his dismissal—for it was that in fact—with good grace. Stating that he was "at all times desirous of restoring peace to the church, on terms honorable and acceptable to his congregation, even at the expense of his feelings and private interest," Hogan, "voluntarily tendered to the Board his formal resignation, accompanied with an intimation that he was about to return to Europe." The trustees then notified Inglesi that they had nominated him to the bishop as the sole pastor of their church and informed William Harold of Hogan's resignation and their selection of Inglesi as a replacement. The trustees expected, they said, that this change would "put to an end all future dissensions in this church."[5]

William Harold refused, however, to cooperate with the trustees' designs. He was determined to secure the pastorship of St. Mary's for himself. He immediately called Inglesi into his presence and threatened him with "*excommunication,* and a thousand dreadful consequences" should he attempt to officiate at St. Mary's. Thoroughly intimidated, Inglesi informed the board of trustees that he could not become their pastor. The trustees were shocked. They denounced Harold as a man so "ambitious, and so violent in his temper, that he has not hesitated to say, that though murder should ensue, he would have possession of the church."[6]

Harold was not content to leave matters as they were. After consultation with Archbishop Maréchal, he began a determined assault on

Inglesi's character, soliciting and publishing criticisms from lay and clerical officials, portraying him as "a renegade (or apostate)" and the dissenters who associated with him as "*Italian* Carbonari." He even went "door to door" to personally denounce the priest to the respectable members of the congregation. Inglesi and his friends countered Harold's attacks with a barrage of testimonials to the priest's good reputation and character, and threatened a law suit against the vicar-general. Soon, astounded and somewhat intimidated by the furor that his attempts to effect a peace had roused, Inglesi withdrew from the affair and left Philadelphia, but even after he left the pamphlet war continued as each side tried to discredit the other.[7]

For William Hogan and St. Mary's lay leadership the entire affair was humiliating. When Inglesi withdrew, the trustees were forced, somewhat sheepishly, to declare that Hogan's resignation had been conditional not final and on August 29 they reinstated him as pastor at St. Mary's. Hogan took his reinstatement, as he had his dismissal, with good grace, but a deep resentment lingered and he determined to escape Philadelphia as soon as possible.[8]

Six weeks later Thadeus O'Meally came to Philadelphia at William Hogan's request to serve as his assistant. O'Meally was a man of respectable demeanor, a good speaker, well-read, and of liberal leanings. He was also a man of impeccable manners. Traditionalist clerics considered him, like Hogan, to have "much the appearance of a dandy." He was, in other words, perfectly suited to serve the congregation at St. Mary's. O'Meally presented his credentials to Bishop Conwell, who initially "made no objection," but on the following day, having been persuaded that O'Meally "came here to abet the schism in St. Mary's Church," forbade him under pain of excommunication "to say mass or perform any priestly functions in the diocese." Ignoring Conwell's order, the trustees of St. Mary's employed O'Meally as pastor. The young priest then wrote to reassure the bishop that he wished only to serve as an "instrument of peace." "I am, and ever shall be," he wrote, "a firm asserter of episcopal rights, and ecclesiastical subordination; . . . I countenance no innovation, even in our church discipline . . . ; I acknowledge, on the part of the laity, no right of interference in spiritual affairs." On October 20 the trustees formally presented the priest to the bishop as "Pastor of St. Mary's Church."[9]

O'Meally preached in St. Mary's on November 2, 1823, and Bishop Conwell immediately issued a formal monition against the priest threatening him with excommunication. To this, O'Meally responded in a long letter that he wished only to serve as a peacemaker, that he found the dissenters' position to be neither unreasonable nor innovative, that Bishop Conwell was sacrificing the interests of religion to his "pride of authority" and "pertinacity of opinion," and that he [O'Meally] had "no . . . superstitious horror of an excommunication" and would not "be at all affected by it." He protested that the bishop was using the threat of excommunication as a "convenient, though rusty, weapon to get rid of an honest and therefore a troublesome adviser."[10]

Through a second and a third monition O'Meally maintained his defiance. He declared excommunication to be a "barbarous" and "*obsolete*" ceremony, "the relic . . . of a barbarous age," the continued use of which would "considerably diminish, if not entirely destroy the respect which the Catholics of this city still entertain for that branch of our discipline. My only offense," he wrote, "is that I was presented to you for institution as pastor of St. Mary's, to the exclusion" of William V. Harold. He called upon the bishop to end the bitter feud at St. Mary's. "Acknowledge me," he wrote, "as *pastor pro tempore,* and by this single act . . . , you will destroy forever the demon of discord that has been scattering so long, and so widely, his deadly and unholy influence amongst your people."[11]

William Hogan viewed the developing situation with deepening suspicion. He had been badly hurt by the trustees' willingness to abandon him during the Inglesi affair, and now that Thadeus O'Meally had been hired his services were again superfluous. What is more, O'Meally, unlike Inglesi, showed no inclination to bow to the threats of William Harold and Henry Conwell. Hogan had also heard that "Mr. Meade and five other gentlemen" had struck a deal with Bishop Conwell, offering to discharge Hogan in exchange for peace. Before he could again be humiliated by being displaced, Hogan suddenly, and without notice, left Philadelphia on November 19, 1823, and took passage for Liverpool on the same ship that had brought Thadeus O'Meally to America. Patrick Kenny was overjoyed. He wrote in his diary, "Wm. Hogan, of vile memory, sailed . . . , May the ship have taken off the scapegoat and all the abominations of the schismatical Trustees and their adherents of St. Mary's Phila[delphia]! May the Kid O'Mealy soon follow."[12]

A consensus had been growing among respectable Catholics on both sides that something had to be done to restore calm to the diocese and to resist the swelling influence of those priests "who work on the minds of the uneducated and excite them to deeds of blood." Many were "tired of this controversy" and wished to end it. "To the terms offered by one [the dissenters]," O'Meally wrote, "the other would cheerfully subscribe, 'if their rulers would let them.'" Now that Hogan was gone, leading figures worked diligently to forge a compromise and "everybody hoped and believed that peace would soon be restored to their distracted Church." Bishop Conwell, William Harold, and the traditionalist clergy, though, were not so minded.[13]

On the day after Hogan's departure O'Meally, accompanied by Richard Meade, asked for an audience with the bishop, hoping to present a defense of his actions and a plea for peace. O'Meally found Conwell, "surrounded by his little conclave." John Ryan, Harold's longtime associate, was "busily engaged in drawing up a paper" that turned out to be a sentence of excommunication. It was an excruciatingly difficult and uncomfortable situation. "After sitting to be stared at for nearly half an hour, during which not one word of mild expostulation was spoken, nor the slightest symptom of kind or charitable feeling shown, the paper was at length finished, and signed, and sealed, and read," after which Meade and O'Meally, "made [their] reverence and left."[14]

That meeting set the tone for relations between St. Mary's congregation and Bishop Conwell for several months to come. Time and again Conwell rejected efforts at conciliation. In December 1823 the dissenters offered "to render our bishop every year, an account of our administration," and promised not to support "priests destitute of legal faculties, or those who are bound by censures (if legal)," nor would they attempt to remove pastors at their pleasure. They would, they said, "harbour no other ministers of the sanctuary, but those who shall be approved of by our Bishops."[15]

The dissenters did ask, though, that no pastors be appointed but those "whom we present in virtue of our right of patronage." This was necessary, they explained, in order that the congregation "have men of talent, and good conduct; men who are capable of supporting our creed; not such as make us the scorn and contempt of our [Protestant] fellow-citizens." They also explained that many would oppose William Harold or John Ryan's appointment to St. Mary's because that would "be hailed as a victory by their followers." They wrote, "In the name of peace, Sir, we beg you to accept this proposal. . . . If we have sinned against each other, let us kneel together before the same altar, and offer up our joint prayers to the 'Father of mercies' for mutual forgiveness. Let us bury all that has passed in silence and oblivion, and dwell together evermore in unity and peace."[16]

Bishop Conwell refused to reply to the dissenters' letter, seeing in it "only a repetition of the same proposals and of the same doctrine, which . . . [he considered to be] incompatible with Catholic principles." "My decisions" he wrote, "can never be changed, because I cannot change the doctrine of the church, which is as unchangeable as truth itself." He advised the dissenters "to desist from ruling in the church, which is by God's appointment the province of bishops alone, and be guided . . . by Catholic principles: attend to the instructions in the brief of the father of the faithful . . . as you would to a voice from heaven."[17]

Conwell's flat refusal of their initiative convinced "the trustees, and the whole congregation of St. Mary's . . . , that there is no longer any room to hope for peace." They "indignantly" gave up "any further attempt to obtain it," but Thadeus O'Meally proceeded on his own. He offered to withdraw from St. Mary's if the bishop promised not to install William V. Harold there. Conwell's response was succinct—a brief note stating, "Mr. O'Meally can have no answer to his letter of yesterday addressed to the bishop!!!" O'Meally then appealed to Archbishop Maréchal. "I conjure you," he wrote, "in the name of peace, to interpose between the Bishop and his harsh advisers, and put an end to this unhappy Schism." He assured the archbishop that "all the congregation asks for is, that a Pastor be given them, who has taken no part in the controversy." Shortly thereafter the trustees, at O'Meally's urging, sent a deputation to meet with the archbishop but Maréchal refused to see them.[18]

Like William Hogan before him, Thadeus O'Meally turned to John England for advice. Early in 1824 he wrote asking England to arbitrate an end to the dispute. In some ways Bishop England was an unlikely candidate for mediator. His earlier experience in Philadelphia had roused the anger and suspicion of both dissenters and Bishop Conwell, and, since returning to Charleston, he had maintained an unrelentingly hostile stance toward the Hoganites. Still, O'Meally saw reasons for hope. In 1822, Bishop England had adopted a written constitution for his diocese in which the reciprocal rights and obligations of bishop, clergy, and laity were carefully delineated. Although England's constitution granted no substantive power to laymen, it did protect the rights of clergy and place constraints on the arbitrary power of bishops, so it did address some of the complaints of St. Mary's dissenters and might therefore serve as a model for the resolution of the Philadelphia troubles.[19]

Shortly after his excommunication Thadeus O'Meally began an extensive correspondence with John England, informing him of his dealings with Bishop Conwell and asking about aspects of the Charleston constitution. To each of these missives Bishop England replied politely, taking no position with regard to the affairs in Philadelphia but supplying information as requested. Bishop Conwell soon learned of the correspondence and was decidedly not pleased. He informed Ambrose Maréchal that "Dr. England . . . is Anxious to embark in the Philadelphia Concerns." He asked that Maréchal refrain from sending information on matters in Philadelphia to Charleston.[20]

On May 20 England informed Bishop Conwell that he had received a letter from O'Meally, "the tenor of which . . . would afford a Basis for terminating the Schism in the very manner in which it must finally if ever be terminated." England agreed that any settlement must include "a full and unequivocal recognition of [the Bishop's] rights," but urged "a Sacrifice on the present instance of feelings on both Sides." He warned, "It will not answer . . . to look for a triumphant victory, in doing so you sacrifice a permanent good to an empty exhibition."[21]

Henry Conwell was outraged by Bishop England's interference in his affairs. He felt that "the schism . . . had been on the brink of being upset" after Hogan's departure but that England's letters had encouraged O'Meally "to continue his wicked course." Speculating as to England's motives, Conwell noted that the southern bishop had a "fertile disposition when properly flattered" and probably had hopes "of raising a name for himself" as the man who ended the Philadelphia conflict. "I cannot have" he wrote, "a good opinion of Dr. E[ngland]'s motives after past experience," and expressed his opinion that the bishop of Charleston was "striving now again to renew the same evils he had created by his former mode of proceeding."[22]

Conwell fired off angry letters to Charleston, Baltimore, and Rome. He forbade England "in plain terms . . . [from] Corresponding with the *Man of Lies* O'M[eall]y." To Archbishop Maréchal he opined that England "kept up [the dissenters'] Spirits for a long time, under the hopes that the *Doctor* would manage for them at Rome in such a manner that they would get their desires accomplished." In succeeding months Conwell's anger and apprehension grew. He came to view Bishop England, his constitution (which he likened to the despised

French Civil Constitution of the Clergy), and his continued calls for a national synod as a positive threat to the American church. In October he wrote, "I consider [England's] Convention and Ecclesiastical Democratic Regimen as bad if not worse than Trusteeship." Two months later he wrote, "The Bishop of Charleston is Still Corresponding with O'Meally and encouraging his cause. . . . For my part I have broken off all correspondence with him Since I have discovered him to be intoxicated in this Business—I hope his democratic Church Regimen will not find favour or be Sanctioned at Rome with his Convention and Civil Constitution of the Church, which is designed to be *Ambulatory* throughout America."[23]

Other members of the American hierarchy were concerned by the course of events in Philadelphia. One of these was William Du Bourg, the bishop of New Orleans. Shortly after O'Meally's excommunication Du Bourg wrote that "Things have in my opinion gone so far, that I see no remedy to the evil but in a mutual sacrifice." He upheld Bishop Conwell's right to discipline O'Meally and his right to appoint pastors for the church, but he also told the dissenters, "I coincide with you, in the principle, that a Bishop never should force upon any of his congregations, a Clergyman disagreeable to a great portion of it." Du Bourg urged O'Meally to again appeal to Archbishop Maréchal and, should that fail, to make "a direct application to the Pope." Bishop Du Bourg also communicated his thoughts on the affair to Propaganda.[24]

Edward Fenwick, the bishop of Cincinnati, also was concerned with the course of the conflict. In November 1824 he passed through Philadelphia and was drawn into the affair. He granted an interview to St. Mary's trustees and they left the meeting convinced that he was sympathetic to their plight and felt that their proposals were reasonable and could be acceded to without harm to religion. John Ashley asserted that Fenwick not only had approved the trustees' proposals but had also promised to argue their case to Archbishop Maréchal.[25]

Despite urgings from his lay advisors and from his episcopal colleagues Bishop Conwell continued to refuse to deal with the dissenters. His disdain for his opponents knew no bounds. "The best of them is worse than Voltaire ever has been," he wrote, "for he was only violent, but they are malicious." He declared that "we shall never more answer any letters from the Trustees or any person connected with them until they demonstrate clearly that they are disposed to be good Catholics and they init[iate] steps toward giving proofs of that disposition." In

March 1824 he demanded as a precondition for any negotiations that they first "send away the Excommunicated Priest [O'Meally] and shut up the Church" and cease writing pamphlets. One month later his position had not changed one whit. He wrote, "I shall for ever refuse all correspondence with them until they become Catholics in reality."[26]

The Failure of Compromise

⎯⎯⎯⎯⎯⎯⎯⎯

By the summer of 1824 it seemed that Bishop Conwell had won the long struggle. Many people abandoned the congregation after William Hogan's departure. Then in June of 1824 the bishopites, despairing of ever being able to gain control of the church through elections, ceased paying their pew rents. "Since that day," the bishop wrote, "the Church is nearly deserted. The men calling themselves Trustees attend there with a few Deists, and women of abandoned Character the number of whom is much declined since Hogan's departure." Those who remained were split into quarreling factions. Hogan still had his partisans among the congregation, as did Inglesi, who had returned to Philadelphia in the spring of 1824. The trustees, along with most of the congregation, though, supported Thadeus O'Meally. Bishop Conwell viewed the situation with delight. "The Schismatics," he wrote in April, 1824, "are now divided into parties and are daily fighting."[1]

Matters reached a crisis in the summer of 1824 when William Hogan suddenly reappeared in Philadelphia and demanded reinstatement as pastor of St. Mary's. Some in the congregation supported his claim, and even hired a lawyer to represent him. The trustees, though, publicly announced that "William Hogan has not authority . . . to preach" and threatened legal action should he attempt to force his way into the pulpit. Bishop Conwell gleefully noted that Hogan's presence caused "great confusion among the schismatics" and "has alarmed them exceedingly."[2]

For several months since the publication of the papal brief at the end of 1822, William Hogan had been articulating ever more radical positions with regard to Catholic authority and discipline. Now his spiritual journey carried him beyond the limits of Catholicity. Ever since his return to America, early in the spring of 1824, he had been accepting invitations to preach in a number of Protestant churches in Charleston, South Carolina, where he resided. The sermons he delivered on these occasions "principally contained invectives against the doctrines and practices of the Roman Catholic Church." Now in Philadelphia he called upon the dissenters to follow him out of the Church.[4]

One month after his return to Philadelphia, Hogan totally repudiated Rome's authority. "The Court of Rome," he declared, has "lost sight of the pure doctrines of the gospel," and has "substituted the traditions and fabulous tales of monks for the revealed will of God." Its doctrines "demoralize the human mind and degrade the understanding of man." Rome, he further declared, "sanctions an evident departure from [the] ancient simplicity of the doctrines and principles of our church." He called on the dissenters to emulate the Greek Catholics and to "declare yourselves independent of the Court of Rome, and insist upon the right of electing your own Bishops and Pastors." "If you consider yourselves on an exact footing with the Greek Catholics," he said, "and will denominate your Church the American Catholic Church, I shall feel pride in being your Pastor."[5]

Hogan asserted the doctrine of salvation by faith rather than the "instrumentality of means." In so doing he trod in the footsteps of Luther and Calvin and completed his estrangement from Catholic doctrine and faith. None among St. Mary's congregation were willing to accompany him. Bishop Conwell might consider the dissenters to be "Heretics & Deists" or "Infidels pretending to be Catholics," but they never renounced their allegiance to Rome. Instead they repudiated William Hogan and soon he left Philadelphia, never to return. In later years he had a career as an anti-Catholic writer. Hogan's radicalism, his instability, and the fact that soon after leaving Philadelphia he married, cost him what little support he had retained in St. Mary's congregation. In December 1824 Bishop Conwell noted that "very few are for Hogan at present." Angelo Inglesi also left Philadelphia after being ordered by Propaganda to return to Europe to do penance for his errors in

America. This left the congregation in relative peace even though none of the initial issues that had driven them into schism had been resolved.[6]

By the end of 1824 it seemed that the revolt could not last for long. Writing in October, Bishop Conwell noted with satisfaction that St. Mary's "church is nearly deserted, [the trustees] will have great difficulty in making $1,000 a year [to pay the salary of] the Apostate Priest." Two months later he wrote that "Some are for giving the Church to the Bishop Without Conditions." At last Thadeus O'Meally offered to withdraw his claim to the pastorship of St. Mary's and challenged the bishop and William Harold to match his effort. He called upon the bishopites, "as Americans jealous of the rights of freemen, as Philadelphians wishing to promote good fellowship, as christians tolerant of each other's errors, and as catholics anxious to uphold the respectability of the name," to make peace and to bury the animosities that had so long sundered them one from another.[8]

Bishop Conwell refused O'Meally's offer, branding his association with the dissenters "Criminal business." He demanded full and unconditional submission. Desperately the dissenters cast about for some means of ending the conflict on honorable grounds. For a while they placed their hopes in the efforts of Luke Tiernan, a close friend of Richard Meade's and a pillar of Baltimore's Catholic community, but Archbishop Maréchal intervened and as a result Tiernan's initiative bore no fruit. The dissenters then sought help from Gabriel Richard, a priest from Detroit and a territorial delegate to Congress who was temporarily in Philadelphia. Richard's efforts at mediation raised hopes on both sides, expressed in a series of well-attended public meetings and several conferences involving lay leaders on both sides, but they ultimately failed. Conwell would not concede his essential point that the laity could have no say in the appointment of pastors, and the dissenters were "fully and firmly determined, not to sacrifice . . . their rights as freemen, and their privileges as Catholics."[9]

While the dissenters cast about for a way to end the schism, Bishop Conwell was preparing to make it permanent. In 1823 Propaganda ordered him to build a new cathedral and directed the other American bishops to contribute money to its construction. Institutional separation, Conwell felt, was necessary lest the dissenters "corrupt the whole Flock" of Philadelphia Catholics. "There is no remedy," he wrote, "but to build a church—for to close with any of those fallen people under any conditions would be to destroy religion by exposing the good people to be corrupted by such contamination." By the spring of 1824 he reported that "Subscriptions for the New Church are progressing prosperously . . . in the success of which [the dissenters] see their own downfall." Buoyed by enthusiasm for the new project, he borrowed $40,000 to purchase a lot on which to build the cathedral. This was an enormous debt to assume, considering the unsettled nature of church affairs in the diocese and Conwell was well aware of the danger his partisans faced as a result of this liability. He wrote, "Those who are engaged for this great sum would be ruined if the Schismatics succeeded in dividing the people, and the cause of Religion would be ruined."[10]

At last Thadeus O'Meally gave up his efforts at reconciliation and resigned his pastorship of St. Mary's. He challenged Conwell, now that he stood out of the way, "to restore of his own motion that 'peace and harmony' which he promises."[11]

Bishop Conwell demanded that the dissenters "renounce publicly [their] communion with the Rev. Mr. O'Meally," and pledge that they would not receive any other minister without his authorization. "These," he wrote, "are points on which it is indispensable that you give a distinct and satisfactory pledge, previously to the discussion of such arrangements as may warrant your restoration to the communion of the Roman Catholic church." To this the trustees responded that O'Meally's resignation made the first point moot and that they could not relinquish their right to have a say in the choice of pastors for their church. The impasse still held and Thadeus O'Meally's withdrawal from St. Mary's had achieved nothing.[12]

More than a year of persistent efforts on the part of prominent laymen and Church officials had failed to sway Bishop Conwell from his course. William Hogan had departed Philadelphia; so had Angelo Inglesi. Now Thadeus O'Meally was gone. All had failed to bring peace to the troubled church. So, too, had Bishops England and DuBourg and Father Gabriel Richard. These repeated failures have usually been ascribed to Bishop Conwell's stubbornness and declining mental faculties, but we should note that throughout this period Conwell enjoyed full support from Archbishop Maréchal and from Propaganda and this would seem to indicate that something more than personality was involved. Fundamental principles were in conflict and these could not be encompassed in an "honourable compromise."

On January 7, 1824, the dissenters made one last appeal to the civil authorities. Their memorial, penned by Augustine Fagan and presented by Richard Meade and John Sullivan, is a coherent exposition of the dissenters' thought. In it they identified one specific principle, popular sovereignty, upon which they and the bishop were at issue. The bishop, they charged, was attempting to rule without regard for "the opinion of a large majority of the congregation," asserting that "his own will should be his only guide in the removal or the appointment of pastors." Conwell and other church authorities argued, moreover, "that the lay members of the Roman Catholic community have no rights whatever; that all is a concession to them on the part of the Holy See and of the bishops," and that such concessions as might be granted to the laity could "only be obtained . . . by giving up to the clergy, for ever, so much property as a church and its revenues may be worth." Such monarchic pretensions, they argued, were incompatible with the protection of American liberties.[13]

In America, the dissenters observed, the principle of divine right was discarded, and instead "political institutions have been all based upon the more correct and rational principle, that the people alone are the true source of power and honour, and the elective franchise was resorted to for the whole formation of the government." Popular sovereignty was the only proper foundation for religious as well as political organization. Only so, they argued, could religious liberties be preserved. In opposition to the corporate interpretation of religious freedom advanced by episcopal authorities, in which religious organizations could organize their affairs free from outside interference, the dissenters asserted a radical individualism. In the new republic, they wrote, "aware that man, as a free agent, was accountable to his creator alone, for the nature or the measure of the homage he might conceive most acceptable to Him, all preference with regard to religious opinions was abolished; and every one left free to act in this respect as his conscience should dictate."[14]

The dissenters grounded their liberalism in an understanding of history that was diametrically opposed to that which informed restoration Catholicism. Unlike those clerics who nursed a romantic longing for things medieval, the dissenters strenuously denounced the authoritarian, universalist culture of the Age of Faith. Against Bishop Conwell's contention that episcopal absolutism was "consistent with the Catholic faith," St. Mary's memorialists argued that such was not "the early practice of our Church"; the ideas dated from the twelfth-century reign of "the ambitious and crafty Hildebrand [Pope Gregory VII]." "Subsequent Pontiffs," they wrote, "did not fail to profit by the example which Gregory [VII] afforded them, until the rights of both the inferior clergy and the laity became a subject of mockery and derision at Rome," and the power of the Holy See had waxed to the point that "various Popes laid claim to the dominion of the whole world; and actually made grants of large portions of it to various monarchs." Such principles, they felt, had no place in the modern age.[15]

The Church's authoritarian doctrines, they said, gained currency in a past age of "ignorance and superstition," when "kings and potentates . . . conceive[d] themselves bound to carry into effect the anathemas of the sovereign pontiff." That was an age of divine-right rulers, hereditary titles, and "barbarous" legal codes "in which destruction, not reclamation, was the ruling principle." "Thus was the order of things," they said, "which the feudal system established in Europe." To the dissenters the medieval world was not the golden age of Christendom for which restoration church reformers yearned; it was pervaded with "the gloom of barbarism and despotism." To them the feudal system meant not the stability of a divinely ordained social order, but "the degradation of the people to the condition of mere slaves, or vassals." The medieval Church they saw as the oppressor, not the comforter or protector, of the people.[16]

The dissenters hailed the "various events that have occurred from the 15th to the present century, [that] have tended partially to ameliorate, and yet could never wholly correct" the evils born in the Age of Faith. The most important of these was the American Revolution. "Forty years have elapsed," they wrote,

> since . . . the complete emancipation of these states from the shackles of European thraldom. . . . Totally disengaged from the corrupt institutions of the old world, and availing themselves of the light which Providence was then pleased to shed upon the human mind, a new order of things was produced among the inhabitants of the United States.[17]

The essential features of this new order of things were popular sovereignty and individual freedom. In America, they wrote, government exists to serve the people and all "branches of the law-making power are elected by, and completely within the control of the people." In this new world there could be:

> no church establishment connected with the state, for the purpose of enslaving the mind as well as the body; no tythes; no compelling one part of the community to support the ministers of another whose doctrines they believe to be erroneous; no religious preferences or persecutions, but every one left free to worship his creator according to the dictates of his own conscience, and all maintain their own ministers as they deem proper.

Individual freedom was, for the dissenters, the essential genius of American society, writ large in the weakness of its civic institutions. They praised the country's "very small standing army . . . , for the protection, not the oppression of the people; a small navy for a similar purpose; a criminal code that is an honour to humanity for its mildness and efficacy; taxation light; national debt small, and contracted for the most justifiable of all purposes—to obtain liberty, and independence, and to defend them."[18]

These were the principles of Jeffersonian Republicanism, but St. Mary's dissenters hardly looked back to an age of agrarian virtue. They were sophisticated urbanites, products of America's new emerging industrial culture. Freedom, they declared, implied responsibility—the republic "imposed new obligations upon its inhabitants; and, whether native or naturalized, none [was] more sacred than the preservation of that civil and religious freedom." Citizenship was a sacred trust. "Every citizen," they declared, reflecting the swelling nationalism of their day, "should consider himself a part of the nation; and should give his consent to nothing which might commit its dignity or welfare."[19]

Suffering a foreign prelate to dictate to American citizens, they held, would be a stain on the dignity and honor of the republic. It was intolerable that "the Roman Catholic citizens of the United States, whose government is precluded from interfering in the religious concerns of any of its citizens, are plainly told that they must be content to receive and support such bishops as foreign influence or intrigue may think fit to intrude upon them." Such was not the case, they pointed out, even in the benighted states of Europe where lay authorities had been granted by the Holy See the right to appoint clergy, and the national churches brooked little interference from

Rome. "The French Church, in particular," the dissenters observed, "has always manifested the utmost jealousy of the encroachments of the Roman See." It was demeaning, they said, that the American church, as a mission church, was "designated as an European colony," rather than as a national church on an equal footing with those of Europe.[20]

St. Mary's dissenters were economic as well as political liberals. They celebrated America's "brilliant prosperity" and saw in the conjunction of political and economic freedoms the ultimate solvent of the social and institutional distinctions so characteristic of the old European cultures from which they had come. The new industrial order had produced immense disparities in wealth and new social distinctions, but the dissenters saw neither injustice nor danger in this. The United States, they said, had abolished hereditary distinctions and had instituted "such a system of [political] equality . . . , as made it probable that [material wealth] should never become dangerous to liberty from its accumulation; and that whatever temporary rank and honours were allowed, should become the reward of virtue and capacity alone." This was a specific repudiation of the leveling rhetoric of the Haroldite movement of just one decade earlier and, like William Harold's earlier paeans to a hierarchy of virtue, it illuminates an important shift in the context and meaning of Catholic dissent.[21]

American historians have documented a decisive change that took place within the urban workforce in the early stages of industrialization. In the traditional culture of preindustrial America master craftsmen had been linked to journeymen and apprentices in their craft by mutual bonds of obligation and professional solidarity. Over time, though, as the structure and content of work changed, these traditional craft bonds were eroded and supplanted by a wage nexus and mounting levels of mutual antagonism between employer and employee. In the early decades of the nineteenth century, as the new industrial order developed, successful master craftsmen, who had once served as acknowledged spokesmen for the "mechanics' interest" in civic affairs, aligned themselves with the emerging middle classes and defined their interests in quite different terms from those of their employees.[22]

A similar process seems to have taken place within St. Mary's congregation as some prominent Haroldites, who had once articulated strongly democratic values and allied themselves with the immigrant working class, became "whiggish" apologists for the inequalities of the new industrial system. Such was the case with Augustine Fagan, a master printer and bookseller who once had been the most prominent and outspoken of the Haroldites. Over time Fagan's attitudes traced a trajectory similar to that of other master craftsmen of his time, and he ceased to denounce the inequities of the American social order. Instead, as secretary of St. Mary's board of trustees and primary author of the memorial, he became an apologist for the inequalities he had once attacked.[23]

The dissenters considered that they lived in a perilous age. "The world," they wrote, "at the present moment, presents an ominous aspect. Our happy country is free from those convulsive and devastating struggles [raging] in different portions of [the West] between the oppressors and the oppressed." But, they said, "how long . . . those despots who dread . . . the example of both . . . our free institutions, and the happiness flowing from them . . . [will] allow us to remain unmolested, is altogether problematical." Already, they claimed, despotism had begun to make inroads. "Dr. Conwell was here but a few days," they wrote, when he named St. Mary's Church as his cathedral, took charge of its finances and, together with members of the traditional elite, voted "no small share" of the revenues to himself. When the people of the congregation attempted "to correct the procedure" by means of "the elective franchise," the bishop rallied his forces in an attempt to abolish elections altogether.[24]

In this effort Conwell was aided by William Harold, whose own words branded him an enemy of freedom. "He . . . praises . . . Edmund Burke . . . , champion of the crusade against French liberty and the rights of man; he [sneers at] patriotic and enlightened Italians . . . , the Carbonari, who endeavoured to emancipate their country; and [declares], that it is a question yet to be decided which is the most conducive to human happiness, the institutions of Great Britain, or those of the United States." They despaired of a man who could not see the difference between America and a system that supported a "hereditary king, . . . an aristocratic nobility, also hereditary, . . . a [corrupt and supine] house of commons . . . , a monster called 'Union of Church and State,' . . . a numerous standing army, and extensive navy, found necessary by the government, in time of peace, to keep the people from making any exertions for their relief, . . . [and] a code of criminal laws, composed in the true spirit of a Draco."[25]

St. Mary's memorial reveals an interesting range of attitudes informing the trustees' protest against episcopal authority. In many ways (the denunciation of aristocracy, the rejection of medievalism, the anticlericalism, the exaltation of reason, references to French liberty and its enemies) the memorial marks its authors as liberal children of the Enlightenment, essentially optimistic about the progress of human affairs, holding values and perspectives consonant with those of the republican revolutionaries of Europe. But in other ways they spoke specifically to the political culture of early nineteenth-century America.

References to a small army and navy, light taxation, an insignificant national debt, the emphasis on popular sovereignty and elective processes, all resonated to the traditional values of Jeffersonian Republicanism. But in other ways the memorial anticipated the emerging political culture of the age of Jackson. Its emphasis on national pride and honor was very much in keeping with the growing nationalism Americans displayed in the wake of the War of 1812, and its insistence on individual freedom of conscience, in both political and religious affairs, anticipated the new "Politics of Individualism" that increasingly informed American political culture in the decades before the Civil War. Finally, the dissenters' view of history, their paeans to American prosperity, and their belief (in an age of increasing economic inequality) that political and institutional equality was sufficient to provide safeguards against economic injustice, places them in the company of liberal economists such as Henry C. Carey who later helped to define what has been called the political culture of the American Whigs.[26]

Once again St. Mary's dissenters were disappointed in their appeal to civil authority. The emergence of a "Catholic interest" in the previous year's debate over the Catholic Bill had made clear to all that Bishop Conwell could, when he chose, rouse significant public support. Under William Harold's direction Conwell took care to remind members of the legislature of this fact. He assembled several pertinent documents and had them printed along with commentary (some of which even he judged to be "obnoxious and perhaps libelous") and sent them to "friends" in the legislature to help them prepare for the coming debate. His efforts paid off—the bill was never reported out of committee. On February 6 a member of the committee considering the petition reported that it was "inexpedient to grant the [dissenters'] request."[27]

"Bishop, Priest and People"

While the trustees petitioned the Pennsylvania legislature, Thadeus O'Meally made yet another appeal to Baltimore in which he attempted to explain why it was necessary that the laity "have some share of influence in the appointment of the Pastors, who are to receive their revenues." Many clergymen, he wrote, were persons for whom the laity "can feel no respect, in whom they can place no confidence." All too often they were "intemperate, impious, illiterate and vulgar"; men "who were utterly incompetent to the duties of the Ministry, and who could not discharge that ministry without disgracing it."[1]

O'Meally's letter underlines just how far the status of the clergy had fallen. Through decades of conflict the clergy had declined from its traditional role as disinterested moral arbiter to become just another among a number of contending interests in the congregation. Now in O'Meally's estimation they had fallen even further. Not even their moral judgment could be trusted. He identified a key point in the dissenters' ecclesiology when he said that they viewed the church as a "mixed" body "composed of Clergy & Laity," each of which acted as a check on the other. "Any undue tendency in either portion," he wrote, "is corrected by the other," and he described the ideal form of church government as "a fair balance of power between them." The dissenters, he said, refused to acknowledge any superior virtue or wisdom in the clergy. Rather, they considered the converse to be true. The people, O'Meally wrote "as a body can have no protégés or nephews—a Bishop may—they cannot be duped (at least not so easily) by the flatteries of the sycophant or the surface virtues of the hypocrite, or the shallow understanding of the ignorant—a Bishop may. The right, therefore . . . , of selecting Pastors, may be safely entrusted to them."[2]

This was an extraordinary view of the Church—one in which the laity exercised power equal to, and were the repository of moral authority and virtue superior to, the clergy. It represented such a complete reversal of roles that to traditionalists it carried the stench of Jacobinism. Even a moderate prelate like John England was shocked. "The more I reflect upon your situation," he wrote to Bishop Conwell, "the more I am inclined to sympathise with you. I know not what to advise." He warned that O'Meally was "a more dangerous foe than Hogan." "If I can judge from what I see," he wrote, "it is no longer an outrageous and open enemy whom you have to contend with, but a man who will give more trouble."[3]

What O'Meally and the dissenters were proposing was far less radical than it seemed at first glance. They were not asserting the will of the people as an absolute imperative. Rather they sought a constitutional relationship that would check the arbitrary power of the bishops and would provide for the sharing of authority among the laity, the lower clergy, and the episcopacy. O'Meally wrote, "so far from harbouring any inclination to shake off episcopal authority and that spiritual allegiance which as catholics we owe to the holy see . . . , our grand ultimate object and our most sincere desire is, to *secure* an obedience to them on the *only* basis on which the obedience of Americans *can* be secured, namely, the frank and explicit acknowledgment of the people's rights and the accurate demarcation of the episcopal prerogative."[4]

O'Meally then published a long *Address Explanatory and Vindicatory* in which he denounced extremists on both sides of the dispute. Borrowing the language of the French Revolution he branded ardent democrats as "*radicals*" and "*sans culottes*"—the most avid of the bishopites he designated "*Ultras.*" He and his supporters were, he said, "the *moderate* party," seeking "the happy medium between the two extremes."[5]

O'Meally's charted his moderate course by fixing on the principle of the rule of law. "If a bishop's will is to be our only law," he wrote, "then, in the name of consistency, let us fling up our creeds and our canons, and let that will be at once the principle of our faith and the rule of our government." He wrote, "I look upon the bishop of this diocese as I do upon the governor of this state—neither has the power to make laws— neither is privileged to break them. . . . The bishop . . . , is himself a subject: the law is the sovereign." Never, he asserted, did the obedience due a bishop require "surrender of [the laity's] honest feelings as men, their rights as citizens, and their principles as republicans." The laity owed their bishop only a "reasonable obedience . . . , the only obedience which freemen should acknowledge; an obedience to the fixed and permanent *authority of law,* not to the *man's* fantastic and fluctuating *will.*"[6]

Once again O'Meally asserted the superiority of the people to those who would govern them. It was not, he argued, the laity's "duty to receive like obedient subjects, whomsoever [the bishop] is pleased to send them . . . , and to hold their tongues." The people were not a "docile flock of sheep" to be so treated. Noting that both sides in the conflict were to some extent animated by stubborn pride, he asked, "In the name of God which pride is the worse? the pride of the *one,* or the pride of the *many,* the pride of the *priest* or the pride of the *people,* the pride of *stubborness,* or the pride of *principle,* the pride of *power* in enforcing its selfish will, or the pride of *resistance* in opposing its despotism?"[7]

O'Meally honored "no aristocracy but the aristocracy of the heart, which is virtue, and the aristocracy of the mind, which is genius" and he felt that virtue and genius were more likely to reside in the people than in their rulers. It was dangerous to concentrate power in one man's hands. A priest, he wrote, is capable of great "mischief . . . ; he may be an angel of light, and lead souls to heaven; [but] he may be a spirit of darkness, and guide them to their ruin." It was therefore necessary that the laity should have a voice in the selection of clergymen and should control their incomes. Much as Adam Smith's "Invisible Hand" ensured optimal results from individual economic choices, the self-interest of the laity, which impelled them to uphold the "respectability of their own creed," would guarantee virtue within the church. To the end of ensuring respectability, he wrote, "is pledged not only [the trustees'] conscience as christians, but also their pride as men, and their predilection as catholics." Therefore they, unlike the bishops, could be counted on "to make the *best* choice in the selection and presentation of pastors."[8]

Despite his insistence on the moral superiority of the people, O'Meally was no more a democrat than had been his predecessor. To him the will of the people, no less than the dictates of bishops, had to be constrained by law. He wrote, "our church cannot exist without a government; that government, to effect its purpose, must be strong; let it be as strong as you will, but let its strength be the stationary strength of law, not the fluctuating stubborness of will." He emphatically repudiated the leveling imperatives of radical republicanism, writing, "I reject with scorn that rank and rancorous radicalism, (whether in church or state,) which disclaims subordination, and whose debasing spirit would reduce all ranks to its own low level," just as he denounced "with as strong a scorn that overweening, out-toping toryism, which would make gods of men, and force the proud and free-born soul to bow itself down before a *golden calf.*" "The middle course is always the best," he proclaimed, "and to that am I attached."[9]

O'Meally envisioned a Church in which power was shared among the clergy, the episcopacy, and the laity. "Is the bishop the church?" he asked. "No!" he answered, "The church is the bishop, priest *and people.* The triumph of the church is the triumph of the whole, and that triumph must be and will be the triumph of reason, of justice and of law, over unfounded pretension and obstinate perverseness." "We contend for the right of the trustees to *present* or *nominate* or *elect* pastors," O'Meally wrote, but he argued that this was not an infringement on the right of bishops "to *appoint* them or give them spiritual faculties." The appointment of clergy, he said, was a cooperative effort in which both episcopacy and the laity participated.[10]

Such a system of government, O'Meally argued, was the only one that would be appropriate in America. The new republic was a place "where 'all things are new,' where the kindling aspirations of the emancipated mind have formed around it a halo of such dazzling glory, as to have startled the world from the slumber of its error." In this land of freedom, he wrote, "Is it wise, is it prudent, that those, who as *men* are the freest that ever lived . . . , should be made to feel that as catholics they must be greater slaves than those of their brethren who live under a tyrant's sway? Is it wise, is it prudent, that those whose voice is *law* in every thing else, should be made to feel, that *in that very thing*, in which they are most deeply interested, they have *no voice at all!*"[11]

O'Meally carried his indictment further, arguing that the American hierarchy was staffed by men who were "utterly incapable of appreciating [the nation's] free institutions, so as to form their conduct upon them." Conwell and other authoritarian prelates he described as "men . . . who having grown old as slaves, *cannot learn to be free!*" Such men, he warned, "who are so highly impregnated with the virus of slavery, as to be utterly incapable of imbibing the pure and healthy spirit of freedom, which mingles in the very air we breathe in this emancipated world, may also have conceived a certain distaste for, a certain repugnance against it." If so, he declared, they are certainly not "fit guardians for the youth of republican freemen." Americans cannot afford to tolerate this, he argued, for "religious freedom is the foundation of civil liberty; and . . . if a man be not free in his intercourse with God, it is farcical to call him free in his intercourse with his fellow man."[12]

Thadeus O'Meally thus turned his critique of the Church into an affirmation of American republican culture, but he rejected many of the nativist implications of American exceptionalism. Like William

Hogan he denounced the role of the Church in Ireland and considered the people of that nation to have been degraded to the point where many of them were incapable of assuming the responsibilities of republican citizenship, but he refused to suggest that Irish immigrants themselves were a threat to the republic. Instead he argued that the threat to liberty in both Ireland and America was the Catholic clergy itself, which he warned, formed a distinct body in the population and were "governed by an *esprit de corps,* rather than by *national* feelings." They cared nothing for America or for the republic, but only for the perpetuation and extension of their wealth and influence. "Catholics of America," he wrote, "open your eyes to this, and *open them in time.*" He continued, "The abuses [of the clergy], most assuredly will not correct themselves;—and, it may be a fatal mistake, instead of plucking them up now, whilst they are young, to suffer them to remain until they become deeply rooted and fully matured."[13]

O'Meally also differed from the nativists in that he restricted his indictment to the clergy and did not extend it to the institutions and doctrines of the Church itself. He rejected the view that republicanism and Catholicism were inherently antagonistic systems of belief. Basing his argument in John England's conciliar concept of the Church, O'Meally advanced the position that the Church was essentially a republican institution. "The pope," he wrote, "is but the *president* of the united *churches* of the *christian* republic. . . . No church can exist without legislative and judicial authorities: those of the catholic church are the most securely bottomed, and the most purely republican of all— the Bible is our constitution." O'Meally pointed out that essential matters of dogma and doctrine were settled by "a general council" over which the pope presided "as the president of these states would a federal congress." Within this council, which represented "all the confederated churches of the christian world," the majority ruled and so, in O'Meally's eyes, "the catholic . . . is actually the freest of all sectarians." "Here," he declared, "is an authority strictly and purely republican—an authority to which the proudest mind need not scorn to bend."[14]

Like Bishop England and the dissenters, Thadeus O'Meally was attempting to reconcile the divergent tendencies of republicanism and restoration Catholicism, and like them he advanced a model of what a republican church should be. His was a constitutional church based firmly on a single principle—"the right of patronage"— which he argued would "not only ensure to the church an honourable body of pastors, but also serve as the groundwork of *a regularly organised, and purely American hierarchy!*" O'Meally expanded the idea of presentation to include what he called, "domestic nomination." "The pastors," he explained,

> chosen by the trustees of the chartered congregations throughout the union, will take care that no bishop be obtruded upon them, unasked for, and unwished for; they will insist upon the right of 'domestic nomination'; so that when a vacancy shall occur, the pastors of that diocese will assemble in diocesan synod, and fill it up by an election from their own body; and as the trustees present the pastor elect to the bishop for institution, so shall the pastors also present the bishop elect to the pope, for the same.

"Thus," he proclaimed, "will there be as beautiful a subordination in your ecclesiastical as in your civil form of government; the people electing trustees, trustees electing pastors, and pastors electing bishops."[15]

Like St. Mary's dissenters before him O'Meally hoped to rouse the support of Catholics throughout the republic: He urged that "the trustees of all the chartered churches throughout the Union" petition Rome for the right to elect their pastors and bishops and for the appointment of a "nuncio or viar apostolic" to whom they could appeal episcopal actions and decisions. O'Meally had no doubt that his plan would find favor in Rome. He wrote, "A people's voice, asking for that which is just, is not to be resisted."[16]

Thadeus O'Meally, no less than the dissenters, placed his critiques in a cosmopolitan context. His points of reference were not merely American society and freedoms but also the intellectual conflicts of Western culture writ large. He supported his assertions with examples from contemporary Ireland, from Chile, and from revolutionary Colombia. He spiced his accounts with references to Newton, Leibniz, Jeremy Bentham, and other great figures of Western philosophy and science. In a remarkable passage he attempted to explain his efforts to resolve the dispute at St. Mary's by likening them to principles of Newtonian physics. He wrote, "I performed to the parties a double service . . . , preventing, on the one hand, a collision that would have been ruinous to both; and, on the other, keeping one of them steady in its orbit, and hindering it from flying off at a tangent, to wander for ever from the centre of attraction." He invoked the images of the French Revolution of 1789. In sum, like his lay supporters, Thadeus O'Meally derived his principles, not just from the American experience, but from the common intellectual heritage of Western culture.[17]

Conwell's Moral Cosmology

Thadeus O'Meally and Henry Conwell, both recent immigrants from Ireland, gazed at each other across an enormous conceptual gulf. A small incident in October of 1824 illustrates the fundamental incompatibility of their views. In that month the Marquis de Lafayette, hero of two continents and the living symbol of liberal reform and revolution, returned to Philadelphia. He was met with exultant celebrations, one of which was a civic procession in which the assembled clergy of Philadelphia marched through the streets of the city to present a memorial honoring the hero. At the head of the procession, walking side by side, were the venerable Protestant Episcopal bishop, William White, and the Roman Catholic bishop, Henry Conwell. Those who follow the current fashion of inferring private attitudes from participation in public demonstrations might see this as a remarkable display of ecumenical amity and republican solidarity. In fact, it was nothing of the kind.

Bishop Conwell was disgusted and disturbed by the entire affair. He hated Lafayette and everything the man stood for and marched only because he had been obliged by the pressure of public opinion to do so. He was particularly upset at having to walk in company with Bishop White and in a letter to Archbishop Maréchal explained that the marching order had been set according to age (placing him and White, as the city's oldest clergymen, at the head of the procession) and without his consent. Although Conwell had publicly assented to a memorial praising Lafayette and the revolutionary tradition he represented, he privately prayed that God would bring about the "complete ruin" of those who agitated for republican causes.[1]

Thadeus O'Meally, by contrast, was hero-struck and rejoiced in Lafayette's second coming. To him the revolutionary hero was "that illustrious man, whose public character (so well sustained by his private virtues) is the purest on which the world's eye can now repose." He was thrilled to think that Lafayette, "who having devoted his stainless honor in his youthful prime, and with a chivalrous enthusiasm to the sacred cause of liberty, has crossed an ocean in the evening of his day, a pious pilgrim to her shrine, to bask once more in the sunshine of her smile, and bless her as he dies."[2]

Like his bishop, O'Meally saw the marquis as the embodiment of revolutionary liberalism; the difference was that Conwell feared, and O'Meally hoped, that "twelve such apostles would regenerate the world!" Here was the source of Bishop Conwell's intransigence. He was absolutely convinced that he was upholding sacred principles and defending an institutional structure without which the world, like revolutionary France, would dissolve into chaos. O'Meally, though, saw the bishop as a tyrant attempting "to make justice, and reason, and authority and law, all succumb to his overruling and overweening will." The priest and the bishop thus stood on opposite sides of a great divide in the history of the Western world. Between their divergent *weltanschauungs* there was little possibility of compromise, and so Thadeus O'Meally's quest to find a "middle course" between his lay supporters and his bishop was doomed to fail.[3]

It is easy to understand the bitterness and frustration of a man who, having served faithfully in subordinate positions in the Irish hierarchy for a half century, had finally been elevated to the episcopacy only to be denied the prerogatives of that office by refractory priests and a rebellious laity. To this can be ascribed some of the current of anger and resentment that runs through Bishop Conwell's correspondence. But to say this is not to exclude matters of principle. In Conwell's letters and published writings all forms of republicanism (conservative, moderate, and radical) Jacobin terror, and Protestantism fused into a single image of the enemy; insidious forces that had slowly but surely eroded the imagined Catholic unity and peace of the premodern era and were now personified by St. Mary's schismatics. For a man who, upon his arrival in Philadelphia had publicly stated, "I am the church for I am bishop," attacks on episcopal prerogatives became personal assaults, and attacks on his personal character became assaults on the faith itself. That is why he could not view his opponents as principled men or as true Catholics. They were, he wrote, "generally Deists or men who never had their first Communion and whose families—wives, Sons & Daughters are Protestants by profession and have Pews in Protestant Churches." He saw the fact that many dissenters had chosen to raise their children outside the faith as confirmation of the essential identity between dissent and the forces of darkness.[4]

In Conwell's view those persons most to be feared were clerical deviationists, men who had betrayed their faith. During the course of the Philadelphia conflict he had been forced to deal with a seemingly endless series of such unreliable and dangerous men—Hogan, Mier, Rico, Inglesi, O'Meally, and, most formidably, John England. Henry Conwell might excuse the involvement of Gabriel Richard and Bishop Fenwick with St. Mary's dissenters; he could not be so charitable with Bishop England. In December he informed Archbishop Maréchal that "The Bishop of Charleston is still corresponding with O'Meally and encouraging his cause." He wrote, "With respect to the Schism, I think nothing can support it any longer, if Dr. England would have the goodness to desist from interfering." Upon reading Thadeus O'Meally's *Address Explanatory and Vindicatory*, he ventured the opinion that "Dr. England has furnished the materials and the Lawyer Ingersoll and Mathew Carey have put it into form—as the speech of Mr. O'Meally."[5]

Henry Conwell thought he saw a grand scheme unfolding with John England at its head: "the Doctor is to be sent to Rome as Envoy from the Catholics of the United States to make a Concordation between the Pope and the Catholics of America—and is to be appointed the Arbiter to regulate and to correct the Clergy and remove them occasionally according to Dr. England's rule and the terms of [England's] Constitution." He felt that "The main way to extinguish the Schism is to obtain from the Holy See an Inhibition to debar Dr. England from intermeddling in any other concerns save his own & those of his own Diocese, and even there from acting on the Civil Constitution . . . until the Propaganda gives their sanction to it, which, I hope, they never do." He confided to Maréchal that "I find myself under the necessity of sending a *caveat* to Rome to frustrate all such ill designs as I consider Dr. England to be meditating," and, "*Entre nous* I really believe that Dr. England's Main Object is to get himself removed from the torrid climes of the Carolinas and Georgia into a more salubrious climate, e.g. into Maryland or Pennsylvania, or perhaps both."[6]

Bishop Conwell's stubborn refusal to negotiate with the dissenters despite several efforts at mediation had become a matter of concern throughout the American episcopacy and even in Rome. In August of

1824 Bishop Cheverus of Boston had even recommended to Propaganda that Conwell should be made to resign because he lacked the necessary qualities for his office. It would be easy to see him as a deviant case, an aberration within the American hierarchy, and indeed he has sometimes been portrayed as such. But his stand on principles was not much more extreme than the opinions of his colleagues and even his critics.[7]

Bishop Fenwick, commenting on the troubles in Philadelphia, attributed them to the long interval between Bishop Egan's death and Conwell's appointment, during which effective episcopal authority had been absent from the diocese. This, he felt, had allowed democracy to spread unchecked, and he urged that steps be taken in all dioceses to ensure the continuity of authority in the event of a bishop's death. He was greatly disturbed by "the republican spirit which prevails [in America, and] gives room to fear an intrusion of Calvinistical independence in the American dioceses and congregations which may involve these in schisms like that which ruins the church in Philadelphia." John England, for all his republican rhetoric, was absolutely opposed to granting the laity a voice in the government of the Church. On the subject of the Philadelphia conflict he wrote to Archbishop Maréchal, "Hogan is not the author of this evil, though he should leave Philadelphia, the evil would not be removed. It is the natural consequence of the [trustee] system upon which Catholicity has been established in Philadelphia." He continued, "If [Archbishop] Carroll did sanction the system of Lay Trusteeship, with all due regard to his memory, *he made a very fatal mistake.* I would not take your Cathedral *free from debt,* with its pews, and Trustees."[8]

Henry Conwell thus differed from his colleagues in the American hierarchy less in substance than in style. It was his unyielding stubbornness they criticized more than his goals. John England might criticize Conwell and others for their intractable hostility to republicanism in all its forms and could find fault with their absolutist sensibilities, but for all that he was no less authoritarian than they. The Catholic "culture of authority" ruled in Charleston no less than in Philadelphia. So long as Henry Conwell held a firm line against republican innovation the criticism was muted and he enjoyed strong support from Baltimore and Rome. It was only when he at long last faltered and conceded some of the dissenters' goals that a serious effort was made to remove him from his position of power.

O'Meally's Submission

In the last month of 1824 St. Mary's dissenters made one last effort to end the schism. They offered, through Thadeus O'Meally, "to waive every question of right or principle . . . , [and] are willing to refer all such questions to a superior tribunal, whose competency to decide is confessed on all hands." All they asked was that the bishop "appoint to St. Mary's, until that decision is obtained, any Clergyman he pleases, who has no interest in the question to be decided upon." John Ashley, speaking for the board of trustees made it clear "that this is the last opportunity that shall be given you by us, for rejecting propositions such as we have lately offered."[1]

Conwell refused to meet with the dissenters until O'Meally had first agreed to "sign an apology, *to be published,* for the scandals and sacrileges you have committed, and the principles you have promulgated to justify your contumacy and usurpation of pastoral jurisdiction in this Diocese." Conwell went on to declare, "no arguments on the ground of expediency shall induce me to shrink from my imperative duty, to require such satisfaction in this case, as the vindication of Catholic principles demands."[2]

O'Meally asked about the content of the letter he would be required to sign and received in reply a form requiring him to declare that he recognized that Henry Conwell, in suspending his faculties, "acted canonically, in virtue of his undoubted right as Bishop of Philadelphia." O'Meally would also state that his conduct "was contrary to the canons of the Roman Catholic church" and that the censures he received "were lawfully and justly inflicted." Further, O'Meally would repudiate his actions as opposed to Catholic principles and, "in [their] tendency subversive of the authority vested in the bishops of the Roman Catholic church, and of that subordination essential to the effective maintenance of ecclesiastical government." Finally, O'Meally would be required to declare "the resistance to authority of the bishop of Philadelphia, made by the persons now in possession of St. Mary's church, to be vexatious, scandalous and schismatical" and to exhort "all those engaged therein to desist.[3]

O'Meally was outraged; not even William Hogan had been treated with such insolence. He wrote, "you are pleased to tell me that I must stand up before the public to confess myself a *knave*, by declaring that I did what I knew I ought not to do, and to bring away with me the honourable cognomen of *fool* for my pains; and you add, that it is only by consenting to all this I can be even admitted into your presence." Indignantly, he washed his hands of the entire affair: "I have offered you peace for your church—I have requested an interview . . . you have rejected that peace, you have declined that interview. Whatever evil therefore may follow, to you, to them, or to the public, the whole blame of it must rest with you, and with you alone, sir."[4]

Now, at last, the long series of negotiations came to an end. At a general meeting on December 23 O'Meally announced that Bishop Conwell was beyond reason. "War is still preferred to peace," he said, "and hatred to love, and discord to harmony, and a stupid and bigoted attachment to the names and forms; to an enlightened and discriminating devotion to the sense and substance of religion!" No longer would he attempt to serve as peacemaker. He said, "my task now is, to shew where the . . . *guilt*, of this unholy preference rests, and to cast it indignantly from my own shoulders." O'Meally pointed to the example of Latin American revolutionary republican governments and urged, "Let not the catholics of the north blush to take a lesson from the catholics of the south, but rather let them blush not to follow the example they have set them."[5]

O'Meally said that only one course now remained for the dissenters. "Philadelphia," he declared, "has been the theatre of those sublime moral movements which have made you, as *Americans*, independent. Let it also originate those movements whose result will be to make you independent as *catholics*." "I do not ask you," he said, "nor do I wish you to disclaim or discard the spiritual authority of the Apostolic See— retain it by all means—but retain it as the bond of a federal union, not as a yoke of servile dependency." He called upon the congregations of St. Mary's, St. Augustine's, St. Joseph's, and Holy Trinity to elect delegates to a local convention which would draw up a memorial and a "joint commission . . . setting forth . . . the wishes of the Catholics of America." This commission would invest Bishop England "with full powers to negotiate a Concordat with the Holy See" which would be modeled on the agreements drawn up between the revolutionary governments of Latin America and Rome. The commission would also establish committees of correspondence to gain signatures from other congregations across the country. In closing, O'Meally declared that he had no fears of reprisal. "The man who dares to advocate liberal principles, must bring to the rostrum that moral courage which spurns alike the anger of the tyrant and the hatred of the slave."[6]

O'Meally's attempt to chart an independent course was no more successful than any of his other efforts. Soon after his appeal to American Catholics was published, John England issued a public letter in which he wrote, "Upon Mr. O'Meally's claim to be pastor of St. Mary's, upon his right to do any clerical duty in Doctor Conwell's Diocese, I never entertained a doubt. His claim is unfounded, he has no right." He continued, "As to the validity of his acts for whose value jurisdiction would be required, no person can raise a question; they are all invalid."[7]

There was no uprising of the American congregations, although many individual laymen expressed sympathy for the principles being articulated by Philadelphia's dissenters. Still there remained an appeal to Rome. O'Meally volunteered to travel to the Holy See and to argue the dissenters' case to Propaganda. On April 12 a general meeting of the congregation formally endorsed his mission and instructed him to argue there for "the establishment of some rational and fair system for the administration of the affairs of the Catholic Church in the United States." Noting the existence of disputes between bishops and laymen in New York, Norfolk, and Charleston "arising chiefly from the ill defined Jurisdiction of the Clergy and the rights of the Congregation" they also invited "the Catholics in this Country, generally" to "cooperate in this important object." Two days later the trustees notified Bishop Conwell of O'Meally's plans and asked him to appoint a priest, one who had no part in the controversy, to serve while the case was pending.[8]

O'Meally carried a paper formally authorizing him to "negotiate a concordat" that would "accurately [define] the boundaries and the rightful powers of" the bishop and the trustees and instructions stating that he could "on no account consent to forego our claim to the right of patronage." Alternatively he should "secure . . . an influence in the appointment of our pastors equivalent to that which [patronage] would secure." His mission had broad popular support. Bishop Conwell complained of this: "The papers [Fr. O'Meally] carries with him have been numerously signed—They depend greatly on . . . numbers to gain their point. . . . They imagine that Rome will [approve] any measure, sooner than lose such immense numbers, who threaten to quit the Church *for ever,* if they are not redressed by the prayer of their petition granted." To counter O'Meally's testimonials Conwell penned a long series of letters to the cardinal prefect of Propaganda denouncing O'Meally, his sponsors, and John England.[9]

O'Meally found Propaganda no more cooperative than Bishop Conwell. He addressed a formal petition to the Sacred Congregation but the secretary refused to accept it. He diligently submitted petitions time and again but Propaganda "refused to have any correspondence with him on the subject of the Schism in Philadelphia." Throughout the controversy O'Meally had consistently declared that he would bow to the decision of what he considered to be a competent tribunal—now he submitted to Propaganda's demands. He signed a document declaring that he was "penitent" for the "perversity" of his actions, regretted the "great scandal" and "evils" he had committed, and repudiated the "schismatical faction of certain Trustees of St. Mary's Church." O'Meally "renounced forever, the [dissenters] and their schismatical proceedings" and "abdicated . . . the usurped right of pastorship in St. Mary's." He asked "pardon and forgiveness" from Bishop Conwell for "all the transgressions . . . committed against his authority" and promised never again to return to the diocese of Philadelphia. Propaganda then sent a copy of the submission to Bishop Conwell, who had it published in papers throughout the diocese.[10]

Two days after his submission Thadeus O'Meally made one last attempt to be heard. In a letter to Propaganda he warned against rejecting the dissenters' petition without even examining it and asked that Bishop Conwell be told to appoint a neutral clergyman to serve at St. Mary's. This letter earned him a stinging rebuke from the secretary of Propaganda, who refused to absolve the priest of his excommunication until he took a solemn oath never to have anything to do with the Philadelphia schism. O'Meally attempted to appeal this decision to the prefect of Propaganda and sent letters to other officials recommending that Propaganda confirm the trustees' right of presentation. None of these brought a response. Finally, on December 28, 1825, after more than six months of futile effort, Thadeus O'Meally signed a formal oath never to involve himself in the affairs of Philadelphia again and was absolved of all censures. With this act his role in the controversy came to an end.[11]

Conwell's Covenant

Thadeus O'Meally's departure left St. Mary's dissenters in a desperate situation. Without a pastor the church was practically deserted. "From the time Mr. O'Meally left here," a prominent bishopite wrote, "the church of St. Mary's had been opened every Sunday morning. . . . There are none who attend . . . but the sexton, who appears to be prime minister, and frequently buries their dead, some of the Trustees, with a few others, who spend some little time in conversation, and then close the doors and retire." This picture is deceptive, though. The "immense numbers" who signed O'Meally's petition showed that the dissenters still enjoyed broad support within Philadelphia's Catholic population. What is more, Bishop Conwell's position was rapidly deteriorating.[1]

Conwell's colleagues in the American hierarchy were beginning to worry about the aging bishop's character and conduct. Rome was beginning to have doubts, too. The Philadelphia conflicts generated an enormous number of reports, petitions, and commentaries, many of them unfavorable to Bishop Conwell—some were quite disturbing. As a matter of principle Propaganda supported Henry Conwell's authority in all things and even praised him for his intransigence, comparing his trials to those of St. Athanasius of Alexandria, but the constant stream of complaints and critical accounts raised serious questions as to the bishop's administrative competence. Conwell was fully aware of this. By 1824 he feared that matters had deteriorated to the point that Propaganda was about to dispatch an agent (a Bishop O'Finan) to investigate him. These reports ultimately proved to be false, but the likelihood of direct Roman interference in the government of the diocese was mounting.[2]

There were troubles, too, with the resident clergy. Some traditionalists, accustomed to a relatively informal and collegial relationship with their ecclesiastical superiors, were beginning to chafe under Conwell's aloof and autocratic regime. At St. Augustine's Michael Hurley flatly refused to pay his share toward the bishop's upkeep. Appeals to Archbishop Maréchal brought no satisfaction, so Conwell carried his complaint all the way to Rome, which in the fall of 1825 finally ordered Hurley to square his accounts with the bishop. Patrick Kenny, for years a bishopite stalwart, was offended by Conwell's failure to respond to his letters or to observe customary civilities during a visit to Delaware. In his diary he wrote, "no letter, no message from Rt. Rev. Bishop Conwell for me!! I have written to him often—no answer." He declared that he would "not trouble the Phila[delphia]. coast hereafter."[3]

Most important was the increasingly strained relationship that was developing between Bishop Conwell and his vicar-general. Since his return to Philadelphia William Harold had been the driving force behind the bishopite movement. "Rev. Mr. Harold," we are told, "was the sole cause of keeping the true catholics of late St. Mary's Church together, he enlighten'd them, he inflamed them to deeds that would do honor to primitive christians." Many American prelates, including Bishop Conwell, considered him a likely candidate for elevation to the episcopacy. Twice Conwell recommended Harold as a candidate to fill vacant episcopal seats. When Bishop DuBourg suggested in 1824 that the only way to resolve the Philadelphia schism was to send Harold and John Ryan out of the diocese, Propaganda wrote that it was unlikely that Bishop Conwell could be persuaded to part with them. In response to a similar inquiry from Archbishop Maréchal, Conwell declared that Harold was "indispensable" where he was.[4]

Despite all of this, things were not well between Conwell and his vicar-general. William Harold at times could be insufferably arrogant and Bishop Conwell was a man of considerable pride. It was perhaps inevitable that they should clash. Over time, as Harold's influence grew among the traditionalist clergy and laity, he began to adopt toward Bishop Conwell an attitude of condescension similar to that he had earlier shown toward Michael Egan. Early in 1824 he began to correspond with John England, and in his letters expressed dissatisfaction with the way in which American dioceses were administered. He even went so far as to invite England to come to Philadelphia to discuss specifics of the reforms he proposed, reforms to which Bishop Conwell was violently opposed. Bishop England declined to come to Philadelphia, but he did consider Harold's charges of administrative incompetence against members of the American hierarchy to be "well-grounded" and wrote that "my opinion coincides with yours."[5]

The break between Harold and Conwell came early in 1826 when the dissenters reopened negotiations to end the long conflict. Although many still nursed resentments against William Harold, "arising . . . from the acrimonious language and haughty tone assumed by him in his publications," they had concluded that his personal popularity was such that "public harmony could not be restored" unless he was restored to the congregation. Accordingly, they grudgingly declared themselves now willing to accept Harold as a pastor of St. Mary's and begged the bishop to appoint another "gentleman, unconnected with the present controversy" as co-pastor. This proposal they then delivered, not to Bishop Conwell, but to the vicar-general, along with a cover letter which declared, "It is now in your hands to restore peace to us, and to allay all angry passions, which have caused so much scandal to religion." Bishop Conwell made no reply to the dissenters' proposals and left Philadelphia on a visitation tour of the western parishes.[6]

When Conwell returned to Philadelphia early in July he found that William Harold had apparently come to an arrangement with the dissenters in his absence. No record of this agreement remains but whatever it was Bishop Conwell found it offensive. He feared that Harold and John Ryan were about to become "successors to Hogan and O'Meally ready to serve [St. Mary's congregation], on the Hoganite principle." The Dominicans, though, would be more dangerous than Hogan or O'Meally for they "could bring in a Considerable faction well disposed to put all authority at defiance and sufficient to support the Principle of the Schism by Physical force." Angrily the bishop fired off a letter to Rome asking the Propaganda to order Harold to obey his bishop and not to take the side of the schismatics. In September Rome responded, admonishing Harold to follow Conwell's direction and assuring the bishop that nothing would be tolerated that would tend to undermine his authority or dignity.[7]

Early in August Conwell's worst fears seemed to be realized. He learned that the bishopite lay leaders were holding a special meeting to discuss the schism. Soon thereafter his lawyer called on him with news that bishopite leaders had "made a Proposition to [the dissenters] to join them—against *Episcopal Authority,* and that all the Parties should Enter the Church *Independently.*" The traditionalist clergy supported the reconciliation. "Several of his clergy," particularly Michael Hurley, advised the bishop that it was absolutely necessary that he come to some agreement with the dissenters. "If he," they said, "created a difficulty in the way of peace and reconciliation . . . , he would have to answer for all the consequences of a protracted and perhaps interminable schism." Conwell was suspicious. He thought that he could see behind this the machinations of Harold and Ryan.[8]

Faced with the possibility of a general revolt against his authority Conwell finally began to make concessions to the dissenters. He was convinced that the situation was perilous. In September he informed Archbishop Maréchal that St. Mary's trustees had finally succeeded in establishing "Active Correspondence" with other "Trustees of the Churches of the United States," and were apparently receiving encouragement. The Philadelphia revolt was threatening to spread to other cities. Already there was an incipient lay revolt against Patrick Kenny's authority in Wilmington, Delaware, and "New York," he wrote, "promises to be a Scene of Confusion." The matter of his age also weighed heavily on Conwell. "If I should happen to die," he asked Archbishop Maréchal, "whom could you find capable of *governing* and correcting the *two Dominicans*? I say you could find *none*."[9]

Once the decision had finally been made to compromise with the dissenters negotiations proceeded rapidly, though not smoothly. One sticking point had to do with the composition of the negotiating teams. The dissenters were willing to accept William Harold as co-pastor of St. Mary's, but they mistrusted him and would not deal with him in the negotiations. Instead they insisted that an independent clergyman be found. Eventually they settled on Patrick Kenny, who had been living in Delaware for some time and so had taken no direct part in the controversy. On October 1 Kenny was surprised to be "called by letter, instantly, to Phila[delphia]" where he was received by Bishop Conwell "as a priest and a friend," despite the coolness that had characterized their relationship for some months.[10]

Conwell informed the astonished priest that "the Schismatical board of Trustees of St. Mary's had made serious proposals of submission. What is more, Kenny understood him to say that these proposals were based "on strict Catholic p[rinci]ples recognizing the divine institution of the Roman Catholic, & Apostolical Episcopacy, unfetter'd by any Lay-intrusion." Kenny was not a well man and suggested that William Harold instead should conclude the business, but Conwell replied that the dissenters would not treat with Harold and cryptically commented that he "had particular reasons" for rejecting the Dominican that he would make clear at a later time.[11]

The negotiators met at the residence of Josiah Randall, the bishop's lawyer. There the dissenters put forth a list of conditions, "1st That the Bishop should not be pastor of St. Mary's—& 2dly that the board of Trustees might present such persons . . . for pastor . . . as they should think acceptable to the congregation; & 3dly that they should enjoy the right of rejecting as pastor or pastors such Priests as would be nominated by the Bishop." All of these were rejected by the bishop's representatives as being subversive of episcopal authority. They declared that unless these provisions "were abandoned by the schismatical board, in their fullest meaning and extent" negotiations could not proceed. They countered by promising that "the Bishop & his successors," would promise to "pay every respectful regard to any request from the Board, or the majority of the congregation on the subject" of clerical appointments. At this point, after about twenty minutes of discussion, Patrick Kenny was "seiz'd with chill, & ague shake, & obliged to go home" and took no further part in the negotiations.[12]

On the following day the dissenters asked that Bishop Conwell appoint Thomas Hayden, currently serving at Bedford in western Pennsylvania, as pastor of St. Mary's. The dissenters had often suggested Hayden as a suitable pastor for St. Mary's, but Bishop Conwell had always insisted that he, William Harold, and John Ryan had already been appointed pastors. Now Conwell was quite "agreeable" to Hayden's appointment. Conwell also made it clear that he "never would dwell in the same house with Rev. W. H. (sic) Harold, who had treated him (Bish[op]-Con[wel]l) most indignantly." Because of the animosity between them it was impossible that William Harold and Henry Conwell serve together and it was very likely that Thomas Hayden would be appointed in the place of John Ryan. Such a resolution would go far toward meeting many of the dissenters' demands. Hearing this, "from the lips of a bishop," shocked and astounded Patrick Kenny—so much that he could not "proceed with any degree of propriety."[13]

Two days later the dissenters presented a draft agreement that stated that the trustees would recommend to the bishop for appointment "such pastors . . . as they may deem proper," and that they reserved the right "to fix the salaries of the Bishop and the pastors in pursuance of the agreement." This was a reiteration of their initial position, articulated many times over the years. In earlier times the proposal would have caused Bishop Conwell to break off all communications with the dissenters. Now he brushed it off and continued with the negotiations. On October 9, 1826, an accord was signed by which "the Bishop of Philadelphia and the congregation of St. Mary's Church . . . agreed amicably, to settle all their disputes and to restore harmony and union to the Roman Catholic Church in [Philadelphia]."[14]

The final agreement between Bishop Conwell and St. Mary's trustees represented a significant concession on the bishop's part. It began innocuously enough, with a declaration that "the faith and doctrines of the Roman Catholic Church shall remain sacred and inviolate, and in accordance with these principles the spiritual concerns of the said Church shall be committed to the care and government of the Bishop, and the temporal concerns to the Board of Trustees." Both sides agreed to drop "all indictments, prosecutions, actions and causes of actions, suits, damages and trespasses" against one another; the trustees agreed to recognize Henry Conwell as bishop and senior pastor of St. Mary's Church "in the same manner as he was at the commencement of the late disputes"; and for his part Conwell "released all claims for arrears of salary and emoluments." The core of the agreement, though, dealt with the means by which clergy would be appointed to serve at St. Mary's, and there Conwell precipitously abandoned the principles for which he had fought so long.[15]

In the fourth section of the agreement Bishop Conwell recognized "the right of the trustees to recommend suitable persons as pastors" subject to a series of conditions. The bishop retained the right to appoint clergy, but the lay trustees were granted the right to raise objections to an appointment. Should the bishop not wish to bow to their objections, a panel, consisting of the bishop, two neutral clergymen, and three laymen selected by the board of trustees, would meet to consider the matter. A majority vote for or against the candidate would be honored by all. Should no majority emerge, a fourth clergyman, determined by lot, would be asked to break the tie. The final sections dealt with the matter of clerical salaries and here again the bishop again made significant concessions. He agreed to leave "the fixing of the salary for himself and the assisting clergy, to the liberality and discretion of the Trustees," but in turn they agreed not to diminish the clerical salaries without the bishop's consent. Finally the trustees agreed to provide a separate living facility for the assistant pastors (by this time the understanding was that Conwell would preside, assisted by Harold and Hayden) so that the bishop would not have to share a roof with William V. Harold.[16]

The concessions made by Bishop Conwell marked a complete abandonment of the absolutist principles to which he had previously adhered. He explained to Archbishop Maréchal that such drastic measures were necessary to forestall a general revolt and to bring the dissenters back into the church. Conwell felt that the concessions had achieved their end; through them he had been able to "receive into the Bosom of the Church a Certain Portion of his flock who had gone astray and admitted them to the fold as *Penitents.*" He saw no danger to religion in the agreement, for both sides understood that it would be submitted to Rome for approval and that "anything contained in [the document] which might militate against the Canons of the Church, or the Act of Incorporation, Should be Considered as *Null and Void.*" Satisfied that he had made the best of a difficult situation Conwell had notices of the agreement printed in the secular press and notified Propaganda that the trustees had yielded and the long schism had finally ended.[17]

The dissenters had a somewhat different view of the matter. They felt that they had not yielded any essential point of principle and they certainly were not penitent. They attached a "Protest" or explanatory note in which they declared that "nothing in the . . . Agreement, should be construed or intended to mean, under any shape or form, a relinquishment or abandonment of . . . [the laity's] *inherent* right of presentation," nor "should [it] be construed as admitting or confirming the principle that the Bishop of Philad[elphia] is in his own right, or can name himself a Pastor in St. Mary's Church." They declared that "peace and harmony can never thoroughly exist 'till this right [of presentation] is acknowledged and practised in these United States." Finally, the trustees declared that they intended "with all their energies" to "prosecute their claim to the See of Rome to allow a Rule or decree against any future Bishop being appointed, unless with the approbation and the recommendation of the Catholic clergy of this diocese."[18]

On October 11, 1826, Bishop Conwell announced a general amnesty and the lifting of all interdicts. He declared the church to be open and he stated that, while the trustees were "to manage the temporalities according to the act of incorporation," the "spiritual concerns shall remain under the care and government of the Bishop." On November 1 the board of trustees ratified the agreement and arranged for the payment of salaries to Bishop Conwell and his assistants, but three days later issued a declaration that the agreement had included an understanding that "no priest should be appointed in [St. Mary's] against whom the congregation, represented by the Trustees, had any reasonable cause of objection." They further declared that Bishop Conwell's acceptance of the agreement on these terms constituted an agreement on his part that lay influence in the appointment of clergy was not "in violation of Catholic principles." They then agreed to submit the agreement to "the Sacred College of the Propaganda for its decision on the points in this settlement, which may affect the canons and general discipline of the Roman Catholic Church."[19]

In the light of their declarations it is impossible to see the dissenters as the submissive penitents Bishop Conwell claimed them to be. They were still defiant and aggressively asserting principles for which they had long fought and their words constituted nothing less than a repudiation of Bishop Conwell's administration. The bishop later claimed that he had never seen the "Protest" of the trustees and never signed it, but it had been published under his name and, together with the concessions in the main document and subsequent declarations made by the trustees, convinced authorities on both sides of the Atlantic that Henry Conwell had compromised essential principles of faith and was no longer competent to rule in Philadelphia.

"This Unhappy Church"

William V. Harold now emerged as Henry Conwell's harshest critic. The personal animosity between the two men had built to the point that Bishop Conwell felt he could no longer tolerate Harold's presence in his diocese. In the same letter that announced the end of the schism Conwell also asked Propaganda to have the superior of the Dominicans reassign Harold and John Ryan out of Philadelphia and into a convent. He repeated this request several times in following months. Harold saw this as a repetition of his experience in 1813 when, after rousing popular opinion in favor of Bishop Egan, he had been displaced by an alliance of the bishop with his former enemies. He was determined to resist.[1]

Harold responded with his own letter to Rome criticizing Bishop Conwell and the terms of agreement at St. Mary's. With it he enclosed a copy of the compact along with a note to the effect that he had nothing to do with the negotiations that had produced it. He followed with a long series of letters to Propaganda in which time and again, he faulted Bishop Conwell for his arbitrary behavior and his concordat with the trustees. "The yearnings of this unhappy church" he wrote in November of 1826, "are directed towards Rome; and whatever happens in Philadelphia will either strengthen the faith or destroy the episcopacy in the United States of America." [2]

On December 1, 1826, Bishop Conwell finally took action against William Harold. He informed the priest that, "In consequence of your insulting language and behavior to me on many occasions, I can no longer recognize you as my Vicar-General, and therefore you are not to consider yourself as such for the time to come." Harold responded as William Hogan had done in similar circumstances. "I demand," he wrote, "at your hands some specific charge; that which you are pleased to allege is too vague and general to be susceptible of examination at the tribunal at which, I fear, I shall have to appeal." Appeal he did, to Baltimore (where Archbishop Maréchal refused to take action) and to Rome. Once more Harold wrote to Propaganda criticizing Bishop Conwell and informing them of the actions taken against him. "It has been brought home to me very forcibly," he wrote, "that . . . unless the Congregation asserts its authority, this church will be totally ruined." Once again Harold mobilized public sentiment to support his cause. He urged his lay supporters to send letters to Rome on his behalf. Some also visited Baltimore to argue Harold's cause personally to the archbishop. [3]

Bishop Conwell countered with a letter to Archbishop Maréchal urging that he "give no credit to the *Respectables* [friends of Harold] who . . . go frequently to Baltimore to disseminate false accounts, with a view to gain over your Grace to make a false report of the Case at Rome." The "main object" of their efforts, he said, was "to procure the Deposition of the Bishop!!!" and "to substitute a favorite [William Harold] in his place." They would, he felt, "be content with nothing, [other] than to make the Dominicans paramount." In letters to the Holy See Conwell repeated his sense of the urgency of the situation and reiterated his request that Harold and Ryan "be removed from this city." [4]

The developing feud between Bishop Conwell and William Harold caused much consternation within the diocesan clergy. Many traditionalists, feeling that the bishop had betrayed them, took Harold's part. "I do not wonder in the least," Patrick Kenny wrote, "that the steady veteran friends of Catholic Bishops' rights during the Hogan schism, should now feel sore." For his own part Kenny was confused and conflicted. When informed of the articles of agreement by disgruntled laymen, he felt that Bishop Conwell had acted "anticatholically as to church discipline" and pronounced the compromise to be a foul business. He angrily denied having any hand in the matter. Still, Kenny was convinced that Bishop Conwell had an absolute right to rule his diocese as he saw fit, and this conflict of principles caused him considerable distress.[5]

Michael Hurley, though, supported Bishop Conwell enthusiastically. He had played an important part in the negotiations that produced the articles of agreement and was even formally thanked by the trustees for his efforts. When Conwell removed Harold from the post of vicar-general Hurley filled the position. Most of the diocesan clergy would seem, like Hurley, to have sided with their bishop, although with considerably less enthusiasm. On April 17, 1827, as criticisms of the bishop swelled, Hurley met with several other clergymen at St. Joseph's Chapel and there they signed a paper, reproaching William Harold for "several acts of impropriety towards Bishop Conwell," which were sufficient to "justify the Bishop to withdraw Mr. Harold's faculties." Richard Baxter, the bishop's secretary, then sent copies of the paper to clergymen outside the city for their signatures and most complied. One of those attending the meeting at St. Joseph's was a newly ordained priest, John Hughes, the future archbishop of New York. To his friend and mentor, Simon Bruté he explained that the purpose of the declaration was to shield Bishop Conwell from "odium" should William Harold's protests to higher authorities bear fruit. Hughes had himself refused to testify to Harold's conduct, since he scarcely knew the man, but later he was persuaded to sign a "milder form" of testimonial asserting that Conwell's withdrawal of Harold's faculties was both proper and canonical.[6]

Like many other clergymen, John Hughes accepted Bishop Conwell's explanation that the concessions made to St. Mary's dissenters were not worth the paper on which they were inscribed because they were sure to be rejected by Propaganda. Hughes assured Simon Bruté that the articles of agreement were "not so bad as they had been represented" because they had voluntarily been "submitted to the *revision* of the court of Rome." "I do not know," he wrote, "whether you will look on this as any relief to the objectionable parts of the articles, but it seemed so to me." It seemed so to Patrick Kenny, too. Upon being assured by Bishop Conwell that the articles of agreement had no force and that their validity would be judged by Propaganda, Kenny wrote that the bishop's letter "quiets, . . . even calms my mind as to the October 1826 'Treaty of Peace.'" Of course, as Kenny noted, Bishop Conwell could hardly make public his reasons for acquiescing to the demands of the dissenters for that would ignite general outrage and a resumption of the schism. Instead his supporters were left ignorant of the real situation, nursing "their deep past wounds, & their deeper present, & worse than bleeding feelings."[7]

As Patrick Kenny's comments suggest, many of the bishop's strongest lay supporters became disaffected from him in the months after the St. Mary's schism ended. To some extent this was due to a feeling of betrayal as they saw Conwell negotiate away principles for which they had long fought, but far more important was the deteriorating relationship between the bishop and William Harold. A crucial turn came on April 3, the day of the annual election for trustees. Prior to the election it had been assumed that a balanced ticket (consisting equally of bishopites and dissenters) would be chosen, but on the day of the election Bishop Conwell, to spite Harold, endorsed a slate of candidates all but one of whom were dissenters. Francis Roloff noted the result with disgust. "None," he wrote, "but the old leaven were made trustees. Election is only a name."[8]

Before the election was concluded Conwell accosted William Harold on the street and "gave him a paper which contained his suspension from all Sacerdotal functions [and] rescinding all faculties given him in writing or by word of mouth." Francis Roloff witnessed the event and predicted that it would "cause a great stir among the people, and bring on a new series of troubles which may appall even the Bishop himself." Already, he noted, people were beginning to talk of "the unsoundness of the Bishop's mind," and this action would only confirm their suspicions. Roloff himself felt threatened, "knowing . . . that [Conwell's] displeasure and that of his Revd. Counsellors in the spurious business of St. Mary's reconciliation extends to all who are not for applauding of what has been done."[9]

As the controversy deepened William Harold took every opportunity to portray himself and John Ryan as wronged men. When most of the diocesan clergy signed a paper supporting Bishop Conwell's actions, Harold obtained a copy, conferred with his lay supporters, and announced that he would promptly institute a suit against the signatories for defamation of character. A delegation of laymen then approached Bishop Conwell and demanded that he order the clergy to retract their signed statements. Conwell refused to do so and protested that he knew nothing of the matter. This was an obvious untruth (Conwell had called the meeting and was present when the paper was signed) and the bishop's behavior on this occasion did much to undermine the confidence placed in him by his former partisans.[10]

Harold and his friends then began to spread the rumor that Bishop Conwell had forced the Dominican's colleagues to denounce him—that Patrick Kenny, Francis Roloff, and another clergyman who refused to sign the paper condemning Harold had been suspended for their defiance. Although this was untrue the story was widely believed in the city. As an alternate explanation Harold charged that the resident clergy had "clubbed together in a conspiracy" against him. Despite such inconsistencies the eloquent Dominican's efforts at influencing lay opinion were, as always, quite effective. Little more than a month after Harold's suspension John Hughes reported that "public opinion is against us here."[11]

Rapprochement

William Harold's suspension brought together formerly antagonistic elements of St. Mary's congregation. Many among the dissenters, despite their personal dislike for Harold, were outraged at Bishop Conwell's arbitrary actions. At the same time William Harold's partisans among the bishopites were aghast at their hero's treatment and began to feel that the dissenters' case against the bishop had not been without merit. Under the circumstances former bishopites and dissenters began to cooperate to resist what they all saw as episcopal tyranny.

The move toward rapprochement was most pronounced among the more affluent elements of the congregation. Several of the "most respectable pewholders . . . old and highly respectable members of the congregation" signed a letter to Bishop Conwell requesting Harold's reinstatement. On April 21, branding the bishop's action "contrary to the plainest principles of justice" and tending "to the debasement and slavery of the clergy," they called for a public meeting of the congregation. Some old dissenters demurred. On the same day, they published a pamphlet urging the laity to remain calm. "Let us avoid all public meetings," they wrote, "it is there where the passions are excited, discontents arise, dissension and ill will produced, and they may probably lead to . . . fatal consequences." They reminded the protesters that Conwell had not violated in any way the terms of his compact with the dissenters and "the Trustees have no cause for complaint." If Harold wished to appeal Conwell's action, he could do so "to the Archbishop; should he obtain no satisfaction from that quarter, the court of Rome is open to him."[1]

Harold's cause, though, was popular. The pewholders of St. Mary's congregation met on April 24, 1827. Mathew Carey chaired the meeting and two former bishopites served as secretaries. The assembled pewholders denounced Harold's suspension as "a dangerous and revolting example of arbitrary power." The system of church government that allowed it was, they said, "an abuse, being contrary to the fundamental principles of justice, and subversive of the rights of clergymen, whom it subjects to the mere caprice of an individual." They stated their determination to "have recourse to all lawful means to obtain from Rome . . . the establishment of the canonical rights of our clergy." To carry on negotiations toward this end the meeting selected a "general committee" of the membership which included several leaders of both the former bishopite and the dissenter factions.[2]

This general committee, in which Richard W. Meade and John T. Sullivan worked side by side with their former enemies John Carrell and Joseph Snyder, illustrates the extent to which the Harold controversy united the congregation in opposition to Bishop Conwell. They composed a petition asking the bishop to reinstate William Harold at St. Mary's and sent the resolutions adopted by the public meeting to all the American bishops. John Hughes (who, along with most of the clergy, still supported the bishop) decried the "unlucky prejudice raised by the cry of persecution and conspiracy against a clergyman [William Harold] in whose favor were enlisted all the benevolent sympathies of such as love eloquence and hate the Bishop, that is to say, of nearly all Philadelphia." Harold's success at swaying public opinion made an impression on Hughes. He was dismayed by the mendacity of all concerned and decided on the basis of what he had seen and heard that "public opinion is credulous, it concludes according to its premises and when it is ill informed its conclusions are rash and often times wrong. It has had to acknowledge this a thousand times, but in every new case its decisions are as dogmatical as before. It is an idiot because it has no memory and of course cannot learn by experience."[3]

In the new spirit of solidarity St. Mary's affluent laymen addressed a number of matters of mutual concern. Not the least of these dealt with questions of order and status within the congregation. In the summer of 1824 many bishopites had refused to pay their pew rents. Six months later their pews had been declared vacant and were reassigned to dissenters. Now the question rose as to who had the right to occupy the choicest pews in the church. This was a matter of some importance because pewholding was the most visible marker of status differentials within the congregation, and conflicting claims threatened to disrupt the agreement right from the beginning. Patrick Kenny noted that many disgruntled bishopites felt that the compact ending the schism was unjust to the "old pew holders." To the dissenter leadership (themselves highly respectable and status-conscious men) the claims of status could not be ignored and they moved quickly to resolve the matter by restoring to the prominent and illustrious bishopites their traditional pews at the head of the congregation.[4]

Respectable Catholics also moved to contain the violence and turmoil that had long characterized elections. Much of the disorder resulted from the practice of "pew packing" instituted by William Harold in 1813 and used again by him in the 1820s. It was Harold's practice to recruit persons from outside the congregation and to pay pew rents for them (often packing four or five people into a single pew), thus entitling them to a vote. Several times the dissenters had proposed revisions to the church's charter that would have eliminated this practice, but the bishopites had successfully blocked them. Now all sides cooperated to propose an amendment that restricted participation in the elections to pewholders who had been registered on the books of the corporation for at least six months. This time the petition passed easily through the legislature and was approved by the State Supreme Court in December 1826. Thus ended the practice of pew packing, and with it much of the influence of the immigrant working class.[5]

A final matter of concern to all respectable Catholics was the reputation of their religion. The bitter conflict that swirled around St. Mary's Church had repeatedly been projected outward into the secular press, into civil institutions, and even into politics. Much critical commentary had ensued and many of St. Mary's congregation were anxious that the respectability of their faith was being impaired. In an attempt to counter the critics of his religion and to unite Catholics against an external foe, Mathew Carey in October 1826 published *A Religious Olive Branch.* In it he lauded "those [Protestants], who, instead of fanning the embers of religious bigotry and intolerance, preach harmony, kind feelings, and good will to all men," but he denounced the "ultra zealots" (by which he meant Scotch-Irish Presbyterians, and in particular a "Society of Irish Orange Men, styling themselves the Gideonite Society") who, knowing that "their ancestors, fined, imprisoned, banished, mutilated, beheaded, tortured, disembowelled, quartered, burned, and drowned, their fellow mortals," had the audacity to reproach Catholics for their intolerance and persecution of dissenters. Even as he reiterated the gruesome atrocities of the past Carey appealed to "his fellow citizens at large, of every denomination and description . . . to inculcate the divine doctrine of mutual forgiveness and forgetfulness of the crimes of ages of barbarous ignorance, insatiate rapacity, blind bigotry, infuriated fanaticism, and bloodthirsty cruelty."[6]

Carey also took the lead in forming, together with William Harold and the leaders of the quarreling factions at St. Mary's, an association of "Vindicators of the Catholic Religion from Calumny and Abuse." Its object was "to publish and distribute . . . such books and pamphlets as may be calculated to refute the calumnious accusations against . . . Catholics." Although the "Vindicators" accomplished little in its brief existence, it did indicate a determined attempt on the part of the lay elite to promote religious solidarity within Philadelphia Catholicism by identifying an outside enemy (Irish Orangemen) against whom all could bend their efforts. It also, by emphasizing the damage to religion ensuing from internecine conflict, helped to promote a more reasoned and less impassioned dialogue within Philadelphia's Catholic community, and in doing so promoted the respectability of the Catholic faith and those who practiced it.[7]

John Hughes noted this new sense of cooperation that pervaded St. Mary's respectable classes. In May of 1827 he wrote, "The opposition is becoming extremely calm and gentle and the fever of passion has in a great measure passed away. It seems [to be] their determination to demean themselves like good Catholics, until the 'Court of Rome' puts all to rights." Many of those who had been prominent in the revolt against episcopal authority retired. Among these was Richard W. Meade, who announced early in 1827 that he would not stand for reelection saying that he felt that his task was over and his efforts had been crowned with success. Resignation from the board of trustees did not, however, mean that Meade's voice was stilled. His profound antipathy to absolutism in all its forms meant that Meade could not condone Bishop Conwell's treatment of William Harold and so, though he personally disliked the former vicar-general and was increasingly incapacitated by ill health, Meade lent his support to several activities on the priest's behalf.[8]

In the April elections of 1827 seven of the eight lay trustees chosen were dissenters. Only Joseph Snyder, the most prominent of the former bishopites and now a harsh critic of Bishop Conwell, represented an alternative perspective. Three weeks later, though, John Ashley, unable to suppress his dislike for William Harold, resigned his position on the board and was replaced by Lewis Ryan, a former bishopite. Then, in July of 1827, John Leamy resigned the board in protest over a decision from the Holy See repudiating the articles of agreement. He was replaced by Richard Meade, who volunteered to serve despite the fact that his health was rapidly failing. Meade remained on the board of trustees and was active on William Harold's behalf through 1827 but was incapacitated after that; on June 28, 1828, he passed away. By the end of 1827, then, Richard Meade's illness and the withdrawal from church affairs of several of his colleagues had virtually eliminated the core of leadership that had sustained the dissenters through long years of controversy.[9]

Resistance to episcopal authority had not, though, ceased at St. Mary's. Even as the old dissenters retired, many former bishopites, now partisans of William Harold, began to question the legitimacy of arbitrary authority. Their resistance, though, was not based in a firm commitment to liberal principles and values. For John Keating, John Carrell, Joseph Snyder, Thomas Maitland, and other former bishopite leaders who took an active part in William Harold's defense Bishop Conwell stood outside even the conservative tradition in American Catholicism. These men were heirs to the long Anglo-American republican Catholic tradition that conceived of liberties in corporate rather than individual terms. Theirs was a middle course that stood in opposition to both the absolutism of restoration Catholicism and the range of republican values represented by St. Mary's dissenters. This was thus a significant shift both in lay leadership and in the ideological perspectives of that leadership, a shift that would powerfully affect the character of Philadelphia Catholicism in years to come.

The Only Tribunal

By the summer of 1827 the burning question occupying the minds of Philadelphia's Catholics was not so much a clash of principles but of men. Bishop Conwell and William Harold were locked in a bitter personal struggle that could only end with the removal of one or the other from the diocese. Still, fundamental matters of principle were not forgotten and both Harold and Conwell grounded their actions in what they considered to be such.

On the day after his initial suspension William Harold appealed to Baltimore, but Archbishop Maréchal told him that there was "no foundation" for such an appeal. "The only tribunal" Maréchal wrote, "which can redress a wrong such as that of which you complain is the Holy See." Harold then set forth a daring argument that ironically incorporated many of the positions earlier taken by the partisans of William Hogan and Thadeus O'Meally. Like them Harold denounced the arbitrary nature of episcopal authority exercised on the American mission. He called Bishop Conwell's actions "unmitigated despotism" and protested that despite "unimpeachable" conduct he (Harold) had been "stigmatized" and stood "exposed to every kind of suspicion with which folly or malice may assail me." Such injustice, and the system that permitted it—one that exalted "the episcopal authority so as to reduce the priesthood in the second order to insignificance, to a state of mere, low servitude"—were, Harold wrote, in accord "neither . . . with the letter nor the spirit of the laws of the Catholic Church."[1]

Like earlier dissenters William Harold proclaimed that "a higher interest is now at issue than that of a persecuted individual"—nothing less than the character and reputation of Catholicism. "It is in the very nature of man," Harold wrote, "when once raised above the level of his fellow creatures, to imagine the short road of absolute power to be the best for attaining the ends of government [,] and the temptation to overlook the sufferings to which others become subjected in the operation of the system . . . is so insidious" that none can resist it. Echoing Thadeus O'Meally's words, Harold argued that those who served as well as their rulers would be corrupted. Priests and laymen would be shorn of "every principle of honest candour," men of high moral stature would be driven out of the Church, and only those who lacked honor and moral sensibilities would willingly submit to "the mere whim of any individual." "Such men," he wrote, "would become fit for any purpose however wicked in the hands of a bishop." Should this ensue, Harold argued, the reputation of the Church must be destroyed. He warned of "the ruinous effects which the present system must produce, on the moral character of our Clergy, on the religious character of our people, and on the reputation of the Catholic religion among the good people of the United States already too much prejudiced against it."[2]

Like others who had served at St. Mary's, William V. Harold proposed constitutional restraints on episcopal power. "I was aware how little defined the system of our ecclesiastical government in the United States is," he wrote to Archbishop Maréchal, "yet no authority exists . . . to check an evil so enormous, as [Bishop Conwell's] avowed act of absolute power, until that authority which is five thousand miles distant from us, can be brought to bear on the case.[3]

Such a system of rule, he argued, was neither "suited to the actual constitution of" the American churches, nor "the most expedient for the interests of religion" in the United States. America was not some primitive land, nor was the Church there a marginal institution staffed by lonely missionaries, Harold wrote: "our bishops are in every canonical sense ordinaries: our Churches are as much diocesan as those of France or Italy." It followed, then, that the same constitutional protections accorded to the lower clergy in the national churches of Europe should be applied in America. He protested, "in no country . . . , *except in these United States,* is it pretended that the clergy of the Second Order are removable at will from their pastoral office." He argued that the need for such constitutional limitations and rights of appeal was imperative because, until such reforms were put into practice, "no Roman Catholic Clergyman in America can be secure against the most wanton outrage on his reputation, on his peace of mind, on every best feeling of his nature."[4]

To this point William Harold's arguments resembled those of John England, with whom he had been in correspondence for some time. Both held that constitutional restraints were necessary and were fully in accord with Catholic doctrine and traditions. Although few members of the American hierarchy would have recognized any effective limits on their own powers and none was willing to follow England's lead in constitution-making, they would not have found Harold's demand that priests be allowed to appeal episcopal decisions to be particularly innovative or threatening. However, William Harold in his anger went far beyond anything that could be tolerated either in the American episcopacy or in Rome—he threatened to take his case into the civil courts.

Harold wrote to Archbishop Maréchal charging him with blatant bias against Irish clergymen and avowing his "firm determination . . . to maintain my rights at a tribunal where I have reason to expect justice and equity." "I am not unknown," he proclaimed, "I am a Citizen of the United States." He declared that "The power of banishing an American citizen under the cloak of spiritual right, is a species of tyranny for which this country is not yet prepared. If this [power] be . . . claimed by the Catholic Bishops in this free land . . . , it will not be endured." Moreover, he argued, his "appointment, as Pastor of St. Mary's," was "a civil contract" which could not be voided by ecclesiastical fiat. Here Harold was treading on dangerous ground and Archbishop Maréchal wrote to warn him that "immovability and irrevocable powers" such as he was claiming, were "inconsistent with the very nature of missions." Once again the archbishop asserted that he had no jurisdiction in the Philadelphia affair and refused to admit Harold's appeal.[5]

Since Archbishop Maréchal refused to involve himself in the affair, participants on all sides increasingly looked to Rome. Bishop Conwell felt that he had nothing to fear from the Holy See. He fully expected Propaganda to disapprove the concessions he had made to the dissenters in October of 1826. In fact, as he explained to Archbishop Maréchal, the certainty that Rome would never tolerate lay interference in the appointment of pastors had provided him with the freedom to make such concessions in the first place. They were, he told Patrick Kenny, "not worth a straw." His actions, Conwell felt, had been fully justified by the circumstances and this would certainly be understood at Propaganda. As for William Harold and his supporters, he wrote, "Rome knows them sufficiently to put no Confidence in them."[6]

Bishop Conwell had been complaining to Propaganda about William Harold and John Ryan since the summer of 1826 and had on several occasions asked that they either be admonished or removed from his diocese. Conwell was convinced that, should William Harold remain in Philadelphia, the schism would resume with even greater disruption than before. After the priest's suspension he began a long correspondence with Rome insisting time and again that Propaganda prevail upon the superior of the Dominicans to reassign the two men out of the diocese. Several members of the diocesan clergy also wrote in support of the bishop's request. Michael Hurley, in particular, was insistent that Harold's ambitions to accede to the episcopacy (which he held to be the root of all the difficulties) be frustrated.[7]

William Harold and his supporters countered these criticisms with appeals to Baltimore, Rome, and to other members of the American hierarchy. On June 14, 1827, Harold officially lodged a protest with Propaganda against the suspension of his faculties, denouncing not only Bishop Conwell but also Archbishop Maréchal, to whom he had appealed in vain. He also protested to the superior of his order who passed his objections on to the Propaganda. "If the authority of Rome restore me," Harold wrote, "it will be in vindication of the *principle,* that no Bishop exercises *legitimate* power when he tramples on the laws of charity, of equity and of justice"[8]

Harold's lay supporters also sent letters. On May 12, a lay committee wrote to Propaganda complaining about Bishop Conwell's conduct in general. They pointed to the bishop's habit of suspending lower clergy without giving reason and raised the question of his competence. They asked that the Sacred Congregation intervene to reinstate William Harold and to remove Bishop Conwell, whom they considered "incapable, and disqualified to exercise the functions, or enjoy the dignity of the episcopal office." Should this result in the see being vacant, they further asked that they not be placed under the direction of Michael Hurley, the bishop's strongest supporter among the clergy and William Harold's most outspoken critic. These specific requests were but the prelude to far more significant ones. They asked that Rome institute regulations that would make clerical appointments permanent. Only by doing so and instituting "a mode of trial" for clerics, they said, could the Holy See "annul the abuse by which it is now sought to hold the Second Order of the Priesthood in a state of servitude, not to the Canons, not to any law, but to absolute mastery." They further protested against the "cabalistic title" of "mission" applied to the American church for it had been invoked to justify the exercise of arbitrary power in ways that would never have been tolerated in Europe.[9]

This petition (signed by prominent dissenters and bishopites alike) marks an important shift in the position of St. Mary's lay leadership. They were no longer relying on democratic procedures and principles such as the right of appointment as a defense against arbitrary authority (that had been denied them by the highest tribunal in the Church). Now they demanded the institution of constitutional safeguards. Their point of reference in making this appeal was no longer the American civil tradition or the liberal movements that were challenging constituted authorities through the West but the national churches of Europe wherein restrictions on episcopal action guaranteed the rights of lower clergy against arbitrary authority.[10]

Once again the indefatigable Richard W. Meade, now in the last months of his life, took arms to battle arbitrary authority. He wrote to Bishop Louis DuBourg of Louisiana enumerating his objections to Bishop Conwell and asked DuBourg to support the petition to Rome asking for Conwell's removal. DuBourg, who had already had some experience with the situation in Philadelphia, passed Meade's objections on to the Propaganda with favorable comments. The fundamental question raised by Richard Meade and others who supported William Harold's cause was that of Bishop Conwell's competence. They argued that the bishop's repeated suspension and excommunication of lower clergy represented a pattern of abuse of his position and possibly indicated mental incompetence. These were matters of some concern to authorities in America and Rome, but they were not sufficient to bring about Conwell's removal. What brought Henry Conwell's rule to an end was a quite different consideration.[11]

"Fatal Articles of Peace"

By July of 1827 St. Mary's lay leadership was largely united in support of William V. Harold. John Hughes, still unswerving in his support of the bishop, observed at the beginning of that month that "the Trustees have nearly all passed over to the opposition and it is not worth while looking after them." At a meeting on July 10 the trustees of St. Mary's passed a resolution declaring that Bishop Conwell was "in direct contradiction to the spirit and intent" of the articles of agreement signed the previous October. In that document the bishop had acknowledged the "right of the Trustees to recommend suitable persons as Pastors" and William Harold had been so recommended and installed and so, they held, could not be removed. They then forwarded the resolution as a petition to Rome.[1]

The trustees' petition illustrated the fundamental weakness of Henry Conwell's position. He had been convinced that concessions made to the dissenters in the October compact were of little consequence since his lay opponents had agreed to abide by the decision of Rome, but several of his colleagues believed, and so informed Propaganda, that the agreement ending the schism at St. Mary's constituted a dangerous precedent of lay interference with episcopal authority. Like Bishop Conwell, his critics were convinced that matters in Philadelphia had reached a point of crisis by 1827, but they absolutely disagreed with his means of dealing with the difficulties. They felt that the "fatal articles of peace," as Simon Bruté termed them, would ultimately exacerbate rather than quell lay dissent. Bruté spoke for many when he opined that "it was evident that, sooner or later, evil would again come out of them." The declaration that William Harold could not be suspended because the articles of agreement prohibited arbitrary actions on the part of the bishop represented, to the minds of many, just such an evil as they had feared. The Holy See, too, saw evil in the accord.[2]

Bishop Conwell's first communications to Propaganda after the accord of October 1826 had not specified the terms of the agreement. He simply informed Rome that peace had been restored in his diocese.

It was not until March of the following year that he finally forwarded a copy of the articles of agreement along with an accompanying document in which the trustees pledged to be bound by Rome's decision. A few days later he followed this with a second copy of the agreement and a note stressing that the pact was conditional and would be rendered null and void if judged to be contrary to the canons of the Church. By this time William Harold had already sent copies of the agreement to the Holy See along with critical commentary, and opposition to it had developed within the American hierarchy.[3]

The first to make his feelings known was Archbishop Maréchal. On November 16 he wrote to Propaganda objecting to the agreement and urging that Bishop Conwell be encouraged "to accept transfer to the first vacant see in Ireland." Other members of the American hierarchy overwhelmingly concurred with Maréchal's opinion. John England wrote in the *Catholic Miscellany* that "the greater number of the American Bishops . . . , immediately upon learning the tenor of the agreement distinctly and unequivocally declared it incompatible with the discipline of the Roman Catholic Church, and the principles contained in it contrary to her doctrine." What is more, England wrote, they believed, "that the Bishop of Philadelphia, . . . exceeded his powers, and acted incompatibly with the constitution of the Church." He denied that the Philadelphia "covenant" had any legal standing within the church.[4]

Over the next several months Archbishop Maréchal kept Propaganda informed concerning the situation in Philadelphia. He was of the opinion that "as long as Bishop Conwell remains bishop there is no ground for hoping that religion can ever flourish; [it] is to be feared . . . that . . . faith and piety will be totally uprooted from the hearts of the faithful." Maréchal was aware that Henry Conwell longed to leave Philadelphia and was awaiting only an opportunity to assume an episcopal chair in Ireland. "I have one in contemplation," Conwell had told the archbishop, "the ordinary is 90 years old—and the majority of priests, 300 in number—will postulate for me if the diocese were vacant." This seemed to Maréchal to be the best solution to the Philadelphia problem and he repeatedly urged Propaganda to reassign Conwell to his homeland. But behind these considerations there lurked in the mind of the archbishop of Baltimore a broader agenda.[5]

Ambrose Maréchal, like John Carroll in his later years, was distressed by the fact that Propaganda had taken complete control of episcopal appointments in America and was constantly extending its influence in the mission. He saw Henry Conwell's failure in Philadelphia as an argument against further Roman appointments to the American episcopacy. Early in April 1827 he wrote to the Holy See decrying the current system of choosing bishops for America. He deplored the fact that most recent appointments had been Irish and strongly urged that some formal set of procedures be established that would allow American bishops some say in future appointments. Time and again in his correspondence with the Holy See Maréchal returned to this theme of the need for formal nominating procedures involving the American bishops, but Rome was following a different agenda.[6]

The constant stream of charges, countercharges, and complaints arising out of the Philadelphia disputes only inclined Propaganda to take a more, rather than a less, active role in American affairs. In the spring of 1827 Michael Egan, president of Mount St. Mary's Seminary in Emmitsburg, Maryland, wrote to John Hughes warning him, "if the bishop and trustees do not change [the articles of agreement], I know from the highest authority that Rome will." He added, "there is a storm, I am afraid, gathering in the Vatican, which will burst on the good old bishop." Soon thereafter Rome moved on the matters in Philadelphia.[7]

What concerned Propaganda most was Bishop Conwell's compact with the dissenters. In March of 1827 a copy of the agreement circulated widely through the Roman Curia and recommendations were solicited. Propaganda agreed with the American bishops that Conwell's pact with the trustees set a dangerous precedent and could not be allowed to stand. The agreement was repudiated by the General Congregation on April 30 and one week later Pope Leo XII approved Propaganda's decision. On May 19 letters were sent from Rome informing Bishop Conwell and all his colleagues that the compact was "altogether reprobated" by both Propaganda and the pope. The letters arrived in America early in July.[8]

On July 20 Bishop Conwell informed the trustees of St. Mary's that the articles of agreement were "formally condemned and declared null and void." Two days later he addressed the congregation to tell them that both Propaganda and pope had declared the articles to be "uncatholic and uncanonical, and consequently null and void." The new, conservative trustees took the condemnation with good grace. They wrote to Pope Leo XII offering their apologies for their actions and proclaiming their loyalty both to him and to the canons of the Church. In the same letter, though, they renewed their petition for the removal of Bishop Conwell and suggested that he be replaced by someone who was "already known" to them and who enjoyed their "confidence and veneration." That person, of course, was William V. Harold.[9]

Rather than being chagrined by Rome's intervention, Conwell was overjoyed. "I have received a document from the Propaganda," he told Archbishop Maréchal, "than which nothing can give me greater pleasure." Conwell believed that the Holy See had vindicated him and the position he had been arguing since his arrival in Philadelphia. Peace had been achieved and no essential principles conceded. The agreement had embodied the dissenters' ideas with regard to church government and now it had been denounced by the highest authorities. Altogether, he considered this to be a satisfactory resolution to the long conflict. He wrote, "indeed the best effects have long since resulted from [the compact], for it has prevented a schism which might have been incurable." To the prefect of Propaganda he expressed his gratitude for the decision and opined that "the rejection of this Pact, will, no doubt, be of great advantage to religion," for, though "evil was done . . . good has certainly resulted. The good that I experience is the possession of St. Mary's Church."[10]

The cardinals of Propaganda did not take so sanguine a view of the situation. The innumerable complaints made against Conwell over several years had finally begun to have an effect. On June 16, 1827, Propaganda informed Conwell that it would be "inexpedient" to remove the two Dominicans from his diocese. Nine days later the papal secretary of state wrote to the prefect of Propaganda regarding Harold's complaints and urging prompt attention to the matter. He enclosed a large packet of materials collected by Harold to bolster his case, including several complaints against Conwell written by prominent laymen. Propaganda acceded to the secretary's wishes and agreed to deal with the entire Philadelphia situation in a General Congregation which met on July 30, 1827. The decision of the cardinals, ratified six days later by the pope, was a devastating defeat for Henry Conwell.[11]

On August 11, 1827, the secretary of Propaganda wrote to inform Bishop Conwell that his oft-repeated desire to return to Ireland could not be allowed unless he first resigned his position as bishop of Philadelphia. Should he decide not to resign and return to Ireland Conwell could alternatively come to Rome. Under no conditions was he to remain in Philadelphia. The administration of his diocese would be assumed by Archbishop Maréchal, who was being ordered to absolve

William Harold and John Ryan of all censures and to reinstate them as pastors of St. Mary's.[12]

Harold Defiant

Propaganda's direct intervention did not resolve matters in Philadelphia, though a deceptive calm descended on the city's Catholic community. Early in 1828 John Hughes noted that "there seems at present a subtraction of that fuel on which the flame of discord has fed so long," but he also wrote that "the parties, and the friends, and the enemies, and above all the approaching election" for trustees all "give just cause of apprehension that disturbance will revive." Hints of troubles to come were already apparent in complications that emerged in the first days after receipt of Rome's instructions.[1]

Propaganda had hoped to transfer administration of the diocese to Ambrose Maréchal, but the archbishop died on January 29, 1828, and his successor, James Whitfield, was not confirmed until March of that year. In this unsettled situation it was impossible for Baltimore to effectively oversee affairs in Philadelphia. Propaganda finally appointed William Matthews, a parish priest from Washington, as "Vicar General Apostolic." Bishop Conwell also complicated matters by refusing to leave Philadelphia. At first he simply took no notice of the order to go to Rome. For several months he remained in the city and his presence confused further the question of administration in the troubled diocese.[2]

Bishop Conwell did comply with Rome's dictates so far as to reinstall William Harold and John Ryan as pastors at St. Mary's and to reinstate their faculties, but even here complications ensued. Harold and Ryan gladly returned to St. Mary's but made it clear that they were not acting at the direction of the bishop. They refused to recognize Conwell's orders because they considered that he had no authority to assign or remove them. In their minds they had never been legally suspended from their posts. The trustees, too, objected. Although they received William Harold and John Ryan as their pastors they insisted that the bishop had no power to order the priests into their church without first consulting with them.[3]

Both Harold and the lay leaders based their claim to independence from Bishop Conwell's authority on the agreement he had earlier signed with the dissenters. Although this had been thoroughly repudiated by the Holy See, Harold argued that it was a civil contract and as such was not subject to review by ecclesiastical authorities. By this logic neither Bishop Conwell nor any other ecclesiastical authority could remove the Dominicans, once installed, from St. Mary's. Needless to say, Propaganda found this line of argument more than a little disturbing. Even more bothersome was Harold's willingness to use civil authority against his clerical critics.[4]

Shortly before suspending Harold's faculties in April 1827, Bishop Conwell had solicited from members of the diocesan clergy a statement approving his actions. Harold had responded with a law suit against his colleagues charging them with defamation of character. These suits were soon dropped but even so they shocked authorities on both sides of the Atlantic. "Philadelphia is in dreadful confusion," Archbishop Maréchal wrote, "Mr. Harold has sued eight young clergymen. . . . This act of violence . . . has given great scandal. [There can be] no peace as long as he remains in Philadelphia." Early in September the secretary of Propaganda wrote to the archbishop expressing the Congregation's dismay at hearing of Harold's suit and urging him to impress on Harold and Ryan the gravity of the matter. Such appeals to civil authority, Propaganda held, must never be sanctioned. Soon officials in Rome were beginning to reconsider their decision to reinstall William Harold and John Ryan in their positions at St. Mary's.[5]

William Harold's return did not bring peace to St. Mary's congregation. No sooner had he been installed than the disparate coalition of interests that had come together to oppose "episcopal despotism" collapsed into what John Hughes termed "petty broils of contending rivals." In general this dispute pitted William Harold's personal following against those who, despite their misgivings about Bishop Conwell, still adhered to the formal strictures of church government. This was not primarily a struggle over ideology; it was far more a matter of class and culture. Harold's strongest support came, as it always had, from the immigrant working classes, and in 1828 he sought once more to rouse them to take control of the temporalities of the church. The election was hotly contested. John Hughes wrote that "the parties . . . looked upon . . . the approaching election . . . with more intense feeling and interest than that for president." This time Harold was stymied by the amendments to the church charter which prohibited pew packing and the "respectable" classes carried the day. In the wake of the election, though, Harold and Ryan began to make preparations for the following year. They personally rented a block of forty pews and distributed them to their friends and so "got a slight advantage . . . in order to have a better election next year.[6]

Through all this contention protests and denunciations continued to pour in to the Holy See. There, doubts concerning Harold and Ryan were mounting and it had become apparent that Henry Conwell intended to remain in Philadelphia so long as the Dominicans were at St. Mary's "because their remaining in Philadelphia after his departure would be considered as a triumph over him." Finally, Rome decided to remove all of the principals from the scene. On March 8, 1828, the prefect of Propaganda informed Bishop Conwell that William Matthews had been appointed as vicar-general apostolic. He wrote, "His Holiness expects you to come to Rome without delay." William Harold and John Ryan were informed that "it is [the pope]s earnest wish, that [you] both depart out of the diocese of Philadelphia [and] that you both proceed to . . . Cincinnati." The vicar-general of the Dominican order also wrote to Harold ordering him to obey the pope's dictates.[7]

Bishop Conwell immediately bowed to superior authority. On June 25 he formally notified the board of trustees at St. Mary's that William Matthews would be serving as their new pastor and on July 15 he set sail from New York for Rome. St. Mary's lay leaders, after some discussion, also accepted the directive of the Holy See without protest. Harold and Ryan, though, decided to resist the order. They appealed to Baltimore, but that gained them no satisfaction. They then personally appealed their case to William Matthews. The vicar, too, gave Harold and Ryan no relief. Then on July 16 they returned to Philadelphia and took up their pastoral duties at St. Mary's in defiance of the Holy See. Five days later William Matthews, in his official capacity as administrator and vicar-apostolic, suspended the two priests' faculties, depriving them "of all jurisdiction in the Diocese of Philadelphia."[8]

In a long letter to Propaganda Harold and Ryan detailed the reasons for their defiance. What concerned them most was their reputation.

They indignantly wrote, "when the Sacred Congregation ordered us to leave the Diocese of Philadelphia and pass to the State of Ohio . . . the Delegate of the Holy See took care to make [our humiliation] public throughout the whole of America. The loss of reputation we will not bear . . . , we will not go forth from Philadelphia branded with the reproach of exile." [9]

Harold and Ryan attempted to take refuge in their status as American citizens. "The sentence of removal" they declared, was something "no foreign prince is allowed to pass upon an American citizen. . . . We could not obey without violating the loyalty we have sworn to the Republic." They raised the bogey of Protestant intolerance. "This people," they wrote, "is English in origin and customs. Though they tolerate, they detest our religion . . . they despise all foreigners as if they were slaves." He warned, "Let the most eminent Fathers be careful, therefore, that nothing be done to excite this people." Already, they said, Roman interference had "greatly disturbed the minds of men, and the enemies of the Holy See made a great outcry." In the circumstances, since Rome "had violated the majesty of the Republic" and brought opprobrium upon the Church, "it became our duty to so act that Catholics might be preserved from any suspicion of a divided allegiance." They therefore determined, on the advice of lawyers, that "the matter should be referred to the President [of the United States], whose place it is to vindicate the majesty of the Republic and to preserve the rights of its citizens uninjured." "This cause is no longer ours," they proclaimed, "but that of our country, which allows no one to be oppressed." [10]

By the time they fired off their protest to Rome, William Harold and John Ryan had already taken steps to protect themselves. On July 2, 1828, Harold wrote to Secretary of State Henry Clay enclosing a copy of the papal mandate which he declared to be an "infraction of [his] rights, as a citizen of the United States." He wrote, "for me . . . to set the example of obeying the mandate . . . would be neither consistent with my principles as a Catholic, nor with the spirit and letter of my sworn allegiance to the Constitution of the United States." If "such an interference in the personal freedom of the citizens of these United States" were to be "obeyed or tolerated" then "the whole order of the priesthood of our church" would be "at the complete and irresponsible disposal of the Court of Rome." [11]

This, Harold argued, was no trivial matter. The injunction implied "consequences which do not belong to religious discipline, so much as they do to political power . . . which the Court of Rome is not without the means of inflicting even in this country." He asked for "the protection of the President against this . . . invasion of [his] private rights"; and he begged the secretary to inform Rome that the United States would protect his "undoubted right" to remain in Philadelphia, and prevent "any attempt to abridge . . . this liberty, by either the menace or the infliction of injury." In a separate attachment John Ryan "humbly claim[ed] the same protection" and denounced the "injunctions from Rome, as interfering with the civil rights and institutions of the United States."[12]

Daniel Brent, assistant secretary of state, handled the appeals. He forwarded copies of Harold and Ryan's letters to President Adams and, since the United States had no representative in Rome, asked James Brown, minister to France, to contact the papal nuncio at Paris regarding the matter. As always the American government was careful not to give offense to or to interfere with the internal integrity of the Church. Brown's instructions specifically warned him against any word or action that could be construed "in the remotest degree [as being] unfriendly to the exercise of the legitimate spiritual authority of the See of Rome over the Catholic Church in the United States." So eager was Brent to please Catholic authorities that when William Matthews asked him for information on the matter he willingly released even confidential letters into the administrator's hands. These materials were then "circulated widely" in Philadelphia, New York, and other places where, Harold and Ryan complained, they were "handed about among the idle, the ignorant, and the malignant and their whole nature and tendency so distorted, that [they were] . . . exposed to every kind of misrepresentations."[13]

News of Harold and Ryan's appeal sent shock waves through the Holy See. Hugh Nolan states that "it is doubtful if any incident in the American Church up to that time caused Rome more consternation and concern than the appeal made to the government of the United States by the two Dominicans." Rome's concerns were twofold: the appeal threatened to rupture the good relations that had prevailed between the Church and the American government, but more importantly Propaganda worried that the government's response to the appeal might set a dangerous precedent "permitting state interference in ecclesiastical appointments in the United States."[14]

The Holy See instructed the nuncio to meet with Brown to explain "how unreasonable and unjust" Harold and Ryan's charges were so that the entire episode might pass "without effect." The matter was considered so urgent that he was to drop all other business until it was settled. The nuncio assured Brown that Rome "had neither the right nor the disposition in any way to abridge the rights, or interfere with the temporal concerns of citizens of the United States, or to exercise any other than spiritual authority over any person under their protection." The pope "neither menaced [Harold and Ryan] with temporal pains nor intended to inflict other than spiritual punishment." He promised that, should Harold and Ryan proceed to Cincinnati, he would take it as his personal responsibility to see that "no evil treatment would await them." Brown explained in turn that, the president had no interest in "any questions touching the doctrines or discipline of the Catholic Church, nor the spiritual supremacy of the Holy See." The nuncio, however, was not reassured. He came away from the meeting with the conviction that William Harold was highly esteemed in America, even by President Adams, who admired the Dominican's literary skills. "The two religious," he wrote, "especially Harold, are regarded as prominent citizens . . . and have great influence and the protection of the government." Alarmed by the nuncio's report, the pope and his secretary of state both held personal interviews with the American consul in Rome in which they "particularly and repeatedly" urged him to assure the government of the United States that Rome "will never interfere in politics."[15]

The Adams administration considered the matter to be "satisfactorily closed," but the Holy See persisted in its efforts to obtain from the government a clear statement recognizing the authority of the pope over American clergy. In addition to formal diplomatic exchanges Propaganda directed American churchmen to use their influence to resolve the matter favorably. At Propaganda's urging William Matthews wrote twice to Henry Clay emphasizing that Rome's action against the Dominicans was "an exercise of purely spiritual jurisdiction." "In no manner," he asserted, was this authority "connected with the rights of the citizen." "Can our [civil] government interfere in matters purely religious?" he asked, and provided the answer, "most certainly not!" Rome also asked Archbishop Whitfield to write directly to President Adams assuring him that "no infringement of civil rights was meant in transferring the two religious since they had vowed obedience to their ecclesiastical superiors." John England was ordered to contact Harold and Ryan to convince them to acquiesce to Rome's dictates.[16]

Bishop England was shocked to learn of William Harold's appeal to civil authority and was dismayed that the government had responded even to the limited extent that it did. In England's opinion President Adams, by even inquiring into the matter and asking the Holy See to review the case, had "interfered in the concerns of the Church in a way in which he neither could nor ought." In order to "guard against similar interference in the future" England fired off a letter to the newly-elected president, Andrew Jackson, in which he put forth the strongest possible argument for a rigid wall of separation between civil and religious authority.[17]

"The spiritual and ecclesiastical supremacy of the Pope," England wrote, "is an essential portion of the Roman Catholic religion. Any attempt to overawe this [exercise of authority] is . . . such an interference with the Roman Catholic religion . . . as the Constitution . . . forbids." Should the pope attempt to exert temporal power within the United States, England said, "the constituted authorities of the several states are fully competent . . . to protect their citizens." Since no state had instituted legal proceedings in the Harold affair, he concluded the federal government had no "constitutional ground for its interference." He declared that should the government intervene in favor of the Dominicans it "would be the commencement of a union of church and state, as well as an unconstitutional meddling with the affairs of our ecclesiastical body, productive of serious mischief to ourselves."[18]

Bishop England even solicited opinions on the matter from eminent jurists. From Roger Taney he obtained an opinion to the effect that since the pope's authority was an essential feature of the Catholic religion interference with the exercise of that authority would violate "the civil rights of those citizens of the United States who are members of the Roman Catholic Church." Taney concluded, the pope's "spiritual jurisdiction should be freely exercised, and the government of the United States has no right to restrain it, nor to interfere with it." William Gaston of North Carolina concurred. He wrote, "The Bishop of Rome is the acknowledged head of the Roman Catholic Church, and as such must have a jurisdiction of some sort over it. Jurisdiction implies obedience." He concluded that "the right of a citizen cannot be infringed by a requisition which he may disobey if his conscience will permit"; therefore, "the aid of the government is not needed to protect him against admonitions addressed to his conscience."[19]

England's last effort was a personal interview with Andrew Jackson on September 27, 1830, during which the bishop was assured by the president that the government's views on the matter coincided with his own.

Taken together with the decisions of other individuals and government agencies, Jackson's statement to Bishop England represented a decisive victory for ecclesiastical authorities. William Harold's appeal to civil authority had ended, like those of earlier dissenters, in a sweeping confirmation of the corporate nature of religious freedoms. The battle had been fought at the local, state, and national level, in the courts, the legislatures, and in the federal executive, and the outcome had always been the same—the regularly constituted leaders of the American church, when faced with challenges from dissenting individuals and groups, had been confirmed in the exercise of their authority. This did not mean that voices of dissent would not be raised in the future, but the hope, cherished by generations of dissenters, that the Church in the United States would be responsive to and could be made to conform to values inherent in the American civil tradition had been dealt a decisive blow.[20]

Conwell Returns

William Harold was bitter in defeat. He protested to Henry Clay that, should Rome prevail, "under the plea of spiritual obedience, it is difficult to perceive within what limits that power can be circumscribed." To a friend in Ireland he confided his understanding that his downfall had been brought about by the "cunning and dishonesty" of the Jesuits. To Bishop England he denounced the American mission as "a Church without law, and a priesthood without rights." Doggedly he resisted any attempts to dislodge him from Philadelphia, where he enjoyed the support of many influential laymen.[1]

On April 21, 1829, Propaganda sent an ultimatum to Harold and Ryan ordering them to leave Philadelphia within fifteen days. John Ryan gave up the fight. He left Philadelphia for Ireland early in August 1829. Harold, however, remained. John Keating, a wealthy textile manufacturer and a former leader of the bishopite faction, offered to build a church for the Dominican in the village of Manayunk, outside the Philadelphia city limits. This, Harold said, would satisfy the technical requirement that he leave Philadelphia, but Propaganda learned of his intentions and again ordered him out of the diocese. Finally, after months of delay, William V. Harold departed Philadelphia never to return. On September 20, 1829, he took ship for Liverpool and from thence to Ireland and there he remained.[2]

Shortly before Harold left the country, forty-two eminent laymen signed a letter praising his "eloquence in the pulpit, the cogency of [his] reasoning, and the impressive manner of [his] preaching." These virtues, they said, placed Harold, "by the common consent of the most intelligent of our citizens, not only of the Roman Catholics, but of all other denominations, among the first class of pulpit orators in this city." Mathew Carey also organized a public meeting of the "Association of the Friends of Ireland" which petitioned the pope to restore Harold to them. These testimonials were significant. They marked the last efforts of the remarkable coalition that had developed to support William Harold after his dismissal. It included members of the old Anglo- and Irish-American elite, many of the "new made gentlemen and ladies," and numerous Irish immigrant workers. This was a tenuous combination, held together by the force of William Harold's personality and a common resentment of arbitrary and absolute authority. It could not long survive Harold's departure.[3]

If the laity were distraught by Harold's fate, the clergy were elated. John Hughes, upon hearing that Harold and Ryan had been ordered out of the diocese wrote, "The shepherds [of the people] . . . have all *preached* obedience to lawful authority, but now it is in their power to *preach effectually* by the practice of their own doctrine. I trust they will." When he heard of the Dominicans' resistance he wrote, "they beg the President to interpose the shield of government between them and their spiritual superiors! Hogan *talked* about it, but they have *done* it. . . . Both are anti-Catholic and diabolical." In similar terms Michael Hurley railed against the Dominicans' "treason . . . against legitimate authority" and applauded the Holy See's actions to bring them to heel.[4]

The clergy overwhelmingly wanted Bishop Conwell to reassume control of his diocese. John Power, a priest in New York who met regularly with his colleagues in Philadelphia, urged Conwell to "come back as quickly as possible." "The only wish," he wrote, "that is uttered by both parties . . . is that you would return." John Hughes was outraged at Bishop Conwell's treatment and worried about the consequences for the church if a bishop could be removed at the request of a faction. The Holy See, he feared, by removing Conwell had "given a precedent to which the restless spirit of republicanism, so prevalent in this country, will appeal on all future similar occasions." Several times in 1829 members of the resident clergy petitioned Rome through William Matthews asking for their bishop's return. Michael Hurley claimed that "the great majority of the people" hoped for Conwell's return.[5]

Upon his arrival in Rome, Henry Conwell had been granted a pension, a servant, new clothing, and living quarters at Monte Citorio. "The S. Cong[ratio].n received me most kindly," he wrote, "and support me in the Style of a Prince." At first he showed no interest in ever returning to Philadelphia and hoped to soon be transferred to a see in Ireland, but communications from America and conditions in Rome soon changed his mind. He found that he could not support himself "like a Prince" on the stipend that had been granted him and he came to resent Propaganda's insistence that he never return to Philadelphia. Harold's behavior, he complained, "was a crime"; his "was a duty." It was unjust that he be subjected "to the same penalty as Harold and Ryan." It was unfair that they "should be equally punished."[6]

Early in April, Propaganda learned of Conwell's dissatisfaction and determined to prevent him from returning to Philadelphia. Soon, Conwell wrote, "everywhere there were rumors, even in America and especially in Washington, that it had been decided to keep me here in Rome for my whole life." When Cardinal Cappellari and William Matthews attempted to dissuade the aged bishop from returning to America, their efforts simply confirmed his suspicions and, he said, "made me afraid." Conwell "made a resolution to leave Rome at [his] first chance." Shortly after midnight on April 19, Easter Sunday, Henry Conwell departed Rome and headed for Paris where he took up residence in the Irish College of that city.[7]

As soon as Conwell was missed, Propaganda sent letters to all his potential destinations warning him that his episcopal jurisdiction would be suspended if he should return to Philadelphia. Conwell received a copy of this notice in Leghorn and again in Paris. Soon thereafter the prefect of Propaganda gave Conwell permission to travel freely anywhere in Europe, but not to America, on penalty of suspension. "Your return to Philadelphia," he wrote, "will contribute to trouble and not to peace. The Sacred Congregation will decide whether and when your return is necessary." Despite these warnings and admonitions, Conwell was determined to return to America which, he wrote (ironically echoing the protests of his old adversaries), "is my country and of whose government I am a citizen." Anywhere else, he said, he would be regarded as a stranger. He declared, "I must go to America, let the consequences be what they may. The people will support me." In August 1829 Henry Conwell took ship for America, whereupon Propaganda immediately fired off a letter to William Matthews ordering him, as administrator of Philadelphia, to suspend Conwell and deprive him of all jurisdiction as soon as he set foot in the country.[8]

The diocese to which Bishop Conwell returned was remarkably quiet. The departure of William Harold and John Ryan, the repudiation of the dissenters' positions by Rome and by American civil authorities, and Conwell's absence had left little to fight about. It was clear that all significant decisions would be made in Rome, not in Philadelphia, and the result was what John Hughes described as "the quietude of suspense" as all awaited word from the Holy See. Still, there was much to worry ecclesiastical authorities. William Matthews, the current administrator, was "not popular with the people and the clergy" in Philadelphia and he spent as little time there as possible. Archbishop Whitfield noted that Matthew "resides almost always in Washington, going to Philadelphia three or four times a year for a few days only." Ecclesiastical authority was thus little felt in Philadelphia and it was feared that "there still exists in [Conwell's] flock, a strong leaven, which, were any imprudence committed, would excite a more dangerous, because, a second fermentation. . . ."[9]

The Provincial Council

━━━➤〉-❍-〈◀━━━

In the spring of 1829 Archbishop Whitfield advised Rome that immediate action was necessary. "The situation in Philadelphia is such that it cannot admit of delay," he wrote. Propaganda responded, "The Sacred Congregation desires nothing more ardently than that the affairs of that diocese be settled as soon as possible so that everything might be put in the correct and lawful order." The prefect then suggested that Archbishop Whitfield consult with his suffragan bishops and "send in writing what you think should be done to restore right order and prosperity to that diocese."[1]

Archbishop Whitfield had already issued a call for his suffragan bishops and administrators to meet in Baltimore in October 1829 for the first provincial council of the American bishops. This was a defining moment in American church history. It has been argued that the council represented an important step toward the emergence of a distinctively American church but it more clearly reflected the growing influence of Rome in America. The bishops were, in James Hennesey's words, "substantially . . . ultramontane," taking direction in all spiritual matters from the Holy See, although (because of William V. Harold's appeal to civil authority which had raised the question of divided loyalty) they were careful to note that this allegiance did not extend to civil matters. It is clear that in their deliberations the bishops followed Rome's lead. In the words of one commentator, the 1829 council was "the momentous hour . . . when regular and strong relations were forged with Rome."[2]

As early as 1819 Propaganda had begun to consider ways to effectively enforce episcopal authority on the mission. Early in the following year a commission of five cardinals issued a series of recommendations that formed the basis upon which were based several "regulations and instructions concerning the choice and direction of trustees." These regulations were issued in 1822 in conjunction with the apostolic brief *Non sine magno*, described by Patrick Carey as "the most important and the foundational papal response to trusteeism in America." *Quo longius*, issued in 1828, elaborated the indictment of trusteeism. Taken together, these briefs and regulations not only repudiated liberalism within the Church but also established procedures to be followed in combating liberal tendencies.[3]

Propaganda recommended that bishops should attempt to influence the election of trustees so as to choose only those men who would be properly subservient to episcopal authority and who would recognize the freedom of clergymen from lay control. Once elected, trustees should be required to take an oath of loyalty to their bishop, to promise to be bound by ecclesiastical laws, and to render an account of their administration to him. When new churches were constructed bishops were to secure title to all church property so as to erect legal barriers to lay interference in church affairs. In churches where the institution of trusteeism was protected by legal charters bishops should attempt to force a change in the charter allowing the clergy to appoint the members of the board. If the congregation insisted on having an elected board of trustees, bishops should require a legal contract that would guarantee episcopal prerogatives as well as free access for the clergy to the church building and all ecclesiastical properties. Should the parishioners object, bishops were instructed to refuse to bless the church or to assign it a pastor.[4]

Propaganda's regulations and the apostolic briefs clearly influenced the 1829 provincial council. The bishops decreed that, "in the future, no church shall be built or consecrated unless, wherever possible, it be given in written deed to the bishop of the diocese in which it is located." They also declared that "no right of patronage . . . is possessed by any person, congregation of laymen, group of trustees or by anyone else in this Province." The council also admonished all bishops to "protect religion, the peace of the Church, and the dignity of the sacerdotal state . . . by revoking immediately the faculties of any cleric [who] . . . has been the author or the accomplice in any fashion [of a lay insurgency]." Finally, the bishops urged that "if [any] congregation or society of trustees should impede the work of the priest as he carries out his sacred duties with the bishop's approval, either confiscating or holding back his customary sustenance" the prelate should "interdict their churches until an end is put to such great evil."[5]

In addition to the formal decrees the bishops assembled in Baltimore adopted a number of "Resolutions" to serve as a guide for uniform discipline. Here Propaganda's influence is unmistakable. The bishops noted many incidents of, "dissensions . . . , scandalous insubordination toward lawful pastors, [and] schisms in favor of priests having no jurisdiction" and attributed them all to "lay trustees usurping the government of the church." As "a general remedy against this evil that tends to the ruin of Catholic discipline to schism and heresy" the prelates recommended that the system of electing lay trustees to control the temporalities of the parish be abolished or at least drastically weakened. They determined that in the future all new churches should be legally deeded to the diocesan bishop who would hold the deeds in trust for the congregations and pass them down to their successors. "It would be of great good to Religion," the bishops said, "if this simple plan were universally adopted, and the system of church trustees entirely abolished."[6]

Charters, however, could not be abolished by episcopal fiat and many of these provided for the election of trustees. In these cases the bishops resolved to place severe restrictions on the powers of trustees and to subvert the elective franchise wherever possible. Henceforth, they decided, trustees should be required to promise that they would in no way attempt to usurp the spiritual authority of their superiors. Whenever possible, clergymen should appoint lay trustees who "by their piety, zeal and prudence [would] promote the good of the church and the peace of the congregation." They also suggested that the clergy exercise a veto over lay elections, nullifying the election of men whom they considered "improper for the trust" and having other, more acceptable individuals elected in their place.[7]

Pastoral letters issued by the council reinforced this stance. To the laity they wrote, "there have been found amongst you, men who, not either fully acquainted with the principles of our church government, either presumed to reform it upon the [Protestant] model . . . , or claimed imaginary rights." "In no part of the Catholic Church," they declared, "does the right of instituting or dismissing a clergyman . . . exist in any one, save the ordinary prelate." "We further declare to you," they wrote, "that no right of presentation or patronage to any one of our churches or missions, has ever existed or does now exist canonically, in these United States." The only concession they were willing to make to lay sensibilities was a general promise to take into consideration lay "wants" and "wishes" in the appointment of clergymen "so far as our conscientious convictions and the just desires and expectations of meritorious priests will permit."[8]

Insubordination on the part of laymen might be excused, like that of children, on the basis of ignorance, but the bishops had nothing but contempt for the "unprincipled priests . . . those usurping and frequently immoral delinquents" who abetted lay insurgencies. "We cannot forget" they wrote, "that it was chiefly through the misconduct of clergymen that several occasions of lamentable schism were given in our province." As a result, "the progress of religion" had "been impeded"; "strife and tumult" had "profaned the sanctuary of the God of peace"; the bishops themselves had "been exposed to the unpleasant observations of [their] fellow citizens"; their "sacred rights" had been "thoughtlessly and criminally invaded"; the Church itself had been "ridiculed and insulted!" The bishops admitted some errors on their part. "It must . . . be confessed," they wrote, "that owing to a variety of circumstances not hitherto under our control, our organization has not been so perfect, nor our observances so exact as we could desire." But now, with the "zealous cooperation" of the clergy they "expect[ed] to make considerable progress toward a more orderly and efficient state of being."[9]

The First Provincial Council in 1829 was, in Patrick Carey's words, "the most important single event in marking the decline of clerical and lay influence and in signaling the beginning of the growth of exclusive episcopal power in the government and management of the church." At Baltimore, "the united voice of the American episcopate . . . , made former Roman decisions against trusteeism effective and helped to sustain an unbending Roman resistance to trusteeism throughout the remainder of the antebellum period." This result was not welcomed by all. John England had long advocated a conciliar approach to the problems of the American church, and advocated regular consultation among all the elements of the church: bishops, clergy and laity. He had hoped that a national council would adopt at least some of his ideas and in so doing demonstrate to American citizens the "republican part of church government" and reassure them that Catholic practice was "in accordance with our National institutions."[10]

At Baltimore, though, Bishop England's hopes were frustrated. "Most of his specific conciliar proposals . . . failed to receive majority support" and "he always voted with the minority on specific controversial issues in the American church." His constitutional schemes were rejected out of hand as "radical" and "innovative." In 1834, after years of frustration, he complained to Rome that his mind and those of the American bishops were "cast in different moulds, and cooperation is out of the question; for I cannot approve of their methods of administration, and at the last Council, they plainly manifested the most distinct want of confidence in me." This was a significant rejection, marking an important intellectual transformation in the American episcopacy, for in spurning John England and his ideas the bishops were rejecting an important alternative in American Catholic thought.[11]

John England exemplified a tradition in American Catholicism that emphasized rationalism, moralism, individualism, and ecclesiastical nationalism. These perspectives, by some accounts, were supplanted in the 1830s by a "romanticized" form of Catholicism that emphasized the organic historical continuity of Catholic traditions and religious subjectivity. Patrick Carey has charted this "shift" in Catholic apologetics and argues that it was related to "a shift in ecclesiastical polity that emphasize[d] . . . the centralization of authority in the Church" and "a shift in piety . . . from the moralism and individualism of the age of reason to . . . medieval forms of piety." By Carey's account the 1829 Baltimore council "provided the institutional basis" for this transformation that produced in the New Republic a Catholic establishment that was opposed to much of what America stood for in the minds of many of its citizens and in the world.[12]

We should not underestimate the hatred felt by most American bishops for the Enlightenment. As they noted in their pastoral to the laity in 1829 many were refugees who had fled the "convulsions of Europe, . . . when the exterminating infidel went forth like to him who sat upon the pale horse of the Apocalypse." "Hell," they said, "followed in his train. . . . many were slain for the word of God . . . , whilst their brethren . . . were scattered to the four winds of Heaven through various regions of the earth." For men such as these, "religious perfection" was to be found, not in science or reason, which had produced the terrors they had witnessed, but "in the unchangeableness of doctrine," which had been "preserved unchanged through the innovations of time and the alterations of ages" and which "neither the improvement of science nor the progress of the arts [could] make false." For them the "new and arbitrary interpretations" associated with the enlightenment-inspired perspectives articulated by John Carroll and John England were merely "the substitution of human opinion for the testimony of God."[13]

The provincial council of 1829 thus represented much more than an administrative action against trusteeism. It was a reaction against the modern world itself. It was a return to the sensibilities associated with medieval mysticism and the institutional imperatives of the Catholic (counter) reformation and it marked the emergence of an

American Catholic establishment organized around Roman universalism, institutional authoritarianism, and intense supernaturalism. It also produced for Philadelphia a new bishop. It would be his task to reconcile the contradictory tendencies of restoration Catholicism and the liberal, nationalist, and materialist values of that city's Catholic lay leadership.

PART THREE

The Construction
of Community

Kenrick

—————»•0•«—————

Francis Patrick Kenrick was raised in Dublin but educated at the Urban College of the Propaganda Fide in Rome. In 1814, one year before Kenrick commenced his studies, Pope Pius VII returned from years of exile and started reconstructing a church that had been ravaged by the liberal regimes of the "age of democratic revolutions." Already anti-liberal, church-centered reforms had emerged in many areas of Catholic Europe; now Pius VII and his successors began to integrate these disparate movements into an international reform imperative. On one level restoration Catholicism can be seen as a reaction against the Enlightenment (counterpoising universalism to nationalism, supernaturalism to secular rationalism, and authoritarianism to liberalism), but it also attempted to reform Catholicity in all its aspects and to recapture the aggressive vitality of the tridentine Church of the sixteenth century. Once more the Church became a militant and transforming force in Western culture.[1]

Francis Kenrick remained in Rome from 1815 to 1821 and imbibed deeply the spirit of restoration reform. By the time he had completed his studies Kenrick had developed "a deep and constant loyalty to the Holy See." "If there was anything," his eulogist declared, "for which [Kenrick] cherished special love and devotion, it may be said to have been the papacy. . . . A decision of that chair . . . , was ever with him decisive of all controversy. . . . He received it with filial docility, and carried it out with childlike obedience." Kenrick was also enthralled with the idea of mission work. Upon his ordination in 1821 he volunteered for the American mission, the first Propaganda graduate to do so, and was assigned to duty at Bardstown, Kentucky. "I love America," he wrote shortly before leaving Rome, "because I know . . . its extreme wants, and because I am convinced that Providence has called me to labor in it."[2]

Few people would have seemed more out of place on the Kentucky frontier than Francis Kenrick. Tall, slender, with a large head, a thick shock of hair, and a round, kindly face, he presented a slightly comical figure. His manner was mild—some thought him effeminate. He had a soft, pleasing voice and was given to understatement. His temperament was that of a scholar. "He was of a retiring, contemplative nature, eager to be alone either with his books or with a few scholarly intimates, or at prayer." Bishop O'Connor described him as unemotional, "never carried away by impulse," reflective, and given to "calm deliberation."[3]

There was nothing calm or unemotional about religion in Kentucky. The "Second Great Awakening" of American Protestantism was in full flower and missionary ministers crisscrossed the region sparking displays of religious enthusiasm wherever they went. Accustomed as he was to the institutional coherence of Roman Catholicism, Kenrick was aghast at the resulting chaos. "These deluded people," he marveled,

> call every doctrine, the word of God. . . . The fanaticism and frenzy of the time are such, that the most illiterate unqualified usurper of the office of Preacher can find hearers, and the doctrines which subvert all Christianity are received as Religious truths confirmed by the divine authority of Scripture. . . . The separated Sects are continually splitting asunder and new Sects arise, all blaspheming the Scripture by adducing it as the foundation of their errors and divisions . . . [and] emitting so many discordant yells of opposition bespeaking the furies of discord.[4]

Kenrick was soon plunged into the welter of religious controversy. In 1825 Pope Leo XII proclaimed a jubilee celebrating his ascension to the papal throne. Public observances opened in Kentucky on September 10, 1826, at the cathedral at Bardstown (attracting large crowds, "embracing Protestants as well as Catholics") and continued in parishes throughout the diocese well into the following year. In each parish the week-long celebrations included sermons expounding "the great truths" of Catholic faith and evening "conferences" in which two Catholic clergymen would debate theological matters. One would pose a question about or make an objection to Catholic belief on "doctrinal and moral subjects," and the other would answer him. These dialectical interchanges were controversial. The questions chosen, "were those that gave the most difficulty to the local Protestant sects and were purposely chosen to show them the errors of their beliefs." Francis Kenrick presided on these occasions and took the part of respondent, explaining points of Catholic belief and illustrating the errors of Protestantism.[5]

The jubilee events were popular, attracting large crowds, "including many Protestants as well as Catholics," and over time the scripted conferences evolved into interdenominational confrontations as Kenrick began to make and accept challenges to debate with Protestant ministers. "It is impossible," Stephen Badin wrote, "for me to tell you all the good which results from these conferences; Protestants relish them even more than Catholics." Soon Kenrick was being invited to speak to Protestant congregations. The young priest seems to have acquitted himself well in these contests. Once, in Springfield, Kenrick so thoroughly "demolished" a Presbyterian minister in debate that the man, when he stood to speak in rebuttal, was pulled down by his friends and prevented from speaking. On another occasion Kenrick's opponent was "abandoned by Protestants as well as Catholics." At other times he is reported to have easily prevailed over a Methodist minister and an Episcopalian priest in debate. All in all, the Jubilee was a great success, resulting in more than twelve hundred confirmations and approximately fifty converts from Protestantism, while many other Protestants "expressed a desire to hear the principles of the Catholic faith again explained."[6]

Kenrick's biographer portrays these episodes as the victory of reason over irrationality, but it is also clear that the young evangelist was a highly effective orator capable of rousing powerful emotions in his listeners. Once a Baptist preacher, hearing Kenrick expound on the sufferings of Christ, "groaned in the spirit." A contemporary noted that Kenrick's "figures [were] striking and appropriate, and his appeals to the heart irresistible"; another account praised his "natural eloquence." His great gift was for lucid exposition. "He sees everything in a clear light," a contemporary said, "and exhibits everything clearly to others."[7]

Kenrick's apologetic efforts soon found their way into print. In 1828 he engaged the Reverend Blackburne, president of Danville Presbyterian College, in an extended debate that was published in the Louisville *Baptist Recorder*. In twenty-one articles Kenrick, writing under the pseudonym "Omicron," outlined essential tenets of Catholic theology while Blackburne, styling himself "Omega," explained the

Protestant position. Far from being a closely reasoned debate the articles were "full of satire and ridicule," but they were effective and they greatly enhanced Kenrick's reputation as a combative Catholic apologist. One year later Kenrick published yet another assault on Protestant theology, his *Sermons on Baptism,* which attacked the Baptists for their practice of total immersion. Years later in Philadelphia he would reissue this work, revised so as to include an attack on Quaker belief and practice.[8]

Francis Kenrick's reputation as an eloquent and effective apologist and controversialist, as well as his scholarship and administrative acumen, recommended him highly to episcopal authorities. Soon bishops were competing for his services. Benedict Flaget, Kenrick's immediate superior, made the young man his secretary, praised him effusively in communications to Propaganda and to Baltimore, and declared his intention to make the young priest his coadjutor and successor. Edward Fenwick, bishop of Cincinnati, in 1824 and again in 1827 attempted unsuccessfully to lure Kenrick to Ohio, even offering to make him coadjutor of that diocese. These efforts resulted in an angry exchange between Flaget and Fenwick in which each argued that Kenrick's presence was absolutely indispensable to the development of Catholicity in his diocese. In 1829, the rest of the American hierarchy got a chance to meet the celebrated young priest when he accompanied his bishop to Baltimore to attend the first provincial council of the American church at Baltimore.[9]

At Baltimore Kenrick continued to impress. The bishops chose him to serve as recording secretary for their meetings and afterwards, in informal discussions, they agreed to recommend to Propaganda that he become the next bishop of Philadelphia. Henry Conwell was in Baltimore while the council met but had been excluded from all formal functions. Still he conferred informally with his colleagues and told them that he concurred in their choice of Kenrick. William Mathews, the administrator apostolic, also indicated that he strongly approved of Kenrick. Only Bishop Flaget protested, arguing that the young priest was too valuable in Kentucky. Shortly thereafter Archbishop Whitfield wrote to the prefect of Propaganda recommending that Kenrick be named coadjutor of Philadelphia diocese "and that the whole administration of the diocese ... be entrusted to [him]." William Matthews also wrote to Propaganda to say that he, too, hoped that Kenrick would be assigned to Philadelphia. Even Henry Conwell wrote to suggest that of all the potential candidates for coadjutor of his diocese "Mr. Kenrick is the most worthy."[10]

The bishops' opinions coincided with those of the Sacred Congregation. As the first Propaganda graduate to be sent to the American mission, Kenrick was "well known and highly esteemed" in Rome and since his assignment to Kentucky he had maintained close contacts with Roman authorities. Each year he sent Propaganda a detailed account of affairs in the American church and he had commented on specific matters from time to time. That his opinion was valued in Rome is shown by the fact that in dealing with the Harold affair Propaganda specifically followed Kenrick's recommendations on the best way to deal with the refractory priest. On January 25, 1830, the cardinals of Propaganda met to discuss the matter and it was agreed that Francis Kenrick was a man of unusual talent who could quiet the troubles in Philadelphia. Propaganda recommended that Kenrick be made titular bishop and coadjutor of Philadelphia with right of succession. One week later the cardinals' decision was ratified by Pope Pius VIII.[11]

There remained the matter of Bishop Conwell. At Baltimore the aged prelate had reassured his colleagues that "he intended to obey the Holy See" and would "abstain from governing the diocese, leaving it to the Apostolic administrator, until the Sacred Congregation decided otherwise." He further promised "not to start any action which would excite animosity; [and] . . . to do everything to preserve the present peace." Conwell said he was "willing to accept a coadjutor . . . to whom he would leave the whole administration of the diocese." All he asked was "to retain the title of bishop of the diocese" and to spend in America among his friends "the remaining days of his life." Benedict Flaget communicated these resolves to Propaganda shortly after the close of the council and soon thereafter Archbishop Whitfield also wrote to urge forgiveness for "this poor old man, weak in mind and body, broken in health, who erred more by levity than by malice."[12]

Once again Propaganda's interests matched those of the American bishops. Both wished to maintain peace in Philadelphia and to preserve the dignity of episcopal authority. It was also clear that effective authority was needed. True to his word, Henry Conwell had refrained from taking any part in the administration of the diocese and his inattention had taken a toll. John Hughes complained that Philadelphia was "really in a deplorable plight. There has been no Jubilee yet—no word of it even now. No oils consecrated for us these two years—no one to tend to it except at the risk of being considered officious." Hughes also feared a recurrence of lay dissent. He wrote, "Nothing but . . . suspense . . . prevents [St. Mary's dissenters] . . . from speaking more loudly still on their pretended, but absurd rights." It was a delicate situation and officials in Baltimore and Rome agreed that taking actions against Conwell might instigate yet another round of protest. It was better, all thought, to leave him in his place.[13]

On March 13, 1830, Propaganda announced that Bishop Conwell had been forgiven and was restored to the pope's grace and favor. Simultaneously Francis Kenrick was named Bishop of Arath and "coadjutor and administrator of the diocese of Philadelphia" with right of succession. He had "the rule of the diocese," and exercised "all authority and power of jurisdiction" there, subject of course to "the good pleasure of the Apostolic see." Propaganda specifically demanded that Bishop Conwell "leave to the coadjutor the whole government of your diocese" and further required, in the interest of preserving peace, that both he and Kenrick conceal the circumstances of the latter's appointment. They were to explain that the transfer of power had been at the elderly bishop's instigation and had been his desire all along.[14]

Francis Kenrick was consecrated at Bardstown in June of 1830. Henry Conwell was in attendance, having come all the way from Philadelphia to present the new bishop to his consecrators. When the ceremonies were concluded, Philadelphia had two bishops and already there were tensions between them. Even before he left Bardstown for the long journey east, Kenrick complained that rumors were circulating to the effect that Bishop Conwell had been reinstated with full powers to rule his diocese. John Hughes had heard the rumors too. He wrote to Archbishop Whitfield to tell him that Henry Conwell had "signified, indeed declared, that he is restored to his former jurisdiction." When confronted on the matter Conwell refused to deny the tales. Moreover Conwell had refused to issue a pastoral letter, as requested by Propaganda, explaining that because of age and ill health he had transferred all jurisdiction to his coadjutor. Kenrick asked permission to make public the fact that episcopal authority had in fact been transferred to him.[15]

Philadelphia's two Irish bishops had little in common. Francis Kenrick knew little of the traditional world in which Henry Conwell had been raised. He was a product of a sophisticated, urban milieu and his church was the ultramontane establishment of the Roman restoration. No less than Conwell he hated the liberal and secular tendencies of the Enlightenment, but he was no defender of the ancien régime. Rather he was a reformer, seeking to nurture into existence a new world order inspired by medieval universalism and the tridentine reforms of the sixteenth century. Whereas Henry Conwell struck a defensive pose, seeking to retain values and ways of life that were not only incompatible with the dominant themes of American culture, but were under assault throughout the West, Francis Kenrick faced the future with the confidence of a reforming evangelist seeking fertile fields within which to spread the values of restoration Catholicism. To what extent those values—universal, supernatural, communal, and authoritarian—could be accommodated within the materialistic, nationalistic, and aggressively liberal environment of Jacksonian America remained to be seen.

The Restoration Church

Through the middle decades of the nineteenth century the Holy See promoted a series of reforms that culminated in a major redefinition of Catholic doctrine and dogma at the First Vatican Council of 1869–70. The reform impulse had its origin in popular resistance movements against national churches controlled by revolutionary regimes in France and elsewhere, but after 1815 these disparate efforts were replaced by a unified international program of reform directed by the Roman Curia. This was no simple attempt to restore the ancien régime, although the restoration reforms were a powerful reaction against liberal, secular, and nationalist tendencies. The reformers envisioned, not a return to the absolutist national establishments of the seventeenth and eighteenth centuries, but a unified moral regime embracing all of Christendom and directed from Rome. Their inspiration derived from the "Age of Faith" rather than the "Age of Absolutism."[1]

In ecclesiastical terms the reforms were ultramontane, promoting a progressive centralization of authority in the Roman Curia and the person of the pope, a tendency legitimated by the doctrine of papal infallibility, which gained broad acceptance within the restoration church and was formally adopted by the Vatican Council. So great was the impact of the ultramontane imperative upon the international Church that one important study has proclaimed that "the transformation of Catholicism by the Ultramontane movement . . . is the content of the history of the Catholic Church in the nineteenth century." Ultramontanism was accompanied by a broad "monarchization" of the Church as episcopal authorities everywhere extended controls over the Catholic laity and parish clergy and systematically suppressed any internal expression of liberal or nationalistic tendencies.[2]

The reform imperative also had a profound effect on religious life, both social and devotional. Under Pius VII and his successors the Church undertook a general redefinition of Catholic life. Inspired by the sixteenth-century Catholic Counter-Reformation and the Council of Trent, restoration churchmen expanded the institutional structures and devotional activities that gave form and substance to Catholic communities throughout the West. Tridentine Catholicism emphasized parish life, and reforming bishops everywhere undertook elaborate and expensive building programs with the intent of making the parish church a physical presence in every community in which Catholics lived. Social institutions were as important as physical. Reformers assiduously promoted the formation of a variety of religious societies, confraternities, sodalities, and devotional associations all of which had as their purpose the involvement of Catholic laymen and women in a comprehensive social network centered on the parish church.[3]

The reformers attacked not only unbelief and Protestantism but also the traditional values and practices of national Catholic churches. The elaborate social and institutional networks constructed by reformers were intended to provide a bulwark against all of these. Within these networks they attempted to nurture a new Catholic milieu (a world of the spirit as well as of social relations) and to this end elaborated and expanded devotional activities. Pius VII increased the number of Marian feasts and instituted new processes for sanctification. He and his successors also called for processions and pilgrimages and other elaborate public displays of devotion as a means of inspiring religious fervor among the faithful. At the same time, reformers greatly elaborated and standardized Catholic liturgies and devotional practices, and everywhere made strenuous efforts to improve the religious instruction of priests.[4]

Reformers also strongly emphasized the apostolic mission of the Church. During the nineteenth century old missionary orders were revitalized and new congregations established and, under the direction of the Propaganda, the Church undertook nothing less than "the restoration of society in a Christian spirit." In addition to the clerical orders, an extensive network of mission and tract societies (similar to those of the Protestant "Benevolent Empire") were founded in an attempt to "rechristianize" the world. The Association for the Propagation of the Faith was founded in 1822 in Lyons and two years later the *Annales de la Propagation de la Foi* began to be distributed internationally. In Vienna the Leopoldine Foundation began its extensive support for foreign missions in 1828 and was soon joined by the Rhenish Xaverius Society and the Bavarian Ludwig Society.[5]

Apostolic zeal involved more than support for missionary orders. Ironically, perhaps, ultramontane reformers were quick to turn modern methods of generating popular enthusiasm to their own purposes. They made extensive use of the popular press and lay organizations, and, in the realm of education, especially at the elementary level, they were absolutely hostile to any education that was not "single-minded" in support of reform. Thus the nineteenth-century Catholic reformation, while politically reactionary and inspired by an idealized conception of medieval society, incorporated within itself some forms of social and political organization that are characteristic of "modern" Western culture.[6]

The impact of the Roman reforms was not everywhere simultaneous, but it was always profound. In Europe the reform impulse generally proceeded from south to north, affecting first the countries adjoining the Mediterranean and spreading northward in the second half of the century. In England the Roman revival did not begin until 1847, when Nicholas Wiseman, rector of the English College at the Propaganda, was appointed pro-vicar apostolic of London. Upon his arrival in England Wiseman instituted a far-reaching program of reform that included a major evangelical campaign, the development of an elaborate network of Catholic associations and devotional societies, and the establishment of myriad schools and churches. Wiseman's efforts generated an enormous revival of Catholic devotional activity. Within one year of his arrival in London some 15,000 Catholics returned to the church as a result of the missions and retreats he sponsored; but this was only the beginning. Over the next eighteen years

Wiseman expanded the number of Catholic institutions and clergy, extended episcopal controls over both clergy and laity, and elaborated devotional exercises. So profound were the changes wrought by Wiseman that upon his death in 1865 it was said that he "found English Catholics a persecuted sect and left them a Church."[7]

Cardinal Wiseman's reform of the English church paralleled the efforts of his contemporary, Paul Cullen, in Ireland. In 1850 Cullen, the rector of the Irish College at the Propaganda, became archbishop of Armagh and soon thereafter assumed the archepiscopacy of Dublin. Over the next quarter century this "Ultramontane of the most uncompromising type," described as a "Counter-Reformation zealot for whom the Council of Trent was still a living reality," remade Irish Catholicism. Like Wiseman he promoted the construction of churches and schools, he standardized and elaborated devotional practices, he fostered the growth of religious associations, he asserted episcopal authority over clergy and laity, and he instigated a major evangelical revival. As a result of this "devotional revolution," according to Emmet Larkin, "the great mass of Irish people became practicing Catholics."[8]

The restoration reforms came to America, too, and it is important to note that they crossed the Atlantic long before they penetrated the Catholic cultures of Northern Europe. As early as the 1820s aspects of the reform were being promoted by French émigré clergy on the Kentucky frontier, and in 1830 Francis Kenrick introduced restoration Catholicism to urban America when he became administrator of Philadelphia. There he and his successors brought about in the three decades before the Civil War a "Reformation of Philadelphia Catholicism" that in its essential features anticipated the later reforms of Paul Cullen in Ireland and Nicholas Wiseman in England.[9]

Reform came early to America for a number of reasons. The American hierarchy was not as deeply entrenched as the national church establishments of Europe and had fewer traditional privileges to defend; nor could it rely upon the support of civil authorities to defend its interests against Roman interference. In America (as William Harold's experience demonstrated) the "wall of separation" between church and state precluded any such intervention. Moreover, since the United States was a mission territory it came directly under the purview of Propaganda, which exercised ever-growing influence over American church affairs. Most important, though, many American prelates were receptive to the Roman reforms because they offered solutions to some of the most pressing problems facing the Church in the New Republic.[10]

Most of the problems that plagued the Church in the United States stemmed from its rapid growth. The number of priests and churches doubled each decade, swelling from sixty-eight priests and eighty churches in 1808 to more than a thousand clergymen serving an equal number of churches and half as many chapels and mission stations at mid-century. But even this rapid expansion was outstripped by Catholic immigration. Most immigrants were, as Propaganda noted, not of "that class of Catholics who are most punctual in the discharge of their religious duties" and many shed their faith in America. Surveying the mission in 1838 Francis Kenrick complained, "Want of opportunity brings on a want of desire to approach the sacraments." As a result, he wrote, "religious exercises are neglected or forgotten; and though the majority profess at least an external respect for some sect or other, there are many who have no creed at all." John England was more evocative in his assessment. America, he wrote, was an "ungrateful land, which seems to devour its Catholic population."[11]

As Kenrick implied, institutional underdevelopment exacerbated apostasy and unbelief. There were never enough priests or churches to serve the swelling and spreading Catholic population, and efforts to close the gap created further problems. The institution of trusteeism (so hated by the prelates) was widespread because in most communities it was the only way in which a church could be built. Often a group of lay-men would build a church on their own initiative and only afterward petition authorities for a priest. The priests available to serve these churches were often inadequate. Many administrators and prelates had to make do with poorly educated or corrupt priests who had left Europe under the cloud of scandal. Because institutional controls were undeveloped, clergymen were often poorly supervised and as a result varieties of religious practice and belief proliferated within the Church.[12]

The restoration reforms, with their emphasis on monarchic authoritarianism, standardization of ritual and doctrine (on a Roman model), institutional development, and aggressive evangelization, directly addressed many of the most pressing needs of the Church in the United States. So thoroughly were they embraced that by the 1860s the archbishop of Baltimore could describe the American church as "Roman to the core." But the "Romanization" of the American church caused as many problems as it solved. Not only did it propel Catholics further from the dominant values of antebellum American civil culture but it also created a gulf between the ecclesiastical establishment and the immigrant population it sought to serve.[13]

Immigration historians have often assumed that the Catholic Church faithfully reflected immigrant values and beliefs. In David Montgomery's words the Church gave "perfect expression [to] . . . the dejection that was the peasant experience and . . . to the insouciant morality of traditionalist culture." To William V. Shannon it was "the one Irish institution the people could regard as peculiarly their own." Lawrence J. McCaffrey has argued that "Catholicism . . . provided a focus for unity in the Irish ghettos, creating an Irish-American community out of a people who arrived in America with diverse loyalties to parish, townland, and county." To Sheridan Gilley it was part of "a true Irish empire beyond the seas."[14]

But American Catholicism as it developed in the middle decades of the nineteenth century owed little to the experience of European peasants. America embraced Roman reforms long before the churches in England, Ireland, and the German states had undergone their own "devotional revolutions," and as a consequence the Church, rather than reflecting the values of immigrant peasants, actively sought to modify them. The disparity between the values promoted by American Catholicism and the traditional churches of Europe was sufficiently great that we might say that mid-century immigrants had to be assimilated not only to American culture but also to American Catholic culture.[15]

In many ways Philadelphia was an extreme example of the difficulties facing the Church everywhere in the United States. At the time of the First Provincial Council the diocese encompassed the states of Pennsylvania and Delaware as well as the western regions of New Jersey. Within that compass lived approximately 100,000 Catholics served by a mere twenty-two churches and thirty-five priests, only one of whom was American by birth. In the city itself only four churches and two schools served a Catholic population of 25,000. Philadelphia was a hotbed of trusteeism and nowhere had the fires of dissent burned hotter; nowhere had lay leaders and members of the lower clergy been more refractory. Apathy, apostasy, and unbelief were also rampant. In 1829 John Hughes estimated that the proportion of Philadelphia's Catholics who made confession during Lent was "hardly one [in] fifteen." A census taken at St. Augustine's two years later showed that of 2,146 adult Catholics living in the parish only 750 were communicants. Testimony from working-class Catholics confirms the statistics. One felt that "all religions are alike;" another was Catholic, but not, he emphasized, "a Roman Catholic." William Loughry was "called a Catholic" but went "to every place" and had "no particular persuasion." Even converts were lukewarm. A young man who had converted to Catholicism, described his religion as being "like the Irishman's horse, works all week and goes idle on Sunday." Apathy, dissent, insubordination, and institutional inadequacy were thus the characteristics of Philadelphia Catholicism when Francis Kenrick entered the city in July of 1830.[16]

"Good Soldiers of Christ Jesus"

Francis Kenrick's first concern was to impose discipline and unity of purpose upon his unruly charges. To him, as for other Propaganda-trained clergymen of his generation, the Church was a "unified, hierarchical society," a "corporate entity" in which rigorous discipline was applied at all levels. His first pastoral letter called upon the clergy to "Labour . . . as good Soldiers of Christ Jesus." In it Kenrick urged them, as "soldiers of God" to "have but one heart and one soul." He praised the priests for their constancy in the past and their efforts to sustain "the sanctity of the priesthood" against the "slander," the "frailty" and the "perversity of some, who proved unworthy of the sacred character." "Be you vigilant" and united, he charged them, "for the time has come when men do not bear sound doctrine, but according to their own desires they heap to themselves teachers, having itching ears; and turn away indeed their hearing from the truth, and are turned to fables."[1]

Bishop Kenrick was a strict superior (John England thought him "a little too sanguine in his zeal") and he held his clergy to high standards. From them he expected "humility, *disinterestedness*, obedience, docility, *temperance*, and purity with zeal, charity, patience and all the train of virtues." These were admirable goals but few among the traditionalist clergy could or even cared to meet all of them. Nevertheless Francis

Kenrick was determined "to inculcate [in the diocesan clergy] . . . the necessity of adopting a line of conduct strictly conformable to the general Rules of the Church, which are so often neglected by individuals whose Rule is their own Sentiment, or the practice of some few others."[2]

Kenrick moved decisively to enforce discipline on the clergy. He had been in Philadelphia for less than two months when he undertook a visitation tour of the diocese and made his presence felt in local communities throughout Pennsylvania. Lest any miss the point he took immediate and personal action to censure and remove from his diocese "evil priests"—men "unworthy of their calling, who had drifted to the United States from Europe." In Westmoreland County he warned a much-hated priest to resign his charge within a month or face removal; in Pittsburgh he withdrew the faculties of a priest from Ohio and forced him to leave the diocese; at Ebensburg he suspended from all priestly functions a Carmelite missionary who then left the diocese; and at Milton he revoked the faculties of yet another priest. By the time he returned to Philadelphia in November 1830 Francis Kenrick had served notice throughout the diocese that a new order of things had arrived.[3]

His efforts to enforce discipline faced two major impediments; the necessity of concealing the source of his authority and Bishop Conwell's opposition. Propaganda insisted that the circumstances of Kenrick's appointment and the fact that his authority derived from Rome be kept secret. This was intended to protect Bishop Conwell's dignity and also to forestall charges that Rome was exercising an unwonted influence in American affairs. Silence on the matter, however, led to confusion, especially since Conwell encouraged people to think that " full authority had been returned to him." John Hughes complained to Baltimore about the ambiguity. He wrote, "It is supposed universally here that the Bishop is restored as before, but still there appears a kind of instinctive impression, that he will leave to his co-adjutor the government of the Diocese—not altogether by his own choice, but by virtue of instructions given to the parties from Rome which they seem to *guess* at." He continued, "The Bishop has signified, indeed declared, that he is restored to his former jurisdiction—but yet no *act* of his, has confirmed the declaration."[4]

For Francis Kenrick, full of reforming zeal and determined to impose his will on the resident clergy, the ambiguities of the situation were intolerable. Members of the traditionalist Irish clergy actively resented him—as his biographer delicately put it, "most of them never got to know him sufficiently well to love him"—and, as they had done with William Hogan and William Harold before, they closed ranks against the intruder and rallied around Henry Conwell. Soon the clergy were divided into two camps. "Some of the priests asked blessing of the old & some of the young Bishop." For his part Conwell did nothing to discourage them—"Old Conwell plays his part like a fox" John England observed. In May of 1831 Conwell issued a public protest which was also communicated to Propaganda on behalf of the clergymen who had suffered suspension at Kenrick's hands. Exasperated, Kenrick wrote to Propaganda asking permission to make public the fact that he alone had jurisdiction in the diocese. "Evil priests," he argued, "could [not] be censured by me if there remained an appeal to the Bishop of Phila-delphia." He also asked that he be sent an "authentic and public instru-ment" specifically naming him as "Apostolic Administrator" with sole jurisdiction so as to make clear to all that his authority derived directly from Rome. In September Propaganda finally gave Kenrick permission to make public the fact that he, and not Conwell, had jurisdiction in Philadelphia, but declined to award him the title he sought.[5]

Kenrick was also determined to bring unity and discipline to the laity. To him the laymen should be "obedient subjects of the ruler." "Fulfill ye our joy," Kenrick admonished them, "that you be of one mind, having the same charity, being of one accord, agreeing in senti-ment." Above all, he urged them "to keep the unity of the spirit in the bond of peace." As Catholics they were, he said, "one body, and one spirit" and as such must serve "one Lord, . . . one God and Father of all," profess "one faith," and honor "one baptism." He denounced the "con-tentions, envyings, animosities, dissensions, detractions, whisperings, swellings, [and] seditions" that had plagued the church in the past and demanded that the laity "all speak the same thing," that they "be perfect in the same mind, and in the same judgment" and "that there be no schisms" among them.[6]

Kenrick moved decisively to establish his authority over the laity. Once more resistance centered at St. Mary's and concerned the question of clerical salaries. Philadelphia's churches had been reluctant to con-tribute funds to support one bishop; now they were expected to support two. At first Kenrick declared that he would not claim any funds due to Bishop Conwell and would instead "depend on all [churches] for support." But many congregations, led by traditionalist Irish clerics, refused to increase their contributions so as to accommodate the new bishop. "Every . . . subsidy for the maintenance of the Episcopal dignity," Kenrick complained in September, "has been denied me." Finally, on

December 27, 1830, Kenrick informed the board of trustees at St. Mary's that he intended to make their church his cathedral and would collect the chief pastor's salary. He further informed them that, as pastor, he would ex officio serve as a member of the board of trustees.[7]

Kenrick's announcement threw St. Mary's congregation into turmoil. The trustees were "displeased." They agreed to increase the congregation's contribution to the bishop's support but balked at paying Kenrick the chief pastor's salary too. As bishop, they argued, he would be expected to administer all the churches in the diocese and could not therefore adequately fulfill the duties of the chief pastor. Their position was far from radical in the context of industrializing America. They held that the bishop could not simply claim a salary as his due; he would have to work for it. Anything else would smack of aristocracy, privilege, and corruption. In their eyes Kenrick's declaration was every bit as arbitrary and unjust as anything Bishop Conwell had done. Kenrick, however, saw the matter differently—as a direct challenge to his authority. To allow laymen to control his salary would be to allow them control over his person and the office he held. That could not be tolerated. Nor could they be allowed to resist his claim to the pastorship of any church he chose.[8]

By 1831 St. Mary's trustees were hardly radicals. Most of them were staunch bishopites who had sustained episcopal authority against radical attacks. They had welcomed Kenrick's arrival and supported his attacks on the traditionalist clergy whose behavior they had always deplored. Prior to Kenrick's announcement, John Hughes tells us, St. Mary's trustees "seemed ready to bear him on their shoulders." But Francis Kenrick could not see the trustees as anything but dangerous insurgents flouting legitimate authority. When they "kicked" at his declaration he saw only willful insubordination. In his mind the trustees' objections were not legitimate but "false principles" and they revealed "schismatic tendencies."[9]

On January 9 Bishop Kenrick took the pulpit to denounce the trustees for resisting his demands. John Hughes wrote that Kenrick's eloquence that day "filled [the trustees] with exasperation, and the people with disgust for *their* proceedings." Matters came to a head three days later when the trustees called a general meeting of the congregation to discuss the matter. Bishop Kenrick, dressed in full regalia, appeared unexpectedly and engaged Archibald Randall, the secretary of the board, in public debate. That night Kenrick's years of disputation on the mission trail served him well and he swayed the audience to his side. "He made them eat their words," John Hughes wrote. He told them they must not dare to control him in the exercise of his episcopal authority." Hughes was elated. *"Gloria in excelsis Deo,"* he wrote, "the neck of the bad principle was *broken* last night. . . . They are under his feet." To Bishop Kenrick, too, "it appeared in this meeting that the wrong ideas which had prevailed about the rights of a congregation to engage and approve the pastor were corrected or repudiated."[10]

Kenrick refused to personalize his struggles with the trustees. At the public meeting, no sooner had they withdrawn their opposition to his claim than Kenrick shook their hands and declared for all to hear that "he wished no other trustees, so long as these gentlemen would confine themselves within their proper limits, and not presume to meddle, directly or indirectly, with his authority." "They were under his feet," John Hughes marveled, "they were fairly beaten; and when they gave up . . . , and when their friends were about to fall on them, he interposed, and set them on their legs again." The reason for Kenrick's magnanimity was simple; he was well aware that his plans for the diocese could not succeed without the support of wealthy and influential men such as his opponents. Eventually he expected to make peace and common cause with them. All he asked was that they not question his authority to rule the diocese and he would support them in all other things. It was a significant gesture. In these handshakes, on the evening of January 12, 1831, we can see the germ of an alliance between the bishop and the bourgeoisie that would change the face of Philadelphia Catholicism.[11]

Interdict

There remained, however, many difficulties to be resolved and Kenrick attacked them ruthlessly. Bishop Conwell still claimed to be chief pastor of St. Mary's, and faced by contending claims from the two bishops the trustees simply refused to recognize either. At first Kenrick tried to secure trustees who would support his claim. At the elections for trustees his friends put forth a "Kenrick" slate of candidates, but the incumbents were reelected. Kenrick then determined to force the victorious trustees into submission. His opportunity came three days later when the trustees called a meeting but neglected to inform him of the fact (although Bishop Conwell was in attendance). This he interpreted as a deliberate challenge. On the following day at mass he announced from the pulpit that "so long as the trustees persevered in opposing [his] authority," he would leave the congregation without any pastor.[1]

Once again the trustees "kicked" and made it known that should Kenrick withdraw his services as pastor he would not be paid. The bishop then threatened to interdict all services in the church if the trustees persevered "in their refusal to recognize me as the chief pastor of this Church." Their actions, he said, were "an aggression on the Episcopal authority [and] . . . an usurpation repugnant to the doctrine and discipline of the Catholic Church." Unless "all opposition be forthwith withdrawn, and the Catholic principles of church government be unequivocally admitted," the most severe measures would be implemented. From the trustees he demanded a written submission and public admission that they had no voice in the selection of pastors.[2]

To this the trustees replied, "we have not assumed or asserted a right to choosing our own pastors." They had no objection to supporting the bishop if he were willing to "withdraw . . . sufficiently from other duties so as to discharge the functions of a pastor here." They agreed to recognize him and his assistant as clerical members of the board. "But to sign a declaration of abstract principles" they said, "would imply an admission that we had violated them and . . . would neither be honorable to us as Catholics nor candid in us as Christians." When the trustees attempted to placate the bishop by paying him his quarterly salary, Kenrick refused it saying, "I can't take the money; you are no board without me." Four days later, on April 16, 1831, he placed St. Mary's Church under interdict. Once more on the following day the trustees tried to reason with him, but as they still refused to give him the public written statement he demanded, the interdict remained.[3]

St. Mary's trustees did not consider themselves to be in defiance of episcopal authority. Bishop Conwell had assured them that he "still enjoyed the rights of the Bishop of Philadelphia" and that Kenrick was guilty of "usurpation." "We know no Bishop of Phila[delphia] but Dr. Conwell," the trustees said, "Dr. K[enrick] is bishop of Arath." Throughout the controversy Conwell encouraged the trustees in this belief. No sooner had Kenrick interdicted St. Mary's than Conwell wrote to the trustees saying, "I have never sanctioned the proceeding [against you], [and] I regret it exceedingly, and entertain feelings of sympathy for the suffering multitude." Again he assured them that "I am the incumbent of this Southern District of Philadelphia and . . . I possess inalienable rights in virtue of this title distinct from the rights which I enjoy as Bishop of Philadelphia." Moreover, he asserted that he had "never abdicated either in the capacity of Parish Priest or of Bishop of Philadelphia, both of which I still adhere to."[4]

Conwell knew that he had no power to oppose his coadjutor directly and took no direct action in the dispute, restricting himself to public denunciations of Kenrick and sending several complaints to Rome. Bishop Conwell was thus an impotent ally and the trustees found themselves alone in a battle against a skilled and implacable foe. Nor was there to be any relief from Baltimore. Archbishop Whitfield strongly disagreed with Kenrick's action. He felt that the bishop's rights had not been violated and that there was no reason for the interdict. In his opinion Kenrick had gone "beyond the boundaries which prudence constitutes," but he refused to overrule Kenrick's actions because to do so would fatally undermine the coadjutor's authority.[5]

Francis Kenrick felt that he was faced with "the new machinations of an anti-Catholic conspiracy" and was determined to drive his opponents into submission. In a pastoral letter he stated that "Catholic principles of church government" admitted no role for laymen beyond "rational and Christian obedience and subjugation . . . to the Prelates of the Church." He expressed surprise that the trustees made his decision to assume the chief pastorship "a matter of deliberation, instead of simply recording it on their books." This was, he averred, an affront to the "God of peace" and the work of "Satan" and he called upon the faithful to "crush" it.[6]

Here exposed was the absolutist core of Kenrick's thought. He expected from laymen and inferior clerics the same "reverence . . . filial docility . . . and childlike obedience" that he showed toward the Holy See. Anything else, any hint of insubordination, was "anti-Catholic." This authoritarian sensibility was a continuing theme in Kenrick's thought. Seven years later he complained bitterly about the peculiarly American "spirit of independence" he had so often encountered. This pernicious spirit, he wrote, "is felt by all [and] fills them with a proud confidence in their own judgments and with a jealous distrust of authority." "Even the children," he lamented, "when receiving catechistical instructions, shew not the docility which might be expected from their age. The adults are willing enough to assist at sermons, but more, it is to be feared, with a view to criticizing than of profiting by the instruction."[7]

Kenrick was surprised at the lay response to his ultimatum. He had expected desperate opposition but the interdict was "not . . . followed by any tumult or excitement." The congregation, weary after years of conflict, simply drifted away to other places. Soon the church was virtually abandoned. "The gates of St. Mary's are thrown open every Sunday," Kenrick wrote, "the few ring leaders and some devoted partisans assemble in the church yard to complain and to plot, whilst the Catholic churches are crowded to excess." There was no general support for defiance. Kenrick reported that "The great body of the Catholics and even Protestants have viewed [the trustees] with disgust."[8]

Kenrick saw his lay opponents as the "miserable remains of the schismatical faction," but they were in no way comparable to the radical republicans who had dominated the board in past times. Essentially conservative themselves, the trustees had no interest in defying legitimate authority. When it became "palpable to all" that Bishop Conwell was not willing to challenge Kenrick's jurisdiction, the trustees gave up the fight. This, too, surprised the coadjutor. He had expected a court challenge (Conwell had threatened one) and even expected to lose it. In anticipation of civil action Kenrick applied to Archbishop Whitfield for official certificates that would remove "every shadow of a doubt . . . but that all power and authority of jurisdiction are vested in me exclusively by the Apostolic See." Kenrick even intended to petition the Holy See to transfer Conwell's title of "Bishop of Philadelphia" to him so as to remove any confusion on that score. But such actions proved to be unnecessary. On May 21, 1831, less than a month after the interdict was imposed, St. Mary's trustees furnished Kenrick with the written statement he had demanded. They sent him a letter in which they "disclaim[ed] all right to interfere in the spiritual concerns of the Church" and specifically stated that these concerns included "the right of appointing, rejecting, and removing Pastors."[9]

Once again Francis Kenrick was magnanimous in victory. In negotiations with the trustees "everything tending to excite the passions was kept back from the question." Although he found the idea "unsavory" Kenrick even conceded to the trustees the right to fix clerical salaries, but insisted that such determinations be made by the full board, including himself and his two assistants as members. Soon thereafter Kenrick reversed himself and declared that "if the temporal support of the priests in charge should be withheld, [he] would without delay" reimpose the interdict, but though the trustees protested, this did not prevent reconciliation. Finally, on May 28 Kenrick removed the interdict and with this act the long series of conflicts between St. Mary's congregation and Philadelphia's bishops came to an end. Henceforth, Kenrick proclaimed, he and the lay leadership would be "one body and one spirit."[10]

Buoyed by his victory over St. Mary's trustees Bishop Kenrick moved to secure his jurisdiction over the rest of the diocese. The First Provincial Council had ruled that wherever possible the deeds to new churches should be made out in the name of the bishop. Kenrick took this provision to its extreme and sought to have all existing church property in the diocese legally transferred to his person. As a first step toward that end he applied for, and on June 29, 1831, was granted, American citizenship. Two months later another impediment was removed when a papal decree publicly deprived Bishop Conwell of all episcopal authority and vested all jurisdiction in Kenrick. Thereafter Conwell withdrew from diocesan affairs; he lived on until 1842 but was never again a factor in the government of the diocese.[11]

Armed with the papal decree and resolved to implement his authority throughout the diocese, Francis Kenrick set out again on a visitation tour of the western parishes. He forbade one local congregation to complete construction of a church until the legal title was redrawn so as to exclude any interference by trustees. At another church where the priest and trustees disagreed as to the disposition of church-owned lands Kenrick proclaimed that unless the trustees renounced all rights to administer church property he would leave them without a pastor. When the trustees acquiesced to his demands Kenrick further required them to petition the state legislature for an act revising the church's charter so as to transfer control of all property to him.[12]

At the recently completed Church of St. Paul in Pittsburgh lay trustees had secured a charter from the state legislature and "had the support and sympathy of the Catholic people at large." Kenrick attacked them directly. In a public address he told the congregation:

> The church is yours. You have a perfect right to do what you please with it. . . . You may make of it, if you will, a factory, and I will not interfere. But . . . if you wish it to be a Catholic

church, you must comply with the requirement of the law
which I have laid before you. Now, do as you please.

Ultimately St. Paul's trustees acquiesced to the bishop's demands, and
so it continued throughout the diocese. Almost everywhere churches
were reorganized "exclusively under ecclesiastical control."[13]

On his return to Philadelphia Bishop Kenrick continued his assault
on lay independence. In May of 1832 at his first diocesan synod he promulgated a decree to the effect that no new church could be begun nor
old one enlarged without his personal sanction. He further required
that in every such case title to the property was to be legally assigned to
his person. Another decree threatened suspension to any priest who
should abet attempts on the part of trustees to infringe his episcopal
authority. Kenrick even carried his campaign into the political arena,
petitioning the Pennsylvania state legislature for a formal recognition
of his personal control of church property. This was granted in
February of 1844 when the legislature specifically empowered the bishops of Philadelphia and the recently created diocese of Pittsburgh to
"take and hold real property for the support and maintenance of . . .
religious or charitable institution[s]."[14]

Bishop Kenrick's attack on lay autonomy went far beyond simply
establishing legal control of church properties. He also attempted to
undermine democratic procedures wherever possible. St. Michael's
Church in Philadelphia's Kensington district is a case in point. In the
spring of 1833 a charter was obtained for the construction of the new
church and, as was customary, the charter provided for annual elections to choose members of a board of trustees to administer the temporal affairs of the parish. Not satisfied with merely holding legal title
to the church, Bishop Kenrick challenged in court the legality of the
electoral provisions in the charter and in 1835 the Pennsylvania
Supreme Court ordered an amendment to the charter permitting the
bishop to appoint members to the board of trustees. This did not end
Bishop Kenrick's involvement with St. Michael's. In 1844 the church
was burned by rioters, and civil courts subsequently awarded damages
of more than $6,000 to the trustees. Kenrick refused to allow the
trustees to accept the award, requiring instead that it be paid directly to
the parish priest who would then be free to spend it as he saw fit. Here
as elsewhere Francis Kenrick was not content simply to establish episcopal absolutism as a general principle; he worked tirelessly to apply
that principle to the government of every parish in the diocese.[15]

Roman Catholics

By June of 1838 it seemed that the battle had been won. Kenrick wrote to inform Pope Gregory XVI that "Almost nothing remains now to bar the free exercise of ecclesiastical jurisdiction. Trustees indeed still exist in a few of the Churches; but they are not now meddling in affairs that belong to the Church." His campaign to tame the traditionalist clergy had also gone well. Beginning with his first diocesan synod in 1832 he promulgated a series of decrees that, in the words of his biographer, "laid the cornerstone of ecclesiastical discipline throughout the diocese." Restrictions were placed on the observance of sacraments, standardized record-keeping procedures were instituted, and controls placed on the behavior of the clergy. Priests were prohibited from administering sacraments outside their own parishes and visiting clergymen from outside the diocese were banned from performing any sacred functions. As a bar to simony and concubinage, priests were forbidden to accept pay for the administration of the sacraments or to hire young girls as servants.[1]

These decrees were supplemented in later synods. In 1844 limits were placed on missionary orders. The Redemptorists were given charge of the German congregations while the Jesuits and Augustinians were prohibited from administering sacraments to persons who were not pewholders in their churches. Guidelines were also established for the division of stipends between pastors and assistants and strict rules were set regulating the administration of confession to women and young girls. Priests were required to keep "perfect parochial registers" on pain of suspension and controls over visiting clergy were also strengthened. Henceforth, all priests entering the diocese were required to present their credentials to the bishop before being allowed to say mass. Finally, in order to overcome the educational deficiencies and "Gallican" tendencies of many of the clergy, quarterly conferences were established, attendance at which was mandatory, during which instruction in dogma and moral theology took place.[2]

Bishop Kenrick's final synod met in 1847. There he standardized bookkeeping procedures throughout the diocese and required parish priests to submit regular financial reports. He also further clarified the rights and responsibilities of missionaries and required priests to adopt a uniform dress—the Roman frock coat. We should also note that it was during this period that priests in Philadelphia, although such was not mandated by episcopal decree, first began to insist upon the title "father." The net effect of these reforms was to force the Philadelphia Catholic clergy away from the traditional practices and intimate relationships between priest and parishioner they had known in their homelands; to systematize, formalize, and regulate their conduct and appearance; and to elevate them above (and in the process distance them from) the Catholic laity.[3]

Francis Kenrick was a "strict liturgist" who found the wide diversity of devotional practices in the United States disturbing. One of his primary objectives in Philadelphia was to bring "attention to the Sacred Rites" into conformity with "the solemn practices of the Universal Church." To this end his synods systematized, elaborated, and regulated devotional practices. According to Kenrick's biographer the decrees of the First Provincial Council had been "openly disregarded" by many of the clergy, who continued to adhere to traditional practices. Kenrick repromulgated those decrees and additionally required that all churches be fitted with baptismal fonts and confessionals and that baptisms only be performed in the church of the parish within which the child's parents lived. The effect of these decrees was to end the former practice of parents choosing to have their children baptized by popular priests of their own nationality, often in their own homes. Marriages, too, were regulated and a new standard, the "Roman ritual" was instituted to replace the popular "English ritual" and other traditional practices that had previously been observed. Kenrick also took steps to increase the mystery and power of the Holy Eucharist, forbidding priests from the common practice of keeping the Blessed Sacrament on their persons at all times, and allowing it to be exposed "only on two occasions, while Mass was being celebrated, viz: 'on the Feast of Corpus Christi and during the Forty Hours' Devotion.'" In the words of Kenrick's biographer, as a result of his efforts "the administration of the Sacraments [was] regulated [and] public worship became more solemn and beautiful by better observance of the liturgy."[4]

This was the first mention in American diocesan legislation of the Forty Hours devotion and it marked a significant movement away from the "simple" and "unadorned" form of Catholic devotion advocated by the republican dissenters. It also represented an important deviation from the traditional practices of the immigrant churches. The Forty Hours ("an exposition of the Blessed Sacrament for a period of forty hours in memory of the forty hours Jesus' body spent in the sepulcher") was the first of several new devotional practices promoted by American prelates in the middle decades of the nineteenth century. Taken together these represented an attempt "to bind the laity more closely to the institutional church . . . and to ensure the orthodoxy of the laity." These expressions of "ultramontane devotionalism" were modeled on the intense and aggressive pietism of the Catholic Counter-Reformation and sought to enhance "the hierarchy's control over the laity . . . by centralizing devotional practices in the parish church and standardizing practices throughout the church as a whole, and . . . by creating symbolical associations and patronage relationships between supernatural beings, the pope, and the institutional church."[5]

Throughout Kenrick's diocese devotions were standardized on the Roman model. He also instituted uniform English and German catechisms for use throughout the diocese. Kenrick further decreed that no religious books could be used unless they had first been approved by him or his authorized representative. It had long been the custom in Philadelphia to include "a great many English hymns and compositions" in Catholic services. Now these were banned. He also required the posting of marriage banns, although this had not been the previous custom, and required that all sacraments, even extreme unction, be administered by priests only in their parish and "revoked all customs to the contrary."[6]

These devotional and liturgical innovations were intended to replace rather than to accommodate immigrant traditions. Rather than tolerating cultural diversity Francis Kenrick and the other American bishops were determined that "every effort [should be made] to see that one and the same discipline is everywhere observed." Ann Taves has described this "desire to standardize practices" as "a reflection of the ultramontane desire to elevate Rome as the center of Catholicism and the pope as arbiter of that which was truly Catholic not only in faith and morals, but also in ritual practice." Joseph Chinnici notes that "at least four of the seven provincial councils of Baltimore between 1829 and 1849 passed regulations enjoining the priests to follow the Roman ritual and ceremonials." Other legislation affected "church ornamentation, confessionals, ecclesiastical dress, music, fasting and devotion to the Blessed Virgin." The result of this Romanization of devotions as well as dress and discipline and liturgy, was to produce in America during the middle decades of the nineteenth century (and particularly in Philadelphia where the attempt began early and was strongly applied) a Roman Catholic church that bore little resemblance to the traditional churches of northern Europe.[7]

Francis Kenrick was relentless in the enforcement of these regulations. Refractory priests were disciplined; some were sent out of the diocese or even driven from the Church. So successful were his efforts that by 1838 he was able to report to Rome that "Generally the life of the secular clergy is without blame: the scandals that can arise by opposition to the exercise of episcopal authority have been removed or punished." He had taken unto himself powers greater than those ever exercised by any of his predecessors during the period of episcopal absolutism, but he exercised that authority toward the end of building and maintaining a coherent system of specified relationships among the various elements of the Church. At all levels conduct was systematized and regularized, bureaucratic controls instituted, and innovative practices established that reinforced visually and behaviorally the formal distinctions among the different elements of the Church. By 1851, when he ascended to the archepiscopacy of Baltimore, Francis Kenrick had gone far toward providing in Philadelphia the "Church of laws, not of men" for which William Harold and Thadeus O'Meally had long before pleaded. It was, however, a Roman, not an American or an Irish or a German church.[8]

The Building Bishop

Like other restoration reformers Francis Kenrick found inspiration in the parish-based organization of the Tridentine Church and placed great emphasis on building programs that made the parish church a physical and social presence in every community in which Catholics lived. When Kenrick arrived in Philadelphia in 1830 the diocese contained only twenty-two churches. Within eight years there were sixty-three, and when he left in 1851, the diocese (much diminished in area by the separation of Pittsburgh) boasted ninety-two churches. During his administration the number of parishes in the city of Philadelphia increased from four to twenty and during his two decades there Bishop Kenrick was responsible for the construction of nineteen churches as well as the early work on the Cathedral of Sts. Peter and Paul, the city's most enduring symbol of Catholic unity.[1]

The extraordinary nature of this growth can be seen in comparison with other dioceses. In 1834, when Boston boasted fourteen Catholic churches and New York but six, Philadelphia already had constructed forty-one. Two years later, Boston had added two churches, New York eight, and Philadelphia seventeen. By 1838 Boston had increased the number of churches to eighteen; New York, under the leadership of John Hughes, had expanded to a total of thirty-eight; but Philadelphia remained far ahead with sixty-three churches. In later years other dioceses gradually closed the gap between themselves and Philadelphia, but Francis Kenrick's primacy among America's "building bishops" was well established.[2]

To staff these churches many new clergymen were brought into the diocese. Kenrick, Propaganda-trained and a committed ultramontanist, considered many of these priests, especially those who had been educated in Ireland, to be of inferior quality and doctrinally suspect. He therefore went to great lengths to obtain properly trained parish clergy. To that end he solicited help from Rome. He induced his friend, Paul Cullen, who at that time was rector of the Irish College at Propaganda, to send priests to Philadelphia and he sent promising young men across the Atlantic to study in Rome. He also established a seminary (named after the Counter-Reformation zealot, Saint Charles Borromeo), housing and teaching theology to the first students in his own home. By 1838 St. Charles Seminary, under the direction of Bishop Kenrick's younger brother, Peter Richard, had produced fifteen priests and had another thirteen in training.[3]

Kenrick's building program established parish churches throughout the diocese. Each of these became the center of a constellation of societies, confraternities, sodalities, and other associations that made it a social center for the local community. In Kathleen Gavigan's words, parish societies "provided the primary affiliation outside the home for generation upon generation of Philadelphia area Catholics." Parish societies sponsored lectures, held balls, mounted charity drives, organized fairs, excursions, and concerts, functioned as insurance companies and savings banks, and in a hundred ways became an indispensable element in the lives of American Catholics. St. Augustine's Church provides us with an excellent example of such a parish network. By 1844, when the church was destroyed by nativist rioters, it boasted a beneficial insurance society, a library society, a Christian Doctrine society, a total-abstinence society, a youth's literary institute, a Confraternity of Our Lady of the Cincture, a Sunday school, a reading-room society, a free school, and an orphan society.[4]

The first provincial council of bishops in 1829 had urged Catholics to withdraw their children from non-sectarian schools and to place them in environments where "their unfolding perceptions" would "be imbued with the mild and lovely tints of religious truth and pure devotion." Priests were told to encourage the development and use of Catholic educational programs and facilities. In this the desires of the council coincided with the efforts of Roman reformers everywhere. Francis Kenrick, following the lead of both Rome and Baltimore, undertook the construction of a broad-based and comprehensive system of Catholic educational institutions. He encouraged the establishment of two Roman Catholic colleges (Villanova and St. Joseph's) and fostered the development of a parochial school system that embraced half the parishes in the diocese. In addition to these he required each parish to establish a Sunday school and a circulating library. Although the Catholic school system depended in its early years on lay support and many schools were administered by laymen, steps were taken to minimize lay interference in the socialization of Catholic youth. Under Kenrick a number of teaching orders entered the diocese and were given charge of the educational facilities.[5]

All this institutional development cost money. A charming myth has developed to the effect that most Catholic institutions were built and maintained by the accumulated contributions and efforts of working-class men and women. John Hughes used to tell a story that epitomizes this myth. He decided, sometime in 1830, to build a new church and, having obtained Bishop Kenrick's approval, announced his intentions one Sunday from the pulpit of St. Joseph's Chapel. He urged all the attending parishioners to give according to their means. Then he went home and waited all day Monday to receive subscriptions. None came. Again on Tuesday he waited, and again no one came. Finally, on Wednesday a humble servant woman appeared. "This is the first day, Father," she said, "since you spoke to us on Sunday, that I have been able to come out. I have brought my contribution for the new church." Whereupon she handed the priest three shillings. "I took the money," Hughes said, "ran to my bedroom, and throwing myself upon my knees, thanked God that the work was done. From that moment I never had a doubt of the success of my enterprise."[6]

Hughes's story, while certainly inspiring, has little truth in it. The imperative for building the church (of St. John the Evangelist) came from Francis Kenrick, who, his biographer tells us, had planned prior to leaving Kentucky to build a new church in Philadelphia without trustees that would serve as an alternative to St. Mary's. On the same day that he announced his intention to assume the pastorship of St. Mary's, Kenrick directed John Hughes to collect funds for the erection of such a church, and while his struggle with the trustees raged, plans for St. John's Church proceeded. While Hughes certainly solicited contributions from members of the working class these amounts were never central to his effort. St. John's was built by the contributions of middle-class and elite Catholics, most importantly by a $40,000 no-interest loan from the prosperous silk merchant and land speculator, Marc Antony Frenaye (who after the church was constructed personally oversaw its financial affairs).[7]

Wealthy and powerful men like Marc Frenaye were the financial foundation upon which Philadelphia's Catholic institutions were erected. They built churches, established schools, endowed orphanages and asylums, and founded and directed a wide range of benevolent associations. In some cases parishes were dominated by a single individual. In Kellyville, west of the city, Dennis Kelly, a textile-mill owner and stockbreeder, underwrote the construction of St. Denis' Church while his son-in-law, Charles Kelly, was the principle support of nearby St. Charles' Church. In addition to being prominent in the affairs of the churches they endowed, both men were actively involved in a wide range of Catholic associations, organizing or serving as directors of local Catholic charities as well as Catholic insurance and savings funds. Similarly, Jerome Keating, who owned a textile mill in Manayunk, paid for the erection of St. John the Baptist's Church there and personally dominated church activities even to the point of teaching confirmation classes and directing the choir.[8]

We can see something of the character of this Catholic elite and trace its influence in the descendants of "Baron" John Keating, an Irish aristocrat who served with the "Irish Brigade" in prerevolutionary France, then emigrated to America and settled in Philadelphia. There he entered into profitable land speculation ventures and over time established himself as a respected member of Philadelphia's merchant and financial community. Keating was also an important civic leader, serving as a trustee of the University of Pennsylvania and as a manager of the Philadelphia Saving Fund Society in addition to being involved in a number of benevolent institutions. Politically he was a Whig and during the Jacksonian "Bank War" he staunchly supported his close friend, Nicholas Biddle.[9]

John Keating was a man of "deep religious faith," and he "was actively interested in all matters pertaining to the well-being of the Church in Philadelphia." His wealth afforded him a great deal of scope for pursuing those interests. After his marriage to his wife, Eulalia, he constructed St. Eulalia's church at Coudersport in her honor. He was a founder of St. Joseph's Hospital and president of the Friends of St. Charles Seminary. He attended mass regularly, holding pews at St. Mary's, St. Joseph's, and St. John the Baptist's churches. He was a strong supporter and good friend of Bishop Kenrick "whom he . . . seconded in all measures affecting [the Church's] growth and development." So great were his services that when he died in 1856 Archbishop Kenrick personally composed his epitaph.[10]

John Keating sought to "surround his children with a Catholic atmosphere" and they mirrored his devotion to the Church. John Keating, Jr., was an attorney and state legislator who married the daughter of Judge Joseph Hopkinson, a prominent local jurist whose father had been a signer of the Declaration of Independence. Like his father, young John was a dedicated "bishopite," rendering legal assistance to the bishop during the long conflict with St. Mary's dissenters. The Baron's second son, William, also a lawyer as well as being a scientist of international repute, was a professor at the University of Pennsylvania and a founder of the Franklin Institute. He served as secretary of the Academy of Natural Sciences, was director of the Board of City Trusts, and was a member of the Philosophical Society. He was also a founder of the Philadelphia and Reading Railroad. Like his father and brother, William Keating was actively involved in Church activities, serving on the boards of a number of Catholic benevolent institutions.[11]

Both of Baron Keating's natural sons died as young men, but there was a third, adopted son—his nephew, Jerome. Jerome Keating became a textile manufacturer and was also a director of the Philadelphia

Saving Fund Society. He, too, was deeply involved in Church activities. He built St. John the Baptist's Church in Manayunk, served on the board of St. Joseph's Orphanage, and until his death in 1832 was active in a number of Catholic charities. His business partner was John J. Borie who campaigned unsuccessfully as a "bishopite" candidate for the board of trustees at St. Mary's Church in 1831. John Borie's son, Adolph, became secretary of the navy in the Grant administration and his daughter married William V. Keating, Jerome's son. William V. Keating in turn was a prominent physician, director of St. Joseph's Hospital, a founder of the Beneficial Saving Fund, and an important contributor to a number of Catholic institutions and charities.[12]

Three generations of the Keating family thus played an important role in Catholic institutional development. Taken together they represented a considerable concentration of power and wealth. They were prominent in politics, the professions, manufacturing and finance, and they were typical of the men and women upon whom Philadelphia's reforming bishops relied. These affluent Catholics were a closely knit community (bound together by intermarriage, friendships, and business relationships) and they were very conscious of their status. As the DeSales Institute stipulated in its constitution, they were "Catholic gentlemen" of "character . . . , piety and intelligence," as well as "elevated social standing." Their outlook was decidedly conservative and was in all major respects indistinguishable from that of their Protestant peers. In 1812, for instance, John Keating, musing on his daughter's first communion, wrote in his diary, "I wish for her a husband sweet and sensible, industrious, well brought up and of the same rank as herself . . . , [and] that they should have between them sufficient income for indulging their simple tastes without ostentation." Except for his stipulation that any suitor must be Catholic, such sentiments could easily have issued from the pen of any wealthy Quaker.[13]

Members of the Catholic elite fused their religion with class interests. Jerome Keating, for instance, was deeply concerned with the religious instruction of his employees. His residence at Manayunk towered over three rows of small dwellings inhabited by employees at his mill and their families. From this vantage point he supervised the most intimate aspects of their lives. He recruited only Catholic workers and required that they regularly attend mass at the church he built adjoining his home. Between services Keating and his wife instructed the "village children" in Christian doctrine as well as proper manners, unquestioning obedience, and devotion to ritual. Not even in their homes could Keating's employees escape his scrutiny. Father Francis Barat, whose father worked for Jerome Keating, remembered an occasion on which Keating visited his parents in their home and asked if the children had studied the Catholic Catechism of Christian Doctrine. "On learning that we had not as yet been supplied with the Catechisms, but that they would be procured without delay, Mr. Keating, turning toward us, said to my father: 'And, unless they study the Catechism we shall have to rap them over their knuckles.'"[14]

Jerome Keating's death in 1832 brought an end to this rigorous discipline, but control of the church in Manayunk remained with others of his class and interests, the McGlinchy family—five brothers and three sisters from County Tyrone who were "active and prominent in local and business affairs," and who provided "strong moral and financial support" to the pastors. Cornelius McGlinchy, the head of the clan, served as chairman of St. John's School Board and director of St. Timothy's Hospital. He listed his occupation as a simple "grocer," but he was also director of the Manayunk Bank, president of the Manayunk Bridge Company, and treasurer and director of the Manayunk and Roxborough Inclined Plane and Railway Company. As such he commanded a large work force of immigrant laborers and, like the Keatings, found the restoration church's emphasis on discipline and submission to authority consonant with his interests.[15]

In a similar manner Dennis and Charles Kelly exercised benevolent control over their coreligionists in Kellyville. Like Jerome Keating, they recruited Catholics to work in their textile factories and on their farms, even importing laborers from Ireland. They housed workers on their own lands and, like Keating, built churches for them and guided their lives with ample "advice" and "counsel." Dennis Kelly, in particular, sought out young, ambitious men and started them in business or farming with cash advances that totaled "an immense sum." In this way the Kellys built up an almost feudal web of dependency and reciprocal obligations in their work forces. In exchange for obsequiousness, respectable behavior, and diligence at the workplace the residents of Kellyville received economic security. Even in difficult times the Kellys kept their mills running at a loss rather than lay off workers.[16]

Except for their devotion to Catholicism there is little to differentiate the attitudes of the Kellys, Keatings, and McGlinchys from those of Protestant industrialists of the period. Anthony F. C. Wallace has brilliantly chronicled the lives of several contemporary Protestant "Cotton

Lords" who established personal fiefdoms in the industrial towns south-
west of Philadelphia. They formed a local oligarchy, bound together in
"loosely overlapping networks of marriage and descent." Their relations
with their workers were paternalistic, informed with a "strong sense of
responsibility for the personal welfare" of their workers while at the
same time demanding from those workers "a recognition of hierarchy."
These "evangelical industrialists" were vitally concerned with questions
of "moral character," and sought to imbue in their work forces a
"Christian Industrialism" that fused the imperatives of Christian evangelism with the practical considerations of industrial discipline. In
short, the major contours of their lives and their social perspectives varied little from those displayed by Catholics of their class.[17]

Romanization was thus not the only imperative shaping Philadelphia Catholicism in the antebellum period. The influence of secular
elites and the demands of industrial discipline also were felt. In many
parishes a small number of very powerful men and women made the
church their own and ran it in cooperation with the local clergy. By and
large, elite interests coincided with and reinforced the authoritarian
tendencies of the Romanizing bishops, but buildings and pews had to
be filled, organizations staffed, and souls saved. Therefore the Church
had to reach out beyond the elite and listen to voices other than those
emanating from Rome and the Catholic Club. Often those voices
expressed interests that would take the Church in directions that were
different from or even opposed to the course that Bishop Kenrick and
his lay supporters sought to chart.

B'hoys and Society Men

The reformation of Philadelphia Catholicism coincided with a period
of rapid social differentiation within the city's Catholic population.
The vertical dimension of this change has been extensively chronicled

but there was a geographic dimension too. As the city grew and spread it became more ecologically diverse. In neighborhoods throughout the city communities formed, each with its own particular set of social relationships and distinctive economic base. Communication between these communities was difficult. As late as 1850 most people still walked to work, shopped near their homes, and associated only infrequently with people from outside their own neighborhood. Occasional trips for shopping, entertainment, or to visit relatives carried people out of their neighborhoods but, except for the few who could afford the time and money necessary for regular travel, life was lived within a very constrained geographical space.[1]

This did not mean that the social life experienced by the residents of these neighborhood communities was necessarily deficient. Notices in mid-nineteenth-century newspapers show that Philadelphians gathered together in their neighborhoods to provide for the poor, to meet emergencies, for entertainment and celebration, for education—for almost any imaginable cause. They held concerts, lectures, balls, fairs, illuminations, parades, demonstrations, political rallies, and all manner of group activities. Philadelphia's neighborhoods in the middle of the nineteenth century were vital social organisms, vibrant with the bustling activities of the local residents. Increasingly, immigrant Catholics were drawn into these multiethnic neighborhood activities and associations.[2]

Some of the intensity of neighborhood attachments can be seen in the Kensington antirailroad riots of 1840–42. For two years residents of that community blocked the construction of a line by the Philadelphia and Trenton Railroad Company along its busiest artery, Front Street. All social classes and ethnic groups within the community were united in this struggle. Irish and German immigrants joined with Native Americans, and "weavers and draymen entered into coalition with their middle-class landlords and employers, as well as professional politicians, to resist the railroad." During the conflict prominent community leaders instituted court appeals, large crowds attended political rallies, and men, women, and children joined in attacking railroad workers and equipment as well as sheriff's posses. Ultimately the resistance was successful and the company's charter was rescinded by the state legislature, an event that was celebrated in Kensington by two days of illuminations and parades.[3]

Neighborhood solidarity such as that displayed by the residents of Kensington in their struggle to control Front Street was not ephemeral;

it was institutionalized in myriad neighborhood-based associations and organizations. The most prominent of these were the volunteer fire companies that proliferated through the city in the second quarter of the nineteenth century. So important was the status conferred by membership in these organizations that it was said that being elected director of a fire company was the "summit of the hope of one-half the clerks, counter-hoppers and quill drivers in the city." These volunteer companies, with their related associations, ladies' auxiliaries, political clubs, street gangs and such, provided a focus for social interaction at the neighborhood level. Their engine and hose houses became local social centers, they sponsored a wide range of social activities, and at election time they were the centers of the local political universe. Bruce Laurie describes them: "Fraternal-clubs-cum-athletic-teams, they offered outlets for recreation and centers of camaraderie. They also conferred upon their impoverished followers the status and recognition denied them by the larger society. Membership in a company was a sign of social acceptance."[4]

In the minds of many respectable Philadelphians, though, the volunteer companies and the neighborhood associations that formed around them epitomized a crisis of violence and disorder that was threatening to destroy the social fabric of the city and of the nation. The volunteers, Sidney George Fisher asserted, were

> a dangerous body of men. They are very numerous, are influenced by an esprit de corps, act together and, being composed of young men and being of the lower classes, have the power to do a great deal of mischief. They defy the law, terrify the magistrates and newspapers, have constantly violent affrays and consider themselves an important body with peculiar rights and privileges.[5]

A popular tract of the time described fire houses as "notorious . . . haunts of the idle and depraved— . . . nurseries of vice— . . . the scene of the ruin of many youths of promise." There was ample reason for alarm. Industrializing Philadelphia was afflicted with ever-rising levels of violence, criminality, and civil disorder that dwarf anything known in American cities today. Between 1828 and 1849 the city witnessed a dozen major riots and hundreds of smaller violent incidents. Holidays, election days, and even weekends became occasions for violent affrays involving fire companies, street gangs, and other neighborhood groups seeking to extend or to defend their turfs. Muggings, robberies, homicides, prostitution, substance abuse, and a host of other social pathologies were rampant on the streets of the city, and as the tide of violence rose so too did cries for a restoration of public order (by any means necessary) and that meant controlling and suppressing indigenous neighborhood associations.[6]

Among the groups most stigmatized by the crisis in civil authority were immigrant Catholics—especially the Irish. This was not a matter of simple bias. Young Irish immigrants were a disruptive element in the city's population and were viewed by respectable citizens, both Protestant and Catholic, as a dangerous class of people. Irish immigrants had been prominent participants in many of the city's worst riots and some of the most notorious volunteer companies and street gangs were led by Irishmen. Immigrants were also considered by many to be a political threat, for they provided strong support for many of the neighborhood-based machines that challenged the legitimacy of elite institutions and central authorities. Even immigrants who did not actively participate in the neighborhood clubs posed a problem for the emerging industrial leadership because they adhered to a traditional culture, many expressions of which (Donnybrook Fairs, pub and tavern carousing, and the like) were inconsistent with the modernizing tendencies of industrial society. There is no reason to suppose that the disorderly gangs of immigrant youths or the men who frequented saloons cared much what proper Philadelphians thought of them, but within the immigrant neighborhoods there were people who were acutely sensitive to the opinions of others.[7]

Immigration created a rising demand for essential services which provided many Catholics with opportunities for economic gain and social advancement. The middle third of the century saw the rise of a new class of small entrepreneurs (grocers, liquor dealers, small contractors and manufacturers, printers, politicians, drygoods merchants, and the like) who specialized in providing essential goods and services to the immigrants and profited from their custom. This emerging Catholic petty-bourgeoisie occupied an extremely tenuous position within the city's social structure. They hovered precariously on the fringes of respectability and, like the "new-made gentlemen and women" of an earlier generation, were quite conscious of their status and sought confirmation of it from the society beyond the bounds of their neighborhoods. Their social aspirations, though, conflicted with their economic interests.[8]

The quest for respectability led the Catholic petty-bourgeoisie to distance themselves from the immigrant workers upon whose custom they depended. At the same time that they were seeking acceptance in the larger world beyond their neighborhoods they were also attempting to build and maintain constituencies within a class of people whose values and behaviors had been repudiated by the dominant culture. Able to neither abandon nor to embrace their disreputable coreligionists, middle-class Catholics were caught in an exquisite dilemma that could be resolved only if the behavior of the immigrant working class could be modified—that is, if the immigrant worker could be made respectable. Many middle-class Catholics therefore had good reasons to attempt to influence the values and behavior of the immigrant working class. So, too, did the Church. Priests and prelates, no less than publicans, publishers, and politicians had an interest in developing constituencies within and shaping the behavior of the immigrant working class.

The rapid expansion of Catholic institutions in Philadelphia after 1830 paralleled, and to some extent competed with, indigenous neighborhood associations. Parish churches and the associations that they promoted presented in each neighborhood a respectable alternative to the unruly volunteer companies and the network of gangs, auxiliaries, and clubs that surrounded them. These Catholic societies were analogous to Protestant and nondenominational self-help associations and like them were the most visible expression of an emerging bourgeois culture in what Arthur Schlesinger called a "nation of joiners."[9]

Like non-Catholic self-help associations, the new Catholic societies were status-defining mechanisms. They distinguished respectable Catholics from their disreputable coreligionists. There was a world of difference between the "society man" and the "volunteer jakey." Church-based societies required that their members adhere to strict standards of conduct. They were to be diligent, temperate, and submissive to both religious and civil authority, and their behavior stood in sharp contrast to that of the "violent volunteers" or the "bhoys" of the street gangs and saloons. Personal standards of behavior thus made the members of church-related societies a distinctive element in the immigrant population, standing somewhat apart from and, in their minds, above the common herd. Friendly societies (as Thomas N. Brown noted) "could transform a nobody into a somebody."[10]

Parish-based societies also provided more tangible benefits. They organized charity within neighborhoods, they established financial institutions, they provided insurance benefits and a variety of consumer services. They also organized recreational and educational activities. Most important, they provided a link between the neighborhood and higher levels of social and political organization.

Society men and women were ambitious; they embraced the striving ethic of industrializing America, but they were not rugged individualists striking out on their own. In these societies like-minded individuals banded together for mutual support and social betterment. In this sense the friendly societies were distinctly superior to the neighborhood-based clubs with which they competed. Volunteer companies and street gangs were potent presences in the local community, but the neighborhood was the extent of their influence. The distinction they conferred on their members was limited. Church-related societies, though, were linked to an overarching structure of associations and institutions that were diocesan, national, and even international in extent. Not only did this enlarged arena provide greater scope for social and material ambition, but it also imbued members of Catholic societies with a sense of participation in a movement that was of great significance to American, and even all of Western culture.

Membership in the parish societies set people apart from their neighbors and enclosed them within a social universe filled with like-minded individuals, but society men and women were by no means disengaged from the world that surrounded them. Members of the friendly societies were tireless proselytizers and living advertisements for the respectable standards of behavior they had adopted. Their goals were twofold and more than a bit contradictory. At the same time that they sought to distinguish themselves from the neighborhood societies in which they lived, they also sought to influence their friends and neighbors into lives of piety, order, and self-discipline. In this latter aspect the goals of the respectable society men and women coincided rather well with Bishop Kenrick's ambitions, but the bourgeois Catholics' drive for distinction in the larger society would pose problems for the Romanizing bishop.

"The Order of the Day"

—————

Nothing exemplified the twin drives for respectability and control more than the total abstinence movement. Bishop Kenrick first addressed the question of temperance in April of 1840. His interest had been sparked by Father Theobald Mathew's temperance crusade in rural Ireland which he saw as a model for evangelizing Philadelphia's immigrants. Through the summer of 1840 Kenrick pressed the issue, preaching temperance sermons and personally administering the total abstinence oath in churches throughout the diocese. The response was enormous. Marc Frenaye declared that "*the temperance reform [is] . . . the order of the day*, it has precedence over everything else." At St. John the Evangelist's at least a thousand individuals had taken the pledge by July, and in the city as a whole five thousand pledged to abstain by the end of August. Soon every parish in the city boasted a total abstinence society.[1]

Bishop Kenrick's count of more than five thousand Catholic abstainers is corroborated by a number of other sources and should be considered to be substantially correct. By way of comparison we should note that the *Public Ledger* in the spring of 1841 boasted that seventeen thousand Philadelphians had taken the pledge. If this figure included, Catholics they would have constituted nearly one-third of the total. If they were not included, Catholics would still have accounted for more than one-fifth of the abstainers in Philadelphia at a time when they made up little more than one-tenth of the city's population. Whatever the reliability of these estimates, and they are questionable, we must still recognize that Catholics in antebellum Philadelphia embraced the temperance reform as enthusiastically as did Protestants.[2]

Catholic temperance reformers proudly displayed their affiliations in public displays that affirmed their commitment to respectability and their loyalty to the American republic. The Independence Day parade in 1841 featured "The banners of S. Patrick, S. Augustine, S. Michael, St. Francis Xavier with the Madonna and Bambino in front borne by the [temperance] societies of these respective churches." One year later the Catholic temperance procession included more than seven thousand adult marchers as well as a number of youth associations. That day George Washington marched alongside the Madonna and the Saints.[3]

On Independence Day of 1843 amid the hoopla of the parades and demonstrations members of the Pennsylvania Catholic Total Abstinence Society gathered to hear an oration by William George Read, a popular Catholic author and lecturer. His subject was American liberty and, like other Catholic apologists of his day, he sought its roots in Catholic culture. He traced the emergence of the idea of liberty from Columbus, through the Calverts, and finally to the Southern planters who, unlike the "bigoted" New Englanders, derived their concepts of liberty from "the classic models [of] . . . balanced government." Aside from its peculiarly Catholic slant, Read's attempt to locate the source of American identity in history rather than principle was remarkably like the perspectives advanced by American Whig politicians and theorists of his day. This was by no means the only similarity.[4]

Like his Whig contemporaries Read associated liberty with material progress. He invited his listeners to "Behold your rivers swarming with the half-animated vehicles of commerce; your land intersected with canals and roads; and the blue of ocean whitened with your sails." He attributed the "progressive multiplication and diffusion of the means of comfort and enjoyment" to that "great secret of American prosperity"—the principle that government is instituted "for the good of the people."[5]

Read also shared with the Whigs an apprehension of imminent catastrophe. The American Revolution, he argued, had represented the triumph of "virtue," born in self-government, over corruption that had ensued from the "insidious intrusion of government patronage." However America had fallen far from that pinnacle and was currently immersed in political corruption, awash in "violence and bloodshed," and imperiled by "Aristocracy" which threatened once again to drain the lifeblood of the community. Like the Whigs, Read located the source of this danger in moral decline. "That which is chiefly lacking in America." he proclaimed, "to the perfect development of . . . the inherent conservatism of republican institutions, is a check to selfishness, and a more complete identification of individuals with the state."[6]

Unrestrained individualism and selfishness, Read said, led to "distinction and plunder" and to the erection of a "profligate and . . . idle" aristocracy not unlike the "crowned and coronetted beggary" of England. Like the noted Whig economist Henry C. Carey (son of

Mathew Carey), Read distinguished between small- to moderate-scale enterprise which resolved, "at last, into mere exchange of one man's production for another's," and large-scale capitalism which was inherently exploitative and reduced free mechanics and laborers to the level of the "naked crawling wretches" who "work in fire" as "in the heart of hell" in British industry.[7]

As a solution he offered a revival of virture and redemption of past pledges. The public, Read observed, "are apt to forget [that there are] . . . certain over-ruling principles of justice and benevolence, which control, or ought to control, the legislative franchise itself." Whole communities, he lamented, "regard their laws as the mere resolutions of an ever varying opinion." Government, he declared, should be "propelled by moral power rather than mischief." Then, in a crucial linkage that stood at the heart of Catholic reform and cemented the alliance between the bishop and the bourgeoisie, Read argued that:

> the only permanent security for American liberty will be found in a more general investigation of the authority and obedience to the teaching of that Divine Religion, which, in her unchanging and unchangeable dogmas, her steady discipline, and sacramental aids, involves the elements of all true morality, all sound politics, all abiding civilization.[8]

Only through submission to the Universal Church, Read explained, would it be possible to "restrain the irregular passions of the multitude, in an age of universal suffrage." Only through the teachings of the Church, he held, would the people "learn, that liberty is not a license to be recklessly enjoyed, but a trust to be scrupulously discharged." The freeman had to understand that his "vote is not a portion of his private property, to be invested for his private emolument, or squandered under the blandishments of personal favour, or the excitements of party rage." Discipline, not coercion, was needed. Social control depended on self-control and only the Church could instill that control by:

> withdrawing [the citizen] from vice and encouraging him to virtue, and by inculcating that fundamental political truth, that he, who would retain the inestimable privilege of self-government, must practice it, not merely in occasional expressions of preference between contending candidates, but in the daily and hourly control of his appetite and passions.[9]

This remarkable document places American Catholicism squarely within the republican tradition of "civic humanism" that had informed colonial criticism of British rule in both Ireland and America in the late eighteenth century. It also places this organic, cooperative view of society in direct contradiction to the acquisitive individualism and competition of democratic liberalism. By doing so it not only provided a link between Catholic culture and the American revolutionary tradition, but it also illuminated a perspective shared by respectable Catholics and those elements of the American polity who still clung to those revolutionary ideals. These, as Daniel Walker Howe has so ably shown, included much of the leadership of the American Whig movement.

If the Whig party, as Howe has suggested, expressed the consciousness and sensibilities of America's antebellum bourgeoisie, then so, too, did Philadelphia's Roman Catholic establishment. A love of order and fear of passion and an emphasis on social and personal control were common to both. This sensibility underlay the cooperation between Catholic bishops and bourgeois elements of the laity, it established ideological connections between the restoration Church and American republican thought, and it advanced a stinging repudiation of the liberal excesses of Jacksonian democracy. This antidemocratic bias was reflected in the political sphere. It has been something of a cliché to say that Irish Catholics were Democrats, but such was not the case in antebellum Philadelphia. There, Irish Catholics constituted "a floating body of voters which never really formed a cohesive group" and were well represented in both the Whig and the Democratic party organizations. There were social ramifications, too.[10]

Late in the afternoon of May 12, 1831, John Hughes, resplendent in his sacerdotal robes, stood in front of a "numerous and respectable" assembly of citizens in Manayunk, a textile village on the Schuylkill River northwest of Philadelphia. More than a hundred conveyances had brought these affluent men and women out from Philadelphia to witness the laying of the cornerstone of St. John the Baptist's Church. Ceremonies began in front of Jerome Keating's home; then Hughes led a procession to the future site of the church where, assisted by three other priests, he held a short religious service. Then, his vestments "glittering" in the "broken rays of the evening sun," Hughes led the largely Protestant assemblage to a nearby Presbyterian church where he preached to "a congregation of all religions" on the importance of ceremony in religious observance. A collection was then taken and the crowd finally dispersed in a festive mood, whips cracking the air, carriages rattling, and "boyhood in all its glee making the most of the holiday."[11]

Such idyllic scenes of interdenominational amity were not uncommon in antebellum Philadelphia. One year after the Manayunk ceremonies John Hughes again presided at the opening of a Catholic church—St. John the Evangelist's in Center City, which supplanted St. Mary's as Philadelphia's elite congregation. Once again many wealthy Protestants were in attendance. Two years previously Protestants had joined with Catholics to celebrate Daniel O'Connell's victory in his crusade for Catholic emancipation in Ireland. Commenting on the extensive support shown by Protestants for a Catholic church fair he attended in the city's Fairmont district in 1842, James S. Buckingham, a visiting British journalist and temperance reformer, noted that:

> there is a very large portion of the community who think that every religious sect and every religious object ought to have a share of their support; and there is another large portion who . . . are perfectly indifferent as to what doctrines they hear. . . . Such persons . . . are very numerous among the wealthy and genteel classes of society here. [To them] a Catholic fair would . . . be as attractive as a Protestant one.[12]

Interdenominational amity and cooperation was by no means restricted to the "wealthy and genteel classes" of Philadelphia society. In the temperance reform we can see a remarkable degree of cooperation that was based on shared sensibilities. Commonly held attitudes could unite people across denominations even in the hothouse atmosphere of the Second Great Awakening. Bruce Laurie has described the antebellum Protestant evangelical crusade in Philadelphia as organized around the principles of "sobriety, industry, economy, peace, and friendship." These ideals, however, were not specific to Protestant reform—they could just as easily apply to the members of Philadelphia's Catholic societies. The impulse toward respectability affected indiscriminately both Protestants and Catholics, uniting them in opposition to the disreputable street and saloon cultures that were flourishing among some elements of the working classes.[13]

In Philadelphia it was never the case, as some scholars have claimed, that "to stand for temperance was to assert a Protestant value in direct opposition to the more liberal drinking habits of Irish Catholics."

Protestant temperance reformers hailed the rise of the Catholic total abstinence movement in the 1840s and many of them crossed denominational lines to seek admission into Catholic associations. Michael O'Connor complained of this in 1842 and noted that, despite the clear Catholic significance of the total abstinence pledge which was "administered before the altar . . . , we cannot refuse to give it to some Protestants in the crowd." The Propaganda-trained priest found such blurring of denominational lines offensive, as did his bishop who, despite entreaties on the part of temperance society members, "declined all official connections with Protestant societies." The laity, however, were not so particular as the priests and commonly admitted Protestants to membership in their societies.[14]

Interdenominational associations were not what Bishop Kenrick had in mind. As he had originally conceived it, the temperance reform was to be a mechanism for drawing unchurched immigrant workers into a Catholic community that spanned the class spectrum. Within this closed society, he hoped, the unruly workers could learn Catholic principles and middle-class values and be isolated from Protestant influence and error. Middle-class Catholic laymen, though, had remade the temperance reform into an affirmation of their respectable status. As such it became more and more a vehicle for the expression of class differences and an occasion for interdenominational cooperation in which distinctions between Protestant and Catholic were muted. Moreover, the intense lay activity associated with the temperance reform represented a degree of empowerment the bishop found disturbing. He was willing to support lay activities only insofar as they did not compromise ecclesiastical authority, and by the early 1840s lay enthusiasm was threatening to burst those bounds.

Lay temperance advocates, Kenrick opined, placed far too much emphasis on the total abstinence pledge in itself and seemed to imply that an individual could redeem himself without clerical assistance. Even Father Mathew, he considered, placed too much emphasis on taking the pledge, and not enough on supernatural assistance, a practice that "seems to detract from religion . . . not without injury to the grace and truth of God." Kenrick also felt that Father Mathew did not do enough to separate himself from Protestant temperance reformers. In Philadelphia, then, he modified Father Mathew's example by insisting upon a complete separation of Catholic and Protestant societies and he refused to accept the validity of any pledge administered by a layman, requiring instead "a spiritual or supernatural approach . . . that would emphasize prayer and frequent reception of the sacraments."[15]

Bishop Kenrick's misgivings about the direction the temperance reform was taking reveal a fundamental tension between the assimilationist goals of the Catholic bourgeoisie and the institutional imperatives of restoration Catholicism. These tensions were brought to the fore by a sudden and overwhelming catastrophe. In 1844 nativism burst like a thunderclap upon Philadelphia's Catholic community. Basking in the atmosphere of interdenominational amity that had prevailed among the city's respectable classes, Catholic leaders were completely unprepared for the violence that erupted first in Kensington and then in Southwark in the spring and summer of that year. In the course of a few short months an "insignificant rivulet" of anti-Catholic sentiment built into "an overwhelming torrent." Suddenly denunciations of Catholicism that had been seldom heard save from some Protestant pulpits became the common currency of political rhetoric and a Native American party that at its founding in 1837 had "amounted to very little" in local politics emerged from obscurity to sweep elections throughout Philadelphia County. Caught unawares, Philadelphia's Catholics, both laity and clergy, were "paralyzed" by "fright and dread."[16]

In the face of nativist violence the Catholic community that Bishop Kenrick had labored so hard to construct fragmented. The anti-Catholic riots of 1844 forced upon respectable Catholics the choice that they had so long avoided; to either embrace or repudiate the unruly immigrant workers. For most the choice was clear. A group of prominent Catholic laymen issued a statement after the May riots (which pitted nativist mobs against Irish gangs in the Kensington District) "disclaim[ing] all sympathy" with the Irish participants and branding them "bands of irresponsible men, some of whom resided in this country only a short time." Speaking, they said, for "the Catholic community at large" these members of the Catholic elite went on to "deprecate all violence, intimidation, and other illegal means" used by the Irish residents of Kensington's Third Ward (where violence first erupted) to disrupt nativist meetings. "It would be most unjust," they continued, "on the presumption, or *'prima facie'* evidence of guilt of a small band of men, to visit their offense on an entire community, from the mere accidental circumstance that most of them are said to hold the religious faith we profess."[17]

Not only the Catholic elite repudiated the "bands of irresponsible men." A large public meeting subsequently endorsed the *Address of the*

Catholic Lay Citizens, and one priest even went so far as to publish a letter in which he warned that "ten or twelve thoughtless rioters will give a bad name to the whole of Irish society. . . . Let your united action compel men either to behave themselves, or to call themselves something other than Irishmen. If they will do neither, hiss them out of town." Some middle-class Catholics took direct action against the rioters. When a second round of nativist riots broke out in Southwark in July, 1844, more than two thousand people, including many Irish Catholics, signed resolutions justifying the firing by militia troops upon citizens. Hundreds of people, including both Protestants and Catholics, joined posses in response to the sheriff's call for help. In neighborhoods throughout the city respectable men of all denominations took steps to protect themselves and their property by forming "committees of safety." While some members of the elite played a role in establishing and leading these neighborhood patrols, they were overwhelmingly staffed by members of the lower middle classes and included both nativists and Irish Catholics.[18]

Rather than separating themselves from the larger society and seeking refuge in a closed, religiously defined community many of Philadelphia's respectable Catholics were impelled by nativist violence to turn their attentions outward. In the wake of the riots many Catholics abandoned parish societies, which now carried a taint of social stigma, and instead sought confirmation of their respectability in more broadly based associations. By 1848 so many Catholics had joined the ranks of the Sons of Temperance and the International Order of Odd Fellows (mistakenly identified by some authors as nativist organizations) that Bishop Kenrick was moved to petition the Congregation of the Inquisition on their behalf, asking that the papal prohibition against membership in oath-bound secret societies be lifted for those fraternal orders on the grounds that both were friendly to Catholics.[19]

Many Protestants, too, found that class ties were stronger than religious solidarity. During the spring riots of 1844 several wealthy Protestants turned out with arms to mount a guard around the property of Philadelphia's most affluent Catholic congregations. Members of the Bar Association camped out in front of St. Mary's while a special militia guard was set at St. John the Evangelist's. A common concern for the sanctity of property and for social order underlay such efforts. An incident reported less than a year after the riots illustrates these common interests that bound respectable Protestants and Catholic together even in the days of "fright and dread." In 1845 construction began on St. Ann's Church located in a working-class neighborhood northeast of center city. Soon thereafter a Sunday school was founded which at first operated out of the home of a lady of the congregation, but this arrangement proved to be inadequate; there were too many children to be accommodated in the private residence. The problem was solved when a Protestant resident of the neighborhood who was a member of the school board, "favorably impressed by the good that was effected in keeping the children from the streets," offered to allow the Catholic Sunday school to meet in the public school building. What is more, his daughters "went weekly to assist their Catholic neighbors in teaching the catechism to the little ones of the parish."[20]

Temperance continued to serve as a bond between middle-class Protestants and Catholics in the years after 1844. In addition to the Catholics who were welcomed into the broader temperance reform, the parish societies still attracted some Protestants as members and continued to do so until 1871, when Bishop James Wood ordered that all societies connected with the Church admit only practicing Catholics to membership. This continuing cooperation was reflected in Philadelphia's response when Father Mathew, in the fall of 1849, visited the city on his American tour. Upon his arrival he was "honored by crowded assemblages of the people," including "men of the highest standing in the city." "Non-Catholics and people of every class," Kenrick noted, "came with great eagerness to visit him." During the two weeks he remained in Philadelphia, at least three thousand men, including many Protestants, knelt before a Catholic altar and took a total abstinence pledge administered by a Catholic priest.[21]

The temperance reform illustrates an important aspect of the mutual accommodation that took place between immigrant Catholics and the dominant American culture in the antebellum years. Respectability counted. The emerging industrial system required a disciplined workforce and bourgeois culture embodied a strong imperative toward both personal and social control. Conspicuous adherence to respectable standards of conduct marked an individual's acceptance of these important imperatives and was a necessary, and in many cases a sufficient, precondition for social acceptance. Many Catholics, especially those who founded and staffed the ever-expanding network of associations and institutions that gave coherence to Philadelphia's Catholic community, enthusiastically embraced those standards. To some extent this sensibility reinforced and complemented elements of the restoration reforms, but the aspirations of middle-class Catholics also posed a serious challenge to the Romanized Church. Reforming bishops sought to accentuate the differences between Catholics and Protestants and to erect barriers to interdenominational interaction, but the quest for respectability carried with it a strong assimilationist imperative. In this respect the interests of Philadelphia's Catholic bourgeoisie ran counter to those of Bishop Kenrick and his successors and posed for them a serious challenge as they sought to form and to maintain a coherent Catholic community in mid-nineteenth-century Philadelphia.

The Church Apostolic

The Catholic community that was emerging in mid-nineteenth-century Philadelphia embodied in its organization and activities the institutional imperatives of the Roman restoration and the class imperatives of American industrial culture, but it did not represent the traditional values of the peasant cultures of rural Europe. Under Francis Kenrick Philadelphia Catholicism was anything but the "Irish plantation" many writers have assumed it to be. Rather it was, to borrow David Doyle's phrase, "Irish in numbers rather than by essential characteristics." The relationship between the bishop and the bourgeoisie was problematic but relations with the immigrant working class were far more so.[1]

We have already noted the lack of religious fervor among immigrants to Philadelphia in the middle decades of the nineteenth century. Bishop Kenrick was determined to do something about it. While in Rome, he had volunteered for mission duty in America and in Kentucky he had distinguished himself as an eloquent and aggressive proselytizer for the Roman Catholic faith. Elevation to the episcopacy in no way diminished his apostolic zeal. Kenrick brought with him to Philadelphia a determination "to visit, as a missionary rather than as a bishop, the most remote places, where no mission has yet been established." "It will afford me great consolation," he wrote, "to carry the light of faith to these people seated in the darkness of error."[2]

There was good reason for Kenrick to be optimistic. William V. Harold and William Hogan had both inspired revivals within the congregations they served and their successes suggested that a more general revival would be met with enthusiasm. The results of Kenrick's first experiment in this direction were encouraging. One of his first acts upon his return to the city was to proclaim the Jubilee commemorating Pius VIII's ascension to the papal throne in the previous year. Spiritual exercises began on November 14, 1830, and continued for two weeks, during which, by Kenrick's account, "a union of hearts was affected . . . which was worthy of the primitive faithful. Piety assumed her ascendancy and *thousands* crowded to the Tribunal of Penance, and to the Divine Banquet." "How many prodigals" he wondered "after 20, 30, 35 years of total abstinence from the Sac[rament]s came with streaming eyes and broken hearts, to deplore their excesses and seek mercy." With satisfaction he concluded that "The jubilee indeed did immense good here."[3]

Encouraged by this enthusiastic reception Bishop Kenrick gathered to him a remarkable body of clergy—men known for their apostolic zeal and their charismatic qualities. They included converts from Protestantism such as Father Charles Carter, a native Kentuckian who brought to his post the evangelical style of a frontier revivalist, and Father Augustine Hewit, the son of a Presbyterian minister who eventually became general of the Paulists (an American missionary order dedicated to the conversion of Protestants). There were also several Jesuits, including Father James Cotting, a speaker of such power that Bishop John Nepomucene Neumann, Kenrick's successor in Philadelphia, was moved to remark that if there were ten more like him the diocese would be completely converted in ten years. Father James Ryder, also a Jesuit and a former president of Holy Cross College, was "one of the country's best speakers, everywhere attracting great audiences." People also flocked to listen to the words of Father Patrick Moriarty, minister at St. Augustine's and "one of the best known Catholic orators of his day."[4]

The "streaming eyes" and "broken hearts" noted by Bishop Kenrick in 1830 testify to the powerful emotional reaction inspired by his efforts. Intense emotionalism such as this was common at Catholic revivals. An eyewitness account of the 1832 Christmas service at St. John the Baptist's Church in Manayunk, conducted by Father Charles Carter, notes that the priest's sermon was so "impressive and interesting" that it "drew tears" from a number of young men and women who were assembled for their first communion and produced "the same effect . . . on many of their parents." At the conclusion of the evening's services a young lady approached the sanctuary and declared "in an audible voice, rendered somewhat tremulous by emotion . . . , her intention to abjure the errors she had been attached to, and to return to the Catholic Church, in whose bosom . . . she was born, but from which she had been seduced by false and deceptive lights." Father Carter responded by exhorting the young woman on the seriousness of pronouncements of faith, telling her that her conviction "should be so strong as to lead her, if necessary, to seal it with her blood." The scene produced "the most breathless silence" in the assembled congregation and Carter took the opportunity to follow her profession of faith with a general address on the subject of Protestant persecution of Catholics.[5]

Conversions such as these were common and testified to the efficacy of Catholic evangelicalism. In 1834 Bishop Kenrick reported to Propaganda that "Many Protestants have . . . renounced the errors of the sects in which they were reared." Apostasy, however, was common. "The number of those who abandon the Faith of their parents," he noted in 1838, "is very considerable." All in all, though, it would appear that gains outnumbered losses. A similar condition can be seen in contemporary Protestant congregations. Bruce Laurie's survey of Protestant church records shows that during the two decades before mid-century "congregations were rather volatile, losing members due to apostasy and out-migration, and replenishing themselves through revivals and transfers."[6]

This extreme fluidity was typical of the period and bred intense competition among those groups, both religious and secular, who sought to organize the general population. Through the middle decades of the nineteenth century Protestant and Catholic clergymen were locked in a fierce evangelical struggle for the souls of a largely unchurched and intermittently responsive working class. Kenrick's earliest efforts were directed at providing institutional facilities to isolated rural settlements and to this end he supported the activities of three missionary orders—the Jesuits, the Augustinians, and the Redemptorists. Then in the last years of his first decade in Philadelphia, Bishop Kenrick began to actively proselytize the city's immigrant working class.[7]

In an attempt to build constituencies among the immigrants Kenrick directed that "free" churches (ones that did not charge pew rents) be established in neighborhoods in which a large number of immigrants lived and toiled. Three such churches (St. Francis Xavier's and St. Patrick's located near the Schuylkill docks, and St. Philip Neri, near the Southwark docks) were built in 1839 and 1840. These efforts to reach out to immigrant traditionalists, though, were limited by the institutional and class imperatives that informed antebellum Philadelphia Catholicism. All three churches soon established temperance societies, reading rooms, Sunday schools, and all the appurtenances of the "new morality" as well as associations that reflected the new style of Catholic devotions. St. Patrick's, for instance boasted a Confraternity of the Scapular, a Rosary Society, a Confraternity of the Sacred Heart, and a Society of Our Lady of Mercy. St. Patrick's first pastor, Daniel Davitt, was anything but an Irish traditionalist (although of Irish descent he was born in America and was a graduate of the Urban College of the Propaganda at Rome) and the financial support upon which he was dependent came from members of the Catholic elite. Periodically the parish would hold fund-raisers, but "there was always a pronounced literary flavor to these money-raising affairs: public lectures . . . band concerts, and exhibits of rare and foreign articles," and they were invariably held outside the impoverished neighborhood in which the church was located.[8]

Bishop Kenrick's evangelical efforts were more than matched by those of Protestants. James S. Buckingham described a "New School" Presbyterian evangelist who in the spring of 1842 "preached three times a day for several weeks in succession!" in churches that "filled an hour before he began; while the doors and windows were surrounded by those who could not find entrance." In the Northern Liberties, Methodists were "effecting wonders among the market-people, butchers, poulterers, and fruitsellers, who quitted the markets at two o'clock, to get placed for the evening service at six." Presbyterians, he noted, "operated in the same way on a higher class, in the more fashionable parts of the city," and in Germantown, to the northwest of the center city, "half the entire population were at the churches, morning, noon, and night; sometimes. . . . till daylight on the following day."[9]

This was all wonderful theater, but no more effective than the Catholic missionaries who, Buckingham noted, were operating more quietly throughout the city at the same time. Catholic gains in these years would seem to have at least matched those of Protestant evangelists. "Religion advances amidst difficulties," Bishop Kenrick informed the Propaganda in the spring of 1843, "conversions are numerous and the eagerness to hear Catholic truth is increasing." Morale within the Catholic community was high. Writing to Propaganda in 1842, Michael O'Connor made reference to "the good spirit that is pervading the whole body of the clergy and people, emanating from the hierarchy and spreading through the whole mass."[10]

Protestants agreed with this assessment. "In former years which it does not require old age to remember," the *Presbyterian* complained in January of 1843, "Popery in the United States was a very quiet unobtrusive thing of which we heard but little and saw less." But now, "every day we hear a bolder tone and see less cautious concealment of its peculiarities. . . . Imposing Catholic ceremonies are becoming common." In November of 1842, confronted by an aggressive Roman Catholic establishment that had "become reimpregnated with the energy and ambition of her earlier days," and unable to rouse public concern over the issue, a broad coalition of Protestant ministers, led by a coterie of Old School Presbyterians, banded together, "on the broad platform of the Reformation" to form the American Protestant Association.[11]

The anti-Catholic riots of 1844 brought this first phase of Catholic evangelical activity in Philadelphia to a halt. Bishop Kenrick was himself thoroughly traumatized by the first outbreak of violence. "What days of dread and trial have come upon us," he lamented in his diary. "I am convinced," he wrote more than a month after the Kensington riots, "that the enemies of our faith have not given up the idea of attack and given the occasion they will try to destroy us and our faith. . . . We have no safety in the law." In desperation, the distraught bishop suspended all worship services in the city and issued a proclamation urging Catholics to go to any extent to avoid antagonizing the Protestant majority. "I earnestly conjure you all to avoid all occasion of excitement," he pleaded, "and to shun all public places of assemblages, and to do nothing that may in any way exasperate."[12]

In the years after the riots Bishop Kenrick refrained from mission activity that might antagonize Protestants, but outside the city the apostolic imperative was building again. The Redemptorists, an Austrian missionary order, had taken up residence in Philadelphia in 1842. Two years later they were charged with the ministry to the Germans. Then in 1847 the order came under the leadership of Giles Smulders, who reoriented them away from the rural missions they had served toward the burgeoning cities. There they proselytized not only Germans but also English-speaking populations, using for this purpose a number of brilliant and aggressive converts from Protestantism. By the mid-1850s this urban reorientation was so complete that the Redemptorists (as well as the Augustinians and the Jesuits, who followed their lead) were unable to attend many of the outlying mission stations they had previously visited. This reorientation of mission activity initiated a second phase of intense evangelical effort in Philadelphia, but by the time it began Francis Kenrick had left the diocese for the archepiscopal chair of Baltimore.[13]

Nationalists

Efforts to reform Philadelphia Catholicism did not end when Bishop Kenrick left the diocese in 1851, nor did the opposition to them. In the last years of his reign Kenrick once again faced determined resistance from lay trustees. Ever since the downfall of the republican leadership at Holy Trinity early in the nineteenth century, the congregation had been led by German "ultra-nationalists" who stoutly resisted any attempt to dilute the distinctive national character of the church. This led to many minor conflicts with members of the resident clergy and with the men who sought to bring order to the troubled diocese.

By the 1830s the nationalist leadership at Holy Trinity was under considerable pressure. Not only was the distinctive German culture that they treasured being eroded, but efforts to transmit that culture to their descendants were failing. By 1835 Bishop Kenrick estimated that of twenty thousand German Catholics in his diocese only five hundred required services in their native language. In an effort to stave off decline, German nationalists attempted to strengthen their ties to traditionalist elements in other German denominations and to purge their own congregation of non-German elements. Both of these efforts brought them into conflict with ecclesiastical authorities.[1]

An incident in 1834 illustrates the ecumenical tenor of German nationalism. In that year Father Peter Henry Lemke, O. S. B., a convert from the Lutheran faith, assumed the pastorship of Holy Trinity and took the occasion of a Lutheran centenary celebration to launch an extended critique of Martin Luther and his doctrines. After the sermon he was approached by members of the board of trustees who objected to his attacks on Luther. "As we wish to live in peace and quiet with our [German] neighbors" they said, "we wish to tell you we will have no more sermons like that." Lemke, an aristocratic Prussian with long military service, was enraged by the trustees' impertinence. Brandishing a poker, he drove them from his house and immediately informed Bishop Kenrick that he would never set foot again in Holy Trinity.[2]

It had long been the custom for pastors at Holy Trinity to preach in English or French on occasion, but nationalists began to demand that these foreign elements be excluded from their services. In 1828 nationalist leaders protested against an attempt to impose on them a pastor of French descent; in 1835 a group of what Bishop Kenrick called "displeased unquiet persons" demanded that no language but German be used in their church and carried their complaint to the director of the Leopoldine Society in Austria with the result that foreign monetary contributions to the Philadelphia missions declined significantly. They also petitioned the state legislature in 1836 to forbid any but German sermons in their church, but Bishop Kenrick intervened and testified against the bill with the result that it was defeated. Kenrick's action outraged the nationalists and in 1837 they petitioned the pope for relief from their "Irish" bishop and their unpopular pastor, Father Francis Guth, and (anticipating a day when they would be a minority of the congregation) secured from the state legislature an amendment to their charter to the effect that Holy Trinity would remain "a German Roman Catholic church . . . , so long as the same should be required, by at least twenty regular contributing members" of the congregation.[3]

In 1841 Bishop Kenrick began construction on a second German church, St. Peter's, which would be administered without trustees by the Redemptorist Fathers. Although this provided an alternative to the ultranationalist orientation of Holy Trinity's leadership, the new church, located to the north of center city, was inconvenient for most Germans to attend. In 1847 Kenrick appealed again to the Redemptorists and asked them to found a church in the vicinity of Holy Trinity, but no funds were available for the project and it was dropped. Finally, in 1850, Kenrick moved directly against the nationalists.[4]

At Kenrick's instigation Father Daniel Oberholzer, the pastor at Holy Trinity, and four sympathetic trustees petitioned the bishop asking him to propose an amendment to the church's charter that would eliminate the annual elections for trustees. Kenrick advised them that all future difficulties could be easily avoided if they simply allowed him to appoint the members of the board. Oberholtzer and his allies then called a public meeting of the congregation to draft a petition to the legislature that would implement Kenrick's recommendations. Nationalists, though, assembled in a nearby tavern and organized a protest. Kenrick personally came to the meeting to argue for the charter change but the nationalists created such a controversy that no business could be done. Kenrick noted in disgust that "much was said and done that is quite subversive of ecclesiastical authority." In his anger he issued a circular letter denouncing the nationalist leaders, then he excommunicated them and placed the church under interdict.[5]

In November of 1850 Kenrick's allies among the trustees resolved to transfer "all the corporated estate, real and personal, under their custody" to three members of the Society of Jesus. They also resolved to petition the state legislature for changes to the charter that would permit this transfer and make it "lawful for the pastors to nominate and appoint trustees." They also produced a petition in support of their actions which they said was signed by a majority of the congregation. Anticipating an easy resolution to the conflict, Kenrick lifted his interdict and the Jesuits made ready to reopen the church for worship. Twenty-five members of the congregation, though, filed suit to block the action, arguing that the trustees had no right to alienate the church property. A court injunction was granted and Kenrick's initiative was defeated. Once more he placed Holy Trinity under interdict.[6]

Elections for trustees were held in the spring of 1851 and the nationalist slate defeated Kenrick's supporters. The newly elected trustees then

went on the offensive, declaring that since the church was under interdict and Father Oberholzer was not holding services there, he had done
nothing to earn his wages. They suspended the priest's salary, whereupon Bishop Kenrick excommunicated "the leading troublemakers." He
also ordered all other Catholic churches in the city to close their doors
to the Germans. Undaunted, the nationalists then threatened to drive
Oberholzer from his residence. Kenrick responded that if the trustees
carried through on their threat he would close the Catholic cemeteries
to them. Writing in his diary Kenrick railed against these impudent
Germans who "entered into a conspiracy to uphold their rights." In a
letter to Propaganda he complained about the offensive "zeal for liberty with which many [Americans] burn" and wished instead that they
could be properly "tenacious to the Faith and most obsequious to the
Holy See."[7]

Thus matters stood when Francis Kenrick became archbishop of
Baltimore in August 1851. His tenure in Philadelphia had started and
ended with battles over the rights of laymen within the restoration
Church. Quite clearly, lay dissent had not been completely quelled, but
the Church in Philadelphia had moved far in the direction of the
monarchic and ultramontane hegemony Kenrick desired. The authority of the hierarchy had been firmly established and legally supported
almost everywhere. Only at Holy Trinity did the laity mount any
significant resistance and there pressures on the congregation were
mounting.

Francis Kenrick's hand-picked successor was John Nepomucene
Neumann, a Bohemian Redemptorist. Although he had not been
trained in Rome, Neumann shared with the restoration reformers a
"corporate and hierarchical view of the Church," a romantic "Counter
Reformation spirituality" and "an ultramontane ecclesiology" that
repudiated the traditions of the Enlightenment. He prosecuted the
campaign against Holy Trinity's nationalists with no less vigor than did
Kenrick. First he demanded that the trustees cede to him the property
rights of the church. The trustees refused and filed suit in court to gain
clear legal title to the church property.[8]

Meanwhile elections for trustees were held once again. Expecting
violence, the bishop's allies came to the polls brandishing clubs.
According to the testimony of the "Marshall's police" the nationalists
easily won, but the "bishopites" charged that their opponents had
packed the electorate "by going into the street and bringing in, as prop-

erty-holders, anyone who would pay $1.33 to obtain a vote." They disputed the votes of these people, saying that they were not "legitimate members" of the congregation, then "adjourned . . . to an upper room" and stationed guards to prevent anyone from interfering with their deliberations. There they appointed a slate of trustees and elected them while downstairs opponents of the bishop held their own election.[9]

Naturally the matter was settled in court. The testimony revealed some important differences in perception between the nationalists and the bishopites. Allies of the bishop ridiculed one of the nationalist leaders, a Dr. Langdorf, because of his low origins. He started as a footman and driver and had risen through his own efforts. The nationalists replied that it was "honor to Langdorf that he has, in this free country, this republican country, this adopted country of his, by the exercise of the talents which the Lord God has given him, risen to the dignity of a doctor himself." These were not the sentiments of peasant traditionalists, clinging to the agrarian culture they had known in Europe. Holy Trinity's "ultra-nationalists" were "self-made men" and hailed the accomplishments of other such upwardly mobile heros as Andrew Jackson, Henry Clay, Elihu Burritt, Martin Van Buren, Millard Fillmore, Zachery Taylor, and even John Hughes.[10]

The nationalists were German chauvinists, but at the same time they were, in their attorney's words, "American citizens, adopted though they be," who had "imbibed from the spirit of our institutions enough of liberty of action, of liberty of thought, and of liberty of speech, not to bow suppliantly before [their] would-be masters." They were Catholics, but at the same time they denounced their opponents as "these trembling, suppliant, unmanly creatures of . . . Jesuitical foreigners—foreigners to your soil, to your blood-bought institutions, and foreigners to the religion of Roman Catholics." Bishop Kenrick's effort to transfer control of the church to the Society of Jesus, they said, was "only one of many instances of [the Jesuits'] desire for universal despotism in ecclesiastical affairs." These men, they declared, "are illiberal in the extreme, the result of their secluded and bigoted education. These are the men who crush to earth the secular priests, and oppose public education, and 'hate with perfect hatred' republican institutions."[11]

The second conflict at Holy Trinity illustrated the modern schism in many of its most important aspects. It posed national assertiveness against Roman universalism, popular sovereignty against authoritarian rule, and individual achievement and mobility against hierarchy and ascribed social status. It also carried strong nativist overtones, portraying the bishops and their followers as a "foreign" influence and a threat to American freedoms. Here, as at St. Mary's earlier, core values of the American civil tradition were embraced by Catholic modernists, many of whom were immigrants, and asserted in contradiction to the changes being promoted by restoration reformers.

The nationalists' arguments prevailed for a time; the jury ruled in their favor, but the court battle was just beginning. Bishop Neumann's attorneys appealed the decision to the State Supreme Court which nearly two years later ruled for the bishop. In March 1854 Neumann recovered full title to all of Holy Trinity's property and the court further ordered that the nationalist board of trustees be dissolved and a new one elected. Once more Pennsylvania's legal authorities had denied a challenge to episcopal rights. The nationalists, however, refused to surrender the church to the bishop and issued an appeal to the state legislature. Bishop Neumann then complained to civil authorities, and on April 8, 1854, several of the nationalist trustees were arrested and thrown into Moyamensing Prison. There they remained for several weeks. Upon their release they were warned that any further intransigence would earn them several years in prison, and with this Holy Trinity's dissenters at last relented and submitted to episcopal authority.[12]

Completing the Devotional Revolution

=►-0-◄=

Bishop Neumann followed his victory with diocesan legislation that further diminished lay independence. In 1855 he required that each parish supply and furnish a rectory for its pastor and curates, thus assuring the clergy of permanent housing. He further directed that all revenues of the parish be deposited with a treasurer appointed by the pastor and that a careful record of receipts and expenses be kept. Other legislation fixed the salaries of pastors and curates so that they could not be modified or suspended by the laity. Laymen were even prohibited from speaking in the church without the bishop's personal permission. The only concession made by Bishop Neumann to lay involvement in church affairs was a provision that two laymen, appointed by the bishop, were to be consulted on matters of importance. A final decree, promulgated in 1855, required that the deeds to all church property in the diocese be physically conveyed to the bishop on pain of forfeiture of the parish.[1]

Like Francis Kenrick, Bishop Neumann closely regulated the quality and behavior of the clergy. At a synod he convened in 1855 he required that any clergy entering the diocese from another place should render an "oath of obedience" and receive permission from his own bishop as well as Neumann before being allowed to perform any sacred function. Priests were also forbidden to visit seaside resorts and curates were prohibited from leaving the rectory for a full day or night without the consent of their pastor or the bishop. Pastors were not allowed to be absent from their rectories or to delegate spiritual duties to their assistants. Neumann also continued Bishop Kenrick's policy of scheduling diocesan retreats and regular conferences to instruct clergy on morals and theology.[2]

Many clergymen chafed under the restrictions placed on them, but while Francis Kenrick ruled the diocese they kept their peace. With Neumann it was another matter. The pious Bohemian was held in "low esteem" by both lay leaders and clergy. His regulations of 1855 raised a storm of criticism among the parish clergy and, when he did not move quickly to discipline them, led to open denunciations. The most vocal of these critics were traditionalist Irish clergymen who barraged Irish prelates with complaints about the German bishop. Michael O'Connor, the bishop of Pittsburgh, received many of these complaints and relayed them to Archbishop Kenrick, and to Rome. Viewing the situation from Baltimore, Francis Kenrick was dismayed at Bishop Neumann's inability to "apply a remedy" to the "manifestly unworthy" priests in his charge. The fact, however, that dissenters took their complaints to the hierarchy rather than openly defying their bishop is a measure of the change that had been effected in Philadelphia Catholicity since 1830.[3]

Bishop Neumann completed the "devotional revolution" that had begun under Bishop Kenrick. Described by his biographer as a "liturgist's ideal," Philadelphia's fourth bishop imposed uniformity on religious life throughout his diocese. He was tireless in this pursuit, "painstakingly" seeking "to observe the smallest prescriptions of the church's law governing her services." He promulgated precise ceremonial rules regarding the administration of the sacraments, even to the point of prescribing the quality of wine used in the Holy Sacrifice. He elaborated services, adding the litany of Our Lady of Loretto to the invocation, and he distributed a uniform ceremonial throughout the diocese.[4]

As devotions became more uniform they also became more elaborate. Neumann, like his predecessor, promoted a "devotional" style of worship centered on the "exercise of piety" either through private devotion to a sacred image or through public communal displays of piety. He encouraged the formation of numerous confraternities as well as apostolic associations such as the St. Vincent DePaul Society, the Society for the Propagation of the Faith, and the Sodality for Conversion to the Faith. In organizations such as these Bishop Kenrick's vision of the church as a unified Army of Christ—"one body, and one spirit"—began to take shape. Devotional associations "helped to form the Catholic body into a 'well-arranged army.'" They "emphasized obedience and sacrifice," bound people into "close-knit . . . units, based on personal contact," and they promoted "acceptance of a corporate definition of the spiritual life."[5]

Devotions were an integral element of the reform effort and the formation of an inclusive Catholic community. Devotional exercises were a conspicuous mark of Catholic identity; they separated members of the community from the Protestant environment in which they lived, bound them together in a common world of symbolic significance and mutual effort, and promoted a Catholic identity "that could unite the rich and the poor, the person and the institution, the male and the female, the Irish, the American, and the German, time and eternity." The most important of the devotional innovations was the Forty Hours, first observed under Bishop Kenrick. John Neumann established a rotating schedule of observances so that the Blessed Sacrament was always on display somewhere in the diocese and the exercises associated with it were expanded to include "confession, Mass, Holy Communion, visits and the deepening of Christian doctrine from . . . sermons." This round of devotions was a powerful focus for Catholic piety and contributed importantly to the "spiritual building up" of the Church in Philadelphia.[6]

Bishop Neumann accelerated the rapid institutional growth begun by Francis Kenrick. During his first thirty-four months in Philadelphia Neumann completed six churches begun by his predecessor, rebuilt six others, and added thirty more of his own. By 1855 he was able to report that his diocese, "in the number of priests caring for souls, and the number of . . . churches . . . , [is] larger than any other diocese or archdiocese" in America. In 1857 alone eleven new churches were constructed. Ultimately, in little more than seven years Bishop Neumann was responsible for the construction of eighty parish churches. Neumann also continued his predecessor's emphasis on the education and moral indoctrination of Catholic youth. By his own account the number of children enrolled in Catholic schools "increased from five hundred to five thousand," during the first year of his reign, and during his seven years in Philadelphia Bishop Neumann oversaw the establishment of thirty parish schools. He also continued Kenrick's policy of slowly shifting control of education away from local congregations and the laity. He established a Diocesan Central Board of Education and charged it with developing and overseeing a general plan of instruction for all parochial schools. This board standardized texts and lessons and priests were instructed to closely supervise classroom activities, especially those conducted by lay teachers. Like his predecessor, Neumann also brought teaching orders into his diocese.[7]

The reformation of Philadelphia Catholicism under Bishops Kenrick and Neumann was an impressive achievement. Together they had brought order out of the chaos and factionalism of the 1820s and restored vigor and instituonal coherence to an establishment that had seemed to be on the verge of dissolution. There were still immense problems, though. The Church continued to rouse intense opposition from Protestants and some Catholics; the assimilationist tendencies of the Catholic bourgeoisie were undermining bishops' attempts to create separate Catholic communities; most important the institutional and class imperatives that were shaping the American church did not reflect the cultural backgrounds of the vast majority of the immigrants who were nominally in its charge, or speak directly to their interests and needs.

1848

On January 6, 1848, at the Chinese Museum, one of the city's most popular assembly halls, several of Philadelphia's most prominent citizens came together in a public meeting. Among the gentlemen attending were John Swift, the current mayor of the city, and three of those who would be his successors: Robert L. Conrad, Richard Vaux, and Morton McMichael. Four judges took part, as did the sheriff of Philadelphia County, members of the Select Council, the head of the Customs Office, and the attorney general of the Commonwealth. National politicians, including current, former, and future presidents, took note of the meeting and sent lengthy letters which were read and published. The fourth estate was amply represented. Among the organizers and participants were the publisher of the *Daily Pennsylvanian*, an editor of the *Philadelphia Inquirer*, an owner and an editor from the *North American and United States Gazette*, an editor of the *Spirit of the Times*, and the owner of the *Saturday Evening Post*. All of the major papers in the city extensively covered the meeting. It was, for its day, a major media event.[1]

Speakers at this affair were drawn from all denominations and included several nativist luminaries as well as a number of important Catholic lay leaders. This was by no means the first time that Catholics and anti-Catholics had shared a stage. Through the 1830s Catholic priests and Protestant ministers had occasionally engaged in public and sometimes acrimonious debates. But this was a purely secular event (no ministers or priests were reported to have been in attendance) and it was not a confrontation, but a celebration. The eminent gentlemen who spoke at the affair were gathered to honor the "great champion of Italian regeneration," the "enlightened" prince who had undertaken "noble efforts" to establish liberal constitutional reforms in that land: Pope Pius IX.[2]

These prominent Philadelphians expressed, "the deepest interest, sympathy, and respect," for the pope and his works. Robert Tyler, the son of President John Tyler and a leading light in Philadelphia's Repeal Association, spoke of the "respect and admiration" of the American people for the "great and virtuous Pontiff." He characterized the pope as a "Great and good philanthropist," a "Noble philosopher," and a "Glorious reformer." "I, for one," he told the pope rhetorically, "(not recognizing your faith), am ever willing to *bow* in *homage* to your genius and patriotism." The audience (an interdenominational assemblage) evidently approved these sentiments, for Tyler was interrupted several times by applause. A communication from George M. Dallas, vice president of the United States, was read. It included a testimonial of "veneration, gratitude, and confidence" for Pius IX, and ended with the exclamation, "God speed the Pope!" an expression reiterated in another letter by secretary of state and future president James Buchanan.[3]

To understand the excitement Pio Nono inspired in Americans we must note that he assumed the throne of Peter after three decades of absolutist excess in Rome. There, after the restoration of papal rule, laymen had been systematically excluded from power. Elections were forbidden, feudal laws reinstituted, and "Government by priests" reestablished. Power was progressively centralized in the Roman Curia, which demonstrated "a narrow minded puritanism which had the aim of governing daily life . . . [and] arrogant indifference toward the constantly increasing stagnation of the political, economic and social life." Controls were ruthlessly imposed on the population. There were "systematic attempts to extinguish all memories [of secular rule]" and "a police state" was instituted, marked by "a spy system . . . and brutal methods of repression."[4]

Revolutionary sentiment grew rapidly in response to repression. Secret revolutionary societies—the infamous *Carbonari*—emerged. In 1831, at the accession of a new Pope, Gregory XVI, these societies, inspired by successful liberal and anticlerical revolutions in France and Belgium, rose to proclaim the end of "priest government." The revolt was quickly crushed by Austrian troops, but the rising of the Carbonari had awakened international concern for conditions in the papal states.[5]

Despite international pressures to institute liberal reforms, Gregory XVI adopted only cosmetic measures. This was sufficient to satisfy the foreign powers but did nothing to ease tensions in central Italy. Revolt broke out anew and was suppressed with military force so brutal that the conflict soon escalated into a general uprising. Again foreign troops were called into central Italy to preserve papal rule, and backed by Austrian bayonets the government ruthlessly rooted out and punished ringleaders of the revolt. Once again the international community, horrified by papal repression, clamored for reform and again the Curia responded with cosmetic changes that only strengthened the centralized administration while yielding nothing to liberal elements within the population.[6]

After 1832 liberal resistance to papal rule fused with nationalism as intellectuals abandoned the secret societies in which they had hatched their earlier schemes and flocked into Giuseppe Mazzini's "Young Italy" movement. There they worked for the establishment of a unified Italian republic with Rome as its capital. By 1843 central Italy was again bubbling with local revolts and as before the government responded with repression. Special military courts were formed and kept in session permanently. "Thousands of people were persecuted, banished, and punished for their political opinions." By 1845 it seemed that a great and unbridgeable gap had opened between the Church and progressive elements of the population it ruled. "Liberty without religion," became a popular rallying cry, and many questioned whether liberalism and Catholicism could ever coexist in Italy or anywhere else.[7]

Gregory XVI's policies had broadened and deepened the resentment against papal rule in Italy and abroad, but his death in 1846 brought hopes for reconciliation between the Roman Curia and the Italian people. The election of Pius IX seemed a godsend. Little was known about the young pope but there were tantalizing hints that he might harbor liberal sentiments. He was known to have recommended in 1845 moderate administrative reforms for the papal dominions and many of his early pronouncements on international relations were couched in ambiguous terms that were widely interpreted as indicating his support for Italian unification and independence from Austrian influence.[8]

In retrospect it is clear that liberal expectations for the new pope were wildly extravagant, but the uncompromising reaction of his predecessor made even minor and moderate gestures seem important. Every action Pius IX took was interpreted in the most favorable light and, for a while, there was reason for optimism. Gregory XVI had instituted a police state, but Pius IX proclaimed amnesty for political prisoners and alleviated censorship. Gregory XIV had banned the construction of railroads; Pius allowed them. The old pope had raised tariff barriers around the papal dominions; the young pope lowered them. Then, in April 1847, Pius IX announced his intention of forming a consultative assembly of laymen. Three months later he authorized a civil guard. In October he appointed a state council and two months later appointed for the first time several laymen to posts in the government ministry.[9]

Liberals everywhere were ecstatic. The "liberal pope" had seemingly shown that Catholicism and republicanism were indeed compatible. For many Catholics throughout the West this resolved a fundamental tension with which they had lived for more than a generation. Whenever Pio Nono appeared in public, adulatory crowds greeted him with "thunderous applause." In the exuberance of the times Great Britain and the United States for the first time opened direct diplomatic relations with the Holy See. By January of 1848, when Philadelphia's political elite met to celebrate him, Pius IX had emerged in the popular imagination as a genuine crusader struggling to bring a reactionary ecclesiastical bureaucracy into harmony with modern Western values. Margaret Fuller Ossoli called him "a man of noble and good aspect . . . , a real great heart, a generous man." The *American Whig Review* praised him as a "great" man. Horace Greeley saw him as a "heaven-appointed instrument" for reform. Robert Tyler called him, a "patron of freedom" and "the author and the leader in a great scheme of constitutional government."[10]

John K. Kane, judge of the United States Circuit Court and chairman of the Philadelphia meeting, delivered a detailed account of the pope's accomplishments which was reproduced in the anti-Catholic journal, the *Daily Sun*. I will quote this account at some length, for it summarizes the prevailing American view of the man and his works at the beginning of the "Year of Revolutions." Prior to the emergence of Pius IX, Kane said,

> All efforts to rise and throw off the galling yoke of despotism, to burst the shackles of tyranny, were uniformly beaten down and a deeper degree of oppression heaped upon the abject people. . . . The people were ruthlessly thrown into prison, and whilst this state of affairs existed the present Pope accepted the pontificate. He looked around over the blasted country—he saw the bleeding people, and though surrounded by enemies on all sides, and insidious friends at home, he humanely and patriotically resolved at once to engage in the glorious and admirable work of reform, which, so far, he has accomplished (applause). The first step he took he opened the prison doors, and set the victims of despotism free, and called home every exiled Roman. (Renewed applause) He gave liberty to the press, and established a municipal guard for sustaining public order and care of the people.

He called around him the friends of humanity. . . . Though
our knowledge of him is limited, yet we know that he can
make Rome happy, and by so doing he contributes to the
happiness of the whole world. (Great applause)[11]

Of course there were skeptics. Some argued that the limited nature
of the reforms instituted by the pope were incommensurate with the
extravagant praise heaped upon him. Philadelphia's nativist organ, the
Daily Sun, after admitting initial enthusiasm for Pius, explained its
reservations this way: "A reformer is one who removes abuses that
destroy or impair the happiness of the people. A reformer is one who
repudiates a pernicious system, and introduces a good one in its place."
The pope, the *Sun* asserted, had done none of these things, for not one
of his supposed reforms had begun to modify the absolute nature of his
reign. Until such fundamental changes took place it was "the most cruel
of mockeries, to flatter [the Italian people] with being governed by a
'liberal reformer.'" Underlying this critique was a profound assumption: that the essential nature of papal government could not be reconciled with liberal principles—that Pius could not be both pope and a
liberal. "Do not, for Heaven's sake," George Perkins Marsh wrote in
1847 to a friend, "commit yourself to the belief in a *liberal Pope!* It is a
contradiction in terms—an impossibility in the very nature of things.
Whatever Pius IX may think now, he will find that he can't be both
Pope and patriot." G. E. Ellis, writing in the *Christian Examiner,* declared that "true reform can triumph in the Roman states only when it
is no longer in the power of a pope to say that it shall or shall not triumph." Comments such as these testify, not to a crude anti-Catholic
bias in American culture, but to a fundamental assumption upon
which much anti-Roman rhetoric was based—the belief that, in its
essential features, Roman Catholicism embodied principles and perspectives that were antithetical to and intolerant of liberal democracy.[12]

As the response to Pius IX's limited reforms shows, a substantial
number of Americans, both Protestant and Catholics, were vitally
interested in the course of events on the far side of the Atlantic. The
gentlemen who met at the Chinese Museum in Philadelphia made reference in their remarks to European class conflicts, the persistence of
feudal constitutions, the course of the liberal revolution in Italy, the
revolt of the Maccabees in ancient Palestine, revolts in France in the
1790s and 1830, the Greek revolt against the Turks, the republican revo-

lutions of South America and Mexico, Caesar's crossing of the Rubicon, and a number of other episodes in ancient and modern European history. What is more, they assumed that their audience and reading public would understand these references. Too often we assume a degree of parochialism in nineteenth-century American consciousness that cannot be sustained by the evidence. Americans were not ignorant of events abroad nor were they insensitive to the political and social contexts within which those events occurred. Moreover their perception of those events colored their understanding of what was happening in the United States. The starkly uncompromising and aggressive nature of Roman absolutism after 1814 had given a degree of plausibility to nativist criticisms of the Church and the progressive Romanization of the American church after 1829 had helped to validate the nativist argument that the forces of reaction were spreading to American shores. But as the 1848 demonstrations show, much nativist apprehension could be assuaged if it seemed that the Church had adopted a political stance that was consonant with core values in America's civic culture.

For decades Catholic dissenters and some "enlightened" members of the episcopacy had struggled to show that their religion was compatible with republicanism, but the 1829 provincial council had charted a course that was aggressively antagonistic to any such efforts. It was therefore with great relief that many Catholics welcomed even the limited liberal reforms instituted by Pius IX. In the early months of 1848 it seemed possible that the powerful tide of Roman absolutism could be reversed, that the Church could be reformed so as to accommodate liberal principles, and that the ideological rift separating Roman Catholics from the rest of American civil culture could at last be breached. Events in Europe, however, soon dashed these hopes.[13]

1848 was the "Year of Revolutions" all over Europe. Revolt erupted in Paris on February 22 and then on March 3 Louis Kossuth rose in the Hungarian Diet to proclaim an "end to absolutism, to centralized bureaucratic government, and . . . to all oppressive measures of the 'Metternich System.'" Ten days later revolution broke out in Vienna and spread rapidly through eastern and central Europe. Meanwhile news of the revolution in France sparked revolts throughout the German states, and on March 18 Frederick Wilhelm IV, the Prussian king, pledged liberal reforms including freedom of the press, a new constitution, and Prussian leadership in the formation of a united Germany.[14]

In Italy insurgents forced the adoption of liberal constitutions in the Kingdom of the Two Sicilies, in Piedmont-Sardinia, and in Tuscany. There ensued a general uprising against Austrian forces of occupation. In March, Milan and Venice gained their independence. Then Sardinia declared war on Austria and for several months republican forces enjoyed an unbroken series of successes. In those heady days many saw Pius IX as a unifying symbol of Italian independence and urged him to lead the crusade against Austria. In the excitement of the times some papal troops, acting on their own initiative and without the pope's consent, joined Sardinia in the war against Austria, seemingly lending substance to these hopes.[15]

For a while the pope delayed making a decision while expectations that he would lead the Italians against the Austrians mounted; then in an allocution on April 29 Pius announced that he would not make war on a Catholic monarch. This bombshell infuriated Italian patriots and in their disillusionment they charged the pope with betraying the national cause. In Rome "agitation against priests, cardinals [who were blamed for influencing the pope's decision not to intervene] and even the Papacy became the order of the day." As the wars continued and Pius stubbornly refused to act, liberal rage mounted and finally, on November 24, the pope was forced to flee the city. From exile in Naples he withdrew his recognition of the liberal government in Rome and issued an appeal to the Catholic rulers of Europe to restore to him his dominions.[16]

Meanwhile, in Rome, the patriots declared the temporal power of the pope to have ended and proclaimed the Roman Republic. On April 27 Garibaldi arrived in Rome and took charge of the defense of the republic. For the moment the forces of secularism, nationalism, and liberalism were ascendant in Rome and liberals rejoiced, but the situation soon began to deteriorate. Within months Austrian counterattacks had driven the liberals from many of their strongholds and by March of 1849 only Rome and Tuscany remained in liberal hands. France then intervened to restore the temporal power of the pope. Republican forces made spirited and tenacious resistance but were gradually overwhelmed. On July 2 the Roman assembly declared further resistance useless and on the July 4, 1849, Rome's experiment in republican government came to an end.

After the events of 1848–49 Pius IX pursued a policy of unrelenting hostility to the "new ideas" that were challenging traditional authorities everywhere throughout the West. The most complete and formal expression of this adamant resistance was the publication in 1864 of the encyclical *Quanta cura* to which was attached the notorious "Syllabus of Errors." In this document the pope condemned rationalism, materialism, and socialism, as well as the ascendancy of secular power over ecclesiastical authority, the interference of laymen in Church affairs, and state-run educational systems. He also denounced the separation of Church and state, freedom of the press, religious toleration, and the failure of civil courts to punish violators of Catholic precepts. The attached syllabus extended the condemnation to include liberal democracy, secret societies, and indifference to religion. Evangelical Protestant societies were denounced as "illa pestis."[17]

The events of the year of revolutions, of course, were high drama for Americans. Newspapers published, and a rapt public read, almost daily reports of the progress of the various movements. Nowhere was American attention more clearly focused than on the struggle in Italy. There the conflict between liberalism and absolutism, between national self-determination and empire, between civic and religous authority, was most sharply drawn. Americans of all denominations treated events there as episodes in a great moral drama with imperial Austria as the chief villain. At first Americans expressed almost universal sympathy for Pius IX in "his constitutional struggle against Austrian bayonets." In this early stage of the conflict the "liberal Pope" was counterposed against Metternich and the Habsburg monarchy. "I believe," Robert Tyler exclaimed in Philadelphia, and many agreed with him, "that the great and virtuous Pontiff is engaged in a Holy War, in which he has been entangled by the wiles of Metternich." "It is the interest of the Austrian government . . . , to crush the seeds of reform that have been sown in Rome . . . , for Metternich fears the Russian bayonets less than he does the power of a single newspaper." "Oh! give liberty to your people," he exhorted the pope to the accompaniment of great applause, "Oh! give liberty to Europe; and if Austrian bayonets threaten you, remember that the heart of the great American republic beats in unison with yours."[18]

Pius IX's refusal in April 1848 to join the war against Austria was a shock and disappointment to many. His flight to Naples and call for the suppression of the Roman Republic caused even greater consternation. Still the image of the "liberal Pope" carried power in American minds. Most editorialists made excuses for Pius and maintained toward him, as a man, "the most benevolent feelings." Howard Marraro notes that the pope's "virtues were estimated by his opponents as highly as by his most ardent admirers" and that "there was a sincere desire to see him restored to all those regular functions, spiritual and moral, which he could legitimately claim as the successor of St. Peter." Most Americans felt that the pope had either been "duped by wily Jesuits bent on gaining a firmer grip on the organizational machinery of the Church" or was a prisoner of his institutional role as infallible arbiter of the Church. It mattered not, they said, what sentiments the pope carried in his heart; he was constrained by his position to act as a despotic ruler. This view, separating the person of the pope from his institutional role, ultimately became the standard American assessment of the man and his work, expressed succinctly by the *New York Times* in its overview of Pius IX's career at his death in 1878; The pope, they said "was liberal from impulse, but absolutist from a sense of duty."[19]

"Keeping the Catholics Steady"

The conflicts of 1848–49 lent substance to the argument that Roman Catholicism and republicanism were fundamentally incompatible and dismayed those Catholics who were struggling to reconcile the two, but far more devastating was the reaction of prominent American prelates to the course of events in Europe. Of all the bishops none was more prominant than John Hughes, archbishop of New York. Possessed of a pugnacious personality and a flair for political theater, "Dagger John" exercised a hold on the public imagination far greater than his influence within the Church itself. In the wake of the pope's flight from Rome he took it upon himself to defend Pius IX and his actions, and the terms in which he did so horrified many Americans, both Protestant and Catholic.

Hughes launched a vicious rhetorical attack on the Roman Republic, accusing the republicans of ingratitude toward the pope. "They wielded the stiletto," he charged, "and sacrificed by assassination the human victims who were to propitiate the goddess of Young Liberty in Italy." They established "a reign of terror over the Roman people, which they called a government." "They had broken and burned," he continued, "the carriages of the cardinals, as if that were heroism. They had plundered the churches; they had extorted money from the people; they had almost legalized assassination wherever their authority prevailed." When Pius IX returned to Rome in April 1850, Hughes ordered that a *Te Deum* be sung in celebration at St. Patrick's Cathedral and he personally offered a sermon giving thanks to God for the restoration of the pope's temporal rule.[1]

Hughes was unrelenting in his public denunciations of republicanism. He characterized the Italians as "corrupt" and "ungrateful" because they insisted "on the transformation of their government from an absolute one into a constitutional one." He denounced Mazzini's "foul Republicanism" and predicted that the triumph of democracy would bring an end to civilization and initiate "an era of promiscuous slaughter and anarchy." He even criticized the founders of the American republic as being "deeply tinged with the indifference, not to say the infidelity of those who figured at the head of the first French Revolution." Hughes held a special hatred for Louis Kossuth, the revolutionary premier of Hungary who triumphantly toured the United States in 1851. Through his organ the *Freeman's Journal* Hughes branded the liberal hero a "humbug," "a demagogue," and "a tyrant and an enemy of Christianity." Millard Fillmore was "an imbecile" for allowing the Hungarian entry into the United States, and his sympathizers were "vipers too pestiferous and disgusting to be longer endured in society."[2]

Such statements by Hughes and other Catholic spokesmen (Orestes Brownson, for instance, traveled all the way to Cincinnati in order to publicly call Kossuth a traitor to his face) were, to say the least, provocative. These were dangerous sentiments, and on first glance they would almost seem to be a deliberate attempt to antagonize the American public at a time when religious tensions were perilously high. What is more, as Horace Greeley was fond of pointing out, such spectacular explosions of invective not only were offensive to most Americans but put the archbishop and other prominent Catholic spokesmen firmly in league with the forces of reaction—with "the Austrian, Neapolitan, Spanish, and (shame to them!) French legions" who crushed freedom in Europe. In other words, they only served to confirm the essential charge of the nativists—that Roman Catholicism was antithetical and hostile to liberty.[3]

John Hughes' statements cannot be excused as angry emotional outbursts, for they were carefully calculated. Nor were they aimed only at sympathetic local audiences; Hughes bragged that "the words which I uttered . . . , were published not only here in New York, but throughout the Country," often rousing hostile comment. In fact, he said, the spectacular exchanges of vituperation between himself and nativist editors were simply a means for spreading his opinions as widely as possible. He explained that such provocation was necessary for "keeping the Catholics *steady.*" He wrote, "I dreaded the influence which [Kossuth's] reception . . . , might exercise on the Catholics, and wished them to be fore-warned."[4]

In Philadelphia, Francis Kenrick, still traumatized by the nativist attacks he had endured, kept a low profile. In the pastoral letter he composed for the provincial council of 1849 he made it clear that the bishops in no way considered the pope to be their "secular ruler." Although he stoutly defended the spiritual primacy of the pope, Kenrick maintained that the bishops were "devotedly attached to the republican institutions" of the United States. He lamented the papal exile but objected to the pope's loss of civil power only on the grounds that the "violence and outrage" of the republican forces had interrupted the development of his "enlightened policy." Kenrick must have been discomfited by Pius IX's seeming liberalism and the close association of Catholic and Protestant lay leaders that enthusiasm for the liberal pope produced, but he knew better than to antagonize either the Protestant mainstream or middle-class Catholics and so kept his peace, showing his displeasure only indirectly. We should note, for instance, that no Catholic clergymen took part in the ceremony at the Chinese Museum to honor the head of their church and the *Catholic Herald,* Kenrick's official organ, ignored the event.[5]

John Hughes had good reason to fear for the steadiness of American Catholics as "Kossuth mania" swept the nation. The revolutions of 1848 had reawakened liberal Catholic dissent. The enthusiasm for "European liberty" was such, Hughes wrote, "that it shook the firmness of not a few of the Catholic Clergy." In the years around mid-century American Catholicism faced one of its greatest crises; not primarily because of Protestant nativism (which had never, as Archbishop

Hughes candidly admitted, posed a real danger and had proven to be useful because "it tended, powerfully to unite the Catholics, and to destroy that spurious liberality . . . , which had prevailed to a great extent"), but from Catholic liberals and nationalists who rose once again to challenge constituted authorities.[6]

For this reason Hughes was particularly hostile to Catholic republicans, even those who fled repression in his beloved Ireland. Thomas D'Arcy McGee, editor of the *Nation*, and an Irish "Forty-Eighter," was to him a "bad Catholic" who "stupidly" imitated Paine and Voltaire. McGee and his comrades were "political confectioners who seal up the poison of their infidelity in sugar plums of flattery to popular prejudices." Thomas Meagher, editor of the *Irish News*, and a self-professed "Liberal Catholic" was a "red republican," and so vituperative were the charges and countercharges that Meagher and the editor of Hughes' organ, the *Freeman's Journal*, came to blows with guns and horsehide whips. When the greatest of the revolutionaries, Giuseppe Garibaldi, arrived in New York in July 1850, plans were made by the city's Italians to honor him at a great public meeting. Hughes brought pressure to bear on local politicians, who advised Garibaldi to shun all public demonstrations; he did so, on the excuse of ill health, and the republican celebration never took place.[7]

No figure disturbed the church more than Alessandro Gavazzi, who arrived in New York in 1853. A former Barnabite priest and chaplain in the papal army, Gavazzi had concluded that "Popery and liberty were incompatible" and joined the liberal revolt. For months Americans had read accounts of the "Hero Priest" and his exploits—of "his march to Rome at the head of 22,000 men; his filling the treasury of the Venetians by speaking daily to thousands; his arrest and imprisonment at Corento, and his work in behalf of the wounded in Rome during the French siege." He had escaped Italy with the assistance of American officials and his subsequent speeches had already appeared in American papers. He was every inch a romantic hero—six feet tall, with "long hair and compelling eyes," "well made, and well developed . . . , with . . . graceful yet impetuous movements . . . , the very symbol of sincerity and power." He wore the "somber garb of a monk with a blazing cross interwoven over his breast. He spoke rapidly, in an excited manner and with an 'almost savage physical energy.' "[8]

On his arrival in New York Gavazzi was feted by the Society of Friends of Civil and Religious Liberty and declared that "Popery cannot be reformed"; it can only be destroyed. "I am a Destroyer" he cried. Gavazzi asked for the support of the American people to aid the Italian struggle against Austrian despotism and denounced the "popish priests" who came to America "preaching popery." Like them he had come to America but for a different purpose. "What do I want here?" he asked. "War! War!— now that we are so quiet, so contented, so friendly, and so united? Yes, I like war; I am a man of war."[9]

Immediately Gavazzi became the target of Catholic spokesmen who construed his words as an attack on immigrants. The editor of the *Irish American* accused him of inciting Protestants to war against the Irish who had found a home in the New World. Gavazzi's supporters rose to his defense, saying that their hero's words had been "cruelly and unjustifiably misrepresented." Although Gavazzi had repeatedly declared war on the "Popish system" and even on the pope himself, they said, never had he made any statement that could be "tortured" into a suggestion that Protestants should attempt to drive out their Catholic fellow-citizens.[10]

The controversy, of course, stirred interest in Gavazzi's appearances and soon large crowds of supporters and detractors appeared night after night at the Broadway Tabernacle to applaud or hiss his pronouncements on despotism in France, Austria, and Italy; on the papal system and the pope's temporal power; on the Inquisition and Catholic "superstitions" such as transubstantiation and veneration of the Virgin and the Saints. Eventually, Gavazzi's provocative attacks on the Catholic establishment roused physical violence. One lecture was interrupted several times by persons outside the hall smashing windows with brickbats and other missiles.[11]

In May and June 1853 Gavazzi took to the road, speaking and drawing large audiences in Baltimore, Quebec, and Montreal. In Quebec he was assaulted while on stage and in Montreal the building in which he was speaking was attacked. Troops were called out to suppress the riot and they fired into the crowd, killing several people. The Canadian outrages were widely reported in the American press, which portrayed Gavazzi "twice a martyr" to Catholic intolerance. Even the nonpartisan Philadelphia *Public Ledger* protested that "Liberty would soon be extinguished were mobs permitted to decide who should and who should not speak in churches and public halls." In June 1853 Gavazzi returned to New York, receiving a hero's welcome from Protestants and from German and Italian immigrants. He continued his lectures, warning Americans that they must "be Protestant, if they would remain Republicans" and urging them to eternal vigilance to ensure that their public institutions would remain "American and not Roman, Protestant and not Papal."[12]

While Gavazzi toured the nation, Holy Trinity's Germans were locked in their struggle with Bishop Neumann. Their rhetoric, like his, reflected the passions and antipathies of the great international drama that had just concluded. In court they argued that they were victims of a Jesuitical conspiracy headed by an "Austrian . . . grand regulator." Their appeals to the Pennsylvania Assembly in the spring and fall of 1854 portrayed Bishop Neumann as the willing tool of a reactionary Austrian cabal, directed by the papal secretary of state, which, they claimed, dominated the Roman Curia, held the pope a virtual prisoner in his palace (thus explaining his sudden change of policy), and now threatened the liberties of Americans.[13]

Holy Trinity's nationalists claimed that Bishop John Neumann was "entirely under Austrian influence." They pointed out that some of his support came from an Austrian mission society, the Leopoldine Foundation, directed by the "Prince Archbishop of Austria." The purpose of the foundation, they said, was to send "monkish missionaries, . . . no secular priest being trusted," to the United States with "politics . . . as much their mission as religion." Their goal was nothing less than "to destroy the heresies of our Republican government," and "[to bring] us back to the true faith of monarchy." A second petition extended these charges. It accused the American hierarchy of "tyranical [sic] and unchristian acts, . . . repugnant to our republican institutions," and of propagating doctrines, "too monstrous and arbitrary to be at all tolerated." A vast conspiracy, it charged, had introduced into America "monks, or jesuits inimical to our republican institutions, [who] sometimes desecrate the pulpit by preaching the divine right of kings, and that the people have no right to govern themselves."[14]

Holy Trinity's protest was not an isolated instance. Other German congregations around the country issued similar statements. One Catholic congregation in Buffalo, New York, denounced the "unscrupulous means . . . ,—all the arts and appliances which Jesuitism knows so well how to employ," which were being used "with persevering malignancy" to advance the "inflexible designs of Romanism in this country." Like Holy Trinity's trustees, the Buffalo congregation petitioned their state legislature to secure legislation limiting episcopal control over the temporalities of the Church and, with the cooperation of Protestant nativists, obtained it. In Phoenixville, near Philadelphia, conflict between German nationalists and the bishop took an ugly turn. There Neumann intervened to settle a dispute between German and English-speaking Catholics and decided against the Germans. When accused of betraying his countrymen, Neumann replied "Thank God I am not a German; I'm a Bohemian." This so incensed the Germans that they tried to kill the bishop by derailing the train in which he was riding. Members of the congregation later traveled to Philadelphia and assaulted Neumann in his home.[15]

While Alessandro Gavazzi was holding forth on the iniquities of Romanism, Gaetano Bedini, archbishop of Thebes, came to America. Like Kossuth and Gavazzi, the monsignor had been a participant in the revolutions of 1848, but unlike them he had served the pope. The archbishop's purposes in coming to the United States were complex and, at the time, unclear. Officially, he had been appointed papal nuncio to Brazil and was merely pausing to pay a courtesy visit to members of the American hierarchy, but he was also charged with investigating and reporting on the state of the Church in the United States, and was instructed to mediate conflicts within the American church. One of the most troubling of these disputes was the revolt at Philadelphia's Holy Trinity.[16]

Word of Bedini's mission preceded him and he was denounced in the press and from pulpits as an agent of the Inquisition and a war criminal who had personally been responsible for the death of several patriots, including Ugo Bassi, an apostate priest who had served with Garibaldi. Bedini's foremost accuser was Gavazzi, who branded him the "Bloody Butcher of Bologna" and charged him with personally torturing Bassi before his death. Gavazzi declared that Archbishop Bedini was "a formidable foe bent on undermining the foundations of American liberty." This theme was picked up and repeated, growing more extravagant over time. In Philadelphia, "A Democratic American" denounced the "blood-stained wretch Bedini, the murderer of Ugo Bassi, who was partly flayed alive, and numerous other Italian patriots."[17]

Catholic spokesmen and journals came to the archbishop's defense, portraying the "martyrs of liberty" as "adventurers, robbers, and assassins." Criticism, however, began to mount, fueled by the periodic arrival of refugees and political exiles from various parts of Italy who told stories of atrocities perpetrated by Italian civil and religious authorities. These complaints provoked riots in the immigrant communities of

New York. Bedini and his mission were endlessly denounced in immigrant journals such as *L'Eco d'Italia,* the *Crusader,* the *Extra Blatt der Reform.* Eventually Protestant ministers and nativist politicians responded to the immigrant agitation and began to denounce Bedini, but the mainstream of Protestant opinion remained favorable to the archbishop and his mission.[18]

Bedini arrived in Philadelphia on July 22, 1853. He intended to intervene in the dispute between Bishop Neumann and Holy Trinity's nationalists and, if possible, to use his influence as official representative of the Holy See to impress on the laity the need to reconcile themselves to the principle of episcopal absolutism. In this he failed absolutely. Bedini refused Bishop Neumann's hospitality, on the excuse that it would compromise his neutrality in the matter. In response Neumann declared that he was too busy with other matters to meet with the monsignor. The dissenters at Holy Trinity denied him entry to their church. Frustrated, Bedini left Philadelphia three days after he arrived. Soon thereafter, accompanied by John Hughes, he embarked on a tour of the American dioceses.[19]

Bedini's tour was a disaster. Everywhere he went he was met by enraged crowds. Several times he was hanged and burned in effigy. In some cities his arrival occasioned riots in which many people were injured. He was verbally and physically assaulted, his life threatened on occasion, and in Baltimore several bullets were fired into his room. His mission a shambles, Archbishop Bedini finally was forced into hiding to avoid hostile mobs and was smuggled out of the country and back to Rome. Riots and demonstrations continued long after Bedini had fled the country. In Boston there was an attempt to burn him in effigy on the Common. In New York Italian immigrants staged a mock trial at which not only Bedini but also American politicians who had defended him were excoriated. A final anti-Bedini meeting was held in Philadelphia at the Chinese Museum on February 11, 1854. There, on the stage that had six years earlier witnessed the interdenominational celebration of the "liberal Pope," resolutions were passed and published condemning the nuncio as well as those members of Congress who had denounced earlier demonstrations, and demanding that the United States sever diplomatic relations with the Holy See.[20]

Bedini's tour of the United States came less than a year after Louis Kossuth's triumphant visit and it is instructive to consider the receptions accorded the two men. Louis Kossuth was given a hero's welcome, not because he was anti-Catholic, although denunciations of the Church and its influence were certainly part of his repertoire. Rather, he was a hero because he stood for a set of ideals—personal freedom, political democracy, and national self-determination—that were strongly cherished by many Americans, both immigrant and native. Conversely, Archbishop Bedini was vilified, not simply because he was a Catholic, but because he was identified in the popular mind as the agent of a Roman regime that, demonstrably, was operating against those ideals. "The religious motive," James F. Connolly concluded in his study of Bedini's ordeal, was,

> secondary to the strong political convictions of the liberals and republicans, whose single passion seemed to be a desire to destroy the established monarchical and autocratic political systems. Every time they rioted against the Papal Nuncio, they were attacking the Papal Government which he represented, and which they believed was dedicated and pledged to maintaining everything to which they were opposed.[21]

It was, then, the Church itself and its policies, rather than Catholics or immigrants, that mainly roused public anger in 1853–54. This point is corroborated by another of Connolly's conclusions: that immigrants were in the forefront of what has usually been considered anti-Catholic, anti-immigrant violence. "The main responsibility," for the disturbances attending Bedini's tour, he says, "must lie with the European exiles . . . , the atheistic Germans and the anti-clerical Italians." To these must be added devout Catholics like Holy Trinity's Germans or the congregation in Buffalo, or the editor of the *Irish-American* who in 1854 denounced as a matter of principle the "ultramontane politico-religious principles" emanating from Rome and embraced by the American prelates. "The whole 'Catholic press' of America," he pointed out, "sang a dismal chorus of unanimity *against* the freedom of European nations—*against* revolutions in Catholic countries . . . , while the entire American press, representing the generous sympathies of the American people, were cheering on the struggle for liberty, and bidding encouragement and hope to the down-trampled and despot-ridden people of the old world."[22]

The political crises of mid-century in Europe and America posed a significant challenge to the Roman Catholic Church in the United States. Not since the days of the French Revolution had the discrepancies between Roman and American political cultures been so apparent or so controversial. What is more, ultramontane internationalism and anti-liberalism alienated important elements of the immigrant population whom the church sought to serve. These ideological conflicts enormously complicated the problems faced by church leaders as they sought to enlarge and strengthen the city's Catholic community.

"Crosses All Over Their Faces"

In the decade before the Civil War Philadelphia Catholicism faced its greatest crisis. Political reaction, aggressively promoted by Rome and by American prelates such as John Hughes, revived a nativist political movement that had been practically moribund at mid-century and had offended and alienated a substantial number of Catholics. The assimilationist tendencies of the Catholic middle classes had undermined the bishops' attempts to separate Catholics culturally and socially from the American mainstream. Most important, the social perspectives of Philadelphia Catholicism, while congenial to the interests of the industrial elites and respectable Catholics of all ranks, distanced the Church from its largest potential constituency—the traditionalist immigrant workers.

Yet, the situation was not hopeless. The excesses of the Know-Nothings repelled many respectable Catholics and the Church was quick to exploit this fact, couching its response to the nativist threat in terms calculated to appeal to the bourgeoisie. The *Catholic Herald* charged nativist politicians with incompetence, intemperance, and corruption and dismissed them as rabble-rousers with lower-class followings. Their arguments were branded anti-American and contrasted with the patriotism of Catholics. When Orestes Brownson criticized working-class immigrants for their clannishness and disreputable behavior, the *Herald*, mindful of its middle-class readership, did not quarrel with his assessment. Arguing that nativist discrimination had severely restricted opportunities for Catholics to advance in the broader society (cut them "off from employment and patronage") the *Herald* recommended that Catholics should band together to "assist one another in business much more than they do" or "[buy] of each other, giving work to their fellow members [of the Church], etc., etc."[1]

The Church's response to the mid-century crisis also included a resumption of evangelical activity. Philadelphia's second Catholic revival began in May of 1852 at St. John the Evangelist's Church when Isaac Hecker, Augustine Hewit, and Clarence Walworth (all of them Redemptorists and converts from Protestantism who would soon be among the founders of the Paulist order) organized a two-week mission that brought thousands back to the faith. Over the next decade parish missions were so frequent that Philadelphia experienced something approaching a perpetual revival.[2]

Missions were extremely emotional affairs. Jay Dolan relates a description of one conducted by Father Walworth during which he "screamed out so the walls of the Cathedral reechoed it back again," and "the people cried, groaned, beat their breasts . . . and . . . when he spoke of the wicked they all cried out Oh Oh Oh My God, My God and then crosses all over their faces." The revivals were also extremely popular. Writing in 1858 Bishop Neumann described a Jesuit mission in one working-class parish which required ten or twelve priests to hear all the confessions of the thousands of penitents who flocked to the services. In addition to these parish missions Bishop Neumann established an elaborate round of devotions that "often took on the proportions of a mission." Sometimes when the Forty Hours was being observed it was necessary to call in priests from adjoining parishes to assist in the administration of sacraments to converts and penitents. An observance of the Forty Hours simultaneous with the Jesuit mission described above but in another working-class parish, attracted nearly as many penitents and required the services of fourteen priests. "And so it goes," Neumann wrote, "the whole year almost without interruption."[3]

Historians of American evangelism have long noted the pronounced bourgeois bias in Protestant revivals. Catholic revivalists, too, tried to instill in their listeners a "rigorous moralism." "Seldom did a mission go by without a sermon on drunkenness or intemperance and throughout the course of the revival the evils of drink were continually alluded to." Dancing, sexual "impurity," novels and magazines, gambling, frivolous entertainments, shows and theaters all came in for condemnation. Mission priests urged their listeners to adopt respectable manners, to submit to authority, and to work diligently to improve themselves and their children. All of this represented a strong repudiation of the "insouciant morality" of traditionalist culture. Nevertheless the revivals were popular with all classes. "Had there been twice as many priests" Bishop Neumann wrote of a revival in a working-class neighborhood, "twice as many would have received Communion . . . , because not half . . . who ask for these exercises can obtain them." Still, he noted, despite the scarcity of clergy the missions "bring abundant fruit." James F. Wood, Neumann's coadjutor, concurred. He bragged that the missions "produced wonderful fruit in our people as well as among Protestants."[4]

As impressive as the parish missions and devotional exercises were, though, their effect on the thousands who thronged to them was transitory. "The religious enthusiasm generated by the revival quickly died down, and there was little evidence of a continued upsurge in piety once the preachers left." Thus, though working-class immigrants could from time to time be induced to involve themselves in demonstrations of extreme religious fervor and devotion, they were not in any great numbers drawn by evangelical efforts into the Catholic community, which continued to be dominated by the most affluent elements of Philadelphia's Catholic population.[5]

We can see evidence of this in the parish records of St. Patrick's Church, built in 1839 to serve immigrant workers on the Schuylkill docks. St. Patrick's had originally been established as a "free" church, but financial difficulties forced the parish to begin collecting pew rents in 1852. A listing of pewholders for that year affords us a profile of the congregation as it stood at mid-century. Numerically, workingmen and women dominated. Only one in five pewholders held a white-collar, proprietary, or professional position. Another third were skilled workers, and nearly two-fifths were unskilled laborers. However, the parish associations (the temperance society, the literary society, the library society, the sodalities, confraternities and the like) were dominated by affluent people such as Thomas E. Cahill, an ice merchant and one of the richest men in the city, and a Mrs. Vermillion, a "gentlewoman" who was the driving force behind several parish associations.[6]

A second list of pewholders from 1859 suggests a reason for this disparity. Nearly 70 percent of the white collar pewholders and 60 percent of those with skilled occupations remained in the congregation over the seven-year period, but two-thirds of the unskilled workers had disappeared from the rolls. This points to a general characteristic of nineteenth-century immigrant populations; they were extremely fluid. Immigrants were not, as some have assumed, trapped in the port cities of the east; they spread throughout the nation's industializing core. Immigrants, especially those who were young and unskilled, moved frequently in search of work, and the immigrant communities that emerged consisted of a core of persistent residents around whom flowed a sizeable stream of transients. Those who persisted usually represented the older and more affluent elements of the immigrant population, and it was these relatively stable individuals who dominated the institutional structures that gave form and substance to the local community.[7]

"This Babylon of Philadelphia"

The enormous institutional expansion undertaken by Bishops Kenrick and Neumann was costly, and the Church incurred heavy debts nearly all of which were owed to wealthy Catholic laymen. The Church in Philadelphia also operated a private savings bank (the "Bishops Bank" it was called), encouraging deposits from the laity and offering as security all the bishop's possessions. By 1858 the deposits in this bank amounted to more than $250,000 and there was a danger that these might be withdrawn at any time.[1]

The Church's financial situation gave wealthy laymen enormous influence. This became apparent in their dealings with John Neumann. Unlike his predecessor, who had been a sophisticated urbanite, Neumann was of peasant stock. Physically diminutive, shy, lacking facility in English, and of limited education, he had little in common with members of the city's Catholic elite. His experience had left him, as he said, without "urbanity—graceful deportment, & all that sort of necessities of life," and therefore "entirely unfitted ... for living as is the vogue in this Babylon of Philadelphia." The city's Catholic elite agreed; so did Propaganda. Gaetano Bedini, after conferring with several locally prominent laymen, reported that because of his "neglect of the fashions" John Neumann was completely unsuited for his constituents, who were "rich, intelligent, [and] full of life and importance." One year later Michael O'Connor reported that Neumann's demeanor occasioned a great deal of dissatisfaction, especially among Catholics "of the higher class."[2]

More important, though, was the fact that Philadelphia's fourth bishop had little understanding of finance. This caused "serious and innumerable complaints" from men to whom the diocese was heavily in debt. Through the middle years of the decade lay leaders frequently demanded that the bishop liquidate the Church's debt, but it continued to mount. Finally, the situation became so serious that Archbishop Kenrick reported to Propaganda that, inasmuch as Bishop Neumann "is unable to carry on the temporal affairs of the diocese," and "does not know how to reduce the debt under which the diocese is laboring . . . all things may become ruined unless the Holy See gives him a coadjutor to handle the financial situation and to check the disorders." Kenrick's fear was that, should the diocese default on its debts, or if the Bishop's Bank would be unable to redeem its notes, properties that had been removed from the control of laymen might again fall into their hands. With dismay he came to agree with those "laymen of zeal and good sense" who insisted that Bishop Neumann was "entirely incompetent."[3]

John Neumann was a devout and humble man. He well knew his shortcomings and was aware of the hostility he had roused among the traditionalist clergy, German nationalists, and members of the Catholic elite. Time and again he petitioned Propaganda to send him away from Philadelphia to a smaller and less sophisticated setting. When Propaganda in response to petitions from all sides named James Frederick Wood to be Bishop of Antigonia and Coadjutor of the Diocese of Philadelphia with right of succession, John Neumann was greatly relieved.[4]

Wood was an ideal choice to manage Philadelphia's affairs. He was a native of the city, of English parentage. He had been raised as a Unitarian and converted to Catholicism as an adult. He had worked in a bank and had extensive financial experience. He was also well educated, having studied at private schools in America and England and trained for the priesthood at the Urban College of the Propaganda. Bishop

Wood was thoroughly ultramontane and an unyielding disciplinarian, but he was also popular with Philadelphia's lay leadership. He was tall and physically imposing, with an outgoing, even ebullient character. He was noted "for his suavity of manners, his learning, and his piety" and was "at ease in any gathering and the master of all the social amenities." Everyone approved of him except the traditionalist Irish clergy and some German nationalists who complained at being placed under an "English" bishop.[5]

Bishops Neumann and Wood divided the rule of the diocese. Neumann spent much of his time traveling in rural areas, administering confirmations and performing symbolic functions. Administrative tasks, especially the control of diocesan finances, were Wood's purview and he performed them admirably, ruthlessly cutting costs and finding new sources of revenues. Even in the depths of a depression the diocesan bank prospered and Wood's fund-raising campaigns and real-estate ventures soon began to reduce the level of diocesan debt. But there were also difficulties.[6]

Bishop Wood was a hard negotiator and sometimes individuals with whom he was dealing would appeal over his head to Bishop Neumann. Wood complained that "money obligations" were "increased without his knowledge" and demanded that he be given authority commensurate with his responsibilities. Other American prelates sympathized with Wood's plight. They recommended to Propaganda that the Philadelphia diocese be divided and that Bishop Neumann be reassigned out of the city. Neumann himself approved this plan, but Rome took no action and American authorities were helpless to act without direction from the Holy See. All awaited word from Propaganda while frustrations mounted. Then, on January 5, 1860, Bishop Neumann died suddenly of apoplexy.[7]

The funeral observances attending John Neumann's death were elaborate and impressive and they illustrate the essential character of the reformed Church that had emerged there. For three days the bishop's body lay in state in the sanctuary of the cathedral chapel while people filed by to pay their respects. It was an impressive setting. The church was "draped in deep mourning. The High Altar was . . . covered with its mantle of black," as was the altar of the Blessed Virgin on the left of the sanctuary. Young men from the Conference of St. Vincent de Paul, stood all day and through the night as a guard of honor around the corpse. The coffin was "surrounded by a number of lighted candles.

At the head was the celebrated Genoa Ivory Crucifix." The bishop's remains were "covered by robes peculiar to the Episcopate" and "rested upon a cushion of white satin, shaded by purple hanging, and surrounded by waxen burners that lit the pallid face of the dead in a manner impressively solemn." Through the day the bell of St. John's Church tolled a funeral knell.[8]

The funeral procession began at the still-incomplete cathedral at 9:00 on the morning of January 9. For nearly two hours crowds had been gathering to witness the spectacle and many more lined the way to St. John the Evangelist's Church. Several Redemptorist fathers bore the body "upon a mattress, covered with purple satin" and placed it in a "large handsome hearse, enclosed with glass" its top "decorated with sable plumes" and drawn by four black horses. The body was carried through the city accompanied by a body of police, a brass band, and the Pennsylvania Rifle Company. Behind them came the Philopatrian Literary Institute, the St. Francis Xavier Institute, St. Francis' Beneficial society, St. Philip's Literary Society, St. Joseph's Literary Society, St. Peter's Literary Society and St. Paul's Literary society followed by seventeen sodalities and confraternities and twelve conferences. Twelve Catholic beneficial societies from Baltimore also marched that day.

"Roofs in every direction were completely covered with spectators, and every window was lined with gazers" to view the spectacle. Here was the Catholic bourgeoisie on display. "Arrayed in beautiful regalia" they bore witness to their numbers, their respectability, their piety, their prosperity, and their prominence within Philadelphia's Catholic community. After nearly an hour the funeral cortege reached St. John's, where six clergymen, acting as pallbearers, conveyed the body into the church and placed it upon a catafalque which was erected before the high altar. The body, "arrayed in the Pontifical robes" with ring, mitre, and a richly gilt crosier prominently displayed was "placed upon an inclined plane on the catafalque, the features openly exposed." The pillars of the building were "shrouded in black, while festoons of the same color depended from the ceiling." "Black lace was suspended in front of all the windows" and "black lace veils tastefully arranged with rosettes" covered the paintings. All the gas fixtures and taper stands were "enveloped in black."[9]

The effect was magnificent and somber and it drew attention to the "beautiful white marble figure of the Blessed Virgin" which was uncovered and lighted for the occasion. A "large and magnificent crucifix" was suspended over the catafalque, which was itself "elegantly adorned with black drapery, and surmounted with a most graceful canopy." Beside the body lay a coffin of "fine black walnut, covered with costly black cloth, and lined with rich purple satin," a silver cross and plaque prominent on its lid. The catafalque was "surmounted by thirty burning consecrated candles and surrounded on the platform by twelve large candles." The corpse itself was placed on an incline "so that the face could be distinctly seen in nearly every part of the church." In attendance were Archbishop Kenrick, Bishop Wood, three other bishops and the provincial of the Redemptorists along with more than seventy priests from all parts of the diocese. James Wood, now bishop of Philadelphia in his own right, celebrated the High Mass of Requiem, assisted by four priests, and Archbishop Kenrick gave the sermon. Two church choirs sang the Requiem Mass accompanied by an organist and an "orchestra of about twenty instruments." The body was then taken in another procession to the Church of St. Peter. That evening the clergy of the diocese assembled again to chant the Office of the Dead and the church remained open through the night while people came in to pray. Finally, on Wednesday, January 11, 1860, John Neumann was buried in the lower chapel of St. Peter's Church.[10]

The pomp and splendor attending the funeral of this shy and humble man was not just an honor to his memory. It was also an expression of the new Catholicity—Romanized, authoritarian, and respectable—that had emerged in Philadelphia in the three decades before the Civil War. With its rich devotional symbolism, extravagant pietism, and clear displays of hierarchy and order it was a far cry from the plain republican church envisioned by St. Mary's dissenters one generation earlier. It was equally distant from the traditionalist churches of Europe, and its celebration of Catholic respectability stood in stark contrast to the disorder and turbulence of Philadelphia's working-class communities. The three bishops of Philadelphia on display—Francis Kenrick, an Irishman; John Neumann, a German; and James Woods, an American of English descent—represented the major nationality elements within the American Catholic church, but all three were ultramontane internationalists who specifically repudiated the ethnic and national enthusiasms that have been given so much prominence in studies of American Catholicism. This was neither the "republican" church nor the "immigrant" church, nor was it a specifically American church. It was a product of the institutional imperatives emanating from restoration Rome and the class imperatives of industrial society.

In the years between the American Revolution and the Civil War, Philadelphia's Catholic community underwent momentous changes. Wracked by social, ideological, and institutional conflicts the small consensual community of the eighteenth century, organized around the principles of hierarchy, deference, and ascribed status, dissolved into a welter of contending factions. Then, gradually, a new Catholic community had begun to emerge. By the middle decades of the nineteenth century its major contours were clear, but it was far from complete. Large elements of the city's immigrant population, most notably the working classes, were not yet integrated into the community, and though institutional and ideological lines were clearly drawn the social boundaries separating Protestant from Catholic were still blurred. These were to be the greatest challenges faced by those who sought to organize Philadelphia's Catholics into a coherent community in the years after the Civil War, but that is another story to be dealt with in another book.

Notes

INTRODUCTION

1. Gordon Wood, *The Radicalism of the American Revolution* (New York, 1991).

2. Martin E Marty, *The Modern Schism: Three Paths to the Secular* (New York, 1969): 11.

"AUTHORS OF DISSENSIONS AND SOWERS OF DISCONTENT"

1. Robert Molyneux to John Carroll, 8 February 1788, Archives of the Archdiocese of Baltimore (hereafter AAB), file 8A T1.

2. John Carroll to Trustee (Joseph Cauffman) of the German Congregation in Philadelphia (November 1787), in Thomas O'Brien Hanley, S.J., ed., *The John Carroll Papers* (Notre Dame, 1982) (hereafter, *Papers*), 1: 234–35. For an account of John Helbron's ministry, see Martin I. J. Griffin, "Church of the Holy Trinity, Philadelphia. Its First Pastor, Rev. John Baptist Charles Helbron. The First Opposition to Ecclesiastical Authority," *Records of the American Catholic Historical Society of Philadelphia* (hereafter *Records*) 21 (1910): 1–45.

3. Carroll was already embroiled in another controversy over the appointment of priests when he received the Germans' petition. See Patrick W. Carey, *People, Priests and Prelates: Ecclesiastical Democracy and the Tensions of Trusteeism* (Notre Dame, 1987), chapter 1, "Trusteeism in New York City, 1785–1790"; John Carroll to Dominick Lynch and Thomas Stoughton, 24 January 1786; to Trustee of German Congregation in Philadelphia (Joseph Cauffman), n.d. [1787], *Papers*, 1:204, 234–35.

4. James Oellers to Bishop John Carroll, 24 November 1787, AAB file 11B P2. Holy Trinity: Minute Book of the Trustees, 1788–1934, in the Archdiocese of Philadelphia and the American Catholic Historical Society of Philadelphia Archives and Historical Collections (hereafter Philadelphia Archives): vol. 1: 15–19; Adam Premir et al. to John Carroll, 23 February 1788, AAB file 11B P3.

5. Adam Premir et al. to John Carroll, 23 February 1788, AAB file 11B P3; Robert Molyneux to John Carroll, 8 February 1788, AAB file 8A T1; Jacob Cline et al. to John Carroll, n.d., AAB file 11B Q2; copy of the subscription appeal, AAB file 11B QA.

6. John Carroll to the German Congregation in Philadelphia, 3 March 1788, *Papers*, 1:276–77, AAB file 9 N1.

7. Vincent J. Fecher, *A Study of the Movement for German National Parishes in Philadelphia and Baltimore (1787–1802)*, (Rome, 1955): 93; Adam Premir et

al. to John Carroll, 23 February 1788, AAB file 11B P3; Holy Trinity, Trustees Minute Book, vol. 1: 18–19.

8. Griffin, "Church of the Holy Trinity," 23, 25–26. On Lutheran contributions to the founding of Holy Trinity, see Anthony Fleming to the *Propaganda Fide*, 3 February 1791, *Scritture Riferite nei Congressi America Centrale 3 (1791–1817)* (hereafter *Congressi*): 17v–18r; Trustees Minute Book 1: 20–21, 35–37. On rural German missions, see Lambert Schrott, *Pioneer German Catholics in the American Colonies (1734–1784)*, (New York, 1933).

9. Adam Premir to John Carroll, 28 May 1788, AAB file 11B Q1. The act of incorporation is reprinted in Francis J. Hertkorn, *Retrospective of Holy Trinity Parish: A Souvenir of the One Hundred Twenty-Fifth Anniversary of the Foundation of the Church* (Philadelphia, 1914): 31–33; the Congregation of Holy Trinity to John Carroll, 22 March 1789, AAB file 11B Q3. On "civic" as opposed to "ethnic" nationalism, see Liah Greenfield, *Nationalism: Five Roads to Modernity* (Cambridge, Mass., 1993).

10. Patrick Smith, *The Present State of the Catholic Missions Conducted by the Jesuits in North America* (Dublin, 1788), cited at length in Griffin, "Church of the Holy Trinity": 29–30; Adam Premir to John Carroll, 28 May 1788, AAB file 11B Q1.

11. Philip Gleason, *The Conservative Reformers: German-American Catholics and the Social Order* (Notre Dame, 1968).

12. On the Anglo-American tradition of Catholic republicanism, see David O'Brien, *Public Catholicism* (New York, 1989), chapter 1, "Republican Catholicism"; Gerald P. Fogarty, "Public Patriotism and Private Politics: The Tradition of American Catholicism," *U.S. Catholic Historian*, vol. 4, no. 1 (1984): 1–48; James Hennesey, "Roman Catholicism: The Maryland Tradition," *Thought*, vol. 51, no. 202 (September 1976): 282–95.

13. Petition, Jacob Cline et al. to John Carroll, n.d., AAB file 11B Q2; Carey, *People, Priests, and Prelates*: 17–19.

14. James Hennesey, *American Catholics: A History of the Roman Catholic Community in the United States* (New York, 1981): 95. For an extensive discussion of the claims of *jus patronatus* made in Philadelphia and elsewhere, see Fecher, *German National Parishes*: 17–19, 120–37, 211–13, 266–68. See also the discussion of *jus patronatus* in Carey, *People, Priests and Prelates*: 27–31.

15. John Carroll to the German Congregation in Philadelphia, 3 March 1788, AAB file 9 N1; to John Helbron, 10 September, 13 October 1789, AAB files 11B R1,11B R3; to the Trustees of Holy Trinity Church, Philadelphia, 11 October 1789, AAB file 9A H1. Carroll also raised the argument that, since "Protestants, Quakers &c." had contributed to the building of Holy Trinity, the logic of the trustees would require that they allow non-Catholics to have a say in the governing of the parish. See John Carroll to John Helbron, November 1789, *Papers*, 1: 391–92. On Carroll as an exemplar of the Anglo-American

Catholic republican tradition, see Hennesey, "The Vision of John Carroll," *Thought*, vol. 54, no. 214 (September 1979): 323–33.

16. On Carroll's moderation, see Patrick Carey, "Two Episcopal Views of Lay–Clerical Conflicts: 1785–1860," *Records* 87 (1976): 85–98. Carroll explicitly laid out the doctrine of apostolic succession to the Philadelphia Germans in 1797. On that occasion he explained that according to Catholic tradition Jesus had invested his apostles with a "sacred commission and authority." The apostles then "appointed Pastors to take charge of the churches formed by their preaching, which Pastors in their turn . . . , constituted others, who have been thus continued to the present time, deriving their power of exercising the holy functions of the Pastoral office, not from human authority, or institutions of civil government, but from the same divine origin as the Apostles themselves." See John Carroll, "Disciplinary Decree to Holy Trinity Congregation," 22 February 1797, *Papers*, 2: 200–201. We may note that Carroll's understanding of the doctrine of apostolic succession locates spiritual authority in the "Pastors of the church." This position is theologically significant for it distinguishes him from the ultramontane reformers of his day who sought to locate spiritual authority within the person of the pope. In terms of the relationship between ecclesiastical authorities and the laity, though, John Carroll's nationalist ("Gallican") vision of the church was no less monarchic and authoritarian than the ultramontane doctrines of the Roman Curia. In fact, throughout Europe, ultramontane reformers often posed as defenders of the rights of the people against the absolutist pretensions of national hierarchs. See Roger Aubert et al., *The Church between Reformation and Restoration*, Peter Becker, trans. (New York, 1981): 108–13.

17. John Carroll to the German Congregation in Philadelphia, 31 March 1788, *Papers*, 1: 294, original and a draft copy in AAB files 9 N2; 11B P5; John Helbron to John Carroll, 28 October 1789, AAB file 11B R3.

18. John Carroll to the German Congregation in Philadelphia, 31 March 1788, *Papers*, 1: 294.

"A SELECT BODY OF CLERGY"

1. Richard Challoner to William Walton, 21 October 1773, cited in John Tracy Ellis, *Catholics in Colonial America* (Baltimore, 1965): 388–89 n.; Ferdinand Farmer (Steinmeyer) to Christian Mayer, 29 January 1778, in Thomas Hughes, ed., *History of the Society of Jesus in North America, Colonial and Federal* (New York, 1907–17), *Documents* 1, part 2: 953–54 n. 6. On the independence of the mission clergy, see Ellis, *Catholics in Colonial America*, 382–83.

2. John Carroll to Francis Beeston, 22 March 1788; to Charles Plowden, 1–25 March 1788, *Papers*, 1: 291–93, 272–76. Carroll nursed a special resentment for

the Capuchins, whom he found to be "most intolerable. To a great deal of ignorance they join most consummate assurance. Add that they seem to have no principles of Religious life." See John Carroll to Charles Plowden, 23 October 1789, *Papers*, 1: 389–91; Leonardo Cardinal Antonelli to John Carroll, 14 August 1790, *Lettere e Decreti della S. Congregazione e Biglietti di Mons. Segretario dell' anno 1790* (hereafter *Lettere*), 258: fols. 501 r and v; John Carroll to Leonardo Antonelli, 27 September 1790, draft in AAB 9A A3.

3. *New Catholic Encyclopedia*, vol. 11: 840–44; Ellis, *Catholics in Colonial America*: 383.

4. Charles Carroll to Richard Challoner, 16 July 1765, in Hughes, *History of the Society of Jesus*, 2: 591–92; Richard Challoner to Christopher Stonor, 12 September 1766, cited in ibid.: 592–93; James Hennessey, "Papacy and Episcopacy in Eighteenth and Nineteenth Century American Catholic Thought," *Records* 77 (1966): 177.

5. John Carroll to Charles Plowden, 20 February 1782, *Papers*, 1: 66; Edward I. Devitt, "Letters of Father Joseph Mosely S.J. and Some Extracts from His Diary, 1757–1786," *Records* 17 (1906): 306.

6. On the first Whitemarsh meeting, see Peter Guilday, *The Life and Times of John Carroll, Archbishop of Baltimore (1735–1815)* (New York, 1922): 169–77; John G. Shea, *Life and Times of the Most Rev. John Carroll, Bishop and First Archbishop of Baltimore, Embracing the History of the Catholic Church in the United States, 1763–1815* (New York, 1888): 207–12. The "Constitution of the Clergy" adopted at these meetings is reproduced in *Papers*, 1: 71–77.

7. These negotiations as well as most of the relevant documents are reproduced in Jules A. Baisnée, *France and the Establishment of the American Hierarchy: The Myth of French Interference, 1783–1784* (Baltimore, 1934). See also Edward I. Devitt, "Propaganda Documents. Appointment of the First Bishop of Baltimore," *Records* 21 (1910): 185–236.

8. John Carroll to Charles Plowden, 18 September 1784; 10 April 1784, *Papers*, 1: 145–47. Plowden had previously warned Carroll that "the foul side of Rome . . . the Propaganda . . . will use every art to extend their own dominion & influence in your country." See Charles Plowden to John Carroll, 4 April 1784, AAB file 6 J1.

9. John Carroll to Charles Plowden, 26 September 1783, *Papers*, 1: 77–79. After consultation with other members of the American clergy, a second, less provocative petition was sent to Rome asking that the ex-Jesuits be allowed to elect their own superior and yet again raising the bogey of Protestant intolerance, arguing that the appointment of a foreign bishop would be unacceptable to the American government. It is unlikely that the Holy See gave this petition much credence in the light of their recent communications with the American Congress. See Peter Guilday, *Life and Times of Carroll*: 170–71. Regarding the motives of the Whitemarsh confreres, Shea, *Life and Times of Carroll*: 242,

states "The restoration of the Society [of Jesus] was the absorbing thought of the American missionaries who had belonged to it, and this is the key to their action, which to some might seem to savor of insubordination and defiance."

10. John Thorpe to John Carroll, 9 June 1784, AAB file 8 H3; Franklin's recommendation of Carroll is cited in Bainsee, *France and the Establishment of the American Catholic Hierarchy*: 67–68; Leonardo Antonelli to John Carroll, 9 June 1784: 117–18; Charles Plowden to John Carroll, 4 July 1784, AAB file 6 J3.

11. John Carroll to Ferdinand Farmer (Steinmeyer) December 1784, *Papers*, 1: 155–58; Leonard Neale to John Carroll, 11 January 1785, AAB file 11 10N.

12. John Carroll to Charles Plowden, 18 September 1784, *Papers*, 1: 149–52.

13. John Carroll to Ferdinand Farmer (Steinmeyer), December 1784, *Papers*, 1: 155–58.

14. Ibid.

15. John Carroll to Leonardo Antonelli, 27 February 1785, *Papers*, 1: 169–79.

16. James Hennesey has argued that Carroll was counterposing to Rome's authority "traditional episcopal arrangements dating from the misty past." However, in other contexts Carroll was perfectly willing to adopt ultramontane positions. See James Hennesey, "Rome and the Origins of the United States Hierarchy," in Bernard Cooke, ed., *The Papacy and the Church in the United States* (New York, 1989): 79–97.

17. Circular letter, Charles Sewell to the American clergy, 24 November 1786, Hughes, *Society of Jesus in North America*, Docs. 1, Pt. 2: 666–67.

18. Leonardo Antonelli to John Carroll, et al., 12 July 1788, 14 November 1789, reprinted in Guilday, *Life and Times of Carroll*: 352, 357; see also 323–26.

"THE PRESERVATION OF DISCIPLINE"

1. John Carroll to John Helbron, November 1789, *Papers*, 1: 391–92.

2. Griffin, "Church of the Holy Trinity": 36.

3. John Carroll to John Helbron, 2 December 1789 (four letters); to Holy Trinity Congregation, 2 December 1789, AAB files 11B R6; 11B R4; 11B S6; 11B T2.

4. John Helbron to John Carroll, 6 December 1789, AAB file 11B S2; Holy Trinity, Trustees Minute Book, 1: 30.

5. Trustees of Trinity Church to John Carroll, 23 December 1789, AAB file 11B S9; "The Preliminaries of Peace & Reunion of the Catholics of the City of Philadelphia Belonging to St. Mary's & Holy Trinity Churches," AAB file 11B S7.

6. John Helbron to John Carroll, December 1789, AAB file 11B S8; John Carroll to John Helbron, 24 December 1789, 29 December 1789, AAB files 11B-T1, 11B-T2.

7. On Helbron's submission, see Fecher, *German National Parishes*: 28–29, 31. The Epiphany service is cited in "Sworn deposition of Bishop John Carroll, Testimony Against Peter Helbron, February 25, 1797," *Papers,* 2: 206–7. See also Griffin, "Church of the Holy Trinity:" 41–42; "Testimony of John Andrews," AAB file 11B W4.

"MARTYR TO THE FAITH"

1. Carey, "Two Episcopal Views of Lay–Clerical Conflicts." John Carroll attributed the turmoil at Holy Trinity exclusively to the "ambition" and "daring spirit" of John Helbron and seems to have completely discounted the laity's role in the affair. See John Carroll to Charles Plowden, 28 December 1789, *Papers,* 1: 397–98.

2. Wood, *Radicalism of the American Revolution:* 56, 109, 156–57.

3. Joseph Chinnici, *Living Stones: The History and Structure of Catholic Spiritual Life in the United States* (New York, 1988): 7. See also C. J. Nuesse, *The Social Thought of American Catholics, 1634–1829* (Westminster, Maryland, 1945): 105–17.

4. John Carroll to John Helbron, 14 August 1791, *Papers,* 1: 510–14, draft in AAB file 11B-U2/1; "Certificate of Travel for John Helbron," 18 October 1791, *Papers,* 1: 525–26, original in AAB file 9A-I1: 25–26. On enthusiasm for the French Republic in Philadelphia, see H. M. Jones, *America and French Culture* (Chapel Hill, 1927): 212–13, 536; Charles D. Hazen, *Contemporary American Opinion of the French Revolution* (Baltimore, 1897): 139–63. John Carroll to Leonardo Antonelli, 23 April 1792, *Papers,* 2: 31; Norbert H. Miller, "Pioneer Capuchin Missionaries in the United States (1784–1816)," *Records and Studies,* 21 (1932): 210–13.

5. On the importance of Oellers' Hotel for émigré political and social life, see Francis S. Childes, *French Refugee Life in the United States, 1790–1800: An American Chapter of the French Revolution* (Baltimore, 1940): 111–12. See also Kenneth Roberts and Anna M. Roberts, trans. and eds., *Moreau de St. Méry's American Journey (1793–1798),* (New York, 1947): 309; Robert Earl Graham, "Taverns of Colonial Philadelphia," in *Historic Philadelphia from the Founding until the Early Nineteenth Century, Transactions of the American Philosophical Society,* new series, 43 (1953): 324; David John Jeremy, ed., *Henry Wansey and His American Journal, 1794* (Philadelphia, 1970): 103. The republican significance of hotels has been noted by Doris Elizabeth King, "The First-Class Hotel and the Age of the Common Man," *Journal of Southern History* 23 (1957): 173–88.

6. John L. Earl III, "Tallyrand in Philadelphia, 1794–1796," *Pennsylvania Magazine of History and Biography* 91 (1967): 284, 293–94; Jeremy, *Henry Wansey:* 104; Ellis Paxton Oberholtzer, *Philadelphia: A History of the City and Its People, A Record of 225 Years* (Philadelphia, 1912): 349–55; Allen J. Barthold, "French Journalists in the United States, 1780–1800," *Franco-American Review*

1 (1938): 25–30; Childes, *French Refugee Life in the United States*, chapter 5, "Aspects of Refugee Life in Philadelphia," chap. 7, "Revolutionary Opinion in Philadelphia."

7. Martin I. J. Griffin, "The Rev. Peter Helbron, Second Pastor of Holy Trinity Church, Philadelphia," *Records* 23 (1912): 3–4. Roberts and Anna M. Roberts, *Moreau de St. Méry's American Journey*: 340; Childes, *French Refugee Life in the United States*: 115–16.

8. John Carroll to Charles Plowden, 23 October 1789; 24 September 1796, to Leonardo Antonelli, 23 April 1792, *Papers,* 2: 188–89, 31.

9. John Carroll to Charles Plowden, 24 September 1796; to John Troy, 12 July 1794, *Papers,* 2: 187–89, 120–21. For a general discussion of Carroll's attitudes, see Thomas O. Hanley, "Archbishop Carroll and the French Revolution," *Records* 71, (1960): 67–72.

10. John Carroll to Charles Plowden, 20 February 1782, *Papers,* 1: 63–67; 27 February 1785, ibid.: 166–69; 25 September 1790, ibid.: 465–66; 21 March 1891, ibid.: 500–501.

11. Cited in Wood, *Radicalism of the American Revolution*: 231. See also Hazen, *Contemporary American Opinion:* 293–98; Robert R. Palmer, *The Age of the Democratic Revolution,* 1: 187–88.

12. John Carroll to Messrs. Zacharie and Latil, 2 December 1791, *Papers,* 1: 546–47.

13. See William M. Sloane, *The French Revolution and Religious Reform, An Account of Ecclesiastical Legislation and Its Influence on Affairs in France from 1789 to 1804* (New York, 1901); Edward E. V. Hales, *Revolution and Papacy, 1769–1846* (New York, 1960); Adrien Dansette, *Religious History of Modern France* (New York, 1961); John McManners, *The French Revolution and the Church* (New York, 1970); Timothy Tackett, *Religion, Revolution and Regional Culture in Eighteenth-Century France: The Ecclesiastical Oath of 1791* (Princeton, 1986).

14. Miller, "Pioneer Capuchin Missionaries": 210–13; S. J. Idzerda, "Iconoclasm during the French Revolution," *American Historical Review* 60 (1954): 13–26; Dansette, *Religious History of Modern France,* 1: 66–90.

"THE EYE OF AN EAGLE"

1. On the distinctive meaning of popular sovereignty within the American republican tradition, see Robert R. Palmer, *The World of the French Revolution* (New York, 1971): 269–70; J. R. Pole, *Political Representation in England and the Origins of the American Republic* (London, 1966): Wood, *Creation of the American Republic*: 344–89, 605–15; Forrest McDonald, *Novus Ordo Seclorum* (Lawrence, Kansas, 1985): 260, 280–93.

2. Oberholtzer, *History of Philadelphia*: 354–55; Julius F. Sachse, *The Religious and Social Conditions of Philadelphia During the First Decade Under the Federal Constitution, 1790–1800* (Philadelphia, 1900): 6–9.

3. Oberholtzer, *History of Philadelphia*: 350–51, *Aurora*, 17 May 1793; J. Thomas Scharf and Thompson Westcott, *History of Philadelphia, 1609–1884* (Philadelphia, 1884) vol. 1: 469, 472.

4. *Aurora*, 15 May 1793, 21 May 1793; Scharf and Wescott, *History of Philadelphia*: 473–82.

5. Henry Kammerer, "Principles of the German Republican Society," in *Aurora*, 15 May 1793.

6. Carey, *People, Priests, and Prelates*: 118–19. On the perspectives of refugee priests, see Leo F. Ruskowski, "French Émigré Priests in the United States (1791–1815)" (Ph. D. dissertation, Catholic University of America, 1940). Justinus Febronius (Johann Nikolaus von Hontheim) (1701–90) argued in *State of the Church and the Legitimate Authority of the Roman Pontiff* that the centralization of authority in the pope was anticanonical and offered instead a conciliar vision of Church government in which all bishops were equal and infallibility resided in the Church as a whole. Paolo Sarpi (1552–1623), priest and scholar, provincial of Venice, who defied papal authority and was excommunicated in 1606. His *History of the Council of Trent* was a devastating and controversial exposé of corruption and hypocrisy in the Roman Curia.

7. Joseph L. J. Kirlin, *Catholicity in Philadelphia from the Earliest Missionaries Down to the Present Time* (Philadelphia, 1909): 129; Griffin, "Rev. Peter Helbron": 4; Miller, "Capuchin Missionaries," 204–5, 213. See also Roberts and Roberts, *Moreau de St. Mery's American Journey*: 191–93.

8. M. Bernetta Brislin, "The Episcopacy of Leonard Neale," *Records and Studies* 24 (1941): 20–111.

9. P. Carey, "Two Episcopal Views of Lay–Clerical Conflicts"; Hennesey, "Papacy and Episcopacy in Eighteenth and Nineteenth Century American Catholic Thought," *Records* 77 (1966): 175–89.

"THE RIGHTS OF THIS GERMAN CATHOLIC CHURCH"

1. James Oellers to John Carroll, 18 August 1796, copy in Holy Trinity, Trustees Minute Book, 1: 69–70.

2. "Letter of the Holy Trinity trustees to the Propaganda," 30 October 1799, German copy in Holy Trinity, Trustees Minute Book, 1: 71–76, English translation in Griffin "Rev. Peter Helbron": 6–8.

3. Ibid.

4. Ibid.

5. Notices reprinted in Griffin, "Rev. Peter Helbron": 8–9; Holy Trinity Trustees to Bishop Carroll, 8 October 1796, AAB file 11B-U4; to Peter Helbron, 5 October 1796, copy in Holy Trinity, Trustees Minute Book, 1: 76.

6. "Proceedings of Meeting of the Trustees of Holy Trinity," 12, 14 October 1796, Holy Trinity, Trustees Minute Book, 1: 78–83; Peter Helbron to the

Congregation of Holy Trinity, 14 October 1796, reprinted in Griffin, "Rev. Peter Helbron": 10–11.

7. Trustees of Holy Trinity to Peter Helbron, 15 October 1796, AAB file 11B-U5.

8. Trustees of Holy Trinity to Peter Helbron, 24 October 1796, copy in Holy Trinity, Trustees Minute Book, 1: 85–6.

9. Peter Helbron to the Trustees of Holy Trinity, 8 November 1796, copy in ibid., 1: 86.

10. James Oellers to John Carroll, 8 September 1806, AAB file 5 Y9.

11. Leonard Neale to John Carroll, 14 November 1796, 4 January 1797, AAB files 11 B5, 11 B2; John Nepomucene Goetz, "Discourse on the Sanctity of Christian Temples," trans by L. F. Flick in *Researches* (1887): 112–33. This sermon was printed in pamphlet form and distributed at James Oellers' hotel. Extracts from the sermon are noted in AAB file 11B V7.

12. Leonard Neale, "To the German Roman Catholics Frequenting Trinity Church in Philadelphia," 8 December 1796, AAB file 11B V3.

13. "Disciplinary Decree for John Goetz," 22 January 1797; "Disciplinary Decree for William Elling," 22 January 1797; "Disciplinary Decree to Holy Trinity Congregation," 22 February 1797; "Testimony Against John Goetz," 23 February 1797, in *Papers*, 2: 195–206. Bishop Carroll's disciplinary decree against the congregation was reprinted and distributed as a pamphlet, *John, By the Grace of God, and with the Approbation of the Holy See, Bishop of Baltimore, to my beloved Brethren, of the Congregation of Trinity Church* (Philadelphia, 1797).

14. Testimony of George Alt, 21 March 1797, AAB file 11B V10; John Carroll to Mathew Carr, 27 July 1797, *Papers*, 2: 219–21; to Thomas Fitzsim[m]ons, 5 September 1797, *Papers*, 2: 222–25.

"THE LAWS OF GOD & THOSE OF THE LAND"

1. Leonard Neale to John Carroll, 4 January 1797, AAB file 11 B2; 7 November 1796, AAB file 11 B4; 13 December 1796, AAB file 11 B7.

2. *The Constitution of the Commonwealth of Pennsylvania, As Altered and Amended by the Convention, For that Purpose Freely Chosen and Assembled, And by Them Proposed for the Consideration of their Constituents* (Philadelphia, 1790).

3. John Carroll to Caesar Brancadoro, 12 October 1799, *Papers*, 2: 286–91. Carroll did emphasize individual conscience in his theology but felt that, if "enlightened by reason & natural law," it in no way conflicted with the institutional imperatives of the Church. The Roman Catholic Church, he argued, embodied the basic truths of "natural religion" and an enlightened individual would therefore, because of a "natural inclination toward religious truth," submit to its corporate dictates. See Chinnici, *Living Stones*: 12–14, 22.

4. John Carroll to James Oellers, 19 November 1801, to Caesar Brancadoro, 12 October, 1799, *Papers*, 2: 367, 286–91. See also Martin I. J. Griffin, "The Reverend John Nepomucene Goetz, and the Reverend William Elling, Assistant of Holy Trinity Church, Philadelphia," *Records* 23 (1912): 122–23. A copy of the writ of attachment is in AAB file 11B-W1.

REUTER'S MISSION

1. Trustees of Holy Trinity to Archbishop Brancadoro, Secretary of the Propaganda, 30 October 1799, *Congressi*, . . . , *3 (1791–1819)*, fols. 110r–115v. See also William Elling to Archbishop Brancadoro, 6 November 1799, which expands on the arguments in the petition, ibid., fols. 125, and 126. The trustees' petition is partially reprinted in Fecher, *German National Parishes*: 155. For Reuter's visit to Philadelphia, see ibid.: 52. By 1799 William Elling succeeded John Goetz as pastor at Holy Trinity. Goetz was fired by the board of trustees after a mysterious incident involving the widow of a former trustee. See Griffin, "John Nepomucene Goetz": 124; William J. McCallen, "Temporary Schism Over the Election of Father William Elling," *Records* 24 (1913): 198–99.

2. Trustees of Holy Trinity to Archbishop Brancadoro, 30 October 1799, in *Congressi*, . . . , *3 (1791–1819)*, fols 110r–115v, 155; William Elling to Archbishop Brancadoro, 5 November 1799, *Congressi*, . . . , *3 (1791–1819)*, fols. 123 and 124.

3. Matthew Carr's appointment as pastor of St. Augustine's Church in Philadelphia was the first time in the United States that parochial rights had been granted to regular clergy outside the Society of Jesus. See Francis E. Tourscher, *Old St. Augustine's in Philadelphia With Some Record of the Austin Friars in the United States* (Philadelphia, 1937): 14; 19.

4. Carey, "Two Episcopal Views," 90–91.

5. John Carroll to William ["Matthew"] Carr, 28 April 1800, *Papers*, 2: 309.

6. Fecher, *German National Parishes* : 163; *Lettere scritte da Padova dell' anno 1799* , vol. 277, fol. 224.

7. James Oellers to John Carroll, 8 September 1806, AAB file 5 Y9.

8. John Carroll to James Oellers, 19 November 1801, *Papers*, 2: 367; James Oellers to John Carroll, 25 November 1801, AAB file 11B W8; 30 November 1801, reprinted in Hertkorn, *Retrospective*: 57.

9. John Carroll to James Oellers, idem, to William Elling, 4 December 1801, *Papers*, 2: 368.

10. William Elling to John Carroll, 6 January 1802, AAB file 11B W11; Submission of William Elling, AAB file 11B W12.

11. Matthew Carr to John Carroll, n.d. [24 November 1801] AAB file 11B W14, 2 December 1801; AAB file 11B W10; William Elling to John Carroll, 8 December 1801, AAB file 11B W9.

12. John Carroll to Matthew Carr, 28 April 1800, *Papers,* 2: 309; to James Oellers, 22 January 1802, *Papers,* 2: 372; to William Elling [n.d.], *Papers,* 2: 370–71; "Act of Submission of the Holy Trinity Trustees," 29 January 1802, AAB file 11 M4.

13. See Peter J. Coleman, *Debtors and Creditors: Insolvency, Imprisonment for Debt, and Bankruptcy, 1607–1900* (Madison, Wis., 1974).

14. Matthew Carr to John Carroll 28, 29 January 1802, AAB file 2 H5, 11B W13; official copy of the trustees' act of submission, 29 January 1802, AAB file 11 M4.

"A REVOLUTION IN OUR SOCIETY"

1. Adam Premir et al., to John Carroll, 22 October 1805, AAB file 11B W15; John Carroll to the trustees of Holy Trinity, 28 October 1805, *Papers,* 2: 496, draft copy in AAB file 11B W15.

2. Holy Trinity, Trustees Minute Book, 1: 122; John Carroll to John Rossitor, 22 September 1806, *Papers,* 2: 531–32; "Appointment of Adam Britt," 4 November 1806, 2: 533. On Stocker, see John Carroll to William Elling, 17 August 1806, 2: 527.

3. "Letter of James Oellers to Bishop Carroll, 14 January 1807," AAB file 5 Y10.

4. James Oellers, Adam Premir, Charles Bouman to John Carroll, 10 December 1809, AAB file 11B W17; Adam Britt to John Carroll, 27 October 1806, AAB file 2 A5; 1 December 1806, AAB file 2 A6.

5. James Oellers, Adam Premir, Charles Bouman to John Carroll, 25 November 1809, AAB file 11B W16.

6. James Oellers, Adam Premir, Charles Bouman to John Carroll, 25 November 1809, AAB file 11B W16; 10 December 1809, AAB letter file 11B W17; Adam Britt to John Carroll, 7 November 1809, AAB file 2A 14; November 1809, AAB file 2A 15.

7. James Oellers to John Carroll, 9 January 1810, AAB file 11B W19.

8. "Earnest Effort Made by the Trustees of the Holy Trinity Church to Bring Missionaries into the New Diocese of Philadelphia," *Records* 23 (1912): 254; "The Reverend Patrick Kenny Appointed English Pastor of Holy Trinity Church. Action of the Trustees on the Appointment": 254–55. Holy Trinity, Trustees Minute Book, 1: 139, 140. Michael Egan to John Carroll, 5 June, 14 October 1811, AAB files 3 I3, 3 I4/1; John Carroll to Charles Neale, 5 November 1811, *Papers,* 3: 159–60. See also Joseph Willcox, "Biography of Rev. Patrick Kenny, A.D. 1763–1840," *Records* 7 (1896): 35.

9. See Peter Guilday, *A History of the Councils of Baltimore, 1791–1884* (New York, 1932): 75. Charles Neale to John Carroll, 28 November 1810, AAB file 5 N9.

10. Anthony Kohlmann to John Grassi, 26 July 1809, B. J. Fenwick to Francis Neale, 10 June 1811, cited in Hughes, *Society of Jesus in North America Docs*. 1, pt. 2: 974, 982; John Carroll to John Grassi, 27 October 1811, to Thaddeus Brzozowski, 25 May 1811, *Papers*, 3: 158–59, 141–42. It is easy to understand the frustration of the old ex-Jesuits. They had elected John Carroll, hoping that his authority would shield them from the Roman Curia. Now Carroll was not only exerting authority derived from Rome, but he had become a spokesman for the Propaganda and its interests. In 1809 Carroll had urged the ex-Jesuit community to effect "most cordial cooperation and understanding with the Directors and alumni of the College of the Propaganda, and other establishments of a similar nature, instead of wrapping up ourselves in our own plans." See John Carroll to Robert Plowden, 2 June 1809, *Papers*, 3: 87. The dispute over the *titulum* reflected differences as to whether members of the ex-Jesuit community could be ordained as members of a religious order. Carroll's position (and that of Propaganda) was that permission to be so ordained had not been granted by the pope. The ex-Jesuits, however, claimed that they had been granted permission to renew their vows to the general in Russia. Carroll's position effectively denied the existence of the Society as a religious order.

11. Michael Egan to John Carroll, 8 October 1811, AAB file 3 I4; John Carroll to Charles Neale, 5 November 1811, *Papers*, 3: 159–60.

12. John Carroll to Charles Neale, 5 November 1811, *Papers*, 3: 159–60.

13. Charles Neale's words to Patrick Kenny are cited in Michael Egan to John Carroll, 14 October 1811, AAB, file 3 I4/1; John Carroll to Anthony Kohlmann, cited in Pierre Malou to Fr. Brzozowski, 20 November 1811, in Hughes, *Society of Jesus in North America*, Docs. 1, pt. 2: 992–93.

14. Pierre Malou to Fr. Brzozowski, 20 November 1811; Fr. Brzozowski to John Grassi, 16 October 1811; to Anthony Kohlmann, 16 October 1811, cited in Hughes, *Society of Jesus in North America*, Docs. 1, pt. 2: 992, 988; John Carroll to Charles Plowden, 20 March, 25 June 1815; to John Grassi, 19 May 1815, *Papers*, 3: 328–31, 337–41, 334–35.

15. John Carroll to Charles Neale, 5 November 1811, *Papers*, 3: 159–60; to Father Marmaduke Stone, cited in Hughes, *Society of Jesus in North America*, Docs. 1, pt. 2, 975n. The first provincial council of the American hierarchy affirmed that "When Priests belonging to Secular or Regular Congregations have with the consent of their Superiors been intrusted with the care of souls, it is our opinion that *Such* Priests ought not to be at the disposal of their Superiors, & be recalled against the will of the Bishop." See *Papers*, 3: 132. John Hennesey notes that as early as 1805, with reference to the selection of bishops in Louisiana, Carroll had adopted a radically ultramontane position. See Hennesey, "Rome and the U.S. Hierarchy": 92. Jay Dolan considers that from the time that Carroll was first elevated to the episcopacy he "became preoccupied with the issue of authority" and "became increasingly dependent on the

Papacy." See Dolan, *The American Catholic Experience: A History from Colonial Times to the Present* (New York, 1985): 113, 117.

THE GERMAN PARTY

1. "Diary of Rev. Patrick Kenny," *Records* 7 (1896): 116–18.
2. John Carroll to William Beschter, 26 October 1811; to Maximillian Rantzau, 14 December 1811, *Papers*, 3: 203–4, 162–63; Maximillian Rantzau to John Carroll, 9 December 1811, AAB file 9 A2. See also Joseph C. Sprenger to Michael Egan, 6 June 1812, copy in AAB file 11 M5; Martin I. J. Griffin, "History of Rt. Rev. Michael Egan D. D., First Bishop of Philadelphia," *Researches* 9 (1892): 84.
3. John Carroll to John Grassi, 22 February, 9 July 1812; to William Beschter, 30 July 1812, *Papers*, 3: 176–77, 185–86, 187–88.
4. "Diary of Rev. Patrick Kenny" *Records* 7 (1896): 117–18.
5. Ibid.: 118; Legal Opinion of A. J. Dallas in Philadelphia Archives (Egan Papers).
6. Miller, "Pioneer Capuchin Missionaries": 213.
7. Patrick Kenny to John Carroll, 9 August 1812, AAB file 4 L1; Griffin, "Diary of Rev. Kenny," *Records* 7 (1896): 122; Patrick Kenny to Michael Egan, 3 August 1812, Philadelphia Archives (Egan Papers).
8. Holy Trinity, Trustees Minute Book, 1: 141–50.
9. Ibid.: 162–72; 179–83. Further investigations uncovered other earlier improprieties that resulted in James Oellers being indebted to the board of trustees to the amount of $356. He agreed to pay this amount over time and no legal proceedings were instituted against him.

ETHNICITY AND IDEOLOGY

1. "Diary of Rev. Patrick Kenny," *Records* 7 (1896): 118; Adam Britt to John Carroll, 31 August 1807, AAB file A-10. Anthony Kohlmann to William Strickland, 23 February 1807, cited in John Gilmary Shea, *Life and Times of Carroll*: 422n. Even under the German Party, Holy Trinity remained culturally diverse. In 1832 the congregation included a variety of Germans, including "Schweizer," "Badenser," "Elsässer," "Lothringer," etc., as well as "French from Bordeaux and other southern cities of France" and refugees from Martinique and San Domingo, "including several negroes." See Francis Guth to the superior of the seminary at Strassburg, 27 June 1832, cited in Hertkorn, *Retrospective of Holy Trinity*: 90–91.
2. Greenfield, *Nationalism: Five Roads to Modernity.*
3. Holy Trinity, Trustees Minute Book, 1: 150–53.
4. Ibid.

THE "IRISH" CHURCH

1. On the founding of St. Mary's, see Scharf and Westcott, *History of Philadelphia,* 2: 1367–71. On the prominence of St. Mary's lay leadership in the Revolution, see Kirlin, *Catholicity in Philadelphia:* 100–113. See also Ellis, *Catholics in Colonial America:* 398; Charles H. Metzger, *Catholics in the American Revolution* (Chicago, 1962): 220–35; C. P. Whittemore, "John Sullivan: Luckless Irishman," in G. A. Billias, ed., *George Washington's Generals* (New York, 1964): 98, 137–62. See also Neusse, *Social Thought of American Catholics:* 84–90.

2. On the influx of "Irish Volunteers," see Dennis Clark, *The Irish in Philadelphia: Ten Generations of Urban Experience* (Philadelphia, 1973): 16. See also Frank McDermot, *Theobald Wolfe Tone: A Biographical Study* (London, 1939): 171–75.

3. William Duane, *A Report of the Extraordinary Transactions which took place at Philadelphia in February, 1799, in Consequence of a Memorial from Certain Natives of Ireland to Congress Praying a Repeal of the Alien Bill* (Philadelphia, 1799); *Aurora,* 12, 13 February 1799; "'The Irish Riot' at St. Mary's Church, Philadelphia, 1799," *Records* 17 (1900): 86–88.

4. Duane, *Report of the Extraordinary Transactions* .

5. "The Irish Riot": 87.

6. Ibid.: 88.

7. Martin I. J. Griffin, "History of Rt. Rev. Michael Egan D. D., First Bishop of Philadelphia," *Researches* 9 (1892): 70–72; John Carrell to John Carroll, 10 March 1802, AAB file 8A D2; Trustees of St. Mary's to John Carroll, 6 February 1803, AAB file 11 J2; Michael Egan to John Carroll, 10 February 1803, AAB file, 3 H1.

8. "A pew holder in St. Mary's" to John Carroll, 24 April 1803, AAB file 11B J3.

9. John Carroll to Cardinal Borgia, 1806, cited in Griffin, "History of Michael Egan," *Researches* 10 (1893): 18; John Carroll to Michele di Pietro 17 June 1807, *Papers,* 3: 27–28.

10. "John Carroll to the Pastors & Trustees of the Several Roman Catholic Churches in Philadelphia," 20 October 1808, copy in AAB file 15 A1.

11. "Meeting of the Trustees of Holy Trinity, St. Mary's & the Rev. Mr. Hurley from St. Augustine," copy in AAB file 15 A1; Griffin, "History of Bishop Egan," *Researches* 10 (1893): 19–20; Kirlin, *Catholicity in Philadelphia:* 189–91, 196. See also John Ashley and Edward Carrell to John Carroll, 2 November 1812, AAB, file 11B K3; "To the Pew Holders of St. Mary's Church," 18 May 1809, in Lawrence F. Flick, ed., "Minute Book of St. Mary's Church, Philadelphia, Pa.," *Records* 4 (1893): 410–11, 412–13.

12. F. Harold Duffee, "Reminiscences of the Rev. William Hogan, Rev. William V. Harold and the Memorial Vow of Rev. Father Carter," *Researches* 8 (1891): 78–79.

13. Ibid.; [Mathew Carey], *Rejoinder to the Reply of the Rev. Mr. Harold, to the Address of a Catholic Layman* (Philadelphia, 1822); "A Catholic Layman" [Mathew

Carey], 15 May 1822, quoted in *A Reply to the Catholic Layman's Rejoinder by William Vincent Harold, Pastor in St. Mary's* (Philadelphia, 1822): 1–2. See also Richard W. Meade, *An Address to the Roman Catholics of the City of Philadelphia, in Reply to Mr. Harold's Address* (Philadelphia, 1823): 4; [The Trustees of St. Mary's] *To the Congregation of St. Mary's Church* (25 March 1822): 5–7.

14. On the democratic imperative in contemporary Protestant evangelism, see Nathan O. Hatch, *The Democratization of American Christianity* (New Haven, 1989). On the link between "popular evangelical Christianity" and democratic movements in American civil society, see Wood, *Radicalism of the American Revolution*: 330–33.

"THE LABORING INTEREST"

1. St. Mary's Trustees, "To the Pewholders of St. Mary's Church," 8 September 1812, in *Sundry Documents, Submitted to the Consideration of the Pewholders of St. Mary's Church, By the Trustees of that Church* (Philadelphia, 1812), AAB file 11B K2. See also Flick, "St. Mary's Minute Book," *Records* 4 (1893), entry of 21 June 1809: 416–17, entry of 7 November 1809: 418–19.

2. Griffin, "History of Bishop Egan," *Researches* 10 (1893): 19, 24; Michael Egan to John Carroll, 16 March 1811, AAB file 3 I2; Flick, "St. Mary's Minute Book," entry of 16 December 1810: 426–27, entry of 20 April 1811: 437–38.

3. Michael Egan to John Carroll, 16 March 1811, AAB file, 3 I2; 14 January 1812, AAB file 3 I5; "Rev. James Harold, the Botany Bay Irish Convict Priest of Philadelphia, 'the Cause' of the Direful Dissension at St. Mary's Church, 1812–13," *Researches* 17 (1900): 17–26.

4. With the exception of John Ashley, president of the Philadelphia Insurance Company, and two "gentlemen," the trustees of St. Mary's prior to the Haroldite revolt were drawn from the proprietary and professional classes. They included master craftsmen, merchants and manufacturers, a few professionals, and a sea captain. John Carrell to John Carroll, 15 September 1812, 2 K4; Michael Egan to John Carroll, 29 December 1812, AAB, file 3 I9. A Catholic Layman [Mathew Carey], *Rejoinder to the Reply of the Rev. Mr. Harold, to the Address to the Right Rev. the Catholic Bishop of Pennsylvania, the Catholic Clergy of Philadelphia, and the Congregation of St. Mary's, in which are Detailed the inflammatory and violent proceedings of the Rev. Mr. H. in the year 1812, whereby discord and disunion were introduced into the Congregation of St. Mary's* (Philadelphia, 1822): 11–12.

5. John Ashley and Edward Carrell to John Carroll, 2 November 1812, AAB file 11B K3.

6. Francis X. Brosius to John Carroll, 3 October 1805, AAB file, 2 B6; Michael Egan to John Carroll, 14 January 1812, AAB file, 3 I5; 17 December 1812, AAB file, 3 I8; John Carrell to John Carroll. 15 September 1812, AAB file, 2 K4; John Ashley and Edward Carrell to John Carroll, 2 November 1812, AAB file 11B K3.

7. Griffin, "History of Michael Egan," *Researches* 10 (1893): 28–29; [A Catholic Layman] *Rejoinder to the Reply of the Rev. Mr. Harold*: 13; "Minute Book of St. Mary's Church, 1812–1829," *Records* 42 (1931) entries of 2 April 1812, 9 April 1812: 206–8.

8. Griffin, "History of Michael Egan," *Researches* 10 (1893): 29–30; "To the Pewholders of St. Mary's Church," 8 September 1812, in *Sundry Documents*: 4.

9. Wood, *Radicalism of the American Revolution*: 24.

10. Ibid.: 33. The fundamental importance of this distinction to Catholic belief was expressed by Pope Pius X when he wrote, "The Church is essentially an unequal society . . . comprising two categories of persons, the Pastors and the flock . . . , the one duty of the multitude is to allow themselves to be led, and, like a docile flock, to follow the Pastors." Cited in Dolan, *The American Catholic Experience*: 222.

11. Wood, *Radicalism of the American Revolution*: 158, 176, 177, 179; "A pewholder in St. Mary's" to John Carroll, 24 April 1803, AAB file, 11B J3.

12. Kim T. Phillips, "William Duane, Philadelphia's Democratic Republicans, and the Origins of Modern Politics," *Pennsylvania Magazine of History and Biography* 101 (1977): 365–87. See also Neusse, *Social Thought of American Catholics*: chap. 7, "The Increase of Democratic Influence": 151–71.

13. [A Catholic] to Michael Egan, 30 January 1813, AAB file 2 M1; Trustees of St. Mary's to John Carroll, 21 April 1813, AAB file 11B N1.

14. Wood, *Radicalism of the American Revolution*: 276–80

15. Ibid.: 280.

16. On Egan's attitude toward the trustees, see John A. Ryan to the Prefect of Propaganda, 14 December 1819, reprinted in Guilday, *Life and Times of Carroll*: 680–85.

17. John Carrell to John Carroll, 15 September 1812, AAB file 2 K4; [Mathew Carey], *Rejoinder to the Reply of the Rev. Mr. Harold*: 20.

18. "True copies of threatening letters addressed to St. Mary's Trustees, 6–8 September 1812," in Philadelphia Archives (St. Mary's Church, Box 1, Folder 5, No. 7).

19. Ibid.; John Carrell to John Carroll, 15 September 1812, AAB file 2 K4; "Letter of the Rev. W. V. Harold of St. Mary's Church, Philadelphia, to the Rev. John Ryan of St. Peter's Church, Baltimore," *Records* 23 (1912): 135–36.

"THE INSTRUMENT OF UNPRINCIPLED MEN"

1. Wood, *Radicalism of the American Revolution*: 290, 294–95; William Elling to John Carroll, 17 September 1806, AAB file 3 O7.

2. "Letter of the Rev. W. V. Harold"; *Sundry Documents*; Trustees of St. Mary's Church to John Carroll, 17 September 1812, AAB file 11 M2; John Ashley and Edward Carrell to John Carroll 2 November 1812, AAB file 11B K3;

John Carrell to John Carroll, 19 September 1812, copy in AAB file 11B L1; "Solemn Protest of the Pewholders of St. Mary's against the late proceedings respecting the Conduct of our Trustees," copy in AAB file 11B L1. Kirlin, *Catholicity in Philadelphia*: 203, notes that the pewholders who signed this document supporting the trustees were "substantial members of the parish."

3. Trustees of St. Mary's to John Carroll, 21 September 1812; John Ashley and Edward Carrell to Michael Egan, 8 October, 15 October 1812, both in AAB file 11B L1; transcript of a meeting of St. Mary's trustees, 22 October 1812, copy in AAB file 11B L1; Michael Egan to John Carroll, 28 September 1812, AAB file 3 I7; 29 December 1812, AAB file 3 I9; 17 December 1812, AAB file 3 I8; Flick, "Minute Book of St. Mary's Church," *Records* 42 (1931), proceedings of meeting, 21 September 1812; [A Catholic Layman], *Rejoinder to the Reply of the Rev. Mr. Harold*: 21–22; John Ashley and Edward Carrell to John Carroll, 5 November 1812, AAB file 2 K6; "Address to the Pewholders of St. Mary's" by Michael Egan, copy in AAB file 11B l3; John Ashley and Edward Carrell to John Carroll, 22 December 1812, AAB file 11B 14.

4. Michael Egan to John Carroll, 28 September 1812, AAB file 3 I7; 29 December 1812, AAB file 3 I9; 7 July 1813, AAB file 3 J3. On the Harolds' interference in trustee elections, see John Carrell to John Carroll, 15 September 1812, AAB file 2 K4.

5. [A Catholic] to Michael Egan, 30 January 1813, AAB file 2 M1.

6. Michael Egan to John Carroll, 24 January 1813, AAB file 11 M3. John Carroll's account of the meeting with William Harold is written on the back of the same document. Michael Egan to John Carroll, 25 January 1812 [1813], AAB file 11B K1; 1 February 1812, AAB file 3 J1; 13 February 1813, AAB file 11 C9; William V. Harold to John Carroll, 16 February 1813, AAB file 11 C10; 22 February 1813, AAB file 11 C12; [A Catholic] to Michael Egan, 30 January 1813, AAB file 2 M1.

7. [A Catholic Layman] *Rejoinder to the Reply of the Rev. Mr. Harold*: 25; *Address of the Lay Trustees to the Congregation of St. Mary's Church on the Subject of the Approaching Election* (Philadelphia, 1822); "Remonstrance of the Roman-catholic inhabitants of St. Mary's parish to John, Archbishop of Baltimore," 14 October 1813, AAB file 11B N5

8. "Remonstrance of the . . . Inhabitants of St. Mary's"; *Report of Committee appointed by a Meeting of St. Mary's Congregation to John Carroll*, 26 February 1813, AAB file 11B L5. John Doyle to John Carroll, 26 February 1813, AAB file 11 C13; "Pennsylvania Catholics (St. Mary's Church) to John Carroll," 10 March 1813, AAB file 11 D15, John Carroll's disdain for the Haroldites' position is revealed by a note he affixed to their report designating them as a "self-created body of malcontents of St. Mary's." Bishop Egan responded to the Haroldite petition by gathering a list of 180 pewholders who supported him. See Michael Egan to John Carroll, 5 March 1813, AAB file 11B M1,2.

9. Michael Egan to John Carroll, 4 March 1813, AAB file 11 O10; 5 March 1813, AAB file 11B M1; 1 April 1813, AAB file 11B M6; 6 April 1813, AAB file 11 O12.

10. [The Trustees of St. Mary's] *To the Congregation of St. Mary's Church* (Philadelphia, 25 March 1822): 11.

11. Griffin, "History of Bishop Egan," *Researches* 10 (1893): 117; Michael Egan to John Carroll, 27 April 1813, AAB file 11 D19.

12. John Carrell to John Carroll 5 May 1813, AAB file 11 D20; [A Catholic Layman] *Rejoinder to the Reply of the Rev. Mr. Harold*: 23.

13. Wood, *Radicalism of the American Revolution*: 294–95.

"INNOVATORS ON ESTABLISHED GOVERNMENTS"

1. Trustees of St. Mary's to John Carroll, 21 April 1813, AAB file 11B N1.

2. Trustees of St. Mary's to John Carroll, 28 April 1813, AAB file 11B N3.

3. "St. Mary's Minute Book," *Records* 42 (1931): entry of 4 May 1813: 224–25.

4. Ibid.; Michael Egan to John Carroll, 28 April 1813, AAB file 11B N2; 5 May 1813, AAB file 11 E27; 7 July 1813, AAB file 3 J3; 13 July 1813, AAB file 3 J4; "Remonstrance of the Roman-Catholic inhabitants of St. Mary's parish to John, Archbishop of Baltimore," 14 October 1813, AAB file 11B N5. The "respectable" men who formed the core of Bishop Egan's support were political as well as religious conservatives. Mathew Carey noted that as late as the 1820s several of them still nursed grudges against him for his attacks on the Federalist party in the early years of the century. See [Mathew Carey] *Review of Three Pamphlets Lately Published by the Rev. W. V. Harold . . . By a Catholic Layman* (Philadelphia, 1822): 14.

5. "To the Congregation of St. Mary's Church," 25 July 1813, AAB file 11 R6.

6. Ibid.; Michael Egan to John Carroll, 26 July 1813, AAB file 3 J3; 15 August 1813, AAB file 11 O13; Michael Doran to John Carroll 11 November 1813, AAB file 11E 22.

7. "Remonstrance to the Archbishop of Baltimore."

8. Ibid. On the pervasiveness of the concept of virtue in republican thought, see Richard Vetterli and Gary Bryner, *In Search of the Republic: Public Virtue and the Roots of American Government* (Totowa, N.J., 1987). On the centrality of the themes of virtue and corruption in contemporary Pennsylvania political discourse, see John M. Murrin, "Escaping Perfidious Albion: Federalism, Fear of Aristocracy, and the Transformation of Corruption in Postrevolutionary America" (paper presented to the Philadelphia Center for Early American Studies, 1990). In his *Sermon Preached in the Catholic Church of St. Peter, Baltimore, November 1st, 1810; On Occasion of the Consecration of the Rt. Rd. Dr. John Cheverus, Bishop of Boston* (Baltimore: G. Dobbins: 1810), William V. Harold argued that episcopal authority, in order to be effective, had to be imbued with virtue.

9. "Remonstrance to the Archbishop of Baltimore"; Michael Doran to John Carroll, 11 November 1813, AAB file 11 E22.

10. "Remonstrance to the Archbishop of Baltimore"; Luis de Onís to John Carroll, 6 March 1813, AAB file, 11B M3; John Carroll to Luis de Onís, 26 March 1813, draft copy in AAB file 11B M4.

11. Michael Egan to John Carroll, 17 November 1813, AAB file 3 J6.

12. Michael Egan to John Carroll, 22 June 1814, AAB file 3 K6; John Carrell to John Carroll, 24 May 1814, AAB file 11 E28; A Catholic Layman, *To the Members of St. Mary's Congregation.*

13. Patrick Kenny to John Carroll, 10 July 1814, AAB file 4 L2; 22 July 1814, AAB file 4 L4; Kirlin, *Catholicity in Philadelphia*: 198. See also John Ashley and Edward Carrell to John Carroll, 2 November 1812, AAB file 11B K3; 22 December 1812, AAB file 11B L4.

14. "Remonstrance to the Archbishop of Baltimore"; Patrick Kenny to John Carroll, 31 July 1814, AAB file 4 L5; John Carrell to John Carroll 5 May 1813, AAB file 11 D20.

15. Patrick Kenny to John Carroll, 31 July 1814, AAB file 4 L5; John Carrell to John Carroll, 5 May 1813, AAB file 11 D20.

"PALTRY INTRIGUES"

1. Trustees of St. Mary's to John Carroll, 24 July 1814, AAB file, 11B N3.

2. Trustees of St. Mary's to John Carroll, 8 August 1814, AAB file 11 F29.

3. John Carroll to The Trustees of St. Mary's, Philadelphia, 16 August 1814, *Papers,* 3: 290–91.

4. Ibid.; John Carroll to Charles Plowden, 25 June 1815, *Papers,* 3: 337–41.

5. John Carroll to William Harold, 20 February 1813, *Papers,* 3: 214; 18 March 1813, AAB Carroll Letterbook III: 105; John A Ryan to the Prefect of Propaganda, 14 December 1819, reprinted in Guilday, *Life and Times of Carroll*: 680–85; Trustees of St. Mary's to John Carroll, 24 July 1814, AAB file, 11B N3.

6. John A. Ryan to the Prefect of Propaganda, 14 December 1819, in Guilday, *Life and Times of Carroll*: 680–85; John Carroll to Archbishop John Troy, [1815], *Papers,* 3: 312–13.

7. Guilday, "Trusteeism": 16. John Carroll to Charles Plowden, 25 June 1815, *Papers,* 3: 337–41; Lorenzo Litta to John Carroll, 11 March 1815, AAB file 5 A5; John Carroll to Lorenzo Litta, 17 July 1815, *Papers,* 3: 344–46.

8. "Provincial Council Resolutions," 15 November 1810, in *Papers,* 3: 132–34. For an overview, see Charles Florence McCarthy, "The Historical Development of Episcopal Nominations in the Catholic Church of the United States (1784–1884)," *Records* 38 (1927): 297–354. See also James Hennesey, "Rome and the Origins of the United States Hierarchy," in Bernard Cooke, ed., *The Papacy and the Church in the United States* (New York, 1989): 79–97, and Guilday, *History of the Councils of Baltimore*: 74.

9. Cardinal Antonelli to the American Clergy, 12 July 1788, reprinted in Guilday, *Life and Times of Carroll*: 352; The bull creating the American dioceses in 1808 is reproduced in *Roman Documents and Letters Pertaining to the See of Baltimore, 1783–1863* [in AAB collections]: 6–9. The failure of Rome to respond to the 1810 request is noted in "John Carroll to the U.S. Bishops," *Papers*, 3: 291–92.

10. John Carroll to Charles Plowden, 25 June 1815; to Lorenzo Litta 10 October 1815, *Papers*, 3: 337–41, 364.

11. Sacred Congregation of the Propaganda to Archbishop Troy, 15 March 1815, cited in Guilday, "Trusteeism": 17; to John Carroll, 11 March 1815, AAB file 5 A5; John Carroll to Lorenzo Litta, 17 July 1815, *Papers*, 3: 344–47; Charles Plowden to John Carroll, 1 September 1815. Plowden had long suspected Archbishop Troy and the Irish Dominicans of conspiring against the Jesuits. See John Carroll to Robert Molyneux, 9 July 1808, to Charles Plowden, 2 June 1809, 5 January 1815, 25 June 1815, *Papers*, 3: 66, 86–88, 316–18, 337–41. See also V. F. O'Daniel, "Concanen's Election to the See of New York (1808–10)," *Catholic Historical Review* 2 (1916–17): 19–46.

12. John Carroll to Archbishop John Troy [1815], to Lorenzo Litta, 17 July 1815, 10 October 1815, to Charles Plowden, 13 October 1815, *Papers*, 3: 312–13, 344–47, 364, 367–69.

13. John Carroll to the Trustees of St. Mary's, 27 July 1814, cited in Guilday, "Trusteeism."

14. Jules C. Foin, "Rev. Louis Barth, A Pioneer Missionary in Pennsylvania and an Administrator of the Diocese of Philadelphia," *Records* 2 (1889): 29–37; John Carroll to Leonard Neale, 27 September 1814, 18 July 1815, *Papers*, 3: 295–97, 348.

15. Louis DeBarth to John Carroll, 24 July 1814, AAB file 3 B10; n.d., AAB file 3 B11.

"THE PRESENT SYSTEM OF ECCLESIASTICAL MISMANAGEMENT"

1. Carey, "Two Episcopal Views of Lay-Clerical Conflicts": 85.

2. Ibid.: 87; Dolan, *The American Catholic Experience:* 112; "Ambrose Maréchal's Report to Propaganda," 16 October 1818, in John Tracy Ellis, ed., *Documents of American Catholic History* (Milwaukee, 1962), 2d ed.: 214. See also Brislin, "The Episcopacy of Leonard Neale"; Ronin John Murtha, "The Life of the Most Reverend Ambrose Maréchal, Third Archbishop of Baltimore, 1768–1828" (Ph.D. diss., Catholic University, 1965).

3. On Leonard Neale's infirmity and incapacity, see Louis DuBourg to Prefect of Propaganda, 1815 *Scritture riferite America Centrale*, vol. 3, fol. 360.

4. Guilday, "Trusteeism": 21; John Carroll to Charles Plowden, 25 June 1815, *Papers*, 3: 337–41.

5. Leonard Neale to Lorenzo Litta, 4 February 1816, AAB file 12 P12; Ambrose Maréchal to Lorenzo Litta, 9 April 1816, cited in Ambrose Maréchal to Leonard Neale, 9 November 1816, AAB file 12B J2; Lorenzo Litta to Ambrose Maréchal, 13 July 1816, AAB file B 13; Ambrose Maréchal to James Whitfield, 10 September 1816, AAB file 12 R3; Ambrose Maréchal to Lorenzo Litta, 1 December 1816, AAB file 21 O4 .

6. Lorenzo Litta to Leonard Neale, 17 August 1816, AAB file 12 Q9; to William Du Bourg, 26 November 1816, cited in Guilday, "Trusteeism": 25, see also p. 27; Leonard Neale to Lorenzo Litta, 20 December 1816, AAB file 12 S1.

7. Louis DeBarth to Ambrose Maréchal, 18 December 1818, AAB file 15 I24.

8. James Gartland to Ambrose Maréchal, 8 January 1818, AAB file 33 J13; "St. Mary's Minute Book," *Records* 43 (1932): 272.

9. Ambrose Maréchal to St. Mary's trustees, 21 January 1818, AAB file 22B P2; "St. Mary's Minute Book," *Records* 43 (1932): 273–74.

10. "Notebook of Bishop Connolly," entry of 23 October 1817, extracts reprinted in J. R. Bayley, *A Brief Sketch of the Early History of the Catholic Church on the Island of New York*, 2d ed. (New York, 1870): 89–90; entry of 25 February 1818: 90–92. Connolly had earlier offered William Harold a position in New York, and parishioners had offered to pay his passage and his salary in advance. See entry of 8 March 1816: 87–88. On Maréchal's anti-Irish prejudices, see "Ambrose Maréchal's Report to Propaganda, October 16, 1818," in Ellis, ed., *Documents of American Catholic History*: 202–20.

11. "St. Mary's Minute Book," *Records* 43 (1932): 275, 276. Bishop Connolly was in Philadelphia in December 1817, at which time he conferred with local Catholic lay leaders. See "Notebook of Bishop Connolly," entry of 7 December 1818: 88–89.

12. "St. Mary's Minute Book," *Records* 43 (1932): 277–79.

13. "Notebook of Bishop Connolly," entry of November 1818: 93–94; Guilday, "Trusteeism": 29, 30–31.

14. "Memorial of the Trustees at St. Mary's to Pope Pius VII, June 15, 1819," reprinted in Francis E. Tourscher, *The Hogan Schism and Trustee Troubles in St. Mary's Church Philadelphia, 1820–1829* (Philadelphia, 1930): Appendix 1: 191–95.

15. Ibid.

16. Ambrose Maréchal to Lorenzo Litta, 19 September 1819; John A. Ryan to Propaganda, 16 June 1819, cited in Guilday, "Trusteeism": 31–32.

17. John A. Ryan to Propaganda, 14 December 1819, reprinted in Guilday, *Life and Times of Carroll*: 679–85.

18. Cardinal F. A. Fontana to Ambrose Maréchal, 11 September 1819, cited in Griffin, "History of Bishop Egan": 189; "Reply of the Sacred Congregation to Mr. Augustine Fagan, Secretary and to all the Congregation of Catholics in

Philadelphia," 11 November 1820, Appendix 2 in Tourscher, *The Hogan Schism*: 196–98.

"A STATE OF CONFUSION"

1. Rev. Mr. Carbry to Fr. Fadaldi, 22 November 1818, cited in Guilday, "Trusteeism": 29. Kirlin, *Catholicity in Philadelphia*: 210–11, 213; Francis Roloff to Ambrose Maréchal, 13 October 1819, AAB file 20 E1.

2. Kirlin, *Catholicity in Philadelphia*: 213; Louis DeBarth to Ambrose Maréchal, 18 May 1820, AAB file 15 M58.

3. Diane Lindstrom, *Economic Growth in the Philadelphia Region, 1810–1850* (New York, 1978).

4. Sam B. Warner, Jr., *The Private City: Philadelphia in Three Periods of Its Growth* (Philadelphia, 1968): 60, 225; Bruce Laurie, *Working People of Philadelphia, 1800–1850* (Philadelphia, 1980), part 2, "The Forging of Working-Class Cultures"; Susan Davis, " 'Making Night Hideous': Christmas Revelry and Public Order in Nineteenth Century Philadelphia," *American Quarterly* 34 (1982): 185–99; *Parades and Power: Street Theatre in Nineteenth-Century Philadelphia* (Philadelphia, 1986); Laurie, "Nothing on Compulsion." See also Theodore Hershberg, ed., *Philadelphia: Work, Space, Family, and Group Experience in the 19th Century: Essays Toward an Interdisciplinary History of the City*: 128–73 (New York, 1981).

5. On changes in Philadelphia's social structure, see John K. Alexander, "Poverty, Fear, and Continuity: An Analysis of the Poor in Late Eighteenth-Century Philadelphia," in Allen F. Davis and Mark H. Haller, *The Peoples of Philadelphia: A History of Ethnic Groups and Lower-Class Life, 1790–1940* (Philadelphia, 1973); Leonard Bernstein, "The Working People of Philadelphia from Colonial Times to the General Strike of 1835," *Pennsylvania Magazine of History and Biography* 74 (1950): 322–39; Eric Foner, *Tom Paine and Revolutionary America* (New York, 1976), "Tom Paine's Philadelphia"; Benjamin J. Klebaner, "The Home Relief Controversy in Philadelphia, 1782–1861," *Pennsylvania Magazine of History and Biography* 76 (1954): 413–23; James T. Lemon, *The Best Poor Man's Country: A Geographical Study of Southeastern Pennsylvania* (Baltimore, 1972); Bruce Laurie, " 'Nothing on Compulsion': Life Styles of Philadelphia Artisans, 1820–1850," *Labor History* 15 (1974): 337–66; Sam B. Warner, Jr., "Innovation and Industrialization in Philadelphia, 1800–1850," in John Burchard and Oscar Handlin, eds., *The Historian and the City* (Cambridge, Mass., 1963).

6. Patrick Jordan, "Annals of St. Joseph's Church," *Woodstock Letters*, 2 (1873): 180, 184; 3 (1874): 3.

7. See Bernstein, "The Working People of Philadelphia"; Klebaner, "The Home Relief Controversy"; Laurie, "Nothing on Compulsion"; Priscilla Ferguson Clement, *Welfare and the Poor in the Nineteenth Century City: Philadelphia, 1800–1854*, (Cranbury, N.J., 1985); Donald R. Adams, Jr., "Wage Rates in the Early National Period: Philadelphia, 1785–1830," *Journal of Economic History* 28 (1968): 404–26.

8. Thompson Westcott, "A Memoir of the Very Rev. Michael Hurley . . . With a Sketch of the History of St. Augustine's Church," *Records* 1 (1884): 172–73.

9. Jordan, "Annals of St. Joseph's Church," *Woodstock Letters* 2 (1873): 185–86, 188; 3 (1984): 2, 3, 10; Westcott, "Memoir of . . . Michael Hurley": 172–73; *An Answer to an "Address by a Catholic Layman to the Roman Catholics of the United States" By a member of St. Mary's Church* (Philadelphia, 27 July 1821). Technically, Matthew Carr was the pastor of St. Augustine's until his death in 1820, but he had been mentally incompetent since 1807. See Francis R. Tourscher, *Old St. Augustine's in Philadelphia* (Philadelphia, 1937): 40–41.

10. Hurley portrayed himself to his parishioners as an immigrant, but his half-sister told Thompson Westcott that he had been born in Philadelphia. See Westcott, "Memoir of . . . Michael Hurley."

11. Ibid.

12. A Layman of the Congregation, *An Inquiry into the Causes Which Led to the Dissentions Actually Existing in the Congregation of St. Mary's, and Observations on the Mode Best Calculated to Prevent Its Increase* (Philadelphia, 1821): 7, 8, 10; William Hogan, *Address to the Congregation of St. Mary's Church, Philadelphia* (Philadelphia, 1821), part 1: 6–7; *The Address of the Ladies of St. Mary's Congregation, presented at the meeting, in Washington Hall, on Wednesday evening* (Philadelphia, 14 February 1821).

13. John Leamy et al., "To the Right Rev. Henry Conwell, Bishop of Pennsylvania" (20 December 1820), cited in Martin I. J. Griffin, "Life of Bishop Conwell," *Records* (1913): 217–19.

14. Kirlin, *Catholicity in Philadelphia*: 215.

15. Mathew Carey, cited in Griffin, "Life of Bishop Conwell," *Records* (1913): 38; A Layman of the Congregation, *An Inquiry into the Causes . . .*: 10; William Hogan, *Address to the Congregation of St. Mary's Church*, part 1: 10–11. In 1816 several prominent Philadelphia Catholics had founded the "Roman Catholic Sunday School Society of Philadelphia" to serve "the children of poor Roman Catholics, who are obliged to work unremittingly on the days of labour [and are therefore] debarred of the advantages of education." This benevolent effort, however, seems to have made little progress until William Hogan's involvement in 1820. See "Constitution of the Roman Catholic Sunday School Society of Philadelphia, 1816," *Researches* 7 (1990): 156–57.

16. Mathew Carey, "Thoughts on Infant Schools" (Philadelphia, 1827); "The Infant School" (28 December 1827), in *Miscellaneous Essays* (Philadelphia, 1830): 309–12; 313–17; A Layman of the Congregation, *An Inquiry into the Causes . . .* : 10.

17. Jordan, "Annals of St. Joseph's," *Woodstock Letters* 3 (1874): 6, 10; A Layman of the Congregation, *An Inquiry into the Causes. . . .*

18. These rumors are recounted by Jordan, "Annals of St. Joseph's," *Woodstock Letters* 3 (1874): 3–9.

19. Ibid., 2 (1873): 183–84; 3 (1874): 10; William Hogan, *Address to the Congregation of St. Mary's Church*, part 1: 12.

20. William Hogan to Benedict Flaget, 11 December 1820, cited in Henry Conwell, *Sundry Documents Addressed to St. Mary's Congregation* (Philadelphia, 1820): 21; William Hogan to Ambrose Maréchal, 17 August 1820, AAB file 17 J9; 31 August 1820, AAB file 17 J10; Ambrose Maréchal to William Hogan, 1820, cited in *Proceedings at a Meeting of the Congregation of Saint Mary's Church, Favorable to the Restoration of the Rev. William Hogan, Held at Washington Hall, Wednesday Evening Feb. 14, 1821 and at an Adjourned Meeting. Held as above, on Wednesday Evening Feb. 28, 1821* (Philadelphia, 1821): 7; Kirlin, *Catholicity in Philadelphia*: 218.

"THAT ABSOLUTE POWER"

1. Griffin, "Life of Bishop Conwell," *Records* (1913): 162–65.

2. Jordan, "Annals of St. Joseph's," *Woodstock Letters*, 3 (1874): 10; Griffin, "Life of Bishop Conwell," *Records* (1913): 166. Conwell's colleagues in Ireland as well as his superiors were of the opinion that he was manifestly unfit for elevation to the episcopacy and were horrified by his appointment. See "Patrick Curtis, President of the Irish College at Salamanca to Monsignor Argenti, Secretary of Propaganda, 14 February 1820," reprinted in *Catholic Historical Review* 6 (1920): 261–63. See also "Testimonial of the Priests of Armagh to Their Vicar General the Revd. Doctor Henry Conwell," in Tourscher, *Hogan Schism*: 227.

3. Kirlin, *Catholicity in Philadelphia*: 266. See also Henry Conwell to Propaganda Fide, 20 November 1829, *Scritture Riferite nei Congressi America Centrale 10, 1829–1832*, fol. 242.

4. Henry Conwell, *Pastoral Charges Delivered by the Right Rev. Bishop Henry, in St. Mary's Church, on the 2d of November [December] 1820 & 11th of Feb. 1821 in Presence of Two Thousand Persons* (Philadelphia, 1821).

5. "To the Gentlemen composing the Committee appointed by a Meeting of the Congregation of St. Mary's Church," reprinted in William Hogan, *Address to the Congregation of St. Mary's Church, Philadelphia*, part 1 : 22–27.

6. Ibid.; Conwell, *Pastoral Charges* ; "Documents Relating to the Case of Rev. William Hogan, and the Schism In St. Mary's Church, Philadelphia," in the General Appendix to *The Works of the Right Rev. John England, First Bishop of Charleston* (Baltimore, 1849), vol. 5: 145.

7. Griffin, "Life of Bishop Conwell," *Records* (1913): 167; A Catholic Layman [Mathew Carey], *Address to the Right Rev., the Bishop of Pennsylvania and the Members of St. Mary's Congregation,* no. 2 (14 February 1821); Henry Conwell to Ambrose Maréchal, 11 December 1820, cited in John Gilmary Shea, *History of the Catholic Church in the United States* (New York, 1886–92), vol. 3: 229; Ambrose Maréchal to William Poynter, 30 March 1821, cited in ibid.: 230; William Hogan, *Address to the Congregation of St. Mary's Church,* part 1: 12–13; Henry Conwell to Ambrose Maréchal, 11 December 1820, cited in Shea, *History of the Catholic Church,* 3: 229.

8. Henry Conwell to Ambrose Maréchal, 11 December 1820, cited in Shea, *History of the Catholic Church,* 3: 229; 2 April 1821, AAB file 14 V5. On the dismissal, see "Notes of Testimony Supplied by J. R. Ingersoll, Counsel for Hogan," in [Mathew Carey] *Address to the Bishop of Pennsylvania,* no. 1; Conwell, *Sundry Documents*: 28. See also Conwell, *Pastoral Charges*: 4–5.

9. William Hogan to Henry Conwell, 18 December 1820, cited in Tourscher, *Hogan Schism*: 15.

10. Ibid.; Trustees of St. Mary's, "Address to the Congregation" (Philadelphia, 1822), cited in Griffin, "Life of Bishop Conwell," *Records* (1913): 176–77; William Hogan, *Address to the Congregation of St. Mary's Church, Philadelphia,* part 1; William Hogan to Ambrose Maréchal, 14 December 1820, AAB file 17 J11; "Affadavit of John T. Sullivan" (12 January 1821), reprinted in William Hogan, *Continuation of an Address to the Congregation of St. Mary's Church, Philadelphia* (Philadelphia, 2 February 1821): 14–16; Henry Conwell to Ambrose Maréchal, 2 April 1821, AAB file 14 V5.

11. William Hogan, *A Brief Reply to a Ludicrous Pamphlet Compiled from the Affidavits, Letters and Assertions of a Number of Theologians, with the Signature of Henry, Bishop, and Entitled Sundry Documents, addressed to St. Mary's Congregation* (Philadelphia, 1821): 7, 9, 39; William Hogan to Ambrose Maréchal, 14 December 1820, AAB file 17 J11; 16 January 1821, AAB file 17 J12; William Hogan, *Continuation of an Address to the Congregation of St. Mary's Church, Philadelphia.*

12. Ambrose Maréchal to William Poynter, December 1820, copy in AAB file 19 Q2; to Henry Conwell cited in Conwell, *Sundry Documents*: 17; to John Leamy, et al., 21 January 1818, AAB file 22B P2; 15 March 1821, cited in Conwell, *Sundry Documents*: 18–19.

13. See Robert Trisco, "Bishops and Their Priests in the United States, part 1, "From the First Bishop to 1850," in John Tracy Ellis, ed., *The Catholic Priest in the United States: Historical Investigations* (Collegeville, Minnesota, 1971):

112–26. John England to Simon Bruté, 4 June 1828, cited in Guilday, *Life of England*, 2: 110 n. 44; William Hogan, *Continuation of an Address to the Congregation of St. Mary's Church, Philadelphia*: 33; John Leamy et al., to Ambrose Maréchal, 13 March 1821, cited at length in Griffin, "Life of Bishop Conwell," *Records* 24 (1913): 242.

14. Conwell, *Pastoral Charges*: 6–7, 8. See also *Sundry Documents*: 28–30. Apologists for the bishop have questioned whether Conwell actually made these statements in the form reported, but at the time it was widely believed that he had and the sentiments are consistent with both his actions and the positions taken by his supporters. Francis Roloff, noting that "the Bishop is no orator and undertook to speak from the altar without preparation," accepted the essential accuracy of the published account. See Francis Roloff to Ambrose Maréchal, 12 March 1821, AAB file 20 E2. See also Richard Poynter to Ambrose Maréchal, 30 July 1821, AAB file 19 Q3.

15. Benedict Flaget to Henry Conwell, n.d., cited in *Sundry Documents*: 22–23.

16. M[arc]. F[renaye]. *An Explanation of Some Canon Laws Concerning Excommunication and Suspension, Respectfully Dedicated to the Congregation of St. Mary's Church, Philadelphia* (Philadelphia, 1821): 7–10.

17. Hogan, *A Brief Reply to a Ludicrous Pamphlet . . .* : 39; William Hogan, *Address to the Congregation of St. Mary's Church, Philadelphia*, part 1 : 4, 14.

18. [Mathew Carey], *Address to . . . the Bishop of Pennsylvania*, no. 1 (21 December 1820); "Affadavit of John T. Sullivan," (12 January 1821), reprinted in William Hogan, *Continuation of an Address to the Congregation of St. Mary's Church*: 15; Henry Conwell to Ambrose Maréchal, 5 February 1821, AAB file 14 V4.

19. A Catholic Laymen [Mathew Carey], *Rejoinder to the Reply of the Rev. Mr. Harold*: 22–23; Tourscher, *Hogan Schism*: 18–19; William Hogan to Ambrose Maréchal, 14 December 1820, AAB file 17 J11; William Hogan, *High and Low Mass*: 215–16; John Leamy, et al., "To the Right Reverend Henry G. Conwell, Bishop of Pennsylvania," 20 December 1820, reprinted in William Hogan, *Address to the Congregation of St. Mary's Church, Philadelphia*, part 1: 19.

20. John Leamy, et al., "To the Right Reverend Henry Conwell, Bishop of Pennsylvania," 20 December 1820, reprinted in William Hogan, *Address to the Congregation of St. Mary's Church, Philadelphia*, part 1: 19–22.

21. Henry Conwell, "To the Gentlemen composing the Committee."

22. Martin E. Marty, *The Modern Schism: Three Paths to the Secular* (New York, 1969): 11.

23. Roger Aubert, "The Catholic Church after the Congress of Vienna," chap. 3 of Aubert et al., *The Church Between Revolution and Restoration*, Peter Becker, trans. (New York, 1981): 85–103, quotes are from 88, 93.

24. Dolan, *The American Catholic Experience*: 224–25. Dolan actually traces the emergence of this reactionary style of Catholicism to the last years of the eigh-

teenth century, while John Carroll still ruled in Baltimore; see pp. 113–17. Joseph P. Chinnici, in "American Catholics and Religious Pluralism, 1775–1820," *Journal of Ecumenical Studies,* 16 (1979): 727–46, argues that a tradition of "Enlightened Catholicism," based in the European Catholic Enlightenment and in the "Maryland experience" of elite minority status, was a significant component of mainstream American Catholic thought as late as the 1820s. In both accounts the period from 1790 to 1830 marked a massive shift in Catholic culture during which liberal tendencies were submerged in a sea of reaction. Six of the men who became bishops in the American church prior to 1850 were refugees from the French Revolution. They were John Dubois, Benedict Joseph Flaget, John Baptist David, Ambrose Maréchal, Louis William BuBourg, and John Cheverus. On their influence in the American Church, see Annabelle M. Melville, "Louis William DuBourg," and Clyde F. Crews, "Benedict Joseph Flaget, First Bishop of the West," in Gerald P. Fogarty, ed., *Patterns of Episcopal Leadership* (New York, 1989).

25. On the aggressive stance of the Roman Catholic Church in mid-nine-teenth century America and the Tridentine critique of American civil culture, see Jay Dolan, "Catholic Attitudes towards Protestants," in Robert N. Bellah and Frederick E. Greenspahn, eds., *Uncivil Religion: Interreligious Hostility in America* (New York, 1987).

26. John Leamy et al., "To the Right Reverend Henry Conwell"; Henry Conwell, "To the Gentlemen composing the Committee."

HOGANITES

1. William Hogan, *A Brief Reply to a Ludicrous Pamphlet*: 24–25; idem, *An Answer to a Paragraph Contained in the United States Catholic Miscellany* (Philadelphia, 1822): 33.

2. On the American revolutionary ideal, see Wood, *Radicalism of the American Revolution.*

3. [Mathew Carey], *Address to the . . . Bishop of Pennsylvania,* no. 1 (21 December 1820).

4. William Hogan, [Second] *Continuation of an Address to the Con-gregation of St. Mary's Church, Philadelphia* [with a Postscript added] (Phila-delphia, 1821): 4–6.

5. [A Layman of the Congregation], *An Inquiry into the Causes . . .* : 9; [An Observer], *A Call to the Catholics; Or, A Word of Conciliation to Both Parties* (Philadelphia, 1822?): 11.

6. William Hogan, *A Brief Reply to a Ludicrous Pamphlet*: 44–45.

7. Ibid.: 45–46; *A Catholic Layman, Address to the . . . Bishop of Pennsyl-vania,* no. 2 (14 February 1821).

8. William Hogan, [Second] *Continuation of an Address . . .* : 28–29.

9. Marty, *The Modern Schism.*

"DAY OF TRYAL"

1. [Mathew Carey], *Address to the . . . Bishop of Pennsylvania*, no. 1 (21 December 1820); "Affadavit of John T. Sullivan," (12 January 1821) reprinted in William Hogan, *Continuation of an Address to the Congregation of St. Mary's Church*: 14–16.

2. On efforts to secure William V. Harold's appointment to Philadelphia, see Augustin Fagan to Daniel Murray, 30 April 1819; to J. McCormick, 14 June 1819; to Pope Pius VII, 1 May 1819; John Ryan to Propaganda Fide, 22 January 1819; in *Congressi, . . . , 3(1791–1819)*, vol. 921, fols. 443r, 431, 444, and 445; 419 and 420r.

3. The non-Haroldite trustees met with Bishop Conwell on 10 February 1821 and issued a protest against the amendments to the charter. The Haroldites responded with a formal protest against the meeting, at which they had not been present, declaring it to be illegal and arguing that since Bishop Conwell and Rev. Terence McGirr had not been duly elected to the board their presence at the meeting was an act of "unconstitutional and unlawful usurpation." See "St. Mary's Minute Book," *Records* 43 (1932): 331–32.

4. An account of the meeting and Bishop Conwell's list of attendees can be found in Griffin, "Life of Bishop Conwell," *Records* 25 (1914): 53–54.

5. Charles Johnson et al. to Ambrose Maréchal, 19 April 1821, AAB file 15 A2.

6. Ibid.

7. The court decision is reported in the *National Gazette*, 21 April 1821. Members of the Anglo-American Catholic elite outside Philadelphia also lent their support to Bishop Conwell. In 1823 wealthy congregations in New York and Baltimore (including no less a personage than Charles Carroll of Carrollton) sent well-publicized expressions of support to the bishop. See *Federal Gazette* (Baltimore), 21 February 1823; *Democratic Press* (Philadelphia): 29 January 1823; George E. Ironside to the Cathedral Trustees (Baltimore), AAB file 22 H10.

8. Henry Conwell to Ambrose Maréchal, 31 January, 5 February 1821, AAB files 14 V3, 14 V4; Bishop Conwell's monition is reproduced in Griffin, "Life of Bishp Conwell," *Records* 24 (1913): 236–37.

9. John Ashley et al. to Ambrose Maréchal, 13 March 1821, AAB file 22 J14; Ambrose Maréchal to John Ashley et al., 15 March 1821, reprinted in Griffin, "Life of Bishop Conwell," *Records* 24 (1913): 243.

10. John Ashley et al. to Ambrose Maréchal, 13 March 1821, AAB file 22 J14.

11. Henry Conwell to Ambrose Maréchal, 2 April 1821, AAB file 14 V5; 8 April 1821, AAB file 14 V6.

12. Henry Conwell to Adam Marshall, 7 April 1821, in Hughes, *Society of Jesus in North America*, Docs. 1: 359. 363; to Ambrose Maréchal, 2 April 1821, AAB 14 V5; *Pastoral Charges*: 6.

13. *Proceedings at a Meeting of the Congregation of Saint Mary's Church, Favorable to the Restoration of the Rev. William Hogan, Held at Washington Hall, Wednesday Evening Feb. 14, 1821 and at an Adjourned Meeting. Held as above, on Wednesday Evening Feb 28, 1821* (Philadelphia, 1821); Joseph Snyder to Adam Marshall, 28 March 1821, reprinted in Griffin, "Life of Bishop Conwell," *Records* 24 (1913): 247–48; John Keating, Jr., to Joseph Strahan, 20 March 1821, reprinted in Griffin, "Life of Bishop Conwell," *Records* 24 (1913): 249.

14. Joseph Snyder to Adam Marshall, 28 March 1821, reprinted in Griffin, "Life of Bishop Conwell," *Records* 24 (1913): 247–48, see also ibid., 253–55; *National Gazette*, 21 April 1821; "St. Mary's Minute Book," *Records* 43 (1932): 345; Francis Roloff to Ambrose Maréchal, AAB file 20 E3; William Tilghman, John B. Gibson and Thomas Duncan, *The Members of St. Mary's Congregation Entitled to Vote . . .* (Philadelphia, 21 April 1821); election results reported in Griffin, "Life of Bishop Conwell," *Records* 25 (1914): 61. There is no report of the vote for the losing slate of candidates but St. Mary's, prior to the expansion of the church in 1821, had about 800 pewholders. Assuming that all of these voted, the dissidents, who received 453 votes, would have gained a margin of about 100 votes or approximately 57% of the congregation. On the payment of clerical salaries in advance, see *A Series of Letters Relating to the Late Attempt at a Reconciliation Between the Members of the Congregations of St. Mary's and St. Joseph's; With a Brief Notice of the Present State of the Controversy Between Them Being an Abstract of an Address Delivered by the Rev. T. J. O'Meally, at the Meeting Held in St. Mary's, On Thursday Evening the 23d Ult.* (Philadelphia, January, 1825).

"THE INTERESTING CATHOLIC QUESTION IN AMERICA"

1. [A Catholic Layman], *Address to . . . the Bishop of Pennsylvania . . .* , no. 3 (10 May 1821); Henry Conwell to Ambrose Maréchal, 8 April 1821, AAB file 14 V6. The public meeting is noted in Griffin, "Life of Bishop Conwell," *Records* 25 (1914): 161–63. "St. Mary's Minute Book," *Records* 43 (1932): 338–40, 346–50.

2. Conwell to Maréchal, 2 April 1821, AAB file 14 V5; 8 April 1821, AAB file 14 V6; 21 April 1821, AAB file 14 V7; 16 May 1821, AAB file 14 V8

3. Henry Conwell to Ambrose Maréchal, 16 May 1821, AAB file 14 V8; 16 May 1821, AAB file 14 V9; Ambrose Maréchal to Henry Conwell, n.d., AAB file 22B S2; Henry Conwell to Ambrose Maréchal, 16 June 1821, AAB file 14 W11/1, reprinted in Tourscher, *Hogan Schism*, Appendix V: 205–6.

4. Henry Conwell to Ambrose Maréchal, 16 May 1821, AAB file 14 V8; 15 June 1821, AAB file 14 W11. It is interesting to note the shift in imagery that took place over time in Bishop Conwell's commentaries. When Conwell

viewed a renegade cleric as his major antagonist his speeches and writings were filled with references to the Protestant Reformation. As his appreciation of the laity's role in the affair awakened Conwell increasingly interpreted events through reference to the French Revolution.

5. Henry Conwell to Ambrose Maréchal, 15 June 1821, AAB file 14 W12.

6. Charles Johnson et al., to Ambrose Maréchal, 4 June 1821, AAB file 22 J11; Ambrose Maréchal to Henry Conwell, 19 June 1821 [copy appended to *Trustees of St. Mary's Church, Philadelphia to Ambrose Marechall [sic] Archbishop of Baltimore* (Philadelphia, 26 June 1821)].

7. "Memorial and Protest of the Appointed Committee of St. Mary's Church, Philadelphia, to Pope Pius VII," (10 April 1821, Philadelphia), Italian translation in *Congressi, 6 Schisma di Filadelfia, 1819–1829*, fols. 38r to 65v, portions cited in Peter Guilday, *The Life and Times of John England, First Bishop of Charleston (1786–1842)* (New York, 1927): 386–87; Augustine Fagan to Cardinal Fontana, 21 April 1821, *Congressi, 6 Scisma di Filadelfia, 1819–1829*, fols. 151 to 152r.

8. "St. Mary's Minute Book," *Records* 43 (1932): 352–56; Propaganda Fide to Henry Conwell, 28 July 1821, *Lettere e Decreti, 1821,* 302, fol. 320.

9. *Address of the Lay Trustees to the Congregation of St. Mary's Church, on the Subject of the Approaching Election* (Philadelphia, 25 March 1822): 19; Marty, *The Modern Schism.* See also Dolan, *American Catholic Experience*: 221.

10. *An Answer to an "Address by a Catholic Layman"*: 20–21.

11. "Letter I," 4 February 1822, in *A Letter to the Roman Catholics of Philadelphia*: 1; Richard W. Meade, *To the Roman Catholics of Philadelphia* (Philadelphia, 1823): 4, 6, 8.

12. Meade, *To the Roman Catholics of Philadelphia*; 10, 18–19; [An Observer], *A Call to the Catholics*: 5, 11, 13, 14, 16.

13. [A Member of St. Mary's Church], *An Answer to an "Address by a Catholic Layman, to the Roman Catholics of the United States"* (Philadelphia, 27 July 1821): 13.

14. Ibid., 13–14.

"THE MAJESTY OF THE PEOPLE"

1. R. W. Meade, "George Meade, Born in Philadelphia, 'Province of Pennsylvania,' February 27th, 1741, Died in Philadelphia, 'United States of America,' November 9th 1808," *Researches* 6 (1889): 98–118. It is perhaps of interest to note that Richard W. Meade's son, George Gordon Meade, was the Union commander at the battle of Gettysburg.

2. Ibid.; Richard W. Meade, *The Case of Richard W. Meade, Esq., A Citizen of Pennsylvania, U.S.A., Seized and Imprisoned, 2d of May, 1816, by the Government of Spain, and Still Detained* (Cadiz, 27 November 1817): 9.

3. Ibid.: 21–23; Griffin, "Rev. John Ricco, Cigar Maker in Philadelphia and Planter in Alabama," *Researches* 7 (1890): 134–37; "Life of Bishop Conwell," *Records* 25 (1914): 147–48.

4. Ibid.

5. Ibid.; *The Opinion of the Rt. Dr. John Rico, of the Order of St. Francis, D.D. and the Vicar General of the Armies of Spain, on the Differences Existing Between the Rt. Rev. Dr. Conwell, and the Rev. Wm. Hogan* (Philadelphia, 1821), AAB file 22B P2; William V. Harold, *An Address to the Roman Catholics of Philadelphia* (Philadelphia, 1823).

6. Testimony of José A. Torrens, *Charge d'Affaires* from Mexico, reprinted in Meade, *To the Roman Catholics of Philadelphia*: 24; Servandus A. Mier, *A Word Relative to an Anonymous Pamphlet Printed in Philadelphia, Entitled, "Remarks on the Opinion of the Rt. Rev. Servandus A. Mier. Doctor of Sacred Theology, &c. on Certain Queries Proposed to Him, by the Rev. Wm. Hogan"* (Philadelphia, 17 August 1821): 6–7, 8.

7. Mier, *A Word Relative to an Anonymous Pamphlet*: 4.

8. *The Opinion of the Rt. Rev. Servandus A. Mier, Doctor of Sacred Theology in the Royal and Pontifical University of Mexico, and Chaplain of the Army of the Right, first Army of the Peninsula, on Certain Queries Proposed to Him by the Rev. William Hogan, Pastor of St. Mary's Church* (Philadelphia, 11 July 1821); Henry Conwell to Ambrose Maréchal, 20 June 1821, AAB file 14 W17; Mier, *A Word Relative to an Anonymous Pamphlet*: 11.

9. *An Answer to an "Address by a Catholic Layman"*: 14.

10. [M. D.], "Letter III," 8 February 1822, in *A Letter to the Roman Catholics of Philadelphia*: 56.

A REPUBLICAN CHURCH

1. *An Answer to an "Address by a Catholic Layman"*: 3–4. Patrick Carey has traced the theological roots of this movement for national autonomy in church affairs, linking it to a number of controversies in the European church. See *People, Priests, and Prelates*: 19–24.

2. *Address of the Committee of St. Mary's Church, of Philadelphia, to Their Brethren of the Roman Catholic Faith Throughout the United States of America, on the Subject of a Reform of Sundry Abuses in the Administration of Our Church Discipline* (New York, 1821).

3. Ibid.

4. Ibid.; *An Answer to an "Address by a Catholic Layman."*

5. *Address of the Committee of St. Mary's*: 4; *An Inquiry into the Causes . . .*: 9; *An Answer to an "Address by a Catholic Layman"*: 13–14.

6. *Address of the Committee of St. Mary's*: 4; William Hogan, *Reply to an Invidious Attack and Calumny of Rev. Wm Harold* (Philadelphia, 1822); *The*

Catechism of Dr. James Butler Revised and Corrected by Rev. William Hogan, Pastor of St. Mary's Church, Philadelphia (Philadelphia, 1821); Henry Conwell to Ambrose Maréchal, 18 June 1821, AAB file 14 W10; Griffin, "Life of Bishop Conwell, *Records* 25 (1914): 163–64 (see also 323).

7. Henry Conwell to Ambrose Maréchal, 22 July 1821, AAB file 14 W13; *An Address to the Catholics of the United States, by a Layman of St. Mary's Congregation, Philadelphia* (Philadelphia, 1821). An Independent Catholic [Francis Roloff], *The True Sentiments of the Writer of the Last Appeal to the Congregation of St. Mary's Church* (Philadelphia, 1821): 8. Contemporaries and some chroniclers of the Hoganite dispute suspected Michael Hurley to be the author of this and other satirical pamphlets. It is clear, though, from Roloff's correspondence that he was the author but insisted on anonymity for fear that the peace of his congregation at Holy Trinity would be disturbed if it were known that he was attacking Hogan. See Francis Roloff to Ambrose Maréchal, 12 March 1821, AAB file 20 E2; 12 April 1821, AAB file 20 E3. [The Detector], *Hoganism Examined According to the Canons of Criticism, Sacred and Profane; Or, A Short Letter To a Late Reverend Pamphleteer on the Republication of his Famous Pamphlet* (Philadelphia, 1821): 5–6.

8. William Hogan, *Continuation of an Address to the Congregation of St. Mary's Church* (2 February 1821): 34; *Continuation of an Address to the Congregation of St. Mary's Church, Philadelphia. Postscript* (26 March 1821): 43.

9. John Cheverus to Henry Conwell, 6 April 1821, *Poulson's Advertiser* 15 April 1821; John England to Henry Conwell, 12 April 1821, both reprinted in *Sundry Documents*; William Hogan to John Cheverus, 13 April 1821, reprinted in Griffin, "Life of Bishop Conwell," *Records* 24 (1913): 354–56, see also William Hogan, "To the Members of St. Mary's Church," *Poulson's Advertiser*, 14 April 1821; William Hogan, "To John England," *Aurora*, 28 April 1821. England's response also appeared in the *Aurora*, reprinted in Griffin, "Life of Bishop Conwell," *Records* 24 (1913): 359–61.

THE STAR OF THE SOUTH

1. Cited in Patrick Carey, *An Immigrant Bishop: John England's Adaptation of Irish Catholicism to American Republicanism* (Yonkers, New York, 1982): 135.

2. Ibid.: 133–60.

3. Ibid.: 152, 153, 155, 156–57, 158; England, *Works*, 4: 233; 5: 95; *United States Catholic Miscellany*, 18 December 1822: 231.

4. Carey, *An Immigrant Bishop*: 146–47, 150, 160.

5. "Diurnal of the Right Rev. John England, First Bishop of Charleston, S.C., From 1820 to 1823," *Records*, 6 (1895): 188; see also Griffin, "Life of

Bishop Conwell," *Records* 25 (1914): 218–19; John England to Ambrose Maréchal, 22 December 1822, AAB file 16 N19.

6. The content of Bishop England's letter to Bishop Conwell was reported in Francis Roloff to Ambrose Maréchal, 27 September 1821, AAB file 20 E7. See also Francis Roloff to Ambrose Maréchal, 11 September 1821, AAB file 20 E4; "Diurnal of John England," 189–90. Although England sympathized with Hogan's predicament, he by no means agreed with the priest's assertion that he was the legal pastor of St. Mary's. See John England, "State of Rev. Wm. Hogan, 22 October 1821," in *Researches* 3 (1887): 139–40.

7. Francis Roloff to Ambrose Maréchal, 11 September 1821, AAB file 20 E4; 15 September 1821, AAB file 20 E5; 27 September 1821, AAB file 20 E7; Guilday, *Life of Bishop England*: 392; "Diurnal of John England": 191–92; "St. Mary's Minute Book," *Records* 49 (1938): 175.

8. "Diurnal of John England": 191–92; see also Griffin, "Life of Bishop Conwell," *Records* 25 (1914): 221; Henry Conwell to Ambrose Maréchal, 13 October 1821, AAB file 14 W14; England, *Works*, 5: 118.

9. Varying accounts of this meeting are to be found in "Diurnal of John England": 192–93; John England to Henry Conwell, 6 September 1822, reprinted in England, *Works*, 5: 118–24; William Hogan, *An Answer to a Paragraph Contained in the United States Catholic Miscellany. Edited by the Bishop of Charleston, Under the Head Philadelphia* (Philadelphia, 1822). See also John England to Henry Conwell, 12 September 1822, reprinted in England *Works*, 5: 125–32.

10. Bishop England claimed to have been misunderstood by all involved. His promise to represent the dissenters' position to Rome was, in his mind, conditional upon his being satisfied that Bishop Conwell had indeed acted irregularly, but the lay leaders interpreted it as a nonconditional pledge that the bishop later repudiated. See Hogan, *An Answer to a Paragraph. . . .* England's assertion that an appeal to Rome would be appropriate was based upon his understanding that only the Holy See was competent in all cases to judge disputes over the meaning of canon law and that only Rome could over- rule decisions made by the American archbishop. He did not welcome Roman interference and hoped that Hogan's departure from Philadelphia would ren- der it unnecessary, but he preferred it to any decision rendered by a civil tri- bunal or legislature. See England *Works*, 5: 140.

11. "Diurnal of John England": 193; John England to Henry Conwell, 6 September 1822, reprinted in England, *Works*, 5: 118–24; Hogan, *An Answer to a Paragraph;* John England to Henry Conwell, 12 September 1822, reprinted in England *Works*, 5: 125–32.

12. "Diurnal of John England": 194–95; On the lay response, at least among the elite, in Charleston to Bishop England's practice of consultation, see Carey, *An Immigrant Bishop*: 157–58; John England to B. J. Fenwick, 11 September 1822, reprinted in England *Works*, 5: 124–25; John England to Henry Conwell, 12 September 1822, reprinted in ibid.: 125–32.

13. "Diurnal of John England": 195–97; letter fragment signed by John England, 22 October 1821, reprinted in ibid.: 228–29; John England to Henry Conwell, 12 September 1822, reprinted in England, *Works,* 5: 125–32.

14. John Power to Joseph Octave Plessis, 9 November 1821, reprinted in Griffin, "Life of Bishop Conwell," *Records* 25 (1914): 236; Jordan, "Annals of St. Joseph's Church," *Woodstock Letters,* 3 (1894).

15. Hogan, *An Answer to a Paragraph*: 31.

16. *U.S. Catholic History Magazine,* vol. iv, no. xiii (1892); England, *Works,* 5: 109–11; *United States Catholic Miscellany,* 18 December 1822: 231.

17. John England to Ambrose Maréchal, 22 December 1822, AAB file 16 N19; 15 January 1823, AAB file 16 J9; "Diurnal of John England": 202.

ANTI-CATHOLICS

1. J. Maitland to William V. Harold, 17 April 1821, *Congressi, 6 Schisma di Filadelfia, 1819–1829,* fols. 148r to 153r; William V. Harold to the Prefect of Propaganda, 2 December 1820, *Acta S. Cong. anni 1821,* vol. 184, fol. 183r. See also ibid., fols. 158, 159, and 161v. On Propaganda's refusal to consult the American hierarchy, see Ambrose Maréchal to Prefect of Propaganda, 24 September 1826, copy in Philadelphia Archives; Guilday, *Life of Bishop England*: 387–90. On Propaganda control of American episcopal appointments, see also Hennesey, "Rome and the Origins of the United States Hierarchy."

2. [Mathew Carey], *A Desultory Examination of the Reply of the Rev. W. V. Harold to a Catholic Layman's Rejoinder, by a Catholic Layman* (Philadelphia, 1822): 46–48; William V. Harold, *Reply to the Catholic Layman's Rejoinder by William Vincent Harold, Pastor in St. Mary's* (Philadelphia, 1822).

3. The leading apologist for the dissenters in this phase of the dispute was Mathew Carey, and he bore the brunt of William Harold's attack. Harold, *Reply to the Catholic Layman's Rejoinder . . .* ; [Mathew Carey], *A Desultory Examination . . .*: 48; *A Review of Three Pamphlets Lately Published by the Rev. W. V. Harold . . . By a Catholic Layman* (Philadelphia, 1822): 39; [An Admirer of Fenelon], *A Letter to the Rev. William Vincent Harold, of the Order of Dominican Friars. On Reading his Late Reply to a "Catholic Layman"* (Philadelphia, 30 March 1822).

4. Harold, *Reply to the Catholic Layman's Rejoinder.*

5. *Strictures on the Strictures of William Hogan, Upon the Rev. Wm. Harold's Pamphlet. By a Catholic "Of the Olden Time."* (Philadelphia, 1822). Patrick Carey has pointed out that Harold and other "anti-trustees" were confusing Catholic doctrine with church discipline, but the distinction, while formally important, was in the context of the trusteeship conflicts of little significance. See his *People, Priests, and Prelates*: 213.

6. Meade, *To the Roman Catholics of Philadelpha*: 3. 5; [An Admirer of Fenelon], *A Letter to the Rev. William Vincent Harold* . . . : 9–10.

7. *Address of the Lay Trustees to the Congregation of St. Mary's Church, on the Subject of the Approaching Election*: 5, 10, 21, 23; [Mathew Carey], *Rejoinder to the Reply of the Rev. Mr. Harold, to the Address to the Right Rev. The Catholic Bishop of Pennsylvania, the Catholic Clergy of Philadelphia, and the Congregation of St. Mary's . . . by a Catholic Layman* (Philadelphia, 1822). The deep social divisions among the dissenters that were submerged in a common opposition to arbitrary authority are indicated by the divergent definitions of "the People" that emerged in the course of the debate. To former Haroldites, the people are identified with the "injured and oppressed" immigrants for whom America is a "natural refuge." By contrast many middle-class Hoganites argued that the people whose rights were violated were those propertied individuals, subscribers and pewholders, who built and contributed to the upkeep of the church.

8. William V. Harold, *Sermon Preached in the Catholic Church of St. Peter, Baltimore, November 1st, 1810; On Occasion of the Consecration of the Rt. Rd. Dr. John Cheverus, Bishop of Boston* (Baltimore, 1810): 18–19.

9. Ibid.: 6–8.

10. William V. Harold, *A Reply to the Catholic Layman's Rejoinder*: 15, 18.

CLUBS AGAINST CUDGELS

1. On the anticipation of violence, see A Catholic Layman [Mathew Carey], *Brief Address to the Roman Catholic Congregation Worshipping at St. Mary's On the Approaching Election for a Board of Trustees* (Philadelphia, 1822): 4; Testimony of Edward Barry, reprinted in *A Graphic Account of the Alarming Riots At St. Mary's Church, in April of 1822 Together With the Most Important Extracts From the Decisions of Chief Justices Tilghman, Duncan and Gibson, Relative to the Charter of Said Church, Including Letters From Hon. J. R. Ingersol & Thos. Kittera, Esq. Compiled By a Reporter* (Philadephia, June 1844): 9–10; J. R. Ingersoll to Thomas Kittera, 5 March 1822; Thomas Kittera to J. R. Ingersoll, 22 March 1822, both reprinted in ibid: 11; *The Battle of Saint Mary's, A Serio comic Ballad, with Desultory Remarks on the Dissensions in that Church, By an Observer, Wholly unconnected with the Parties, But Wishing Well to Liberty and Peace* (Philadelphia, 1822).

2. Years later William Hogan claimed that the Conwell had blessed the cudgels that the bishopites bore into battle. Historians have ridiculed this assertion and claimed that it shows Hogan's tendency to embroider his accounts, but a contemporary song, written to celebrate the dissenters' victory states that "Their clubs were blest, and they caress'd, By a Bishop quite the

dandy," and concludes "Consecrated sticks shall never shine, While Hoganites are handy." See "The Battle of St. Mary's," *Researches* 15 (1898): 139–40; *Democratic Press*, 10 April 1822; Testimony of Edward Barry in *A Graphic Account*: 9; Jordan, "Annals of St. Joseph's Church," *Woodstock Letters*, 3 (1874); *The Ballad of Saint Mary's*.

3. *Democratic Press*, 10 April 1822, Henry Conwell to Joseph Octave Plessis, 4 July 1822, cited in Griffin, "Life of Bishop Conwell, *Records* 25 (1914): 310–11; Testimony of Edward Barry, in *A Graphic Account*: 9; Philip Smith et al., "To the Public" in ibid.: 11–14; *The Battle of Saint Mary's*.

4. *Democratic Press*, 10 April 1822; Testimony of Edward Barry, in *A Graphic Account*: 9–10; Philip Smith et al., "To the Public" in ibid: 11–14; "The Battle of St. Mary's": 140.

5. Testimony of Edward Barry, in *A Graphic Account*: 9–10; Philip Smith et al., "To the Public," in ibid.: 11–14; "St. Mary's Minute Book," *Records* 49 (1938): 254–55. General Cadwallader's decision is noted in Griffin, "Life of Bishop Conwell," *Records* 25 (1914): 314.

6. *A Graphic Account*: 14–15.

7. Ibid.

8. [Mathew Carey], *A Desultory Examination . . .* : 36; Harold, *A Reply to the Catholic Layman's Rejoinder* (Philadelphia, 1822): 17; *An Address of the Roman Catholics of Philadelphia* (Philadelphia, 1823): 27–29; *Address of the Lay Trustees to the Congregation of St. Mary's Church*: 5; "The Catholic Advocate and Irishman's Journal," *Researches* 7 (1890): 40; [Augustine Fagan], *Reflections On the Dissension Actually Existing in St. Mary's Congregation: Respectfully Addressed to His Excellency the Governor of the State of Pennsylvania. To Which are Added, Notes On the Right of Patronage and Presentation, As Established In the Roman Catholic Church. By a Roman Catholic* (Philadelphia, January 1824).

9. *A Short Address To the Roman Catholic Congregation of St. Mary's Church, On the Approaching Election for Trustees. Written in consequence of two late Addresses from the Pastor and Lay Trustees of the Said Church. By an Irish Catholic* (Philadelphia, 1822): 7; Philip Smith et al., "To the Public," in *A Graphic Account*: 13–14.

10. "Letter from The Right Reverend Doctor England, Catholic Bishop of Charleston, To the Proprietor of the Charleston Mercury," in *Letters, &c. viz From Bishop England On Captain Rock's Proclamation; From the Rev. W. Hogan, In Reply to the Rev. Bishop; From an Irishman, To the Rev. William Hogan; And From An Irish Catholic To an Irishman: Copied from The Charleston Mercury, The Columbian Observer, and The Democratic Press* (Philadelphia, 1823): 3–7.

11. William Hogan, "To the Editors of the Columbian Observer," in *Letters, &c.*: 7–11.

12. Ibid.

13. Ibid.

14. "To the Rev. William Hogan," and "A Lady" to "Mr. William Hogan," in *Letters, &c.*: 11–14, 17. See also William V. Harold, *An Address to the Roman Catholics of Philadelphia. By the Rev. W. V. Harold, Pastor of St. Mary's and Vicar General* (Philadelphia, 1823): 27.

15. "To the Rev. William Hogan.—No. II," in *Letters &c.*: 17–22.

16. Willcox, "Diary of Rev. Patrick Kenny," *Records* 9 (1898): 430–31, entry of 9 April 1822.

17. Tourscher, *Hogan Schism*: 57n.

COURTS OF APPEAL

1. [An Observer], *A Call to the Catholics*: 6; Charles O'Hara et al. to John Leamy et al., 6 July 1822, reprinted in Griffin, "Life of Bishop Conwell," *Records* 25 (1914): 314–16; Henry Conwell to Joseph O. Plessis, 6 January 1822, reprinted in *Researches* 28 (1911): 103. Meade, *To the Roman Catholics of Philadelphia*: 5. *A Compendious Trial of the Rev. William Hogan, Pastor of the Roman Catholic Church of St. Mary's, On an Indictment For an Assault and Battery, On the Person of Mary Connwell. By a Listener* (Philadelphia, 1822). See also Griffin, "Life of Bishop Conwell," *Records* 25 (1914): 338–40; Henry Conwell to Joseph O. Plessis, 4 July 1822, reprinted in ibid.: 312; Henry Conwell to Ambrose Maréchal, 19 March 1823, 15 A7. The paternity suit against the bishop is described in *Concatenation of Speeches, Memoirs, Deeds, and Memorable References Relative to St. Mary's Church in Philadelphia* (Philadelphia, 1824): 85–91.

2. The petition of St. Mary's trustees to the Pennsylvania Supreme Court, dated 5 April 1821 is reprinted in "St. Mary's Minute Book," *Records* 49 (1938: 334–35.

3. "Decision of the Supreme Court of Pennsylvania," in *The National Gazette and Literary Register*, 1 January 1822; [William] Tilghman, *Decision of the Supreme Court of Pennsylvania in the Case of the Corporation of St. Mary's Church (Roman Catholic) in the City of Philadelphia, on a Proposed Alteration of its Charter* (Philadelphia, 1822?)

4. *The National Gazette*, 1 January 1822.

5. Henry Conwell to Joseph O. Plessis, 6 January 1822, reprinted in *Researches* 28 (1911): 102, 103. See also Conwell to Plessis, 25 October 1821, reprinted in Griffin, "Life of Bishop Conwell," *Records* 25 (1914): 297.

6. *The National Gazette*, 2 January 1822.

7. Ibid.

8. *Freeman's Journal*, 15 January 1822; *Relf's Advertiser*, 18 January 1822.

9. On Petitions to Rome, see "Memorial of the Trustees of St. Mary's, "10 April 1821, copy in Philadelphia Archives; "St. Mary's Minute Book," *Records*

43 (1932): 351–56, entry of 11 June 1821; *Congressi, 6, Scisma di Filadelfia. 1819–1829*, fols. 38r to 65v, 151, and 152r; *Address of the Committee of Saint Mary's Church . . . to their Brethren*: 6, 12. The Latin form of the papal brief is reprinted in Tourscher, *Hogan Schism*, Appendix 7: 207–11. An English translation was published as *The Brief of His Holiness, Pope Pius the Seventh, Addressed to Ambrose, Archbishop of Baltimore, To His Suffragan Bishops, To the Administrators of the Temporalities of the Churches, and To All the Faithful In the United States of America* (no publisher listed, 1822): 9–10.

10. Ibid.: 10–11, 13–14 .

11. Ibid.: 12; Cardinal Consalvi to Henry Conwell, 7 September 1822, cited in Griffin, "Life of Bishop Conwell," *Records* 25 (1914): 321–22.

12. *Brief of His Holiness*: 12; Henry Conwell to Ambrose Maréchal, 19 March 1823, AAB file 15 A7; *Propaganda Fide* to Ambrose Maréchal 27 July 1822, *Congressi: 7, 1821–22*, fols. 834r to 838r.

13. The correspondence among Bishop Conwell, William Hogan, and John Keating relating to Hogan's attempt to submit on his own terms is reprinted in "Bishop Conwell and Father Hogan," *Researches* 3 (1887): 34–35. The correspondence between William Harold and William Hogan and an account of their meetings was published in the *National Gazette*, 18 December 1822. Robert Walsh, the Catholic editor of the *Gazette*, printed only William Harold's comments on the communications and refused to print William Hogan's commentaries. Hogan's rebuttal was printed in the *Aurora*, 1 January 1823, and the *Democratic Press*, 3 January 1823. See also Henry Conwell to Ambrose Maréchal, 10 December 1822, AAB file 15 A4; *Aurora*, 12 December 1822, 1 January 1823; *Democratic Press*, 11 December 1822. William Hogan to William V. Harold, 14 December 1822, reprinted in the *National Gazette*, 18 December 1822; Henry Conwell to Ambrose Maréchal, 13 December 1822, AAB file 15 A5.

14. *Griffin*, "Life of Bishop Conwell," *Records* 25 (1914): 331–32; F. Harold Duffee, "Reminiscences of the Rev. Wm. Hogan, Rev. William V. Harold and the Memorial Vow of Rev. Father Carter," *Researches* 8 (1891): 76–78; "Letter of Rev. B. Fenwick to Mr. George Fenwick at the Gesu, Rome, 1823," ibid.: 79–80.

15. *Aurora* 1, 3 January 1823.

16. Ibid.

17. William Harold to William Hogan, 16 December 1822, reprinted in the *National Gazette*, 18 December 1822.

THE CATHOLIC BILL

1. Although support for Hogan at least remained constant and may have even grown within St. Mary's Church, the size of the congregation declined

precipitously after the publication of the papal brief. Between the fall of 1822 and the spring of 1824 the number of pewholders declined by approximately fifty percent. For the most part, though, this represents bishopites abandoning their pews, not a decline in the numbers of the dissenters. See "St. Mary's Treasurer's Account Book, 1821–1826," in Philadelphia Archives, "St. Mary's Church," Box 1, Folder 1.

2. The text of the petition is recorded in "St. Mary's Minute Book": 257–61.

3. Ibid.

4. Ibid.

5. *Journal of the Thirty-Third House of Representatives of the Commonwealth of Pennsylvania Commenced at Harrisburg, Tuesday the Third of December, in the Year of Our Lord, One Thousand Eight Hundred and Twenty Two* (Harrisburg, 1822–23): 141; *Journal of the Senate of the Commonwealth of Pennsylvania Which Commenced at Harrisburg, the Third Day of December, in the Year of Our Lord One Thousand Eight Hundred and Twenty Two* (Harrisburg, 1822–23): 84; *Aurora*, 9 January 1823; *National Gazette*, 9 January 1823; 11 January 1823. William Harold's speech is cited in *A View of the Application for an Amendment of the Charter of Incorporation of St. Mary's Church* (Harrisburg, 1823): 5. See also the references to Harold's testimony in "Mr. Duncan's Speech on the Roman Catholic Question, In the Senate of Pennsylvania," in *Concatenation of Speeches . . . ,*: 51–55. On Augustine Fagan's speech, see ibid.: 82; *A View of the Application*: 9.

6. See Philip S. Klein, *Pennsylvania Politics, 1817–1832, A Game Without Rules* (Philadelphia, 1940); William C. Armor, *Lives of the Governors of Pennsylvania, with the Incidental History of the State, From 1609 to 1872* (Philadelphia, 1872): 340; Philip S. Klein and Ari Hoogenboom, *A History of Pennsylvania*, 2d ed. (University Park, Pennsylvania, 1986): 134. It is indicative of the unsettled nature of politics in this era that the reform coalition that elected Governor Heister in 1820 campaigned under different names in different parts of the state. In Philadelphia, where William Duane and Michael Leib led the effort, they called themselves "Old School Democrats" to emphasize their Jeffersonian origins. Elsewhere, in addition to the reformist label "Independent Republicans," they also adopted the name "Federal Republicans" in some areas where Federalist influence still lingered. During the debate in 1823 over the Catholic Bill they styled themselves "Constitutionalists" to emphasize their opposition to what they considered to be an unconstitutional assumption of authority by the legislature. See the *Aurora*, 20 March 1823.

7. Henry Conwell to Ambrose Maréchal, 23 January 1823, AAB file 15 A6; Henry G. Ganss, *History of St. Patrick's Church, Carlisle*, cited in Griffin, "Life of Bishop Conwell," *Records* 26 (1915): 135; *National Gazette*, 21 January 1823. Remonstrances from Catholic congregations are noted in *Journal of the House*

... (1822–23): 378, 426, 498, 505; *Journal of the Senate* ... (1822–23): 93, 129, 168, 173, 180, 186, 204, 206, 210, 224, 291, 294, 398, 435.

8. *Concatenation of Speeches* ... ,: 51–55; A *View of the Application*: 13.

9. Thomas Earle, *The Right of States to Alter and Annul Charters, Considered, and the Decisions of the Supreme Court of the United States Thereon, Examined, By the Principles of the American Constitution, Common Law, and Common Sense. With Some Observations on the Dispute Concerning the Alteration of the Charter of St. Mary's Church, Philadelphia* (Philadelphia, 1823): 27.

10. Ibid., 30; *Aurora*, 25 February 1823; *National Gazette*, 3 February 1823. On the battles over the judiciary early in the century, see Kim Phillips, "William Duane, Philadelphia's Democratic Republicans, and The Origins of Modern Politics"; Elizabeth K. Henderson, "The Attack on the Judiciary in Pennsylvania, 1800–1810," *Pennsylvania Magazine of History and Biography* 16 (1937): 113–36. The various motions and the votes taken on them are reported in *A Fair and Full View of the Votes of John Andrew Shulze, In the Senate of Pennsylvania, Respecting the Charter of the Roman Catholic Congregation, Worshiping at St. Mary's Church, In the City of Philadelphia* (np., 1823).

11. *View of the Application*; 4–5, 10; *National Gazette*, 3 February 1823.

12. Earle, *The Right of States* ... : 28.

13. *View of the Application*, 13; Duncan's speech was published in *Concatenation of Speeches* ... Throughout the debate over the Catholic Bill the American hierarchy concealed the existence of detailed regulations from Propaganda on the administration of the American church for fear that the public would construe them as proof of the dissenters' claims. At the height of the debate Bishop Conwell wrote "If we succeed at Harrisburg by preventing the Change of the Charter, it may not be then any longer necessary to Conceal the Regulations of his Holiness & the Sacred Congregation." See Henry Conwell to Ambrose Maréchal, 23 January 1823, AAB file 15 A6.

14. "Mr. Duncan's Speech," in *Concatenation of Speeches* ... : 26.

15. *Aurora*, 24, 25 February 1823; "A Sketch of Mr. Wirts' Speech," in *Concatenation of Speeches* ... : 29–39.

16. *Aurora*, 20, 21 February 1823; "remarks of Mr. W. R. Smith," in *Concatenation of Speeches* ... : 39–45.

17. Ibid.

"AN INTERESTED UNION OF RELIGION AND POLITICS"

1. *A Full and Fair View* ... : 24–25. "Opinion of the Attorney General," cited in Griffin, "Life of Bishop Conwell, *Records* 26 (1915): 76; *Aurora*, 20 March 1823.

2. Heister's veto message is reprinted in *Aurora*, 31 March 1823; *Concatenation of Speeches . . .* : 46–48.

3. *Aurora*, 31 March 1823; *A Full and Fair View . . .* was published by the Republicans in order to present a full account of the circumstances of Shulze's votes.

4. *Aurora*, 16, 21 June, 8 July, 1 August 1823.

5. *Aurora*, 16, 20 June, 1823; *Address of the Trustees of St. Mary's Church, To Their Fellow-Citizens; Containing a Correspondence Between Them and the Right Reverend Bishop Conwell, On A Late Attempt At A Reconciliation Between the Contending Parties of the Congregation of Said Church* (Philadelphia, September 1823): 3–4; Henry Conwell to Joseph Octave Plessis, 25 July 1823, reprinted in Griffin, "Life of Bishop Conwell," *Records* 49 (1938): 161–62.

6. *Aurora*, 1 August 1823.

7. Henry Conwell to Ambrose Maréchal, 19 March 1823, AAB file 15 A7; Griffin, "Life of Bishop Conwell," *Records* 49 (1938): 135–36. Kenny's reference to Nag's Head repeats a slander made by English Catholics to the effect that early Anglican bishops were consecrated in a London tavern, the Nag's Head. His use of the term implies a comparison between the proponents of the Catholic Bill and the schism that produced the Church of England and so reinforces the identification of St. Mary's dissenters with Protestant schismatics.

PASTOR OF ST. MARY'S

1. The election results and the turmoil that accompanied them, as well as pew transfers, are reported in "St. Mary's Minute Book," *Records* 49 (1938): 334–35, 338, 341–42, 346, 353–54; *St. Mary's Account Book*, in Philadelphia Archives, "St. Mary's Church," Box 1, Folder 2; "Summons to Appear in the Case of the Catholic Society Worshiping at the Church of St. Mary's in Philadelphia vs John Maitland and Others," 29 March 1823, in ibid., Box 2, Folder 4.

2. R. W. Meade, et al. to Henry Conwell, 5 June 1823, in *Address of the Trustees . . . To Their Fellow-Citizens*: 5–7; "St. Mary's Minute Book," *Records* 49 (1938): 351–53; Henry Conwell to Ambrose Maréchal, 1 August 1823, AAB file 15 B12; *Address of the Trustees . . . To Their Fellow-Citizens*: 22, 23. Financial pressures on both sides were also mounting. By the summer of 1823 Bishop Conwell was receiving no income from St. Mary's and Michael Hurley at St. Augustine's was withholding that church's contribution to the bishop's upkeep. Hurley by this point was in the advanced stages of alcoholism and was frequently debilitated by drink. Conwell wrote to Archbishop Maréchal to inform him that "*Entre nous* Mr Hurley is retrogressing in every respect. He is becoming a perfect Sot." See Henry Conwell to Ambrose Maréchal, 25 July 1823, AAB file 15 A10. So desperate was his situation that Conwell was forced to solicit funds from the bishop of Quebec. See Joseph Octave Plessis to Henry Conwell,

13 August 1823, reprinted in Griffin, "Life of Bishop Conwell," *Records* 26 (1915): 240–41. St. Mary's congregation was also heavily in debt, largely due to the actions of the last bishopite board of trustees in 1820 who, in the last days before leaving office, mortgaged the church property heavily in order to pay the clergy's salaries in advance. In 1822 the debt burden had been increased "due to the forcible entry into and possession of the church" by bishopite forces which had forced the trustees to install a permanent guard on the building. Revenues were also declining since many bishopite pewholders were withholding their pew rents. Now, in 1823, the debts were coming due and efforts to raise money proved to be unsuccessful. Finally, John Leamy personally advanced the congregation $1,200 to keep it solvent. See Griffin, *Life of Bishop Conwell*: 143, "St. Mary's Minute Book," *Records* 49 (1938): 336–37, 346–47, 353.

3. Henry Conwell to Ambrose Maréchal, 29 June 1823, AAB file 15 A8.

4. *Address of the Trustees . . . To Their Fellow-Citizens*: 20–22; Henry Conwell to Joseph Octave Plessis, 13 September 1823, translated and reprinted in Griffin, "Life of Bishop Conwell," *Records* 26 (1915): 247–49.

5. *Address of the Trustees . . . To Their Fellow-Citizens*: 21; John Leamy and Archibald Randall to Rev. A. Inglesi, 28 August 1821, reprinted in Address of the Trustees . . . To Their Fellow-Citizens: 22; Harold, *Address to the Roman Catholics of Philadelphia*: 18; "St. Mary's Minute Book," *Records* 49 (1938): 355.

6. Angelo Inglesi to St. Mary's Board of Trustees, 29 August 1823, reprinted in *Address of the Trustees . . . To Their Fellow-Citizens*: 23, 25; Angelo Inglesi, *An Address to the Public of Philadelphia: Containing, A Vindication of the Character and Conduct of the Reverend Mr. Inglesi From Charges and Strictures Lately Reported and Published Against Him By the Reverend Mr. Harold* [translated from the French] (Philadelphia, 1824): 6, 7f.

7. Inglesi, *Address . . . Containing A Vindication of the Character*; Henry Conwell to Joseph Octave Plessis, 15 October 1823, translated and reprinted in Griffin, "Life of Bishop Conwell," *Records* 27 (1916): 76–79; Harold, *Address to the Roman Catholics of Philadelphia*: 5, 6; *Democratic Press*, 22 November 1823; *Address of the Trustees . . . To Their Fellow-Citizens*; Appendix to *The Address of the Lay Trustees of St. Mary's Church To Their Fellow-Citizens* (Philadelphia, 1823); Meade, *Address To the Roman Catholics of Philadelphia*: 25–31.

8. "St. Mary's Minute Book," *Records* 49 (1938): 356.

9. Ibid.: 356–58; Thadeus J. O'Meally, *An Address Explanatory and Vindicatory, to Both Parties of the Congregation of St. Mary's* (Philadelphia, 1824): 6–7, contains a description of the initial meeting between O'Meally and Conwell; Henry Conwell to Thadeus O'Meally, 15 October 1823, Thadeus O'Meally to Henry Conwell, 18 October 1823, reprinted in ibid.: 6–8; Henry Conwell to Ambrose Maréchal, 16 October 1823, AAB file 15 B13; John Leamy and Archibald Randall to Henry Conwell, 20 October 1823 in *Address*

Explanatory and Vindicatory . . . : 8. For a description of O'Meally, see a contemporary account by Joseph Snyder, reprinted in Griffin, "Life of Bishop Conwell," *Records* 28 (1917): 80–82.

10. William Harold to Archibald Randall, 22 October 1823; Thadeus O'Meally to William Harold, 27, 30 October 1823; Henry Conwell to Thadeus O'Meally, 3 November 1823; Thadeus O'Meally to Henry Conwell, 6 November 1823, all reprinted in *Address Explanatory and Vindicatory*: 8–15.

11. Thadeus O'Meally to Henry Conwell, 6 November 1923, *Address Explanatory and Vindicatory*: 14.

12. William Hogan, "Address To the Congregation of St. Mary's Church," *National Gazette*, 24 July 1824; Willcox, "Diary of Rev. Patrick Kenny," *Records*, 9 (1898): 437–38, entries of 2, 5 September, 23 October 1824.

13. R. W. Meade et al. to Henry Conwell, 5 June 1823, in *Address of the Trustees . . . To Their Fellow-Citizens*: 5–7; Thadeus O'Meally to Ambrose Maréchal, 30 January 1824, AAB file 19 S4. *Address Explanatory and Vindicatory*: 41–42. On the general problem of rising levels of civil disorder, see Alan M. Zachary, "Social Disorder and the Philadelphia Elite Before Jackson," *Pennsylvania Magazine of History and Biography* 99 (1975): 288–308. On elite attitudes toward Irish immigrants, see Edward C. Carter, "A Wild Irishman Under Every Federalist's Bed," *Pennsylvania Magazine of History and Biography* 94 (1974).

14. Bishop Conwell's sentence of excommunication, dated 20 November 1823, is reprinted *Concatenation of Speeches* . . . : 92–93 and in *Address Explanatory and Vindicatory*: 21–22. O'Meally's description of his meeting with Conwell is presented in ibid .: 20–21, 22.

15. Richard W. Meade to Henry Conwell, 8 December 1823, reprinted in *Address Explanatory and Vindicatory*: 27–29.

16. Ibid.

17. Henry Conwell to Richard W. Meade, 18 December 1823, reprinted in ibid.: 29–31, copy in AAB file 22B R1, encl. 1.

18. Thadeus O'Meally to Henry Conwell, 23 December 1823, reprinted in ibid.: 37–40, copy in AAB file 22B R1, encl. 2; Thadeus O'Meally to Ambrose Maréchal, 15 December 1823, AAB file 22B R1; *Address Explanatory and Vindicatory*: 40.

19. *Address Explanatory and Vindicatory*: 41–42; John England to Henry Conwell, 4 October 1822, reprinted in England, *Works*, 5: 145–47. On England's constitution, see ibid.: 91–108; P. Carey, *An Immigrant Bishop*: 111–26.

20. John England to Henry Conwell, 3 March 1824, reprinted in Guilday, *Life of John England*, 1: 413–14; Henry Conwell to Ambrose Maréchal, 17 March 1824, AAB file 15 B18; 20 March 1824, AAB file 15 B19; *Address Explanatory and Vindicatory*: 40–41.

21. John England to Henry Conwell, 20 May 1824, cited at length in Henry Conwell to Ambrose Maréchal, 28 May 1824, AAB file 14 W15.

22. Henry Conwell to Ambrose Maréchal, 28 May 1824, AAB file 14 W15.

23. Henry Conwell to Ambrose Maréchal, 10 July 1824, AAB file 15 B22; 3 October 1824, AAB file 15 C24; 14 December 1824 [misdated as 6 June 1824], AAB file 15 C22, to "The Cardinal-Prefect of Propaganda," 8 June 1824, reprinted in Guilday, *Life of John England*, 1: 416–17.

24. Louis William Du Bourg to Richard W. Meade, 19 December 1823, copy in Richard W. Meade to Ambrose Maréchal, 4 February 1824, AAB file 16 A15; Henry Conwell to Ambrose Maréchal, 28 May 1824, AAB file 14 W15; to the Cardinal-Prefect of Propaganda, 8 June 1824, copy in Philadelphia Archives; Louis William DuBourg to Propaganda Fide, 8 March 1824, 10 May 1824, *Congressi 6, Scisma di Filadelfia. 1819–1829*, fols. 412 and 413r; 418, and 419. Thadeus O'Meally also noted Bishop Plessis of Quebec as one of the bishops who were urging Conwell to make sacrifices to end the schism. See Thadeus O'Meally to Ambrose Maréchal, 3 March 1824, AAB file 19 S1.

25. Thadeus O'Meally to Ambrose Maréchal, 3 March 1824, AAB file 19 S1; Henry Conwell to Ambrose Maréchal, 14 December 1824, AAB file 15 C26.

26. Henry Conwell to Ambrose Maréchal, 12 January 1824, AAB file 15 B14; 17 March 1824, AAB file 15 B18; 19 April 1824, AAB file 15 B20.

THE FAILURE OF COMPROMISE

1. Henry Conwell to Ambrose Maréchal, 3 October 1824, AAB file 15 C24. Henry Conwell to Ambrose Maréchal, 17 March 1824, AAB file 15 B18; 19 April 1824, AAB file 15 B24; *A Series of Letters Relating to the Late Attempt at a Reconciliation Between the Members of the Congregations of St. Mary's and St. Joseph's; With a Brief Notice of the Present State of the Controversy Between Them Being an Abstract of an Address Delivered by the Rev. T. J. O'Meally, at the Meeting Held in St. Mary's, On Thursday Evening the 23d Ult.* (Philadelphia, January 1825): 28.

2. Henry Conwell to Ambrose Maréchal, 10 July 1823, AAB file 15 B22; to Joseph Octave Plessis, 11 July 1824, cited in Griffin, "Life of Bishop Conwell," *Records* 27 (1916): 359.

3. Henry Conwell to Ambrose Maréchal, 10 July 1824, AAB file 15 B22; to Joseph Octave Plessis, 11 July 1824, cited in Griffin, "Life of Bishop Conwell," *Records* 27 (1916): 359.

4. "St. Mary's Minute Book," *Records* 49 (1938): 363; *U.S. Catholic Miscellany,* 19 May 1824; William Hogan, "Address to the Congregation of St. Mary's Church," *National Gazette,* 24 July 1824.

5. Hogan, "Address to the Congregation."

6. Henry Conwell to Ambrose Maréchal, 29 June 1823, AAB file 15 A8; 1 August 1823, AAB file 15 B12; 5 October 1824, AAB file 15 C25; 20 March 1824, AAB file 15 B19; 11 December 1824, AAB file 14 W16. Hogan's career after he left Philadelphia is sketched in Griffin, "Life of Bishop Conwell," *Records* 27 (1916): 369–78.

7. Griffin, *Life of Conwell*: 84.

8. Henry Conwell to Ambrose Maréchal, 3 October 1824, AAB file 15 C24; 11 December 1824, AAB file 14 W16; O'Meally, *Address Explanatory and Vindicatory*: 74–75.

9. Henry Conwell to Ambrose Maréchal, 3 October 1824, AAB file 15 C24; 1 December 1824, AAB file 15 C27; 11 December 1824, AAB file 14 W16; Richard W. Meade, "To the Editor of the Democratic Press," reprinted in *Series of Letters*: 5, 6; Minutes 1821–29, St. Mary's Church, Phila. Pa.: 93; "Abstract of the proceedings of a general meeting of the Congregation now worshipping at St. Mary's Church, held at their schoolroom, on Wednesday evening, the 24th instant," in *Series of Letters*: 3; Henry Conwell, "To the Editor of the Democratic Press," 2 December 1824, in ibid.: 7; Minutes 1821–29, St. Mary's Church, Phila. Pa.: 97. "Minutes of a General Meeting of the Congregation now Worshipping at St. Mary's Church," 24 November 1824, Philadelphia Archives, "St. Mary's Papers," Box 1, folder 8, No. 2; "Abstract of the Proceedings": 4.

10. Griffin, "Life of Bishop Conwell," *Records* 27 (1916): 275. Henry Conwell to Ambrose Maréchal, 1 August 1823, AAB file 15 B12; 12 January 1824, AAB 15 B14; 17 March 1824, AAB file 15 B18; to Joseph Octave Plessis, 15 October 1823, translated and cited in Griffin, "Life of Bishop Conwell," *Records* 27 (1916): 76–79.

11. Thadeus O'Meally, "To the Editor of the Democratic Press," 3 December 1824 in *Series of Letters*: 7–12.

12. "From Dr. Conwell to the Trustees," 8 December 1824, in ibid.: 12; "From the Trustees to Dr. Conwell" in ibid: 12–13.

13. Minutes 1821–29, St. Mary's Church, Phila. Pa.: 87, entry of 7 January 1824; [Fagan], *Reflections On the Dissension . . .* : 3, 4–6.

14. [Fagan], *Reflections on the Dissension . . .* : 4–6.

15. Ibid.: 6–8. The identification of absolutism with medieval culture is, of course, profoundly ahistorical, although it was accepted by both Catholic liberals and ultramontane reformers. Absolutism was far more a product of the "Age of Reason" than of the "Age of Faith."

16. Ibid.: 7, 10, 12.

17. Ibid.: 10–11.

18. Ibid.: 18–19.

19. Ibid.: 13.

20. Ibid.: 12–13.

21. Ibid.: 11.

22. For representative studies, see Laurie, *Working People of Philadelphia*; Alan Dawley, *Class and Community: The Industrial Revolution in Lynn* (Cambridge, Mass. 1976); Paul Faler, *Mechanics and Manufacturers in the Early Industrial Revolution: Lynn, Massachusetts, 1780–1860* (Albany: 1981); Sean Wilentz, *Chants Democratic: New York City and the Rise of the American Working Class, 1788–1850* (New York, 1984).

23. On the authorship of the memorial, see *Concatenations*: 82; Henry Conwell to Ambrose Maréchal, 12 January 1824, AAB file 15 B14. This was to be Fagan's last contribution to the dissenters' cause. He died within hours of completing his work on the memorial. Bishop Conwell was unsure as to whether Fagan's death was a consequence of his depraved character (he attributed it to an overdose of laudanum) or God's judgment on a wicked soul.

24. [Fagan], *Reflections On the Dissension*: 14.

25. Ibid.: 14–15, 18.

26. See Lawrence Frederick Kohl, *The Politics of Individualism: Parties and the American Character in the Jacksonian Era* (New York, 1989); Daniel Walker Howe, *The Political Culture of the American Whigs* (Chicago, 1979). H. L. Carey's father was Mathew Carey.

27. Henry Conwell to Ambrose Maréchal, 16 March 1824, AAB file 15 B18; *Concatenation*: 102 (in this published version of Bishop Conwell's political manual, the offensive and libelous passages were "blotted out").

"BISHOP, PRIEST AND PEOPLE"

1. Thadeus O'Meally to Ambrose Maréchal, 3 March 1824, AAB file 19 S1.

2. Ibid.

3. John England to Henry Conwell, 3 March 1824, reprinted in Guilday, *Life of John England*, 1: 413–14.

4. *Congressi, 6, Scisma di Filadelfia. 1819–1829*, fols. 414 and 416r.

5. *Address Explanatory and Vindicatory*: 77.

6. Ibid.: 47–48.

7. Ibid.: 60, 62. Henry Conwell, as was the practice for Old World aristocrats, had used his position to provide employment for a number of his relatives. This was much resented by the dissenters.

8. *Address Explanatory and Vindicatory*: 64, 78.

9. Ibid.: 48.

10. Ibid.: 48, 63.

11. Ibid.: 48–49, 64.

12. Ibid.: 68–70.

13. Ibid.: 56, 72–73.

14. Ibid.: 79–80.

15. Ibid.: 66–67.
16. Ibid.: 70–72.
17. Ibid.: 24, 25–26, 67; *A Series of Letters.*

CONWELL'S MORAL COSMOLOGY

1. Henry Conwell to Ambrose Maréchal, 5 October 1824, AAB file 15 C25.
2. *Address Explanatory and Vindicatory*: 69–70.
3. Ibid.: 84.
4. Henry Conwell to Ambrose Maréchal, 14 December 1824, AAB file 15 C26.
5. Ibid.; Henry Conwell to Ambrose Maréchal, 4 January 1825, AAB file 15 C28.
6. Henry Conwell to Ambrose Maréchal, 14 December 1824, AAB file 15 C26; 4 January 1825, AAB file 15 C28; Henry Conwell to Julius Cardinal Somaglia, pro-prefect of Propaganda Fide, 1 January 1825, copy in Philadelphia Archives. See also Conwell to Propaganda Fide, 9 March 1825, copy in Philadelphia Archives. Bishop Conwell's complaints led Propaganda to formally censure John England on August 27, 1825, for his role in the Philadelphia schism. This brought a spirited reply from Charleston in which England said that Propaganda was obviously ignorant concerning conditions in America, especially the genius of the American people and their mode of government. See Guilday, *Life of John England*, 1: 422–23, John England to Julius Cardinal Somaglia, 4 November 1825, *Congressi, 6, Scisma di Filadelfia. 1819–1829*, fol. 561.
7. Jean L. Cheverus to Propaganda Fide, 21 August 1824, *Congressi, 8, 1825*, fols. 377, 378, 376r.
8. Fenwick cited in Griffin, "Life of Bishop Conwell," *Records* 25 (1914): 337–38; John England to Ambrose Maréchal, 22 December 1822, AAB file 16 N9; 15 January 1823, AAB file 16 J9.

O'MEALLY'S SUBMISSION

1. "From the Committee of the Trustees to Dr. Conwell," 15 December 1824, in *Series of Letters*: 15–17; Thadeus O'Meally, "To the Congregation of St. Mary's," 19 December 1824, in ibid.: 17–19; Thadeus O'Meally to Henry Conwell, 21 December 1824, in ibid: 19–20.
2. Henry Conwell to Thadeus O'Meally, 21 December 1824, in ibid.: 20.
3. Thadeus O'Meally to Henry Conwell, 21 December 1824 [second letter], in ibid: 21; Henry Conwell to Thadeus O'Meally, 22 December 1824, in ibid.: 21–22.

4. Thadeus O'Meally to Henry Conwell, 22 December 1824, in ibid.: 22–23.

5. Thadeus O'Meally, "Address to the Congregation of St. Mary's Church," 23 December 1824, in ibid.: 24–42.

6. Ibid.

7. John England to the Roman Catholics of the Diocese of Philadelphia, 12 January 1825, reprinted in Guilday, *Life of John England*, 1: 417–20.

8. O'Meally's proposal to travel to Rome is recorded in Minutes 1821–29, St. Mary's Church, Phila. Pa.: fol. 96r, entry of 11 April 1825. Extracts from the proceedings of the meeting of the congregation held 12 April 1825 are recorded in ibid.: fol. 96, entry of 14 April 1825. Committee of the Board of Trustees to Henry Conwell, 14 April 1825, *Congressi, 6, Scisma di Filadelfia. 1819–1829*, fol. 481r.

9. Minutes 1821–29, St. Mary's Church, Phila. Pa.: 97r, entry of 15 April 1825; G. Deabbate to Propaganda Fide, 18 April 1825, *Congressi, 6, Scisma di Filadelfia. 1819–1829*, fols. 487, 488r.; Henry Conwell to Julius Cardinal Somaglia, 20 May 1825, 20 August 1825, ibid., fols. 489, 490, 496, 497; 20 June 1825, copy in Philadelphia Archives; Henry Conwell to Ambrose Maréchal, 2 July 1825, AAB file 15 C30.

10. Cardinal Prefect of Propaganda to Henry Conwell, 30 July 1825, reprinted in Griffin, "Life of Bishop Conwell," *Records* 28 (1917): 77–78. See also ibid.: 79; Thadeus O'Meally to Henry Conwell, 25 July 1825, reprinted in *Philadelphia Gazette*, 4 Nov. 1825.

11. Thadeus O'Meally to P. Caprano, Secretary of Propaganda Fide, 27 July 1825, to Julius Cardinal Somaglia, 25 August, 31 October 1825, to Cardinal Zurla, 18 November 1825, to Propaganda Fide, 28 December 1825, *Congressi, 6, Scisma di Filadelfia. 1819–1829*, fols. 514, 515, 521, 529, 533, 534r, 538r.

CONWELL'S COVENANT

1. Contemporary account by Joseph Snyder, reprinted in Griffin, "Life of Bishop Conwell," *Records* 28 (1917): 80–82. See also Henry Conwell to Ambrose Maréchal, 2 July 1825, AAB file 15 C30.

2. See Henry Conwell to Ambrose Maréchal, 25 July 1823, AAB file 15 A10; July 1823, cited in Griffin, "Life of Bishop Conwell," *Records* 26 (1915): 239–40.

3. Henry Conwell to Ambrose Maréchal, 19 December 1825, AAB file 14 Y21; "Diary of Rev. Patrick Kenny," *Records* 9 (1898): 97, entry of 17 September 1826.

4. "Diary of Rev. Patrick Kenny," *Records* 9 (1898): 100, entry of 2 October 1826; Henry Conwell to Propaganda Fide, 6 June 1824, *Congressi: 7*, fols. 297

and 298, copy in Philadelphia Archives; 20 July 1825, *Scritture originali riferite nelle congregazioni generali del 1825* (hereinafter *Scritture originali*) vol. 938, fols. 95 and 96 r. See also ibid., vol. 934, fols. 390 and 391r; Propaganda Fide to Bishop DuBourg, 24 July 1824, *Lettere e decreti, 1824*, vol. 305, fol. 495.

5. John England to William V. Harold, 24 February 1824, AAB file 16 J11; Guilday, *Life of John England*: 412–14.

6. Griffin, "Life of Bishop Conwell," *Records* 28 (1917): 154–55.

7. Henry Conwell to Ambrose Maréchal, 12 February 1827, AAB file 14 Y27; Michael Hurley to Anthony Kohlmann, 22 January 1827, *Scritture originali, 1827*, vol. 940, fols. 616r–639r; Propaganda Fide to Henry Conwell, 16 September 1826, *Lettere, 1826*, vol. 307, fol. 607v; to William V. Harold, 23 September 1826, copy in Philadelphia archives. Conwell was convinced that William Harold and John Ryan intended to "establish themselves as independent pastors." See Henry Conwell to Francis P. Kenrick, 1827, cited in Tourscher, *Hogan Schism*: 155.

8. Henry Conwell to Ambrose Maréchal, 2 August 1826, AAB file 14 Y24.

9. Henry Conwell to Ambrose Maréchal, 30 September 1826, AAB file 14 Y25; 12 February 1827, AAB file 14 Y27; John England, *Works*, 5: 207. On the Wilmington troubles, see "Diary of Rev. Patrick Kenny," *Records* 9 (1898): 97, 106, entries of 18 September and 12 November 1826. The trustees of St. Mary's specifically named Michael Hurley and Josiah Randall as persons who worked to effect the compromise. See Minutes 1821–29, St. Mary's Church, Philadelphia, Pa.: 103v, 104r, entry of 7 November 1826.

10. Henry Conwell to Ambrose Maréchal, 30 September 1826, AAB file 14 Y25; "Diary of Rev. Patrick Kenny," *Records* 9 (1898): 99, entry of 1 October 1826.

11. "Diary of Rev. Patrick Kenny," *Records* 9 (1898): 99, 100, entries of 2, 3 October 1826.

12. Ibid.: 100–101, entry of 3 October 1826; Michael Hurley to Anthony Kohlmann, 22 January 1827, *Scritture originali, 1827*, vol. 940, fols. 616r–639r.

13. "Diary of Rev. Patrick Kenny," *Records* 9 (1898): 101, entry of 4 October 1826.

14. Minutes 1821–29, St. Mary's Church, Phila. Pa.: 100v, entry of 29 September 1826; "Proclamation of Agreement between the Bishop of Philadelphia and St. Mary's Trustees," 9 October 1826, copy in AAB file 14 Y26.

15. Ibid.

16. Ibid.

17. Henry Conwell to Ambrose Maréchal, 12 February 1827, AAB file 14 Y27; *Democratic Press*, 11 October 1826; *National Gazette*, 14 October 1826; Henry Conwell to Propaganda Fide, 20 October 1826, *Scritture originali, 1827*, vol. 940, fols. 579 and 580r.

18. "Proclamation of Agreement between the Bishop of Philadelphia and St. Mary's Trustees," 9 October 1826, copy in AAB file 14 Y26.

19. *Democratic Press,* 11 October 1826; *An Address . . . by a Worshipper at St. Mary's* (Philadelphia, 1827); Minutes 1821–29, St Mary's Church, Phila. Pa.: 101, 102, 103, entry of 1 November 1826; "Petition of the Trustees of St. Mary's Church to the Propaganda Fide," 4 November 1826, enclosure in Henry Conwell to Cardinal Cappelari, Prefect of Propaganda Fide, 17 March 1827, *Congressi, 6, Scisma di Filadelfia, 1819–1829,* fols. 576r–578r.

"THIS UNHAPPY CHURCH"

1. Henry Conwell to *Propaganda Fide,* 20 October 1826, *Scritture originali, 1827,* vol. 940, fols. 579 and 580r; 20 November 1826, ibid., fol. 642r; to Cardinal Cappellari, 17 March 1827, *Congressi, 6, Scisma di Filadelfia. 1819–1829,* fol. 576r to 578r; 20 April 1827, ibid., fol. 591r; 1 August 1827; ibid., fol. 605; 14 September 1827, ibid., fols. 622 and 623r.

2. Henry Conwell to *Propaganda Fide,* 1 February 1827, *Scritture originali, 1827,* vol. 940, fol. 599; William V. Harold to *Propaganda Fide,* 1 November 1826, ibid., fols. 581, 582r, 583, 584r, 585r to 587v.; 29 November 1826, ibid., fols. 589 and 590r; 30 January 1827, fols. 591, 593r to 595v, 597r and 598r; 14 June 1827, *Congressi, 6, Scisma di Filadelfia. 1819–1829,* fols. 595 and 596; John England, *Works,* 5: 266.

3. William V. Harold to *Propaganda Fide,* 30 January 1827, *Scritture originali, 1827,* vol. 940, fol. 591; Henry Conwell to William V. Harold, 1 December 1826, enclosure in ibid, 593r to 595v, William V. Harold to Henry Conwell, n.d., enclosure in ibid. 597r and 598r; Petition of the Trustees of St. Mary's Church to Pope Leo XII, 12 July 1827, *Congressi, 6, Scisma di Filadelfia. 1819–1829,* fols. 602 and 603r; Trustees of St. Mary's Church to Pope Leo XII, 7 August 1827, ibid., fols. 617, 618r.

4. Henry Conwell to Ambrose Maréchal, 12 February 1827, AAB file 14 Y27; Henry Conwell to Propaganda Fide, 1 February 1827, *Scritture originali, 1827,* vol. 940, fol. 599, undated, *Congressi, 6, Scisma di Filadelfia. 1819–1829,* fol. 564; "Diary of Patrick Kenny," *Records* 9 (1898): 120, entry of 16 April 1827.

5. "Diary of Rev. Patrick Kenny," *Records* 9 (1898): 117, entry of 14 March 1827; 106, entry of 11 November 1826.

6. Minutes 1821–29, St. Mary's Church, Phila. Pa.: 103v, 104r, entry of 7 November 1826; "A Statement of facts which took place between Bishop Conwell and Lewis Ryan, Dennis McCredy & Joseph Snyder," Philadelphia Archives, "St. Mary's Church," Box 1, fol. 8, no. 3; John Hughes to Simon Bruté, 7 May 1827, reprinted in Griffin, "Life of Bishop Conwell," *Records* 28 (1917): 251–55; "Diary of Patrick Kenny," *Records* 9 (1898): 120, entry of 16 April 1827. See also J. Smith to Richard Baxter, 9 April 1827, *Congressi, 7, 1823–1826,* fols. 589 and 590.

7. John Hughes to Simon Bruté, 7 May 1827, reprinted in Griffin, "Life of Bishop Conwell," *Records* 28 (1917): 251–55; "Diary of Rev. Patrick Kenny," *Records* 9 (1898): 117, entry of 14 March 1827.

8. Francis Roloff to Ambrose Maréchal, 3 April 1827, AAB file 20 E9.

9. Ibid.; account of meeting in Griffin, "Life of Bishop Conwell," *Records* 28 (1917): 256.

10. "Statement of . . . Joseph Snyder," Philadelphia Archives, "St. Mary's Church," Box 1, fol. 8, no. 3; John Hughes to Simon Bruté, 7 May 1827, reprinted in Griffin, "Life of Bishop Conwell," Records 28 (1917): 251–55.

11. Ibid.

RAPPROCHEMENT

1. Minutes 1821–29, St. Mary's Church, Phila. Pa.: fols. 110v, 111, entry of 19 April 1827; "Notice of Public Meeting," 21 April 1827, reprinted in Griffin, "Life of Bishop Conwell," *Records* 28 (1917): 258; *Address to the Pewholders and Congregation of St. Mary's*. John Ashley spoke for those "members of the 'contracting parties' [who] were averse to the appointment of Mr. Harold." Shortly thereafter he resigned his position on the board of trustees and withdrew from church affairs.

2. John England, *Works*, 5: 203.

3. Minutes 1821–29, St. Mary's Church, Phila. Pa.: fols. 110v, 111, entry of 19 April 1827; John Hughes to Simon Bruté, 7 May 1827, reprinted in Griffin, "Life of Bishop Conwell," *Records* 28 (1917): 251–55.

4. "Diary of Rev. Patrick Kenny," *Records* 9 (1898): 106, entry of 11 November 1826. On pewholder discontent, see also "Statement of . . . Joseph Snyder," Philadelphia Archives, "St. Mary's Church" Box 1, fol. 8, no. 3.; Minutes 1821–29, St. Mary's Church, Phila. Pa.: fols. 106v, 107r, entry of 28 December 1826; 107, entry of 12 February 1827; 108v, 109, 110r; entry of 2 April 1827.

5. Minutes 1821–29, St. Mary's Church, Phila. Pa.: 103v, 104r, entry of 7 November 1826. The proposed amendments are noted in ibid. 104v, 105, 106r. See also ibid. 106v, 107r, entry of 28 December 1826. See also *Act to Incorporate the Members of the Religious Society of Roman Catholics, belonging to the Congregation of St. Mary's Church, in the City of Philadelphia. As Amended* (Philadelphia, 1826). The final form of the charter as passed by the state legislature is reprinted in Griffin, "Life of Bishop Conwell," *Records* 28 (1917): 175–79.

6. A Catholic Layman [Mathew Carey], *A Religious Olive Branch* (Philadelphia, 7 October 1826).

7. The records of the first meeting of the "Vindicators of the Catholic Religion" and its constitution were reprinted in *Researches* 6 (1889): 158–59. See also "An Early Philadelphia Catholic Truth Society—1827," *Records* 38

(1927): 8–14, which contains a list of the members of the association. See also *Constitution of the Society for the Defense of the Catholic Religion* (Philadelphia, 1826). See also [Mathew Carey] *Letters on Religious Persecution: Proving, that That Most Heinous of Crimes, Has Not been Peculiar to Roman Catholics . . . , By a Catholic Layman* (Philadelphia, 1 January 1827).

8. John Hughes to Thomas Hayden, 19 May 1827, reprinted in John R. G. Hassard, *Life of the Most Reverend John Hughes, D.D., First Archbishop of New York, With Extracts from his Private Correspondence* (New York: 1866): 60. Patrick Connell's resignation and Richard Meade's refusal to serve as a trustee are noted in Griffin, "Life of Bishop Conwell," *Records* 28 (1917): 255. Meade died on June 25, 1828, in Washington, D.C..

9. John Ashley's retirement is noted in Minutes 1821–29, St. Mary's Church, Phila. Pa.: fol. 112, entry of 5 July 1827.

THE ONLY TRIBUNAL

1. William Harold to Ambrose Maréchal, 14 April 1827, AAB file 22 D6. For a brief account of William Harold's protest that places it within the context of the general problem of episcopal authority in the early republic, see Trisco, "Bishops and Their Priests": 118–19.

2. William Harold to Ambrose Maréchal, 14 April 1827, AAB file 22 D6; 23 April 1827, AAB ref 17 H4.

3. William Harold to Ambrose Maréchal, 14 April 1827, AAB file 22 D6.

4. Ibid.; William Harold to Ambrose Maréchal, 23 April 1827, AAB file 17 H4.

5. William Harold to Ambrose Maréchal, 14 April 1827, AAB file 22 D6; 23 April 1827, AAB ref 17 H4; Ambrose Maréchal to William Harold, 7 April 1827, AAB file 17 H3.

6. Henry Conwell to Ambrose Maréchal, 12 February 1827, AAB file 14 Y27; "Diary of Rev. Patrick Kenny," *Records* 9 (1898): 120, entry of 17 April 1827. See· also the account of the negotiations in Michael Hurley to Anthony Kohlmann, 22 January 1827, *Scritture originali, 1827*, vol. 940, fols. 616r to 639r. William Harold even went so far as to take up a collection to send himself and John Ryan to Rome to personally plead their case to Propaganda. See Henry Conwell to Cardinal Capellari, August 1827, cited in Tourscher, *The Hogan Schism*: 165. See also Conwell to Capellari, 22 September 1827, *Congressi, 6, Scisma di Filadelfia. 1819–1829*, fols. 624 and 625.

7. Henry Conwell to Propaganda Fide, 14 July 1826, *Scritture originali, 1827*, vol. 940, fol. 644; 20 November 1826, fol. 642r; to Cardinal Cappelari, Prefect of Propaganda, n.d., [probably May 1827], *Congressi, 6, Scisma di Filadelfia. 1819–1829*, fol. 564; 17 March 1827, fols. 576r to 578r; 20 April 1827, fol. 591r; J. Farnum to Henry Conwell, 20 April 1827, fol. 593; Michael Hurley to

Anthony Kohlmann, 22 January 1827, *Scritture originali, 1827*, vol. 940, fols. 616r to 639r. Demetrius A. de Gallitzin to Henry Conwell, August 1827, *Congressi, 9, 1827–1828*, fol. 307; to the Prefect of Propaganda, 4 February 1828, fol. 569. We should note that four years later Cardinal Cappelari, the recipient of most of this correspondence, became Pope Gregory XVI.

8. William V. Harold to Julius Cardinal Somaglia, 14 June 1827, *Congressi, 6, Scisma di Filadelfia. 1819–1829*, fols. 595 and 596.

9. J. Savage to J. Leahy, 13 December 1826, ibid., fols. 608 and 609; Mathew Carey et al., to Propaganda Fide, 12 May 1827, *Scritture originali, 1827*, vol. 940, fols. 732r to 737v.

10. Ibid.

11. Richard W. Meade to Louis DuBourg, 12 May 1827, *Scritture originali, 1827*, vol. 940, fols. 692r to 694r; Louis G. V. DuBourg to Propaganda Fide, 13 June 1827, fol. 690.

"FATAL ARTICLES OF PEACE"

1. John Hughes to Thomas Hayden, 3 July 1827, reprinted in Hassard, *Life of . . . John Hughes*: 61–62; St. Mary's Minute Book, fol. 113; "Petition of the trustees of the Church of St. Mary . . . to . . . Pope Leo XII," 12 July 1827, *Congressi, 6, Scisma di Filadelfia. 1819–1829*, fols. 602 and 603r. Thomas Hayden's departure from St. Mary's was quite voluntary. He was dissatisfied with his position there and asked to be allowed to return to his rural mission at Bedford where his parents resided. The reasons for his request are unclear. In addition to the disturbances accompanying the feud between William Harold and Bishop Conwell, there seems to have been some dissatisfaction with the allocation of clerical salaries at St. Mary's. See Hassard, *Life of . . . John Hughes*: 56–57. Hughes briefly served as a replacement for Harold at St. Mary's, but found the experience intolerable and soon he too resigned his pastorship. See John Hughes to Thomas Hayden, 3 July 1827, reprinted in ibid., 61–62.

2. Simon Bruté to John Hughes, 22 March 1827, cited in ibid.: 57.

3. Henry Conwell to *Propaganda Fide*, 20 October 1826, *Scritture originali, 1827*, vol. 940, fols. 579 and 580r; 20 November 1826, ibid., fol. 642r; to Cardinal Cappelari, 17 March 1827, *Congressi, 6, Scisma di Filadelfia. 1819–1829*, fols. 576r to 578r; Henry Conwell to Cardinal Cappelari, 20 March 1827, ibid., fol. 586r.

4. Ambrose Maréchal to Propaganda Fide, 16 November 1826, *Scritture originali, 1827*, vol. 940, fols. 601r to 603v; John England, *Works*, 5: 204, 207. See also Louis DuBourg to Propaganda Fide, 13 June 1827, *Scritture originali riferite nelle congregazioni generali 1827*, vol. 940, fol. 690; B. J. Flaget to Propaganda Fide, 20 August 1827, *Congressi, 9, 1827–1828* fols. 120 and 121; 24 March 1827, ibid., fol. 224.

5. Ambrose Maréchal to Propaganda Fide, 6 April 1827, *Scritture originali, 1827*, vol. 940, fol. 640; Henry Conwell to Ambrose Maréchal, 16 October 1823, AAB file 15 B13. See also Henry Conwell to Propaganda Fide, 14 July 1826, in which he requests reassignment to Ireland, *Scritture originali, 1827*, vol. 940, fol. 644.

6. Ambrose Maréchal to Propaganda Fide, 6 April 1827, *Scritture originali, 1827*, vol. 941, fols. 771r to 774v; see also Marechal to Prefect of Propaganda, 24 September 1826, copy in Philadelphia Archives, 28 September 1826, *Congressi, 8, 1823–1826*: fol. 665r to 667v.

7. Michael Egan to John Hughes, 1827, cited in Hassard, *Life of . . . John Hughes*: 58.

8. Memorandum of Guiseppe Cardinal Fesch, 30 April 1827, copy in Philadelphia Archives; Cardinal Cappellari to the American prelates, 19 May 1827, reprinted in Kirlin, *Catholicity in Philadelphia*: 257–58; Cardinal Cappelari to Henry Conwell, 19 May 1827, reprinted in Griffin, "Life of Bishop Conwell," *Records* 28 (1917): 311–13.

9. Henry Conwell to the Trustees of St. Mary's Church, 20 July 1827, reprinted in Kirlin, *Catholicity in Philadelphia*: 259; "Address to the Congregation of St. Mary's Church," 22 July 1827, in Griffin, "Life of Bishop Conwell," *Records* 28 (1917): 316; Trustees of St. Mary's to Pope Leo XII, 7 August 1827, *Congressi, 6, Scisma di Filadelfia. 1819–1829*, fols. 617r and 618.

10. Henry Conwell to Cardinal Capellari, July, 1827 cited in Tourscher, *The Hogan Schism*, 163; to Ambrose Maréchal, 19 July 1827, reprinted in Griffin, "Life of Bishop Conwell," *Records* 28 (1917): 311.

11. Propaganda Fide to Henry Conwell, *Lettere, 1827*, vol. 308, fol. 374; Julius Cardinal Somaglia to Cardinal Cappelari, 25 June 1827, *Congressi, 6, Scisma di Filadelfia. 1819–1829*, fol. 598; Propaganda Fide to Julius Cardinal Somaglia, 30 June 1827, *Lettere, 1827*, vol. 308, fols. 407 and 408r; Secretary of Propaganda to the Cardinals of Propaganda, ibid., fol. 487r.

12. Secretary of Propaganda to Henry Conwell, 11 August 1827, *Lettere, 1827*, vol. 308, fols. 511 and 512r; Henry Conwell to the Trustees of St. Mary's Church, 19 October 1827, cited in Tourscher, *Hogan Schism*: 169–70.

HAROLD DEFIANT

1. John Hughes to Simon Bruté, 31 January 1828, reprinted in Hassard, *Life of Hughes*: 64–66.

2. Cardinal Cappelari to Henry Conwell, 8 March 1828, reprinted in Griffin, "Life of Bishop Conwell," *Records* 28 (1917): 325–26; to William Harold, ibid.: 326–27. Word of Matthews's appointment did not reach Philadelphia until June of 1828. Henry Conwell to Cardinal Cappelari, 14 November 1827, copy not found but its contents are discussed in Cardinal

Cappelari to Henry Conwell, 8 March 1828, reprinted in Griffin, "Life of Bishop Conwell" *Records* 28 (1917): 325–26.

3. Henry Conwell to Archibald Randall, 17 October 1827, reprinted in Griffin, "Life of Bishop Conwell," *Records* 28 (1917): 319. This letter was published in the *Aurora* on 22 October 1827. John Ryan to Henry Conwell, 17 October 1827, *Congressi, 6, Scisma di Filadelfia. 1819–1829*, fol. 626. The trustees' conference with Bishop Conwell is noted in Griffin, "Life of Bishop Conwell," *Records* 28 (1917): 320. The trustees even went so far as to appoint a committee to investigate the bishop's selection of pastors for their church. On November 7 the committee reported back that William Harold and John Ryan were acceptable appointments. Bishop Conwell, who had been presiding at the meeting, left in protest whereupon Richard Meade took his seat as president of the board. See ibid.: 321.

4. William Harold to Ambrose Maréchal, April 1827, cited in ibid.: 257–58.

5. The circumstances surrounding the denunciation of William Harold are detailed in Hassard, *Life of Hughes*: 57–58. John Hughes was a reluctant signatory to this document. The suit is discussed on 58–59. See also Henry Conwell to Cardinal Cappelari, 1827, *Congressi, 6, Scisma di Filadelfia. 1819–1829*, fol. 564; "Legal summons to Baxter," 6 July 1827, ibid., fol. 604; "Legal summons to Rev. B. Keenan," 30 July 1827, ibid., fol. 696; Ambrose Maréchal to Dr. Gradwell 22 June 1827, cited in Hughes, *Jesuits in North America*, Documents 1: 574; Propaganda Fide to Ambrose Maréchal, 8 September 1827, *Lettere*, 1827, vol. 308, fol. 573v.

6. John Hughes to Simon Bruté, 31 January 1828, 2 May 1828, reprinted in Hassard, *Life of Hughes*: 64–66, 66–67. The slate of candidates elected in 1828 is noted in Griffin, "Life of Bishop Conwell," *Records* 28 (1917): 324.

7. For representative complaints from Philadelphia to Rome, see Henry Conwell to Cardinal Cappelari, 1827, *Congressi, 6, Scisma di Filadelfia. 1819–1829*, fol. 604; Committee of Philadelphia Catholics to Julius Cardinal Somaglia, 14 November 1827, ibid., fols. 628 and 629r; Henry Conwell to Anthony Kohlmann, 1 December 1827, ibid., fols. 630 and 631. Bishop Conwell's reluctance to leave Philadelphia is discussed in Secretary of Propaganda to Luigi Lambruschini, papal nuncio in Paris, 6 September 1828, cited in Nolan, *Kenrick*: 71. On Propaganda's concern about Harold and Ryan, see Cardinal Cappelari to Archbishop Maréchal, 24 November 1827, AAB file 22 S9. According to the papal nuncio at Paris, "it was believed in the Holy See that [the Philadelphia] disputes could only be settled, and harmony restored, by calling the bishop to Rome, and requesting Messrs. Harold and Ryan to reside for a short time at Cincinnati." See James Brown to Henry Clay, 13 October 1828, in England Works, 5: 222. The letters from Cardinal Cappelari to Henry Conwell and William Harold are reprinted in Griffin, "Life of Bishop Conwell," Records 28 (1917): 325–26.

8. Henry Conwell, *To the Public in General Who May Feel Interested in the Case Herein Specified* (Philadelphia, 22 May 1828); Henry Conwell to the

Board of Trustees, 25 June 1828, reprinted in Griffin, "Life of Bishop Conwell," *Records* 28 (1917): 320; see also 331, 333. The appeal to Baltimore is noted in Shea, *History of the Church in the United States*, 3: 259. See also William V. Harold and John Ryan to Cardinal Cappellari, 30 June 1828 [incorrect date], in Griffin, "Life of Bishop Conwell," *Records* 28 (1917): 334–39; *Exemplar Authenticum Epistolae, quam Dominus Harold simul cum Joanne Ryan Scripsit, ad Eminentissianum Cardinalem Cappellari . . .* (Philadelphia, 1828).

9. William V. Harold and John Ryan to Cardinal Cappellari, 30 June 1828. We should note that this was precisely the same reason given by William Hogan for his refusal to leave Philadelphia eight years earlier.

10. Ibid.

11. William V. Harold, *Letter to the Hon. Henry Clay, Sec'y of State. With Letter of Daniel Brent to Mr. Brown* (Philadelphia, 2 July 1828), copy in Philadelphia Archives, reprinted in England, *Works*, 5: 214–16, and Tourscher, *Hogan Schism*: 222–25.

12. Ibid.; John Ryan to Henry Clay, 2 July 1828, in England, *Works*, 5: 216; to Michael Ryan, 28 October 1828, reprinted in Nolan, *Kenrick*: 73.

13. Daniel Brent to James Brown, 9 July 1828, in England *Works*, 5: 219–20, copy in Philadelphia Archives; also reprinted in *Researches* 28 (1911): 184–86. When informed of the use to which these materials were being put, Daniel Brent apologized to William Harold and John Ryan and expressed his disapproval of the administrator's conduct, but still said that he felt that he had done the right thing in provoding Matthews with the information he sought. See Daniel Brent to William Harold and John Ryan, ibid.: 220.

14. Nolan, *Kenrick*: 73; William Matthews to Luigi Lambruschini, 11 July 1828, *Congressi, 6, Scisma di Filadelfia. 1819–1829*, fol. 728r; to Anthony Kohlmann, 11 July 1828, ibid., 729r; Luigi Lambruschini to Cardinal Bernetti, Papal Secretary of State, 11 August 1828, ibid., fols. 727; to Cardinal Cappellari, 27 August 1828, ibid. fol. 715.

15. Cardinal Bernetti, Papal Secretary of State to Luigi Lambruschini, 6 September 1828, cited in ibid.: 74; James Brown to Henry Clay, 13 October 1828, reprinted in England, *Works*, 5: 221–23; Luigi Lambruschini to Cardinal Cappellari, 26 September 1828, *Congressi, 6, Scisma di Filadelfia. 1819–1829*, fols. 747 and 748, English translation in Nolan, *Kenrick*: 75–76.

16. On the attitude of the Adams administration see Henry Clay to James Brown, 22 November 1828, reprinted in England, *Works*, 5: 223. William Matthews to Henry Clay, 10 October, 11 October 1828, reprinted in ibid.: 220–21. Archbishop Whitfield's letter to John Adams is cited in Nolan, *Kenrick*: 74, as are John England's contacts with Harold and Ryan.

17. John England to William Harold, 17 September 1829, reprinted in *Works*, 5: 225–26.

18. John England to Andrew Jackson, 26 September 1830, reprinted in ibid.: 227–28.

19. "Opinion of Mr. Taney" and "Opinion of Mr. Gaston" reprinted in ibid.: 231–32.

20. Bishop England's interview with President Jackson is reported in ibid.: 228.

CONWELL RETURNS

1. William Harold to Michael Ryan, 7 November 1828, cited in Nolan, *Kenrick*: 77; to John England, reprinted in *Works*, 5: 226; to Henry Clay, reprinted in ibid.: 224–25. On the apprehension of a Jesuit conspiracy against the Dominicans, see also John Ryan to John Savage, n.d., cited in Nolan, *Kenrick*: 77.

2. Propaganda's ultimatum to Harold and Ryan was simultaneously communicated to William Matthews and Archbishop Whitfield. See Cardinal Cappellari to James Whitfield, 21 April 1829, AAB file 23 Q6. Nolan, *Kenrick*: 79, notes Harold's delaying tactics through the summer of 1829. See also William Matthews to the Prefect of Propaganda, 27 August 1829, *Congressi, 10, 1829–1832*, fol. 163. William Matthews delivered Propaganda's "final decision" to Harold on July 23. See William Matthews to William Harold, 23 July 1829, ibid., fol. 151. Ryan's departure is noted in William Matthews to Secretary of Propaganda Fide, 27 August 1829, ibid., fol. 161. See also William Matthews to Propaganda Fide, 26 October 1829, ibid., fol. 231. Harold's departure is noted in "Diary of Patrick Kenny," *Records* 9 (1898): 318, entry of 20 September 1829.

3. "Catholics of Philadelphia" to William Harold, 16 September 1829, cited in Nolan, *Kenrick*: 79. The public meeting is noted in Shea, *History of the Church in the United States*, vol. 3: 259. See also Association of the Friends of Ireland to Pope Pius VIII, 3 November 1829. *Congressi, 6, Scisma di Filadelfia. 1819–1829*, fols. 775r to 778v. See also Michael Hurley to Henry Conwell, 30 August 1828, ibid. 736r to 741v.

4. John Hughes to Simon Bruté, 14 May 1828, reprinted in Hassard, *Life of Hughes*: 68; to Patrick Hayden, 31 October 1828, reprinted in ibid.: 69–70; Michael Hurley to Henry Conwell, 30 September 1828, *Congressi, 6, Scisma di Filadelfia. 1819–1829*, fol. 677. See also Michael Hurley to Henry Conwell, 31 July 1828, ibid., fols. 709 and 710r.

5. Michael Hurley to Henry Conwell, January 1829, *Congressi, 10, 1829–1832*, fols. 51 and 52r; 30 January 1829, *Congressi, 6, Scisma di Filadelfia. 1819–1829*, fol. 674; J. Power to Henry Conwell, 20 September 1928, fols. 645 and 646r; 14 January 1829, fols. 649 and 650r; John Hughes to Henry Conwell, 29 January 1829, ibid., fols. 670 and 671r; Michael Hurley et al. to the Prefect of Propaganda, 19 February 1829, *Congressi, 10, 1829–1832*, fols. 70 and 72; B. Keenan et al. to Propaganda Fide, 8 March 1829, copy in Philadelphia Archives; Terence M'Girr to Propaganda Fide, 28 December 1828, ibid., fols.

262 and 263r. Matthews was of the opinion that Henry Conwell had instigated these petitions; see William Matthews to Henry Conwell, 26 February 1829, ibid., fol. 73r; to Cardinal Cappellari, 26 February 1829, ibid., fols. 74 and 75r; 27 November 1829, ibid., fol. 239.

6. Tourscher, *Hogan Schism*: 180; Nolan, *Kenrick*: 79–80; Henry Conwell to James Whitfield, 1 January 1829, AAB file 23 C6; to Anthony Kohlmann, 10 July 1829, *Congressi, 10, 1829–1832*, fols. 147r to 150v, English translation in Tourscher, *Hogan Schism*: 182; Propaganda Fide report to the Pope, 12 April 1829, *Congressi, 6, Scisma di Filadelfia. 1819–1829*, fol. 716. On Bishop Conwell's attempts to secure a see in Ireland, see Patrick Kelly to Henry Conwell, 5 November 1828, *Congressi, 10, 1829–1832*, fol. 1; 9 January 1829, ibid.: fols 3 and 4; 29 January 1829, ibid., fol. 5; 30 April 1829; ibid., fol. 99, Henry Conwell to the Prince of Musignano, 8 May 1829, ibid., fol. 103.

7. Henry Conwell to Cardinal Cappellari, 11 May 1829, cited in Nolan, *Kenrick*: 81. William Matthews to Cardinal Cappellari, 26 February 1829, copy in Philadelphia Archives.

8. Propaganda Fide report to the Pope, 12 April 1829, *Congressi, 6, Scisma di Filadelfia. 1819–1829*, fol. 716; Propaganda Fide Memoir, n.d., *Congressi, 10, 1829–1832*, fols. 292r to 294v; Cardinal Cappellari to Henry Conwell, 30 May 1829, summary printed in Nolan, *Kenrick*: 82–83. Henry Conwell to Anthony Kohlmann, 10 July 1829, *Congressi, 10, 1829–1832*, fols. 147r to 150v; Luigi Lambruschini to Propaganda Fide, 31 August 1829, ibid., fol. 171; Frederic Résé to Propaganda Fide, 5 October 1829, ibid., fols. 209 and 210r. (Résé, who four years later became bishop of Detroit, and Bishop Portier travelled with Conwell on his return journey.)

9. John Hughes to John Purcell, 21 December 1829, reprinted in Hassard, *Life of Hughes*: 96–97; James Whitfield to Cardinal Cappellari, 24 October 1829, cited in Nolan, *Kenrick*: 87; John Larkin to Nicholas Wiseman, 12 February 1827, reprinted in *Catholic Historical Review*, 43 (1957): 460–70, quote is from 467.

THE PROVINCIAL COUNCIL

1. James Whitfield to Mauro Cardinal Cappellari, 26 March 1829, cited in Nolan, *Kenrick*: 83. Cappellari to James Whitfield, 18 July 1829, AAB file 23 Q7; Whitfield to Nicholas Wiseman, 28 September 1829, *Congressi, 10, 1829–1832*, fol. 191.

2. Archbishop Whitfield had first requested permission to call a council in the spring of 1828, shortly after Archbishop Maréchal's death. Permission was granted by Pope Leo XII in August of that year. Letters announcing the council were sent to the suffragans in December 1828 and the council met on October 20, 1829. On the council itself, see Peter Guilday, *A History of the*

Councils of Baltimore (1791–1884) (New York: 1932): 81–99. James Hennesey, "Papacy and Episcopacy in Eighteenth and Nineteenth Century American Catholic Thought" *Records* 77 (1966): 177–89. On Rome's greater involvement in American affairs after 1820, see Carey, *People, Priests, and Prelates*: 243–65. Carey sees a marked change in the Holy See's policy toward the institution of trusteeism taking place around 1820 and links it specifically to petitions from American bishops and a secret trip to Rome by Ambrose Maréchal in 1822. I would argue for a much greater degree of continuity in Rome's policy. Prior to 1820 the Holy See made limited concessions to lay and clerical sensibilities, but these were confined to the creation of new sees and the appointment of Irish bishops over the protests of the French Archbishop Maréchal and at no time suggested any attempt on Rome's part to accommodate republican or liberal ideas or practices. As I have argued elsewhere, Catholic church officials were always sensitive to difficulties arising out of national differences while maintaining hostility to liberal innovations. After 1820 the Holy See extended ever-greater controls over American bishops, prescribing and modifying policies and even (in the case of Henry Conwell) removing persons they deemed incompetent, but the general policy of unrelenting hostility to liberal and republican innovations was unchanged, and may even have intensified. At the same time the continuing sensitivity of Propaganda to ethnic and national differences is reflected in the choice in 1828 of James Whitfield as Archbishop Maréchal's coadjutor and successor. According to Peter Guilday, the choice of Whitfield was dictated to some extent by the fact that he was of English descent and thus not a participant in the continuing controversies among French, German, and Irish Catholics. See Guilday, *Life of England*, 2; 112. On the relationship of Rome to the American church, see also Thomas F. Casey, *The Sacred Congregation de Propaganda Fide and the Revision of the First Provincial Council of Baltimore (1829–1830)* (Rome, 1957), quote is from p. v.

3. "Papal Audience of 8 August 1819," *Udienze di N. S.: Foglio per l'udienzam* no. 26, items 5, 7, vol. 57, fols. 675, 676v; Carey, *People, Priests, and Prelates*: 260, 262. G. Mazzetti to Propaganda, 26 January 1820, cited in ibid.: 262; *The Brief of His Holiness, Pope Pius the Seventh, Addressed to Ambrose, Archbishop of Baltimore, To His Suffragan Bishops, To the Administrators of the Temporalities of the Churches, and To All the Faithful In the United States of America* (no publisher listed, 1822).

4. Propaganda Fide to Ambrose Maréchal 27 July 1822, *Congressi, 3, 1821–22*, fols. 834r to 838r; Carey, *People, Priests, and Prelates*: 261–62.

5. Guilday, *History of the Councils of Baltimore*: 90–93; Casey, *Propaganda . . . and the First Provincial Council*: 71, 77, 81, 84.

6. "Resolutions of Archbishop and Suffragans," n.d. [1829], AAB file 23 V6.

7. Ibid.

8. Ibid.; Peter Guilday, *The National Pastorals of the American Hierarchy (1792–1919)* (Washington, 1923): 33.

9. Ibid.: 33, 50–51.

10. Carey, *People, Priests, and Prelates*: 214, 253. On England's hopes for the 1829 council, see *An Immigrant Bishop*: 144.

11. Carey, *An Immigrant Bishop*: 146–47, John England to Paul Cullen, 13 May 1834, "Papers Relating to the Church in America, from the portfolios of the Irish College at Rome," *Records* 7 (1896): 481; also cited in Guilday, *Life of England*, 1: 537.

12. Patrick W. Carey, "American Catholic Romanticism, 1830–1888," *Catholic Historical Review*, 74 (1988): 590–606, quote is from 593 n. 7; Margaret Mary Reher, *Catholic Intellectual Life in America: A Historical Study of Persons and Movements* (New York, 1989), chap. 1, "Enlightenment and Episcopal Leadership, 1780–1830"; David O'Brien, *Public Catholicism*, chap. 2, "Republican Catholicism"; James Hennessey, "Roman Catholicism: The Maryland Tradition."

13. Guilday, *National Pastorals*: 23, 29.

KENRICK

1. Francis Kenrick's early life and education are treated in Nolan, *Kenrick*: 1–33, and in John J. O'Shea, *The Two Kenricks: Most Rev. Francis Patrick, Archbishop of Baltimore; Most Rev. Peter Richard, Archbishop of St. Louis* (Philadelphia, 1904): 1–39.

2. Nolan, *Kenrick*: 31; O'Shea, *The Two Kenricks*: 31; Francis Kenrick to his mother, 8 May 1821, reprinted in ibid.: 31–33. Michael O'Connor, *Archbishop Kenrick and His Work* (Philadelphia, 1867): 7. Several of Kenrick's writings, especially his *Theological Dogmatica* (Philadelphia, 1840) and *The Primacy of the Apostolic See . . . Vindicated*, advance ultramontane positons. Kenrick's desire to be assigned to the American mission is noted in Propaganda Fide to Archbishop Troy, 5 May 1821, *Lettere*, 1821, vol. 302, fols. 186v and 187; to Bishop Flaget, ibid.: fols. 193 and 194r.

3. On Kenrick's physical appearance and demeanor, see Nolan, *Kenrick*: 29, 39, 41; O'Connor, *Kenrick and His Work*: 5, 7.

4. Francis Kenrick to his mother, 1 August 1827, reprinted in Nolan, *Kenrick*: 47–48.

5. Nolan, *Kenrick*: 46–47; Martin J. Spalding, *Sketches of the Life, Times and Character of the Rt. Rev. Benedict Joseph Flaget, First Bishop of Louisville* (New York, 1852): 257.

6. Ibid: 50; M. Spalding, *Life of Bishop Flaget*: 259–60; *Sketches of the Early Catholic Missions of Kentucky from their Commencement in 1787 to the Jubilee in 1826–7* (Louisville, 1844): 293, 298–99.

7. Nolan, *Kenrick*: 46–50, 52; John Spalding, *The Life of the Most Reverend M. J. Spalding, D.D., Archbishop of Baltimore* (New York, 1873), Bishop Joseph Flaget to Rev. Stephen Badin, 29 September 1826, cited in M. Spalding, *Early*

Catholic Missions of Kentucky: 291–92; M. Spalding, *Life of Bishop Flaget*: 258–59; Benjamin Webb, *The Centenary of Catholicism in Kentucky* (Louisville, 1884): 99 ff.

8. Robert Gorman, *Catholic Apologetic Literature in the United States (1784–1858)* (Washington, D.C., 1939), 51; Nolan, *Kenrick*: 50–51; Spalding, *Catholic Missions of Kentucky*: 298; Francis Kenrick, *Sermons on Baptism* (Bardstown, 1829). A revision of this work, expanded to include an attack on the beliefs of the Society of Friends, was published under the title *Treatise on Baptism and a Treatise on Confirmation* in Philadelphia in 1843.

9. Nolan, *Kenrick*: 53, 56–60.

10. James Whitfield to Cardinal Cappellari, 24 October 1829, reprinted in ibid: 87–88; William Matthews to Cardinal Cappellari, 27 November, 1829, *Congressi, 10, 1829–1832*, fol. 239; Henry Conwell to Cardinal Cappellari, 30 November 1829, ibid., fols. 245 and 246r. On Bishop Flaget's protest, see Benedict Flaget to Propaganda Fide, 14 April 1830, ibid., fol. 352.

11. Francis Kenrick to Cardinal Cappellari, 22 February 1827, copy in Philadelphia Archives; 20 October 1828, *Congressi, 6, Scisma di Filadelfia*: fols. 750 and 751; "Undated memorandum on the Philadelphia affair," ibid., fols. 756r to 758r; Cardinal Cappellari to Francis Kenrick, ibid., 759r and 760v. See also Francis Kenrick to Cardinal Cappellari, 20 May 1827, copy in Philadelphia Archives, in which he denounces Bishop Conwell's agreement with the trustees of St. Mary's and suggests that the bishop be removed from Philadelphia. Propaganda solicited regular reports from Kenrick on "the state of the American Church." See Propaganda Fide to Francis Kenrick, 29 June 1822, *Lettere*, 1830, vol. 303, fol. 496. See also James Whitfield to John England, April 1830, reprinted in Griffin, "Life of Bishop Conwell," *Records* 29 (1918): 171–72. In Kentucky and later in Philadelphia Kenrick recruited young men for the priesthood and sent many of them to Propaganda for education. See Francis Kenrick to Propaganda Fide, 26 March 1830, *Congressi, 10, 1829–1832*, fol. 332r; 1 April 1830, ibid., 342. The general convocation of the cardinals of Propaganda is discussed in Nolan, *Kenrick*: 90–91.

12. Benedict Flaget to Cardinal Cappellari, 11 October 1829, reprinted in Nolan, *Kenrick*: 85–86; James Whitfield to Cardinal Cappellari, 24 October 1829, cited in ibid.: 86–87.

13. John Hughes to John Purcell, 24 March 1830, reprinted in Hassard, *Hughes*: 97–98; to James Whitfield, 5 May 1830, AAB file 23 J9.

14. Cardinal Cappellari to James Whitfield, 13 March 1830, AAB file 23 Q 10; James Whitfield to John England, April 1830, reprinted in Griffin, "Life of Bishop Conwell," *Records* 29 (1918): 171–72; Cardinal Cappellari to Francis Kenrick, 13 March 1830, reprinted in Nolan, *Kenrick*: 92–93; to Henry Conwell, 13 March 1830, cited in Nolan, *Kenrick*: 91–92.

15. Details concerning Francis Kenrick's consecration are presented in Nolan, *Kenrick*: 98–99. Francis Kenrick to Cardinal Cappellari, 5 May 1830,

Congressi, 10, 1829–1832, fols. 369 and 370r; 6 May 1830, ibid., fol. 371r; 11 June 1830, ibid., fols. 388 and 389r; John Hughes to James Whitfield, 5 May 1830, AAB file 23 J9.

THE RESTORATION CHURCH

1. There are several excellent treatments of the reorganization of the Roman Catholic Church in the nineteenth century. My account draws heavily from J. Derek Holmes, *The Triumph of the Holy See: A Short History of the Papacy in the Nineteenth Century* (London, 1978); Cuthbert Butler, *The Vatican Council* (London, 1962); Roger Aubert et al., *Between Revolution and Restoration;* and Friedrich Heyer, *The Catholic Church from 1648 to 1870* (London, 1969), trans. D. W. D. Shaw, especially chap. 7.
2. Heyer, *The Catholic Church from 1648 to 1870*: 151.
3. On Tridentine Catholicism, see John Bossy, "The Counter-Reformation and the People of Catholic Europe," *Past and Present* 47 (1970): 51–70. For an excellent exposition of the parish orientation of Tridentine reforms as they were applied in America, see Jay P. Dolan, *The Immigrant Church: New York's Irish and German Catholics, 1815–1865* (Baltimore, 1975).
4. Aubert, *Between Revolution and Restoration*: 92–93. For a systematic treatment of the conflict between ultramontane reformers and Gallican church establishments, see Richard F. Costigan, *Rohrbacher and the Ecclesiology of Ultramontanism* (Rome, 1980). See also Roger Aubert, "Progressive Centralization on Rome," in Aubert et al., *The Church in A Secularized Society,* vol. 5 in *The Christian Centuries,* Janet Sondheimer, trans.: 56–69. Jonathan Sperber describes in a cleric's protest against restrictions on religious celebrations in Münster what he calls "a classic formulation of the ultramontanist mentality" as "a priest defends popular holidays and the pious common people against the attack of an economically calculating bureaucracy, without missing the opportunity to take a sideswipe at the Protestants"; see his *Popular Catholicism in Nineteenth-Century Germany* (Princeton, 1984): 23. By contrast the "enlightened" clerics found support among the bourgeoisie and the elite [22].
5. Aubert, *Between Revolution and Restoration*: 192–93.
6. Ibid., 92; Roger Aubert, "Les Progres de l'Ultramontanisme," in Augustin Filche and Victor Martin, eds., *Le Pontificat de Pie IX,* vol. 21 of *Histoire de l'Eglise* (Paris, 1963), 262–310; Costigan, *Rohrbacher.* On the relationship between revivalism and ultramontanism in nineteenth-century Prussia, see Sperber, *Popular Catholicism in Nineteenth-Century Germany*: 96–97. On the decline of religious standards in the first half of the nineteenth century and mid-century revivals in Germany and France, see J. Michael Phayer, *Sexual Liberation and Religion in Nineteenth-Century Europe* (London, 1977). On the

devotional revolution in France after 1850, see Thomas A. Kselman, *Miracles & Prophecies in Nineteenth-Century France* (New Brunswick, N.J., 1983).

7. J. Derek Holmes, *More Roman than Rome: English Catholicism in the Nineteenth Century* (London, 1978), 72, 84. For a criticism of Holmes's interpretation, see Gerard Connolly, "The Transubstantiation of Myth: towards a New Popular History of Nineteenth-Century Catholicism in England," *Journal of Ecclesiastical History*, 35 (1984): 78–104. See also Brian Fothergill, *Nicholas Wiseman* (London, 1963), and Denis R. Gwynn, *Cardinal Wiseman* (London, 1929). For contemporary reforms in the German states, see Sperber, *Popular Catholicism in Nineteenth-Century Germany*.

8. Desmond Brown, *Paul Cardinal Cullen and the Shaping of Modern Irish Catholicism* (Dublin, 1983): vii, viii; Emmet Larkin, "The Devotional Revolution in Ireland, 1850–1875," *American Historical Review* 77 (1972): 625–52.

9. Dale B. Light, "The Reformation of Philadelphia Catholicism, 1830–1860," *Pennsylvania Magazine of History & Biography*, 112 (1988): 375–405.

10. Ann Taves, *The Household of Faith*: 116, notes that "There is not much evidence of opposition to the Romanization of religious practice on the part of American bishops and priests." I would agree with regard to the bishops but would note the animosity expressed by traditionalist priests toward reforming bishops and would suggest that this feeling, at least in part, was a reaction against devotional innovations that changed the nature of Catholic worship in a fundamental way from the modes to which they were accustomed.

11. Statistics on the institutional growth of the Church are from the *Metropolitan Catholic Almanac, and Laity's Directory, for the United States . . . 1860* (Baltimore, 1860): 266. Francis Kenrick and John England are quoted in "The Missions of the United States in 1838," originally published in *Annals of the Propagation of the Faith* (September 1838), reprinted in *Researches* 8 (1891): 161–67. A recent study argues that most nineteenth-century immigrants from Catholic countries in Europe "were at best *potential* American Catholic parishioners." See Roger Finke and Rodney Stark, *The Churching of America 1776–1990: Winners and Losers in Our Religious Economy* (New Brunswick, 1992): 109.

12. On the origins of trusteeism, see Dolan, *American Catholic Experience*: 163–68. The inadequacy of many of the clergy was a subject of much discussion at the first provincial council of bishops in 1829.

13. Archbishop Martin J. Spalding's description of the mid-nineteenth century American church is reported in Robert D. Cross, *The Emergence of Liberal Catholicism in America* (Cambridge, Mass., 1958): 19.

14. The point that the Romanization of American Catholicism distanced it from the mainstream of American secular culture is made by Ann Taves in *The Household of Faith*: 113–14. David Montgomery, "The Shuttle and the Cross: Weavers and Artisans in the Kensington Riots of 1844," *Journal of Social History* 5 (1972): 378; William V. Shannon, *The American Irish: A Political and*

Social Portrait (New York, 1974): 20; Lawrence J. McCaffrey, *The Irish Diaspora in America* (Bloomington, 1976): 8; Sheridan Gilley, "The Roman Catholic Church and the Nineteenth-Century Irish Diaspora," *Journal of Ecclesiastical History* 35 (1984): 188.

15. On traditional Catholic practices in England, Ireland, and Germany, see Lynn H. Lees, *Exiles of Erin: Irish Emigrants in Nineteenth Century London* (New York: 1979); David Miller, "Irish Catholicism and the Great Famine," *Journal of Social History* 9 (1975): 81–98; S. J. Connolly, *Priest and People in Pre-Famine Ireland, 1780–1845* (Dublin, 1982); Larkin, "Devotional Revolution"; Sperber, *Popular Catholicism in Nineteenth-Century Germany.*

16. Statistics on churches and Catholic population from Nolan, *Kenrick*: 105–6; John Hughes to John Purcell, 23 April 1829, reprinted in Hassard, *Hughes*: 90. The St. Augustine parish census is reported in Kirlin, *Catholicity in Philadelphia*: 292–93. Testimony on religious attitudes was recorded in *A Full and Accurate Report of the Trial for Riot Before the Mayor's Court of Philadelphia on the 13th of October, 1831, Arising out of a Protestant Procession on the 12th of July . . .* (Philadelphia, 1831).

"GOOD SOLDIERS OF CHRIST JESUS"

1. "Bishop Kenrick's First Pastoral Letter," Nolan, *Kenrick*, Appendix B: 439–50. For comparison see Joseph Chinnici's description of Martin John Spalding's "corporate" view of the Church in *Living Stones*: 38–45. Chinnici suggests that Spalding's vision of the Church was inspired in large part by his reactions to Protestant bigotry and immigrant poverty in the United States. I would suggest rather that Spalding's training at the Urban College of the Propaganda was a major influence on his thinking and that he is fairly representative of restoration reformers throughout the Western world.

2. John England to Edward Fenwick, 22 September 1830, UNDA; Francis Kenrick to John Purcell, 24 August 1830, cited in Nolan, *Kenrick*: 112.

3. Francis Patrick Kenrick, *Diary and Visitation Record, 1830–1851*, Francis E. Tourscher trans. (Lancaster, Pa.: 1916): 31–44; see also Bishop J. Carroll McCormick, "The Difficulties of Bishop Conwell," manuscript, cited in Nolan, *Kenrick*: 109; Francis Kenrick to Propaganda Fide, 7 January 1831, *Congressi, 10, 1829–1832*, fols. 491 and 492; public Letter of Henry Conwell, 15 May 1831, original in Latin, English translation in Griffin, "Life of Bishop Conwell," *Records* 29 (1918): 181–82, 250–51.

4. Francis Kenrick to Propaganda Fide, 15 July 1830, *Section X, 10, 1829–1832*, fols. 411 and 412; John Hughes to James Whitfield, 5 May 1830, AAB file 23 J9.

5. Nolan, *Kenrick*: 112; Nolan also notes that the Irish clergy in Philadelphia made fun of Kenrick for his effeminate manner. John England

to Edward Fenwick, 22 September 1830, UNDA; Public Letter of Henry Conwell, 15 May 1831, original in Latin, English translation in Griffin, "Life of Bishop Conwell," *Records* 29 (1918): 181–82, 250–51; William Matthews to John Purcell, 25 September 1831, UNDA; Francis Kenrick to Propaganda Fide, 15 July 1830 *Congressi, 10, 1829–1832*, fols. 411 and 412; 9 August 1830, ibid., fols. 421 and 422.

6. "Bishop Kenrick's First Pastoral Letter"; Chinnici, *Living Stones*: 38.

7. Kenrick, *Diary*: 44, 45; Nolan, *Kenrick*: 117; the bishop's letter to the trustees is printed in *Address of the Trustees of St. Mary's Church to the Congregation, April 16, 1831* (Philadelphia, 1831). See also O'Connor, *Kenrick and His Work*: 8–9. Propaganda had assigned Bishop Conwell the income from the parish in Lancaster in 1826 in an attempt to make him financially independent of the trustees at St. Mary's. See Julius Cardinal Somaglia to Henry Conwell, 16 September 1826, copy in Philadelphia Archives.

8. *Address of the Trustees*; Kenrick, *Diary*: 45–46.

9. Francis Kenrick to Propaganda Fide, 7 January 1831, *Congressi, 10, 1829–1832*, fols. 491 and 492; John Hughes to John Purcell, 13 January 1831, reprinted in Hassard, *Hughes*: 113–14.

10. Kenrick, *Diary*: 46; John Hughes to John Purcell, 13 January 1831, reprinted in Hassard, *Hughes*: 114.

11. John Hughes to John Purcell, 13 January 1831, reprinted in Hassard, *Hughes*: 114.

INTERDICT

1. Kenrick, *Diary*: 47–50; Kirlin, *Catholicity in Philadelphia*: 268.

2. Francis Kenrick to Edward Fenwick, 17 May 1831, UNDA; Francis Kenrick, "(Circular.) To the Pewholders of St. Mary's Church," 12 April 1831, in Philadelphia Archives.

3. Kenrick, *Diary*: 48; Trustees statements cited in "The Cessation at St. Mary's," *Researches* 1 (1887): 83–89.

4. Francis Kenrick to Bishop Rosati, 17 May 1831, translated and reprinted in Nolan, *Kenrick*: 120; to James Whitfield, 17 May 1831, AAB file 23 K7; Henry Conwell to Archibald Randall, 13 May 1831, reprinted in *Researches* 1 (1887): 88–89. On Conwell's obstruction of his authority, see also Francis Kenrick to Propaganda Fide, 7 January 1831, *Congressi, 10, 1829–1832*, fols. 491 and 492.

5. James Whitfield to Propaganda Fide, 17 October 1831, *Congressi, 10, 1829–1832*, fols. 596 and 597r.

6. Francis Kenrick to James Whitfield, 17 May 1831, AAB file 23 K7; *Pastoral Address of the Right Rev. Dr. Kenrick to the congregation of St. Mary's, 22 April 1831* (Philadelphia, 1831).

7. O'Connor, *Archbishop Kenrick and His Work*: 7; Kenrick, "Missions of the United States": 162.

8. Francis Kenrick to James Whitfield, 17 May 1831, AAB file 23 K7.

9. Ibid.; Francis Kenrick to Bishop Rosati, 17 May 1831, cited in Nolan, *Kenrick*: 120; Henry Conwell to Archibald Randall, 13 May 1831, reprinted in *Researches* 1 (1887): 88–89; Francis Kenrick to John Keefe et al., 21 May 1831, reprinted in Kenrick, *Diary*: 50.

10. John Hughes to John Purcell, 24 May 1831, reprinted in Hassard, *Hughes*: 113; Kenrick to John Keefe, et al., 21 May 1831, reprinted in Kirlin, *Catholicity in Philadelphia*: 273–74; Kenrick, *Diary*: 51. Kenrick's methods left some residual anger among members of the board of trustees and this resulted in some minor skirmishes between them and the bishop. Through the summer of 1831 they refused to hold any meetings, and without their approval salaries could not be paid. Finally, Bishop Kenrick threatened to withdraw from the church and to turn it over to the Jesuits, who had their own sources of income and would not be dependent on the trustees. This brought an offer from the trustees to pay salaries on a quarterly basis. Kenrick refused this and demanded payment in a lump sum. At last, on December 6, 1831, the trustees capitulated to Kenrick's demand and granted him his full salary which he accepted "with bad grace." See Kenrick, *Diary*: 52–57.

11. Kenrick, *Dairy*: 52; Connelly, *History of the Archdiocese of Philadelphia*: 126–27. Henry Conwell lived on until 1842, surrounded by a bevy of relatives and cared for by the Jesuits who had taken charge of St. Joseph's Chapel. For income he was dependent upon occasional stipends voted him by St. Mary's trustees in lieu of the salary which, he continued to claim, had been "usurped" by Bishop Kenrick. See Griffin, "Life of Bishop Conwell," *Records* 29 (1918): 252–62, 360–73. Propaganda Fide to Francis Kenrick, 27 August 1831 *Lettere, 1831*, vol. 312, fols. 649 and 650.

12. Kenrick, *Diary*: 59, 63; Nolan, *Kenrick*: 127.

13. O'Connor, *Archbishop Kenrick and His Work*: 12; O'Shea, *The Two Kenricks*; Francis P. Kenrick, *Substance of a Sermon Preached in St. Patrick's Church, Pittsburgh, Pa. . . . (Pittsburgh, 1832)*. Kenrick, *Diary*: 63.

14. Nolan, *Kenrick*: 143–44; "Philadelphia's First Diocesan Synod, May 13–15, 1832," *Records* 54 (1943): 28–43; Kirlin, *Catholicity in Philadelphia*: 277–78.

15. Kirlin, *Catholicity in Philadelphia*: 285.

ROMAN CATHOLICS

1. "Report on the Condition of the Church of Philadelphia Made to Our Holy Father Pope Gregory XVI, June 1, 1838, by Francis Patrick Kenrick, Bishop of Arath and Coadjutor to the BsÊhop of Philadelphia," *Records* 38 (1927): 211. Francis Kenrick to Cardinal Cappellari, 15 July 1830, *Congressi*,

10, 1829–1832, fols. 411 and 412; to John Purcell, 13 August 1830, cited in Nolan, *Kenrick*: 112–13; "Philadelphia's First Diocesan Synod."

2. Nolan, "Philadelphia's First Diocesan Synod."

3. Nolan, *Kenrick*: 381–83; there is a discussion of the usage of the term "father" in *Researches* 18 (1901): 83, 174–75. There the title is described as an "innovation" of the time, "after the church in the United States had begun to shake off the trammels of Protestant surroundings and influence and the laity had become more Catholic in spirit; say about 1840, the period of the decline of the Trustee system." We may note that the sharp distinction between clergy and laity was also a repudiation of John Carroll's view of the church as a community of all believers. By Joseph Chinnici's account, Carroll "never described the priesthood in isolation from the community as a 'state' or 'independent' office, nor did he refer to the 'dignity of episcopal authority.'" See, *Living Stones*: 24.

4. Francis Kenrick to Propaganda Fide, 10 June 1829, cited in Casey, *Revisions of the First Provincial Council*: 45; to John Purcell, 24 August 1830, reprinted in Nolan, *Kenrick*: 112–13; ibid.: 56, 142, 143, 146; "Philadelphia's First Diocesan Synod": 42.

5. Taves: *Household of Faith*: 30, 89.

6. Nolan, *Kenrick*: 145, 281–82, 382; on the elaboration of music in the Church under Kenrick and his successors, see Michael H. Cross, "Catholic Choirs and Choir Music," *Records* 2 (1886): 115–26.

7. *Acta et decreta sacrorum conciliorum recentiorum collectio lacenses* 3: 502, cited in Joseph Chinnici, "Organization of the Spiritual Life: American Catholic Devotional Works, 1791–1866," *Theological Studies* 40 (1979): 231, 233–34. Taves, *Household of Faith*: 118. See also Guilday, *History of the Councils of Baltimore*: 255–70.

8. Kenrick, "Report on the Condition of the Diocese . . . 1838": 212.

THE BUILDING BISHOP

1. The Tridentine emphasis on parish organization is discussed in Dolan, *The Immigrant Church*. Figures on the institutional status of Philadelphia at the time of Kenrick's arrival and when he left are from Nolan, *Kenrick*: 433 and were originally compiled from various sources. See also Dennis Clark, "A Pattern of Urban Growth: Residential Development and Church Location in Philadelphia," *Records* 82 (1971): 158–70.

2. Comparative statistics for Philadelphia and other dioceses are from the *Catholic Directory* (Baltimore, 1833–1843).

3. Bishop Kenrick was particularly averse to having Irish clergymen in his diocese. He considered them to be poorly educated and infected with Gallican tendencies. Thus, despite his incessant pleading to Rome for more clerics and his active recruitment of German missionaries, Kenrick was extremely

reluctant to accept Irish missionaries into his domain. See Lawrence F. Flick, "Biographical Sketch of Rev. Peter Henry Lemke," *Records* 9 (1898): 145–46; Richard J. Purcell, "Missionaries From All Hallows (Dublin) to the United States, 1842–1865," *Records* 53 (1942): 204–49. See also Nolan, *Kenrick*: 13–14. Kenrick's suspicion of the missionary orders is noted in John P. Marschall, "Kenrick and the Paulists: A Conflict of Structures and Personalities," *Church History* 38 (1969): 88–105. Translations of the extensive correspondence between Bishop Kenrick and Cardinal Cullen are in the Philadelphia Archives. See also George E. O'Donnell, *St. Charles Seminary, Philadelphia* (Philadelphia, 1964).

4. On the importance of parish associations, see Dolan, *The Immigrant Church*. On the development of parish societies in Philadelphia, see D. H. Mahoney, *Historical Sketches of the Catholic Churches and Institutions of Philadelphia* (Philadelphia, 1895). See also Kathleen Gavigan, "The Rise and Fall of Parish Cohesiveness in Philadelphia," *Records* 86 (1975): 107–31; J. Thomas Scharf and Thompson Westcott, *History of Philadelphia*, 2: 1376–79; Tourscher, *Old St. Augustine's*; *Constitution of the St. Augustine's Catholic Temperance Beneficial Society, 1840* (Philadelphia, 1840); *The Constitution and By Laws of the St. Augustine Reading Room Society of Philadelphia* (Philadelphia, 1853).

5. Nolan, *Kenrick*: 385–92. Guilday, *Pastorals of the American Hierarchy*: 24–25, 28. Once again the reform in Philadelphia proceeded in advance of similar efforts elsewhere. Kathleen Gavigan has pointed out that prior to 1844 Philadelphia already had eight free parochial schools and added six more by 1851 and another twelve by 1866. By contrast Boston in 1850 had only one parochial school, had added only two more by 1860, and finally began to construct large numbers of schools only after that date. She concludes that Boston was "moving in the direction of alternative institutions for Roman Catholics twenty years later than Philadelphia." See, "Rise and Fall of Parish Cohesiveness": 114.

6. The story of the serving woman is recounted in Hassard, *Hughes*: 117.

7. Kirlin, *Catholicity in Philadelphia*: 275; Nolan, *Kenrick*: 125–27; Kenrick, *Diary*: 50; Francis E. Tourscher, *The Kenrick-Frenaye Correspondence, 1830–1862* (Philadelphia, 1920): viii. Tourscher, in "Marc Antony Frenaye—A Sketch," *Records* 38 (1927): 132–43, gives the amount of the loan at $30,000. No interest was paid on it and forty years after it was made the loan still was unpaid. Frenaye was also involved in a number of other building projects. Tourscher notes his contribution, saying, "After years of schisms and unrest Church government and Catholic social life were taking a better form during the twenty-one years of Bishop Kenrick's stay in Philadelphia. The generosity of Frenaye laid a material foundation for much that was done." See Tourscher, "Frenaye": 143.

8. Short biographies of both Charles and Dennis Kelly are found in John H. Campbell, *History of the Friendly Sons of St. Patrick and of the Hibernian Society for the Relief of Emigrants from Ireland* (Philadelphia, 1892): 442–43. See also Dennis Clark, "Kellyville: Immigrant Enterprise," *Pennsylvania History* 39 (1972): 40–49. A fascinating account of Catholic life in Manayunk during the years when Jerome Keating dominated the community is "Reminiscence Pertaining to the Early History of Our Own Dear Manayunk Church of St. John the Baptist" by Francis Barat. This manuscript is reprinted in Eugene Murphy, *The Parish of St. John the Baptist, Manayunk: The First One Hundred Years* (Philadelphia, 1931): 39–54.

9. On John Keating's life and accomplishments, see J. Percy Keating, "John Keating and His Forbears," *Records* 39 (1918): 289–335.

10. Ibid.: 326, 333.

11. Ibid.; See also William and John J. Keating's biographies in Campbell, *Hibernian Society*.

12. Keating, "John Keating and His Forbears."

13. *Constitution and By-Laws of the DeSales Institute of Philadelphia* (Philadelphia, 1872): Keating, "John Keating and His Forbears": 326–27. Twenty-seven individuals who were noted in various sources as being strong supporters of Bishop Kenrick in his conflict with lay trustees were linked to city directories. They included six merchants, five "gentlemen," two manufacturers, two attorneys, two contractors, one doctor, one professor at the University of Pennsylvania, and five small proprietors. Only three members of this group listed occupations that could be considered working-class and they were by no means typical. They were Timothy Desmond, a "painter" whose father was a prominent attorney; Patrick Hayes, a "mariner" who was the nephew of Commodore John Barry, the Revolutionary War hero, and Michael Magrath, a "chandler" who was affluent enough to leave $30,000 to the church upon his death in 1853.

14. Barat, "Reminiscence": 41, 43–44, 46–47.

15. Kenrick, *Diary*: 47; Murphy, *Parish of St. John the Baptist*: 37; Campbell, *Hibernian Society*: 478.

16. Campbell, *Hibernian Society*: 442–43; Dennis Clark, "Kellyville: An Immigrant Enterprise"; Stephen N. Winslow, *Biographies of Successful Philadelphia Merchants* (Philadelphia, 1864): 158–61.

17. Anthony F. C. Wallace, *Rockdale: The Growth of an American Village in the Early Industrial Revolution* (New York: 1978).

B'HOYS AND SOCIETY MEN

1. On social stratification and differentiation associated with the impact of industrialism in Philadelphia, see Laurie, *Working People of Philadelphia*,

especially chap. 1, "The Sources of Industrial Diversity." See also Warner, *The Private City*, pt. 2, "The Big City." On neighborhood communities, see Light, "Class, Ethnicity and the Urban Ecology." On travel in the city, see Roger Miller, "Time-Geographic Assessment of the Impact of Horse-Car Transportation in Philadelphia, 1850–1860" (Ph.D. dissertation, University of California, Berkeley, 1979); Theodore Hersherg, Dale B. Light et al., "The 'Journey-to-Work': An Empirical Investigation of Work, Residence and Transportation, Philadelphia, 1850 and 1880," in Hershberg, ed., *Philadelphia: Work, Space, Family, and Group Experience in the Nineteenth Century* (New York, 1981).

2. The multiethnic nature of neighborhood associations is discussed in Light, "Class, Ethnicity, and the Urban Ecology."

3. Michael Feldberg, "Urbanization as a Cause of Violence: Philadelphia as a Test Case," in Davis and Haller, *Peoples of Philadelphia*: 53–69.

4. Ellis Paxton Oberholtzer, *Philadelphia: A History of the City and Its People* (Philadelphia, 1911), 2: 89. Bruce Laurie, *Working People of Philadelphia*: 60; See also Laurie, "Fire Companies and Gangs in Southwark: the 1840's," in Davis and Haller, *Peoples of Philadelphia*: 71–88, and Andrew Neilly, "The Violent Volunteers: A History of the Volunteer Fire Department of Philadelphia, 1763–1871" (Ph. D. dissertation, University of Pennsylvania, 1959). On the political importance of fire companies, see Harry C. Silcox, "William McMullen, Nineteenth Century Political Boss," *Pennsylvania Magazine of History and Biography*, 110 (1986): 389–412.

5. Nicholas B. Wainwright, ed., *A Philadelphia Perspective: The Diary of Sidney George Fisher, Covering the Years 1834–1871* (Philadelphia, 1967).

6. See Warner, *The Private City*, especially chap. 7, "Riots and the Restoration of Public Order"; David R. Johnson, *Policing the Urban Underworld: The Impact of Crime on the Development of the American Police, 1800–1887* (Philadelphia, 1979); Howard Gillette, Jr., "The Emergence of the Modern Metropolis: Philadelphia in the Age of Consolidation," in William W. Cutler III and Howard Gillette, eds., *The Divided Metropolis: Social and Spatial Dimensions of Philadelphia, 1800–1975* (Westport, 1980), 3–26; Elizabeth Geffen, "Industrial Development and Social Crisis, 1841–1854," in Russell F. Weigley, ed., *Philadelphia: A 300-Year History* (New York, 1982), 307–62; Marcia Carlisle, "Disorderly City, Disorderly Women: Prostitution in Antebellum Philadelphia," *Pennsylvania Magazine of History and Biography*, 110 (1986): 549–68; David R. Johnson, "Crime Patterns in Philadelphia, 1840–1870," in Davis and Haller, *Peoples of Philadelphia*: 89–110.

7. The clash between traditionalist cultures and the modernizing imperatives of industrial society are emphasized by many authors. The most important statement of this thesis is Herbert G. Gutman, "Work, Culture, and Society in Industrializing America, 1815–1919," *American Historical Review* 78 (1973): 531–87. For a treatment specific to Philadelphia, see Laurie,

Working People of Philadelphia, especially chap. 3, "Traditionalists: 'The Boys of Pleasure.'" See also Michael P. McCarthy, "The Philadelphia Consolidation of 1854: A Reappraisal," *Pennsylvania Magazine of History and Biography*, 110 (1986): 531–48. H. C. Watson, *Jerry Pratt's Progress or Adventures in the Hose House* (Philadelphia, 1855): 5. For another such alarmist tract, see Anon., *Life and Adventures of Charles Anderson Chester, the Notorious Leader of the Philadelphia "Killers"* (Philadelphia, 1850). On the prominence of the saloon in neighborhood communities, see Jon M. Kingsdale, "The 'Poor Man's Club': Social Functions of the Urban Working-Class Saloon," *American Quarterly* 25 (1973): 472–89.

8. See Light, "Class, Ethnicity and the Urban Ecology," especially chap. 3, "Economic Differentiation"; "The Role of Irish-American Organisations in Assimilation and Community Formation," in P. J. Drudy, ed., *Irish Studies 4: The Irish in America* (New York: 1985): 113–41.

9. Arthur M. Schlesinger, "Biography of a Nation of Joiners" *American Historical Review* 50 (1944): 1–25.

10. Thomas N. Brown, *Irish-American Nationalism* (Philadelphia, 1966): 34.

"THE ORDER OF THE DAY"

1. The pastoral letter was reprinted in the *Catholic Herald*, 25 June 1840. References to temperance sermons and conversions are found in Kenrick, *Diary*: 191–92, 196–97, 209, 212. On the popularity of temperance societies, see the *Catholic Herald*, 10 February, 28 April 1842. Marc A. Frenaye to Francis Kenrick, 24 July 1840, reprinted in Tourscher, *The Kenrick-Frenaye Correspondence*.

2. Bishop Kenrick's estimate is from his *Diary*: 191. For corroborating estimates on turnouts for Catholic temperance processions, see Edith Jeffrey, "Reform, Renewal and Vindication: Irish Immigrants and the Catholic Total Abstinence Movement in Ante-Bellum Philadelphia," *Pennsylvania Magazine of History and Biography*, 112 (1988): 407–32. We should also note that, following the example of Father Mathew in Ireland, Philadelphia churches issued a certificate to each person taking the pledge and therefore an accurate accounting would have been available to the bishop. On estimates for the city, see *Public Ledger*, 20 March 1841. On the proportion of Catholics in Philadelphia's population, see Michael Feldberg, *The Philadelphia Riots of 1844: A Study of Ethnic Conflict* (Westport, Conn., 1975): 20. The total abstinence reform also compares favorably to other movements that sought to organize the immigrant population. On July 4, 1841, for instance, Father Patrick Moriarty delivered a temperance sermon to benefit the city's Catholic orphanages that raised more than $1,000. Later in the same day he spoke on Irish

independence at a rally sponsored by the Philadelphia Repeal Association for the benefit of the same charities. This time he raised only $145.

3. Michael O'Connor to Paul Cullen, 6 July 1841, "Papers Relating to the Church in America": 348–49; Jeffrey, "Reform, Renewal and Vindication."

4. William George Read, *An Oration Delivered Before the Pennsylvania Catholic Total Abstinence Society at Philadelphia on the 4th of July, 1843* (Philadelphia, 1843). For a comparison with Whig thought, see Daniel Walker Howe, *The Political Culture of the American Whigs* (Chicago, 1979), especially chap. 4, "The Whig Interpretation of History." This was not the first occasion on which Read had addressed Philadelphia's Catholic bourgeoisie. See also *An Oration Delivered at the Second Commemoration of the Pilgrims of Maryland, at Philadelphia, May 10th, 1843* (Philadelphia, 1943); see also *Oration, Delivered at the First Commemoration of the Landing of the Pilgrims of Maryland; Celebrated May 10th, 1842, Under the Auspices of the Philodemic Society of Georgetown College* (Baltimore, 1842?).

5. Read, *Oration*: 7–8; Howe, *American Whigs*: 101–3.

6. Read, *Oration*: 15, 17, 21; Howe, *American Whigs*: 76–79.

7. Read, *Oration*: 8, 17, 20; Henry C. Carey, *Essay on the Rate of Wages: With an Examination of the Causes of the Differences in the Condition of the Laboring Population Throughout the World* (Philadelphia, 1835). Carey's distinction between normal commerce and exploitative capitalism and his relation to Whig economic theory are treated in Howe, *American Whigs*: 108–22.

8. Read, *Oration*: 2, 21–22. Compare to Howe, *American Whigs*: 19, 30–35, 52–53, 270–71.

9. Read, *Oration*: 22–23. Compare to Howe, *American Whigs*, 32, 35–37, 300–301.

10. P. B. Sheridan, Jr., "The Immigrant in Philadelphia, 1827–1860: The Contemporary Published Report" (Ph.D. dissertation, Georgetown University, 1957): 214. It might be argued that the temperance movement, because it was directly inspired by an Irish example, Father Mathew, was an authentic expression of traditional Irish culture, but within the context of nineteenth-century Ireland Mathew represented a "modernizing" rather than a traditionalist imperative. See H. F. Kearney, "Father Mathew: Apostle of Modernization," in Art Cosgrove and Donal McCarthey, eds., *Studies in Irish History* (Dublin, 1979).

11. *United States Gazette*, 13 May 1831.

12. James S. Buckingham, *The Eastern and Western States of America*, 3 vols. (London, 1842), 1: 567–68; Scharf and Westcott, *History of Philadelphia*, 2: 1380; Hassard, *Hughes*: 222; *Public Ledger*, 11 August 1842; 15 June 1843.

13. Laurie, *Working People of Philadelphia*: 46.

14. Ibid., 150. The classic statement of this position is Joseph R. Gusfield, *Symbolic Crusade: Status Politics and the American Temperance Movement* (Chicago, 1963). See also Paul E. Johnson, *A Shopkeeper's Millennium: Society*

and Revivals in Rochester, New York, 1815–1837 (New York, 1978); Howe, *American Whigs*, chap. 7, "The Evangelicals." Paul Kleppner, *The Cross of Culture, A Social Analysis of Midwestern Politics, 1850–1900* (New York, 1970). On Protestant members in Catholic associations, see Michael O'Connor to Paul Cullen, 8 July 1842, in Philadelphia Archives; *Catholic Herald*, 8 July 1841; Joan Bland, *Hibernian Crusade: The Catholic Total Abstinence Union in America* (Washington, 1951).

15. Francis Kenrick to Peter Richard Kenrick, 9 September 1843, reprinted in Nolan, *Kenrick*: 412–14; *Catholic Herald*, 27 August 1840; 25 March, 6 May 1841; 1 February 1844.

16. Alan Nevins, ed., *The Diary of Philip Hone* (New York, 1927), 2: 691; Scharf and Westcott, *History of Philadelphia*, 1: 663; Nolan, *Kenrick*: 316; Kenrick, *Diary*: 223–24. On the sudden emergence of a politically viable nativist movement in Philadelphia, see Leonard Tabachnik, "Origins of the Know-Nothing Party: A Study of the Native American Party in Philadelphia, 1844–1852" (Ph.D. dissertation, Columbia University, 1973): 12–43.

17. *Address of the Catholic Lay citizens, of the City and County of Philadelphia, to Their Fellow Citizens . . .* (Philadelphia, 1844). See also *Catholic Herald*, 24 June 1844. For an alternative view of the effect of nativism on Catholic community formation, see Thomas T. McAvoy's enormously influential article, "The Formation of the Catholic Minority in the United States, 1820–1860," *Review of Politics* 10 (1948): 13–34. See also the criticism of McAvoy in Taves, *Household of Faith*: 113–14.

18. Posses formed on July 7 and 8 included a number of Irishmen of respectable means. They included two attorneys, one trader, a grocer, a "collector," a printer, two tailors, an upholsterer, and a postman. See Raymond Schmandt, "A Selection of Sources Dealing with the Nativist Riots," *Records* 80 (1969): 74–77. Names from Schmandt's lists were manually linked to city directories for 1844. See also Feldberg, *Philadelphia Riots*: 121. The "Southwark Citizen's Committee of Safety" organized in response to the July riots included in its leadership two grocers, one merchant, a bank clerk, a cabinet maker, a corder, a plumber, and a ship carpenter. See *Public Ledger* (August 23, 1845); Feldberg, *Philadelphia Riots*: 185, notes the presence of nativists among these men, but Irishmen such as Michael M'Goff, Michael Kirby, and Edward Kelly were also present. The priest's letter is cited without attribution in George Potter, *To the Golden Door: the Story of the Irish in Ireland and America* (Boston, 1960): 367.

19. Kenrick's petition is reprinted in Nolan, *Kenrick*: 398–99.

20. Martin I. J. Griffin, "Historical Notes of St. Ann's Church and Mission, Philadelphia (1845–1895)," *Records* 6 (1895): 426–49.

21. Kenrick, *Diary*: 257; *Rules for the Government of Beneficial Societies Issued by Bishop Wood* (Philadelphia, 1871).

THE CHURCH APOSTOLIC

1. David Doyle, *Irish-Americans, Native Rights and National Empires: The Structure, Divisions and Attitudes of the Catholic Minority in the Decade of Expansion* (New York, 1976).

2. F. T. Furey, trans., "Letter from Dr. Kenrick to the Annals of the Propagation of the Faith, (Philadelphia) 14 January 1834," reprinted in *Researches* 8 (1891): 137; Kenrick, *Diary*: 30.

3. Nolan, *Kenrick*: 15; Francis Kenrick to John Purcell, 16 December 1830, UNDA.

4. Michael J. Curley, *Bishop John Neumann, C.SS.R., Fourth Bishop of Philadelphia* (Philadelphia, 1952): 187–88; *Catholic Herald*, 10 January 1833; Joseph George, "The Very Rev. Dr. Patrick E. Moriarty, O.S.A., Philadelphia's Fenian Spokesman," *Pennsylvania History* 48 (1981): 399–421. We should also note that until 1838 John Hughes, himself a stunningly effective orator, was also a parish priest in Philadelphia.

5. *Catholic Herald*, 10 January 1833, also reprinted in *Records* 30 (1919): 334–38.

6. Furey, "Letter from Dr. Kenrick": 140; Laurie, *Working People of Philadelphia*: 50; Kenrick, "Report to the Propaganda ... in 1838": 162–63. For confirmation of Laurie's impressions, see Robert Adair, *Memoir of Rev. James Patterson, Late Pastor of the First Presbyterian Church, Northern Liberties, Philadelphia* (Philadelphia, 1840).

7. John F. Byrne, "The Redemptorists in America, Part 5," *Records* 42 (1931): Michael Drennan, "The Early History of the Congregation of the Missions in Philadelphia," *Records* 20 (1904): 4–21; Tourscher, *Old St. Augustine's*: 61–76.

8. Nolan, *Kenrick*: 250–51; *Souvenir Sketch of St. Patrick's Church* (Philadelphia, 1892); *A Century of Faith: Church of St. Patrick, Philadelphia* (Philadelphia, 1935): 15, 17–18. *How Unsearchable His Ways. One Hundred Twenty Fifth Anniversary of Saint Patrick's Church* (Philadelphia, 1965).

9. Buckingham, *Eastern and Western States*, 1: 564–65. See also Robert F. Doherty, "Social Bases of the Presbyterian Schism, 1837–1838: The Philadelphia Case," *Journal of Social History* 9 (1976): 466–80; Laurie, *Working People of Philadelphia*: 43–49, 120.

10. Buckingham, *Eastern and Western States*, 1: 567; Francis Kenrick to Paul Cullen, 28 March 1843, copy in Philadelphia Archives; Michael O'Connor to Paul Cullen, 14 January 1842, copy in Philadelphia Archives.

11. *Presbyterian*, 14 January 1843; *An Address of the Board of Managers of the American Protestant Association* (Philadelphia, 1843). For comments on the effectiveness of Catholic missions and Protestant discomfiture, see *Catholic Herald*, 15 October 1840; 9 June, 27 October 1842; 21 December 1843.

12. Kenrick, *Diary*: 223–24; *Public Proclamation of Bishop Kenrick* (7 May 1844).

13. Michael Curley, *John Neumann*: 83, notes that "many of the foundations the Redemptorists received in those early years came as a result of the fact that the trustee trouble existed in the parishes before they took them over. . . . The American prelates were only too glad to let the Redemptorists have the places, thus ridding themselves of many of the annoyances and vexations growing out of trusteeism." On the Redemptorists in Philadelphia, see John F. Byrne, *The Redemptorist Centenaries* (Philadelphia: 1932), passim.

NATIONALISTS

1. Francis Kenrick to M. Roess, Director of the Seminary at Mainz, 14 May 1835, cited in Nolan, *Kenrick*: 190.

2. O'Shea, *The Two Kenricks*: 47–49; Hertkorn, *Retrospective of Holy Trinity Parish*: 94.

3. Francis Kenrick to M. Roess, 14 May 1835, cited in Nolan, *Kenrick*: 190. In this correspondence Kenrick noted that there were three pastors at Holy Trinity and that one of them preached one Sunday a month in English and once in French. See also "Letter from Dr. Kenrick to the Annals . . . 1834"; John Hughes to Simon Bruté, 2 May 1828, Hassard, *Hughes*: 66; Nolan, *Kenrick*: 415; Cardinal Franzioni to Francis Kenrick, 25 September 1837, AAB file 28 L1; William Baker, *Speech of William D. Baker in the German Roman Catholic Trinity Church Case* (Philadelphia, [1851]) (this is a transcript of the arguments in the case "In the Court of Common Pleas for the City and County of Philadelphia," 24 January 1851).

4. Curley, *John Neumann*: 223.

5. Ibid.: 221–22; Nolan, Kenrick: 415–16; Kenrick, *Diary*: 261; Dignan, "Legal Incorporation of Catholic Church Property": 182–83.

6. Baker, *The Trinity Church Case*; Curley, *John Neumann*: 222.

7. Dignan, "Legal Incorporation of Catholic Church Property": 188; Hertkorn, *Retrospective of Holy Trinity*: 100–101; Kenrick, *Diary*: 251; Francis Kenrick to Cardinal Franzoni, 25 November 1850, cited in Nolan, *Kenrick*: 418–19; "The Opening of Holy Trinity Parish," *Researches* 22 (1905): 57.

8. On John Neumann's view of the Church, see Chinnici, *Living Stones*: 70–71. See also Curley, *John Neumann*; John A. Berger, *Life of Right Rev. John N. Neumann, D.D., of the Congregation of the Most Holy Redeemer. Fourth Bishop of Philadelphia*, Eugene Grimm, trans. (New York, 1884); Joseph Wüst, "John N. Neumann, a Saintly Bishop," *Catholic World* 56 (1892): 322–38; Richard Andrew Boever, "The Spirituality of St. John Neumann, C.SS.R., Fourth Bishop of Philadelphia," (Ph.D. dissertation, St. Louis University, 1983).

9. Baker, *The Trinity Church Case*: 43–45, 51; *Public Ledger*, 11, 13, 21 May 1852.

10. Baker, *The Trinity Church Case*: 42.

11. Ibid: 51, 54–55; *Public Ledger*, 27 May 1852.
12. Curley, *John Neumann*: 227–28.

COMPLETING THE DEVOTIONAL REVOLUTION

1. Curley, *Bishop John Neumann, C.SS.R.*: 286–87, 350.
2. Ibid.: 354–55.
3. Ibid.: 286–87; Michael O'Connor to Cardinal Franzoni, 16 August 1855; Francis Kenrick to Gaetano Bedini, 23 July 1856, cited in Alfred C. Rush and Thomas J. Donaghy, "The Saintly John Neumann and His Coadjutor Archbishop Wood," chap. 4 of Connelly, *History of the Archdiocese of Philadelphia*: 238–40.
4. Curley, *John Neumann*: 219–20; 350; *Catholic Herald*, 9 June 1853; Kirlin, *Catholicity in Philadelphia*: 359. Neumann also contributed two catechisms that were used throughout the diocese. See Mary Charles Bryce, "An Accomplished Catechist: John Nepomucene Neumann," *Living Light* 14 (1977): 327–37.
5. Dolan, *American Catholic Experience*: 208–11; Taves, *The Household of Faith*; Nolan, *Kenrick*: 147; Connelly, *History of the Archdiocese*: 216–18; Curley, *John Neumann*; 219–20, 350, 352; Kenrick, "Condition of the Church in Philadelphia, 1838": 212; Chinnici, *Living Stones*: 79–80.
6. On the significance of the Forty Hours devotion as a unifying symbol for American Catholics, see Ann Taves, "Content and Meaning: Roman Catholic Devotion to the Blessed Sacrament in Mid-Nineteenth Century America," *Church History* 54 (1985): 482–95. On Bishop Neumann's reforms, see Curley, *John Neumann*: 219–20, 352; John F. Byrne, "The Redemptorists in America, Part 8, The Venerable Bishop John Neumann," *Records* 43 (1932): 51–52; Martin I. J. Griffin, "Who Introduced the Forty Hours Devotion into the United States?" *Researches* 29 (1912): 41. Neumann's devotional innovations are discussed in Rush and Donaghy, "Neumann and His Coadjutor": 214–20. On the significance of devotions for community formation, see Chinnici, *Living Stones*: 78.
7. Curley, *John Neumann*: 211, 215–16, 262–63, 375, 378; Clark, "A Pattern of Urban Growth": 167; John Neumann to Cardinal Franzoni, 28 May 1855, in Philadelphia Archives; Kirlin, *Catholicity in Philadelphia*: 356–59; Rush and Donaghy, "Neumann and His Coadjutor": 220–31.

1848

1. *Proceedings of a Public Meeting of the Citizens of the City and County of Philadelphia, Held January 6, 1848, to Express their Cordial Approval of the Liberal Policy of Pope Pius IX in His Administration of the Temporal Government of Italy* (Philadelphia, 1848). A short account of this meeting as well as

a reproduction of the printed "Proceedings" can be found in Raymond H. Schmandt, "A Philadelphia Reaction to Pope Pius IX in 1848," *Records* 88 (1977): 63–87.

2. Ibid.: 85. A similar meeting honoring the pope had been held at the Broadway Tabernacle in New York on 29 November 1847. See *United States Catholic Magazine* 7 (January 1848): 49–50; H. Nelson Gay, *Proceedings of the Public Demonstration of Sympathy with Pope Pius IX, and with Italy* (New York, 1847). For other similar demonstrations, see Loretta Clare [Feiertag], *American Public Opinion on the Diplomatic Relations between the United States and the Papal States: 1847–1867* (Washington, D.C., 1933): 8–14.

3. Ibid., pp. 72, 74, 75; *Public Ledger*, 7 January 1848; *Daily Sun*, 7 January 1848.

4. Aubert et al., *The Church Between Revolution and Restoration*: 3, 73, 101–4.

5. Ibid.: 310–11. Gregory XVI was formerly Cardinal Cappellari, Prefect of Propaganda, and as such had been intimately involved in the Philadelphia disputes.

6. Aubert, *Between Revolution and Restoration*: 311–13.

7. Ibid.: 314, 327.

8. Heyer, *The Catholic Church from 1648 to 1870*: 152–53.

9. For a summary in English of Pius IX's early reforms, see George F. C. Berkeley, *Italy in the Making* (Cambridge, 1934), part 2, chap. 4; the amnesty proclamation and commentary can be found in Denis Mack Smith, ed., *The Making of Italy, 1796–1870* (New York, 1970): 112–14.

10. *Public Ledger*, 7 January 1848; *America Whig Review* 6 (November 1847): 546; Margaret Fuller Ossili to Ralph Waldo Emerson, May 1847, cited in Howard Marraro, *American Opinion on the Unification of Italy, 1846–1861* (New York: Columbia, 1932): 12; *Proceedings of the Public Demonstration.* . . .

11. *Daily Sun*, 7 January 1848.

12. *Daily Sun*, 14 January 1848; Caroline C. Marsh *Life and Letters of George Perkins Marsh* (New York, 1888), 1: 116; *Christian Examiner* 34 (March, 1848): 263.

13. For a general survey of republican positions taken by Catholic lay spokesmen and enlightened bishops, see Patrick Carey, "Republicanism in American Catholicism, 1785–1860," *Journal of the Early Republic* 3 (1983): 413–37.

14. For a survey of the events of 1848, see William L. Langer, *Political and Social Upheaval, 1832–1852* (New York, 1969): 319–465; R. F. Leslie, *The Age of Transformation, 1789–1871* (New York, 1966): 245–85. On the implications of the revolutions, see Eric J, Hobsbawm, *The Age of Capital, 1848–1875* (New York, 1984).

15. For a general survey of events in Italy, see Luigi Salvatorelli, *The Risorgimento: Thought and Action*, Mano Domandi, trans. (New York, 1970). For an

American expression of neo-Guelf sentiment, see the *United States Catholic Magazine and Monthly Review* 6 (September and October, 1847): 457–67, 513–22. On neo-Guelphism in Italy, see Salvatorelli, *The Risorgimento*: 112–14.

16. Leslie, *Age of Transformation*: 280–81; Langer, *Political and Social Upheaval*: 377–79.

17. Heyer, *The Catholic Church*: 162–65.

18. *Public Ledger*, 7 January 1848; *Daily Sun*, 7 January 1848. For similar sentiments from other cities, see *Brownson's Quarterly Review*, January 1848, p. 134; *New York Herald*, 7 January 1848; *Daily National Intelligencer* (Washington, D.C.), 26 April 1848.

19. Marraro, *American Opinion*, p. 63; *New York Times*, 8 February 1878, cited in Samuel J. Thomas, "The American Press Response to the Death of Pope Pius IX and the Election of Pope Leo XIII," *Records* 86 (1975): 44. See also Theodore Dwight, *The Roman Republic of 1849; with Accounts of the Inquisition and the Siege of Rome* (New York, 1851).

"KEEPING THE CATHOLICS *STEADY*"

1. Marraro, *America Opinion*: 54, 58–60. On John Hughes' pugnacity, see Richard Shaw, *Dagger John: The Unquiet Life and Times of Archbishop John Hughes of New York* (New York, 1977).

2. Marraro, *American Opinion*: 123–29; Browne, "Memoir of Archbishop Hughes": 168–74; Hassard, *Hughes*: 342–44; Donald S. Spencer, *Louis Kossuth and Young America, a Study of Sectionalism and Foreign Policy, 1848–1852* (Columbia, Mo., 1977): 127; *Freeman's Journal and Catholic Register* (27 December 1851); John Hughes, "Report to the Vatican," 23 March 1858, in John Tracy Ellis, ed., *Documents in American Catholic History* (Milwaukee, 1962): 341–43. Archbishop Hughes to Horace Greeley, 21 November 1851, see Hassard, *Hughes*: 342. Merle Curti attributed the extraordinary invective launched at Kossuth by American Catholic leaders to the influence of the Austrian chargé d'affaires on the American bishops; see "Austria and the United States, 1848–1852," *Smith College Studies in History*, 11 (April, 1926): 177.

3. Marraro, *American Opinion*: 60, 63, 100; The *Catholic Telegraph* of Cincinnati branded Kossuth an enemy of the Roman Catholic Church; the *Citizen*, another Catholic journal, was repeatedly critical of Kossuth. See Carl Wittke, *The Irish in America* (Baton Rouge, 1956): 86.

4. Browne, "Memoir of Archbishop Hughes": 172–73. See also, Hassard, *Hughes*: 342–46.

5. Guilday, *National Pastorals*: 176.

6. Browne, "Memoir of Archbishop Hughes": 173, 178–79.

7. Carl Wittke, *The Irish in America*: 81–87; Browne, "Memoir of Archbishop Hughes": 168–74; Lawrence Kehoe, *The Complete Works of the Most Reverend John Hughes*, 2: 22–24, 790–93; Skelton, *The Life of Thomas D'Arcy McGee*: 166; Josephine Phelan, *The Ardent Exile, the Life and Times of D'Arcy McGee*; Robert G. Ahern, *Thomas Francis Meagher, An Irish Revolutionary in America*. For antiepiscopal comments by McGee, see D'Arcy, *The Fenian Movement*: 4; Marraro, *American Opinion*: 167–68; *New York Herald*, 8 August 1850: *Daily Tribune*, 8 August 1850; *American Whig Review*, 13 (February, 1851): 173–77.

8. Marraro, *American Opinion*: 169–70; Ray A. Billington, *The Protestant Crusade, 1800–1860* (New York, 1938); 300–301; *New York Daily Tribune*, 28 May 1851; Alessandro Gavazzi, *The Life of Father Gavazzi* (London, 1851): 1– 64; *Philadelphia Daily Sun*, 1–4 March 1853; *The Lectures Complete of Father Gavazzi as Delivered in New York; Reported by an Eminent Stenographer and Revised and Collected by Gavazzi Himself; to which is Prefixed the Life of Gavazzi by G. B. Nicolini* (New York, 1853).

9. *New York Evening Post*, 24 March 1853; *New York Daily Times*, 25 March 1853; *New York Observer*, 31 March 1853.

10. *New York Daily Times*, 25 March 1853.

11. Marraro, *American Opinion*: 171–72; *New York Evening Post*, 26, 29, 30 March, 7, 11, 17 April 1853.

12. *Pilot*, 18 June 1853; *New York Observer*, 18 June 1853; Philadelphia *Public Ledger*, 13 June 1853. Peter Guilday, "Gaetano Bedini, An Episode in the Life of Archbishop Hughes," *Historical Records and Studies* 23 (1933): 109 notes the prominent support given to Gavazzi by "Italian and German radicals and infidels." On 114 he cites John Hughes, in a letter to Rev. Bernard Smith, Rector of the Irish College at the Propaganda, 25 November 1853, noting the support for Gavazzi among New York's Italian "desperados." For accounts of Gavazzi's lectures in New York, see *New York Times*, 15 November 1853; *New York Tribune* 7 January 1854; *Lectures Complete of Father Gavazzi*. For an account of a riot accompanying one of Gavazzi's speeches, see Allan Nevins and Milton Halsey Strong, eds. *The Diary of George Templeton Strong* (New York, 1952), vol. 2, 15 December 1853.

13. *Public Ledger*, 27 May 1852; *To the Honorable the Members of the Senate and House of Representatives of the Commonwealth of Pennsylvania in General Assembly Met. The Petition of the Undersigned Citizens of Pennsylvania Respectfully Sheweth* (Philadelphia, n.d. [1854]) in Philadelphia Archives.

14. *The Petition of the Undersigned Citizens*; *To the Honorable the Members of the Senate and House of Representatives of the Commonwealth of Pennsylvania in General Assembly Met. The Petition and Remonstrance of the undersigned members of the Holy Trinity Church, worshipping at the N. W. corner of 6th and Spruce Streets in the City of Philadelphia* (Philadelphia, n.d. [1854]) in

Philadelphia Archives, reprinted under the title, "Petition to the Legislature of Pennsylvania to Prohibit Charters to Churches not having Lay Trustees, Debarring Bishops from Appointing Other than Lay Trustees and the Clergy from Receiving Legacies," *Researches* 11 (1894): 129–32.

15. Cited in Carey, *People, Priests, and Prelates*: 51, 54–55. On the Phoenixville incident, see Curley, *John Neumann*: 216–17. Curley notes that there was yet another attempt on Neumann's life in 1859, but does not identify the assailants. See 449 n. 134.

16. For general accounts of Bedini's visit, see Guilday, "Gaetano Bedini," and James F. Connolly, *The Visit of Archbishop Gaetano Bedini to the United States of America (June, 1853–February, 1854)* (Rome, 1960).

17. For denunciations of Bedini's mission, see the *New York Observer*, 25 August 1853 and 10 November 1853, 16 February 1854; *Popery as it Was and Is* (Hartford, Conn., 1856): 361; W. S. Tisdale, *The Controversy between Senator Brooks, and John, Archbishop of New York, over the Church Property Bill* (New York, 1855): vii; *Pope or President? Startling Disclosures of Romanism as Revealed By its Own Writers* (New York, 1859): 290–91; *The Sons of the Sires; a History of the Rise, Progress and Destiny of the American Party* (Philadelphia, 1855): 32; [A Democratic American], *An Alarm to "Heretics"; Or an Exposition of Some of the Evils, Villanies and Dangers of Papacy* (Philadelphia, 1854).

18. On Catholic defense of Bedini, see Guilday, "Gaetano Bedini": 102; *Milwaukee Sentinel*, 5 September 1853. On Italian refugees, see Marraro: 174–78; for an account of the assassination attempt see *Historical Records and Studies* 3 (1908): 155–67. On the generally benign reception given Bedini by Protestants, see Guilday: 110, 113. See also John Hughes to Bernard Smith, 25 November 1853, reprinted in Guilday: 114–15.

19. *Catholic Herald*, 28 July 1853; Connolly, *Visit of Archbishop Gaetano Bedini*: 22–24. Patrick Carey, *People, Priests and Prelates*: 272–75, notes that Bedini was anything but neutral. He had prejudged all the conflicts in favor of episcopal authority, which he held was superior even to civil laws.

20. Marraro, *American Opinion*: 140–43; 146–49; Guilday, "Gaetano Bedini" : 140–41; *New York Tribune*, 7 February 1854; Connolly, *Visit of Archbishop Gaetano Bedini*: 158. For accounts of specific incidents on Bedini's tour, see *Freeman's Journal* 17 December 1853; *Pittsburgh Catholic*, account reprinted in the *Freeman's Journal*, 31 December 1855; Cincinnati *Daily Gazette*, 16, 20 January 1854; Cincinnati *Unionist*, 16 January 1854; *Hochwächer*, article reprinted in Connolly, *Visit of Archbishop Gaetano Bedini*: 98–100; *Public Ledger*, 7 January 1854; *New Orleans Times Picayune*, 10 January 1854; *New Orleans Crescent*, 9 January 185.

21. Connolly, *Visit of Archbishop Gaetano Bedini*: 182.

22. Ibid.: 181–82. Robert F. Hueston, *The Catholic Press and Nativism, 1840–1860* (New York, 1976): 235–53, describes a protracted dispute between

immigrant papers and the Catholic press in which Catholic leaders claimed that immigrant clannishness promoted nativist reactions and immigrant editors responded that nativism was provoked by the reactionary political stance of the Church. *Irish-American*, 8 July 1854, quoted in Hueston: 251.

"CROSSES ALL OVER THEIR FACES"

1. *Catholic Herald*, 22 March, 12 April, 17 May, 21 June, 20 July, 4, 25 October, 27 December 1855, 12 January 1856. Brownson's articles on nativism and the *Herald's* response to them are discussed in Hueston, *Catholic Press*: 242–44.

2. Martin I. J. Griffin, "A History of the Church St. John the Evangelist, Philadelphia, from 1845 to 1853," *Records* 21 (1910): 133, 137.

3. John Neumann to his sister, 15 March 1858, cited in Curley, *John Neumann*: 353; Dolan, *Catholic Evangelism*: 69–70. Rush and Donaghy, "Neumann and His Coadjutor": 218, note that the Redemptorists held missions in twenty-six parishes during Neumann's seven years as bishop.

4. Dolan, *Catholic Evangelism*: 109–12; John Neumann to his sister, 15 March 1858, cited in Curley, *John Neumann*: 353; James Wood to Alessandro Barnabo, 2 March 1858, reprinted in *Records* 83 (1972): 52–53.

5. Dolan, *Catholic Evangelism*: 141.

6. Society lists as well as lists of pewholders are from *Souvenir Sketch of St. Patrick*.

7. Several years ago Stephen Thernstrom described the plight of a "floating proletariat" of unskilled and semiskilled workers that flowed through nineteenth-century cities, unable to put down roots and to fully participate in the organizations and institutions that defined neighborhood communities. John Modell and Lynn Lees have since traced the migration of young Irish immigrants through the American urban hierarchy. Even more recently, in my own work I have discussed the implications of this phenomenon for Philadelphia's Irish community in the second half of the nineteenth century. See Stephen Thernstrom and Peter Knights, "Men in Motion, Some Data and Speculations upon Population Mobility in Nineteenth Century America," *Journal of Interdisciplinary History* 1 (1970); Lynn Lees and John Modell, "The Irish Countryman Urbanized: A Comparative Perspective on the Famine Migration," *Journal of Urban History* (1977): 391–408; Light, "Class. Ethnicity and the Urban Ecology": 15–23. Pennsylvania Railroad Statistics are reported in P. B. Sheridan, Jr., "The Immigrant in Philadelphia, 1827–60; the Contemporary Published Report" (Ph.D. dissertation, Georgetown University 1957): 25–26. For an overview of the problem of geographical mobility, see David Ward, *Cities and Immigrants: A Geography of Change in Nineteenth-Century America* (New York, 1971).

"THIS BABYLON OF PHILADELPHIA"

1. James F. Woods to Cardinal Alessandro Barnabo, 15 September 1858, reprinted in *Records* 83 (1972): 53–56; Martin I. J. Griffin, "A History of the Church of St. John the Evangelist, Philadelphia, from 1845 to 1853," *Records* 21 (1910): 133.

2. John Neumann to Francis Kenrick, 7 June 1855, reprinted in Byrne, "Venerable John Neumann": 56–57, AAB file 30 U14; to Hermann Dichtl, August 1856, cited in Curley, *John Neumann*; "Report of Archbishop Gaetano Bedini to the Cardinal Prefect of the Propaganda" (1855); Michael O'Connor to Cardinal Franzioni, 16 August 1855, cited in Curley, *John Neumann*: 293. See also ibid.: 281, 284.

3. Michael O'Connor to Gaetano Bedini, 1 September 1856, Francis Kenrick to Cardinal Barnabo, 25 August 1856; cited in Curley, *John Neumann*, 295, 298.

4. Curley, *John Neumann*, chap. 15, "Travail of Soul," details in terms sympathetic to Neumann the controversies that led to the appointment of a coadjutor. See also Rush and Donaghy, "Neumann and His Coadjutor": 238–41.

5. Richard H. Clarke, *Lives of Deceased Bishops of the Catholic Church in the United States* (New York, 1888): 533–40. Curley, *John Neumann*: 307–14; Rush and Donaghy, "Neumann and His Coadjutor": 263.

6. Francis Kenrick to Peter Kenrick, 14 July 1859, cited in Curley, *John Neumann*: 327.

7. On the continuing troubles between Bishops Neumann and Wood, see ibid.: 321–36; Rush and Donaghy, "Neumann and His Coadjutor": 241–49; see also 215–16. As a measure of the degree to which Wood supplanted Neumann in administering the diocese, we should note that he, rather than the bishop of Philadelphia, presided at the diocesan synod of 1857.

8. *Funeral Obsequies of the Rt. Rev. John N. Neumann, Fourth Bishop of Philadelphia* (Philadelphia, 1860): 6. By contrast, in 1814 Bishop Egan's body lay in state only one night, then on the day after his death a Requiem Mass was said and he was buried in an unmarked grave in St. Mary's churchyard. It was not until 1830, Bishop Kenrick's first year in the diocese, that a tomb was built to house the body. See Kirlin, *Catholicity in Philadelphia*: 208.

9. *Funeral Obsequies*: 11–14, 16.

10. Ibid.: 14–17; Rush and Donaghy, "Neumann and His Coadjutor": 250–51.

Bibliography

COLLECTIONS

Archdiocese of Philadelphia, Archives and Historical Collections (Philadelphia Archives). Includes the Historical Collections of the American Catholic Historical Society of Philadelphia.

Archives of the Archdiocese of Baltimore (AAB)

Historical Society of Philadelphia (HSP)

University of Notre Dame Archives (UNDA)

Archives of the Sacred Congregation de Propaganda Fide (APF). Microfilm copies of documents relating to the American mission can be found at UNDA. Photocopies of many of the materials relating specifically to Philadelphia are on file at the Philadelphia Archives.

UNPUBLISHED SOURCES

Holy Trinity: Minute Book of the Trustees, 1788–1934 (Philadelphia Archives)

Minutes 1821–29, St. Mary's Church, Phila. Pa. (Philadelphia, Archives)

Roman Documents and Letters Pertaining to the See of Baltimore, 1783–1863 (AAB)

St. Mary's Treasurer's Account Book, 1821–1826 (Philadelphia Archives)

PUBLISHED SOURCES

Concilia Provincialia, Baltimore habita ab anno 1829, usque ad annum 1849. Baltimore: apud Joannen Murphy et socium, 1851.

Devitt, Edward I. "Letters of Father Joseph Mosely S.J. and Some Extracts from His Diary, 1757–1786." *Records* 17 (1906).

———. "Propaganda Documents. Appointment of the First Bishop of Baltimore." *Records* 21 (1910): 185–236.

"Diurnal of the Right Rev. John England, First Bishop of Charleston, S.C., From 1820 to 1823." *Records* 6 (1895): 29–55, 184–224.

"Earnest Effort Made by the Trustees of the Holy Trinity Church to Bring Missionaries into the New Diocese of Philadelphia." *Records* 23 (1912): 254.

Ellis, John Tracy, ed. *Documents of American Catholic History.* 2d ed. Milwaukee: Bruce, 1962.

England, John. "'State of Rev. Wm. Hogan,' 22 October 1821." In *Researches* 3 (1887): 139–40.

Flick, Lawrence F., ed. "Minute Book of the Board of Trustees of St. Mary's Church, 1812–1829," *Records* 4 (1893): 243–443; 42 (1931): 197–232; 43 (1932): 246–79, 320–59; 49 (1938): 171–87, 249–61, 334–69.

Furey, F. T., trans. "Letter from Dr. Kenrick to the Annals of the Propagation of the Faith (Philadelphia), 14 January 1834." Reprinted in *Researches* 8 (1891).

Goetz, John Nepomucene. "Discourse on the Sanctity of Christian Temples." Trans L. F. Flick in *Researches* (1887): 112–33.

Griffin, Martin I. J., ed. "Extracts from the Diary of Rev. Patrick Kenny; from March 25, 1805 to November 11, 1813." *Records* 7 (1896): 94–137; "From 1816 to 1819," 9 (1898): 64–76.

Guilday Peter. *The National Pastorals of the American Hierarchy (1792–1919).* Washington, D.C.: National Catholic Welfare Council, 1923.

Hanley, Thomas O., ed. *The John Carroll Papers.* 3 vols. Notre Dame: University of Notre Dame Press, 1976.

Kenrick, Francis Patrick. *Diary and Visitation Record, 1830–1851.* Francis E. Tourscher, trans. Lancaster, Pa.: Wickersham Printing Co. 1916.

Kehoe, Lawrence, ed. *The Complete Works of the Most Reverend John Hughes, D.D., Archbishop of New York, comprising his sermons, letters, lectures, speeches, etc.* 2 vols. New York: American News Co. 1865.

"Letter of the Rev. W. V. Harold of St. Mary's Church, Philadelphia, to the Rev. John Ryan of St. Peter's Church, Baltimore." *Records* 23 (1912): 135–36.

"The Missions of the United States in 1838." Originally published in *Annals of the Propagation of the Faith* (September 1838), reprinted in *Researches* 8 (1891): 161–67.

"Papers Relating to the Church in America, from the portfolios of the Irish College at Rome." *Records* 7 (1896): 283–388, 454–92; 8 (1897): 195–240, 294–329, 450–512; 9 (1898), 1–34.

"Patrick Curtis, President of the Irish College at Salamanca to Monsignor Argenti, Secretary of Propaganda, 14 February 1820." Reprinted in *Catholic Historical Review* 6 (1920): 261–63.

"Petition to the Legislature of Pennsylvania to Prohibit Charters to Churches not having Lay Trustees, Debarring Bishops from Appointing Other than Lay Trustees and the Clergy from Receiving Legacies."*Researches* 11 (1894): 129–32.

"Report on the Condition of the Church of Philadelphia Made to Our Holy Father Pope Gregory XVI, June 1, 1838, by Francis Patrick Kenrick, Bishop of Arath and Coadjutor to the Bishop of Philadelphia." *Records* 38 (1927).

Reynolds, Ignatius O., ed. *The Works of the Rt. Rev. John England, First Bishop of Charleston.* 5 vols. Baltimore: John Murphy and Co., 1849.

Roberts, Kenneth, and Anna M., trans. and eds. *Moreau de St. Méry's American Journey* [1793–1798]. New York: Doubleday, 1947.

Schmandt, Raymond. "A Selection of Sources Dealing with the Nativist Riots of 1844." *Records* 80 (1969): 68–113.

Shearer, Donald C., ed. *Pontificia Americana. A Documentary History of the Catholic Church in the United States, 1784–1884.* Washington, D.C.: Catholic University of America Press, 1933.

———. *The Kenrick-Frenaye Correspondence; Letters of Francis Patrick Kenrick and Marc Antony Frenaye, 1830–1862.* Philadelphia: 1920.

Wainwright, Nicholas B., ed. *A Philadelphia Perspective: The Diary of Sidney George Fisher, Covering the Years 1834–1871.* Philadelphia: Historical Society of Pennsylvania, 1967.

Willcox, Joseph. "Extracts from the Diary of Rev. Patrick Kenny." *Records* 9 (1898), "from June 23, 1827 to February 6, 1829": 223–56; "from February 13, 1829 to March 26, 1833": 305–36; "from 1821 to 1825": 422–58.

Willcox, Joseph. "Further Selections from the Diary of the same Missionary [Patrick Kenny]." *Records* 9 (1898): 77–128.

NEWSPAPERS AND JOURNALS

American Catholic Historical Researches (*Researches*)
Aurora (Philadelphia)
Catholic Herald (Philadelphia)
Daily Sun (Philadelphia)
Democratic Press (Philadelphia)
Journal of the Irish Catholic Benevolent Union (*ICBU Journal*)
National Gazette (Philadelphia)
Public Ledger (Philadelphia)
Records of the American Catholic Historical Society of Philadelphia (*Records*)
Relf's Advertiser (Philadelphia)
United States Catholic Historical Society, Historical Records and Studies (*Records and Studies*)
United States Catholic Miscelleny (Charleston)

PAMPHLETS

Act to Incorporate the Members of the Religious Society of Roman Catholics, belonging to the Congregation of St. Mary's Church, in the City of Philadelphia. As Amended. Philadelphia, 1826.

An Address of the Board of Managers of the American Protestant Association. Philadelphia, 1843.

Address of the Catholic Lay Citizens, of the City and County of Philadelphia, to Their Fellow Citizens. . . . Philadelphia, 1844.

Address of the Committee of Saint Mary's Church of Philadelphia, To Their Brethren on the Roman Catholic Faith Throughout the United States of America, On the Subject of A Reform of Sundry Abuses In the Administration of Our Church Discipline. New York, 1821.

The Address of the Ladies of St. Mary's Congregation, presented at the meeting, in Washington Hall, on Wednesday evening. Philadelphia, 14 February 1821.

Address of the Lay Trustees To the Congregation of St. Mary's Church, On the Subject of the Approaching Election. Philadelphia, 1822.

Address of the Trustees of St. Mary's Church, To Their Fellow-Citizens; Containing a Correspondence Between Them and the Right Reverend Bishop Conwell, On A Late Attempt At A Reconciliation Between the Contending Parties of the Congregation of Said Church. Philadelphia, September 1823.

Address to the Pewholders and Congregation of St. Mary's Church, by A Worshipper at St. Mary's. Philadelphia, 21 April 1827.

An Address to the Roman Catholics of the United States. By a Layman of St. Mary's Congregation. Philadelphia, 1821.

[An Admirer of Fenelon]. *A Letter to the Rev. William Vincent Harold, of the Order of Dominican Friars. On Reading his Late Reply to a "Catholic Layman."* Philadelphia, 30 March 1822.

An Answer to an "Address by a Catholic Layman," To the Roman Catholics of the United States." By a member of St. Mary's Church. Philadelphia, 27 July 1821.

Baker, William. *Speech of William D. Baker in the German Roman Catholic Trinity Church Case.* Philadelphia, [1851].

The Battle of Saint Mary's, A Serio comic Ballad, with Desultory Remarks on the Dissensions in that Church, By an Observer, Wholly unconnected with the Parties, But Wishing Well to Liberty and Peace. Philadelphia, 1822.

The Brief of His Holiness, Pope Pius the Seventh, Addressed to Ambrose, Archbishop of Baltimore, To His Suffragan Bishops, To the Administrators of the Temporalities of the Churches, and To All the Faithful In the United States of America. No place listed, 1822.

Brief Remarks, Addressed to a Catholic Layman, on his late "Address to the Right Reverend the Bishop of Pennsylvania, the Catholic Clergy of Philadelphia, and the Congregation of St. Mary's in this City." Philadelphia, 1822.

A Call To the Catholics; Or, A Word of Conciliation to Both Parties, By an Observer. Philadelphia, 1822?

[Carey, Mathew]. *Address to the Right Rev. Bishop Conwell and the Members of St. Mary's Congregation.* Philadelphia, 1821.

———. *Address to the Right Rev., the Bishop of Pennsylvania and the Members of St. Mary's Congregation, No. II.* N.p., 14 February 1821.

———. *Address to the Right Reverend, the Bishop of Pennsylvania, the Catholic Clergy of Philadelphia, and the Congregation of St. Mary's in this City.* Philadelphia, 1822.

———. *Brief Address to the Roman Catholic Congregation Worshipping at St. Mary's On the Approaching Election for a Board of Trustees.* Philadelphia, 1822.

———. *A Desultory Examination Of the Reply Of the Rev. W. V. Harold To a Catholic Layman's Rejoinder. By a Catholic Layman. To Which is Annexed An Appendix, Containing the Above Reply Verbatim.* Philadelphia, 1822.

———. *Letters on Religious Persecution: Proving, that That Most Heinous of Crimes, Has Not been Peculiar to Roman Catholics . . . , In reply to a libellous attack on the Roman Catholics, in an Address delivered to a Society of Irish Orange Men, styling themselves the Gideonite Society . . . , by a Catholic Layman.* Philadelphia, 1 January 1827.

———. *Miscellaneous Essays.* Philadelphia, 1830.

———. *Rejoinder to the Reply of the Rev. Mr. Harold, to the Address to the Right Rev. the Catholic Bishop of Pennsylvania, the Catholic Clergy of Philadelphia, and the Congregation of St. Mary's, In which are Detailed The inflammatory and violent proceedings of the Rev. Mr. H. in the year 1812, whereby discord and disunion were introduced into the Congregation of St. Mary's, By a Catholic Layman.* Philadelphia, 1822.

———. *Rejoinder to the Reply of the Rev. Mr. Harold, to the Address to the Right Rev. the Catholic Bishop of Pennsylvania, the Catholic Clergy of Philadelphia, and the Congregation of St. Mary's in this City,* 2d ed. Philadelphia, 1822.

———. *A Religious Olive Branch, to Inculcate the Divine Doctrine of Mutual Forgiveness and Forgetfulness of the Crimes of Ages of Barbarous Ignorance, Insatiate Rapacity, Blind Bigotry, Infuriated Fanaticism, and Bloodthirsty Cruelty, by a Catholic Layman.* Philadelphia, 7 October 1826.

———. *Review of Three Pamphlets Lately Published by the Rev. W. V. Harold. By A Catholic Layman.* Philadelphia, 1822.

———. *To the Congregation of St. Mary's Church.* Philadelphia, 27 March 1814.

———. *To the Congregation of St. Mary's Church, "On the Banks of the Rubicon."* Philadelphia, 1821.

The Case of Richard W. Meade, Esq., A Citizen of Pennsylvania, U.S.A., Seized and Imprisoned, 2d of May, 1816, by the Government of Spain, and Still Detained. Cadiz, 27 November 1817.

A Clear View of the State of the Roman Catholic Succursal Church, Styled St. Mary's in Philadelphia; Deduced From Facts Connected with the Schism in that Church. N.p., 1822.

A Compendious Trial of the Rev. William Hogan, Pastor of the Roman Catholic Church of St. Mary's, On an Indictment For an Assault and Battery, On the Person of Mary Connwell. By a Listener. Philadelphia, 1822.

The Constitution of the Commonwealth of Pennsylvania, As Altered and Amended by the Convention, For that Purpose Freely Chosen and Assembled,

And by Them Proposed for the Consideration of their Constituents. Philadelphia, 1790.

Constitution of the Society for the Defense of the Catholic Religion. Philadelphia, 1826.

[Conwell, Henry].*Concatenation of Speeches, Memoirs, Deeds, and Memorable References Relative to St. Mary's Church in Philadelphia.* Philadelphia, 1824.

———. *Sundry Documents Addressed to St. Mary's Congregation.* Philadelphia: Bernard Dornin, 1821.

———. *To the Public in General Who May Feel Interested in the Case Herein Specified.* Philadelphia, 22 May 1828.

[The Detector]. *Hoganism Examined According to the Canons of Criticism, Sacred and Profane; Or, A Short Letter To a Late Reverend Pamphleteer on the Republication of his Famous Pamphlet.* Philadelphia, 1821.

Duane, William. *A Report of the Extraordinary Transactions which took place at Philadelphia in February, 1799, in Consequence of a Memorial from Certain Natives of Ireland to Congress Praying a Repeal of the Alien Bill.* Philadelphia, 1799.

Earle, Thomas. *The Right of States to Alter and Annul Charters, Considered, and the Decisions of the Supreme Court of the United States Thereon, Examined, By the Principles of the American Constitution, Common Law, and Common Sense. With Some Observations on the Dispute Concerning the Alteration of the Charter of St. Mary's Church, Philadelphia.* Philadelphia, 1823.

Exemplar Authenticum Epistolae, quam Dominus Harold simul cum Joanne Ryan Scripsit, ad Eminentissianum Cardinalem Cappellari. . . . Philadelphia, 1828.

[Fagan, Augustine]. *Reflections On the Dissension Actually Existing in St. Mary's Congregation: Respectfully Addressed to His Excellency the Governor of the State of Pennsylvania. To Which are Added, Notes On the Right of Patronage and Presentation, As Established In the Roman Catholic Church. By a Roman Catholic.* Philadelphia, January, 1824.

A Fair and Full View of the Votes of John Andrew Shulze, In the Senate of Pennsylvania, Respecting the Charter of the Roman Catholic Congregation, Worshiping at St. Mary's Church, In the City of Philadelphia. N.p., 1823.

F[renaye?], M[arc?]. *An Explanation of Some Canon Laws Concerning Excommunication and Suspension, Respectfully Dedicated to the Congregation of St. Mary's Church, Philadelphia.* Philadelphia, 1821.

A Full and Accurate Report of the Trial for Riot Before the Mayor's Court of Philadelphia on the 13th of October, 1831, Arising out of a Protestant Procession on the 12th of July. . . . Philadelphia, 1831.

Funeral Obsequies of the Rt. Rev. John N. Neumann, Fourth Bishop of Philadelphia. Philadelphia, 1860.

Gay, H. Nelson. *Proceedings of the Public Demonstration of Sympathy with Pope Pius IX, and with Italy.* New York, 1847.

A Graphic Account of the Alarming Riots At St. Mary's Church, in April of 1822 Together With the Most Important Extracts From the Decisions of Chief Justices Tilghman, Duncan and Gibson, Relative to the Charter of Said Church, Including Letters From Hon. J. R. Ingersol & Thos. Kittera, Esq. Compiled By a Reporter. Philadephia, June, 1844.

Harold, William V. *An Address to the Roman Catholics of Philadelphia. By the Rev. W. V. Harold, Pastor of St. Mary's and Vicar General.* Philadelphia, 1823.

————. *Letter to the Hon. Henry Clay, Sec'y of State.* With: *Letter of Daniel Brent to Mr. Brown.* Philadelphia, 2 July 1828.

————. *A Postscript to the rev. Mr. Harold's Address to the Roman Catholics of Philadelphia.* Philadelphia, 1823.

————. *Remarks on the Catholic Layman's Desultory Examination.* Philadelphia, 1822.

————. A Reply to a Catholic Layman. . . . Philadelphia, 1822.

————. *Reply to the Catholic Layman's Rejoinder by William Vincent Harold, Pastor in St. Mary's.* Philadelphia, 1822.

————. *Sermon Preached in the Catholic Church of St. Peter, Baltimore, November 1st, 1810; On Occasion of the Consecration of the Rt. Rd. Dr. John Cheverus, Bishop of Boston.* Baltimore: G. Dobbins & Co., 1810.

Hogan, William, *An Address to the Congregation of St. Mary's Church.* Philadelphia, 1821.

————. *An Answer to a Paragraph Contained in the United States Catholic Miscellany. Edited by the Bishop of Charleston, Under the Head Philadelphia.* Philadelphia, 1822.

————. *A Brief Reply to a Ludicrous Pamphlet Compiled from the Affidavits, Letters and Assertions of a Number of Theologians, with the Signature of Henry, Bishop, and Entitled Sundry Documents, addressed to St. Mary's Congregation.* Philadelphia, 1821.

————. *Continuation to an Address to the Congregation of St. Mary's Church, Philadelphia: Part I.* Philadelphia, 1821.

————. *Continuation to an Address to the Congregation of St. Mary's Church, Philadelphia, Part II.* Philadelphia, 1821.

————. *A Reply to the Sundry Letters of the Right Rev. Dr. England to the Bishop of Philadelphia.* Philadelphia, 1822.

————. Strictures on a Pamphlet written by William Vincent Harold Entitled "A Reply to a Catholic Layman." Philadelphia, 1822.

Hoganism Defended; or the Detector Detected. . . . Philadelphia, 1821.

Inglesi, Angelo. *An Address to the Public of Philadelphia: Containing, A Vindication of the Character and Conduct of the Reverend Mr. Inglesi From Charges and Strictures Lately Reported and Published Against Him by the Reverend Mr. Harold.* Philadelphia, 1824.

An Inquiry Into the Causes Which Led to the Dissentions Actually Existing in the Congregation of St. Mary's, and Observations on the Mode Best Calculated to Prevent its Increase, by a Layman of the Congregation. Philadelphia, 1821.

John, By the Grace of God, and with the Approbation of the Holy See, Bishop of Baltimore, to my beloved Brethren, of the Congregation of Trinity Church. Philadelphia, 1797.

Kenrick, Francis P. *Address to the Trustees of St. Mary's Church to the Congregation, April 16, 1831.* Philadelphia, 1831.

———. *Pastoral Address of the Right Rev. Dr. Kenrick to the congregation of St. Mary's, 22 April 1831.* Philadelphia, 1831.

———. *Substance of a Sermon Preached in St. Patrick's Church, Pittsburgh, Pa. . . .* Pittsburgh, 1832.

———. *To the Pewholders of St. Mary's Church.* 12 April 1831.

The Lectures Complete of Father Gavazzi as Delivered in New York; Reported by an Eminent Stenographer and Revised and Collected by Gavazzi Himself; to which is Prefixed the Life of Gavazzi by G. B. Nicolini. New York, 1853.

A Letter to the Rev. William Vincent Harold, Of the Order of Dominican Friars, On reading his late Reply to a "Catholic Layman." By an Admirer of Fenelon. Philadelphia, 30 March 1822.

A Letter To the Roman Catholics of Philadelphia and the United States of America By a Friend To the Civil and Religious Liberties of Man. Philadelphia: Robert DeSilver, 1822.

Letters, &c. viz From Bishop England On Captain Rock's Proclamation; From the Rev. W. Hogan, In Reply to the Rev. Bishop; From an Irishman, To the Rev. William Hogan; And From An Irish Catholic To an Irishman: Copied from The Charleston Mercury, The Columbian Observer, and The Democratic Press. Philadelphia, 1823.

Meade, Richard W. *An Address to the Roman Catholics of Philadelphia in Reply to Mr. Harold's Address.* Philadelphia, 1823.

———. *Continuation of an Address to the Roman Catholics of the City of Philadelphia in Reply to Mr. Harold's Address.* Philadelphia, 1823.

Mier, Servando de. *A Word Relative to an Anonymous Pamphlet Printed in Philadelphia, Entitled "Remarks on the Opinion of the Rt. Rev. Servandus A. Mier, Doctor of Sacred Theology, &c. On Certain Queries Proposed to Him, by the Rev. Wm. Hogan."* Philadelphia, 17 August 1821.

[An Observer]. *A Call to the Catholics; Or, A Word of Conciliation to Both Partie.* Philadelphia, 1822?

O'Connor, Michael. *Archbishop Kenrick and His Work.* Philadelphia, 1867.

O'Meally, Thadeus J. *An Address, Explanatory and Vindicatory, to Both Parties of the Congregation of St. Mary's.* Philadelphia, 1824.

———. *A Series of Letters Relating to the Late Attempt at a Reconciliation Between the Members of the Congregations of St. Mary's and St. Joseph's; With a Brief Notice of the Present State of the Controversy Between Them Being an*

Abstract of an Address Delivered by the Rev. T. J. O'Meally, at the Meeting Held in St. Mary's, On Thursday Evening the 23d Ult. Philadelphia, January, 1825.

The Opinion of the Rt. Rev. Servandus A. Mier, Doctor of Sacred Theology in the Royal and Pontifical University of Mexico, and Chaplain of the Army of the Right, first Army of the Peninsula, on Certain Queries Proposed to Him by the rev. William Hogan, Pastor of St. Mary's Church. Philadelphia, 11 July 1821.

The Opinion of the Rt. Dr. John Rico, of the Order of St. Francis, D.D. and the Vicar General of the Armies of Spain, on the Differences Existing Between the Rt. Rev. Dr. Conwell, and the Rev. Wm. Hogan. Philadelphia, 1821.

Pastoral Charges Delivered by the Right Rev. Bishop Henry, in St. Mary's Church, on the 2d of November [December] 1820 & 11th of Feb. 1821 in Presence of Two Thousand Persons. Philadelphia, 1821.

Proceedings and Addresses at the Grand Demonstration Held Under the Auspices of the Catholic Total Abstinence Union of the Diocese of Philadelphia. Philadelphia, 1875.

Proceedings at a Meeting of the Congregation of Saint Mary's Church, Favorable to the Restoration of the Rev. William Hogan, Held at Washington Hall, Wednesday Evening Feb. 14, 1821 and at an Adjourned Meeting. Held as above, on Wednesday Evening Feb. 28, 1821. Philadelphia, 1821.

Proceedings of a Public Meeting of the Citizens of the City and County of Philadelphia, Held January 6, 1848, to Express their Cordial Approval of the Liberal Policy of Pope Pius IX in His Administration of the Temporal Government of Italy. Philadelphia, 1848.

Public Proclamation of Bishop Kenrick. Philadelphia, 7 May 1844.

Read, William George. *An Oration Delivered Before the Pennsylvania Catholic Total Abstinence Society at Philadelphia on the 4th of July, 1843.* Philadelphia, 1843.

Reflections On the Dissension Actually Existing in St. Mary's Congregation: Respectfully Addressed to His Excellency the Governor of the State of Pennsylvania. To Which are Added, Notes On the Right of Patronage and Presentation, As Established In the Roman Catholic Church. By a Roman Catholic. Philadelphia, January, 1824.

Remarks on the Opinion of the Right Rev. Servandus A. Mier, Doctor of Sacred Theology, &c. On Certain Queries, Proposed to Him by the Rev. Wm. Hogan. Philadelphia: Bernard Dornin, 1821.

[Roloff, Francis]. *Last Appeal to the Congregation of St. Mary's Church by an Independent Catholic.* Philadelphia, 1821.

———. *The True Sentiments of the Writer of the Last Appeal to the Congregation of St. Mary's Church by A Sincere Catholic, and no Traitor.* Philadelphia, 1821.

A Republication of Two Addresses, Lately Published in Philadelphia, the First by a Committee of St. Mary's Church on Reform of Church Discipline, the Second by a Layman of St. Mary's Congregation in Reply to the Same with Introductory Remarks by a Layman of New York. New York, 1821.

Rules for the Government of Beneficial Societies Issued by Bishop Wood. Philadelphia, 1871.

Semi-annual Report of the Catholic Total Abstinence Union of the Archdiocese of Philadelphia. Philadelphia, 1880.

A Series of Letters Relating to the Late Attempt at a Reconciliation Between the Members of the Congregations of St. Mary's and St. Joseph's; With a Brief Notice of the Present State of the Controversy between Them Being an Abstract of an Address Delivered by the Rev. T. J. O'Meally, at the Meeting Held in St. Mary's on Thursday Evening the 23d Ult. Philadelphia, January, 1825.

A Short Address To the Roman Catholic Congregation of St. Mary's Church, On the Approaching Election for Trustees. Written in consequence of two late Addresses from the Pastor and Lay Trustees of the Said Church. By an Irish Catholic. Philadelphia, 1822.

Strictures on the "Strictures of William Hogan, Upon the Rev. Wm. Harold's Pamphlet." By a Catholic "Of the Olden Time." Philadelphia, 1822.

Sundry Documents, Submitted To the Consideration of the Pewholders of St. Mary's Church, By the Trustees of That Church. Philadelphia, 1812.

Tilghman [William]. *Decision of the Supreme Court of Pennsylvania in the Case of the Corporation of St. Mary's Church (Roman Catholic) in the City of Philadelphia, on a Proposed Alteration of its Charter.* Philadelphia, 1823.

———. John B. Gibson and Thomas Duncan, *The Members of St. Mary's Congregation Entitled to Vote.* . . . Philadelphia, 21 April 1821.

To the Honorable the Members of the Senate and the House of Representatives of the Commonwealth of Pennsylvania General Assembly Met. The Petition of the undersigned citizens of Pennsylvania respectfully Sheweth. Philadelphia, n.d. [1854].

To the Honorable the Members of the Senate and House of Representatives of the Commonwealth of Pennsylvania in General Assembly Met. The Petition and Remonstrance of the undersigned members of the Holy Trinity Church, worshiping at the N. W. corner of 6th and Spruce Streets in the City of Philadelphia. Philadelphia, n.d. [1854].

[The Trustees of St. Mary's]. *To the Congregation of St. Mary's Church.* 25 March 1822.

Trustees of St. Mary's Church, Philadelphia to Ambrose Marechall [sic] *Archbishop of Baltimore.* Philadelphia, 26 June 1821.

The Trial of the Rev. William Hogan, Pastor of St. Mary's Church, for an Assault and Battery on Mary Connell. Tried Before the Mayor's Court in and for the City of Philadelphia, on Monday, the first of April, 1822, and Succeeding Days. . . . Philadelphia, 1822.

A View of the Application for an Amendment of the Charter of Incorporation of St. Mary's Church. Philadelphia, 1823.

BOOKS

Aubert, Roger, et al. *The Church between Reformation and Restoration.* Peter Becker, trans. New York: Crossroad, 1981.

———. *The Church in A Secularized Society.* Janet Sondheimer, trans. New York: Paulist Press, 1978.

Baisnée, Jules A. *France and the Establishment of the American Hierarchy: The Myth of French Interference, 1783–1784.* Baltimore: The Johns Hopkins University Press, 1934.

Bayley, J. R. *A Brief Sketch of the Early History of the Catholic Church on the Island of New York.* 2d ed. New York: Catholic Publication Society, 1870.

Berger, Johann A. *Life of Right Rev. John N. Neumann, D.D., of the Congregation of the Most Holy Redeemer. Fourth Bishop of Philadelphia.* Eugene Grimm, trans. New York: Benziger Brothers, 1884.

Berkeley, George F. C. *Italy in the Making.* Cambridge: The University Press, 1934.

Billington, Ray A. *The Protestant Crusade, 1800–1860.* New York: Macmillan, 1938.

Bland, Joan. *Hibernian Crusade: The Catholic Total Abstinence Union in America.* Washington, D.C.: Catholic University of America Press, 1951.

Blumin, Stuart M. *The Emergence of the Middle Class: Social Experience in the American City, 1760–1900.* New York: Cambridge University Press, 1989.

Bowen, Desmond. *Paul Cardinal Cullen and the Shaping of Modern Irish Catholicism.* Dublin: Gill and Macmillan, 1983.

Boyer, Paul. *Urban Masses and Moral Order in America: 1820–1920.* Cambridge: Harvard University Press, 1978.

Bradsher, Earl L. *Mathew Carey: Editor, Author and Publisher: A Study in American Literary Development.* New York: Columbia University Press, 1912.

Brown, Thomas N., *Irish-American Nationalism.* Philadelphia: Lippincott, 1966.

Bryner, Gary. *In Search of the Republic: Public Virtue and the Roots of American Government.* Totowa, N.J.: Rowman, Littlefield, 1987.

Buckingham, James S. *The Eastern and Western States of America.* 3 vols. London: Fisher, Son & Co., 1842.

Butler, E. Cuthbert. *The Vatican Council, Based on Bishop Ullathorne's Letters.* Westminster, Md.: Newman Press, 1962.

Byrne, John F. *The Redemptorist Centenaries; Founding of the Congregation of the Most Holy Redeemer; 1832 Establishment in the United States.* Philadelphia: Dolphin Press, 1932.

Campbell, John H. *History of the Friendly Sons of St. Patrick and of the Hibernian Society for the Relief of Emigrants from Ireland.* Philadelphia, 1892.

Carey, Henry C. *Essay on the Rate of Wages: With an Examination of the Causes of the Differences in the Condition of the Laboring Population Throughout the World.* Philadelphia: Carey, Lea & Blanchard, 1835.

Carey, Patrick. *An Immigrant Bishop: John England's Adaptation of Irish Catholicism to American Republicanism.* New York: United States Catholic Historical Society, 1982.

———. *People, Priests, and Prelates: Ecclesiastical Democracy and the Tensions of Trusteeism.* Notre Dame: University of Notre Dame Press, 1987.

Casey, Thomas F. *The Sacred Congregation de Propaganda Fide and the Revision of the First Provincial Council of Baltimore (1829–1830).* Rome: Apud Aedes Universitatis Gregorianae, 1957.

A Century of Faith: Church of St. Patrick, Philadelphia. Philadelphia, 1935.

Childs, Francis S. *French Refugee Life in the United States, 1790–1800: An American Chapter of the French Revolution.* Baltimore: The Johns Hopkins University Press, 1940.

Chinnici, Joseph P. *Living Stones: The History and Structure of Catholic Spiritual Life in the United States.* New York: Macmillan, 1988.

Clare, Loretta [Feiertag]. *American Public Opinion on the Diplomatic Relations between the United States and the Papal States: 1847–1867.* Washington, D.C.: Catholic University of America Press, 1933.

Clark Dennis, *The Irish in Philadelphia: Ten Generations of Urban Experience.* Philadelphia: Temple University Press, 1973.

Clarke, Richard H. *Lives of Deceased Bishops of the Catholic Church in the United States:* New York: P. O'Shea, 1888.

Connelly, James F., ed. *The History of the Archdiocese of Philadelphia.* Philadelphia: Archdiocese of Philadelphia, 1976.

———. *The Visit of Archbishop Gaetano Bedini to the United States of America (June, 1853–February, 1854).* Rome: Libreria Editrice dell'Universita Gregoriana, 1960.

Connolly, Sean J. *Priests and People in Pre-Famine Ireland, 1780–1845.* Dublin: Gill and Macmillan, 1982.

Cooke, Bernard, ed. *The Papacy and the Church in the United States.* New York: Paulist Press, 1989.

Costigan Richard F. *Rohrbacher and the Ecclesiology of Ultramontanism.* Rome: Universita Gregoriana, 1980.

Cross, Robert D. *The Emergence of Liberal Catholicism in America.* Cambridge: Harvard University Press, 1958.

Curley, Michael J. *Bishop John Neumann, C.SS.R., Fourth Bishop of Philadelphia.* Philadelphia: Bishop Neumann Center, 1952.

Cutler, William W. III and Howard Gillette, eds. *The Divided Metropolis: Social and Spatial Dimensions of Philadelphia, 1800–1975.* Westport, Conn., 1980.

Dansette, Adrien. *Religious History of Modern France.* 2 vols. New York: Herder & Herder, 1961.

Davis, Allen F. and Mark H. Haller. *The Peoples of Philadelphia: A History of Ethnic Groups and Lower-Class Life, 1790–1940.* Philadelphia: Temple University Press, 1973.

Davis, Susan. *Parades and Power: Street Theatre in Nineteenth-Century Philadelphia.* Philadelphia: Temple University Press, 1986.

Dignan, Patrick J. *A History of the Legal Incorporation of Catholic Church Property in the United States (1784–1930).* New York: P. J. Kennedy & Sons, 1935.

Dolan Jay P. *The American Catholic Experience: A History from Colonial Times to the Present.* New York: Doubleday, 1985.

———. *Catholic Revivalism.* Notre Dame: University of Notre Dame Press, 1978.

———. *The Immigrant Church: New York's Irish and German Catholics, 1815–1865.* Baltimore: The Johns Hopkins University Press, 1975.

Doyle, David. *Irish-Americans, Native Rights and National Empires: The Structure, Divisions and Attitudes of the Catholic Minority in the Decade of Expansion.* New York: Arno Press, 1976.

Ellis, John Tracy. *American Catholicism.* 2d ed. rev. Chicago: University of Chicago Press, 1969.

Ellis, John Tracy, ed. *The Catholic Priest in the United States: Historical Investigations.* Collegeville: Saint John's University Press, 1971.

———. *Catholics in Colonial America.* Baltimore: Helicon, 1965.

Fecher, Vincent J. *A Study of the Movement for German National Parishes in Philadelphia and Baltimore (1787–1802).* Rome: Apud Aedes Universitatis Gregorianae, 1955.

Feldberg, Michael, *The Philadelphia Riots of 1844: A Study of Ethnic Conflict.* Westport, Conn.: Greenwood Press, 1975.

Finke, Roger and Rodney Stark, *The Churching of America, 1776–1990: Winners and Losers in Our Religious Economy.* New Brunswick: Rutgers University Press, 1992.

Fogarty, Gerald P., ed. *Patterns of Episcopal Leadership.* New York: Macmillan, 1989.

Foner, Eric. *Tom Paine and Revolutionary America.* New York: Oxford University Press, 1976.

Fothergill, Brian. *Nicholas Wiseman.* London: Faber and Faber, 1963.

Frost, J. William. *A Perfect Freedom: Religious Liberty in Pennsylvania.* University Park, Pa., 1990.

Geffré, Claude and Jean-Pierre Jossua, eds. *1789: The French Revolution and the Church.* Edinburgh: T. & T. Clark, 1989.

Gibbs, Joseph C. *History of the Catholic Total Abstinence Union of America.* Philadelphia: Penn Printing House, 1907.

Gleason, Philip, ed. *Catholicism in America.* New York: Harper & Row, 1970.

———. *The Conservative Reformers, German-American Catholics and the Social Order.* Notre Dame: University of Notre Dame Press, 1968.

———. *Keeping the Faith: American Catholicism Past and Present.* Notre Dame: University of Notre Dame Press, 1987.

Gorman, Robert. *Catholic Apologetic Literature in the United States (1784–1858).* Washington, D.C.: Catholic University of America Press, 1939.

Greenfeld, Liah. *Nationalism: Five Roads to Modernity.* Cambridge: Harvard University Press, 1993.

Griffin, Martin, I. J. *History of Rt. Rev. Michael Egan, D.D., First Bishop of Philadelphia.* Philadelphia, 1893.

———. *History of St John's Church. Philadelphia.* Philadelphia: I.C.B.U., 1882.

Guilday Peter. *A History of the Councils of Baltimore (1791–1884).* New York: Macmillan, 1932.

———. *The Life and Times of John Carroll, Archbishop of Baltimore (1735–1815).* Westminster, Md.: The Newman Press, 1922.

———. *The Life and Times of John England.* 2 vols. New York: America Press, 1927.

Gusfield, Joseph R. *Symbolic Crusade: Status Politics and the American Temperance Movement.* Urbana: University of Illinois Press, 1963.

Gwynn, Denis R. *Cardinal Wiseman.* London: Burns Oates & Washbourne, 1929.

Hales, Edward E. V. *Revolution and Papacy, 1769–1846.* New York: Hanover House, 1960.

Hassard, John R. G. *Life of the Most Reverend John Hughes, D.D., First Archbishop of New York, With Extracts from his Private Correspondence.* New York: D. Appleton & Co., 1866.

Hatch Nathan O. *The Democratization of American Christianity.* New Haven: Yale University Press, 1989.

Hazen, Charles D. *Contemporary American Opinion of the French Revolution.* Baltimore, The Johns Hopkins University Press, 1897.

Hennesey, James. *American Catholics, A History of the Roman Catholic Community in the United States.* New York: Oxford University Press, 1981.

Hershberg, Theodore, ed. *Philadelphia: Work, Space, Family, and Group Experience in the Nineteenth-Century City.* New York: Oxford University Press, 1981.

Hertkorn, Francis J. *Retrospective of Holy Trinity Parish: a Souvenir of the One Hundred Twenty-Fifth Anniversary of the Foundation of the Church.* Philadelphia: 1914.

Heyer, Friedrich. *The Catholic Church from 1648 to 1870.* D.W.D. Shaw trans. London: Black, 1969.

Holmes, J. Derek. *More Roman than Rome: English Catholicism in the Nineteenth Century.* London: Burns and Oates, 1978.

———. *The Triumph of the Holy See: A Short History of the Papacy in the Nineteenth Century.* London: Burns and Oates, 1978.

How Unsearchable His Ways. One Hundred Twenty-Fifth Anniversary of Saint Patrick's Church. Philadelphia: 1965.

Howe, Daniel Walker. *The Political Culture of the American Whigs.* Chicago: University of Chicago Press, 1979.

Hueston, Robert F. *The Catholic Press and Nativism, 1840–1860.* New York: Arno, 1976).

Hughes Thomas, ed. *History of the Society of Jesus in North America, Colonial and Federal.* 4 vols. New York: Longmans, Green, 1907–17.

Jeremy, David John, ed. *Henry Wansey and His American Journal, 1794.* Philadelphia, American Philosophical Society, 1970.

Johnson, David R. *Policing the Urban Underworld: The Impact of Crime on the Development of the American Police, 1800–1887.* Philadelphia: Temple University Press, 1979.

Johnson, Paul E. *A Shopkeeper's Millennium: Society and Revivals in Rochester, New York, 1815–1837.* New York: Hill & Wang, 1978.

Jones, H. M. *America and French Culture.* Chapel Hill: University of North Carolina Press, 1927.

Kennealy, Finbar. *United States Documents in the Propaganda Fide Archives: A Calendar.* 10 vols. Washington, D.C., Academy of American Franciscan History, 1966.

Kirlin, Joseph L. J. *Catholicity in Philadelphia from the Earliest Missionaries Down to the Present Time.* Philadelphia: John Joseph McVey, 1909.

Klein, Philip S. and Ari Hoogenboom. *A History of Pennsylvania.* 2d ed. University Park: Pennsylvania State University Press, 1986.

———. *Pennsylvania Politics, 1817–1832, A Game without Rules.* Philadelphia: Porcupine Press, 1940.

Kohn, Hans. *Prelude to Nation States: The French and German Experience, 1789–1815.* Princeton: Princeton University Press, 1967.

Kohl, Lawrence Frederick. *The Politics of Individualism: Parties and the American Character in the Jacksonian Era.* New York: Oxford University Press, 1989.

Kleppner, Paul. *The Cross of Culture: A Social Analysis of Midwestern Politics, 1850–1900.* New York: The Free Press, 1970.

Kselman, Thomas A. *Miracles & Prophecies in Nineteenth-Century France.* New Brunswick: Rutgers University Press, 1983.

Langer, William L. *Political and Social Upheaval, 1832–1852.* New York: Harper & Row, 1969.

Laurie, Bruce. *Working People of Philadelphia, 1800–1850.* Philadelphia: Temple University Press, 1980.

Lees, Lynn H. *Exiles of Erin: Irish Emigrants in Nineteenth Century London.* New York: Cornell University Press, 1979.

Lemon, James T. *The Best Poor Man's Country: A Geographical Study of Southeastern Pennsylvania.* Baltimore: The Johns Hopkins University Press, 1972.

Leslie, R. F. *The Age of Transformation, 1789–1871.* New York: Humanities Press, 1966.

Lindstrom, Diane. *Economic Growth in the Philadelphia Region, 1810–1850.* New York: 1978.

Mahoney, D. H. *Historical Sketches of the Catholic Churches and Institutions of Philadelphia.* Philadelphia: 1895.

Marraro, Howard. *American Opinion on the Unification of Italy, 1846–1861.* New York: Columbia University Press, 1932.

Marty, Martin E. *The Modern Schism: Three Paths to the Secular.* New York: Harper and Row, 1969.

McAvoy, Thomas T. *A History of the Catholic Church in the United States.* Notre Dame: University of Notre Dame Press, 1969.

McCaffrey, Lawrence J. *The Irish Diaspora in America.* Bloomington: Indiana University Press, 1976.

McDonald, Forrest. *Novus Ordo Seclorum.* Lawrence: University Press of Kansas, 1985.

McManners, John. *The French Revolution and the Church.* New York: Church Historical Society, 1970.

Melville, Annabelle M. *John Carroll of Baltimore, Founder of the American Catholic Hierarchy.* New York: Scribner's, 1955.

Metzger, Charles H. *Catholics in the American Revolution.* Chicago: 1962.

Murphy Eugene. *The Parish of St. John the Baptist, Manayun: The First One Hundred Years.* Philadelphia: 1931.

Neusse, Celestine Joseph. *The Social Thought of American Catholics, 1634–1829.* Washington, D.C.: Catholic University of America Press, 1945.

Nolan, Hugh J. *The Most Reverend Francis Patrick Kenrick, Third Bishop of Philadelphia, 1830–51.* Philadelphia: American Catholic Historical Society of Philadelphia, 1948.

Oberholtzer, Ellis Paxton. *Philadelphia: A History of the City and Its People, A Record of 225 Years.* Philadelphia: S. J. Clarke, 1912.

O'Brien, David. *Public Catholicism.* New York: Macmillan, 1989.

O'Donnell, George E. *St. Charles Seminary, Philadelphia.* Philadelphia: American Catholic Historical Society, 1964.

O'Ferrall, Fergus. *Catholic Emancipation: Daniel O'Connell and the Birth of Irish Democracy.* Dublin: Gill and Macmillan, 1985.

O'Shea, John J. *The Two Kenricks: Most Rev. Francis Patrick, Archbishop of Baltimore; Most Rev. Peter Richard, Archbishop of St. Louis.* Philadelphia: J. J. McVey, 1904.

Palmer, Robert R. *The Age of the Democratic Revolution: A Political History of Europe and America, 1760–1800.* 2 vols. Princeton: Princeton University Press, 1959–64.

———. *Catholics and Unbelievers in Eighteenth-Century France.* Princeton: Princeton University Press, 1940.

———. *The World of the French Revolution.* New York: Harper & Row, 1971.

Phayer, J. Michael. *Sexual Liberation and Religion in Nineteenth-Century Europe.* London: Croom Helm, 1977.

Pole, J. R. *Political Representation in England and the Origins of the American Republic.* London: Macmillan, 1966.

Potter, George. *To the Golden Door: The Story of the Irish in Ireland and America.* Boston: Little, Brown, 1960.

Reher, Margaret Mary. *Catholic Intellectual Life in America: A Historical Study of Persons and Movements.* New York: Macmillan, 1989.

Roberts, Kenneth and Anna M. Roberts, trans and eds. *Moreau de St. Méry's American Journey [1793–1798].* New York: Doubleday, 1947.

Ruskowski, Leo. *French Emigré Priests in the United States (1791–1815).* Washington, D.C.: Catholic University of America Press, 1940.

Salvatorelli, Luigi. *The Risorgimento: Thought and Action.* Mano Domandi, trans. New York: Harper & Row, 1970.

Scharf, J. Thomas and Thompson Westcott. *History of Philadelphia, 1609–1884.* 3 vols. Philadelphia: L. H. Everts, 1884.

Schrott, Lambert. *Pioneer German Catholics in the American Colonies (1734–1784).* New York: United States Catholic Historical Society, 1933.

Shannon,William V. *The American Irish: A Political and Social Portrait.* New York: Macmillan, 1974.

Shaw, Richard. *Dagger John: The Unquiet Life and Times of Archbishop John Hughes of New York.* New York: Paulist Press, 1977.

Shea, John G. *Life and Times of the Most Rev. John Carroll, Bishop and First Archbishop of Baltimore, Embracing the History of the Catholic Church in the United States, 1763–1815.* New York: McBride, 1886–92.

Sloane, William M. *The French Revolution and Religious Reform, An Account of Ecclesiastical Legislation and Its Influence on Affairs in France from 1789 to 1804.* New York: Scribner's, 1901.

Smith, Denis Mack, ed. *The Making of Italy, 1796–1870.* New York: Macmillan, 1970.

Souvenir Sketch of St. Patrick's Church. Philadelphia, 1892.

Spalding, John. *The Life of the Most Reverend M. J. Spalding, D.D., Archbishop of Baltimore.* New York: Christian Press Association, 1873.

Spalding, Martin J. *Sketches of the Early Catholic Missions of Kentucky From their Commencement in 1787 to the Jubilee in 1826–7.* New York: Arno, 1972.

————. *Sketches of the Life, Times and Character of the Rt. Rev. Benedict Joseph Flaget, First Bishop of Louisville.* New York: Christian Press Association, 1852.

Spencer, Donald S. *Louis Kossuth and Young America, a Study of Sectionalism and Foreign Policy, 1848–1852.* Columbia: University of Missouri Press, 1977.

Sperber, Jonathan. *Popular Catholicism in Nineteenth-Century Germany.* Princeton: Princeton University Press, 1984.

Tackett, Timothy. *Religion, Revolution and Regional Culture in Eighteenth-Century France: The Ecclesiastical Oath of 1791.* Princeton: Princeton University Press, 1986.

Taves, Ann. *The Household of Faith: Roman Catholic Devotions in Mid-Nineteenth Century America.* Notre Dame: University of Notre Dame Press, 1986.

Tourscher, Francis E. *The Hogan Schism and Trustee Troubles in St. Mary's Church Philadelphia, 1820–1829.* Philadelphia: Peter Reilly, 1930.

———. *Old St. Augustine's in Philadelphia With Some Record of the Austin Friars in the United States.* Philadelphia: Peter Reilly, 1937.

Wallace, Anthony F. C. *Rockdale: The Growth of an American Village in the Early Industrial Revolution.* New York: Knopf, 1978.

Ward, David. *Cities and Immigrants: A Geography of Change in Nineteenth-Century America.* New York: Oxford University Press, 1971.

Warner, Sam B., Jr. *The Private City: Philadelphia in Three Periods of Its Growth.* Philadelphia: University of Pennsylvania Press, 1968.

Weigley, Russell F., ed. *Philadelphia: A 300-Year History.* New York: W. W. Norton, 1982.

Winslow, Stephen N. *Biographies of Successful Philadelphia Merchants.* Philadelphia: 1864.

Wittke, Carl. *The Irish in America.* Baton Rouge: Louisiana State University Press, 1956.

Wood, Gordon. *The Radicalism of the American Revolution.* New York: Knopf, 1991.

ARTICLES AND CHAPTERS OF BOOKS

Adams, Donald R. Jr. "Wage Rates in the Early National Period: Philadelphia, 1785–1830." *Journal of Economic History* 28 (1968): 404–26.

Agonito, Joseph. "Ecumenical Stirrings: Catholic-Protestant Relations During the Episcopacy of John Carroll." *Church History* 45 (1976): 358–73.

Alexander, John K. "Poverty, Fear, and Continuity: An Analysis of the Poor in Late Eighteenth-Century Philadelphia." In Allen F. Davis and Mark H. Haller, eds. *The Peoples of Philadelphia: A History of Ethnic Groups and Lower-Class Life, 1790–1940.* Philadelphia: Temple University Press, 1973.

Aubert, Roger. "Progressive Centralization on Rome." In Aubert et al., *The Church in a Secularized Society,* Janet Sondheimer, trans. New York: Paulist Press, 1978.

———. "Les Progres de l'Ultramontanisme." In Augustin Filche and Victor Martin, eds., *Le Pontificat de Pie IX:* 262–310. Paris, 1963.

Barat, Francis. "Reminiscence Pertaining to the Early History of Our Own Dear Manayunk Church of St. John the Baptist." In Eugene Murphy, *The Parish of St. John the Baptist, Manayunk: The First One Hundred Years:* 39–54. Philadelphia, 1931.

Barthold, Allen J. "French Journalists in the United States, 1780–1800." *Franco-American Review* 1 (1938): 25–230.

Bernstein, Leonard. "The Working People of Philadelphia from Colonial Times to the General Strike of 1835." *Pennsylvania Magazine of History and Biography* 74 (1950): 322–39.

Blumin, Stuart M. "Mobility and Change in Antebellum Philadelphia." In Stephan Thernstrom and Richard Sennett, eds., *Nineteenth-Century Cities: Essays in the New Urban History*: 165–208. New Haven: Yale University Press, 1969.

Bossy, John. "The Counter-Reformation and the People of Catholic Europe." *Past and Present* 47 (1970): 51–70.

Brislin, M. Bernetta. "The Episcopacy of Leonard Neale." *Records and Studies* 24 (1941): 20–111.

Browne, Henry J., ed. "The Archdiocese of New York a Century Ago; A Memoir of Archbishop Hughes, 1838–1858." *United States Catholic Historical Society, Historical Records and Studies* 39 (1952).

Bryce, Mary Charles. "An Accomplished Catechist: John Nepomucene Neumann." *Living Light* 14 (1977): 327–37.

Byrne, John F. "The Redemptorists in America, Part 8, The Venerable Bishop John Neumann." *Records* 43 (1932).

Carey, Patrick W. "American Catholic Romanticism, 1830–1888." *Catholic Historical Review* 74 (1988): 590–606.

———. American Lay Catholics' Views of the Papacy, 1785–1860." *Archivum Historiae Pontificiae* 21 (1983): 105–30.

———. "Arguments for Lay Participation in Philadelphia Catholicism, 1820–1829." *Records* 92 (1981): 43–58.

———. "The Laity's Understanding of the Trustee System, 1785–1860." *Catholic Historical Review* 64 (1978): 357–77.

———. "Republicanism in American Catholicism, 1785–1860." *Journal of the Early Republic* 3 (1983): 413–37.

———. "Two Episcopal Views of Lay-Clerical Conflicts: 1785–1860." *Records* 87 (1976): 85–98.

Carlisle, Marcia. "Disorderly City, Disorderly Women: Prostitution in Antebellum Philadelphia." *Pennsylvania Magazine of History and Biography* 110 (1986): 549–68.

Carter, Edward C. "A Wild Irishman Under Every Federalist's Bed." *Pennsylvania Magazine of History and Biography* 94 (1970).

"The Cessation at St. Mary's." *Researches* 1 (1887): 83–89.

Chinnici, Joseph P. "American Catholics and Religious Pluralism, 1775–1820." *Journal of Ecumenical Studies* 16 (1979): 727–46.

———. "Organization of the Spiritual Life: American Catholic Devotional Works, 1791–1866." *Theological Studies* 40 (1979).

Clark, Dennis. "Kellyville: Immigrant Enterprise." *Pennsylvania History* 39 (1972): 40–49.

———. "A Pattern of Urban Growth: Residential Development and Church Location in Philadelphia." *Records* 82 (1971): 158–70.

Connolly, Gerard, "The Transubstantiation of Myth: Towards a New Popular History of Nineteenth-Century Catholicism in England." *Journal of Ecclesiastical History* 35 (1984): 78–104.

Cross, Michael H. "Catholic Choirs and Choir Music." *Records* 2 (1886): 115–26.

Davis, Susan. "'Making Night Hideous': Christmas Revelry and Public Order in Nineteenth Century Philadelphia." *American Quarterly* 34 (1982): 185–99.

Doherty, Robert F. "Social Bases of the Presbyterian Schism, 1837–1838: The Philadelphia Case." *Journal of Social History* 9 (1976): 466–80.

Drennan, Michael. "The Early History of the Congregation of the Missions in Philadelphia." *Records* 20 (1904): 4–21.

Duffee, F. Harold. "Reminiscences of the Rev. William Hogan, Rev. William V. Harold and the Memorial Vow of Rev. Father Carter." *Researches* 8 (1891).

Earl, John L. III. "Talleyrand in Philadelphia, 1794–1796." *Pennsylvania Magazine of History and Biography* 91 (1967).

Ellis, John Tracy. "Religious Freedom and American Catholicism." *Cross Currents* 13 (Winter, 1963).

Ennis, Arthur J. "The New Diocese of Philadelphia." In James F. Connelly, ed., *The History of the Archdiocese of Philadelphia* (Philadelphia, 1976).

Feldberg, Michael. "Urbanization as a Cause of Violence: Philadelphia as a Test Case." In Allen F. Davis and Mark H. Haller, *The Peoples of Philadelphia: A History of Ethnic Groups and Lower-Class Life, 1790–1940.* Philadelphia, 1973.

Flick, Lawrence F. "Biographical Sketch of Rev. Peter Henry Lemke." *Records* 9 (1898): 129–92.

Fogarty, Gerald P. "Public Patriotism and Private Politics: The Tradition of American Catholicism." *U.S. Catholic Historian*, vol. 4, no. 1 (1984): 1–48.

Foin, Jules C. "Rev. Louis Barth, A Pioneer Missionary in Pennsylvania and an Administrator of the Diocese of Philadelphia." *Records* 2 (1889): 29–37.

Gavigan, Kathleen. "The Rise and Fall of Parish Cohesiveness in Philadelphia." *Records* 86 (1975): 107–31.

Geffen Elizabeth. "Industrial Development and Social Crisis, 1841–1854." In Russell F. Weigley, ed., *Philadelphia: A 300-Year History:* 307–62. New York, 1982.

George, Joseph. "The Very Rev. Dr. Patrick E. Moriarty, O.S.A., Philadelphia's Fenian Spokesman." *Pennsylvania History* 48 (1981): 399–421.

Gillette, Howard, Jr. "The Emergence of the Modern Metropolis: Philadelphia in the Age of Consolidation." In William W. Cutler III and Gillette, eds., *The Divided Metropolis: Social and Spatial Dimensions of Philadelphia, 1800–1975:* 3–26. Westport, 1980.

Gilley, Sheridan. "The Roman Catholic Church and the Nineteenth-Century Irish Diaspora." *Journal of Ecclesiastical History* 35 (1984): 188–207.

Gorman, M. Adele Francis. "Evolution of Catholic Lay Leadership, 1820–1920." *Historical Records and Studies* 50 (1964): 130–65.

Graham, Robert Earl. "Taverns of Colonial Philadelphia." In *Historic Philadelphia From the Founding Until the Early Nineteenth Century, Transactions of the American Philosophical Society,* n.s., 43 (1953): 318–25.

Griffin, Martin I. J. "The Church of Holy Trinity, Philadelphia. Its First Pastor, Rev. John Baptist Charles Helbron. The First Opposition to Ecclesiastical Authority." *Records* 21 (1910): 1–45.

————. "Historical Notes of St. Ann's Church and Mission, Philadelphia (1845–1895)." *Records* 6 (1895): 426–49.

————. "History of Rt. Rev. Michael Egan D. D., First Bishop of Philadelphia." *Researches* 9 (1892): 65–80, 113–28, 161–76; 10 (1893): 17–32, 81–96, 113–28, 161–92.

————. "A History of the Church St. John the Evangelist, Philadelphia, from 1845 to 1853." *Records* 21 (1910): 129–38.

————. "The Life of Bishop Conwell." *Records* 24 (1913): 16–42, 162–78, 217–50, 348–61; 25 (1914): 52–67, 146–78, 217–48, 296–341; 26 (1915): 64–77, 131–65, 227–49; 27 (1916): 74–87, 145–60, 275–83, 318–59, 28 (1917): 64–84, 150–83, 244–65, 310–47; 29 (1918): 170–82, 250–61, 360–84.

————. "The Reverend John Nepomucene Goetz, and the Reverend William Elling, Assistant of Holy Trinity Church, Philadelphia." *Records* 23 (1912): 94–124.

————. "Rev. John Ricco, Cigar Maker in Philadelphia and Planter in Alabama." *Researches* 7 (1890): 134–37.

————. "The Rev. Peter Helbron, Second Pastor of Holy Trinity Church, Philadelphia." *Records* 23 (1912): 1–21.

————. "Who Introduced the Forty Hour Devotion into the United States?" *Researches* 29 (1912): 41.

Guilday, Peter. "Gaetano Bedini, An Episode in the Life of Archbishop Hughes." *U.S. Catholic Historical Society, Records and Studies* 23 (1933): 87–170.

————. "Trusteeism." *U.S. Catholic Historical Society, Records and Studies* 18 (1928): 7–73.

Gutman, Herbert G. "Work, Culture, and Society in Industrializing America, 1815–1919." *American Historical Review* 78 (1973): 531–87.

Hanley, Thomas O. "Archbishop Carroll and the French Revolution." *Records* 71 (1960): 67–72.

Hastings, William S. "Philadelphia Microcosm." *Pennsylvania Magazine of History and Biography* 91 (1967): 164–80.

Henderson, Elizabeth K. "The Attack on the Judiciary in Pennsylvania, 1800–1810." *Pennsylvania Magazine of History and Biography* 16 (1937): 113–36.

Hershberg, Theodore, Harold E. Cox, Dale B. Light, and Richard R. Greenfield. "The 'Journey to Work': An Empirical Investigation of Work, Residence and Transportation, Philadelphia, 1850 and 1880." In Theodore Hershberg, ed., *Philadelphia: Work, Space, Family, and Group Experience in the 19th Century: Essays Toward an Interdisciplinary History of the City.* New York: Oxford, 1981.

Hennesey, James J. "An Eighteenth Century Bishop: John Carroll of Baltimore." *Archivum Historiae Pontificiae* 16 (1978): 171–205.

———. "Papacy and Episcopacy in Eighteenth and Nineteenth Century American Catholic Thought." *Records* 77 (1976): 175–89.

———. "Roman Catholicism: The Maryland Tradition." *Thought*, vol. 51, no. 202 (September 1976): 282–95.

———. "Rome and the Origins of the United States Hierarchy." In Bernard Cooke, ed., *The Papacy and the Church in the United States:* 79–97. New York: Paulist Press, 1989.

———. "The Vision of John Carroll." *Thought*, vol. 54, no. 214 (September 1979): 323–33.

Hutt, M. G. "The Curés and the Third Estate, The Ideas of Reform in the Pamphlets of the French Lower Clergy in the Period 1787–89." *Journal of Ecclesiastical History* 8 (1957): 74–92.

Idzerda, S. J. "Iconoclasm during the French Revolution." *American Historical Review* 60 (1954): 13–26.

" 'The Irish Riot' at St. Mary's Church, Philadelphia, 1799." *Records* 17 (1900): 86–88.

Jeffrey, Edith. "Reform, Renewal and Vindication: Irish Immigrants and the Catholic Total Abstinence Movement in Ante-Bellum Philadelphia." *Pennsylvania Magazine of History and Biography*, 112 (1988): 407–32.

Johnson, David R. "Crime Patterns in Philadelphia, 1840–1870." In Allen F. Davis and Mark H. Haller, *The Peoples of Philadelphia: A History of Ethnic Groups and Lower-Class Life, 1790–1940*: 89–110. Philadelphia, 1973.

Jordan, Patrick. "Annals of St. Joseph's Church." *Woodstock Letters* 2 (1873); 3 (1874).

Kearney, H. F. "Father Mathew: Apostle of Modernization." In Art Cosgrove and Donal McCarthey, eds., *Studies in Irish History.* Dublin, 1979.

Keating, J. Percy. "John Keating and His Forbears." *Records* 39 (1918): 289–335.

Klebaner, Benjamin J. "The Home Relief Controversy in Philadelphia, 1782–1861." *Pennsylvania Magazine of History and Biography* 76 (1954): 413–23.

King, Doris Elizabeth. "The First-Class Hotel and the Age of the Common Man." *Journal of Southern History* 23 (1957): 173–88.

Kingsdale, Jon M. "The 'Poor Man's Club': Social Functions of the Urban Working-Class Saloon." *American Quarterly* 25 (1973): 472–89.

Krugler, John D. "Lord Baltimore, Roman Catholics and Toleration: Religious Policy in Maryland during the Early Catholic Years, 1634–1647." *Catholic Historical Review* 65 (January 1979): 87–170.

Larkin, Emmet. "The Devotional Revolution in Ireland, 1850–1875." *American Historical Review* 77 (1972): 625–52.

Laurie, Bruce. " 'Nothing on Compulsion': Life Styles of Philadelphia Artisans, 1820–1850." *Labor History* 15 (1974): 337–66.

———. "Fire Companies and Gangs in Southwark: the 1840's." In Allen F. Davis and Mark H. Haller, *The Peoples of Philadelphia: A History of Ethnic Groups and Lower-Class Life, 1790–1940*: 71–88. Philadelphia, 1973.

Lees, Lynn H. and John Modell. "The Irish Countryman Urbanized: A Comparative Perspective on the Famine Migration." *Journal of Urban History* (1977): 391–408.

Light, Dale B. "The Reformation of Philadelphia Catholicism, 1830–1860." *Pennsylvania Magazine of History and Biography* 112 (1988): 375–405.

———. "The Role of Irish-American Organisations in Assimilation and Community Formation." In P. J. Drudy, ed., *Irish Studies 4: The Irish in America*: 113–41. Cambridge, 1985.

Maier, Eugene F. J. "Mathew Carey, Publicist and Politician (1760–1839)." *Records* 39 (1928): 71–154.

Marschall, John P. "Kenrick and the Paulists: A Conflict of Structures and Personalities." *Church History* 38 (1969): 88–105.

McAvoys, Thomas T. "The Formation of the Catholic Minority in the United States, 1820–1860." *Review of Politics* 10 (1948): 13–34.

McCallen, William J. "Temporary Schism Over the Election of Father William Elling." *Records* 24 (1913).

McCarthy, Charles Florence. "The Historical Development of Episcopal Nominations in the Catholic Church of the United States (1784–1884)." *Records* 38 (1927): 297–354.

McCarthy, Michael P. "The Philadelphia Consolidation of 1854: A Reappraisal." *Pennsylvania Magazine of History and Biography* 110 (1986): 531–48.

McNamara, Robert F. "Trusteeism in the Atlantic States, 1785–1855." *Catholic Historical Review* 30 (1944): 135–54.

Meade, R. W. "George Meade, Born in Philadelphia, 'Province of Pennsylvania,' February 27th, 1741, Died in Philadelphia, 'United States of America,' November 9th 1808." *Researches* 6 (1889): 98–118.

Miller, David. "Irish Catholicism and the Great Famine." *Journal of Social History* 9 (1975): 81–98.

Miller, Norbert H. "Pioneer Capuchin Missionaries in the United States (1784–1816)." *Records and Studies* 21 (1932): 210–13.

Moltmann, Jürgen. "Revolution, Religion and the Future: German Reactions." In Claude Geffré and Jean-Pierre Jossua, eds., *1789: The French Revolution and the Church* (Edinburgh, 1989): 43–50.

Montgomery, David. "The Shuttle and the Cross: Weavers and Artisans in the Kensington Riots of 1844." *Journal of Social History* 5 (1972).

Nolan, Hugh J. "Philadelphia's First Diocesan Synod, May 13–15, 1832." *Records* 54 (1943): 28–43.

O'Daniel, V. F. "Concanen's Election to the See of New York (1808–10)." *Catholic Historical Review* 2 (1916–17): 19–46.

Phillips, Kim T. "William Duane, Philadelphia's Democratic Republicans, and the Origins of Modern Politics." *Pennsylvania Magazine of History and Biography* 101 (1977): 365–87.

Purcell, Richard J. "Missionaries from All Hallows (Dublin) to the United States, 1842–1865." *Records* 53 (1942): 204–49.

"Rev. James Harold, the Botany Bay Irish Convict Priest of Philadelphia, 'the Cause' of the Direful Dissension at St. Mary's Church, 1812–13." *Researches* 17 (1900): 17–26.

"The Reverend Patrick Kenny Appointed English Pastor of Holy Trinity Church. Action of the Trustees on the Appointment." *Records* 23 (1912): 254–55.

Schmandt, Raymond H. "A Philadelphia Reaction to Pope Pius IX in 1848." *Records* 88 (1977): 63–87.

Silcox, Harry C. "William McMullen, Nineteenth Century Political Boss." *Pennsylvania Magazine of History and Biography* 110 (1986): 389–412.

Taves, Ann. "Content and Meaning: Roman Catholic Devotion to the Blessed Sacrament in Mid-Nineteenth Century America." *Church History* 54 (1985): 482–95.

Thernstrom, Stephen, and Peter Knights. "Men in Motion, Some Data and Speculations upon Population Mobility in Nineteenth Century America." *Journal of Interdisciplinary History* 1 (1970).

Thomas, Samuel J. "The American Press Response to the Death of Pope Pius IX and the Election of Pope Leo XIII." *Records* 86 (1975).

Tourscher, Francis E. "Marc Antony Frenaye—A Sketch." *Records* 38 (1927): 132–43.

Trisco, Robert. "Bishops and Their Priests in the United States, Part I, From the First Bishop to 1850." In John Tracy Ellis ed., *The Catholic Priest in the United States: Historical Investigations*: 112–26. Collegeville, Minn., 1971.

Waibel, Alfred H. "Venerable John Nepomucene Neumann, Fourth Bishop of Philadelphia." *Records* 52 (1941): 25–33.

Warner, Sam B., Jr. "Innovation and Industrialization in Philadelphia, 1800–1850." In John Burchard and Oscar Handlin, eds., *The Historian and the City*. Cambridge, Mass. 1963.

Westcott, Thompson. "A Memoir of the Very Rev. Michael Hurley . . . With a Sketch of the History of St. Augustine's Church." *Records* 1 (1884): 165–212.

Whittemore, C. P. "John Sullivan: Luckless Irishman." In G. A. Billias, ed., *George Washington's Generals*: 137–62. New York, 1964.

Willcox, Joseph. "Biography of Rev. Patrick Kenny, A.D. 1763–1840." *Records* 7 (1896): 27–79.

Wüst, Joseph. "John N. Neumann, a Saintly Bishop." *Catholic World* 56 (1892): 322–38.

Zachary, Alan M. "Social Disorder and the Philadelphia Elite Before Jackson." *Pennsylvania Magazine of History and Biography* 99 (1975): 288–308.

DISSERTATIONS AND PAPERS

Boever, Richard Andrew. "The Spirituality of St. John Neumann, C.SS.R., Fourth Bishop of Philadelphia." Ph.D. dissertation, St. Louis University, 1983.

Light, Dale B. "Class Ethnicity and the Urban Ecology: Philadelphia's Irish, 1830–1890." Ph.D. dissertation, University of Pennsylvania, 1979.

Miller, Roger. "Time-Geographic Assessment of the Impact of Horse-Car Transportation in Philadelphia, 1850–1860." Ph.D. dissertation, University of California, Berkeley, 1979.

Murrin, John M. "Escaping Perfidious Albion: Federalism, Fear of Aristocracy, and the Transformation of Corruption in Postrevolutionary America." Paper presented to the Transformation of Philadelphia Project, University of Pennsylvania, 1990.

Murtha, Ronin John. "The Life of the Most Reverend Ambrose Maréchal, Third Archbishop of Baltimore, 1768–1828." Ph.D. dissertation, Catholic University of America, 1965.

Neilly, Andrew. "The Violent Volunteers: A History of the Volunteer Fire Department of Philadelphia, 1763–1871." Ph.D. dissertation, University of Pennsylvania, 1959.

Ruskowski, Leo F. "French Émigré Priests in the United States (1791–1815)." Ph.D. dissertation, Catholic University of America, 1940.

Sheridan, P. B., Jr. "The Immigrant in Philadelphia, 1827–60: The Contemporary Published Report." Ph.D. dissertation, Georgetown University, 1957.

Szarnicki, Henry. "The Episcopate of Michael O'Connor, First Bishop of Pittsburgh, 1843–1860." Ph.D. dissertation, Catholic University of America, 1971.

Tabachnik, Leonard. "Origins of the Know-Nothing Party: A Study of the Native American Party in Philadelphia, 1844–1852." Ph.D. dissertation, Columbia University, 1973.

Index

About the Author

Dale B. Light teaches at Penn State University. He is the author of a number of articles on American and American Catholic history, including many on Philadelphia.